AN ANSWERE VNTO
SIR THOMAS MORES
DIALOGE

THE INDEPENDENT WORKS OF

WILLIAM TYNDALE

THE INDEPENDENT WORKS OF

WILLIAM TYNDALE

VOLUME 3

AN ANSWERE VNTO SIR THOMAS MORES DIALOGE

EDITED BY

ANNE M. O'DONNELL, S.N.D.

AND JARED WICKS, S.J.

THE CATHOLIC UNIVERSITY OF
AMERICA PRESS
WASHINGTON, D.C.

Cover emblem: Armorial bearings of Hugh, Baron de Tyndale, from
The New Testament, reprint of William Tyndale's translation, 1526
(London, 1836).

Printed in the United States of America

The paper used in this publication meets the minimum require-
ments of American National Standards for Information Science—
Permanence of Paper for Printed Library materials ANSI A39.48-
1984.

∞

Library of Congress Cataloging-in-Publication Data

    Tyndale, William, d. 1536

        An answere vnto Sir Thomas Mores Dialoge.

        p.   cm. — (The independent works of William Tyndale;
        v. 3)

        Includes bibliographical references (p.   ) and indexes.

        1. More, Thomas, Sir, Saint, 1478–1535. Dyaloge.

    2. Catholic Church Controversial literature.   I. Title.   II. Series:
    Tyndale, William, d. 1536. Selections. 2000; v. 3.

    BX1752.M6453T96 2000

    230' .2—dc21

    99-23501

    ISBN 0-8132-0820-3 (alk. paper)

CONTENTS

To

John O'Donnell, S.J.

Philip O'Donnell, M.D.

"brethern and very saruauntes for Christes sake"

Answer to More, 57/20–21

ACKNOWLEDGMENTS

I give heartfelt thanks to the many individuals and institutions who helped me complete this critical edition, especially the following:

Sister Wilfred Parsons SND (1881–1970), translator of Augustine's complete letters;

Richard S. Sylvester (1926–1978), founder of the Yale edition of the Complete Works of St. Thomas More, who first planned a Tyndale Project in 1976;

the editors of *Dialogue Concerning Heresies* (CWM 6) and *Confutation of Tyndale* (CWM 8), who led the way by first annotating the cross-references to *Answer to More;*

the Southeast Institute of Medieval and Renaissance Studies for a fellowship to the University of North Carolina, Chapel Hill in Summer 1979;

David C. Steinmetz of the Duke Divinity School, for post-graduate courses in Luther and in the English Reformation during my sabbatical in 1980–81;

Donald J. Millus, whose prompting helped bring about the revival of the Tyndale Project in October 1986, the 450th anniversary of Tyndale's death;

Jared Wicks SJ for his sections "Theology" and "Principal Contents" in the "Introduction"; for his knowledge of seven languages, especially Latin and German; and for his patience with the slow progress of *Answer* ever since he became theological co-editor in 1987;

the Centre for Reformation and Renaissance Studies, Victoria University, University of Toronto, for a Senior Fellowship in 1988–89;

the National Endowment for the Humanities for a travel grant in Spring 1989 and for another grant in Summer 1989;

the Folger Shakespeare Library, the British Library, Cambridge

University Library, and Trinity College of Dublin for use of their copies of *Answer to More;* and to their staffs for devoted service;

the theological libraries of the Catholic University of America and the Dominican House of Studies, Washington DC;

Antanas Suziedelis, Dean of Arts and Sciences, and the Richard Foley Fund at Catholic University for travel grants to professional meetings;

the Chairs of the English Department of Catholic University in the order of their tenure: Joseph M. Sendry, Stephen K. Wright, and Ernest Suarez;

the Sisters of Notre Dame de Namur and the University Research Fund for grants for a research assistant;

Mariann McCorkle Payne, research assistant from 1990 to 1993, especially for typing on disk the text, the glossary, the index of proper names, and references to the works of More and Tyndale into the commentary;

Jennifer Bess, administrative assistant for the Tyndale Conference in 1994 and research assistant from 1995 to 1998, especially for changing all the page and line references from the facsimile of *1531* to the critical edition of *2000;*

Chad A. Engbers, research assistant in 1999, especially for updating the Scripture index and for compiling the index of post-scriptural authors and the general index;

Charlotte Fromshon SND, Ann Gormly SND, Catherine Horan SND, and Timothy Reitz for short-term editorial assistance;

James Andrew Clark, Stephen J. Mayer and Anne Richardson, for helping correct the typescript and/or pageproofs of the text of *Answer;*

Peter W.M. Blayney, for reviewing the bibliographical descriptions;

all those who read the introduction and/or commentary: James Andrew Clark, David Daniell, John T. Day, John A.R. Dick, Richard L. Greaves, Germain Marc'hadour, Stephen J. Mayer, Susan Needham, and William S. Stafford;

Susan Needham, Managing Editor of the CUA Press, for her warm encouragement during our eight years of collaboration on *Word, Church, and State* (1998) and *Answer to More* (2000);

David J. McGonagle, Director of the CUA Press, for his dedication to producing handsome and weighty scholarly books;

Richard C. Marius (1933–1999) of the Advisory Board for chairing Tyndale panels at two national conventions and for serving on the editorial board of *Word, Church, and State;*

the Sisters of Notre Dame de Namur, the Gregorian University, and the Detroit Province of the Society of Jesus for subsidies toward the publication of *Answer to More;*

for prayers: the Carmelites of Baltimore and countless SNDs; for hospitality: the Sisters of Mercy of Baggot Street, Dublin; the Sisters of St. Joseph of Wellesley Street West, Toronto; the Sisters of Notre Dame of Woodstock Road, Oxford and Nightingale Lane, London; for community: Mary Hayes SND, Catherine Horan SND, and Claire McCormick SND—sisters and true servants of Christ.

During the years of working on *Answer to More,* when "the laboure semed to[o] tediouse and paynfull" (72/9–10), my flagging energies were renewed by the warmth of Tyndale's biblical prose, the support of friends and colleagues, and the anticipation of future readers.

ANNE M. O'DONNELL SND
Washington, DC

ABBREVIATIONS

ACW. *Ancient Christian Writers*. Ed. Johannes Quaesten and Joseph C. Plumpe. Westminster, MD: Newman; New York: Paulist, 1946–.

ANF. *The Ante-Nicene Fathers*. Ed. Alexander Roberts and James Donaldson. 10 vols. including Index. 1867–72; Grand Rapids, MI: Eerdmans, 1950.

ASD. *Opera omnia Desiderii Erasmi Roterodami*. Amsterdam: North Holland, 1969–.

CC. *Corpus Catholicorum*. Münster in Westfalen: Aschendorff, 1919–.

CCL. *Corpus Christianorum, Series Latina*. Turnhout: Brepols, 1953–.

CIC. *Corpus Iuris Canonici*. Ed. Emil Friedberg. 2 vols. Leipzig, 1879–81.

CSEL. *Corpus Scriptorum Ecclesiasticorum Latinorum*. Vienna: Gerold, 1866–.

CWE. *Collected Works of Erasmus*. U of Toronto P, 1974–.

CWM. Complete Works of St. Thomas More. 15 vols. New Haven: Yale UP, 1963–97. CWM 1, *English Poems, Life of Pico, The Last Things*. Ed. Anthony S.G. Edwards, Katherine Gardiner Rodgers, and Clarence H. Miller, 1997. CWM 2, *The History of King Richard III*. Ed. Richard S. Sylvester, 1963. CWM 3, Part 1, *Translations of Lucian*. Ed. Craig R. Thompson, 1974. CWM 3, Part 2, *Latin Poems*. Ed. Clarence H. Miller, Leicester Bradner, Charles A. Lynch, and Revilo P. Oliver, 1984. CWM 4, *Utopia*. Ed. Edward Surtz SJ and J.H. Hexter, 1965. CWM 5, *Responsio ad Lutherum*. Ed. John M. Headley, 1969. CWM 6, *A Dialogue Concerning Heresies*. 2 parts. Ed. Thomas M.C. Lawler, Germain Marc'hadour, and Richard C. Marius, 1981. CWM 7, *Letter to Bugenhagen, Supplication of Souls, Letter Against Frith*. Ed. Frank Manley, Germain Marc'hadour, Richard Marius, and Clarence H. Miller, 1990. CWM 8, *The Confutation of Tyndale's Answer*. 3 parts. Ed. Louis A. Schuster, Richard C. Marius, James P. Lusardi, and Richard J. Schoeck, 1973. CWM 9, *The Apology*. Ed. J.B. Trapp, 1979. CWM 10, *The Debellation of Salem and Bizance*. Ed. John Guy, Ralph Keen, Clarence H. Miller, and Ruth McGugan, 1987. CWM 11, *The Answer to a Poisoned Book*. Ed. Stephen Merriam Foley and Clarence H. Miller, 1985. CWM 12, *A Dialogue of Comfort Against Tribulation*. Ed. Louis L. Martz and Frank Manley, 1976. CWM 13, *Treatise on the Passion, Treatise on the Blessed Body, Instructions and Prayers*. Ed. Garry E. Haupt, 1976. CWM 14, *De Tristitia Christi*. Ed. and trans. Clarence H. Miller, 1976. CWM 15, *In Defense of Humanism: Letters to Dorp, Oxford, Lee, and a Monk*. Ed. Daniel Kinney, 1986.

DThC. *Dictionnaire de Théologie catholique.* Ed. A. Vacant et al. 15 vols. plus Indices. Paris: Letourzey et Ané, 1903–72.

EETS. Early English Text Society

DS. Heinreich Denziger and Adolph Schönmetzer SJ, eds. *Enchiridion symbolorum, definitionum et declarationum de rebus fidei et morum.* 34th ed. Barcelona: Herder, 1967. References are to paragraph number.

FJO. *Fontes Juris Orientalis.* Series I, Fascicolo IX. *Disciplina Generale Antica* (Sec. II–IX). Rome: Tipografia Poliglotta Vaticana, 1933.

FOTC. Fathers of the Church

GL. Voragine, Jacobus de. *The Golden Legend: Readings on the Saints.* Tr. William Granger Ryan. 2 vols. Princeton UP, 1993.

KJV. King James Version. *The Holy Bible.* A Facsimile in a reduced size of the Authorized Version published in the year 1611. Intro. A. W. Pollard. Oxford UP, 1911.

LB. *Desiderii Erasmi Roterodami opera omnia.* Ed. Jean LeClerc. 10 vols. Leiden, 1703–6; Hildesheim: Olm, 1961–62.

LCC. Library of Christian Classics

LP. *Letters and Papers, Foreign and Domestic, of the Reign of Henry VIII.* Ed. J.S. Brewer, J. Gairdner, and R.H. Brodie. 21 vols. 1862–1932; Vaduz: Kraus, 1965.

LThK. *Lexikon für Theologie und Kirche.* 2d ed. Ed. Josef Höfer and Karl Rahner SJ. 10 vols. Freiburg: Herder, 1957–65. References are to volume and column-number.

LW. *Luther's Works.* American Edition. Ed. Jaroslav Pelikan and Helmut T. Lehmann. 55 vols. St. Louis: Concordia; Philadelphia: Fortress, 1955–1986.

MRTS. Medieval & Renaissance Texts & Studies

NCE. *New Catholic Encyclopedia.* 19 vols. including supplements. New York: McGraw-Hill, 1967–96.

1NPNF. *A Select Library of the Nicene and Post-Nicene Fathers of the Christian Church, First Series.* Ed. Philip Schaff. 14 vols. 1886–90; Grand Rapids, MI: Eerdmans, 1956.

2NPNF. *A Select Library of the Nicene and Post-Nicene Fathers of the Christian Church, Second Series.* Ed. Philip Schaff and Henry Wace. 14 vols. New York: Christian Literature, 1890–1916.

NT. New Testament

ODEP. *The Oxford Dictionary of English Proverbs.* 3d ed. Ed. F.P. Wilson. Introduction by Joanna Wilson. Oxford: Clarendon, 1970.

OED. *The Compact Edition of the Oxford English Dictionary.* Complete Text Reproduced Micrographically. 2 vols. Oxford UP, 1971.

———. *The Oxford English Dictionary* Second Edition [1989] *on Compact Disk.* Ed. J.A. Simpson and E.S.C. Weiner. Oxford UP, 1994.

OER. *The Oxford Encyclopedia of the Reformation.* Ed. Hans J. Hillerbrand. 4 vols. New York: Oxford UP, 1996.

OT. Old Testament

PG. *Patrologiae cursus completus: Series Graeca.* Ed. J.P. Migne. 161 in 166 vols. plus Indices. Paris, 1857–87.

PL. *Patrologiae cursus completus: Series Latina.* Ed. J.P. Migne. 221 vols. Paris, 1844–82.

PN. Pater Noster

PS 1. Tyndale, William. *Doctrinal Treatises and Introductions to Different Portions of the Holy Scriptures.* Ed. Henry Walter. Parker Society 42. Cambridge UP, 1848.

PS 2. Tyndale, William. *Expositions and Notes on Sundry Portions of the Holy Scriptures Together with the Practice of Prelates.* Ed. Henry Walter. Parker Society 43. Cambridge UP, 1849.

PS 3. Tyndale, William. *An Answer to Sir Thomas More's Dialogue, . . . And Wm. Tracy's Testament Expounded.* Ed. Henry Walter. Parker Society 44. Cambridge UP, 1850.

Reeve 1. *Erasmus' Annotations on the New Testament: Gospels.* Facsimile of the final Latin text (1535) with all earlier variants (1516, 1519, 1522 and 1527). Ed. Anne Reeve. Intro. M.A. Screech. Calligraphy by Patricia Payn. London: Duckworth, 1986.

Reeve 2. *Erasmus' Annotations on the New Testament: Acts – Romans – I and II Corinthians.* Facsimile of the final Latin text with all earlier variants. Ed. Anne Reeve and M.A. Screech. Calligraphy by Patricia Payn. Studies in the History of Christian Thought 42. Leiden: Brill, 1990.

Reeve 3. *Erasmus' Annotations on the New Testament: Galatians to Revelation.* Facsimile of the final Latin text with all earlier variants. Ed. Anne Reeve. Intro. M.A. Screech. Calligraphy by Pamela King. Studies in the History of Christian Thought 52. Leiden: Brill, 1993.

STC. *A Short-Title Catalogue of Books Printed in England, Scotland, and Ireland and of English Books Printed Abroad 1474–1640.* 1st ed., A.W. Pollard and G.R. Redgrave. 2d ed., begun by W.A. Jackson and F.S. Ferguson, completed by Katharine F. Pantzer. 3 vols. London: Bibliographical Society, 1976, 1986, 1991.

TNT. *Tyndale's New Testament.* A modern-spelling edition of the 1534 translation, with an introduction by David Daniell. New Haven: Yale UP, 1989.

TOT. *Tyndale's Old Testament.* A modern-spelling edition of the Pentateuch (1530), Joshua to 2 Chronicles (1537) and Jonah (1531), with an introduction by David Daniell. New Haven: Yale UP, 1992.

TRE. *Theologishe Realenzyklopädie.* Ed. Gerhard Krause, Gerhard Müller et al. Berlin and New York: Walter de Gruyter, 1976–.

TRP. *Tudor Royal Proclamations, Vol. 1, The Early Tudors (1485–1553)*. Ed. Paul
L. Hughes and James F. Larkin CSV. New Haven: Yale UP, 1964.

UD. *Unio Dissidentium*. Ed. Hermannus Bodius. 2 vols. Cologne: [Antwerp:
Martin de Keyser], 1527 [?].

WA. *D. Martin Luthers Werke, Kritische Gesamtausgabe*. Ed. J.K.F. Knaake et al.
Weimar: Hermann Bohlaus, 1883– .

WA/DB. *D. Martin Luthers Werke. Kritische Gesamtausgabe. Die Deutsche Bibel*.
Ed. P. Pietsch et al. II vols. Weimar: Hermann Bohlaus, 1906–1960.

WCS. *Word, Church, and State: Tyndale Quincentenary Essays*. Ed. John T. Day,
Eric Lund, and Anne M. O'Donnell SND. Washington, DC: Catholic
University of America P, 1998.

BIBLIOGRAPHY

The following bibliography includes the titles of all works cited frequently in the Introduction and Commentary. The titles of works referred to only once or occurring in a brief cluster of references are given in full as they occur. References are to volume and page unless otherwise noted.

Ackroyd, Peter. *The Life of Thomas More*. London: Chatto & Windus, 1998.

Allen, P.S., H.M. Allen, and H.W. Garrod, eds. *Opus epistolarum Des. Erasmi Roterodami*. 12 vols. including Index. Oxford: Clarendon, 1906–58.

Aquinas, St. Thomas. *Summa Theologica*. 3 vols. New York: Benziger, 1947. Cited as "*Summa*."

Assertio. See Henry VIII.

Augustine, St. *Letters*. Tr. [Elsie] Wilfred Parsons SND. 5 vols. FOTC 12, 18, 20, 30, 32. New York: Fathers of the Church, 1951–56. Cited as "Parsons 1–5."

———. *Sermons*. Gen. ed. John E. Rotelle OSA. Brooklyn, NY: New City, 1990–. Cited as "Rotelle."

Bainton, Roland H. *Here I Stand: A Life of Martin Luther*. New York: New American Library, 1950.

Barlowe, Jerome, and William Roye. *Rede Me and Be Nott Wrothe*. Ed. Douglas H. Parker. U of Toronto P, 1992.

Berschin, Walter. *Greek Letters and the Latin Middle Ages: From Jerome to Nicolas of Cusa*. Rev. ed. Tr. Jerold C. Frakes. Washington, DC: Catholic University of America P, 1988.

Biblia Latina cum Glossa Ordinaria. Facsimile Reprint of the Editio Princeps: Adolph Rusch of Strassburg 1480/81. 4 vols. Turnhout: Brepols, 1992.

Biblia Sacra juxta Vulgata Clementinam [1592]. Paris: Descleé, 1947.

The Book of Concord. Ed. Theodore Tappert et al. Philadelphia: Fortress, 1959.

Bradshaw, Brendan, and Eamon Duffy, eds. *Humanism, Reform and the Reformation: The Career of Bishop John Fisher*. Cambridge UP, 1989.

Bray, Gerald, ed. *Documents of the English Reformation*. Minneapolis: Fortress, 1994.

Brigden, Susan. *London and the Reformation*. Oxford: Clarendon, 1989.

Cavendish, George. *The Life and Death of Cardinal Wolsey*. Ed. Richard S. Sylvester. EETS 243. London: Oxford UP, 1959.

Die Confutatio der Confessio Augustana. Ed. Herbert Immenkötter. CC 33. Münster: Aschendorff, 1979.

*Contemporaries of Erasmus: A Biographical Register of the Renaissance and the Re-
    formation.* Ed. P.G. Bietenholz and T.B. Deutscher. 3 vols. U of Toronto P,
    1985–87.

Chaucer, Geoffrey. *The Riverside Chaucer.* 3d ed. Ed. Larry D. Benson.
    Boston: Houghton Mifflin, 1987.

Daniell, David. *William Tyndale: A Biography.* New Haven: Yale UP, 1994. Cit-
    ed as "Daniell."

Deanesly, Margaret. *The Lollard Bible and Other Medieval Biblical Versions.*
    Cambridge UP, 1920.

Delumeau, Jean. *Rassurer et protéger: Le sentiment de sécurité dans l'Occident
    d'autrefois.* Paris: Fayard, 1989.

Duffy, Eamon. *The Stripping of the Altars: Traditional Religion in England
    c.1400–c.1580.* New Haven: Yale UP, 1992.

Duns Scoti, Joannis. *Opera Omnia.* 26 vols. 1891–95; Farnborough, Hants.:
    Gregg, 1969.

Eck, Johann. *Enchiridion locorum communium adversus Lutherum et alios hostes ec-
    clesiae (1525–1543).* Ed. Pierre Fraenkel. CC 34. Münster: Aschendorff,
    1979. Cited as "Fraenkel."

———. *Enchiridion of Commonplaces: Against Luther and Other Enemies of the
    Church.* Tr. Ford Lewis Battles. Grand Rapids, MI: Baker, 1979. Cited as
    "Battles."

Eire, Carlos M.N. *War against the Idols: The Reformation of Worship from Eras-
    mus to Calvin.* Cambridge UP, 1986.

Erasmus, Desiderius. *Enchiridion Militis Christiani: An English Version.* Ed.
    Anne M. O'Donnell SND. EETS 282. Oxford UP, 1981.

———. *Novum Instrumentum, Basel 1516.* Faksimile-Neudruck mit . . . Ein-
    leitung von Heinz Holeczek. Stuttgart: Frommann-Holzboog, 1986.

Fisher, John. *The English Works of John Fisher.* Ed. John E.B. Mayor. EETS,
    Extra Series no. 27. 1878; London: Oxford UP, 1935. Cited as "Fisher."

Foxe, John. *The Acts and Monuments.* 2d ed. Ed. George Townsend. 8 vols.
    1843–49; New York: AMS, 1965.

Friedman, Jerome. *The Most Ancient Testimony: Sixteenth-Century Christian-
    Hebraica in the Age of the Renaissance.* Athens: Ohio UP, 1983.

Frith, John. *The Work of John Frith.* Ed. N.T. Wright. Courtenay Library of
    Reformation Classics 7. Appleford, UK: Sutton Courtenay, 1978. Cited as
    "Wright."

Gleason, John B. *John Colet.* Berkeley: U of California P, 1989.

Gogan, Brian. *The Common Corps of Christendom: Ecclesiological Themes in the
    Writings of Sir Thomas More.* Studies in the History of Christian Thought
    26. Leiden: Brill, 1982.

Gregory the Great, St. *Dialogues.* Tr. Odo John Zimmerman OSB. FOTC 39.
    New York: Fathers of the Church, 1959.

Haigh, Christopher. *English Reformations: Religion, Politics, and Society under the Tudors.* Oxford: Clarendon, 1993.

Henry VIII. *Assertio septem sacramentorum.* Ed. Pierre Fraenkel. CC 43. Münster: Aschendorff, 1992.

Holborn, Hajo and Annemarie, eds. *Desiderius Erasmus Roterodamus: Ausgewählte Werke.* Munich: Beck, 1933.

Hudson, Anne, ed. *Selections from English Wycliffite Writings.* Cambridge UP, 1978. Cited as "Hudson."

Jedin, Hubert, and John Dolan, eds. *History of the Church.* 10 vols. New York: Seabury, 1980–82. Cited as "Jedin and Dolan."

Jones, G. Lloyd. *The Discovery of Hebrew in Tudor England: A Third Language.* Manchester UP, 1983.

Jungmann, Joseph A., SJ. *The Mass of the Roman Rite.* Tr. Francis A. Brunner. 2 vols. New York: Benzinger, 1951–55.

Langland, William. *Piers Plowman: The B Version.* Ed. George Kane and E. Talbot Donaldson. U of London: Athlone, 1975.

Latomus, Jacobus. *Confutationum adversus Guilielmum Tindalium libri tres.* In *Opera.* Louvain: B. Gravius, 1550. Facsimile in *Reformation* 1 (1996) Appendix. Cited as "*Confutationum* in *Opera.*"

―――. "His Three Books of Confutation Against William Tyndale." Tr. James A. Willis. *Reformation* 1 (1996) 345–73. Cited as "Tr. Willis."

Lunt, William E. *Financial Relations of the Papacy with England, 1327–1534.* Studies in Anglo-papal Relations during the Middle Ages 2. Cambridge, MA: Medieval Academy of America, 1962. Cited as "Lunt, *Papacy.*"

MacCulloch, Diarmaid. *Thomas Cranmer: A Life.* New Haven: Yale UP, 1996. Cited as "MacCulloch, *Cranmer.*"

Marc'hadour, Germain. *The Bible in the Works of St. Thomas More.* 5 vols. Nieuwkoop: De Graaf, 1969–72. Cited as "Marc'hadour, *Bible.*"

Marius, Richard. *Thomas More: A Biography.* New York: Knopf, 1984.

Markish, Shimon. *Erasmus and the Jews.* Tr. Anthony Olcott. Afterword by Arthur A. Cohen. U of Chicago P, 1986.

Marlowe, Christopher. *The Complete Works of Christopher Marlowe.* Ed. Roma Gill. Oxford: Clarendon, 1987–. Cited as "Gill."

Marshall, Peter. *The Catholic Priesthood and the English Reformation.* Oxford: Clarendon, 1994.

Milton, John. *The Riverside Milton.* Ed. Roy Flannagan. Boston: Houghton Mifflin, 1998.

Mombert, J.I., ed. *William Tyndale's Five Books of Moses Called the Pentateuch [1530].* Intro. F.F. Bruce. Carbondale: Southern Illinois UP, 1967.

More, St. Thomas. *The Correspondence of Sir Thomas More.* Ed. Elizabeth Frances Rogers. Princeton UP, 1947. Cited as "More, *Correspondence.*"

―――. *Selected Letters. St. Thomas More: Selected Letters.* Ed. Elizabeth Frances

Rogers. New Haven: Yale UP, 1961. Cited as "More, *Selected Letters.*"

Mozley, J.F. *William Tyndale.* 1937; Westport, CT: Greenwood, 1971.

Neuner, Joseph, and Jacques Dupuis, eds. *The Christian Faith in the Doctrinal Documents of the Catholic Church.* New York: Alba House, 1982. Cited as "Neuner-Dupuis." References are to paragraph number.

Oberman, Heiko Augustinus, ed. *Forerunners of the Reformation: The Shape of Late Medieval Thought.* Tr. Paul L. Nyhus. 1966; Philadelphia: Fortress, 1981. Cited as "Oberman, *Forerunners.*"

———. *The Harvest of Medieval Theology: Gabriel Biel and late Medieval Nominalism.* 1963; Durham, NC: Labyrinth Press, 1983. Cited as "Oberman, *Harvest.*"

———. *Luther: Man between God and the Devil.* Tr. Eileen Walliser-Schwarzbart. New Haven: Yale UP, 1989. Cited as "Oberman, *Luther.*"

The Oxford Companion to Classical Literature. Ed. Sir Paul Harvey. Oxford: Clarendon, 1974.

The Oxford Dictionary of Popes. Ed. J.N.D. Kelly. Oxford UP, 1986.

O'Donnell, Anne M., SND. "Cicero, Gregory the Great, and Thomas More: Three Dialogues of Comfort." In *Miscellanea Moreana: Essays for Germain Marc'hadour.* Ed. Clare M. Murphy et al. Binghamton, New York: MRTS, 1989. 169–97. Cited as "O'Donnell, 'Three Dialogues of Comfort.'"

Parsons. See Augustine, St. *Letters.*

Payne, John B. *Erasmus: His Theology of the Sacraments.* Richmond, VA: John Knox, 1970.

Peter Lombard. *Sententiae in IV Libris Distinctae.* 2 vols. Grottaferrata (Rome): Collegii S. Bonaventurae, 1971, 1981.

Roper, William. *The Lyfe of Sir Thomas Moore, knighte.* Ed. Elsie Vaughan Hitchcock. EETS, Original Series no. 197. 1935; London: Oxford UP, 1958.

Rotelle. See Augustine, St. *Sermons.*

Rubin, Miri. *Corpus Christi: The Eucharist in Late Medieval Culture.* Cambridge: UP, 1991.

Shakespeare, William. *The Norton Shakespeare.* Ed. Stephen Greenblatt et al. New York: Norton, 1997.

Smalley, Beryl. *The Study of the Bible in the Middle Ages.* Notre Dame UP, 1964.

Statutes of the Realm. Ed. A. Luders et al. London, 1810–28. 11 vols. Cited as "*Statutes.*"

Surtz, Edward, SJ. *The Works and Days of John Fisher (1469–1535).* Cambridge: Harvard UP, 1967.

Thomas, Keith. *Religion and the Decline of Magic.* London: Weidenfeld & Nicolson, 1971.

Tilley, Morris P. *A Dictionary of the Proverbs in England in the Sixteenth and*

Seventeenth Centuries. Ann Arbor: U of Michigan P, 1950.

Tudor England: An Encyclopedia. Ed. Arthur F. Kinney. New York: Garland, forthcoming.

Tyndale, William. *A briefe declaration of the sacraments*. London: R. Stoughton, 1548? STC 24445. Cited as *Sacraments*.

———. "A Critical Edition of William Tyndale's *The Obedience of a Christian Man*." STC 24446. Ed. Anne Richardson. Diss. Yale, 1976. Xerox University Microfilms 76–29,182. Cited as *Obedience*.

———. "A Critical Edition of William Tyndale's *The Parable of the Wicked Mammon*." STC 24454. Ed. John Alexander Russell Dick. Diss. Yale, 1974. Xerox University Microfilms 75-1351. Cited as *Mammon*.

———. "A Critical Edition of *An exposicion vpon the .v .vi .vii chapters of Mathew* by William Tyndale." STC 24440. Ed. Stephen J. Mayer. Diss. Yale, 1975. Xerox University Microfilms 76–13,210. Cited as *Matthew*.

———. "An Edition of William Tyndale's *Exposition of the Fyrste Epistle of Seynt Ihon*." STC 24443. Ed. Donald J. Millus. Diss. Yale, 1973. Xerox University Microfilms 74–11,618. Cited as *1 John*.

———. *A path way into the holy scripture*. London: Thomas Godfray, 1536? STC 24462. Cited as *Pathway*.

———. *The practyse of prelates*. Antwerp: J. Hoochstraten, 1530. STC 24465. Cited as *Prelates*.

Wallis, N. Hardy, ed. *The New Testament, translated by William Tyndale, 1534*. Intro. Isaac Foot. Cambridge UP, 1938.

Watkins, Oscar D. *A History of Penance: The Whole Church to A.D. 450*, Vol. 1; *The Western Church from A.D. 450 to A.D. 1215*, Vol. 2. 1920; New York: Burt Franklin, 1961.

Wicks, Jared, SJ. *Luther's Reform: Studies in Conversion and the Church*. Mainz: Philipp von Zabern, 1992. Cited as "Wicks, *Luther's Reform*."

———. "Abuses under Indictment at the Diet of Augsburg 1530." *Theological Studies* 41 (1980) 253–302. Cited as "Wicks, 'Abuses.'"

Wilkins, David. *Concilia Magnae Britanniae et Hiberniae: AD 446–1718*. 4 vols. London, 1737.

Williams, Glanmor. *The Welsh Church from Conquest to Reformation*. Rev. ed. Cardiff: U of Wales P, 1976.

Zwingli, Huldreich. *Sämtliche Werke*. Corpus Reformatorum 88–91, 94–97. Ed. Emil Egli and Georg Finsler. Vol. 1, Berlin: Schwetschke, 1905. Vol. 2–10, Leipzig: Heinsius, 1908–29.

INTRODUCTION

1. Composition

The humanist Desiderius Erasmus published for learned readers a bilingual edition of the New Testament: a corrected text of Latin facing the Greek, the latter circulating in print for the first time. The Greek NT had been printed at Alcalá in 1514, but Erasmus released his version first, at Basel in 1516, followed by revised editions in 1519, 1522, 1527, and 1535. Inspired to address a lay audience, the reformer William Tyndale resolved to make the first English translation of the Bible from the original languages. Because of strictures against the Lollards in the late 14c and the Lutherans in the early 16c, Tyndale went into self-imposed exile in the Low Countries in 1524. Using the third edition of Erasmus' Greek NT and Luther's German translation (both 1522), he published the first complete English NT in 1526 and a major revised edition in 1534. Using a Hebrew Bible from Venice (1488, 1517) or Alcalá (1522), Tyndale published his English translation of the Pentateuch in 1530 and Jonas in 1531. After his execution for heresy in 1536, his translation of Joshua through 2 Chronicles was published posthumously in 1537. While Tyndale was cut off before fulfilling his dream of translating all of Scripture, he rendered half the Hebrew Bible and all the Greek New Testament into clear and vivid English.[1]

The English bishops and king were not responsible for Tyndale's

1. Significant biographers of Tyndale include John Foxe (5.114–34), Robert Demaus (1886; Amsterdam: Gieben, 1971), J.F. Mozley, and David Daniell. Cf. Erroll F. Rhodes, "The Complutensian Polyglot (1514–1517)"; Robert G. Bratcher, "Tyndale and His Successors" in *The Oxford Companion to the Bible,* ed. Bruce M. Metzger and Michael D. Coogan (New York: Oxford UP, 1993) 601, 758–59. For knowledge of Greek and Hebrew by 16c Christians, cf. 75/5nn.

Tyndale's scriptural translations include: Matthew up to 22.12 (Cologne, 1525) STC 2823; complete NT (Worms, 1526) STC 2824; revised editions of NT (Antwerp, 1534) STC 2826, and (Antwerp, 1535) STC 2828; Pentateuch (Antwerp, 1530) STC 2350; Jonas (Antwerp, 1531) STC 2788; Joshua through 2 Chronicles in Matthew's Bible (Antwerp, 1537), STC 2066.

death outside Brussels, but they restricted the importation of his biblical, polemical, and exegetical works from the Continent. On 24 October 1526, Cuthbert Tunstall, then Bishop of London, published a list of prohibited books which included Tyndale's 1526 NT and his Introduction to Paul's Epistle to the Romans printed separately (Foxe 4.667). Ten days later, on 3 November 1526, these same books and others were banned by William Warham, Archbishop of Canterbury (Wilkins 3.706–7). Tunstall further commissioned Thomas More on 7 March 1528 to read heretical works and to dispute them in the vernacular (Ep. 160 in More, *Correspondence* 386–88). While More read Cochlaeus' Latin digest of thirty-six sermons by Luther (CWM 6/2.544 and n3), as well as Tyndale's English translation of the NT, Tyndale published the tracts of *Mammon* and *Obedience* in May and October 1528. Then in June 1529, More, the pseudonymous author of *Responsio ad Lutherum* (December 1523), published *A Dialogue Concerning Heresies,* addressed, not so much to Protestant leaders, as to Catholic layfolk.

For the reader still affectionately united to the Church of Rome, *Dialogue* has its charms: the study and arbor in Chelsea where the *dramatis persona* of More as Mentor advises the Messenger; the miracle of childbirth granted to the young couple from St. Stephen's Walbrook (Bk. 1, Ch. 10); the Vulgate version of Ps. 67.7, *qui facit vnanimes in domo* (CWM 6/1.166/28, 191/21, 253/31–32); and the extended family of the Fathers and the saints who constitute "the comen corps of crystendome" (CWM 6/1.413/30).

For the reader separated from Rome by the Reformation, *Dialogue* is hardly convincing, not the least because More does not come to grips with major Protestant issues. He devotes over half of Bk. 1 to post-apostolic miracles and more than half of Bk. 2 to veneration of saints, concerns which were marginal to his own Christocentric piety. The tolerant author of *Utopia* defends the religious prosecution of Thomas Bilney (Bk. 1, Ch. 2; Bk. 3, Ch. 2–5) and Richard Hunne (Bk. 3, Ch. 15). More does not discuss Tyndale on vernacular Scripture until Bk. 3, nor Luther on the bondage of the will until Bk. 4. On the other hand, the Messenger, who is attracted by Reformation criticisms of medieval Catholicism, anticipates the development of the Anglo-American tradition of civil liberties. He

affirms that Christ "wolde neuer haue any man compelled by force
and vyolence to byleue vpon his fayth" (CWM 6/1.32/3–4); and
"And better were yt the fauty to be quytte / than the fautles to be
punysshed" (CWM 6/1.265/26–27). More as Mentor overwhelms
the Messenger, if not the critical reader, with affable rhetoric.

It is surprising to learn that the dialogue form was used in religious controversy, not only by More, but by Augustine, the Protestant Ulrich von Hutten, and the Catholic Thomas Murner.[2] Whatever your religious persuasion, you must be wide awake when reading *Dialogue Concerning Heresies.* Little harm is done by wrongly attributing the bawdy tale of the shrine of St. Valery to More instead
of the Messenger (Bk. 2, Ch. 10). But you will be lost in the
labyrinth if you let go of the argument on faith and works in the
cross-questioning of a Lutheran sympathizer (Bk. 4, Ch. 11). In this
dialogue-within-a-dialogue More as Mentor tells the Messenger
about the interrogation of Robert Forman by church authorities
who frequently repeat the words of the accused to him (CWM
6/1.379/17–399/10). More does not return to this ecumenical form
until he writes *Dialogue of Comfort against Tribulation* in the Tower.

Meanwhile, the secular government showed alarm at Tyndale's ac-
tivities. A royal proclamation published before 6 March 1529 (Old
Style) prohibited his Genesis, Deuteronomy, and *Practice of Prelates*
(TRP no. 122). Another, of 22 June 1530, condemned Tyndale's
Mammon and *Obedience* as well as the Bible in English, French, and
German (TRP no. 129). In *Prelates* (1530), Tyndale indirectly refers to
More as the author of *Supplication of Souls* (F5, K2v) and *Dialogue
Concerning Heresies* (K2v). After the latter attacked the 1526 NT, Tyn-
dale undertook a defense of his translation and its underlying theol-
ogy of justification by faith in his terse *[A]nswere vnto sir Thomas
Mores dialoge.* On 26 January 1531, Stephen Vaughan, undercover
agent for Henry VIII in Antwerp, wrote to the king that he could
"neither get a copy of his answer to More, . . . nor ascertain whether
it is published" (LP 5, no. 65). Two months later, on 25 March 1531,
Vaughan reported some success to Cromwell: "I obtained a copy of

2. Cf. Rainer Pineas, "More and the Dialogue Form," *Thomas More and Tudor Polemics*
(Bloomington: Indiana UP, 1968) 80–92.

the third part of Tyndall's book against my Lord Chancellor's book. I
have been obliged to rewrite it; and when that is done, I will jointly
write the other part in a fair book, and send them to the King. The
three parts filled three quires of paper thoroughly written" (LP 5,
no. 153). O'Donnell believes that these "three parts" refer to Tyndale's creed (later the six gatherings of A–F), Answer to Bk. 1 and 2
(approximately the four gatherings of G–K), and Answer to Bk. 3
and 4 (approximately the seven gatherings of L–R). On 18 April
1531, Vaughan wrote again to Cromwell that he was shipping a fair
copy of part of Tyndale's *Answer to More* (LP 5, no. 201), and on 20
May 1531, Vaughan reported to Henry VIII that it was too late to
stop publication (LP 5, no. 246).

The Yale editors believe that Vaughan sent Cromwell the last third
(CWM 6/2.557), but more probably he sent the first third of *Answer*
(pp. 5–78). This opening section is striking for the clarity and force
of its arguments, so much so that Jared Wicks has aptly named it the
"Foundational Essay." Here Tyndale advances his own agenda and
does not merely respond to More's priorities, as he does in the later
two-thirds of the work. Vaughan's description of the excerpt best fits
the Foundational Essay: "It is but a third or fourth part of his whole
work, but comprehends the pith of the other parts, in which he answers every chapter of my Lord's book with the grounds he has laid
in the first part. I will also write and send the second part with all
convenient speed" (LP 5, no. 201). Vaughan's reference to "a third or
fourth part of his whole work" arguably means a percentage of the
whole, while his reference to "first" and "second" means parts in order of succession. Why would Vaughan forward Tyndale's Answer to
Bk. 3 and 4 and not the Foundational Essay? A secret agent would
be eager to convey, not fragments of shrapnel but the blueprint of
the warhead.

This pre-publication excerpt from Tyndale's *Answer* may have
prompted More to reinforce the second version of *Dialogue* with
five major additions (CWM 6/2.556–58). In Bk. 1, these include six
folio pages in defense of images (CWM 6/1.39/26–47/22), a passage
in defense of miracles (CWM 6/1.90/1–29), and some lines on Peter's recognition of Christ's sonship (CWM 6/1.143/15–29). In Bk.
4, there are three new folio pages on Gregory's defense of images

(CWM 6/1.355/28–359/33), and more than a folio page on the meaning of Jas. 2.19 (CWM 6/1.386/18–388/34). The Yale editors argue that More made these additions after reading the last third of *Answer,* especially the reference to Gregory in Answer to Bk. 4 (184/2–6). But More could have been responding to the first third, which has three sub-sections on images (57/26ff, 63/26ff, 68/6ff), and glances at miracles (e.g., 25/3). Vaughan sent the partial manuscript of *Answer* on 18 April 1531; William Rastell published the second edition of *Dialogue* in May 1531 (CWM 6/2.554); Simon Cock brought out the printed version of *Answer* about July 1531 (CWM 8/2.1081). But whether it was the last or the first third of *Answer* that influenced the second edition of *Dialogue,* the heart of Tyndale's argument beats in the Foundational Essay. The Answers to Bk. 1 through Bk. 4 contain mere capillaries.

From the time of its publication, there has been some debate about the authorship of *Answer to More.* In *An apologye made . . . to satisfye w. [sic] Tindale . . .* (1535) STC 14820, George Joye claimed that John Frith wrote *Answer* and published it in Amsterdam not Antwerp: "Frith wrote tindals answers to More for tindale / and corrected them in the prynte / and printed them to[o] at Amelsterdam . . ." (E1r-v, quoted by CWM 8/3.1234). In 1937 J.F. Mozley (200–1) reported Joye's assertion but suspended judgment. In 1964 William A. Clebsch[3] took Joye's words literally and supposed that Frith had drafted the refutations of Bk. 1–4 while Tyndale had composed the Foundational Essay. In 1973 Louis A. Schuster agreed with Clebsch's position and cited one instance where *Answer* refers uncharacteristically to Tyndale in the third person (CWM 8/3.1234n3). Richard Marius in 1984 (CWM 7.cxxiv) and Carl R. Trueman[4] in 1994 accepted as probable Clebsch's conclusion about Frith's partial authorship of *Answer.*

On the other hand, Clebsch himself noted that in *A disputation of purgatorye* (Antwerp, 1531) STC 11386.5, Frith had twice credited Tyndale with writing against More about error in the church: "Wil-

3. William A. Clebsch, *England's Earliest Protestants, 1520–1535* (New Haven: Yale UP, 1964) 81, 96–97.

4. Carl R. Trueman, *Luther's Legacy: Salvation and English Reformers, 1525–1556* (Oxford: Clarendon, 1994) 15 and n21.

liam Tyndall hath declared aboundantly in a treatise which by Goddes grace you shall shortly haue"; "a woorke that William Tyndal
hath written agaynst M. More" (Clebsch 96 and n35 citing *Whole
Works* 46, 56; modern spelling in Wright 174, 196). But in 1978 N.T.
Wright countered that "in Tyndale's *Answer* the flow of statement
and refutation proceeds as a rapid fire argument, whereas in Frith's
Purgatory the replies are far more discursive and drawn out" (Wright
11). Recalling Tyndale's rage over the several changes of "resurrection" in his 1526 NT to "life after this" in Joye's 1534 NT, Wright
added, "Joye's personal animosity against Tyndale accounts fully for
the fact that Joye may well have intended to slight him" (Wright 11).

Like Wright, O'Donnell believes that Frith did not write the last
two-thirds of *Answer to More*. First, the writer of *Answer* claims authorship of *Obedience* and of the 1526 NT. He argues against intercession by the saints in Answer to Bk. 2, Ch. 8: "I haue answered you
vn to that and manye thynges moo in the obedience and other
places" (119/12–13). He defends his English NT in Answer to Bk. 3,
Ch. 9: "For if he wold haue any wyse man to beleue that my translacion wold destroye the masse any other wyse then the latine or
greke texte / he shuld haue alleged the place and howe" (148/24–
27). Admittedly, the writer does not assert authorship of *Mammon* in
Answer to Bk. 4, Ch. 11: "And when he allegeth S. Iames / it is answered him in the mammon" (201/29–30). Perhaps he avoided the
active, "I answered him," and chose the passive, "it is answered him,"
because *Mammon* is a translation and expansion of a sermon by
Luther (148/22n).

Second, Mozley (345) claimed that Tyndale never speaks of himself in the third person. But Mozley made this observation when
commenting on a Lollard tract, *A compendious olde treatyse . . .*
(Antwerp, 1530) STC 3021, not *Answer to More*. Also, Tyndale might
refer to himself in the third person when countering a polemic
which frequently does so. In Answer to Bk. 3, Ch. 8, Tyndale simply
quotes More, "And when he sayth Tindale was confederatt with
Luther that is not trueth" (148/21–22). In twice responding to Bk. 4,
Ch. 16, the writer parodies More's language on Tyndale: "he sware
not nether was there any man that required an oth of him" (214/
1–2); "he entendeth to purge here vn to the vttermost of his power

and hopeth that deeth wyll ende and fynish his purgacion" (214/16–18). The one example cited by Schuster (CWM 8/3.1234n3), from *Answer* to Bk. 3, Ch. 13, bristles with the active verbs typical of Tyndale, "There [More] biteth / sucketh / gnaweth / towseth / and mowseth tindale" (152/3–4).

Third, where Clebsch argued that *Answer* does not quote the 1526 NT verbatim, other scholars note that Tyndale habitually makes ad hoc translations of Scripture in his independent works. Donald J. Millus (166) judges that Tyndale made a new translation for his *Exposition of the Fyrste Epistle of Seynt Ihon,* cf. Mozley 203. Stephen J. Mayer (327–29) concludes that Tyndale follows Luther's NT rather than his own in writing *An exposicion vpon the .v .vi .vii chapters of Mathew* (72/18–19n).

Frith may have culled arguments out of More's *Dialogue Concerning Heresies* for Tyndale, but he did not actually write the last two-thirds of *Answer.* It is more likely that Frith shared his knowledge of the Fathers with Tyndale, perhaps even recommending *Unio Dissidentium* (188/3, 213/22), a patristic anthology on Reformation themes. Schuster (CWM 8/3.1237n2) thought that Frith might have contributed the passage from Gregory to *Answer* (184/2n). Frith will write *A boke . . . answeringe vnto M mores lettur* (Antwerp, 1533) STC 11381, but Tyndale wrote *An answere vnto Sir Thomas Mores dialoge* (Antwerp, 1531) STC 24437.

As for *Confutation of Tyndale,* has it ever had more than a dozen readers in any generation? *Confutation* is both the longest work by More (CWM 8/3.1260) and the longest religious polemic in English (Ackroyd 299). The reformers protested it was too long, as More himself admitted in his next book, *The Apologye:* "For they fynde fyrste for a great fawte, that my writyng is ouer longe, and therfore to[o] tedyouse to rede" (CWM 9.5/7–8). More explains that *Confutation* is repetitious because he intended each chapter to stand on its own so the inquirer would "not nede to rede ouer any chapyter but one . . ." (CWM 9.10/1–2).[5] How many laymen could afford to buy the two bulky folios?

5. For comments on the repetitious style of *Confutation,* cf. C.S. Lewis, *English Literature in the Sixteenth Century Excluding Drama* (Oxford: Clarendon, 1954) 173–74; Louis L. Martz, *Thomas More: The Search for the Inner Man* (New Haven: Yale UP, 1990) 31–32.

A Catholic reader of *Confutation* will sift through bushels of sand to find a few nuggets of gold. It is inspiring to read More's prayers for his readers (CWM 8/1.142/3–9), for Tyndale (8/1.130/9–14), for Barnes (8/2.920/35), and for the reformers in general (8/1.249/4, 438/37–439/1). A Rabelaisian list of infinitives and nouns wittily mimics the polemic of reformers against papists (CWM 8/1.59/13–22). We finally arrive at the best part with Bk. 8, the last section of *Confutation* published in More's lifetime. More devotes nearly twenty folio pages of Chaucerian humor to the rout of Friar Barnes by two laywomen. The Merchant's Wife (CWM 8/2.883/28–896/27, 903/19–905/18) defends the necessity of a visible church, and the Hostess of the Bottle (CWM 8/2.896/34–903/14) rejects arbitrary salvation and damnation.

A Protestant reader of *Confutation* will discard the flints lurking in the soil. Besides offering prayers for their conversion, More curses the Lutherans (CWM 8/1.453/26–27) and Tyndale (CWM 8/1.471 /36–37). He twice objects to Tyndale's vivid diction by asking, "[Y]f all Englande lyste now to go to scole wyth Tyndale to lerne englyshe . . ." (CWM 8/1.187/26–27, cf. 8/1.212/12–13). The answer to this rhetorical question is "Yes" because of the large influence of Tyndale's biblical translations on the KJV. The worst part comes at the beginning of Bk. 5, halfway through *Confutation,* where More as hammer of heretics foretells their future, "And for heretikes as they be / the clergy dothe denounce them. And as they be well worthy, the temporaltie dothe burne them. And after the fyre of Smythfelde, hell dothe receyue them / where the wretches burne for euer" (8/2.590/3–7).

If Tyndale ever read *Confutation,* he would have been pleased by the care with which it reprints *Answer* from the Preface through the first five of his six major topics in the Foundational Essay (5/1–54/ 12; CWM 8/1.41/5 to 8/2.805/38). The Yale edition records virtually all the substantive variants between *Answer* and *Confutation,* occasionally remarking on the fidelity of More's transcription (8/3.1491, 1495, 1514). Yale might have praised *Confutation* for reproducing an entire sub-section (52/18–54/12; CWM 8/2.773/13 to 774/37) with one minor variant: "readynge in bokes" (53/24) given as "redynge of bokes" (CWM 8/2.774/16). Yale's most negative judgment targets

More's verbosity: "Without impairing Tyndale's content, More snips a few phrases from the extended passage with mock light-heartedness and makes his point quickly—a noteworthy deviation from his usual practice" (8/3.1574). As textual editor, O'Donnell here notes the few places where *Confutation* weighs a puzzling word in *Answer,* where *Confutation* adds or omits a clause, and where a theological difference prompts a variant.[6] Rather than crush *Answer to More,* the thousand pages of *Confutation* preserve the major articles of Tyndale's creed.

ii. Theology

William Tyndale's rebuttals and counterpositions to Thomas More's *Dialogue Concerning Heresies* emerge from a coherent cluster of doctrinal convictions. Tyndale argues from consistent views on major theological themes such as the church, the Bible, true teaching in the heart by the Holy Spirit, fallen humankind, God's gracious work to save his elect, and the sacramental rites by which the elect are instructed and formed. The theological commentary that accompanies this edition of Tyndale's *Answer* will draw attention to these theological positions, but the notes are unavoidably scattered and diffuse because they follow the text in its unsystematic movements of response to More. Here, we offer an ordered sketch of Tyn-

---

6. Textual problems: "profession" (30/31) > "possession" (8/1.420/24, 8/3.1596) restored to "professyon" (8/1.446/5); "kyndes" (33/7) > "kyndnes" (8/1.490/4, 8/3.1604) [*1573* agrees with More, but see the Glossary for "kynd"]; "thou reade" (36/5) > "thou reder" (8/1.542/5, 8/3.1610); "thy fall" (42/9 and n) > "thy fatte" (8/2.634/26, 8/3.1627); "refuge / to flight" (44/2) > "refuge to flyght" (8/2.675/24, not in 8/3); "wordly wisdome" (48/6 and n) > "worldly wysdome" (8/2.730/16, not in 8/3).

Clarifications: "offeringe" (29/11) > "offerynge of Crystes body and bloude" (8/1.409/30, 8/3.1594); "then thys" (29/23) > "then thys fayth that saynte Peter confessed" (8/1.417/4–5, not in 8/3); "if some" (31/13) > "If some of them (that is to wytte the trew membres of the electe chyrche)" (8/1.472/28–29, 8/3.1602).

Omissions: "when I had beleved it" (26/13–14) > (om. 8/1.282/27, not in 8/3); "and all hys werkes" (37/11) > (om. 8/1.548/21, 8/3.1610); "that the ypocritish wolues can not heare (47/27) > (om. 8/2.718/14, 727/1; restored at 8/2.728/23, 8/3.1648–49); "so that all is open" (98/6) > (om. 8/1.336/27, not in 8/3).

Emendations: "congregacion" (25/8) > "generacyon" (8/1.271/34, not in 8/3); "oure ypocrites" (41/23) > "the clergye" (8/2.613/35, 8/3.1621); "Paul and Peter" (99/12) > "Peter and Paule" (8/1.334/10, not in 8/3).

dale's thought to orient one's reading of *Answer* as an expression of Reformation thought, teaching, and argument.

Setting

Tyndale understands the history of the church in accord with a biblical pattern that has been realized once more in his own day. Scripture tells of the People of God repeatedly falling from their original devout obedience into error and corrupt worship. But a recurrent, counteractive series of events also took place. Moses and the prophets initiated reform and restored some of the people to their pristine faith and life. When later Judaism declined under the scribes, Pharisees, and high priests, then John the Baptist and Jesus himself led a small group out of the corrupt multitude. But Christianity too has degenerated into a religion of erroneously understood ceremonies, especially under the papacy (40/21–43/20).

The Reformation has resulted from God's new intervention to create a small prophetic community. Among members of a true church of elect believers, the Holy Spirit has inscribed upon docile hearts a renewed faith in Christ, love of the law of God, and insight into the true meaning of both Scripture and Christian rites and sacraments. But, alas, a further element of the biblical typology is also realized, namely, the persecution by the carnal multitude of this Little Flock of believers spiritually taught (104/29–105/10). Master Thomas More writes for this powerful majority, while Tyndale exerts himself to respond with an account of the faith that the Spirit has instilled in the Little Flock of believers.

Sources

The *Answer* that Tyndale gave to More, strange to say, draws upon two sources of doctrinal truth. This of course is not the duality of Scripture and ecclesial tradition, for Scripture has no need of supplemental oral revelations that the church later certifies. Scripture in fact suffices for instruction on what Christians are to believe and do (24/25–30). It gives a full account of the meaning of rites and sacraments in their relation to Jesus and his saving death for humankind. Scripture has been validated by miracles occurring in the early Christian centuries to confirm the true books of God's revelation.

But still Tyndale is a "two-source" theologian because of the importance he also attributes to the Holy Spirit's work in the heart to inscribe God's law at the center of the person. In fact, he formulates the key to understanding the Scripture as twofold. Biblical interpretation must proceed first from the doctrine of justification by faith as Paul formulated this at the center of Scripture. Secondly, true comprehension of Scripture also needs the Holy Spirit's interior writing of God's truth upon the hearts of docile believers (170/13–21). Public instruction is to rest on the biblical texts in their original meaning, but the individual needs the Spirit's internal guidance to attain faith and godly living in love (54/1–55/5).

The unreformed church must be confronted and overcome because of the hierarchy's opposition to Scripture, both to its teachings and to its diffusion among the people. Accurate rendering into the vernacular, as in Tyndale's English New Testament, improves on the misleading language that has been obscuring the truth. *Answer,* however, has much more to say about biblically grounded doctrine beyond its defense of the new translation (10/1–23/11).

God's Salvation Given to Fallen Humankind

Thomas More charged the Reformation with error in its doctrine of the bondage of the will. Tyndale responds that while human beings have the power of voluntary action as a good gift from the Creator, sad to say, "the God of this world hath blinded the wittes of the vnbeleuers" (2 Cor. 4.4, 191/24–25). This blindness is the cause of all evil (212/5), for by it men and women find themselves inevitably caught in error and sin. What More proposes about free choice cannot apply to our fallen race.

The way out of the human predicament is the grace of God that brings light to our "wittes" and judgment. God comes in this way to his elect out of a love that precedes any good effort on their part. A person's will cannot act to predispose itself for God's grace or to collaborate with it. An outward ministry of the true Word does work in tandem with God's interior enlightenment, but it is the latter that impresses upon the heart a new-found appreciation for the divine law. Faith then is new sight given to those who were blind. God's Spirit writes upon the heart so that it perceives the sweetness of

God's law, from which springs a heartfelt consent (175/10–26). The "wit" comes before the will and in salvation this means that a "feeling faith" in God, given by God, precedes one's assent to God's law.

Interior agreement with the law is, however, central to justification in Tyndale's account. Faith lays hold of God's mercy and forgiveness given because of Christ, but faith's full form includes explicit assent to God's law as good. Here Tyndale has moved beyond Luther regarding a key element of justification. Assent to the law is essential to conversion and the reversal of sin's blindness. God thus creates in the elect a good will, consequent upon faith, and from it a new practice buds forth. Assent to the law gives rise spontaneously to good deeds of loving service. These deeds, however, are not perfect and the righteous person is *simul iustus et peccator,* for the norm of one's action is the loving dedication of Jesus Christ, beside which all love and works are radically deficient (174/22–25, 209/2–6).

God's elect are taught interiorly to look for salvation solely by the grace of Christ. Their lives then unfold under the rod of God's tribulation, so as to overcome the evil remaining in them. Their faith is not held in peaceful possession but is ever tried and tempted, as they are schooled in the knowledge of their own infirmity. For a while sin and error may even get the upper hand, but this is a step toward purging out pride and self-reliance. God is present in these trials to restore and heal (32/11–33/29).

Tyndale is eloquent on the new freedom from calculating self-regard that marks the life of the elect. Right faith instilled by the Holy Spirit issues in right love, a love that treats the neighbor without thought of gain and acts with a spark of the same gratuitous love God has shed forth upon oneself. Serving God in the Spirit, the elect see Christ in everyone and serve him in everyone with love and gratitude (107/2–14).

Sacraments and Worship

In the biblical pattern of decline and prophetic reform, the fall of God's people was especially evident in their life of ritual worship. What God instituted for the schooling of Israel, such as circumcision, the paschal lamb, the sabbath, and the Temple sacrifices, degenerated into good works to win divine favor (63/27–68/5). In Christianity an analogous development took place, as Christians lost the signification of their sacraments.

Tyndale underscores the original didactic and inspirational purpose of sacraments. They do not cause grace, as medieval theology and the Council of Trent hold, but instead they represent significations central to living in the light of faith. Baptism shows forth the death and new life of repentance from sin, while the Lord's Supper signifies that Christ's body was broken and his blood shed for our sins (96/23–26, 150/10–17).

Sacraments are not specially qualified good works but instead instructional reminders about God's saving work in Christ and about the right pattern of living in the sphere of this salvation. It is not enough, however, to have the right theology of sacraments. Here, too, the Holy Spirit must inscribe faith and love in the heart, and then one will approach sacraments rightly (54/13–29).

Regarding the Lord's Supper, Tyndale's *Answer* voices the Reformation rejection of eucharistic sacrifice offered by the priest to God as a renewal of Christ's passion. The movement of the Supper is instead toward the people. But Tyndale has also accepted the Zwinglian critique of a giving of the body and blood of Christ for true eating and drinking by believers. Faith is misplaced if directed to a miraculous presence of Christ in and with the bread and wine. At the Supper one should eat and drink in the Spirit, and this means to hearken to the signification of the broken bread and shared cup, as they represent Christ's death. In his death for sinners, faith finds its true object (150/9–30, 179/12–180/7).

Tyndale's *Answer* offers in brief the Reformation arguments against Catholic claims for other sacraments such as confirmation (71/1–73/7), penance (172/10–173/24), marriage (176/17–177/4), and ordination (177/5–13). But the treatment of the role of images in worship and the invocation of the saints is more extensive. Images of Christ, his mother, and the other saints should bring the believer to loving recollection of God's saving mercy, his promises, and his call to obedient living. An image is not a way to gain protection against bodily harm, and giving honor to it is not a good work that will be rewarded. Images are creatures at a lower level than human beings and so they should serve the human spirit (59/7–16).

The saints loom large in the More-Tyndale dispute. Tyndale proposes limiting their role in Christian life and prayer. There is no biblical word that justifies invoking their intercession, no matter how hard More may strain to find textual openings to such prayer. But the saints, for Tyndale, can serve as models of faith in God even unto martyrdom, of heroic love of others, and of patience in suffering. Images that remind us of them in this sense can be of service (59/3–16). Along with Mary and the saints, believers are being schooled under God's hand in faith and life (185/8–11).

But these sacramental and devotional practices have under the papacy been vitiated by misconceptions that leave believers bereft of the true meaning of rites and ceremonies. Here reform has a primary target.

The Church

The term "church" can stand for the great multitude of all those professing Christianity. But this group can be divided into the carnal multitude and the Little Flock of the elect. The latter then are "the church" in the strict sense, being the congregation of those who trust in God's promises and assent interiorly to his law. Members of the right church of the elect have repented because the Holy Spirit has inscribed faith and the law upon their hearts. Their faith is not belief about past history or submission to a present authority but "feeling faith" by which they spy out God's true word and the voice of their shepherd (47/6–22).

In the church of the elect, the significations of rites are taught and God's law is affirmed as good. But the elect, once they are instructed in true piety by the Holy Spirit, have to face a hostile adversary. The carnal multitude is always a persecutor, as it defends its traditions, meritorious works, and image-worship. From Tyndale's vantage point the truly Christian people have been oppressed by the papal hierarchy for eight hundred years. The carnal multitude has institutionalized itself in a structure of power claiming to be normative for the church. The New Testament had foreseen the rise of this "Antichrist," that is, a vicious opponent of the elect (100/6–104/29).

This then is William Tyndale's understanding of the ecclesial situation in which he writes his *Answer to More*. His adversary's *Dialogue* had in fact made only brief mention of the papacy, but Tyndale saw behind More's accusations and arguments an errant and obdurate enemy of biblical teaching and authentic faith.

III. Principal Contents

We offer here an initial guide to reading in the form of a brief resumé of the main topics of argument that Tyndale developed in *Answer*. The detailed commentary on the text contains further content-analyses of the sections, which the reader can identify within the Foundational Essay and in each of the four books of Tyndale's *Answer*.

Tyndale's preface first urges the reader to exercise a discerning judgment in virtue of the Holy Spirit's empowerment promised in John 16.8 and 1 Cor. 2.15 (5/7–29, also 8/19–28). Second, examples are given of such judgment, and of the lack of it, regarding the true intent of laws of God (5/29–6/14 and 7/15–34) and human, ecclesiastical laws (6/15–7/14 and 7/34–8/19). A third section anticipates the main topics of *Answer* by briefly listing the opposing views on the church and the authority of its hierarchy, exhorting the reader to exercise judgment on certain Catholic sacraments and devotional practices, and referring to eight hundred years of error and self-aggrandizement by the higher clergy (8/29–9/17). The preface concludes with an admonition that such a reign of hypocrisy calls for everyone to awaken and exercise personal judgment "with his awne yies" before it is too late (9/17–31).

Answer begins with a foundational treatise before responding to particular arguments advanced in each of the four books of More's *Dialogue*. A first section (10/1–23/11) turns back the charge that Tyndale has insinuated with "mischevouse minde" (13/13–14) a set of heresies by his choice of English words for crucial terms in the translated New Testament. The next section (23/12–28/9) sets forth two essential aspects of the relationship between the word of God and the congregation of believers. The preached gospel is prior in time and nature to the believing congregation. Furthermore, "euery thinge necessarie vn to oure soules health" (24/25–26) was set down in Scripture so as to render superfluous any teaching or practice alleged to have come from Christ's apostles solely by oral transmission. A third foundational section (28/10–37/32) explains how the elect of God are simultaneously sinners and repentant, and as well erring and firm in faith, during their lives of adversity, temptation, and ongoing struggle. Fourth (38/1–47/5), Tyndale argues that the pope and his prelates are not "the right church." The fifth section (47/6–55/5) explains how the elect perceive the word addressed to them and accept it, not with "faythlesse fayth made by the persuasyon of man" (53/11–12), but with a "feeling faith" about what is written in their hearts. The sixth foundational section (55/6–78/13) is Tyndale's account, with abundant examples, of what is right and wrong in the worship of God and practice of piety, leading to the conclusion that error about "ceremonies" is rampant and cries out for reform.

Tyndale answers Book 1 of More's *Dialogue* in three steps. A long first section (79/3–100/5) relates numerous arguments made by More and refutes each with short counterarguments. *Answer* first dismantles More's defense of the cult of the saints, treating miracles occurring at saints' shrines (83/13–84/3, 87/10–15, 89/6–91/28) and the shrines themselves as special places of worship (84/4–32, 86/1–88/21). Then (92/2), the refutation shifts to two principles with which More sustained the rightfulness of venerating saints. *Answer* excludes any power vested in the church's hierarchy to interpret inerrantly what Scripture and tradition imply for Christian worship (92/2–94/5). Tyndale rejects unwritten traditions alleged to come from the apostles, which would justify beliefs and practices not mandated by Scripture (94/28–97/8, 98/5–100/5). A second section (100/6–104/29) argues from the New Testament that the papal hierarchy is in fact the foreseen Antichrist. Third (104/29–109/5), Tyndale describes the profound enmity between the carnal multitude in the church and the "small flocke of them that be electe and chosen" (105/7).

Tyndale's response to Book 2 of More's *Dialogue* breaks down into some fifty-five rebuttals of particular arguments advanced by More. Many are brief, because they restate points already developed in *Answer*. The main issues are, first, the contrast between the church of the multitude, which is no sound guide to Scripture, and the church of the elect, which God instructs in true spiritual worship (e.g.,

111/3–113/34, 121/14–122/10, 124/6–22), and, second, the role of the saints in prayer, about which Tyndale concludes, "I may haue no trust therfore in the saintes" (116/19–20). In warding off More's arguments in favor of prayer to the saints, *Answer* calls into question whether any of the departed are living and attending to our needs during the interval between their death and the final resurrection (117/15–118/8). More's appeal to miracles allegedly certifying the saints gives rise to an extensive treatment of the true function of miracles in the Christian dispensation (127/3–131/21).

Answer's response to Book 3 of *Dialogue* moves through four major sections. First (133/3–145/33), Tyndale counters ten points made by More concerning church teaching as an authoritative source of doctrine in addition to Scripture. Tyndale concedes that a believer does begin with a global adherence to the authority that certifies the biblical books (136/25–31). But further study sows suspicion of the hierarchy when it diverges from Scripture (136/32–137/14). Furthermore, Tyndale finds key texts of Scripture witnessing to the Holy Spirit writing the law of God directly upon the believing heart (137/15–28). In response to More's claim that the will can move the wit (i.e., the intellect) to accept Scripture and tradition, Tyndale asserts that the Holy Spirit speaking through Scripture alone moves the will to accept God's saving love (140/27–141/7). A second section (146/1–151/30) counters numerous assertions found in Bk. 3, Ch. 2–12, especially about the examination of accused heretics. Third (152/2–167/10), Tyndale argues against the obligation of clerical celibacy. The final section (167/12–170/21) attacks the hierarchy's measures to suppress a vernacular Bible.

In response to Book 4 of *Dialogue,* Tyndale begins with a series of rapid counterarguments, some fifty-five in all, to More's syllabus of the errors held by Luther or Tyndale (171/22–191/9). Then the issue of God's influence on the human will in sin occasions an account of the will's functioning in both evil and good (191/9–193/31) and of the steps by which God mercifully brings a person to faith, repentance, love of the law, and good works beneficial to one's neighbor (195/21–207/26). Finally, there follows a set of thrust-and-parry exchanges in which Tyndale counters further accusations advanced by More (207/27–215/19).

Bibliographical Descriptions

Answer to More, STC 24437

[Hand] An answere vnto Sir Thomas Mores |[1] dialoge made by Vvillyam Tindale. | ¶ First he declareth what the church is / and | geveth a reason of certayne wordes which | Master More rebuketh in the transla= | cion of the newe Testament. [Hand] | ¶ After that he answereth particularlye vn | to everye chaptre which semeth to haue | anye apperaunce of truth thorow | all his .iiij. bokes. | [Hand] Awake thou that sle= | pest and stonde vpp | from deeth / and | Christ shall | geue the | light E | phesi= | ans. | v.

Colophon: None

Collation: Octavo. A–R8, S4

Signatures: The first five leaves of each gathering are signed except the following: A1 (title-page), D5, H4, K5, N5, O5, R4, S4; O3 is missigned O5. Arabic numbers are used except for C ij, C iij, E iij, H iij, I iij.

Foliation: 140 leaves numbered Fo(l). ij. to C.xxxiij. recto only. Exceptions are Fo. 14 and Foli. xx. Title-page (Fol. 1) and Table of Contents (Fol. 134–39) lack folio numbers.

Contents: Title-page (A1), Preface (A1v–A4v), Foundational Essay (A5r–F8r), Answer to Book 1 (G1r–I3v), Answer to Book 2 (I4r–L2r), Answer to Book 3 (L2v–O1v), Answer to Book 4 (O2r–R5v), Table of Contents (R6–S3v), blank (S4r–v).

Running-titles:
Wi(y)llyam Tindale (A1v, A2v, A3v, A4v)
To the reader (A2r, A3r, A4r)
What(e) the church is (A5r–v, A6r–v, B5r–v; B6v–C5v [verso only])
Why he vsed thys worde congregacion (A7r)
Why he vsed congregacyon (A7v)
In translatinge the new T(t)estament (A8r, B1r, B2r, B3r)
Why he vsed this worde elder (A8v); . . . vseth (B1v)

---

1. The end of a line of print or handwriting is indicated by a vertical line (|).

Why he vseth this worde loue (B2v)
Why fauoure and not grace (B3v)
Why he vsed knowlege and not confession (B4r–v)
Whether the apostles left what vnwriten (B6r, B7r)
And whether the church can erre (B8r)
And whether it maye erre (C1r–C6r) (recto only)
Whether the pope and his secte (C6v–C7v, D1v–D8v) (verso only)
Be christes church or not (C7r, C8r); . . . or no (C8v)
Be the church of god or no (D1r–E1r) (recto only)
Of worshuppinge (E1v, E2r–v, E3r, E4r–v, E5r–v)
Of pilgrimages (E6r–v, E7r)
Of S(s)acramentes and ceremoni(y)es (E7v–F4v) (recto and verso)
The cere(i)moni(y)es of the masse (F5r–v, F6r–v, F7r–v, F8r)
An answere vnto (G1v–H4v, I3v–R5v) (verso only)
Master Mores first boke (G2r–H5r) (recto only)
A sure token that (H5v–I2v) (verso only)
The pope is Antichrist (H6r–I3r) (recto only)
Master Mores second(e) boke (I5r–K4r, K6r–L2r) (recto only)
Master Mores seconde (K5r)
Master Mores thirde boke (L3r–O1r) (recto only)
Master Mores fourth boke (O2r, O5r–Q2r, Q5r–R5r) (recto only)
M. Mores fourth boke (O3r–4r, Q3r–4r) (recto only)
The table of the boke (R6r)
The T(t)able (R6v–S3v) (verso only)
Of the boke (R7r–S3r) (recto only)

Editorial Comments on STC 24437: The title-page is no. 3988 in
Nijhoff and Kronenberg.[2] Thirty-six lines per page, seven ornamental capitals (A1v, A5, E1v, G1, I4, L2v, O2), running-titles, text and
sidenotes all in 68 textura, catchwords except before the beginning
of major divisions (A4v, C1v, F8, I3v, R5v, S3v). There is no run-
ning-title on E3v, F8v, G1, I4. In the preceding list of running-titles,
O'Donnell has included the variants in parentheses and has silently
corrected the following errors: wheter (C3), ceremonys (F2), cer-
monies (F3v), Mastes (G7), angenst (G7v), answeere (H1v and I7v),

2. Wouter Nijhoff and M.E. Kronenberg, *Nederlandsche Bibliographie van 1500 tot 1540,* 3
vols. plus index (The Hague: M. Nijhoff, 1923–71) no. 3988 in Vol. 2, 1940.

his (I1), More (I6). In the running-titles, all initial "w"s have been capitalized; "Vw" has been normalized as "W"; all final periods have been removed.

There are only four extant copies of STC 24437. A2–4 were collated against a reproduction of A1.

A1, Folger Shakespeare Library, bound with Tyndale's *The practyse of Prelates,* STC 24465. The title-pages of *Prelates* and *Answer* each contain the signature "Iohan bale." R8r–v is missing and has been supplied by a xerox from the British Library. There are marginalia written in secretary hand.

A2, British Library, C.37–a.26.

A3, Cambridge University Library, Syn.8.53.43, used by Henry Walter for the Parker Society edition. This copy is bound with John Frith's *A disputacion of purgatorye,* STC 11386.5.

A4, Trinity College Library, Dublin, FF.mm.32. As in Cambridge, this copy is bound with John Frith's *A disputacion of purgatorye,* STC 11386.5. A1–8, F4–5, N1–8 are missing. The outer margins have been trimmed, cutting away portions of notes in secretary hand.

The error "beius" for "eius" (A8, 7 lines from bottom), which occurs in Folger and Cambridge, is corrected in London; gathering A is missing in Dublin. Sidenote 2 on D6 reads right to left in Folger and London, but is corrected in Cambridge and Dublin. D7v is erroneously reprinted without sidenotes on F8v in Folger and London; F8v is blank in Cambridge. In Dublin a blank page is pasted on F8v, but it can be partially lifted to reveal D7v. In Folger the "u" in "must" (Q4, line 14) has slipped down to the next line (which is half blank), but is firmly in place in London, Cambridge and Dublin. A blank (S4r–v) is missing in Folger and London, but is present in Cambridge and Dublin.

Whole Works

The Folger distinguishes between two issues: "Folger 24435.8," in which the date on the title-page is printed as "1572" but changed by hand to "1573"; "Folger 24436," in which the date on the title-page is printed as "1573." The revised STC lists all copies as "24436 . . .

1573 (1572)" and notes, "Several copies . . . have the gen. tp dated 1572 and altered in ink to 1573."

Whole Works, Folger 24435.8

Architectural border, McKerrow and Ferguson, no. 76.[3] Within a frame (251 mm x 143 mm) enclosing a compartment (121 mm x 65 mm): ¶ THE WHOLE | workes of W. Tyndall, Iohn | Frith, and Doct. Barnes, three | worthy Martyrs, and principall | teachers of this Churche of England, | collected and compiled in one Tome to= | gither, beyng before scattered, & now in | Print here exhibit-ed to the Church. | To the prayse of God, and | profite of all good Chri= | stian Readers. | [rule] | Mortui resurgent. | [rule] | AT LONDON | Printed by Iohn Daye, | and are to be sold at his shop | vnder Aldersgate. | An. 1572. | [rule] | ¶ Cum gratia & Priuilegio | Regiae Maiestatis. Lines 1–2, 14–17 and 20 are in roman type; lines 3–11 are in textura; lines 12–13, 18–19 are in italic.

Title of Answer to More (Hh2, p. 247): [Leaf] An aunswere vnto Syr Thomas Mores | Dialogue, made by William Tyndall. 1530. | [Hand] First he declareth what the Church is, and geueth a rea= | son of certaine wordes which Master More rebuketh in the | trans-lation of the new Testament. | ¶ After that he aunswereth particular-ly vnto euery Chapter | which semeth to haue any appearaunce of truth | thorough all his foure bookes. | ¶ Awake thou that slepest and stand vp from death, and Christ shall | geue the light. Eph-esians. 5. Lines 1–2, 9–10 are in roman type; lines 3–8 are in textura; "Master More" in line 4 is in roman.

Colophon for Works of Tyndale (GG2, p. 495): [Leaf] Imprinted at London by Iohn Daye, | dwellyng ouer Aldersgate. | An. 1572. | ¶ Cum gratia & Priuilegio Regiae Maiestatis. [Tailpiece with medal-lion bearing John Day's initials] Lines 1–3 are in italic type; line 4 is in roman.

Colophon for Whole Works: (RRr4, p. 379): AT LONDON | Printed by Iohn Daye, and are to bee sold | at hys shop vnder

---

3. R.B. McKerrow, and F.S. Ferguson, *Title-page Borders used in England & Scotland 1485–1640,* Bibliographical Society, Illustrated Monographs, no. 21 (London: Oxford UP, 1932 [for 1931]) 79, 81.

Aldersgate. | An. 1572. | ¶ Cum gratia & Priuilegio Regiae Maiestatis. | [rule] Lines 1 and 5 are in italic type; lines 2 and 4 in roman.

Collation for Whole Works: Folio. A–Y4, Aa–Yy6, AA–EE6, FF–GG4, HH–XX6, YY4, *AAa4*, AAa–QQq6, RRr4. Three leaves (probably blanks) are lacking: B4, HH1, AAa1; CC3 is a cancel.

Collation for Answer to More: Folio. Hh2r–Pp6r, pp. 247–339

Signatures for Answer to More: First five leaves of six are signed; Kk3 missigned K3; HH4v missigned Hh5.

Contents for Works of Tyndale: Title-page (A1r, p. i), Table of Contents (A1v, p. ii), Preface (A2r, p. iii to A3v, p. vi), Life (A4r, p. vii to B3r, p. xiii), Protestation on Resurrection of the Body (B4v, p. xiv), Biblical Prefaces (C1r, p. 1 to K2r, p. 59), *Mammon* (K2r, p. 59 to O4v, p. 96), *Obedience* (P1r, p. 97 to Bb6r, p. 183), *Exposition of Matthew* (Bb6v, p. 184 to Hh2r, p. 247), *Answer to More* (Hh2r, p. 247 to Pp6, p. 339), *Prelates* (Pp6v, p. 340 to Tt1r, p. 377), *Pathway* (Tt1r, p. 377 to Tt5v, p. 386), *Exposition of 1 John* (Tt6r, p. 387 to AA3r, p. 429), *Tracy* (AA3r, p. 429 to AA6r, p. 435), *Sacraments* (AA6v, p. 436 to CC2v, p. 452), first Letter to Frith (CC3r–v, pp. 453 [corrected] to p. 454), second Letter to Frith (CC4r–v, pp. 455–56), [George Joye's] *Supper of the Lord* (CC5r, p. 457 to EE3v, p. 478), Index (EE4r, p. 479 to GG2r, p. 495), blank (GG2v, p. 496).

Contents for Answer to More: Preface (Hh2r–Hh3r, pp. 247–49), Foundational Essay (HH3r–Kk6r, pp. 249–79), Answer to Book 1 (Kk6r–Mm1r, pp. 279–93), Answer to Book 2 (Mm1r–Mm5v, pp. 293–302), Answer to Book 3 (Mm5v–Oo2r, pp. 302–19), Answer to Book 4 (Oo2r–Pp6r, pp. 319–39).

Running-titles for Answer to More:
Preface to the Reader. (Hh2r–v, pp. 247–48)
What the church is. (Hh3r, Hh6r; pp. 249, 255)
Of the worde congregation. (Hh3v, p. 250)
Of this worde Elder. (Hh4r–v, pp. 251–52)
Of this word loue. (Hh5r, p. 253)
Knowledge and not confession. (Hh5v, p. 254)

Of thinges written. (Hh6v, p. 256)

Whether the Church can erre. (Ii1r, p. 257)

All men sinne, and all flesh doth erre. (Ii1v, p. 258)

Faith is assaulted. (Ii2r, p. 259)

The order of our election. (Ii2v, p. 260)

What the Church is, and whether it may erre. (Ii3r, p. 261)

Whether the Pope and his secte (Ii3v, Ii4v, Ii5v, Ii6v; pp. 262, 264, 266, 268)

be Christes Church or not. (Ii4r, Ii6r; pp. 263, 267)

be the Church of God or no. (Ii5r, p. 265)

Of worshippi(y)ng. (Kk1r–v, Kk2r; pp. 269–71)

Of worshippyng, and Pilgrimages. (Kk2v, p. 272)

Of Sacramentes and Ceremonies. (Kk3r–v, Kk4r–v; pp. 273–76)

The ceremonies of the Masse. (Kk5r–v, pp. 277–78)

An answere vnto M. Mores first booke. (Kk6r–v, Ll2r–v; pp. 279–80) 283–84

An aunswere vnto maister Mores first booke. (Ll1r–v, pp. 281–82)

maister Mores first booke. (Ll3r, Ll4r; pp. 285, 287)

An aunswere vnto (Ll3v, Ll4v; pp. 286, 288)

A sure token that the Pope is Antichrist. (Ll5r–v, Ll6r–v; pp. 289–92)

An answere vnto M. Mores second booke. (Mm1r–v, Mm3r–v, Mm4r–v, pp. 293–94, 297–300)

An aunswere vnto M. Mores ij. booke. (Mm2r–v, Mm5r–v, pp. 295–96, 301–2)

An answere vnto M. Mores third booke. (Mm6r–v, Nn2r–v, Nn5r–v, Oo1r–v; pp. 303–4, 307–8, 313–14, 317–18)

An aunswere vnto M. Mores iij. booke. (Nn1r–v, Nn3r–v, Nn4r–v, Nn5r–v, Nn6r–v; pp. 305–6, 309–12, 315–16)

An aunswere vnto M. Mores iiij. booke. (Oo2r–v, Oo5r–v, Pp1r–v, Pp3r–v, Pp4r–v, Pp6r; pp. 319–20, 325–26, 329–30, 333–36, 339)

An answere vnto M. Mores fourth booke. (Oo3r–v, Oo4r–v, Oo6r–v, Pp2r–v, Pp5r–v, pp. 321–24, 327–28, 331, 332 [corrected], 337 [corrected], 338)

Copy 1: The title-page is inscribed in ink, "D. Basilius fyldyngg ex dono I. Foxi | 16. Ianuarij. 1573." [period after date]. The Folger card catalogue lists as "Feilding family library copy." At the bottom of the title-page is added, "Sine me nihil potestis facere | W^t out me ye can doo nothyng | Ioan. 15." The pages have been trimmed.

Copy 2: The Folger card catalogue lists as "Marshall Clifford Lefferts copy." There is a slip cancel on RRr4v.

Whole Works, Folger 24436

Copy 1: Signature "William Laud: /" is written on the title-page for *The Workes of . . . Iohn Frith* (GG3r, p. 1). The second inscription is: "The scarce Portrait inserted is from 'Holland's Heroologia' [sic]. A copy on a | reduced scale of this head is prefixed to 'Anderson's Annals of the English Bible'."[4] This portrait has been pasted on the page facing the title-page.

Copy 2: On the title-page a name at the top right has been heavily crossed out; the central compartment and the printer's motto have been tinted ochre; the title-page has been repaired. Many topics relevant to the political situation in the mid 17c have been added to the indices, e.g.: "Kings not to be obey'd against Conscience" (EE4r, p. 479); "Bps. should be liberal" (YY3, p. 173); and "Ministers should be no Lords" (RRr4r, p. 379). The last page before the final index is signed: "376 | 1649 | J. Poole" and "J. Nevill Poole" (RRr2v, p. 376).

Copy 3: John T. Beer, a previous owner, made the painting on the fore-edge similar to the engraving of the martyrdom of Tyndale (A4r, p. vii). An extra leaf before the title-page is inscribed in red ink: "Rhod Gwylim Alaw | iw Nai | Rhinallt Navalaw ap Ioan Pughe | 1853 | [arabesque]". Another page is stamped "IOAN AP RUW / FEDDY G[?]" (A3v, p. vi). This owner added in red ink "Tyndall was a Welshman" next to "that we cal Iohn, the Welshman call Euan" (C3, p. 5). Another hand has written in brown ink: "Alphabet | Libri | Lexe" (PPp5v, p. 358).

---

4. Henry Holland, *Herωologia Anglica* (Arnhem: J. Jansson, 1620) STC 13582. For a discussion of this collection of portraits of the Reformers, see Arthur M. Hind, *Engraving in England in the Sixteenth & Seventeenth Centuries,* Part II, The Reign of James I (Cambridge UP, 1955) 145ff. See also Christopher Anderson, *Annals of the English Bible* (London: J. Pickering, 1845). Volume I is devoted to Tyndale. According to a review of Lewis Lupton, *Tyndale: Translator* and *Tyndale: The Martyr* (London: The Olive Tree, 1986 and 1987), "[T]he commonly accepted likeness of Tyndale is most probably a mis-labelled portrait of John Knox"; Donald Dean Smeeton, *Moreana* 97 (March 1988) 172.

Editorial Comments on Folger 24435.8 *and* Folger 24436: There are two series of paginations, one for works of Tyndale and another for works of Frith and Barnes. *Answer to More* is found on pp. 247–339 of works of Tyndale; p. 332 is misnumbered 337 and vice versa. There are seventy-two lines per column in preface, sixty-two lines in main text, and two columns per page throughout. Main text is in 72 textura; prologue and sidenotes are in 63 textura.[5] Running-titles, Latin quotations and some proper names are in italic. A few Greek words are given in Greek letters. Chapter and section headings, most proper names, biblical references in sidenotes (but not in text), and quotations from More's *Dialogue Concerning Heresies* are in roman. There are three large engravings: martyrdom of Tyndale (A4r, p. vii), martyrdom of Barnes and two companions (★AAa1★v, p. 178), and allegorical Judgement weighing Verbum Dei against papal decretals (RRr4v, p. 380). Within *Answer to More,* there are large ornamental capitals introducing: Preface (Hh2r, p. 247), Foundational Essay (Hh3r, p. 249), Answer to Book 1 (Kk6r, p. 279), Answer to Book 2 (Mm1r, p. 293), Answer to Book 3 (Mm6r, p. 303), Answer to Book 4 (Oo2r, p. 319), and an arabesque tailpiece (Pp6r, p. 339). Catchwords are added to second columns only.

Editorial Comments on Folger 24435.8: There are two copies, each of which has been collated against *Answer to More,* STC 24437. Copy 1 has "c" in "ceremonie," but "c" is missing in Copy 2 (Hh6v, p. 256, column 2, 14 lines from the bottom). Copy 1 has handwritten notes for adding "r" to "hauest" and striking final "l" from "vntill" (Ii2v, p. 260, column 1, 9 lines from the bottom). Copy 2 prints "haruest, vntil".

Editorial Comments on Folger 24436: The library contains three copies, each of which has been collated against the two copies of Folger 24435.8 in the twenty-some places where the latter contains errors. The three copies of Folger 24436 give the "c" in "ceremonie" (Hh6v, p. 256, column 2, 14 lines from the bottom) as in Folger 24435.8, Copy 1. They print the corrected "haruest, vntil"

---

5. The type sizes are based on the examples given in F.S. Isaac, *English and Scottish Printing Types, 1501–35, 1508–41; 1535–58, 1552–58;* Bibliographical Society no. 2, 3 (Oxford UP, 1930, 1932).

(Ii2v, p. 260, column 1, 9 lines from the bottom) as in Folger 24435.8, Copy 2. Otherwise, they repeat the errors of Folger 24435.8.

v. Editorial Procedures

This edition of the *1531* edition of *Answer to More* is based on the copy in the Folger Shakespeare Library, Washington, DC in consultation with the other surviving copies: London, Cambridge, and Dublin. Signature marks enclosed in square brackets have been inserted into the text of this edition to indicate the beginning of a new page in the original printed text. Abbreviations have been expanded except for the ampersand (&). Characteristic Tyndalian spellings are preserved, and the emendations of *1573* noted: "bedged" (36/32 etc.) for "begged," "mischeue" (44/3 etc.) for "mischief," and "wordlie" (7/25 etc.) for "worldly."

A marked feature of *1531* is its habit of joining the modifier to a modified word: noun plus noun, e.g., "imageseruice" (63/26 etc.); noun plus gerund, e.g., "trucebreakynge" (104/5); auxiliary plus verb, e.g., "becalled" (31/17). Because this practise of joining related words seems deliberate, other compounds are left unchanged: adjective plus noun, e.g., "preciousstones" (61/12); article plus noun, e.g., "awaight" (35/1); copulative plus adjective, e.g., "bewise" (17/31); verb plus adverb: "vnseneto" (78/4); article plus adjective: "agreate" (68/24 etc.); adjective plus pronoun: "etherother" (171/23); even verb plus preposition: "bewith out" (165/21 etc.). Following the preference of *1531* for joining compounds, this edition silently links parts which run on to the next line as if a hyphen were given. In a few cases, compound words are separated to remove a stumbling-block, e.g.: "goodwin sandes" (78/10), "popysh eyes" (197/5), "put to" (45/15), "Teynterden steple" (77/S1 etc.), "We be" (117/32). These latter emendations are recorded.

Because *1531* frequently treats the space at the end of the line as a marker, this edition supplies the missing punctuation, especially a virgule in a series (11/17 etc.), and records the emendations. It regularizes final periods by keeping or adding them after a complete sentence to headings, sidenotes, and entries in the "The table of the boke." It adds a period after numbers in the sidenotes and silently removes the occasional period before an abbreviation, e.g.: ".M." for "Master", ".S." for "Saint". Twice, it changes the exclamation point to the anachronistic question mark to alert readers to the different modality; the emendations are recorded (17/13, 140/29). "Vv" is changed to "W" throughout *1531* (except in the bibliographical description of the title-page), and the first letter of the sidenotes is capitalized. Roman numbers are regularized: "j" is given for "i" as the only or the last letter in a series, and a final period is added to the number.

The 1531 edition of *Answer to More* frequently signals the end of a major section by arranging the conclusion of a paragraph in a pendant: title-page (A1), end of preface (A4v), end of section (B8, C1v, C2v, D6v, E1v), end of division (F8, I3v, L2), but no apparent reason (B3v, E2, G2, O5v, O6, P1v, P3, R2v). This edition keeps the pendant only on the title-page but indicates the beginning of the Foundational Essay, the Answers to the First through the Fourth Books, and "The table of the boke" by starting a new page. Less handily, *1531* places a section-head at the end of the page instead of with new material on the next page (C2v, F1v, H4, I7, K5v, M3v, M4, N7v, P4). Even a division-head is separated from its proper material (L2v). Here the format is improved by uniting heads to bodies.

Since this edition is intended for theologians as well as literary historians, it corrects biblical citations and notes the emendations (23/S4, 67/S2, 87/S4). For the sidenotes line references are given where they actually occur in *1531*, not where they ought to occur. In a few cases the sidenote is placed on the page where the topic occurs, but the line numbers (73/31, 120/33–121/1, 124/1, 124/33–125/1, 136/33–137/6) refer to the preceding or following page. Thus, modern readers can still use the marginalia to find topics in the text.

The edition of *Answer to More* in *Whole Works* (1573) commands respect. John Foxe reproduces Tyndale's subject matter faithfully, but he makes a few changes relevant to the doctrine and discipline of the Elizabethan church: "Masse" to "Christes Supper & not Masse" (95/S2), and "altare" to "body & bloud of Christ" (164/S2) to remove the idea of sacrifice from the Eucharist; "Faith" to "Faith is the gift of God & commeth not by free wil." (192/S1) to emphasize justification by faith; he removes "oure" from "prelates" (94/3) to distinguish Anglican from Roman bishops; he omits "Prestes maye haue wives." (152/S1) probably because the queen disapproved of a married clergy.

In the spirit of Tyndale, Foxe also makes a number of polemical emendations in the sidenotes: "Place" to "M. More teacheth false doctrine." (87/S1); "[Hand]" to "The Pope selleth sinne and paine & all that can be solde." (101/S1); "Purgatory" to "Purgatory profitable to the Pope" (143/S5); "[Hand]" to "Money dispatcheth Purgatory." (144/S1); "Pope" to "Pope forbiddeth matrimony & the eatyng of meates." (171/S9); "Sectes," i.e., "religious orders," to "The sectes in the popishe church are almost innumerable." (127/S3).

Because the Henrician and Elizabethan editions of *Answer to More* are separated by forty-odd years of human speech, Foxe "modernizes" Tyndale's language: verb forms, e.g., "beleuen" to "beleued" (36/28); diction, e.g., "endoted" to "endowed" (16/30–31); syntax, e.g., "maner workes" to "maner of workes" (100/23–24). Foxe also misreads Tyndale's coinage of names. He changes "litle flocke" to "the little flocke" (107/29 etc.), "quod youre frend" to "quoth your frend" (18/28), "quod he" to "quoth he" (194/14–15). All these changes are recorded in the variants.

In 1850 the Parker Society published a modern-spelling version of *Answer to More,* conscientiously edited by Henry Walter. He used the Cambridge University copy of *1531* collated with a copy of *1573* (PS 3.3). His worst fault is to bowdlerize the text, cf. 60/6–7n and 165/30n. He frequently, though not always, identifies sidenotes from *1531* with "W.T." He adds some scriptural references, especially those identified in the text of *1531.* His documentation of other sources is also limited but helpful, cf. his annotation on Augustine and prayers to the saints (126/2–4n). When weary from rowing through Tudor spelling, the reader can steam ahead by consulting *Answer* in its Victorian form.

Since the editions of 1531, 1573, and 1850 offer few problems in regard to text, this critical edition is noteworthy for providing the context. The introduction presents the history of the composition and the principles of theology in *Answer to More.* The text reproduces the Early Modern spelling of 1531 with the variants of 1573.

In an appendix, sidenotes from the *Whole Works* of 1573 show how *Answer* was received in Elizabethan England after the queen was excommunicated by Pius V (pope, 1566–72) in 1570. The glossary alerts the reader to the subtle differences between Renaissance and Modern English. The indices to Scripture, Jerome, Augustine, Aquinas, Erasmus, More, and Luther provide access to the rich theological background. Most helpful of all, the commentary spans fifteen hundred years of church history from the New Testament to Tyndale's works of polemic and exegesis.

AN ANSWERE VNTO
SIR THOMAS MORES
DIALOGE

In answere vnto Sir Thomas Mores
dialoge made by Wyllyam Tindale.

First he declareth what the church is/and
geueth a reason of certayne wordes which
Master More rebuketh in the translacion of the newe Testament.

After that he answereth particularlye vn
to euerye chaptre which semeth to haue
anye apperaunce of truth thorow
all his .iiij. bokes.

Awake thou that sle-
pest and stonde vp
from deeth/and
Christ shall
geue the
light Ep-
hesi-
ans.
v.
Johan bale

Title page, Tyndale's *Answer to More,* 1531
(courtesy of the Folger Shakespeare Library)

[A1] [Hand] An answere vnto Sir Thomas Mores
dialoge made by Willyam Tindale.

¶First he declareth what the church is / and
geveth a reason of certayne wordes which
Master More rebuketh in the transla= 5
cion of the newe Testament. [Hand]

¶After that he answereth particularlye vn
to everye chaptre which semeth to haue
anye apperaunce of truth thorow
all his .iij. bokes. 10

[Hand] Awake thou that sle=
pest and stonde vpp
from deeth / and
Christ shall
geue the 15
light E
phesi=
ans.
v.

---

2 Tindale.] Tyndall. 1530. *1573*

3

[A1v] The grace of oure lorde / the light of his spirite to se and to iudge / true repentaunce towardes goddes lawe / a fast faith in the mercifull promises that are in oure savioure Christ / fervent loue towarde thy neyghboure after the ensample of Christ and his sayntes / be with the o reader and with all that loue the trouth and longe for the redempcion of goddes electe. Amen.

Oure savioure Ihesus in the .xvj. chaptre of Iohan at his last souper when he toke his leaue of his disciples / warned them sayenge / the holye gost shall come and rebuke the worlde of iudgement. That is / he shall rebuke the worlde for lacke of true iudgement and discrecyon to iudge / and shall proue that the taste of their mouthes is corrupte / so that they iudge swete to be sowre and sowre to be swete / and their yies to be blinde / so that they thinke that to be the verye service of god which is but a blinde supersticyon / for zele of which yet they persecute the true service of god: and that they iudge to be the lawe of god which is but a false imaginacion of a corrupte iudgement / for blinde affeccyon of which yet they persecute the true lawe of god & them that kepe it. And this same is it that Paule sayeth in the seconde chaptre of the first epistle to the Corinthians / how that the naturall man that is not borne agayne and created anew with the spirite of god / be he never so great a philosopher / never so well sene in the lawe / never so sore studyed in the scripture / as we haue ensamples in the pharises / yet he can not vnderstonde the thinges of the spirite of god: but sa[A2]yeth he / the spirituall iudgeth all thinges and his spirite sercheth the depe secretes of god / so that what so ever god commaundeth him to do / he never leveth serchinge till he come at the botome / the pith / the quycke / the liffe / the spirite / the marye and verye cause why / and iudgeth all thinge. Take an ensample / in the greate commaundement / loue god with all thyne herte / the spirituall sercheth the cause and loketh on the benefites of god and so conceaveth loue in his herte. And when he is commaunded to obeye the powers and

---

7 Ioa. 16.   20 I. Cor. 2.   30 Mat. 22.   32 Rom. 13.

7 chaptre] *om. 1573*   13 their] the *1573*   18–19 is it] it is *1573*
19–20 in the seconde chaptre of the first epistle to the Corinthians] I. Corinth. ij. *1573*

5

rulers of the worlde / he loketh on the benefytes which god sheweth
the worlde thorow them and therfore doth it gladlye. And when he
is commaunded to loue his neyghboure as him silfe / he sercheth
that his neyghboure is created of god and bought with Christes
5   bloude and so forth / and therfore he loveth him out of his harte /
and if he be evell forbereth him and with all loue and pacience draweth him to good: as elder brothren wayte on the younger and serve
them and sofre them / and when they will not come they speake
fayre and flater and geue some gaye thinge and promise fayre and
10   so drawe them and smite them not / but if they maye in no wyse be
holpe / referre the punishment to the father and mother and so forth.
And by these iudgeth he all other lawes of god and vnderstondeth
the true vse and meaninge of them. And by these vnderstondeth he
in the lawes of man / which are right and which tirannie.
15   If god shulde commaunde him to drinke no wyne / as he commaunded in the olde testament that the preastes shulde not: when
they ministred in the temple and forbade diverse meates / [A2v] the
spirituall (because he knoweth that man is lorde ouer all other creatures and they his servauntes made to be at his pleasure / and that it
20   is not commaunded for the wyne or meate it silfe that man shuld be
in bondage vnto his awne servaunt the inferioure creature) ceaseth
not to serch the cause. And when he findeth it / that it is to tame the
flesh and that he be alwaye sobre / he obeyeth gladlye / and yet not
so supersticiouslye that the tyme of his disease he wolde not drinke
25   wyne in the waye of a medicyne to recouer his helth / as David ate
of the halowed breed and as Moses for necessite lefte the children
of Israel vncircumcysed .xl. yeares / where of likelyhod some died
vncircumcysed & were yet thought to be in no worse case then they
that were circumcysed / as the children that died with in the eyght
30   daye were counted in as good case as they that were circumcysed /
which ensamples might teach vs manye thinges if there were spirite
in vs. And likewyse of the holye daye / he knoweth that the daye is
seruaunt to man / and therfore when he findeth that it is done be-

2 Mat. 22.   27 I. Reg. 21.

25 helth] *ed.*, helts *1531*, health *1573*; ate] eat *1573*   26 Moses] *1573*, Mose *1531*

cause he shulde not be lette from hearinge the worde of god / he
obeyeth gladlie / and yet not so supersticiouslye that he wolde not
helpe his neyghboure on the holye daye and let the sermon alone
for one daye / or that he wolde not worke on the holydaye / neade
requyringe it / at such time as men be not wont to be at church / and   5
so thorow out all lawes. And even likewyse in all ceremonyes and
sacramentes he sercheth the significations and wil not serve the visible thinges. It is as good to him / that the preast saye masse in his
goune as in his other apparell / if they teach him not some whate
and that his soule be edefyed therbye. And as sone [A3] will he gape   10
while thou puttest sonde as holysalt in his mouth / if thou shewe him
no reason therof. He had as lefe be smered with onhalowed butter as
anoynted with charmed oyle if his soule be not taught to vnderstonde some whate therbye / and so forth.

But the worlde captyvateth his witte and aboute the lawe of god   15.
maketh him wonderful imaginacions vnto which he so fast cleaveth
that ten Iohan Baptistes were not able to dispute them out of his hed.
He beleveth that he loveth god because he is readie to kille a turcke
for his sake that beleveth better in god then he / whom god also
commaundeth vs to loue and to leave nothinge vnsought / to winne   20
him vnto the knowlege of the truth / though with the losse of oure
lyves. He supposeth that he loveth his neyghboure as moch as he is
bounde / if he be not actuallye angrye with him / whom yet he wil
not helpe frelye with an halfpenye but for avantage / or vaynglorye
or for a wordlie purposse. If any man haue displeased him / he kep-   25
eth his malice in and will not chafe him silfe aboute it till he se an
occasion to avenge it craftelye and thinketh that well ynough. And
the rulars of the worlde he obeyeth thinketh he / when he flatereth
them and blindeth them with giftes and corrupteth the officers with
rewardes and begyleth the lawe with cautels and sotiltyes. And be-   30
cause the loue of god & of his neyghboure which is the spirite and
the liffe of all lawes and wherfore all lawes are made / is not writen
in his harte / therfore in all inferioure lawes and in all worldlye ordinaunces is he betell blinde. If he be commaunded to absteyne from

_____

25 wordlie] worldly *1573*

wyne / that will he observe vnto the deeth to / as the charter house
monkes [A3v] had lever dye then eate flesh: and as for the sobrenesse
and chastisinge of the membres will he not loke for / but will powre
in ale and bere of the strongest with out measure and heate them
5 with spices and so forth. And the holidaye will he kepe so strayte
that if he mete a flee in his bed he dare not kill hir / and not once
regarde wherfore the holidaye was ordained to seke for goddes
worde / & so forth in al lawes. And in ceremonyes & sacramentes /
there he captiuateth his witte & vnderstondinge to obey holye
10 church with out askinge what they meane or desiringe to knowe but
onlye careth for the kepinge and loketh ever with a payre of narow
yies and with all his spectacles vppon them / lest ought belefte out.
For if the preast shulde saye masse / baptize or heare confession with
out a stole aboute his necke / he wolde thinke all were marred and
15 doute whether he had power to consecrate / & thinke that the vertue
of the masse were lost / & the childe not wel baptized or not baptized
at all / & that his absolucion were not worth a myte. He had leuer
that the bisshope shuld wagge .ij. fingers ouer him / then that a
nother man shulde saye god saue him and so forth. Wherfore be-
20 loved reader in as moch as the holye gost rebuketh the worlde for
lacke of iudgement / and in as moch also as their ignoraunce is with
out excuse before whose faces ynough is sette to iudge by / if they
wolde open their yies to se / and not captiuate their vnderstondinge
to beleue lyes: and in as moch as the spirituall iudgeth all thinge /
25 even the verye botome of goddes secretes / that is to saye / the causes
of the thinges which god commaundeth / how moch more ought
we to iudge oure holye fathers secrettes and not to be as an oxe [A4]
or an asse with out vnderstondinge.

Iudge therfore reader whether the pope with his be the church /
30 whether their auctorite be aboue the scripture: whether all they
teach with out scripture be equalle with the scripture: whether they
haue erred / and not onlye whether they can. And agenst the mist
of their sophistrye take the ensamples that are past in the olde testament and autentike storyes and the present practise which thou seist

2 then] *1573*, them *1531*   7 ordained] *ed.*, ordined *1531*, ordayned *1573*

before thyne yies. Iudge whether it be possible that any good shuld
come out of their domme ceremonies and sacramentes in to thy
soule. Iudge their penaunce / pilgrimages / pardons / purgatorye /
prayinge to postes / domme blessinges / domme absolucyons / their
domme pateringe and howlinge / their domme straunge holye ges-   5
tures with all their domme disgysinges / their satisfaccions and ius-
tefyinges. And because thou findest them false in so manye thinges /
trust them in nothinge but iudge them in al thinges. Marke at the
last the practise of our fleshlye spiritualtye and their wayes by which
they haue walked aboue .viij. hundred yeares / how they stablish   10
their lyes / first with falsifiynge the scripture / then thorow cor-
ruptinge with their riches wher of they haue infinite treasure in
store: and last of all with the swerde. Haue they not compelled the
emperoures of the erth and the great lordes and hie officers to be
obedient vnto them / to dispute for them and to be their tor-   15
mentoures / and the samsumims them selves do but imagen mis-
chefe and inspire them. Marke whether it were ever truer then now /
the scribes / pharises / Pilate / Herode / Caiphas & Anna / are gathered to gether agenst god & Christ. But yet I trust in vayne / and
that he that brake the [A4v] counsell of achitophell shall scater   20
theirs. Marke whether it be not true in the hyest degre / that for the
sinne of the people hypocrites shall rayne over them. What shewes /
what faces and contrarie pretenses are made / and all to stablish them
in their thefte / falsehed and dampnable lyes / and to gather them to
gether for to contryve sotiltye to oppresse the truth and to stoppe   25
the light & to kepe all still in darkenesse. Wherfore it is tyme to
awake and to se everye man with his awne yies and to iudge / if we
will not be iudged of Christ when he cometh to iudge. And remem-
bre that he which is warned hath none excuse / if he take no hede.
Here with fare well in the lorde Iesus Christ whose spirite be thy   30
gyde and doctrine thy light to iudge with all. Amen.

19–20 and that] and 1573   28–29 remembre] ed., rebembre 1531, remember
1573   31 thy] and the 1573

[A5] ¶What the church is

Thys worde church hath dyuerse significacions. First it signifyeth a
place or housse / whether christen people were wont in the olde time
to resorte at tymes conuenient / for to heare the worde of doctryne /
5   the lawe of God and the faith of oure sauioure Ihesus christ / and
how and what to praye and whence to axe power and strength to
lyue goodly. For the officers therto appoynted preached the pure
worde of god onlye and prayed in a tonge that all men vnderstode.
And the people herkened vnto his prayers / and said therto Amen
10   and prayed with him in their hertes / and of him lerned to praye at
home and every where / and to instructe euery man hys howsholde.

Where now we heare but voyces with out significacion and buzsinges / howlinges and crienges / as it were the halowenges of foxes
or baytinges of beres / and wonder at disguisinges and toyes wheroff
15   we know no meaninge.

By reason wherof we be fallen in to soch ignorauncye / that we
know of the mercie and promyses which are in christe nothynge at
all.

And of the lawe of god we thinke as do the turkes / and as did the
20   olde hethen people / how that it is a thinge which euery man maye
doo of his awne power / and in doynge therof becometh good and
waxeth rightuouse and deserueth heven: ye and are yet more mad
then that. For we ymagen the same of phantasyes and vayne ceremonies of oure awne makynge / neyther nedefull vn to the tamynge
25   of oure awne flesh / neyther profytable vn to oure neyboure /
neyther honoure vnto god.

[A5v] And of prayer we thynke / that no man can praye but at
church / and that it is nothinge else but to saye pater noster vnto
a post. Wherewith yet and with other obseruaunces of oure awne
30   imagininge / we beleue / we deserue to be sped of all that oure blinde
hertes desyre.

In a nother significacion it is abvsed and mystaken for a multitude

---

1 ¶] *ed.*, What the church is] *running title 1531*, ¶] What the Church is
1573   7 goodly] godly *1573*

of shaven shorn and oyled whych we now calle the spirytualtye and
clergye. As when we reade in the chronicles Kinge wyllyam was a
great tyrant and a weked man vnto holy church and toke moch
landes from them. Kinge Iohan was also a perylouse man and a
weked vnto holy church / and wold haue had them punyshed for   5
theft / murther and what soeuer mischeue they did / as though they
had not bene people annoynted / but euen of the vile rascall
and comen laye people.

And Thomas bekett was a blessed and an holy man for he died for
the liberties (to do all mischeue vnpunished) and priuileges of the   10
church. Is he a laye man or a man of the church? Soch is the liuynge
of holy church. So saye men of holy church. Ye must beleue in holy
church and do as they teach you. Will ye not obeye holy church?
will ye not do the penaunce enioyned you by holy church? wyll ye
not forswere obedience vnto holy church? Beware lest ye fall in to   15
the indignacion of holy church / lest they curse you and so forth.
In which all we vnderstonde but the pope / cardenalles / legates /
patriarckes / archbisshopes / bisshopes / abbotes / priours /
chauncelers / archedecons / commissaries / officiales / prestes /
monkes / freres / blacke / whit / pied / grey / & so forth / by (I   20
trowe) a thousand names of blasphemy & of ypocrisie & as many
sundrie facions of disgysinges.

[A6] It hath yet or shuld haue a nother signifycacyon litle knowen
amonge the comen people now a dayes. That is to witt / it signifieth
a congregacion / a multitude or a company gathered to gether in   25
one / of all degrees of people. As a man wold saye / the church of
london / meaninge not the spiritualtie only (as they wilbe called for
their diligent saruinge of god in the sprite & so sore eschuynge to
medle wyth temporall maters) but the hole body of the cytye / of all
kyndes condicions and degrees. And the church of bristow / al that   30
pertayne vnto the towne generally. And what congregacion is

2–3 Kinge Willyam   4–5 Kynge Iohan   9–11 S. Thomas of canter-
burye

---

7 bene] 1573, haue bene 1531   12 saye men] men say 1573   14 wyll ye]
will yet 1573   17 pope /] ed., pope 1531, Pope, 1573   21 ypocrisie] hypocri-
sies 1573   27 spiritualtie] 1573, spirituallie 1531

ment / thou shall all waye vnderstonde by the mater that is entreted
of and by the circumstaunces therof.

And in this thrid significacion is the church of god or christ taken
in the scripture / euen for the whole multytude of all them that re-
5   ceaue the name of christe to beleue in him / and not for the clergye
onlye. For paul saith Galatiens .i. I persecuted the church of God a
boue measure. Which was not the preachers only / but all that beleued generally / as it is to se actes .xxij. where he saith / I persecuted
this waye / euen vnto the deeth bindinge and puttinge in preson
10 both men and wemen. And Galath. i. I was vnknowen concernynge
my person vnto the congregacyons off the Iewes which were in
chryste. And Roma. xvj. I commende vnto you phebe the deaconysse of the church of cenchris. And the churches of Asia salute
you .i. Coryn. the laste.

15   And yf a man can not rule hys awne howsse / how shall he take
the care of the church of God .i. Tymothe .iij? yf any faythfull man
or woman haue wedoowes / let them fynde them / that the church
be not charged .i. Tymothe .v. [A6v] And Matt. xviij. if thi brother
heare the not tell the church or congregacion and so forth. In which
20 places and thorowout al the scripture / the church is taken for the
hole multitude of them that beleue in christ in that place in that parish towne / citie / prouince / londe or thorowout all the worlde / and
not for the spiritualitie only.

Notwithstondinge yet it is some times taken generally for all that
25 embrace the name of Christe though their faythes be nought or
though they haue no fayth at all. And some times it is taken specially
for the electe only in whose hertes God hath written his lawe with
his holy spirite and geuen them a felinge faith of the mercy that is in
christe Iesu oure lorde.

---

6 Gala. i.   8 Actes .22.   11 Gala. i.   12 Ro. xvj.   15 i. Cor.
16.   16 i. timo. 3.   18 i. timo. 5.   24–27 A double significacion of
this word church

---

1 shall] shalt *1573*   18 brother] *1573*, broter *1531*   24 all] all them
1573   25 nought] naught *1573*

¶Why Tindale vsed this worde congregacion rather then church in the translacion of the new testament

Wherfore in as moch as the clergye (as the nature of those hard & indurat adamandstones is / to draw all to them) had appropriat vn   5
to them selues the terme that of right is comen vnto all the hole congregacion of them that beleue in christe and with their false and sotle
wyles had begyled and mocked the people and brought them in to
the ignoraunce of the worde / makynge them vnderstonde by this
word church / nothinge but the shauenflocke / of them that shore   10
the hole world: therfore in the translacion of the new testament
where I found this word ecclesia / I enterpretated it / bi this worde
congregacion. Even therfore did I it / and not of any mischevouse
minde or purpose to stablishe heresie / as master More vntrulye reporteth of me in his dialoge where he rayleth on the translacion of   15
the new testament.

[A7] And when M. More saith / that this word church is knowen
well ynough / I reporte me vnto the conscyences of all the londe /
whether he saie truth or otherwise / or whether the laye people
vnderstonde by church the hole multytude of all that professe   20
christe / or the iuglinge sprytes onlye. And when he saith that congregacion is a moore generall terme / iff yt were yt hurteth not. For
the circumstaunce doeth ever tell what congregacyon ys ment.
Neuerthelesse yet sayth he not the truth. For whersoeuer I maye
saye a congregacyon / there maye I saye a church also as the church   25
of the deuell / the church of sathan / the church of wretches / the
church of wekedmen / the church of lyers and a church of turkes
therto.

For M. More must graunt (if he will have ecclesia translated
thorowte all the new testament by thys word church) that church   30
is as comen as ecclesia. Now is ecclesia a greke worde and was in
vse before the tyme of the apostles and taken for a congregacyon

---

4 as the clergye (as] *ed.,* (as the clergye as *1531,* (as the clergy, as *1573*
12 enterpretated] enterpreted *1573*   14 heresie] *1573,* he- heresie *1531*

amonge the hethen / where was no congregacion of god or of christ.
And also Lucas hym selfe vseth ecclesia for a church or congregacyon of hethen people thrise in one chapter even in the .xix. of the
actes / where Demetrius the goldsmyth or syluersmyth had gath-
5   ered a companie agenst paul for preachynge agenst ymages.

How be it M. More hath so longe vsed hys figures of poetrie / that
(I suppose) when he erreth most / he now by the reason of a longe
custome / beleueth him selfe / that he saith most true. Or else (as the
wyse people whych when they daunce naked in nettes beleve that
10   no man seyth them) even so M. More thynketh that his erroures
[A7v] be so subtilly cowched that no man can espye them. So blinde
he counteth all other men in comparison of his great vnderstondinge. But charitablye I exhorte him in chryste to take hede for
though Iudas were wilier then his felowes to get lucre / yet he
15   proued not most wise at the last ende. Nether though Balam the
false prophete had a clere sighte to bringe the curse of God vppon
the chyldern of Israel for honoures sake / yet his couetousenesse did
so blynd his prophesie / that he coude not se his awne ende. Let therfore M. More and hys company awake be tymes ere ever their sinne
20   be rype lest the voyce of theyr wekednesse ascende vp and awake
God out of his slepe / to loke vppon them and to bow his eares vnto
their cursed blasphemies agenst the open truth / and to send hys her-
uestmen and mowares of vengeaunce to repe yt.

But how happeth it that M. More hathe not contended in lyke
25   wise agaynst hys derelynge Erasmus all this longe while? Doeth not
he chaunge this worde ecclesia in to congregacyon and that not sel-
den in the new testament? peraduenture he owithe him fauoure because he made Moria in his housse. Which boke if were in englishe /
then shulde euery man se / how that he then was ferre other wise
30   minded than he nowe writeth. But verelie I thinke that as Iudas be-
traid not christ for any loue that he had vnto the hie prestes / scribes
and phareses / but only to come by that wherfore he thirsted: euen

4 Actes .19.   13 Iudas   15 Balaam

3 chapter] *ed.*, chapther *1531*, Chapter *1573*   16 prophete] *ed.*, phophete *1531*,
Prophet *1573*   20 wekednesse] *ed.*, wekenesse *1531*, wickednesse *1573*   28 if
were] *1531*, if it were] *1573*

so M. More (as there are tokens evident) wrote not these bokes for any affeccyon that he bare vnto the spiritualtie or vnto the opinions which he so barelie defendeth / but to obtayne only that which he was an hongred fore: I praie God that he eate not to hastely lest he be cho[A8]ked at the later end / but that he repent and resyst not the 5 spirite of god whych openeth lyght vnto the worlde.

¶Why he vseth thys word elder and not prest

Another thinge which he rebuketh ys that I interprete thys greke word presbiteros by this word senior. Of a truth senior is no veri good english / though senior and iunior be vsed in the vniuersities: 10 but there came no better in my mynde at that tyme. How be it I spyed my faute sens / longe yer M. More told it me / and haue mended it in all the workes which I sens made and call it an elder. And in that he maketh heresie of it / to call presbiteros an elder he condemneth their awne olde latine texte of heresye also / which they 15 vse yet dayly in the church and haue vsed / I suppose / this .xiiij. hundred yeres. For that texte doeth call it an elder lykewyse. In the .v. chaptre of the first of peter / thus standeth it in the laten texte. Seniores qui in vobis sunt / obsecro ego consenior / pascite qui in vobis est gregem christi. The elders that are amonge you I besech 20 whych am an elder also that ye fede the flocke of christe / whych is amonge you. There ys presbyteros called an elder. And in that he saith fede christes flocke / he meaneth euen the ministres that were chosen to teache the people and to enforme them in gods worde and no laye persones. And in the seconde epystle of Ihon saith the texte / 25 senior electe domine et filijs eius. The elder vnto the electe ladye and to here chylderen. And in the .iij. epystle of Ihon. Senior Gaio dilecto. The elder vnto the beloued Gaius. In these .ij. pystles presbiteros ys called an elder. And in the .xx. of the actes / the texte sayth:

15–17 M. More condempneth the laten texte.   18 1. petri .5.   25 ij. Iohan   27 iij. Iohan   29 Actes .20.

18 .v. chaptre of the first of peter] .1. Pet. 5. _1573_   22 presbyteros] _ed._, presyteros _1531_, Presbyteros _1573_   25 seconde] 2. _1573_   26 eius] _1573_, beius _1531_   28 pystles] Epistles _1573_

paule sent for maiores natu ecclesie / the [A8v] elders in birth of the
congregacion or church / and said vnto them / take hede vnto youre
selues and vnto the hole flocke / ouer which the holy gost hath made
you episcopos ad regendum ecclesiam dei / bisshopes or ouersears
5   to gouerne the church of god. There is presbiteros called an elder in
birth which same is immediatly called a bisshope or ouersear / to
declare what persons are ment. Herof ye se that I haue no moare
erred then there awne texte which they haue vsed sens the scripture
was first in the latine tongue / and that their awne texte vnderstond-
10   eth by presbiteros nothinge saue an elder. And they were called elders / because of their age / grauite and sadnesse / as thou maist se
by the texte: and bisshopes or ouersears by the reason of their offices. And all that were called elders (or prestes if they so will) were
called bisshopes also / though they haue diuided the names now /
15   Which thinge thou maist euidently se by the first chapter of titus.
And the .xx. of the actes and other places moo.
    And when he layeth Timothe vn to my charge / how he was
younge / then he weneth that he hath wonne his gylden spores. But
I wolde praye him to shew me where he readeth that Paul calleth
20   him presbiteros / preast or elder. I durst not then call him Episcopus
propirly. For those ouersears which we now call bisshopes aftir the
greke worde / were all waye bydynge in one place / to gouerne the
congregacion there. Now was Timothe an apostle. And Paul also
writeth that he will come shortly agayne. Wel / will he saye / it com-
25   eth yet all to one. For if it becometh the lower ministre to be of a sad
and discrete age / moch more it becometh the hyer. It is trueth. [B1]
But .ij. thinges are with out lawe / god and necessite. Yf god to
shew his power shall shede out his grace moare vppon youth then
vppon age at a tyme / who shall lett him? wemen be no mete vesseles
30   to rule or to preach (for both are forboden them) yet hath god endoted them with his spirite at sondrie tymes and shewed his power

27 Note   29 Wemen

2 church] *ed.*, curch *1531*, Church *1573*   4 or] *om. 1573*   6 is] *om.*
1573   10 were] *1573*, vere *1531*   16 the .xx. of the actes] Actes xx.
1573   24 will come] *ed.*, come *1531*, came *1573*   30 forboden] forbidden
1573   30–31 endoted] endowed *1573*

& goodnesse vppon them and wrought wonderfull thinges by them / because he wold not haue them dispised. We reade that wemen haue iudged all Israel and haue bene greate prophetisses and haue done mightie deades. Yee and if stories be true / wemen haue preached sens the openynge of the new testament.   5

Doo not oure wemen now christen and ministre the sacrament of baptim in tyme of neade? Might they not by as good reason preach also / if necessite required? If a woman were dreuen in to some Ilande / where Christ was neuer preached / might she there not preach him / if she had the gyfte therto? Mighte she not also baptise?   10 And why might she not / by the same reason ministre the sacramente of the body & bloude of Christe / and teach them how to chose officers & ministres? O pore wemen / how despice ye them! The viler the better welcome vnto you. An hore had ye lever than an honeste wife. If only shauen & annoynted maye doo these   15 thinges / then Christe did them not ner any of his apostles / ner any man in longe time after. For they vsed no soch ceremonyes.

Notwithstondinge though god be vnder no law & necessite lawlesse: yet be we vnder a lawe & ought to preferre the men before the wemen and age before youth / as nye as we can. For it is agenst the   20 lawe of nature that younge men shul[B1v]de rule the elder / and as vncomely as that wemen shulde rule the men / but when nede requireth. And therfore if paul had had other shifte & a man of age as mete for the rowme / he wold not haue put Timothe in the office. He shuld no doute haue bene kepte backe vntyll a fuller age and haue   25 lerned in the meane tyme in silence. And what soeuer thou be / that readest this / I exhorte the in oure lorde / that thou reade both the epistles of Paul to Timothe / that thou maist se how diligently (as a mother careth for hir child / if it be in perell) Paul writeth vnto Timothe / to enstructe him / to teach him / to exhorte / to corage   30 him / to stere him vpp / to bewise / sobir / diligent / circumspecte / sad / humble and meke sayenge: these I write / that thou maist know how to behaue thy selfe in the howsse of god which is the church or congregacion. Avoyde lustes of youth / beware of vngodly fables

6 now] 1573, nov 1531   13 them!] ed., them? 1531, 1573

and old wiues tales / & auoyde the companye of men of corrupte
myndes which wast their braynes aboute wranglynge questions. Let
no man dispise thyne youth. As who shulde saye / youth is a dispised thinge of it selfe / where vnto men geue none obedience natu-
5   rally or reuerence. Se therfore that thy vertue excede / to recompence thy lacke of age / and that thou so behaue thy selfe / that no
faute be founde with the. And agayne / rebuke not an elder sharpe-
ly / but exhorte him as thy father / and yongemen as thy brethern / and the elder wemen as thy mothers / and the younge wemen
10 as thy sisters and soch like in euerye chapter. Admitte none accusa-
cion agenst an elder vnder lesse then .ij. wittenesses. And Paul
chargeth him in the sight of god and of the lorde Iesus christe and of
his electe angeles / to doo nothynge rashly or of af[B2]feccion. And
shortely where vnto youth is most prone and ready to fall / therof
15 warneth he him with al diligence / even al most or all to gether halfe
a dosen tymes of someone thynge. And fynally as a man wold teach
a childe that had neuer before gone to scole / so tenderly & so care-
fully doeth paul teach him. It is a nother thynge to teach the people
and to teach the preacher. Here Paul teacheth the preacher / younge
20 Timothe.

   And when he affirmeth that I saye / how that the oylinge and
shauinge is no parte of the presthode. That improueth he not ner
can do. And therefore I saye it yet. And when he hath enserched
thuttermost that he can this is al that he can laye agenst me / that
25 of an hundred there be not .x. that haue the propirties which paul
requireth to be in them. Wherefore if oylinge and shauinge be no
parte of their presthod / then euermore of a thousand .ix. hundred
at the lest shuld be no prestes at all. And quod youre frend wold
confirme it with an oth and swere depely / that it wold folowe and
30 that it must nedes so be. Which argument yet / if there were no
nother shifte I wold solue aftir an oxforde facion / with concedo
consequenciam et consequens. And I saye morouer that their annoyntynge is but a ceremonie borowed of the Iewes / though they

4–5 naturally or reuerence] or reuerence naturally *1573*   28 quod] quoth
1573

haue somewhat altered the maner / & their shauinge borowed of the
hethen prestes / & that they be no more of their presthode / then the
oyle / salte / spittell / taper & chresom cloth of the substaunce of
baptim. Which thinges / nodoute / because they be of their coniur-
ynge / they wold haue preached of necessite vnto the saluacion of   5
the childe / excepte necessite had dreuen them vn to the contrarye.

[B2v] And seinge that the oyle is not of necessyte / let M. More
tell me what moare vertue is in the oyle of confyrmacion / in as
moch as the bysshope sacrithe the one as well as the other: ye and
let hym tell the reason why there shulde be more vertue in the oyle   10
where wyth the bysshope annoynteth hys prestes. Let him tell you
from whence the oyle cometh / how it is made / and why he selleth
it to the curates wher with they anoynte the syke / or whether thys
be of lesse vertue then the other.

And finally whi vsed not the appostles this greke worde hiereus or   15
the interpreter thys laten worde sacerdos / but all waye thys worde
presbiteros and senior / by which was at that tyme nothynge sygny-
fyed then an elder? And it was no doute taken of the custome of
the hebrues / where the offycers were ever elderly men as nature
requireth. As yt appereth in the olde testament and also in the newe.   20
The scrybes / pharises and the elders of the people sayth the texte /
which were the officers and rulars / so called by the reason of theyr
age.

¶Why he vseth loue rather then cheryte

He rebuketh also that I translate thys greke word agape in to loue /   25
and not rather in to charite so holy and so knowen a terme. Verely
charite is no knowen Englesh in that sens whych agape requireth.
For when we saye / geue youre almes in the worshepe of God and
swete saint charite / and when the father teacheth his sonne to saye
blissinge father for saint charite / what meane they? In good faith   30
they wot not. Morouer when we saye / God helpe you / I haue done

15 [Hand]
_____

18 then] but *1573*

my charite for this daye / doo we not take it for almes? And the man
is euer chidinge and out of charyte / [B3] and I beshrew him sauinge
my charyte / there we take it for pacyence. And when I saye a charitable man / it is taken for mercifull. And though mercifulnesse be a
5 good loue or rather springe of a good loue / yet ys not euery good
loue mercifulnesse. As when a woman loueth her husbonde godly
or a man his wife or his frend that is in none aduersitie / it is not
allwaye mercifulnesse. Also we saie not this man hath a greate charite to god / but a greate loue. Wherefore I must haue vsed this gener-
10 all terme loue / in spite of mine herte often tymes. And agape and
charitas were wordes vsed amonge the hethen yer chryste came /
and signified therfore more then a godly loue. And we maye saye
well ynough and haue hearde it spoken that the turkes be charitable
one to a nother amonge them selues and some of them vnto the
15 chrysten to. Besydes all thys agape ys comen vnto all loues.

And when Master More saith euery loue ys not charyte / no more
is every appostle chrystes appostell ner every angell gods angell /
ner euery hope chrysten hope nor euery faith or beleffe chrystes beleffe / and so by an hundred thousande wordes. So that yf I shulde all
20 waye vse but a worde that were no moore generall then the worde I
enterprete / I shulde interprete no thynge at all. But the mater yt
selfe and the circumstaunces doo declare what loue / what hope and
what fayth ys spoken of. And finally I saye not charite god or charite
youre neyboure but loue God and loue youre neyboure ye and
25 though we saye a man ought to loue hys neyboures wife and his
doughter / a christen man doeth not vnderstonde / that he ys commaunded to defyle hys neyboures wife or hys doughter.

[B3v] ¶Why fauoure and not grace

And wyth lyke reasons rageth he because I turne charis in to fa-
30 uoure and not in to grace / sayenge that euery fauoure is not grace
and that in some fauoure there is but litle grace. I can saye also in

22 circumstaunces] 1573, circumestaunces 1531   28 ¶] ed., Why fauoure and
not grace] running title 1531, ¶] Why fauour and not grace 1573

some grace there is lytle goodnesse. And when we saye / he stondeth well in my ladis grace / we vnderstonde no greate godly fauoure. And in vniuersities manye vngracious graces are goten.

¶Why knowlege and not confessyon / repentaunce and not penaunce

And that I vse this word knowlege and not confession / and this repentaunce and not penaunce. In whych all he can not proue / that I geue not the ryghte englishe vnto the greke worde. But yt ys a ferre other thynge that payneth them and byteth them by the brestes. There be secret panges that pinch the very hertes of them / where of they dare not complayne.

The sekenesse that maketh them so impacyent ys / that they haue lost theyr iuglinge termes. For the doctours and preachers were wont to make many deuisyons / distinccyons and sortes of grace / gratis data / gratum faciens / preueniens and subsequens. And wyth confessyon they iugled / and made the people / as ofte as they spake of yt: vnderstonde shryft in the eare. Wherof the scripture maketh no mencyon: no it is cleane agenst the scrypture as they vse yt and preach yt / and vn to god an abhominacyon and a foule stinkynge sacrifice vnto the filthy ydole priapus. The losse of those iuglinge termes ys the mater where all these bottes brede / that gnawe them by the belies and make them so vnquiet.

[B4] And in lyke maner / by this word penaunce / they make the people vnderstonde holy dedes of their enioynynge / with which they must make satisfaccion vnto godwarde for their synnes. When al the scripture preacheth that christ hath made full satisfaccyon for oure synnes to godwarde / and we must now be thankefull to god agayne and kyll the lustes of oure flesh wyth holy workes of gods enioynynge and to take pacientlye all that god layeth on my backe. And if I haue hurte my neyboure / I am bounde to shriue my selfe vnto hym and to make hym a mendes / yf I haue where with / or if

23 Penaunce
_____

6 and this] and this word *1573*   13 doctours and] *1573*, doctours
1531   16 and] & so *1573*

not then to axe him forgeuenesse / and he is bounde to forgeue me. And as for their penaunce the scripture knoweth not of. The greke hath Metanoia and metanoite / repentaunce and repente / or forthynkynge and forthynke. As we saye in english it forthynketh me
5 or I forthynke / and I repent or yt repenteth me and I am sory that I dyd yt. So now the scripture sayeth repent or let yt forthynke you and come and beleue the gospell or glad tydynges that ys brought you in chryst / and so shall all be forgeuen you / and henceforth lyue a new lyfe: And yt wyll folowe yf I repent in the herte / that I shall doo
10 no moore so wyllyngely and of purpose. And yf I beleued the gospell / what God hath done for me in christe / I shuld suerly loue hym agayne and of loue prepare my selfe vnto hys commaundementes.

These thinges to be euen so M. More knoweth wel ynough. For he vnderstondeth the greke / and he knew them longe yer I. But so
15 blinde is couetousenesse and dronken desire of honoure. Giftes blinde the eies of the seinge and peruerte [B4v] the wordes of the righteous Deut. xvij. When couetousenesse findeth vauntage in seruinge falshed / it riseth vpp in to an obstinat malise agenst the trouth and seketh all meanes to resiste it and to quench it. As Balam
20 the false prophete / though he wiste that god loued Israhel & had blessed them and promised them greate thinges / and that he wold fulfyll his promises / yet for couetousenesse and desyre of honoure / he fell in to soch malice agenst the trueth of god / that he sought how to resiste it and to curse the people. Which when god wold not
25 let him doo / he turned him selfe a nother waye and gaue pestilent counsell / to make the people synne agenst god wherbye the wrath of god felle vppon them / and many thousandes perished. Notwithstondinge gods trueth abode fast and was fullfilled in the reste. And Balam as he was the cause that many perished / so escaped he not
30 him selfe. No moare did any that maliciously resisted the open trueth agenst his awne conscience / sence the world beganne / that euer I red. For it is sinne agenst the holy gost / which Christ saith

16 Deut. 17.   17 [Hand]   20 Balam   22/31–23/2 The sinne
agenst the holye gost

1 bounde] 1573, bouude 1531   13 be] 1573, be be 1531   30 maliciously]
1573, maliciousy 1531

shall neyther be forgeuen here nor in the worlde to come / which
texte maye this wise be vnderstonde that as that sinne shalbe punished with euerlastinge damnacion in the life to come: even so shall
it not escape vengeaunce here. As thou seist in Iudas / in Pharao / in
Balam and in all other tirantes which agenst their consciences re-   5
sisted the open trueth of god.

So now the cause why oure prelates thus rage / and that moueth
them to call master More to helpe / is not that they finde iust causes
in the translacion / but because they haue loste their iugglynge and
fayned termes / wherwith Peter [B5] prophisied they shuld make   10
marchaundice of the people.

¶Whether the church were before the gospell
or the gospell before the church

Another doute there is / whether the church or congregacion be
before the gospell or the gospell before the church. Which question   15
is as hard to solue / as whether the father be elder then the sonne or
the sonne elder then his father. For the hole scripture and all beleuinge hertes testifye that we are begotten thorow the worde. Wherfore if the worde begette the congregacion / and he that begetteth is
before him that is begotten then is the gospell before the church.   20
Paul also Romano. ix. sayth / how shall they call on whom they
beleue not? And how shall they beleue with out a preacher? That is /
Christ must first be preached yer men can beleue in him. And then
it foloweth / that the worde of the preacher must be before the faith
of the belevar. And therfore in as moch as the worde is before the   25
faith / and faith maketh the congregacion / therfore is the word or
gospell before the congregacion. And agayne as the ayre is darke of
it selfe and receaueth all hir light of the sonne: even so ar all mens
hertes of them selfe darke with lies & receaue al their trueth of gods
worde / in that they consent therto. And morouer as the darke ayre   30
geveth the sonne no lighte / but contrary wise the light of the sonne

3 [Hand]   10 ij. Pet. ij.   17 j. Petr. j.   21 Ro. 10.

21 on] *1531*, on him] *1573*   29 them selfe] themselues *1573*   S3 j. Petr. j.]
om. 1573   S4 Ro. 10.] *ed.*, Ro. 9. *1531*, Rom. 9. *1573*

in respecte of the ayre is of it selfe and lighteneth the ayre and
purgeth it from darkenesse: even so the lienge herte of man can geue
the word of god no trueth / but contrary wise the trueth of gods
worde is of hir selfe and [B5v] lyghteneth the hertes of the beleuers
5   and maketh them true / and clenseth them from lies / as thou readest
Ihon .xv. ye be cleane by reason of the word. Which is to be vnderstond / in that the word had purged their hertes from lies / from
false opinions and from thynkynge evell good / and therfore from
consentinge to synne. And Ihon .xvij. sanctifie them o father
10 thorow thy trueth. And thy word is trueth. And thus thou seist that
gods trueth dependeth not of man. It is not true because man so saith
or addmitteth it for true: But man is true because he beleueth it /
testifieth and geueth wittenesse in his hert that it is true. And Christ
also saith him selfe Ihon .v. I receaue no wittenesse of man. For if
15 the multitude of manswittenesse might make ought true / then were
the doctrine of Mahomete truer then Christes.

¶Whether the appostles left ought vnwritten / that is of necessite to be beleued

But did not the appostles teach ought by mouth that they wrott
20 not? I answere / because that many taught one thinge / and every
man the same in diuers places and vnto diuers people / and confirmed euery sermon with a sondry miracle: therfore Christ and his
appostles preached an hundred thousand sermons and did as many
miracles which had bene superfluous to haue bene all written. But
25 the pith and substaunce in generall of euery thinge necessarie vn to
oure soules health / both of what we ought to beleue & what we
ought to doo / was written / and of the miracles done to confirme
it / as ma[B6]ny as were nedefull. So that what soeuer we ought to
beleue or doo / that same is written expresly or drawen out of that
30 which is written.

For if I were bounde to doo or beleue vnder payne of the losse of
my soule any thynge that were not written / ner depended of that

6 Iohan .xv.   10 Iohan .17.

_____

32 not] _om._ 1573

which is written / what holpe me the scripture that is written? And therto in as moch as Christ and all his apostles warned vs that false prophetes shuld come with false miracles / even to disceaue the electe / if it were possible / where with shuld the true preacher confounde the false / excepte he brought true miracles to confounde the false or else autentycke scripture of full auctorite all ready amonge the people.

Some man wolde axe / how did god continue his congregacion from Adam to Noe / & from Noe to Abraham / and so to Moses / with out wrytynge / but with teachynge from mouth to mouth. I answere first that there was no scripture all the while / they shall proue / when oure lady hath a new sonne. God taught Adam greater thinges then to write. And that there was writynge in the world longe yer Abraham ye and yer Noe doo stories testifie.

Notwithstondinge / though there had bene no writynge / the preachers were euer prophetes glorious in doynge of miracles / where with they confirmed their preachynge. And beyonde that god wrote his testament vn to them all waye / both what to doo and to beleue / even in sacramentes. For the sacrifices which god gaue Adams sonnes were no dumme popetrie or supersticious [B6v] mahometrie / but signes of the testament of god. And in them they red the worde of god / as we do in bokes / and as we shuld doo in oure sacramentes / if the weked pope had not taken the significacions a waye from vs / as he hath robbed vs of the true sens of all the scripture. The testament which god mad with Noe / that he wolde no moare droune the world with water / he wrote in the sacrament of the raynebowe. And the appoyntement made betwene him and Abraham / he wrote in the sacrament of circumcision. And therfore saide Steuen Actes .vij. he gaue them the testament of circumcision. Not that the outwarde circumcision was the hole testament / but the sacrament or signe therof. For circumcision preached gods word vnto them / as I haue in other places declared.

But in the tyme of Moyses when the congregacion was en-

29 Actes .7.

---

19 sacramentes] the sacramentes 1573   31 therof] there 1573

creased / that they must haue many preachars and also rulars temporall / then all was receaued in scripture / in so moch that Christ and
his appostles might not haue bene beleued with out scripture for all
their miracles. Wherfore in as moch as Christes congregacion is
5   spred a brode in to all the world moch broder then Moseses / and in
as moch as we haue not the old testament only but also the new /
wherin all thinges are opened so richly and all fulfilled that before
was promised / and in as moch as there is no promise behinde of
ought to be shewed moare saue the resurreccion: yee and seinge that
10   Christ and all the appostles with all the angels of heuen / if they were
here / coude preach no moare then is preached / of necessite vnto
oure soules: How then shuld we receaue a new article of the faith /
with out scripture / as profitable [B7] vnto my soule / when I had
beleved it / as smoke for sore eyes. What holpe it me to beleue that
15   oure laidies bodie is in heuen? what am I the better for the beleffe
of purgatorye? to feare men thou wilt saye. Christ & his appostles
thought hell ynough. And yet (besydes that the fleshly imaginacion
maye not stonde with gods worde) what greate feare can there be
of that tereble fire which thou maist quench all most for .iij. halfe
20   pence?

    And that the apostles shuld teach ought by mouth which they
wold not write / I praye you for what purpose? because they shuld
not come in to the handes of the hethen for mockynge / saith M.
More. I pray you what thinge moare to be mocked of the hethen
25   coude they teach / then the resurreccion / and that Christ was god
and man and died betwene .ij. theves / and that for his dethes sake /
all that repent and beleue therin / shuld haue their sinnes forgeuen
them. Ye and if the apostles vnderstode therby as we doo what madder thinge vnto hethen people coude they haue taught then that bred
30   is Christis body and wine his bloude. And yet all these thynges they
wrote. And agayne purgatory / confession in the eare / penaunce
and satisfaccion for synne to godward with holy deades / and prayenge to saintes with soch like / as dome sacramentes and ceremo-

16–17 Purgatorye

5 then] *1573*, them *1531*; Moseses] Moses *1573*   26 man and] *ed.*, man an *1531*,
man, and *1573*   29 people] *1573*, people / *1531*

nies / ar marvelouse agreable vn to the supersticion of the hethen
people / so that they neaded not to absteyne from writynge of
them / for feare lest the hethen shuld haue mocked them.

Morouer what is it that the appostles taught by mouth and durst
not write? The sacramentes? As for baptim and the sacrament of the   5
body & [B7v] bloud of Christ they wrote / and it is expressed what
is signified by them. And also all the ceremonies and sacramentes
that were from Adam to Christ had significacions / and all that are
made mencion of in the new testament. Wherfore in as moch as the
sacramentes of the olde testament haue significacions / and in as   10
moch as the sacramentes of the new testament (of which mencion is
made that they were deliuered vn to vs by the verye appostles at
Christes commaundement) haue also significacions / and in as moch
as the office of an appostle is to edifie in Christe / and in as moch as
a dumme ceremonie edifieth not / but hurteth all to gether (for iff it   15
preach not vn to me / then I can not but put confidence therin / that
the dede it selfe iustifieth me / which is the denyenge of Christes
bloude) & in as moch as no mencion is made of them / as well as of
other / ner is knowen what is ment by them: therfore it appereth
that the appostles taught them not / but that they be the false mar-   20
chaundice of wilye ypocrites. And therto presthode was in the tyme
of the appostles an office which if they wold do truely / it wold
moare profitt then all the sacramentes in the worlde. And agayne
gods holinesses striue not one agenst a nother ner defile one a nother.
Their sacramentes defile one a nother. For wedlocke defileth   25
presthode moare then horedom / thefte / murther or any sinne
agenst nature.

They wyll happly demaunde where it is written that wemen shuld
baptise. Verely in this commaundement loue thy neyboure as thy-
selfe it is written / that they maye and ought to ministre not only   30
baptim / but all other in time of neade / iff they be so necessarie as
they preach them.

[B8] And finally though we were sure that god him selfe had

6–8 Sacramentes haue significacions.   23 [Hand]

20 that the] 1573, thar the 1531   26 presthode] ed., preshode 1531, priesthode
1573   29 thy] 1573, they 1531

geuen vs a sacrament / what soeuer it were / yet if the significacion
were once lost we must of necessite / ether seke vpp the significacion
or put some other significacion of gods word therto / what we
ought to doo or beleue therby / or else put it downe. For it is impossible to obserue a sacrament with out significacion / but vnto oure
damnacion. If we kepe the faith purely and the law of loue vnde-
filed / whych are the significacions of all ceremonies there is no ieoperdy to alter or chaunge the facion of the ceremonye or to put it
doune / if nede requyre.

¶Whether the church can erre

There is a nother question whether the church maye erre. Which
if ye vnderstonde of the pope and his generacion / it is verely as hard
a question as to axe / whether he which hath both his eyes out be
blynd or no / or whether it be possible for him that hath one legge
shorter then a nother / to halt. But I said that Christes electe church
is the hole multitude of all repentynge synners that beleue in Christ
and put all their trust and confidence in the mercye of god / felynge
in their hertes / that god for Christes sake loueth them and wilbe or
rather is mercifull vn to them and forgeueth them their synnes of
which they repent / and that he forgeueth them also all the mocions
vn to synne of which they feare lest they shuld therby be drawen in
to synne agayne. And this faith they haue with out all respecte of
their awne deseruynges / yee and for no nother cause then that the
mercifull trueth of god the father which can not lye / hath so promised and so sworne.

[B8v] And this faith and knowlege is euerlastynge life / and by
this we be born a new and made the sonnes of god and obtayne
forgeuenesse of synnes and are translated from deeth to life and from
the wrath of god vn to his loue and fauoure. And this faith is the
mother of all trueth. And bryngeth with hir the spirite of all trueth.
Which spirite purgeth vs / as from all sinne / even so from all lyes

15–18 What the very church is & what faith saveth

3 other] *om.* *1573*   4–5 impossible] *1573*,   impossibible   *1531*
16 multitude] *1573*, multititude *1531*

and erroure noysome and hurtefull. And this faith is the fundacion layd of the appostles and prophetes wheron Paul saith Ephe. ij. that we are bylt / and therby of the household of god. And this faith is the rocke wheron Christ bilt his congregacion. Christ axed the appostles Matth. xvj. whom they toke him for. And Peter answered 5 for them all sayenge I saye that thou art Christ the sonne of the liuinge god that art come in to this worlde. That is / we beleue that thou art he that was promised vn to Abraham / shuld come and blesse vs and deliuer vs. How be it Peter yet wist not by what meanes. But now it is opened thorow out all the world / that thorow 10 the offerynge of his body and bloude. That offeringe is a satisfaccion for the sinne of all that repent and a purchasynge of what so euer they can axe / to kepe them in fauoure. And that they sinne no moare. And Christ answered vppon this rocke I will byld my congregacion: that is / vppon this faith. And agenst the rocke of this 15 faith can no sinne / no hell / no deuell / no lies nor erroure preuayle.

For what soeuer any man hath committed / if he repent and come to this rocke / he is saffe. And that this faith is the only waye bi which the church of Christ goeth vn to god and vn to the enheretaunce of all his riches / testifie all the ap[C1]postles and prophetes 20 and all the scripture / with signes and miracles / and al the bloud of marters. And who soever goeth vnto God and vnto forgeuenesse of synnes or saluacion / by any other waye then thys / the same is an heretike out of the rightwaye and not of Christes church.

For this knowlege maketh a man of the church. And the church is 25 christes body Collossen. j. and every person of the church is a member of christ. Ephe. 5. Now it is no member of christ that hath not christes spirite in it. Roma. viij. as it is no parte of me or member of my body wherin my soule is not present and quikeneth it. And then iff a man be none of christes / he is not of his church. 30

2 Ephe. 2.   4 Mat. 16.   26 Col. j.   27 Ephe. 5.   29 Rom. 8.

4 bilt] build *1573*   8 shuld come and] that should come *1573*

¶How a true member of christes church synneth not / and how he is yet a synner

Furthermoare / he that hath this faith can not sinne / and therfore can not be disceaved with damnable erroures. For by this faith we be (as I saide) borne of God. Now he that is born of god can not synne / for his seed dwelleth in him / and he can not therfore synne / because he is born of God .j. Ihon .iij. which seed is the holygost that kepith a mans hert from consentinge vnto sinne. And therfore it is a false conclusion that master More holdeth / how that a man maye haue a righte faith ioyned with all kyndes of abhominacion and synne.

And yet every membir of Christes congregacion is a synner and sinneth dayly / some moare and some lesse. For it is written .j. Ihon .j. if we saye we haue no synne / we disceaue oure selues and the trueth is not in vs. And agayne iff we saye / we haue not sinned / we make him a liar [C1v] and his worde is not in vs. And Paul .Roma. vij. saith / that good which I wold / that do I not / but that evell which I wold not / that do I. So it is not I that doo it (saith he) but synne that dwelleth in me. Thus are we synners and no synners. No synners / if thou loke vn to the profession of oure hertes towarde the law of God / on oure repentaunce and sorow that we haue / both because we haue synned and also because we be yet full of synne still / and vn to the promises of mercie in oure sauioure christe / and vn to oure fayth. Synners are we / iff thou loke vn to the frailtie of oure flesh / which is as the weakenesse of one that is newly re-couered out of a greate disease / by the reason wherof oure dedes are imperfett. And by the reason where of al so / when occasions be greate / we fall in to horrible dedes / and the frute of the synne which remayneth in oure membirs breaketh out. Notwithstondynge yet the spirite leaveth vs not / but rebuketh vs and bringeth vs home agayne vn to oure profession / so that we never cast off the yocke of God from oure neckes nether yeld vpp oure selues vn to synne / for to serue it / but fighte afresh and begynne a new batayle.

7 j. Ioha. 3.   9–12 Faith and synne can not stond to gether.

[C2] ¶How a christen man can not erre /
and how he maye yet erre

And as they synne not / so they erre not. And on the other syde
as they synne / so they erre: but never vn to deeth and damnacion.
For they never synne of purpose ner holde any erroure maliciously /   5
synnynge agenst the holygoste / but of weakenesse and infirmitie.
As good obedient childern / though they loue their fathers commaundementes / yet breake them oft / by the reason of their wekenesse. And as they can not yelde them selves bond vn to synne / to
serue it: even so they can not erre in any thynge that shuld be agenst   10
the promises which are in christe. And in other thynges their erroures
be not vn to damnacion / though they be neuer so greate / because
they hold them not maliciously. As now / if some when they reade in
the new testament of Christes brethern / wold thynke that they were
oure ladies childern aftir the birth of christe / because they know not   15
the vse of speakynge of the scripture or of the hebrues / how that nye
kinsmen becalled brethren / or happly they might be Iosephes
childern / by some first wife / neyther can haue any to teach him for
tiranny that is so greate / yet coude it not hurte him / though he died
therin / because it hurteth not the redempcion that is in christes   20
bloude. For though she had none but christ / I am therfore neuer the
moare saued / neyther yet the lesse / though she had had. And in soch
like an hundred that plucke not a mans faith from Christ / they might
erre / and yet beneuer the lesse saued no though the contrary were
written in the gospel. For as in other synnes / [C2v] as sone as they be   25
rebuked / they repent: even so here / assone as they were better taught /
they shuld immediatly knowlege their erroure and not resiste.

But they which maliciously maynetene opinions agenst the scripture / or that that can not be proued by the scripture / or soch as
make no mater vn to the scripture and saluacion that is in christ   30
whether they be true or noo / and for the blinde zele of them make
sectes / breakinge the vnite of christes church / for whose sake they
ought to suffre all thynge / and rise agenst their neyboures / whom
they ought to loue as them selues / to slee them / soch men I saye

---

34 / soch] *ed.*, (soch *1531*, (such *1573*

are fallen from christe and make an Idole of their opinions. For except they put trust in soch opinions and thought them necessarie vn
to saluacion / or with a cankred conscience went about to disceaue /
for some filthie purpose / they wold never breake the vnite of faith
5 or yet slee their brethern. Now is this a playne conclusion / that both
they that trust in their awne workes / and they also that put confidence in their awne opinions / be fallen from Christe and erre from
the waye of faith that is in christes bloude / and therfore are none of
christes church / because they be not bilt vppon the rocke of faith.

10   ¶Faith is ever assayled and fought with all.

[C3] Morouer this oure faith which we haue in Christ / is euer
fought agenst / euer assaylled and beten at with disperacion: not
when we sinne only / but also in all temptacions of adversite in to
which God bringeth vs / to nurtoure vs and to shew vs oure awne
15 hertes / the ypocrisie and false thoughtes that there lye hidd / oure al
most no faith at all and as litle loue / even then happly when we
thought oure selues most perfecte of all. For when temptacions come
we can not stond / when we haue synned faith is feble / when wronge
is done vs we can not forgeue / in sickenes / in losse of goodes and in
20 all tribulacions we be impacient: when oure neyboure neadeth oure
helpe / that we must departe with him of oures then loue is colde.

And thus we lerne and fele that there is no goodnesse ner yet
power to doo good / but of God only. And in all soch temptacions
oure faith perisheth not vtterly neyther our loue and consent vnto
25 the law of God / But they be weke / sycke and wounded and not
cleane deed. As a good child whom the father and mother haue
taught nurtoure and wisdom / loueth his father and all his commaundementes / and perceaueth of the goodnesse shewed him / that
his father loueth him and that all his fathers preceptes are vnto his
30 welth and profitt / and that his father commaundeth him nothinge
for any neade that his father hath therof / but seketh his profitt only /

5 brethern] *ed.*, bretern *1531*, brethren *1573*   26 good] *1573*, Good
1531   27 nurtoure] *1573*, nurtourne *1531*

and therfore hath a good faith vn to all his fathers promises and
loueth al his commaundementes and doeth them with good wyll
and with good will goeth to scole. And by the waye haply he seeth
companie playe and with the sight is taken and raveshed of his
me[C3v]mory and forgetteth him selfe and stondeth and beholdeth   5
and falleth to playe also / forgettynge father and mother / all their
kyndes / all their lawes and his awne profitt therto. How be it the
knowlege of his fathers kyndnesse / the faith of his promises and the
loue that he hath agayne vn to his father and the obedient mynde are
not vtterly quenched / but lye hyd / as all thynges do when a man   10
slepeth or lieth in a traunce. And assone as he hath played out all his
lustes or be warned in the meane season / he cometh agayne vn to
his olde profession. Neuer the later many temptacions goo ouer his
herte / and the law as a right hangman tormenteth his conscience
and goeth nye to persuade him that his father will cast him a waye   15
and hange him if he ketche him so that he is like a greate while to
runne awaye rather then to returne vn to his father agayne. Feare and
dreade of rebuke and of losse of his fathers loue and of punishment
wrastell with the trust which he hath in his fathers goodnesse and as
it were geue his faith a fall. But it riseth agayne assone as the rage of   20
the first brount is past and his mynd moare quiett. And the goodnesse of his father and his old kindnesse cometh vn to remembraunce / eyther of his awne corage or by the comforte of some
other. And he beleueth that his father will not cast him a waye or
destroye him / and hopeth that he will no moare doo so.   25

    And vppon that he geteth him home / dismayed. But not all to
gether faythlesse. The old kyndneses wyll not lett him dispayre. How
be it all the world can not sett his hert at rest / vntill the payne be past /
and vntyll he haue herd [C4] the voyce of his father that all is forgeuen.

¶The maner and ordre of oure election   30

    Even so goeth it with gods electe. God choseth them first and they
not god / as thou readest Ihon .xv. And then he sendeth forth and

32 Ioan .15.

---

7 kyndes] kindnes 1573

calleth them / and sheweth them his goodwyll which he beareth vn
to them / and maketh them se / both their awne damnacion in the
lawe and also the mercie that is layd vpp for them in christes bloude /
and therto what he will haue them doo. And then when we se his
5 mercie / we loue him agayne and chose him and submitte our selues
vn to his lawes to walke in them. For when we erre not in witt /
reason and iudgement of thinges / we can not erre in wil and choyse
of thynges. The choyse of a mans will doeth naturally and of hir
awne accorde folowe the iudgement of a mans reason / whether he
10 iudge righte or wronge. So that in teachinge only resteth the pith of
a mans liuynge. How be it there be swine that receaue no lerninge
but to defile it. And there be dogges that rent all good lerninge with
their teth. And there be pope holy whych folowynge a ryghtewesnes of their awne faynynge resiste the rightwesnesse of god in
15 Christe. And there be that can not attend to herken vn to the trueth
for rage of lustes / which when lustes abate / come and obeye well
ynough.

And therfore a Christen man must be pacient and sofre longe to
wynne his brother to Christ / that he whych attendeth not to daye /
20 maye receave grace and heare to morowe: [C4v] we se some at their
very later ende / when colde feare of deeth hath quenched the heet
of their appetites / lerne and consent vnto the trueth / where vnto
before they coude geue none eare / for the wylde rages of lustes that
blinded their wittes.

25 And though gods electe can not so faull that they rise not agayne /
because that the mercy of god euer wayteth vppon them / to deliuer
them from euell / as the care of a kind father wayteth vppon his
sonne / to warne him and to kepe him from occasions and to call
hym bake agayne yf he begonne to ferre: yet they forgett them
30 selues oftymes and synke downe in to traunces and fall aslepe in
lustes for a season. But assone as they be awaked they repent and
come agayne wyth out resistaunce. God now and then withdraweth
his hande and leueth them vnto their awne strength / to make them
feale that there is no power to do good but of god only lest they
35 shulde be proude of that which is none of theirs. God layd so sore

25–28 Mercye waiteth euer on the electe.

awaight of persecucion vppon Dauids backe that passed his strength
to beare. So that he cried oft out in his psalmes / sayenge that he had
liued well and folowed the right waye off God in vaine. For the
moare he kepte him selfe from sinne / the worse yt went with hym /
as he thought / and the better with his enemie Saull the worse he   5
was. Yet god left hym not there / but comforted him and shewed
him thynges which before he wist not of / how that the saintes must
be pacyent and a byde gods heruest / vntyll the wekedenesse of
vngodly synners befull ripe / that god maye repe it in dew season.
    God also suffered occasyons stronger then [C5] Dauid / to faull   10
vppon him and to carie him cleane out of the waye. Was he not readye for a churlysshe answere to haue slayn naball and all the males
of his housse / so moch as the chyld in the cradell? how be it God
with helde hym and kepte hym backe from that evell / thorow the
wisdome of Abegall. How longe slomberd he / or rather how hard   15
in slepe was he in the adulterye of Bathseba. And in the murther of
her husbond Vriah / But at both tymes assone as he was rebuked
and his faulte told him / he repented immedyatly & turned agayne
mekely. Now in all that longe tyme / from the adulterye of Bathsabe
vntyll the prophete Nathan rebuked him he had not lost his faith nor   20
yet his loue vnto the lawes of god / no moare then a man loseth hys
wittes when he ys a slepe. He had forgott hym selfe only and had
not malycyously cast of the yocke of gods commaundementes from
off his necke. There is no man so good / but that there cometh a
tyme vppon hym / when he fealeth in hym selfe no moare faith or   25
loue vnto god / then a sycke man oftymes feleth the tast of his meate
which he eateth.
    And in lyke maner the apostles of chryst at hys passyon were as-
tonyed and amased and in soch a storme of temptacyons / for the
soden chaunge from soo great glorye in to so vyle and shamfull   30
deeth / that they had forgott all the myracles and all the wordes
whych he had told them before / how that he shulde be betrayed
and delyuered on the same maner vnto deeth. Morouer they neuer

1 Dauid

2 in] of *1573*   9 repe] ripe *1573*   12 churlysshe] *ed.*, churlysse *1531*,
1573   21 loseth] looseth *1573*   31 forgott] forget *1573*

vnderstode that sayenge of hys deeth because their hertes were all
waye hevie and ouer lade wyth erthely [C5v] thoughtes. For though
they saw him reyse vpp other / yet who shulde reyse hym vpp /
when he were deed / they coude not comprehende.

5   Reade what thou reade canst / and thou shalt fynd no temptacyon lyke vnto that from the creacyon of the world / or so greate as
yt by the hundred parte. So that the wonderfull soden chaunge and
the tereble syght of hys passyon and of hys most cruell and most
vile deeth / and the losse of whom they so greatly loued / that theyr
10   hertes wolde fayne haue died wyth hym / and the feare of their awne
deeth / and the impossibilite that a man shulde ryse agayne of his
awne power / so occupyed theyr myndes and so astonyed them and
amased them / that they coude receaue no comforte / ether of the
scrypture or of the miracles which they had sene christ doo / nor of
15   the monicions and warnynge wherewith he had warned them before / nether of the women that brought them tydynges that he was
rysen. The swerd of temptacyons wyth feare / sorow / mornynge
& wepynge / had depely perced theyr hertes / and the cruell syght
had so combred their mindes / that they coude not beleue / vntyll
20   chryst hym selfe came / deeth put off and ouercome / ye and when
they first saw him / they were astonied for wonderinge and ioye to
gether that thoughtes a rose in theyr hertes / alas ys thys he or doeth
some spirite mocke vs? he was faine to lett them feale him and to
eate with them / to strength theyr faythes.

25   How be yt there was none of them that was fallen in hys hert from
chryste. For assone as the wemen brought worde / Peter and Ihon
ran vnto the sepulchre and saw and wondred and wold fayne haue
beleuen that he was [C6] risen and longed for hym? But coude not
beleue the wound of temptacyon beinge greater then that it coude be
30   healed wyth the preachynge of a woman with out any other miracle.
     Ioseph of Arimathea and Nicodemus which while he yet liued
durst not be a knowen of hym assone as he was deed / bedged his

15 warnynge] warnings 1573   17 feare /] ed., feare 1531, 1573
27 wondred] 1573, wonred 1531   28 beleuen] beleued 1573; risen] 1573, rosen
1531   32 bedged] begged 1573

bodie and buried hym boldly. And the wemen assone as yt was lawful to worke prepared their annoyntmentes with all diligence. And
the hertes of the dysciples that went to Emaus burned in their brestes
to heare speake of hym.

And thomas had not forsaken Christ / but coude not beleue vntyll   5
he sawe hym / and yet desyred and longed to se hym and reioysed
when he saw hym and for ioye cryed out / my lorde my god. There
was none of them that euer railed on hym and came so ferre forth /
to saye / he was a disceauer and wrought wyth the dyuels craft all
thys whyle / and se where to he ys come in the ende? we defye hym   10
and all hys werkes false wretch that he was and hys false doctrine
also. And therto must they haue come at the last / when feare /
sorow and wonderynge had bene past / yf they had not bene preuented and holpe in the meane tyme.

Yee and peter assone as he had denied chryst came too hym selfe   15
immedyatly and went out and wepte bytterly for sorow. And thus
ye se / that peters fayth fayled not / though yt were oppressed for a
tyme: so that we neade to seke no gloses for the texte that Chryst
sayd to peter how that hys fayth shulde not fayle. Yes sayth Master
More yt fayled in hym selfe / but was reserued in our ladye.   20

[C6v] But lat vs se the texte and their glose to gether. Christ saith
Luke .xxij. Simon / Simon / sathan seketh you to sifte you as men
sifte whete: but I haue prayed for the / that thy faith shall not faile /
werfore when thou art come vn to thy selfe agayne strength thy
brethern. Now put this wise glose therto and se how they agre to   25
gether. Simon / satan seketh to sift you as whete / but I haue prayd
for the / that my mothers faith shall not faile / wherfore when thou
art come to thy selfe agayne / acordynge as my prayar hath obtayned for the / that my mothers faith shall not faile / strength thy
brethern. How saye ye / is not this a propir texte and well framed to 30
gether? Do ye not thinke that there is as moch witte in the heed of
mad colens / as in the braynes of soch expositoures?

15–17 Peters fayth fayled not.   19 [Hand]   22 Lu. 22.   28 [Hand]

4 speake of hym] him spoken of *1573*   21 But] *1573*, but *1531*

¶Whether the pope and his secte be Christes church or no

That the pope and his spirites be not the church maye this wise be proued. He that hath no faith to be saued thorow Christe / is not of
5   Christes churche. The pope beleueth not to be saued thorow Christe. For he teacheth to trust in holy workes for the remission of sinnes and saluacion: as in the workes of penaunce enioyned / in vowes / in pilgremage / in chastite / in other mens prayars and holy liuynge / in freres and freres cotes / in saintes merites / and the sig-
10 nificacions put out / he teacheth to beleue in the dedes of the ceremo-nies and of the sacramentes ordeyned at the begynnynge to preach vn to vs and to do vs seruice / and not that we shuld beleue in them and serue them. And a thousand such supersticiousnesses setteth he before vs in steade [C7] of Christ / to beleue in / nether Christ ner
15 gods worde / nether honourable to god ner serviceable vnto our neyboure ner profitable vn to our selues for the tamynge of the flesh / which all are the denyenge of Christes bloud.

A nother reason is this. Whosoeuer beleueth in Christ / consent-eth that gods lawe is good. The pope consenteth not that gods lawe
20 is good. For he hath forboden lawfull wedlocke vn to all his / ouer whom he raigneth as a temporall tirant with lawes of his awne mak-ynge and not as a brother exhortynge them to kepe Christes. And he hath graunted vnlaufull horedom vn to as many as bringe money. As thorow all doucheland / euery prest payenge a gulden vn to the
25 archedecon shall frely and quietly haue his hore and put hir awaye at his pleasure & take a nother at his awne luste. As they doo in wales / in yerland / Scotland / Fraunce & Spayne. And in Englond therto they be not few whych haue licences to kepe hores / some of the pope and some of their ordinaries. And when the parishes goo
30 to law with them to put a waye their hores / the bisshopes officers mocke them / poll them and make them spend their thryftes / and

3 1.   4 Pope   18 2.

---

18 reason] *1573*, rason *1531*   20 forboden] forbydden *1573*   24 all] *om.* *1573*; gulden] *ed.*, gelden *1531*, gildren *1573*   27 Englond] *ed.*, Euglond *1531*, En-gland *1573*

the prestes kepe their hores still. How be it in very dede sens they
were rebuked by the preachynge of wicleffe / oure englesh spiritualtie haue layd their snares vn to mens wiues / to couer their abhominacions / though they byde not all waye secret.

Ther to all Christen men if they haue done amisse repent when   5
their fautes be told them. The spiritualtie repent not / but of very
lust and consent to synne persecute both the scripture wherwith
they be rebuked and also them that [C7v] warne them to amend &
make heretikes of them and burne them. And besydes that / the
pope hath mad a playne decre in which he commaundeth sayenge /   10
though the pope synne neuer so greuously and draw with him to
hell by his ensample thousandes innumerable / yet let no man be so
hardye to rebuke him. For he is heed ouer all & none ouer him distinct .xl. Si papa.

And Paul saith Roma. xiij. let euery soule obey the hier powers   15
that are ordeyned to punysh synne. The pope will not / ner let any
of his.

And Paul chargeth .i. Corin. v. if he that is a brother be an horekeper / a dronkerd / couetouse / an extorsioner or a raylar and so
forth / that we haue no felowsheppe with him: No not so moch as   20
to eate in his companie. But the pope with violence compelleth vs
to haue soch in honoure / to receaue the sacramentes of them / to
heare their masses and to beleue all they saye / and yet they wyll not
lett vs se whether they saye trouth or no. And he compelleth .x.
parishes to paye their tithes and offeringes vn to one soch to goo and   25
runne at riott at their cost & to doo noughte therfore. And a thousand soch like doeth the pope contrarie vn to Christes doctrine.

¶The argumentes where with the pope wold proue
him selfe the church / are solued.

Notwithstondinge because as they be all shauen they be all shame-   30
lesse to affirme that they by the right church & can not erre / though

5 3.   15 4.   16 Rom. 13.   18 5.   20 1. Cor. 5.

2 rebuked] 1573, rekuked 1531

all the world seeth that not one of them is in the right waye and that
they haue with vtter defiaunce forsaken both the doctrine and
livinge of [C8] Christe and of all his appostles / lat vs se the sophistrie where with they wold persuade it. One of thier hie reasons is
5 this. The church / saye they / was before the heretikes / and the heretikes came euer out of the church and left it. And they were before
all them which they now call heretikes and lutherans / and the luth-
eranes came out of them. &c. Wherfore they be the right church and
the other heretikes in dede as they be called. Well / I will like wise
10 dispute. First the right church was vnder Moses and Aaron & so
forth in whose rowmes satt the scribes phareses and hye prestes in
the time of Christ. And they were before Christe. And Christ and
his apostles came out of them and departed from them and left them.
Wherefore the scribes phareses and hie prestes were the right
15 church / and Christ and his appostles and disciples heretikes and a
damnable secte. And so the Iewes ar yet in the right waye and we in
erroure. And of trueth if their blynd reason be good / then is this
argument so to. For they be like and are both one thynge.

But in as moch as the kingdom of god stondeth not in wordes /
20 as paul sayth .1. Co. iiij. but in power / therfore loke vn to the mary
and pith of the thinges selfe / and lett vayne wordes passe. Vnder
Abraham / Isaac / and Iacob was the church greate in faith and small
in numbre / And as it encreased in numbre / so it decreased in faith
vntyll the tyme of Moses. And out of those vnbeleuers god stered
25 vpp Moses & brought them vnto the right faith agayne. And Moses
left a glorious church and in faith and cleauinge vn to the word of
god / and deliuered them vn to Iosuah Eleazer / Phineas and Caleb.

[C8v] But assone as the generacion of them that saw the miracles
of god were deed / they fell to Idolatrie immediatly as thou seist in
30 the bible. And god when he had delyuered them in to captiuite for
to chastise their wekednesse / stered them vpp a prophete euer
moare / to call them vn to his testament agayne. And so he did well-
nye an hundred tymes / I suppose / yer Christ came / for they neuer

---

5–6 Their first reason   9–10 A like reason   19–20 The solucion

19 of] *1573*, af *1531*   20 but] *1573*, But *1531*   25 them] *1573*, then *1531*;
right faith] faith right *1573*   26 church and] Churche, both *1573*

bode any space in the right faith. And agenst the comynge of Christ
the scribes / Phareses / Caiphas / Anna / and the elders / were crepte
vpp in to the sete of Moses / Aaron and the holy prophetes and patriarkes and succeded them linially and had the scripture of god but
euen in captiuite / to make marchaundice of it and to abvse it vn to   5
their awne glorie & profitt. And though they kepte the people from
outward Idolatrie of worshepynge of images with the hethen: yet
they brought them in to a worse inward Idolatrie of a false fayth
& trust in their awne dedes and in vayne tradicions of their awne
faynynge. And they had put out the significacions of all the cereme-   10
nies and sacramentes of the olde testament and taught the people to
beleue in the workes selfe / and had corrupte the scripture with false
gloses. As thou maist se in the gospell / how Christ warneth his disciples to be warre of the leuen of the phareses which was their false
doctrine and gloses. And in a nother place he rebuked the scribes   15
and the phareses sayenge: wo be to them / because they had taken
awaye the keye of knowlege and had shutt vpp the kingdome of
heven and neyther wold entre in them selues ner sofre them that
wolde. How had they shutt it vpp? verely with their tradicions and
false gloses whych [D1] they had sowed to the scripture in playne   20
places and in the takynge a waye the meaninge of the ceremonies
and sacrifices and teachinge to beleue in the worke.

   And oure ypocrites are in like maner crept vpp in to the sete of
Christ and of his apostles / by succession: not to doo the dedes of
Christ and his appostles / but for lucre only (as the nature of the   25
wilye foxe is / to gett him an hole made with a nother beestes laboure) and to make marchaundice of the people with fayned
wordes / as Peter warned vs before / & to doo acordinge as Christ
and all his apostles prophesyed / how they shuld begyle and leade
out of the right waye / all them that had no loue to folow and liue   30
aftir the trouth.

   And in like maner haue they corrupte the scripture / and blinded
the right waye with their awne constitucions / with tradicions of

---

15 Mat. 16.   16 Mat. 23.   26 2. Pet. 2.

10 they] *om. 1573*   18 heven] *ed.,* even *1531,* heauen *1573*   24 apostles]
ed., ppostles *1531,* Apostles *1573*

domme ceremonies / with takynge awaye the significacions of the
sacramentes / to make vs beleue in the worke of the sacramentes
first / where by they might the better make vs beleue in workes of
their settynge vpp aftirwarde / and with false gloses which they haue
5   patched to the scripture in playne places to destroye the litterall sens
for to sett vp a false fayned sens of allegories / when there is none
soch. And therby they haue stopte vpp the gates of heven / the true
knowlege of Christ / and haue made their awne belies the dore. For
thorow their belies must thou crepe and there leave all thy fall be-
10   hynde the.

And soch blynd reasons as oures make agenst vs / made they
agenst Christe sayenge: Abraham is our father / we be Moses disciples / how knoweth he the vnderstondinge of the scripture / seinge
he neuer lerned of any of vs? only the cursed [D1v] vnlerned people
15   that know not the scripture beleue in him. Loke whether any of the
rulars or phareses doo beleue in him.

Wherfore the scripture truely vnderstond aftir the playne places
and generall articles of the faith which thou findest in the scripture /
and the ensamples that are gonne before / wyll all waye testifie who
20   is the right church. Though the phareses succeded the patriarkes and
prophetes and had the scripture of them / yet they were heretikes
and fallen from the faith of them & from their lyuynge. And Christ
and his disciples & Ihon the Baptist departed from the phareses
which were heretikes / vn to the right sens of the scripture & vn to
25   the faith & liuinge of the patriarkes & prophetes and rebuked the
phareses. As thou seist how Christ calleth them ypocrites / dissim-
ulars / blynd gydes & paynted sepulchres. And Ihon called them the
generacion of vipers & serpentes. Of Ihon the angell said vn to his
father Luke .j. he shall turne many of the children of Israel vn to
30   their lord god. Which yet before Ihon beleued after a fleshly vnderstondynge in god & thought them selues in the right waye. And he
shall turne the hertes of the fathers vn to the childerne. That is / he
shall with his preachynge & true interpretynge of the scripture make

---

11 Ioan .8.   23 Christ   24–25 Ioan baptist   29 Luce .1.

9 thy] that *1573*   17 vnderstond] vnderstode *1573*   20 right] *om. 1573*

soch a spirituall hert in the children as was in their fathers / Abraham / Isaac / & Iacob. And he shall turne the disobedient vn to the
obedience of the rightteouse & prepare the lorde a perfecte people.
That is / them that had sett vpp a rightewysnesse of their awne &
were therfore disobedient vnto the rightewysnesse of faith / shall   5
he conuerte from their blyndnesse vn to the wisdome of them that
beleued in god to be made righ[D2]tewysse / and with those fathers
shall he geue the childern egles eyes to spie out Christ & his rightewysnesse and to forsake their awne and so to become perfecte.

And aftir the same maner / though oure popish ypocrites succede   10
Christ and his appostles and haue their scripture / yet they befallen
from the faith and liuinge of them and are heretikes and had nede of
a Ihon Baptist to conuerte them. And we departe from them vn to
the true scripture and vnto the faith and liuynge theirof / and rebuke
them in like maner. And as they which departe from the faith of the   15
true church are heretikes / even so they that departe from the church
of heretikes and false fayned faith of ypocrites / are the true church /
which thou shalt all waye know by their faith examined by the scripture and by their profession and consent to liue acordynge vn to the
lawes of god.   20

¶A nother argument

Another like blynd reason they haue where in is all their trust. As
we come out of them & they not of vs / so we receaue the scripture
of them & they not of vs. How know we that it is the scripture of
god and true but because they teach vs so? How can we that beleue /   25
excepte we first beleue that they be the church and can not erre in
any thynge that perteyneth vn to oure soules health. For if a man tell
me of a marvelouse thynge / wherof I can haue no nother knowlege
then by his mouth only / how shuld I geue credence excepte I beleued that the man were so honest that he coude not lye or wold not   30
lye. Wherefore we must beleue that they be the right church that can
not erre or else we can beleue nought at all.

---

1 [Hand]   22–23 Their seconde reason

25 that] *om. 1573*

[D2v] This wise reason is their shoteancre and al their hold / their
refuge to flight and chefe stone in their fundacion / wheron they
haue bilt all their lies and all their mischeue that they haue wrought
this .viij. hundred yeres. And this reason do the Iewes laye vn to
5   oure charge this daye / and this reason doeth chefely blynd them and
hold them still in obstinacie. Oure spirites first falsifie the scripture
to stablish their lyes. And when the scripture cometh to light and is
restored vn to the true vnderstondinge and their iuglinge spied / and
they like to sofre shippwracke / then they cast out this ancre / they
10 be the church and can not erre / their auctorite is greater then the
scripture / and the scripture is not true / but because they saye so
and admitte it. And therfore what soeuer they affirme / is of as
greate auctorite as the scripture.

    Notwithstondinge / as I saide / the kingdome of heuen stondeth
15 not in wordes of mans wisdome / but in power and spirite. And
therfore loke vn to the ensamples of the scripture and so shalt thou
vnderstonde. And of an hundred ensamples betwene Moses and
Christe / where the Israelites fell from god and were euer restored
by one prophete or other / let vs take one: even Ihon the Baptiste.
20 Ihon went before Christ to prepare his waye / that is / to brynge
men vn to the knowlege of their sinnes and vn to repentaunce /
thorow true expoundynge of the lawe / which is the only waye vn
to Christe. For excepte a man knowlege his sinnes and repent of
them / he can haue no parte in Christe / of Ihon Christ saith Matt.
25 xvij. that he was Elias that shuld come and restore all thynge. That
is / he shuld restore the scripture vn to the right sens agayne / which
[D3] the phareses had corrupte with the leuen of their false gloses
and vayne fleshly tradicions. He made croked thynges streyght / as
it is written / and rough smoth. Which is also to be vnderstonde of
30 the scripture / which the phareses had made croked wrestynge them
vn to a false sens with weked gloses / and so rough that no man
coude walke in the waye of them. For when god said / honoure fa-

---

12–13 The solucion   24 Mat. 17.

2 refuge to flight and] *ed.*, refuge / to flight and *1531*, refuge, to flye vnto
1573   3 their mischeue] the mischief *1573*   14 kingdome] *ed.*, kingdone
1531, kyngdome *1573*

ther and mother / meaninge that we shuld obey them and also helpe
them at their nede / the phareses put this glose therto / out of their
awne leuen sayenge: God is thy father and mother. Wherfore what
soeuer nede thy father & mother haue / iff thou offer to god / thou
art hold excused. For it is better to offer to god / then to thy father   5
and mother and so moch moare meritorious as god is greater then
they: yee and god hath done moare for the then they and is moare
thy father and mother then they. As oures now affirme / that it is
moare meritorious to offer to god and his holy deed saintes / then
vn to the pore liuynge saintes. And when god had promised the peo-   10
ple a sauioure to come and blesse them and saue them from their
synnes / the phareses taught to beleue in holy workes to be saued by
as if they offered and gaue to be prayd for. As oures / as ofte as we
haue a promise to be forgeuen at the repentaunce of the herte thorow
Christes bloud shedynge / put to / thou must first shriue thy selfe to   15
vs of euery sillable / & we must laye oure handes on thine heed and
whistell out thy synnes and enioyne the penaunce to make satisfaccion. And yet art thou but loused from the synne only that thou
shalt not come in to hell / but thou must yet sofre for every synne
.vij. yeres in purgatory which is as whott as hell / ex[D3v]cepte thou   20
bye it out of the pope. And if thou aske by what meanes the pope
geueth soch pardon. They answere out of the merites of christ. And
thus at the last they graunt agenst them selues / that Christ hath not
only deserued for vs the remission of oure synnes / but also the
forgeuenesse of that grosse and fleshly imagined purgatory / saue   25
thou must by it out of the pope. And with soch tradicions they toke
awaye the keye of knowlege and stopped vpp the kingdome of
heuen that no man coude entre in.

  And as I said / they taught the people to beleue in the dedes of the
ceremonyes whych god ordeyned not to iustifie but to be signes of   30
promises by which they that beleued were iustified. But the phareses
put out the significacions and quenched the faith and taught to be
iustified by the worke / as oures haue serued vs.

---

20 Purgatory

15 put to] *1573*, putto *1531*

For oure sacramentes were onse but signes partely of what we shulde beleue / to stere vs vp vn to faith / and partely what we shuld doo / to stere vs vpp to doo the law of god / and were not workes to iustifie.

5   Now make this reason vn to Ihon and vn to many prophetes that went before him & did as he did / ye and vn to Christ him selfe and his appostles / and thou shalt finde them all heretikes / and the scribes and phareses good men / iff that reason be good. Therfore this wise thou maist answere. No thankes vn to the heedes of that church that the scripture was kepte / but vn to the mercie of god. For as they had destroyed the right sens of it for their lucre sake / even so wold they haue destroyed it also had they coude / rather then the people shuld haue come vn to the right vnderstondinge of it / as they slew [D4] the true interpretours and preachers of it. And even so no thankes vn to oure ypocrites that the scripture is kepte / but vn to the botomlesse mercie of god.

For as they haue destroyed the right sens of it with their leuen / and as they destroye dayly the trewe preachers of it / and as they kepe it from the laye people / that they shuld not se how they iugle with it / even so wolde they destroye it also / coude they brynge it aboute / rather then we shuld come by the true vnderstondynge of it were it not that god prouided other wise for vs. For they haue put the stories that shuld in many thynges helpe vs / cleane out of the waye / as nye as they coude. They haue corrupte the legend and liues all most of all sayntes. They haue fayned false bokes and put them forth / some in the name of S. Hierome / some in the name of saynt Augustine / in the name of S. Ciprian / S. Deonise & other holy men. Which are proued none of theirs / partly by the stile & latine / & partly by autenticke stories. And as the Iewes haue sett vpp a boke of tradicions called talmud / to destroye the sens of the scripture / Vn to whych they geue faith & vn to the scripture none at all be it never so playne / but saye it can not be vnderstonde / saue by that talmud: even so haue oures set vpp their dunce / their Thomas & a

---

30 Talmud   33 Dunce

12 had] if *1573*   32 that] the *1573*

thousand like draffe / to stablish their lies / thorow falsifienge the
scripture / & saye that it can not be vnderstonde with out them / be
it never so playne. And if a man allege an holy doctoure agenst them
they glose him out as they doo the scripture / or will not heare / or
saye the church hath other wise determined.   5

Now therfore when they aske vs how we kno[D4v]we that it is
the scripture of god / aske them how Ihon Baptiste knew and other
prophetes which god stered vpp in all soch times as the scripture was
in like captiuite vnder ypocrites? Did Ihon beleue that the scribes /
phareses and hie prestes were the true church of god / and had his   10
spirite and coude not erre? who taught the egles to spie out their
praye? euen so the children of god spie out their father and Christes
electe spie out their lorde / and trace out the pathes of his fete and
folowe / ye though he goo vppon the playne and liquide water
which will receaue no steppe: and yet there they find out his foote / 15
his electe know him / but the world knoweth him not Ihon .1. If the
world know him not / and thou call the world pride / wrath / envie /
couetousnesse / slowth / glotonnye and lecherie / then our spiritualtie know him not. Christes shepe heare the voyce of Christ Ihon
.x. where the world of ypocrites as they know him not / even so the   20
wolues heare not his voyce / but compell the scripture to heare them
and to speake what they luste. And therfore excepte the lorde of Sa-
baoth had left vs seed / we had bene all as Sodom and Gommor said
Esaias in his first chapter. And even so saide Paule in his tyme. And
even so saye we in oure tyme / that the lord of the hostes hath saued 25
him seed and hath gathered him a flocke to whom he hath geuen
eares to heare / that the ypocritish wolues can not heare / and eyes
to se / that the blynde leadars of the blynd can not se / and an hert
to vnderstonde / that the generacion of poysoned vipers can nether
vnderstonde ner knowe.   30

If they allege sent Augustine which saith / I had not beleued the
gospell / excepte the auctorite [D5] of the church had moued me. I

5 Question   6 Answere   16 Ioan   .1.   17 [Hand]   19 Ioa.
10.   24 Esa. 1.   26 Rom. 9.   31–32 Augustinus

18 couetousnesse /] ed., couetousnesse 1531, couetousnesse, 1573   24 in his
first chapter] .1. 1573   32 auctorite] ed., auciorite 1531, authoritie 1573

answere / as they abuse that sayenge of the holy man / even so they
allege al the scripture and all that they bringe for them / even in a
false sens. S. Augustine before he was conuerted was an hethen man
and a philosopher full of worldly wisdome vn to whom the preachinge of christe is but folishnesse / saith paul .j. Corin. j. And he disputed with blynd reasons of wordly wisdome agenst the christen.
Neuerthelesse the ernest liuinge of the christen acordinge vn to their
doctrine and the constant soferinge of persecucion and aduersite for
their doctrines sake moued him and stered him to beleue that it was
no vayne doctrine / but that it must nedes be of god / in that it had
soch power with it. For it happeneth that they which will not heare
the worde at the begynninge / are aftir warde moued by the holy
conuersation of them that beleue. As Peter warneth christen wiues
that had hethen husbandes that wold not heare the trueth preached /
to liue so godly that they might winne their hethen husbandes with
holy conuersacion. And Paul saith how knowest thou christen wife /
whether thou shalt winne thine hethen husbande / with holy conuersacion ment he. For many are wonne with godly liuynge / which
at the first ether will not heare or can not beleue. And that is the
auctorite that S. Augustine ment. But if we shall not beleue / tyll
the liuynge of the spiritualtie conuerte vs / we belike to byde longe
ynough in vnbeleffe.

And when they aske whether we receaved the scripture of them?
I answere / that they which come after receaue the scripture of them
that go before. And when they aske whether we bele[D5v]ue not
that it is gods worde by the reason that they tell vs so. I answere /
that there are .ij. maner faythes / an historicall faith and a felynge
faith. The historical faith hangeth of the trueth and honestie of the
teller or of the comen fame and consent of many. As if one told me
that the turke had wonne a citie and I beleved it moved with the
honestie of the man. Now if there come a nother that semeth moare
honest or that hath better persuasions that it is not so / I thynke immediatly that he lied and lose my faith agayne. And a felynge faith

---

4 1. Cor. 1.   13 1. P. 3.   16 1. Cori. 7.

6 wordly] worldly *1573*   13 beleue] *1573*, belue *1531*

is / as iff a man were there present whan it was wonne and their were wounded and had there lost all that he had and were taken presoner there also. That man shuld so beleue that all the world coude not turne him from his faith. Even like wise iff my mother had blowen on hir finger and told me that the fire wold burne me / I shuld haue 5 beleued hir with an historicall faith / as we beleue the stories of the worlde / because I thought she wold not haue mocked me. And so I shuld haue done / if she had told me that the fire had bene cold and wold not haue burned / but assone as I had put my fingre in the fire / I shuld haue beleued / not by the reason of hir / but with a felynge 10 faith / so that she coud not haue persuaded me aftir warde the contrarie. So now with an historicall faith I maye beleue that the scripture is Gods by the teachynge of them / and so I shuld haue done though they had told me that roben hode had bene the scripture of God. Which faith is but an opinion and therfore abideth euer frute- 15 lesse and fauleth a waye / iff a moare gloriouse reason be made vnto me or iff the preacher liue contrarye.

[D6] But of a felynge faith it is written. Ihon .vj. They shalbe all taught of God. That is / God shall write it in their hertes with his holy spirite. And Paul also testifieth Romano. viij. the spirite 20 beareth recorde vn to oure spirite / that we be the sonnes off God. And this faith is none opinion / but a sure felynge / and therfore euer frutefull. Neyther hangeth it of the honestie of the preacher but of the power of God and of the spirite / and therfore iff all the preachers of the world wold goo a boute to persuade the contrary / it wold 25 not preuayle / no moare then though they wold make me beleue the fire were cold / aftir that I had put my fingre therin.

Of this ye haue an ensample Ihon .iiij. of the Samaritanish wife / which left hir pitcher and went in to the citie and said / come and se a man that hath told me all that euer I did / is not he Christe and 30 many of the Samaritanes beleued because of the sayenge of the woman / how that he had told hir all that euer she did / and went out vn to him and desyred him to come in / which faith was but an

18 Ioh. 6.　　　20 Rom. 8.　　　29 Ioan .4.

10 the reason] reason *1573*　　　26 preuayle] *1573*, preualye *1531*　　　S2 Rom.
8.] *1573*, *type reversed for* Rom. 8. *1531*

opinion and no faith that coude haue lasted or haue brought out
frute / but when they had herd Christ / the spirite wrought and
made them fele. Wheruppon they came vn to the woman and saide:
we beleue not now because of thy sayenge / but because we haue
5   harde our selues and know that he is christ the sauioure of the
worlde. For christes preachinge was with power and spirite that maketh a man feale and knowe and worke to / and not as the scribes
and phareses preached and as oures make a man ready to cast his
gorge [D6v] to heare them raue and rage as mad men. And therfore
10 saith the scripture cursed is he that trusteth in man and maketh flesh
his arme / that is to saye / his strength. And euen so cursed is he that
hath no nother beleffe but because men so saye. Cursed were he that
had no nother why to beleue then that I so saye. And even so cursed
is he that beleueth only be cause the pope so saith / and so forth
15 thorow oute all the men in the worlde.

¶The faith that dependeth of a nother mans mouth is weke.

If I haue no nother fealynge in my faith then because a man so
saith / then is my faith faithlesse and frutelesse. For if I haue no
20 nother felynge that lecherie is synne then that the pope so preacheth / whom I se before my face sett vppe in Rome a stues of .xx. or
.xxx. thousand hores / takynge of every pece tribute yerly / and his
bisshopes with all other his disciples folowynge the ensample
mightily / and the pope therwith not content / but to sett vpp therto
25 a stues of younge boyes agenst nature / the committers of which
synne be burnt at a stake amonge the turkes / as Moses also commaundeth in his lawe / and the pope also to forbid all the spiritu-
alltie / a multitude of .xl. or .l. hundred thousand to mary / & to
geue them licence to kepe euery man his whore who so wyll: if I
30 saye / I haue no nother felynge in my faith that lechery is synne then
this mans preachinge / I thynke my faith shuld be to weake to beare

20 Lecherye

---

11 strength] 1573, strengh 1531

moch frute. How coude I beleue a man that wold saye he loued me /
if [D7] all his dedes were contrary? I coude not beleue God him selfe
that he loued me / if in all my trybulacions I had of him no nother
comforte then those bare wordes.

And in like maner if I had no nother felynge in my fayth that 5
couetousnesse were synne / then that the spiritualtie so sayth / my
faith coude be but weake and faintie / when I se how the pope wyth
wiles hath thrust downe the emproure / and how the bisshopes and
prelates be cropt vpp an hye in all regyons aboue their kinges and
haue made them a seuerall kingdome and haue goten in to their 10
handes all most the one halfe of euery realme whiche they diuide
amonge them selues / geuinge no laye man ony parte wyth them /
and hepynge vpp bisshoperike vppon bisshoperike / promocyon
vppon promocion / benefice vppon benefice / with vnions and tot
quottes robbinge in euery parish the soules of their fode and the pore 15
of their due sustynaunce: ye and some preachinge that it were lesse
sinne to haue .ij. wyues then .ij. benefices / but whyle they be yet
younge & hote / and therfore thynke couetousnesse greater synne
then lecherye: which same / when they be waxed elder and their
complexcyon some what altered / thinke that couetousnesse is as 20
small a synne as lechery / and therfore take all that cometh. And if
any man cast theyr preachynge in their tethes / they answere that
they be better lerned and haue sene further. If I saye / I haue no
nother felinge that couetousnesse is synne / then the preachynge of
these holy fathers / my faith were bilt but vppon a weke rocke or 25
rather on the soft sonde. And therfore oure defenders do ryght well
to fome out their awne shame and to vtter the secret thoughtes
[D7v] of their hertes. For as they write / so they beleue. Other felynge of the lawes of god and feyth of chryst haue they none / then
that theyr God the pope so sayth. And therfore as the pope preach- 30
eth with hys mouth only / even soo beleue they wyth theyr mouth
only what soeuer he preacheth / with out moare a doo / be it neuer
so abhominable / and in theyr hertes consent vnto all their

---

fathers wekednesse and folow hym in theyr dedes as fast as they can runne.

The turkes beinge in numbre .v. tymes mo then we knowlege one God and beleue many thynges of God moued only by the auctoryte
5   of theyr elders and presume that God wyll not let so greate a multitude erre so longe tyme. And yet they haue erred and bene faythlesse thys .viij. hundred yeres. And the Iewes beleue thys daye / as moch as the carnall sorte of them euer beleued / moued also by the auctoryte of theyr elders only / and thynke that yt ys impossyble for them
10   to erre / beynge Abrahams seed and the chyldern of them to whom the promysses of all that we beleue were made. And yet they haue erred and bene faythlesse thys .xv. hundred yeres. And we of lyke blyndnesse beleue only by the auctoryte of our elders and of lyke pryde thynke that we can not erre / beynge soch a multytude. And
15   yet we se how God in the olde testament did lett the greate multitude erre / reseruynge al waye a litle flocke to call the other backe agayne and to testifie vnto them the right waye.

¶How this word church hath a double interpretacyon

20   This ys therfore a sure conclusyon / as paul sayth .Ro. ix. that not all they that are of Israel are Israelites / neyther because they [D8] be Abrahams seed / are they all Abrahams chyldren: but they only that folow the faith of Abraham. Euen so now none of them that beleue wyth theyr mouthes moued wyth the auctoryte of theyr elders only:
25   that ys / none of them that beleue wyth Master Mores fayth / the popes fayth and the deuels fayth whych maye stonde (as Master More confesseth) with al maner abhominacyons / haue the ryght fayth of christ or are of hys church. But they only that repent and fele that the law is good / And haue the law of god written in their
30   hertes and the fayth of oure sauioure Iesus / even wyth the sprite of God. There is a carnall Israel and a spirituall. There ys Isaac and Is-

---

3 Turkes   8 Iewes   20 Ro. 9.   26 [Hand]

3 we] we are *1573*   7 thys .viij.] these eight *1573*   21 they be] *1573*, rhey be *1531*

mael / Iacob and Esau. And Ismael persecuted Isaac and Esau Iacob
and the fleshly the spiritual. Wherof paul complayned in hys tyme
persecuted of hys carnall brethern / as we doo in oure tyme and as
the electe euer dyd and shall doo tyll the worldes ende. What a multitude came out of Egypte vnder Moses of whych the scripture testi-   5
fyeth that they beleued / moued by the miracles of Moses / as Simon
magus beleued by the reason of philippes miracles actes .viij. Neuer
the lesse the scripture testyfieth that .vj. hundred thousand of those
beleuers peryshed thorow vnbeleffe and lefte theyr carcasses in the
wildernesse and neuer entred in to the lond that was promysed   10
them. And euen so shall the childern of Master Mores faythlesse
fayth made by the persuasyon of man / leppe shorte of the rest
whych oure sauioure Iesus is rysen vnto. And therfore lett them en-
brace thys present worlde as they doo / whose chyldern they are
though they hate so to be called.   15

[D8v] And hereby ye se that it is a playne and an evident conclusion as bright as the sonne shyninge that the trueth of gods worde
dependeth not of the trueth of the congregacion. And therfore when
thou art asked / whi thou beleuest that thou shalt be saved thorow
christ and of soch like principles of oure faith / answere thou wottest   20
and felest that it is true. And when he asketh how thou knowest that
it is true / answere because it is written in thine herte. And if he aske
who wrott it / answere the sprite of God. And if he aske how thou
camest first by it / tel him / whether by readynge in bokes or hear-
ynge it preached / as by an outward instrument / but that inwardly   25
thou wast taught by the spirite of God. And if he aske whether thou
beleuest it not because it is written in bokes or because the prestes
so preach / answere no / not now / but only because it is written in
thine hert and because the spirite of god so preacheth and so testifieth vn to thi soule. And saye / though at the begynnynge thou wast   30
moued by readynge or preachynge / as the Samaritanes were by the
wordes of the woman / yet now thou beleuest it not therfore any
lenger / but only because thou hast herde it of the spirite of God and
red it written in thyne herte.

7 Actes .8.   19 Questions   20 Answeres   32 Ioh. 4.

24 camest] came *1573*   29 and so] *1573*, aud so *1531*

And concerninge outwarde teachynge we allege for vs scripture
elder then any church that was this .xiiij. hundred yeres / and old
autenticke stories which they had brought a slepe where with we
confounde their lies. Remembir ye not how in oure awne tyme / of
5   all that taught grammer in England not one vnderstode the latyne
tongue? how came we then by the latyne tongue agayne? not by
them / though we lerned certay[E1]ne rules and principles of them
by which we were moued and had an occasion to seke further / but
out of the old auctours. Even so we seke vpp old antiquities out of
10   which we lerne and not of oure church / though we receaved many
principles of oure church / at the beginninge / but moare falshed
amonge then trueth.

It hath pleased God of his exceadynge loue where with he loued
vs in christ (as Paul saith) before the world was made and when wee
15   were deed in synne and his enemies in that we did consent to synne
and to liue evell / to write with his spirite .ij. conclusions in oure
hertes / by which we vnderstond all thynge: that is to wete / the
faith of Christ and the loue of oure neyboures. For whosoeuer feleth
the iust damnacion of synne and the forgeuenesse and mercie that is
20   in christes bloud for all that repent and forsake it and come and beleue in that mercie / the same only knoweth how God is to behon-
oured and worsheped and can iudge betwene true seruinge of God
in the spirite and false imageseruinge of God with workes. And the
same knoweth that sacramentes / signes ceremonies and bodyly
25   thynges can be no seruice to God in his person but memorials vnto
men and a remembraunce of the testament wherewith god is serued
in the spirite. And he that feleth not that / is blynd in his soule and
of oure holy fathers generacion & maketh god an image and a creature and worshepith him with bodyly seruice. And on the other
30   syde he that loueth his neyboure as him selfe vnderstondeth all lawes
and can iudge betwene good and evell right and wronge / godly and
vngodly in all conuersacion / dedes / lawes / bargens / [E1v]
couenauntes / ordinaunces and decrees of men / & knoweth the of-

---

24–26 The vse of signes & ceremonyes

---

12 amonge] *om.* 1573   29 worshepith] *ed.*, vorshepith 1531, worshippeth
1573   31 and can] 1573, an can 1531

fice of euery degre and the due honoure of euery person. And he that
hath not that written in his herte is popish and of the spiritualtie
which vnderstondeth nothynge saue his awne honoure his awne
profit and what is good for him selfe only: and when he is as he wold
be / thinketh that al the world is as it shuld be.   5

¶Of worshepinge and what is to be vnderstonde by the worde

Concerninge worshepinge or honouringe (which .ij. termes are
both one) M. More bringeth forth a difference / a distinccion or diui-
sion of greke wordes / fayned of oure scolemen which of late nether   10
vnderstode greke / latine or hebrue / called dulia / yperdulia and latria. But the difference declareth he not ner the propirties of the
wordes / but with confused termes leadeth you blindfold in his
mase. [E2] As for yperdulia I wold fayne wete where he readith of
it in all the scripture and whether the worshuppe done to his lorde   15
the cardinalles hatte were dulia / yperdulia or idololatria. And as for
dulia and latria we fynde them both referred vn to god in a thousande places.

Therfore that thou be not begyled with falshed of sophisticall
wordes / vnderstond / that the wordes which the scripture vseth in   20
the worshepynge or honouringe of god are these: loue god / cleaue
to god / dreade / serue / bowe / praye and cal on god beleue and trust
in god and soch like. Which wordes al we vse in the worshepinge of
man also / how be it diuersly and the difference therof doeth all the
scripture teach.   25

God hath created vs and made vs vnto his awne likenes / and our
sauioure christ hath bought vs with his bloude. And therfore are we
Gods possession of dutie and right and Christes saruauntes only / to
wayte on his wil and pleasure / and ought therfore to moue nether
hand ner fote ner any other membir / other hert or mynd other wise   30
then he hath appoynted. God is honoured in his awne person / when
we receaue all thynge both good and bad at his hande / and loue his

30–31 What it is to honoure God
_____

32 all thynge] al things *1573*

lawe with al oure hertes / and beleue hope and long fore all that he
promiseth.

The officers that rule the world in Gods stede / as father / mother /
master / husband / lorde and prince are honoured / when the law
5   which almightye God hath committed vnto [E2v] them to rule
with / is obeyed. Thi neyboure that is out of office / is honoured /
when thou (as god hath commaunded the) louest hym as thi selfe /
countest him as good as thy selfe thinkest him as worthy of any
thynge as thy selfe and comest louyngly to helpe him at all his nede /
10   as thou woldest be holpe thy selfe / because God hath made him like
vnto his awne image as well as the and christ hath bought him as
well as the.

Yf I hate the lawe / so I breake it in myne hert / and both hate and
dishonoure God the maker therof. If I breake it outwardly / then I
15   dishonoure God before the world and the officer that ministreth it.
Yf I hurte my neyboure / then I dishonoure my neyboure and him
that made him and him also that bought him with his bloude. And
even so iff I hate my neyboure in myne herte / then I hate him that
commaundeth me to loue him and him that hath deserued that I
20   shuld at the lest way for his sake loue him. If I be not ready to helpe
my neyboure at his nede / so I take his due honoure from him / and
dishonoure him / and him that made him / and him also that bought
him with his bloude / whose saruant he is. Yf I loue soch thinges as
God hath lent me and committed vn to mine administracion / so
25   that I can not find in myne hert to bestow them on the vses which
God hath appoynted me / then I dishonoure god and abuse his creature in that I geue moare honoure vn to it then I shuld do / And
then I make an Idole of it in that I loue it moare then god and his
commaundment and then I dishonoure my neyghboure from whose
30   nede I withdraw it.

3–4 What it is to honoure rulars   6–9 What it is to honoure a mans
neyghboure   13–17 What it is to dishonoure God / christ a ruler or a mans neyboure

3 Gods stede] 1573, Gods / stede 1531   4 husband / lorde] ed., husband- lorde
1531, husband, Lord 1573   7 hym] 1573, hem 1531   22 dishonoure] ed.,
dish- honoure 1531, dishonour 1573   S3 christ a ruler or a mans] and dishonour
our 1573

[E3] In like maner if the officer abusynge his power / compell the subiecte to doo that which god forbiddeth or to leue vndone that which god commaundeth / so he dishonoureth god / in withdrawenge his seruaunt from him / and maketh an Idole of his awne lustes / in that he honoureth them a boue god / and he dishonoureth 5
his brother in that he abuseth him contrary vn to the right vse which God hath created him for and christ hath bought him for / which is to wayte on gods commaundementes. For iff the officer be other wise minded then this / the worst of these subiectes is made by the hondes of him that made me / and bought with the bloude of him 10
that bought me / and therfore my brother and I but his saruaunt only / to defende him and to kepe him in the honoure that god and christ hath sett him / that no man dishonoure him: he dishonoureth both God and man. And therto if any subiecte thynke any otherwise of the officer (though he be an emperoure) then that he is but a sar- 15
vaunt only / to ministre the office indifferently / he dishonoureth the office and god that ordeyned it. So that all men / what so euer degre they be of are every man in his rowme / saruauntes to other / as the hand sarueth the foote and every membre one a nother. And the angels of heuen are al so oure brethern and very saruauntes for 20
Christes sake / to defend vs from the power of the deuels.

And finally all other creatures that are nether angels ner man / are in honoure lesse then man / and man is lorde ouer them / & they created to sarue him / as scripture testifieth / and he not to serue them / but only / his lord god and his sauioure Christe. 25

[E3v] ¶Of worshepinge of sacramentes / ceremonies / images / reliques and so forth

Now let vs come to the worshepynge or honourynge of sacramentes ceremonies images and reliques. First images be not god / and therfore no confidence is to be geuen them. They be not made 30
after the image of god ner are the price of christes bloude / but the

---

8–10 A true officer in the sight of God   31 Images

19 membre] *ed.*, menbre *1531*, member *1573*   27 ceremonies] *1573*, cer-mo-
nies *1531*   30 geuen] put in *1573*

werkmansheppe of the craftes man and the price of money and therfore inferioures to man.

Wherfore of all right man ys lord ouer them and the honoure of
them is to doo man seruyce and mans dishonoure yt ys to doo them
5 honorable seruyce / as vnto hys better. Images then and reliques ye
and as christ saith / the holy daye to are seruantes vnto man. And
therfore it foloweth that we can not / but vnto oure damnacion put
one a cote worth an hundred cotes / vppon a postes backe / and let
the ymage of god and the price of christes bloude goo vpp &
10 downe / therby naked. For yf we care more to cloth the deed image
made by man and the pryce of seluer then the liuely image of god
and pryce of christes bloude / then we dishonoure the image of god
and hym that made him and the price of chrystes bloude and hym
that bought hym.

15 Wherfore the right vse / office and honoure of al creatures inferi-
ores vnto man / is to do man seruice / whether they be images /
reliques / ornamentes signes or sacramentes / holidayes / ceremonies
or sacrifices. And that maie be on this maner and no doute it so once
was. If (for an ensample) I take a pece of the crosse of christe and
20 make a litle crosse therof and beare it aboute me / to loke theron
with a repentinge hert / at tymes when I am moued therto / to put
me in remembraunce that the body of christ was broken and his
bloud [E4] shed theron / for my sinnes / and beleue stedefastly that
the mercyfull trueth of god shall forgeue the sinnes of all that repent
25 for his deeth sake and neuer thinke on them moare then it seruith me
and I not it and doeth me the same seruice as yf I red the testament in
a boke / or as iff the preacher preached it vnto me. And in like maner
if I make a crosse in my forehed / in a remembraunce that god hath
promised assistence vnto al that beleue in him / for his sake that died
30 on the crosse / then doeth the crosse serue me and I not it. And in
like maner if I beare on me or loke vppon a crosse of what soeuer
mater it be / or make a crosse vppon me / in remembraunce that
whosoeuer wilbe christes disciple must sofre a crosse of aduersite

---

8 [Hand]   15–17 The vse of creatures inferyours to man   19–21 The
worshepinge of the crosse

---

23 shed] *1573*, hed *1531*

tribulacions and persecucion / so doeth the crosse serue me and I not
it. And this was the vse of the crosse once / and for this cause it was
at the begynnynge set vpp in the churches.

And so yf I make an image of christ or of any thinge that christ
hath done for me / in a memory / it is good and not euel vntill it be   5
abvsed.

And euen so / yf I take the true life of a saynt and cause it to be
painted or carued / to put me in remembraunce of the saintes life /
to folow the saynt as the saint did christe / and to put me in remembraunce of the greate faith of the saint to god and how true god was   10
to helpe him out of al tribulacion / and to se the saintes loue to warde
his neyboure / in that he so paciently sofered so paynefull a deeth
and so cruell marterdome to testifie the trueth for to saue other / and
all to strength my soule with all and my faith to god and loue to my
neyboure / then doeth the image serue me and I not it. And this was   15
the vse of images at the beginninge and of reliques also.

[E4v] And to knele before the crosse vnto the word of god which
the crosse preacheth is not euell. Neyther to knele doune before an
image in amans meditacions to cal the lyuinge of the saint to minde
for to desyre god of lyke grace to folow the ensample / is not evell.   20
But the abuse of the thynge is euell / and to haue a false fayth: as to
beare a pece of the crosse aboute a man / thynkynge that so longe as
that ys aboute hym / spyrytes shall not come at him / his enimies
shall do him no bodyly harme / all causes shall go on his side euen
for beringe it aboute him / and to thynke that yf it were not aboute   25
him yt wold not be so / & to thinke / if any misfortune chaunce /
that it came for leauynge it of or because this or that ceremonie was
lefte vndone / and not rather because we haue broken Gods commaundementes / or that God tempteth vs to proue oure pacyence.
Thys ys playne ydolatrie / and here a man ys captyue / bonde and   30
seruaunt vnto a false faith and a false ymaginacyon / that ys nother
god ner hys worde. Now am I Gods only and ought to serue nothynge but god and hys worde. My bodye must serue the rulars of

4–6 The worshepynge of images   21–22 False worshepynge

10 to] *1573*, co *1531*   11 to warde] towardes *1573*

thys world and my neyboure (as god hath appoynted it) & so must
all my goodes: but my soule must serue God only / to loue hys law
and too trust in hys promyses of mercye in all my nedes. And in like
maner yt ys that thousandes / whyle the prest patereth Saynt Ihons
5   Gospell in latine ouer theyr heedes / crosse them selues wyth / I
trow / a legyon of crosses / behynde and before and wythe reuerence
on the very arses and (as Iack off napis when he claweth him selfe)
ploucke vp theyr legges and crosse so moch as their heeles and the
very soles of their fete / & beleue that if it be done in [E5] the tyme
10 that he readeth the gospell (and else not) that there shall no mis-
chaunce happen them that daye / because only of those crosses. And
where he shuld crosse him selfe / to be armed and to make him silfe
stronge to beare the crosse with Christe / he crosseth him selfe to
driue the crosse from him / and blesseth him selfe with a crosse from
15 the crosse. And if he leaue it vndone / he thynketh it no small synne /
and that god is hyly displeased with him and if any misfortune
chaunce / thinketh it is therfore / which is also Idolatrie and not gods
worde. And soch is the confidence in the place or image or what
soeuer bodyly obseruaunce it be: soch is S. Agathes letter written in
20 the gospell tyme. And soch are the crosses on palmesondaye made
in the passion tyme. And soch is the beryng of holy waxe aboute a
man. And soch is that some hange apece of S. Ihons gospell aboute
their neckes. And soch is to beare the names of god with crosses
betwene ech name aboute them. Soch is the sayenge of gospels vn
25 to wemen in childbed. Soch is the limeteriers sayenge of in principio
erat verbum from housse to housse. Soch is the sayenge of gospells
to the corne in the feld in the procession weke that it shuld the better
growe. And soch is holy bred holy water and seruinge of all ceremonies and sacramentes in generall with out significacion. And I praye
30 you how is it possible that the people can worshepe images / reliques / ceremonies and sacramentes / saue supersticiously / so longe
as they know not the true meaninge / nether wil the prelates sofre

4–5 S. Ioans gosspell   19–20 Supersticiousnesse

3 nedes] deedes *1573*   6 trow /] *ed.*, trow *1531, 1573*   9 tyme] *ed.*, thyme
1531, time *1573*   27 procession] *1573*, precession *1531*
S2 Supersticiousnesse] A great number of supersticious baggages *1573*

any man to tell them: yee and the very meanynge of some and right
vse no man can tell?

And as for the riches that is bestowed on ima[E5v]ges and reliques
they can not proue but that it is abhominable / as longe as the pore
are dispised and vncared for and not first serued / for whose sakes   5
and to fynd preachers / offeringes tithes / londes rentes and all that
they haue was geuen the spiritualtie. They will saye we maye do
both. Maye or not maye / I se that the one most necessary of both /
is not done: But the pore are bereued of the spiritualtie of all that
was in tyme passed offered vn to them. Morouer though both were   10
done / they shall neuer proue that the sight of gold and siluer and of
preciousstones shuld moue a mans hert to dispice soch thynges aftir
the doctrine of Christe. Nether can the riche cote helpe to moue thy
mind / to folow the ensample of the saint / but rather if he were
purtrayde as he sofred / in the most vngoodly wise. Which thinge   15
taken awaye / that soch thynges with all other seruice / as stekynge
vpp candels / moue not thy mynde to folow the ensample of the
saint / ner teach thy soule any godly lernynge: then the image serueth not the / but thou the image / and so art thou an Idolater / that
is to saye in English / a serueimage. And thus it appereth that youre   20
vngodly and bely doctrine where with ye so magnifie the dedes of
youre ceremonies and of youre pilgremages and offerynge for the
dede it selfe / to please god and to obtayne the fauoure of deed
saintes (and not to moue you and to put you in remembraunce of
the law of god & of the promises which are in his sonne and to folow   25
the ensample of the saynte) is but an exhortynge to serue images /
and so are ye imageseruers / that is / Idolaters / And finally the more
deuocion men haue vn to soch dedes / the lesse they haue vn to gods
commaundement / [E6] in so moch that they which be most wontte
to offer to images and to shewe them / be so colde in offerynge to   30
the pore / that they wyll scace geue them the scrappes which must
else be geuen dogges / or their old shone / iff they maye haue new
bromes for them.

3–6 Riches bestowed on images or reliques   7 Obiection   8 Solution

31 scace] scarce *1573*

¶Pilgrimages

To speake of pilgrimages / I saye / that a christen man / so that he
leaue nothinge vndone at home that he is bounde to doo / is fre to
goo whother he will / only aftir the doctrine of the lorde / whose
5 seruaunte he is and not his awne. If he goo and viset the pore / the
secke and the presoner / it is well done and a worke that god commaundeth. If he goo to this or that place / to heare a sermon or because his mynd is not quiet at home / or if because his hert is to moch
occupied on his worldly businesses bi the reasons of occasions at
10 home / he gett him in to a moare quiett and styll place / where his
minde is moare abstracte and pulled from worldly thoughtes it is
well done. And in all these places if what soeuer it be / whether
liuely preachynge / ceremonie / relique or image stere vpp his herte
to god and preach the worde of god and the ensample of oure sau-
15 ioure Iesus moare in one place then in a nother / that he thither goo /
I am content. And yet he bydeth a lorde and the thynges serue him
and he not them / Now whether his entent be so or no / his dedes
wil testifie / as his vertuouse gouernynge of his housse and louynge
demeanoure to warde his neyghboures: yee and gods worde wilbe
20 all waye in his hert and in his mouth & he euery daye perfecter then
other.

[E6v] For there can nothinge edifie mans soule saue that which
preacheth him gods worde. Only the worde of god worketh the
health of the soule. And what someuer preacheth him that / can not
25 but make him perfecter.

But to beleue that god wilbe sought moare in one place then in a
nother / or that god will heare the moare in one place then in a
nother / or moare where the image is / then where it is not is a false
faith and Idolatrie or imageseruice. For first god dwelleth not in
30 temples made with handes Actes .xvij. Item steuen died for the contrary and proued it by the prophetes Actes .vij. And Salomon in the
.viij. off the thirde of the kinges / when he had byld his temple /

27 [Hand]   29–32 God dwelleth not in any place. Actes .7.

_____

32 byld] built *1573*   S2 any place. Actes .7.] Temples made with mennes handes. *1573*

testified the same and that he had not byld it for god to dwell in / ye and that god dwelleth not in the erth / but that he shuld out of heuen heare the prayars of them that prayed there. And the prophetes did often testifye vn to the people that had soch a false faith that god dwelt in the temple / that he dwelt not their. Morouer god in his   5
testament byndeth him selfe vn to no place ner yet the: But speaketh generally (concerninge where and when) sayenge psalme .xlix. in the daye of the tribulacion thou shalt call on me and I wil deliuer the / and thou shalt glorifie me. He setteth nether place ner tyme / But whersoeuer and when soeuer: so that the prayar of Iob vppon   10
the dongehyll was as good as Poules in the temple. And when oure sauioure saith Ihon .xvj. Whatsoeuer ye axe my father in my name / I will geue it you / he saith not in this or that plase / or this or that daye: but whersoeuer & when soeuer / as well in the feldes as in the toune and on the Monedaye as on the sondaye. God [E7] is a   15
spirite and wilbe worsheped in the spirite Ihon .iiij. That is / though he be present euery where / yet he dwelleth liuely and gloriously in the myndes of angells only and hertes of men that loue his lawes and trust in his promises. And whersoeuer god findeth soch an hert / their he heareth the prayar in all places and   20
tymes indifferently. So that the outward place nether helpeth or hindred / excepte (as I said) that a mans minde be moare quiett and still from the rage of wordely businesses / or that some thynge stere vpp the worde of god and ensample of our sauioure moare in one place then in a nother.   25

¶Whence Idolatrie or imageseruice springeth

Now that thou maist se whence all this Idolatrie or imageseruice is sprounge / marke a litle / and then I will answere vn to the argumentes which these imageseruars make agenst the open trueth. All the ceremonies ornamentes and sacrifices of the olde testament were   30
sacramentes. That is to wete / signes preachinge vn to the people

---

7 Psal. 49.   12 Ioan .16.   16 Iohan .4.   30–31 Sacramentes

1 byld] built *1573*   9 shalt] *1573*, salt *1531*   18 angells] *ed.*, angell *1531*, aungels *1573*   22 hindred] hindreth *1573*   30 ceremonies] *1573*, cerrmonies *1531*

one thynge or a nother. As circumcision preached vn to them / that
god had chosen them to be his people / and that he wold be their
god and defende them and encrease and multiplie them and kepe
them in that londe and blesse the frutes of the erth and all their pos-
5 sessions. And on the other syde it preached / how that they had
promised god agayne to kepe his commaundementes / ceremonies
and ordinaunces. Now when they saw their younge children circumcised / iff they consented vn to the appoyntement made betwene god and them / moued by the pre[E7v]achinge of that same /
10 then were they iustified thereby. How be it the dede in it selfe / the
cuttynge off of the foreskyn of the manchildes priuey membir iustified them not ner was a satisfaccion for the childes synnes / but the
preachynge only did iustifie them that receaued the faith theroffe.
For it was a bage geuen indifferently as well vn to them that neuer
15 consented in their hertes vn to gods lawe / as vn to the electe in
whose hertes the lawe was written. And that this was the meaninge
of circumcision maye be proued many wayes: But namely by Paul
Romans .ij. where he saith / circumcision is moch worth / if thou
kepe the lawe (whose signe it was) and else not. And Roma. iij.
20 where he saith that god did iustifie the circumcised of faith (whose
signe it was on the other syde) and else not.

And the paschall lambe was a memoriall of their deliueraunce out
of Egypte only and no satisfaccion or offeringe for synne.

And the offeringe of their first frutes preached how they had re-
25 ceaued all soch frutes of the hand of god / and that it was god that
gaue them that land and that kepte them in it / and that did blesse
and make their frutes grow. In token wherof as vn to a lorde roiall
they brought him the first ripe frutes of their herueste. Which remembraunce as longe as it abode in their hertes / it moued them to
30 loue god againe and their neyboure for his sake / as he so oft desyred
them. And out of this ceremonye was fett the blessynge of oure new
ripe frutes for like purpose / though we haue lost the significacion.

And their other offeringes / as the sacrifices of doues / turtles /

1–2 Circumcision   22–23 Paschall   lambe   24–25 Firste   frutes
33 Sacrifices

11 cuttynge] ed., cuttynhe 1531, cuttyng 1573

lambes / kyddes / shepe / calues / gottes and oxen were no satisfaccions for syn[E8]ne / but only a signe and token / that at the repentaunce of the hert / thorow an offeringe to come and for that
seedes sake that was promised Abraham / their synnes were
forgeuen them.   5

And in like maner the ornamentes and all other ceremonies were
eyther an open preachynge or secrett prophisies and not satisfaccions or iustifienges. And thus the workes did serue them and preach
vnto them and they not the workes ner put any confidence therin.

¶False worshepynge   10

But what did the children of Israel and the Iewes? They latt the
significacions of their ceremonyes goo and lost the meanynge of
them and turned them vn to the workes to serue them / sayenge that
they were holy workes commaunded of god and the offerars were
therby iustified and obtayned forgeuenesse of synnes and therby be-   15
came good: as the parable of the pharesey and publican declare Luke
.xviij. and as it is to se in Paul and thoroute all the Byble: and became
captiue to serue and put their trust in that which was nether god ner
his worde. And so the better creature agenst nature did serue the
worse. Where of all likelyhode god shuld haue accepted their worke   20
by the reason of them / if their hertes had bene right / & not haue
accepted their soules for the bloudes sake of a calfe or shepe / for as
moch as a man is moch better then a calfe or shepe / as Christ testifieth Matth. xij. For what pleasure shuld god haue in the bloud of
calues or in the light of oure candeles? his pleasure is onlye in the   25
hertes of them that loue his commaundementes.

[E8v] Then they went further in the imagination of their blynd
reason sayenge / in as moch as god accepteth these holy workes /
that we be made righteous therby / then it foloweth that he whyche
offereth most / is most rightewesse and the best man: ye and it is   30
better to offer an oxe then a shepe / because it is more costly. And

6–7 Ornamentes   12 [Hand]   17 Luc. 18.

_____

1 calues /] ed., calues 1531, Calues, 1573   15–16 became] become 1573
S2 [Hand]] om. 1573

so they stroue who might offer most / and the prestes were well
apayde. Then went they further in their fleshly wisdome sayenge: if
I be good for the offeringe of a doue and better for a shepe and yet
better for an oxe / and so euer the better thynge I offer / the better I
5   am / Oh how accepted shuld I be if I offered a man / and namelye
him that I most loued? And vppon that imaginacion / they offered
their awne children and burnt them to asshes before images that they
had imagined.

And to confirme their blyndnesse they layde for them (nodoute)
10 the ensample of Abraham which offered his sonne Isaac and was so
accepted / that god had promised him / how that in his seed / all the
world shuld be blessed. Herof ye se vn to what abhominacion blynd
reason bryngeth a man / when she is destitute of gods worde.

And to speake of the sabbath / which was ordeyned to be their
15 saruaunte & to preach & be a signe vn to them / that god thorow
his holy spirite & worde did sanctifie them / in that they obeyed his
commaundementes & beleued and trusted in his promises (& therfore were charged to leaue workynge and to come on the holy daye
& heare the worde of god by which they were sanctified) vn to it
20 also they became captiue and bonde to sarue it / sayenge that they
were iustified by absteynynge from bodyly laboure (as oures thinke
al so) in so moch that though they bestowed not the [F1] holy day
in vertue prayer and hearinge the worde of god / in almosdede / in
visitynge the sycke / the nedie and comfortelesse and so forth / but
25 went vp & downe ydlye / yet what soeuer nede his neyghboure had /
he wolde not haue holpe hym on the saboth daye / as thou mayst
se by the ruler of the synagoge which rebuked christ for healinge the
people on the holy daye luke .xiij.

And of like blyndnesse they went and fett out the brasen serpent
30 (which Moses commaunded to be kepte in the arcke for a memorie)
and offered before it: thinkynge (no doute) that god must be there

---

1 [Hand]   14 Holyday   15 Exo. 31.   28 Luke. 13.
29–30 The brasen serpent

---

14 / which] ed., (which 1531, 1573   19 were] 1573, vere 1531
23 almosdede] ed., almosede 1531, almosedede 1573   S5 serpent] ed., serpens
1531, Serpent 1573

present / for else how coude yt haue healed the people that came not
nye yt / but stode afarre off and beheld yt only. And a thousand soch
madnesses did they.

And of the temple they thought that god herd them there better
then any were else: ye and he hearde them nowhere saue there. And 5
therfore they coude not praye but there / as oures can no where but
at church and before an ymage. For what prayar can a man praye /
when the woorde of god is not in the temple of hys herte: ye and
when soch come to church / what is their prayer and what is their
deuocyon / saue the blynde imageseruice of their hertes. 10

But the prophetes euer rebuked them for soch faythlesse workes
and for soch false fayth in theyr workes. In the .xlix. psalme saith
the prophete / I wil receaue no calues of youre houses ner gottes out
of youre foldes / thinke ye that I will eate the flesh of oxen or drynke
the bloude of gottes? And Esaias saith in his first chaptre / what care 15
I for the multitude of your sacryfyces sayth the lorde. I am full. I
haue [F1v] no lust in the burnt offeringes of youre rammes or in the
fatt of fatt beestes or bloud of calues / lambes or gottes: offer me
no moare soch false sacryfyce. And therto youre swete cense ys an
abhominacion vnto me. And thus he said because of the false fayth 20
and peruertynge the ryght vse of them.

And for their false fastinge / not referrynge theyr fast vnto the
tamynge and subduynge of theyr flesh vnto the spirite / when they
complayned vnto god iustifienge them selues and saynge / how happeneth it / that we haue fasted and thou woldest not loke vppon it / 25
we haue humbled oure soules and thou woldest not know it. God
answered them by the prophete Esayas in the .lviij. chaptre / behold / in the daye of youre fast / ye doo youre awne lustes and gather
vpp all youre dettes. And how soeuer ye fast / ye neuer the later
striue and fight and smyte with fyste cruelly. I haue chosen no soch 30
faste and humblynge of soule. &c. But that ye louse weked bondes
and lett the oppressed goo fre / and to breake breed vnto the hon-
grye and to cloth the naked and so forth.

4–5 The temple   11 Psal. 49.   22 Fastynge   27 Esai. 58.

---

3 madnesses] *ed.*, madnessesse *1531*, madnesse *1573*   29 neuer the later]
neuerthelesse *1573*   S2 Psal. 49.] *ed.*, Psal. 46. *1531, 1573*

And concerninge the temple / Esaias sayth in hys last chaptre.
What housse wyll ye bild for me or in what place shall I rest? heuen
is my sete and the erth my fote stole. As who shuld saye I am to
greate for any place that ye can make / and (as steuen sayth actes .vij.
5   and paul actes .xvij.) I dwell not in a temple made with handes.

¶How ceremonies sprange amonge vs

[F2] Vnderstond also (to se how we came yn to like blyndenesse)
that before the comynge of christe in the flesh / the Israelites and
Iewes were scatered thorow out all the world / to punish theyr im-
10 ageseruice / both eest / west south and north / as ye reade in the
chronicles how Englonde was once full: so that there was no prouince or greate citie in the world where no Iewes were: god so pro-
uydynge for the spedie preachynge of the gospell amonge the
hethen thorow out the worlde. Now chryst / as he was promised /
15 so was he sent / vnto the Iewes or Israelites. And what by chrystes
preachynge and the appostles after his resurrexion / there were innumerable Iewes conuerted haply an hundred thousand or moo in Ierusalem and Iewry and in the contres aboute / and abode still in the
londe. Then paul rose vpp and persecuted them in Iherusalem and
20 thorow out al Iewry and Damasco / sleynge all that he coude catche
or makinge them forswere christe. For feare of which persecucion
they fled in to all costes and preached vnto the Iewes that were scatered / prouinge that Iesus was christ the sauioure of the worlde /
both by the scripture and also by myracles: so that agreate parte of
25 the Iewes came to the faith euery where / and we hethen came in
shortely after / and parte a bode styll in vnbeleffe as vnto this
daye.
Now the Iewes beynge born & bred vp / roted and noseld in ceremonyes as I haue shewed and as ye maye better se in the .v. bokes
30 of Moses / if ye wold reade them / coude but with greate difficultie /

---

1 Temple   3 Actes .7.   4 Actes .17.   19 Paule

5 .xvij.)] ed., .xvij.(1531, .xvij. 1573   9 to punish] for 1573
19 Iherusalem] ed., Ihernsalem 1531, Ierusalem 1573   28 bred vp / roted] ed.,
bred vp roted 1531, bred vp, rooted 1573   S4 Paule] Paule a cruell persecutor 1573

depart from them as it is to se in al the epistles of paul / how he
fought agenst them. But in processe [F2v] they gatt the vpperhand.
And therto the fyrst that were christened and all the offycers and
bisshopes of the church / euen so moch as the greate God of Rome
were Iewes for the most parte a great season.   5

And Morouer / as paul saith .Ro. ix. not al that came of Israel are
ryght Israelites nether are al they Abrahams sonnes that are Abrahams seed. Whi so? because they folowed not the steppes of the
fayth of their graundfathers. Even so / not all they that were called
and also came vnto the mariage whych god the father made betwene   10
christ hys sonne and all sinners / brought their maryage garment
wyth them / that is to wete / true faith wherwyth we be maryed
vnto chryste and made his flesh and hys bloude and one spirite with
hym / his brethren and heyres with him and the sonnes of god also.
But many of them (to fulfyll the sayenge of christ / that the kyng-   15
dome of heuen / which is the gospell / is like a net that ketcheth good
and bad) were dreuen in to the net and compelled to confesse that
Iesus was christ and that seed that was promised Abraham and Mes-
sias that shuld come: not off any inward fealinge that the spirite of
god gaue them / nether of any louely consent that they had vnto the   20
law of god that it was good / mornynge / both because they had
broken it and because also they had no power to fulfill it and therfore
to obtayne mercie and power came to christ and vnto the father
thorow him / with the hert of naturall childern which receaue all
thinge frely of their fathers bounteous lyberalitie and of loue become   25
saruauntes vnto theyr brethren for theyr fathers sake: But were
compelled only [F3] with violence of the scripture which everiwhere
bare wittenesse vn to christe and agreed vn to al that he did / and
ouercome also with the power of miracles that confirmed the same.
That is to saye / they came with a storifaith / a popish faith / a faith-   30
lesse faith & a fayned faith of their awne makinge / and not as God
in the scripture describeth the faith / so beleuinge in christ / that they
woldbe iustified by theyr awne dedes / which is the denienge of

---

11 Matt. 22.

---

2 But] *ed.*, but *1531*, and *1573*; they] *om. 1573*   33 denienge] *ed.*, deinenge *1531*,
denying *1573*

christe. As oure papistes beleue. Which moare mad then those
Iewes / beleue nothynge by the reason of the scripture / but only
that soch a multitude consent therto / compelled with violence of
swerde / with falsyfienge of the scripture and fayned lyes. Which
5   multitude yet is not the fifte part so many as they that consent vn to
the lawe of Mahomete. And therfore by their awne argumentes / the
faith of the turkes is better then theirs. And their faith therto maye
stond by theyr awne confession / with all misheue (as it well appereth by them) and with yeldynge them selues to worke all weked-
10   nesse with full delectacion / aftir the ensample of the faith of their
father the deuell / and with out repentaunce and consent vn to the
law of god / that it is good. Which popish therto so beleue in Christ /
and so wilbe his saruauntes / that they wilbe bond vn to domme
ceremonies and deed workes puttynge their trust and confidence in
15   them & hopinge to be saued by them and ascribynge vn to them the
thanke of their saluacion and righttewysnesse.

And therfore because / as I saide / the Iewes ye and the hethen to /
were so accustomed vn to ceremonies and because soch a multitude
came with a faithelesse faith / they went and cleane [F3v] contrary
20   vnto the mynde of paul / set vp ceremonies in the new testamente /
partely borowynge them of Moses and partely imageninge like / as
ye now se / and called them sacramentes: that is to saye / sygnes (as
yt ys playne in the storyes) the sacrament of holy water / of holy
fyre / holy bred / holy salt and so forth. And they gaue them sig-
25   nificacions. As holy water signifyed the sprinclinge of christes
bloude for our redempcyon. Which sacrament or sygne (though yt
seme superfluous / in as moch as the sacrament of christes body and
bloud signifieth the same dayly) yet as longe as the significacion
bode / it hurted not. And the kyssynge of the pax was sett vpp to
30   signifie / that the peace of christ shuld be euer amonge vs / one to
loue an other after hys ensample as the word yt selfe well declareth.
For pax ys as moch to saye as peace.

---

1 [Hand]   25–27 What holy water sygnyfyeth   30 The pax

8 misheue] mischiefe *1573*   12 Which . . . therto] And the . . . also do
1573   13 bond] bound *1573*   19–20 went and . . . paul /] went . . . Paul,
and *1573*   24 holy bred /] *ed.*, holy bred *1531*, holy bread, *1573*   S1 [Hand]]
om. 1573

And as for confirmacion / it is no doute / but that it came this wise
vp and that thys was the vse / which the word it selfe well declareth.
We reade in the stories / that they wich were conuerted vnto the faith
of the age of discrecion / were ful taught in the law of god (as right
is) and in the fayth of oure sauiour Iesus / yer they were baptised /   5
and vppon the profession or promisinge to kepe that law and fayth /
were baptised. And then for the socure and helpe of younge
childern / baptised before the age of discrecion / to know the law of
god and faith of christe / was confirmacion institute that they shuld
not be all waye ignoraunt and faithlesse / but be taught the pro-   10
fessyon of theyr baptim. And thys / no doute / was the maner / as
we maye wel gather by probable coniectures and euident tokens.
When the childern were of [F4] .vj. or seuen yeres olde / their elders
brought them vnto the preest or deacon in euery parish / which officer taught the children what their baptim ment & what they had   15
professed therin: that is to wete / the law of god & their dutie vn to
all degrees / and the faith of oure sauiour. And then because it shuld
not be neglecte or lefte vndone / an hier officer as the archdeacon
(for it hath not bene I suppose in the bisshopes handes all waye as
now / nether were it mete) came aboute from parish to parish / at   20
tymes conuenient. And the prestes brought the children vn to him
at .xj. or .xij. yere olde / before they were admitted to receaue the
sacrament of Christes body haply. And he apposed them of the law
of god & faith of Christe / and axed them / whether they thought
that law good / and whether their hertes were to folow it. And they   25
answered ye.

And he apposed them in the articles of oure faith / and axed them /
whether they put their hope and trust in Christ / to be saued thorow
his deeth and merites. And they answered ye. Then confirmed he
their baptim sayenge: I confirme you / that is / I denunce and de-   30
clare / by the auctorite of gods worde and doctrine of Christ / that
ye be truely baptised within in youre hertes and in youre spirites /
thorow professynge the lawe of god and the faith of oure sauioure

1–2 Confirmacyon

6 to] to to *1573*   9 institute] instituted *1573*   15 taught] *1573*, taughr
1531   18 officer] *1573*, officerr *1531*   19 bene] bene as *1573*

Iesu / which youre outwarde baptim doeth signifie / and thervppon
I put this crosse in youre forehedes that ye goo and fight agenst the
deuell / the world and the flesh / vnder the standarde of oure sauioure / in the name of the father / the sonne / and the holy gost.
5   Amen. Which maner I wold to god for his tender mercie were in vse
this daye.

[F4v] But aftir that the deuell was broken lowse and the bisshopes
beganne to purchace / and the deacons to scratch all to them / and
the spiritualtie to clime an hye: then because the laboure semed to
10 tediouse and paynfull / to appose the childern one by one / they axed
the prestes that presented them only / whether the childern were
taught the profession of their baptim. And they answered ye. And
so vppon their wordes they confirmed them with out apposinge.
When they no lenger apposed them / the prestes no lenger taught
15 them / but committed the charge to their godfather and godmoth-
ers / and they to the father and mother / dischargynge them selues
by theyr awne auctorite with in halfe an houre.

And the father and mother taught them a monstrous laten pater
noster and an Aue and a crede. Which gibbresh euery popiniaye
20 speaketh with a sundrye pronunciacion and facion / so that one pater
noster semeth as many languages all most as there be tonges that
speake it. How be it / it is all one / as longe as they vnderstonde it
not. And in processe as the ignoraunce grewe / they brought them
to confirmacion streight from baptim: so that now oftimes they be
25 volowed and bysshoped both in one daye / that is / we be confirmed
in blindenesse to be kept from knowlege for euer. And thus are we
come in to this damnable ignoraunce and ferce wrathe of god
thorow oure awne deseruinge / because when the trueth was told vs
we had no loue therto. And to declare the full & sett wrath of god
30 vppon vs / our prelates whom we haue exalted ouer vs to whom we
haue geuen al most al we had / haue perswaded the wordly princes
(to whom we haue [F5] submitted our selues and geuen vpp our
power) to deuoure vpp body and soule / and to kepe vs / downe in
darkenesse / with violence of swerde / and with all falshed and gyle.

---

14 When] So when *1573*   28 when] *1573*, wh/en *1531*   31 wordly]
worldly *1573*   33 deuoure] deuour vs *1573*

In so moch that if any do but lift vpp his nose to smell aftir the trueth / they swapp him in the face with a fire brande to sengge his smellynge / or if he open one of his eyes to once loke towarde the light of gods worde / they bleare and dase his sight with their false iuglynge: so that if it were possible / though he were gods electe / he coude not but be kepte doune and perish for lacke of knowlege of the trueth.

And in like maner / because christ had institute the sacrament of his body and bloude / to kepe vs in remembraunce of his bodye breakinge and bloud shedynge for oure synnes / therfore went they and sett vpp this facion of the masse and ordeyned sacramentes in the ornamentes therof to signifie and expresse all the rest of his passion. The amice on the heed is the kercheue that Christ was blyndfolded with / when the soudioures buffeted him and mocked him sayenge: prophete vn to vs who smote the? But now it maye well signifie that he that putteth it on / is blynd and hath professed to leade vs aftir him in darkenesse / acordynge vn to the begynnynge of his playe. And the flappe theron is the croune of thorne. And the albe is the white garment that herode put on him / sayenge he was a fole because he held his peace and wold not answere him. And the .ij. flappes on the sleues and the other .ij. on the albe beneth ouer agenst his fete behind and before / are the .iiij. nayles. And the fanon on his hand / the cord that his handes were bound with: And the stole the rope where with he was [F5v] bounde vn to the piler / when he was scorged: And the corporiscloth / the sindon wherin he was buryed: & the altare is the crosse or haply the graue and so forth. And the castynge abrode of his handes / the splayenge of Christ vppon the crosse. And the light and stickinge vpp of candels and beringe of candels or tapers in procession happlye signifyed this texte. Mat. v. ye be the light of the worlde / and let youre light so shyne before men / that they maye se youre good workes & glorefye

13 Amice   17–19 The flappe on the amice   20 The albe
21–22 The flappes on the albe   23 The fanon   24 The stole
24–25 The corporescloth   26 The altare   28 Candels   30 Mat. 5.

3 to once loke] once to looke *1573*   15 prophete] prophecie *1573*

youre father which is in heven. And the salt signifyeth the wysdome
of Christes doctrine / and that we shulde therwith salt oure dedes
and do nothinge with out the auctorite of goddes worde. So that in
one thynge or other / what in the garmentes and what in the gestures
5   all is playde / in so moch that before he will goo to masse / he wilbe
sure to sell him / lest Iudases parte shuldbe left out.

And so thorow out all the sacramentes / ceremonies or signes (.iij.
wordes of one significacion) there were significacions vn to them at
the beginninge. And so longe as it was vnderstond what was ment
10 by them and they did but serue the people and preach one thinge or
a nother vn to them / they hurted not greatly / though that the fre
seruaunt of Christ ought not to be brought violently in to captiuite
vnder the bondage of tradicions of men. As S. Augustine com-
playneth in his dayes / how that the condicion & state of the Iewes
15 was moare easy then the christens vnder tradicions: so sore had the
tyranny of the shepardes invaded the flocke all redy in those dayes.
And then what iuste cause haue we to complayne oure captiuite
now / vn to whose yocke [F6] from that tyme hitherto / even .xij.
hundred yeres longe / hath euer some what moare wayght bene
20 added to / for to kepe vs downe and to confirme vs in blindnesse?
how be it / as longe as the significacions bode / they hurted not the
soule / though they were paynful vnto the body. Neuer the later I
impute this oure greuous faull in to so extreme and horrible blyndnesse (wher in we are so depe and so dedly brought a slepe) vn to
25 nothinge so moch as vn to the multitude of ceremonies. For assone
as the prelates had sett vpp soch a rable of ceremonies / they thought
it superfluous to preach the playne texte any longer and the law of
god / feith of Christ / loue toward oure neyboure and the ordir of
oure iustifienge & saluacion / for as moch as all soch thynges were
30 playd before the peoples faces dayly in the ceremonies and euery
child wist the meanynge: but gott them vn to allegories / faynynge
them euery man aftir his awne brayne / with out rule / all most on

5 is] *ed.*, his *1531, 1573*   22 Neuer the later] *ed.*, Neuer the lather *1531*, Neuerthelesse *1573*

euery silable / and from thence vnto disputynge and wastinge their
braynes aboute wordes / not attendynge the significacions vntyll at
the last the laye people had lost the meaninge of the ceremonies and
the prelates the vnderstondynge of the playne texte / and of the
Greke Latine and specially of the Hebrue which is most of nede to   5
be knowen / and of all phrases / the propir maner of speakynges and
borowed speach of the Hebrues.

Remembir ye not how with in this .xxx. yeres and ferre lesse /
and yet dureth vn to this daye / the olde barkynge curres dunces
disciples and like draffe called scotistes / the childern of darkenesse /   10
raged in euery pulpyt agenst [F6v] Greke Latine and Hebrue / and
what sorow the scolemastirs that taught the true Latine tonge had
with them / some betynge the pulpyt with their fistes for madnesse
and roringe out with open and fominge mouth / that if there ware
but one tirens or virgill in the world and that same in their sleues   15
and a fire before them / they wold burne them therin / though it
shuld cost them their liues / affirmynge that all good lerninge de-
cayed and was vtterly lost sens men gaue them vn to the Latine
tonge? ye and I dare saye / that there be .xx. thousand prestes curattes this daye in Englond and not so few / that can not geue you the   20
right English vn to this texte in the pater noster / fiat voluntas tua
sicut in celo & in terra and answere therto.

And assone as the significacion of the ceremonies was lost / and
the prestes preached christ no lenger / then the comen people began
to wax mad and out of their mindes vppon the ceremonies. And that   25
trust and confidence which the ceremonies preached / to be geuen
vn to Gods worde and Christes bloude / that same they turned vn
to the ceremonie it selfe as though a man were so mad to forgett that
the bosh at the tauern dore did signifie wine to be solde within / but
wold beleue that the bosh it selfe wold quench his thirste. And so   30
they became seruantes vn to the ceremonies / asscribynge their iustifienge and saluacion vn to them supposynge that it was nothynge
else to be a christen man / then to serue ceremonies / and him most

25 [Hand]

---

8 Remembir] *ed.*, Remenbir *1531*, Remember *1573*   18 them] *1573*, then
1531   19 dare] day *1573*

christen that most serued them / and contrary wise him that was not
popish & ceremoniall / no christen man at all. For I pray you / for
what cause worshepe we our spiritualtie so hiely or wherfore thynke
[F7] we their prayars better then the pore laye mens / then for their
5   disgysynges and ceremonies? ye and what other vertue se we in the
holiest of them / then to wayte vppon dumme supersticious ceremonies?

Yee and how cometh it that a poore laye man hauinge wife and
.xx. children and not able to fynde them / though all his neybours
10 know his necessite / shall not gett with bedgynge for Christes sake /
in a longe somers daye / ynough to fynde them .ij. dayes honestly /
when iff a disgysed monster come / he shall with an houres lyenge
in the pulpit / gett ynough to fynde .xxx. or .xl. sturdy lubboures a
moneth longe / of which the weakest shalbe as stronge in the bely
15 when he cometh vn to the manger / as the mightiest porter in the
weyhousse or best courser that is in the kynges stable? Is ther any
other cause then disgisynge and ceremonyes? For the dedes of the
ceremonies we count better then the dedes which god commaundeth to be done to our neyboure at his nede. Who thinketh it as good
20 a dede to fede the pore / as to stecke vpp a candle before a poste or
as to sprencle him selfe with holy water? Nether is it possible to be
other wise / as longe as the significacion is lost. For what other
thinge can the people thinke / then that soch deades beordeyned of
god / and because as it is euident / they serue not our neyboures
25 nede / to be referred vn to the person of god and he though he be a
spirite / yet serued therwith? And then he can not but forth on dispute in his blynde reason / that as god is greater then man / so is that
dede that is appoynted to serue god greater than that whych serueth
man. And then when it is not possible to thinke them ordeyned for
30 nought / what can I [F7v] wother wise thynke then that they were
ordeyned to iustifie and that I shuld be holy therby / acordynge to
the popis doctrine / as though god were better pleased when I sprin-
kle my selfe with water or sett vpp a candle before a blocke / then
iff I fedde or clothed or holpe at his nede him / whom he so tenderly

loueth that he gaue his awne sonne vn to the deeth for him / and commaunded me to loue him as my selfe?

And when the people beganne to runne that waye / the prelates were glad & holpe to heue aftir with sotle allegories & falsifienge the scripture / & went & halowed the ceremonies / to make them moare 5 worshepful / that the laye people shuld haue them in greater estimacion & honoure / & be afrayde to twich them for reuerence vn to the holy charme that was saide ouer them / & affirmed also that christes deeth had purchased soch grace vn to the ceremonies to forgeue sinne & to iustifye. O monstre / Christes deeth purchased grace for 10 mans soule / to repent of euell & to beleue in Christ for remission of synne / & to loue the lawe of god and his neyboure as him selfe / which is the true worshepynge of god in the spirite / & he died not to purchesse soch honoure vn to vnsensible thynges / that man to his dishonoure / shuld doo them honourable seruice & receaue his 15 saluacion of them.

This I haue declared vn to you / that ye mighte se & fele euery thinge sensibly. For I entend not to leade you in darkenesse. Nether though twise .ij. cranes make not .iiij. wild gees / wold I therfore that ye shuld beleue that twise .ij. made not .iiij. Nether entend I to 20 proue vn to you that Paules steple is the cause whi temes is broke in about Erith / or that teynterden steple is the cause of the decaye of sandwich hauen as Master Mo[F8]re iesteth. Neuer the lesse this I wold were persuaded vn to you (as it is true) that the bildynge of them & soch like / thorow the false faith that we haue in them / is 25 the decaye of all the hauens in Englande & of all the cities / townes / hie wayes & shortly of the hole comen wealth. For sens these false monstres crope vpp in to oure consciences & robbed vs of the knowlege of oure sauioure Christe / makynge vs beleue in soch pope holy workes & to thynke that ther was no nother waye vn to heuen / 30 we haue not ceased to bylde them abbayes / cloysters / coleges / chauntrees and cathedrall churches with hie steples / striuinge & enuienge one a nother / who shuld do most. And as for the dedes / that

22–23 Teynterden steple

pertayne vn to oure neyboures and vn to the comen wealth / we
haue not regarded at all / as thinges which semed no holy workes
or soch as god wold once loke vppon. And therfore we left them
vnseneto / vntyl they were past remedie or past our power to re-
5   medie them / in as moch as our slowbelies with their false blessynges
had iugled a waye from vs / that wherwith they might haue bene
holpen in dew season. So that that syly pore man / though he had
haply no wisdome to expresse his mynde / or that he durst not / or
that master More fascioneth his tale as he doeth other mennes to iest
10   out the trouth / sawe that nether goodwin sandes ner any other cause
alleged was the decaye of sandwich hauen / so moch as that the people had no lust to maynetene the comen wealthe / for blynde deuocion which they haue to popeholy workes. [F8v] [blank]

---

3 wold] woulde not *1573*   10 goodwin sandes] *ed.*, goodwin- sandes *1531*,
Goodwinsandes *1573*

[G1] ¶The solutions and answeres vn to M. Mores first boke

In the first Chapter to beginne the boke with al / to bringe you goodlucke and to geue you a saye or a taste what trueth shall folowe / he fayneth a letter sent from no man.   5

ij.

In the seconde chapter / besydes that it is vntrue this vse to haue bene euer sens the tyme of the appostles / he maketh many sophisticall reasons about worshepinge of sayntes reliques and images / and yet declareth not with what maner worshepe / but iugleth with the   10
terme in comune / as he doeth with this worde church and this word faith / when the wordes haue diuers significacions: for al faythes are not one maner faith and so forth / and therefore he begylyth a mans vnderstondinge. As if a man said / the boyes will was good to haue geuen his father ablowe / and a nother wold inferre / that a good   15
wyll coude be no synne / and conclude / that a man might lawfully smite his father. Now is good wyll taken in one sens in the maior and in a nother in the minor / to vse scolars termes / & therfore the conclusion doeth mocke a mans witte. Then disputeth he / the seruaunt is honowred for the masters sake / and what is done to the   20
pore is done to Christ (as the popish shall once fele / for their so robbynge them). And the .xij. appostles shall haue their setes and sitte and iudge with christe (as shall all that here preach him truely as they did) and Mary that powred the oyntement on christes heed before his passion / [G1v] hath hir memoriall / and therfore we   25
ought to sett candles before images. First I axe him by what rule his argument holdeth. And secondaryly I answere that the true worshepynge of saintes is their memorial / to folow them as they did christe. And that honoure we geue them and so do not ye popish /

7–8 Worshepinge   27–29 True worshepynge of saintes

6 ij.] The second Chapter. 1573   29 popish] papists 1573

but folow the steppes of youre father the pope / as he doeth the
steppes of his father the deuell. And as for stekinge vpp of candels /
I answere that God is a spirite and in the spirite must be worsheped
only. Faith to his promises and loue to his lawes and longynge for
5   the life that is in his sonne are his due honoure and seruice. All
bodyly seruice must be referred vn to oure selues and not vn to the
person of God immediatly. All outward thynges which we receave
of god ar geuen vs / to take oure partes with thankes and to bestow
the rest vppon oure neyboures. For god vseth no soch thinges in his
10   awne person / but created them for to geue them vs / that we shuld
thanke him / and not to receaue them of vs / to thanke vs: for that
were our prayse and not his. Fastynge / watchynge / wolward
goinge / pilgrimage and all bodyly excercice must be referred vn to
the taminge of the flesh only. For as god deliteth not in the tast of
15   mete / drinke / or in the sighte of gold or seluer / no moare doeth
he in my fast and soch like / that I shuld referre them vn to his person / to do him a pleasure with all. For god in him selfe is as good
as he can be and hath all the delectacion that he can haue. And therfore to wish that god were better then he is or had moare pleasure
20   then he hath / is of a worldely imaginacyon.

And al the spirites that be in heuen are in [G2] as good case as they
can be & haue all the delectacion they can haue / & therefore to wish
them in better case or to studie to doo them more pleasure then they
haue / is fleyshly minded popishnesse. The pleasure of them that be
25   in heuen is / that we herken to God and kepe his commaundementes / which when we doo / they haue all the pleasure that they
can haue in vs. If in this life / I sofre hell gladly / to winne my brother
to folow god / how moch moare if I were in heuen shuld I reioyce
that he so did? If in this world when I haue nede of my neyboure /
30   by the reason of mine infirmites / yet I seke nought of him / saue his
wealth only / whate other thynge shuld I seke of him / if I were in
heuen / where he can do me no seruice ner I vse any pleasure that he
can do me?

5–7 True worshuppinge of god   13–14 Bodelye exercyse

15 mete /] ed., mete 1531, meat, 1573; sighte] ed., sigthe 1531, sight 1573
S1 god] ed., go 1531, God 1573

The deuel desyred to haue his imaginacions worsheped as god /
& his popish childern desyre the same / and compell men so to honoure them / and of their deuelish nature describe they both God and
his saintes. And therfore I saye / al soch fleshly imaginacions / as to
fast the wenisdaye in the worshepe of S. Ihon or of S. katerine or   5
what saynt it be / or to fast sayntes euens or to goo a pilgremage
vnto their images or to offer to them / to doo them pleasure /
thinkynge therby to obteyne their fauoure and to make speciall ad-
uocates of them / as a man wold winne the fauoure of a nother with
presentes and giftes / and thinkynge that if we did it not / they wold   10
be angrie / are playne Idolatrye and [G2v] imageseruice / for the
saint deliteth in no soch. And when thou stekest vpp a candle before
the image / thou mightest with as good reason make an holow bely
in the image and powre in meate and drincke. For as the saynt nether
eateth ner drincketh / so hath he no bodyly eyes to delyte in the light   15
of a candle.

A nother is this / god geueth not the promises that are in Christ
for bodyly seruice / but of his mercy only / vn to his awne glorie.
Ye and of the fathers goodnesse doo all naturall childern receaue.
Axe a litle boye / who gaue him his gaye cote / he answereth / his   20
father. Axe him whi / and he answereth / because he is his father and
loueth him / and because he ys his sonne. Axe him whether his father loue him / and he saith ye. Ax him how he knoweth it and he
saith / because he geueth me this or that. Axe him whether he loue
his father / he saith ye. Axe him whi / he saith / for his father loueth   25
him and geueth him all thynge. Axe him why he worketh / he answereth / his father will so haue it. Axe him whi his father geueth
not soch and soch boyes cotes to. Nai saith he / they be not his
sonnes / their fathers must geue them as myne doeth me. Goo now
ye popish bond seruauntes and receaue youre rewarde for youre   30
false workes and robbe youre brethern & raigne ouer them with violence and cruell tiranny and make them worshepe youre pilars / polaxes images and hattes. And we will receaue of the mercifull kynd-

13 Candle

───────────

6 euens] eues *1573*   31 brethern] *ed.*, bethern *1531*, brethren *1573*

nesse of oure father and will serue our brethern frely / of very loue
and wilbe their seruauntes and sofre for their sakes. And therto oure
good dedes which we do vn to oure neybours nede / springe out of
oure rightwysenesse or iustifienge / which is the forgeuenesse of
5   [G3] oure synnes in Christes bloude / and of other rightwysnesse
knowe we not before god. And contrari wise youre rightwysnesse
or iustifienge which stondeth / as youre faith doeth / with all wekednesse / springeth out of youre holy workes which yee doo to no
man frely saue vn to paynted postes.

10   And when he allegeth the sacrifices of the old law / I saye they
were sacramentes and preached vn to the people (as no dout / oure
candels once were) and were no holy werkes to be referred vn to
gods person to obtayne his favoure / and to iustifie the people / and
that the people shuld doo them for the werkes selues. And when the
15   people had lost the significacions and loked on the holynesse of the
dedes / to be iustified therby / they were imageseruice and hatefull
to god and rebuked of the prophetes / as it is to se thorow out all the
old testament.

Then he iugleth with a texte of S. Paule Rom. xiiij. let eueriman
20   for his parte abounde / one in this Idolatrie and a nother in that:
when the sens of the texte is / let euery man be sure of his awne
conscience / that he doo no thinge / excepte he know well and his
conscience sarue him that it maye be lawfully done. But what care
they to abuse gods worde and to wrest it vn to the contrary?

25   And in the last end / to vtter his excellent blindnesse / he saith /
the wiseman Luther thinketh that if the gold were taken from the
reliques / it wold be geuen vnto the pore immediatly / when he seith
the contrary / that they which haue their purses full will geue the
pore (if they geue ought) ether an halfe peny or in his contre the .iiij.
30   parte of a ferthynge. Now I axe master [G3v] Mores conscience /
seinge they haue no deuocion vn to the poore which are as christes
awne person and for whom Christe hath sofered his passion that we
shuld be kynd to them and whom to visett with oure almes is gods
commaundement / with what minde doo they offer so great trea-
35   sure / to the garnessinge of shrines / images and reliques? It is man-

---

10 Sacrifices   30–34 A sure token of a false faith and imageseruice

yfest that they which loue not gods commaundement / can do nothynge godly. Wherfore soch offeringes come of a false faith / so
that they thinke them better then workes commaunded by god and
beleue to be iustified therby. And therfore are they but imageseruice.   5

And when he saith / we might as well rebuke the powringe of the
annoyntment on Christes heed. Nay / Christe was then mortall as
well as we / and vsed soch thinges as we doo / and it refreshed his
body. But and if thou woldest now powre soch on his image to doo
him pleasure / I wold rebuke it.   10

iij.

In the third Chapter he bringeth in miracles done at S. Steuens
tombe. I answere that the miracles done at saintes tombes / were
done for the same purpose that the miracles which they did when
they were aliue / were done: even to prouoke vn to the faith of their   15
doctrine / and not to trust in the place or in bones or in the saint. As
Paul sent his napken to heale the seke / not that men shuld put trust
in his napkin / but beleue his preachinge.

And in the olde testament Eliseus healed Naaman the hethen man
in the water of Ior[G4]dayne / not to put trust in the water or to   20
praye in that place / but to wonder at the power of god and to come
and beleue / as he also did. And that his bones / when he was deed /
reysed vpp a deed man / was not done that men shuld pray to him:
for that was not lawfull then / by their awne doctrine / nether to put
trust in his bones. For god to avoyd all soch Idolatrie / had poluted   25
all deed bones / so that whosoeuer twitched a deed bone / was
vncleane and all that came in his companye / vntyll he had washed
him selfe: in so moch that if a place were abvsed with offeringe vn
to Idoles / there was no beter remedie then to scater deed bones
there / to driue the people thence / for beinge defiled and poluted.   30
But his bones did that miracle / to testifie that he was a true prophete
and to moue men vn to the faith of his doctrine.

12 Miracles   19 Heliseus

11 iij.] The third Chapter. *1573*   25 trust] theyr trust *1573*

And even so miracles done at the holy crosse / were done / to
moue men vn to the faith of him that died theron / and not that we
shuld beleue in the wodde.

He saith that pilgrimes put no trust in the place / as necromancers
5   doo in their circles / and saieth he wotteth not what / to mocke out
the texte of our sauioure of prayenge in the spirite. And in the ende
he confoundeth him selfe sayenge / we reken oure prayers moare
pleasaunt in one place then in a nother. And that must be by the reason of the place / for god is as good in one place as in a nother and
10 also the man. Morouer where a man pleaseth god best / thither is he
most bounde to goo. And so that imaginacyon bindeth a man to the
place with a false faith / as nicromancers trust in their circles.

[G4v] And agayne if god had said that he wold moare heare in one
place then in a nother / he had bound him selfe to the place. Now as
15 god is like good euery where generally so hath he made his testament generally / whersoeuer mine hert moueth me and am quiet to
pray vn to him / there to heare me like graciously.

And if a man laye to oure charge / that god bound them vn to the
tabernacle and aftir to the temple in the old testament. I saye that he
20 did it not for the places sake / but for the monumentes and testimonies / that their preached the worde of god vn to them / so that
though the prestes had bene negligent to preach / yet shuld soch
thynges that there were haue kepte the people in the remembraunce
of the testament made betwene god and them. Which cause and soch
25 like only shuld moue vs to come to church / and vn to one place
moare then a nother. And as longe as I come moare to one place then
a nother by cause of the quietnesse or that some thynge preacheth
gods worde moare liuely vn to me there than in a nother / the place
is my seruaunte and I not bonde to it: which cause and soch like
30 taken awaye / I can not but put trust in the place as necromancers
doo in their circles / & am an imageseruer and walke aftir myne
awne imaginacion and not aftir gods worde.

And when he saith / we might as well mocke the obseruaunce of

5–6 Pilgrimages   18 Temple

2 the faith] fayth 1573   4 no] not 1573   29 bonde] bound 1573

the paschall lambe. I answer / Christ oure paschall lambe is offered for vs and hath deliuered vs as Paul saith .1. Cor. v. whose signe and memoriall is the sacrament of his body and bloude. Morouer we were not deliuered out of Egypte. And therfore in as [G5] moch as we be ouerladen with our awne / I se no cause why we shuld become   5
Iewes / to obserue their ceremonies to.

And when he saith holy straunge gestures. I answere / for the holynesse I wyll not swere: but the straungenesse I dare well avowe. For euery prest maketh them of a sundrie maner and many moare madly then the gestures of Iackanapes. And when he saith that they   10
were left from hand to hand sens the appostles tyme / it is vntrue. For the appostles vsed the sacrament as Christ did / as thou maist se .1. Corin .xj. Morouer the appostles left vs in the light and taught vs all the counsell of God / as Paule wittenesseth Actes .xx. and hid nothinge in straunge holy gestures and apes playe the significacions   15
wherof noman might vnderstonde.

And a Christen man is moare moued to pitie saith he / at the sight of the crosse / then with out it. If he take pitie as English men doo / for compassion / I saye / that a Christen man is moued to pitie when he seith his brother beare the crosse. And at the sight of the crosse /   20
he that is lerned in god / wepith not Christe with ignoraunt wemen / as a man doeth his father when he is deed: but morneth for his synnes / and att the sight of the crosse comforteth his soule with the consolacion of him that died theron. But their is no sight whether of the crosse or ought else / that can moue you to leue youre wek-   25
ednesse / for the testament of god is not written in youre hertes.

And when he speaketh of prayenge at church who denyeth him that men might not praye at church or that the church shuld not be a place of prayar? But that a man coude not praye sa[G5v]ue at church / and that my prayars were not hearde as wel elsewhere / If   30
I prayed with like feruentnesse and stronge faith / is a false lye.

84/33–85/1 Paschall lambe   2 I. Cor. v.   7–9 Holy straunge gestures
13 I. Co. II.   18 Pitie

6 ceremonies] 1573, ceromonies 1531   21 Christe] om. 1573   22 doeth]
doth for 1573   S1 Paschall] 1573, Phascall 1531   S3 gestures] gestures is like
an apes play. 1573

And when he speaketh of the presence of god in the temple. I answere that the prophetes testified / how that he dwelt not there /
and so doeth Paul Actes .xvij. and so doeth Steuen Actes .vij. and
Salomon .iij. Of the kinges .viij. And no doute as the mad Iewes
5   ment / he dwelt not there / ner as we moare mad suppose also. But
he dwelled there only in his signes sacramentes / and testimonies
which preached his worde vn to the people. And finally for their false
confidence in the temple / god destroyed it. And no doute for oure
false faith in visitynge the monumentes of Christe / therfore hath god
10 also destroyed them and geuen the place vnder the infideles.

And when he speaketh of the piler of fire & cloude. I answere /
that god was no nother wise present there then in all fire and in all
cloudes saue that he shewed his power there specially by the reason
of the miracle / as he doeth in the eyes of the blynde whom he mak-
15 eth se / and yet is no nother wise present in those eyes then in other /
ner moare there to be prayde to then in other. And in like maner he
is no moare to be prayed to where he doeth a miracle then where he
doeth nonne. Nether though we can not but be in some place /
ought we to seke god in any place / saue only in oure hertes and that
20 in verite / in faith hope and loue or charite acordynge to the worde
of his doctrine.

And oure sacramentes / signes / ceremonies / images / reliques
and monumentes ought to be [G6] had in reuerence so forforth as
they put vs in minde of gods worde and of the ensample of them
25 that liued therafter and no further.

And the place is to be sought and one to be preferred before a
nother for quietnesse to praye and for liuely preachynge and for the
preachynge of soch monumentes and so furth. And so longe as the
people so vsed them in the olde testament / they were acceptable and
30 plesaunt to god and god was saide to dwell in the temple. But when
the significacions beinge lost / the people worsheped soch thynges
for the thinges selues / as we now doo / they were abhominable to
god and god was saide to be no lenger in the temple.

---

3 Actes .17.   4 Actes .7.   5 3. Regum .8.   11–12 The piler of fire

22 ceremonies /] *ed.*, ceremonies *1531*, ceremonies, *1573*   23 ferforth] *ed.*, fer-
foth *1531*, farforth *1573*

iiij.

And in the .iiij. he saith / that god setteth moare by one place then a nother. Which doctrine besydes that it shuld bynde vs vn to the place and god therto and can not but make vs haue confidence in the place / is yet false. For first god vn to whose worde we maye adde   5
nought / hath geuen no soch commaundement ner made any soch couenaunte. Nether is Christ here or there saith the scripture / but in oure hertes is the place where god dwelleth by his awne testimonie if his word be there.

And when he proueth it / because god doeth a miracle moare in   10
one place then in a nother I answere / if god wyll doo a miracle / it requireth a place to be done in. How be it he doeth it not for the place but for the peoples sakes whom he wold call vn to the knowlege of his name / and not to worshepinge him moare in one place then in a nother.   15

[G6v] As the miracles done in Egipte / in the red se / in mount Sinay and so forth were not done that men shuld goo in pilgremage vnto the places to praye there / but to prouoke them vnto the true knowlege of god / that after warde they myght euer praye in the spryte / where soeuer they were. Christ also did not his miracles   20
that men shuld praye in the places where he did them / But to stere vpp the people to come and heare the worde of their soules health. And when he bringeth the miracle of Siloe / I answere / that the sayde miracle and that christ sent the blynd thither to receaue his sight / were not done / that men shuld praye in the pole: but the   25
seconde miracle was so done / to declare the obedient faith of the blinde and to make the miracle moare knowen / and the first for the worde of God / that was preached in the temple / to moue the contre aboute to come thither and lerne to knowe God / and to become a liuely temple / out of which they might euer praye and in all places.   30
Nether was the miracle of lazarus done / that men shuld moare praye

---

2 Place   7 Mat. 24.   23 Siloe   24–25 Ioan 5 .&. 9.

1 iiij.] The fourth chapter. *1573*   2 .iiij.] fourth *1573*
14 worshepinge] worshippe *1573*   S1 Place] M. More teacheth false doctrine.
1573   S4 Ioan 5] *ed.*, Ioan 4 *1531*, Ioh. 4 *1573*

in that place then in a nother / but to shew christes power and to
moue the people thorow wonderinge at the miracle / to herken vnto
gods worde and beleue it / as it is to se playnly.

Morouer God so loueth no church / but that the parish haue liber-
5   tie to take it downe and to byld it in a nother place: ye and yf it be
tymbre to make it of stone and to alter it at their pleasure. For the
places / ye and the images must serue vs and not god which is a spirite and careth for none moare then other ner is other wise present in
one then in a nother. And likewise ys yt of sayntes bones we maye
10   remoue them whother we will / ye and breake all images therto and
[G7] make newe / or yf they be abused / put them out of the waye
for euer / as was the brasen serpent / so that we be lordes ouer all
soch thynges and they oure seruauntes. For if the sayntes were oure
seruauntes / how moch moare their bones. It is the hert and not the
15   place that worshepeth god. The kechen page turninge the spitt maie
haue a purer hert to god / then his Master at church / and therfore
worshepe God better in the kechen / then his master at church. But
when wyll M. More be able to proue that miracles done at sayntes
tombes / were done that we shuld praye vnto the sayntes / or that
20   miracles done by deed saintes whych a liue nether preached gods
worde ner coude doo miracle are done of god?

God loueth none angell in heuen better then the greatest sinner in
erth that repenteth and beleueth in christ. But contrary wyse careth
most for the weakest and maketh all that be perfecte their sar-
25   uauntes / vntyll as paul saith .Eph. iiij. they be growen vpp in the
knowlege of god in to a perfecte man and in to the measure of age
of the fullnesse of christ / that is / that we know al the misteries and
secretes that god hath hyd in christ / that we be no moare childern
wauerynge with euery wynde of doctrine / thorow the sotiltie and
30   wilinesse of men that come vppon vs to bringe vs in to erroure or
begile vs. So ferre it is of that he wold haue vs kept downe to serue
images. For with bodyly seruice we can serue nothinge that is a spirite. And therto if it were possyble that all the angeles of heuen coude

22–25 The father careth most for the youngest.   26 Ephe. 4.

9 one] one place *1573*   10 breake] *1573*, kreake *1531*   12 serpent / so] *ed.*,
serpent So *1531*, serpent, so *1573*

be mine enimies: yet wold I hold me by the testament that my mercyfull and true father hath made me in the bloude off my sauyoure /
and so come vnto [G7v] all that is promised me and christ hath purchased for me / and geue not a straw for them all.

v.

5

In the .v. chapter he falleth from al that he hath so longe swette to
proue & beleueth not by the reason of the miracles / but by the
comen consent of the church and that many so beleue. This man is
of a ferre other complexion then was the prophete Elias. For he beleued a lone as he thought / agenst the consent by all likelyhod / of   10
.ix. or .x. hundred thousand beleuers. And yet M. Mores church is
in no nother condicion vnder the pope / then was that church agenst
whose consent Elias beleued a lone vnder the kinges of Samary.

vj.

In the .vj. chapter & vnto the .xviij. he proueth all most nought   15
saue that which neuer man denied him / that miracles haue bene
done. But how to know the true miracles from the false were good
to be knowen which we shal this wise do if as we take those for true
sacramentes and ceremonies which preach vs gods worde / euen so
we count them true miracles only which moue vs to herken therto.   20

xvj.

Concerninge his .xvj. chapter of the mayde of Ipswich / I answere / that Moses warned hys Israelites that false miracles shuld be
done to proue them / whether their hertes were fast in the lorde.
And euen so christ and the apostles shewed vs before that lienge mir-   25
acles shuld come / to peruerte the very electe / if it were possyble.

22–23 The mayde of Ipswich

5 v.] The fift chapter. *1573*   6 .v.] fift *1573*; that] *om. 1573*   14 vj.] The
sixt chapter. *1573*   15 .vj.] sixt *1573*   18 as] *om. 1573*   21 xvj.] The xvj.
Chapter. *1573*   22 Ipswich] *ed.*, Ipshwcih *1531*, Ipswiche *1573*

And therfore we must haue a rule to know the true miracles from
the false / or else it were impossible that any man shuld scape vndis-
ceaued and continue in the true [G8] waye. And other rule then thys
ys there not: that the true are done / to prouoke men to come and
5   herken vnto gods worde / and the false to confirme doctrine that ys
not gods worde. Now yt ys not Gods worde if thou reade all the
scripture thorowe out / but contrary therto / that we shuld put soch
trust and confidence in our blissed lady as we doo / and cleane agenst
the testament that is in christes bloude. Wherfore a man nede not to
10 feare / to pronounce that the deuell dyd yt to mocke vs with all.

Neuer the later let vs compare the mayde of Ipswich and the
maide of kent to gether. First they saye that the maide of Ipswich
was possessed with a deuell & the maide of kent with the holy goste.
And yet the tragedies are so lyke the one to the other in all poyntes /
15 that thou cowdest not know the holy gost to be in the one and the
deuell in the other by any dyfference of workes. But that thou
mightest with as good reason saye that the deuell was in both / or
the holy gost in both / or the deuell in the mayde of kent and the
holy gost in the mayde of Ipswich. For they were both in like traun-
20 ses / both raueshed from them selues / both tormented a lyke / both
disfigured / lyke terreble ougly and grysely in sight / and theyr
mouthes drawen a syde / euen vnto the very eares of them / both
enspyred / both preach / both tell of wonders / wilbe both caryed
vnto our lady / and are both certified by reuelacyon that our lady in
25 those places and before those images shuld deliuer them.

Now as for the mayde of Ipswych was possessed off the deuell by
theyr awne con[G8v]fession. Whence then came that reuelacion /
that she shuld be holpe and all hir holy preachinge? Iff of the deuell /
then was the myracle and all of the deuell. Iff of the holy gost / then
30 was she inspired with the holy gost and had the deuell within hir
both at tonce. And in as moch as the mayd of kent was inspired by
the holy gost by their confession / whence came that stoppynge of

---

3–4 True miracles   12–13 The mayde of kent   31–32 The mayde of kent

32 stoppynge] *ed.*, stopppnge *1531*, stoppyng *1573*   51 miracles] miracles are
done to prouoke vs to the hearing of Gods worde, and the false do the contrary. *1573*

hir throte / that rauinge / those greuouse panges / that tormentynge / disfigurynge / drawing of hir mouth awrye and that fer-
full and terreble countenaunce? If of the holy gost / and then whi
not the revell and gamboldes of the maide of Ipswich also? and then
what mater maketh it whether a man haue the deuell or the holy 5
gost in him. If ye saye of the deuell / then had she likewise both
the deuell and the holy gost both at tonce. Morouer those possessed
which Christ holpe avoyded christ and fled from him / so that other
which beleued were fayne to bringe them vn to him agenst their
willes. For which causes and many moo that might be made / thou 10
maist conclude / that the deuell vexed them and preached in them / to
confirme fayned confession and dome ceremonies and sacramentes
with out significacion and damnable sectes / and shewed them those
reuelacions. And assone as they were brought before oure ladies image / departed out of them / to delude vs and to turne oure faythes 15
from Christ vn to an old blocke. As we reade in the legend of S. Bartholomewe / how the deuels hurte men in their lymmes and assone as
they were brought in to a certayne temple before an Idole / their they
departed out of them and so begyled the people makynge them beleue that the Idole had healed them of some naturall diseases. 20

[H1] How be it let it be the holy gost that was in the maide of kent.
Then I praye you what thinge worthy of so greate prayse hath oure
ladye done? Our lady hath deliuered her of the holy gost & emptyed
her of moch hie lerninge which as a goodly poetisse / she vttered in
rimes. For appose her now of christ / as scripture testifieth of him / 25
and thou shalt finde her clene with out ryme or reason. The mayde
was at home also in heuenly pleasures / and our lady hath deliuered
her out of the ioyes of Orestes and brought her in to the miseries of
middell erth agayne.

xvij. 30

As for dulia / yperdulia and latria / though he shew not with
which of them he worsheped the cardinalles hatt / ys answered vnto
hym all ready.

17–18 S. Bartholomewe   28 Orestes

1 panges/] *ed.*, panges *1531, 1573*   12 confirme] confirmed *1573*   30 xvij.]
The xvij. Chapter. *1573*

xviij.

In the .xviij. where he wold faine proue that the popes church can
not erre / he allegeth thynges wherof he myght be asshamed / yf he
were not past shame / to proue that the bisshopes haue auctorite to
5   lade vs with tradicions nether profitable for soule nor body. He
bringeth a false allegorie vppon the ouerplus that the Samaritane if
it were layde out / promised to paye when he came agayne / for the
bysshopes tradicions. Nay M. More / besydes that allegories which
euery man maye fayne at his pleasure can proue nothynge / Chryst
10   interpreteth it him selfe / that it betokeneth a kynde mynde and a
louinge neyboure / whych so loued a straunger / that he neuer left
carynge for hym / both absent as wel as present / vntyll he were full
hole and comen out of all necessite.

It signifieth that the prelates / if they were [H1v] true apostles and
15   loued vs after the doctrine of christ / wold sell their myters / croses /
plate / shrynes / iuels and costly showes to socoure the pore and not
robbe them / of all that was offered vn to them / as they haue done:
and to repare thynges fallen in decaye and ruine in the comen welth /
and not to bedger the realmes wyth false Idolatrye and imageser-
20   uice / that they haue not lefte them where wyth to beare the cost of
the comen charges.

And Morouer when the scribes and phareses taught their awne
doctrine / they satt not vppon Moses sete / but on their awne. And
therfore christ (so far it is off that he wold haue vs herken vnto mans
25   doctryne) sayde / bewarre of the leuen of the scribes / phareses and
saduces which is their doctrine and rebuked them for their doctrine
and brake yt hym selfe and taught hys dysciples so to doo and excused them / and sayd of all tradicions / that what soeuer his heuenly
father had not planted / shuld be plucked vp by the rotes. And therto
30   all the persecucion that the apostles had of the Iewes / was for
breakynge of tradycyons.

2–3 Tradycyons   8 Allegory

1 xviij.] The xviij. Chapter. *1573*   8 besydes] *ed.*, b sydes *1531*, besides
1573   11 whych] *ed.*, whych / *1531*, which, *1573*   19 bedger] begger *1573*; the
realmes] *1573*, the / realmes *1531*

Oure prelates ought to be oure saruauntes as the appostles were / to teach vs christes doctrine / and not lordes ouer vs / to oppresse vs with theyr awne. Peter calleth it temptynge of the holy goste actes .xv. to lade the hethen with ought a boue that whych necessite and brotherly loue required. And paul rebuketh his corinthians for their ouer moch obedience and the galathyans alsoo and warneth all men to stonde fast and not to sofre them selues to be brought in to bondage. 5

[H2] And when he sayth peter and paul commaunded vs / to obey oure superioures. That ys trouth / they commaunded vs to obey the temperall swerde whych the pope wyll not. And they commaunded to obey the bysshopes in the doctrine of christe and not in their awne. And we teach not to breake all thynges rashly / as M. More vntrulie reporteth on vs (which is to be sene in oure bokes / if men wil loke vppon them). Of tradicions therfore vnderstond generally. He that maye be fre is a fole to be bonde. But yf thorow wilinesse / thou be brought in to bondage: then yf the tradicion hurte thy soule and the fayth / they are to be broken immediatly / though wyth the losse of thy lyfe. If they greue the body only / then are they to be born tyll god take them off / for breakynge the peace and vnite. 10

15

Then how sore maketh he christes burthen. If yt be so sore / why is Master More so cruell to helpe the bysshopes to lade vs with moare? But surelye he speaketh verye vndiscretelye. For christ did not lade vs with one sillable moare then we were euer bounde to / nether did he saue interpret the law trulye. And besides that / he geueth vn to al his / loue vnto the law: which loue maketh all thynges easye to be born that were before impossible. 20

25

And when he saith / ye be the salt of the erth was spoken for the bysshops and prestes only yt ys vntrue / but yt was spoken generally vn to all that beleue and know the trueth / that they shulde be salt vnto the ignoraunt / and the perfecter vn to the weker / ech to other euery man in hys measure. And Morouer yf yt be spoken vn to the 30

4 Actes .15.   12–13 Tradycyons   27 Matt. 5.

13–14 (which . . . them).] *ed.*, (which . . . them *1531,*   ) whiche . . . them. *1573*   15 be bonde] *1573,* bonde *1531*   17 the fayth] thy faith *1573* 24 saue] any thyng but *1573*   26 to] *om. 1573*   27 erth] earth that it *1573* S3 Matt. 5.] *ed.*, t.Mat 5. *1531,* Math. 5. *1573*

prelates only / how fortuneth yt that Master More ys so busye to
salte the [H2v] world with his hie lernynge? And last of all the salt
of oure prelates which ys theyr tradycions and ceremonyes wyth out
sygnificacion ys vnsauerye longe a goo / and therfore no moare
5   worth but to be cast out at the dores and to be troden vnderfote.

And that he sayth in the ende that a man maye haue a good faith with
euell liuinge / I haue proued it a lie in a nother place. Morouer fayth /
hope and loue be .iij. sisters that neuer can departe in this worlde /
though in the worlde to come loue shal swalowe vp the other two.
10 Nether can the one be stronger or weker then that other. But as moch
as I beleue so moch I loue and so moch I hope: ye and so moch I worke.

xix.

In the .xix. he proueth that prayinge to saintes is good & miracles
that confirme it are of god or els the church saith he doeth erre. It
15 foloweth in dede or that the popis church erreth. And when he saith
it is sinne to beleue to moch I saie we had the moare nede to take
hede what we beleue and to serch gods worde the moare dylygently
that we beleue nether to moch ner to litle.

And when he saith god is honoured by prayenge to saintes be-
20 cause it is done for hys sake: I answere / if it sprange not out of a
false faith but of the loue we haue to god / then shuld we loue god
moare. And morouer in as moch as all oure loue to god spryngeth
out of faith / we shulde beleue and trust god. And then if oure fayth
in god were greater then oure feruent deuocyon to sayntes / we
25 shulde praye to no sayntes at all / seynge we haue promyses of all
thynges in oure sauyoure Iesu and in the sayntes none at all.

[H3] xxv.

In the .xxv. how iugleth he / to proue that al that perteyneth vn
to the faith / was not written / alleginge Ihon in the laste / that the

---

1 [Hand]   8 iij. sisters   29 Ioan .21.

2 salte] fault 1573   3 oure] om. 1573   10 that] the 1573   12 xix.] The
xix. Chapter. 1573   27 xxv.] ed., om. 1531, The xxv. Chapter. 1573   29 laste]
ed., laite 1531, last 1573   S2 iij. sisters] Fayth, loue [sic], & charitie, are iij. sisters.
1573

world coude not conteyne the bokes / if al shuld be written. And Ihon meaneth of the miracles which Iesus did and not of the necessarie poyntes of the faith.

And how bringeth he in the perpetuall virginite of oure ladye which though it be neuer so true / is yet none article of oure faith / to be saued by. But we beleue it / with a story faith / because we se no cause resonable to thinke the contrary.

And when he saith many misteries are yet to be opened / as the cominge of antichriste. Naye verelye the babe is knowne well ynough and al the tokens spide in him which the scripture describeth him by.

And when he allegeth Paules tradicions to the tessalo. / to proue his phantasye. I haue answered rochester in the obedience / that his tradicions were the gospell that he preached.

And when he allegeth Paul to the corin. I saye that Paul neuer knew of this word Masse. Nether can any man gather there of any straunge holy gestures / but the playne contrary and that there was no nother vse there then to breake the breed amonge them at soper / as christ did. And therfore he calleth it christes soper and not Masse.

There was lerned the maner of consecracion. A greate doute / as though we coude not gather of the scripture how to do it. And of the water that the prest mingleth with the wine. A gre[H3v]ate doute also and a perelouse case if it were left out. For ether it was done to slake the hete of the wine or put to after / as a ceremonie / to signifie that as the water is chaunged in to wine / so are we chaunged thorow faith as it were in to christe and are one with him / how be it all is to their awne shame / that ought shuld be done or vsed amonge vs christen / where of noman wist the meaninge. For if I vnderstonde not the meaninge / it helpeth me not .i. corin. xiiij. and as experience teacheth. But if oure sheperdes had bene as wel willynge to fede as to shere / we had neded no soch dispicience / ner they to haue burnt so many as they haue.

5

10

15

20

25

30

---

9 Pope   15 Masse   22 Water   30 1. Cori. 14.

12 tessalo.] *ed.*, tessalo *1531*, Thessalo. *1573*   29 meaninge] *ed.*, meanige *1531*, meaning *1573*   S1 Pope] Antichrist is knowen. *1573*   S2 Masse] Christes Supper & not Masse *1573*   S3 Water] Water mixed with the wyne *1573*

And as for that he allegeth out of the epistle of Iames for the iustifienge of workes. I haue answered in the Mammon agenst which he
can not hisse / and will speake moare in the .iiij. boke.

And as for the Saboth / agreate mater / we be lordes ouer the sa-
5   both and maye yet chaunge it in to the monedaye or any other daye /
as we se nede / or maye make euery tenth daye holy daye only if we
se a cause why / we maye make .ij. euery weke / if it were expedient
& one not ynough to teach the people. Nether was there any cause
to chaunge it from the saterdaye then to put difference betwene vs
10   and the Iewes and lest we shuld become seruauntes vn to the daye
aftir their supersticion. Nether neded we any holydaye at all / if the
people might be taught with out it.

And when he axeth by what scripture we know that a woman
maye christen. I answere / if baptim be so necessary as they make
15   it / then [H4] loue thy neyboure as thy selfe doeth teach wemen to
baptise in tyme of neade: ye and to teach and to rule there husbandes
to / if they be besydes them selues.

And when he saith that of likelyhode / the laye people vnderstode
the gospell of Ihon and Paules pistles better then greate clerkes now.
20   I answere / the moare shame is theirs. How be it ther be .ij. causes
why: the one is their diligent sheringe: and a nother / they denye the
iustifienge of faith where of both Paule and Ihon doo entreate and all
most of nothynge else / if the significacyon of oure baptime which
is the lawe of god and faith of christ / were expounded trulye vnto
25   vs / the scripture wolde be easye to all that exercised them selues
there in. And sir in as moch as the prelates care so litle for the losse
of the vnderstondynge of the scripture and to teach the people / how
happeneth it / that they care so sore for a bald ceremonie / which the
significacion lost / though christ him selfe had institute it / we coude
30   not obserue with out a false faith & with out hurtynge of oure
soules?

And finally to rocke vs a slepe with all / he saith / that he shall

4 Saboth   13–14 Whi wemen baptise   21–24 Whi the prelates vnderstond not the scripture

5 or] or or 1573   6 holy daye] 1573, holy dage 1531   15 selfe doeth teach]
ed., selfe doeth / teach 1531, selfe, doth teach 1573   19 pistles] Epistles 1573

neuer spede wel / that wil seke in the scripture whether our prelates
teach vs a true faith / though ten preach ech contrary to other in one
daye. And yet christ for all his miracles sendeth vs to the scripture.
And for all Paules miracles / the Iewes studied the scripture the diligenterly / to se whether it were as he saide or no. How be it he   5
meaneth / that soch can not spede wel because the prelates will
burne them excepte M. More helpe them and make them forswere
christ before hande.

xxvij.

[H4v] In the .xxvij. he bringeth Paul exhortynge to agre & to tell   10
al one tale in the faith which can not be saith Master More / excepte
one beleue by the reason of a nother. Yes verelye we al beleue that
the fyre is hotte and yet not by the reason of a nother and that with
a moch surer knowlege then if we beleued it the one by the tellynge
of a nother. And euen so they that haue the law of god written in   15
their hertes and are taught of the spirite to know synne and to abhorre it / and to fele the power of the resurreccion of christ / beleue
moch surer then they that haue no nother certente of their faith /
then the popis preachynge confirmed with so godly liuinge.

And it is not vnknowne to M. More that the churches of late dayes   20
and the churches now beinge haue determined thinges in one case
the one contrarye to the other / in soch wyse that he can not denye
but the one hath or doth erre: the which case I coulde shewe him if
I so were minded. The olde popes / cardinalles and busshopes sayed
yee to the thinge that I meane / where vnto these that now raigne   25
saye naye. Now sir if you gather a generall counsell for the matter /
the churches of fraunce and Italye will not beleue the churches of
spayne & douchlonde because they so saye: but will aske how they
proue it. Neyther will Louayne beleue Parise / because they saye that
they can not erre / but will heare first their probacion. Also how shal   30
we know that the old pope & his prelates erred / because these that

2–8 Ye can not spede wel if ye trye the doctrine of oure prelates by the scripture.   23–26 The church must shewe a reason of their doctrine.

9 xxvij.] The xxvij. chapter. *1573*   14 moch] more *1573*

are now so saye? When the old pope liued we were as moch bound
to beleue that he coude not erre / as we be now that this can not:
wherfore you must graunt me / that god must shew a miracle for
the tone parte / or else they must brynge autenticke scripture.

5   [H5] Now sir god hath made his last and euerlastinge testament /
so that all is open / and no moare behynde then the apperinge of
Christe agayne. And because he will not stere vpp euery daye a new
prophete with a new miracle to confirme new doctrine or to call
agayne the old that was forgotten / therfore were all thynges neces-
10   sarye to saluacion comprehended in scripture euer to endure. By
which scripture the counseles generall and not by open miracles /
haue concluded soch thinges as were in them determined / as stories
make mencion. And by the same scripture we know which
counseles were true and whych false. And by the same scripture
15   shall we / if any new question arise / determine it also. Abraham
answered the rich man / they haue Moses and the prophetes / let
them heare them / and saide not / they haue the scribes and the
phareses whom they shuld heare preachynge out of the sete of their
awne doctrine with out scripture.

20   And when he allegeth / he that heareth you heareth me / and if
any man heare not the church take him for an hethen / concludynge
that we must beleue whosoeuer is shauen in all that he affirmeth
with out scripture or miracle / I wold fayne wete in what figure that
silogismus is made. Christes disciples taught Christes doctrine con-
25   firmynge it with miracles / that it might be knowen for gods and
not theirs. And euen so must the church that I will beleue shew a
miracle or bringe autenticke scripture that is come from the appostles which confirmed it with miracles.

xxix.

30   In the .xxix. he allegeth that christ saide not the holy gost shall
write / but shall teach. It is [H5v] not the vse to saye / the holy

15 Luk. 16.   20 Luke .x.   21 Mat. 18.

1 saye? When] *ed.*, saye? .When *1531*, say? When *1573*   23 wete] know
1573   29 xxix.] The xxix. Chapter. *1573*

gost writeth / but inspireth the writer. I maruayle that he had not
brought / as many of his brethren doo / Matthew in the last / where
Christ commaunded the appostles to goo and teach all nacions / and
saide not write. I answere / that this precepte / loue thy neyboure
as thy selfe and god aboue all thynge went with the appostles and   5
compelled them to seke gods honoure in vs / and to seke al meanes
to continue the faith vn to the worldes ende. Now the appostles
knewe before that heresies shuld come / and therfore wrote / that it
might be a remedie agenst heresies / as it well appereth Ihon .xx.
where he saith / these are written / that ye beleue and thorow beleffe   10
haue life. And in the seconde of his first pistle he saith / these I write
because of them that deceaue you. And Paul and Peter therto warne
vs in many places. Wherfore it is manifest / that the same loue compelled them to leue nothynge vnwritten that shuld be necessarily re-
quyred / and that if it were left out / shuld hurte the soule.   15

And in the last Chaptre to make all fast / he bringeth in the kinges
grace how he confuted Marten Luther with this conclusion / the
church can not erre: where vn to I will make none answere for feare
to displease his grace / neuerthelesse because Marten coulde not
soyle it / if his grace loke well vppon the matter / he shall finde that 20
god hath assoyled it for him in a case of his owne.

And vppon that master More concludeth his first boke / that
whatsoeuer the church / that is to wete / the pope and his brode
saye / it is gods worde / though it be not written ner confirmed with
miracle ner yet good liuinge / ye and [H6] though they saye to daye   25
this and to morow the contrarie / all is good ynough and gods
worde: ye and though one pope condemne a nother (.ix. or .x.
popes arow) with all their workes for heretikes / as it is to se in the
stories / yet all is right & none erroure. And thus good night and
good rest / Christ is brought a slepe and layde in his graue and the   30
dore seled to / and the men of armes aboute the graue to kepe him
doune with polaxes. For that is the surest argument / to helpe at nede
and to be rid of these babillinge heretikes / that so barke at the holy

---

3 Mat. 28.   9 Ioan .20.   10 1. Ioan .2.   28 [Hand]

11 pistle] Epistle *1573*   22 boke] *ed.*, koke *1531*, booke *1573*
27 condemne] *1573*, condeme *1531*   S2 Ioan] *ed.*, Iona *1531*, Iohn *1573*

spiritualtie with the scripture / beinge therto wretches of no reputacion / nether cardenales ner bisshopes ner yet greate benefised men /
ye and with out totquottes and pluralities / hauynge no holde but
the very scripture / whervnto they cleaue as burres so fast that they
5   can not be pulled awaye saue with very singgynge them of.

¶A sure token that the pope is antichriste.

And though vn to all the argumentes & persuasions which he
wold blinde vs with / to beleue that the pope with his secte were the
right church / and that god for the multitude will not sofre them
10   erre / we were so simple that we saw not the sotiltie of the argumentes ner had wordes to solue them with / but oure bare faith in oure
hertes yet we be sure and so sure that we can therin not be disceaued / and doo both feale and se that the conclusion is false and
the contrary true.

15   For first Peter saith .ij. Peter .ij. there shalbe false teachers amonge
you whych shall secretly brynge in damnable sectes / denyenge the
lorde that bought them / and many shall [H6v] folow their damnable wayes / by whom the waye of trouth shalbe evel spoken of / and
with fayned wordes they shall make marchaundice ouer you. Now
20   saith Paul Roma. iiij. the law speaketh vn to them that are vnder the
law. And euen so this is spoken of them that professe the name of
christe. Now the pope hath .x. thousand sectes cropen in / as pied
in their consciences as in their cotes / settynge vpp a thousand maner
workes to be saued by / whych is the denyenge of Christe. And we
25   se many and all most all to gether folow their damnable wayes. And
in that Peter said that they shall rayle and blaspheme the trueth / it
foloweth that there shalbe a litle flocke reserued by the hand of god
to testifie the trueth vn to them or else how coude they rayle on it?
And it foloweth that those raylars shalbe the mightier parte in the
30   world / or else they durst not do it. Now what truth in christ doeth
not the pope rebuke and in settynge vpp false workes denie all to
gether? And as for their fayned wordes / where findest thou in all

---

7 Antichrist   15 2. Pet. 2.   20 Rom. 3.

7 persuasions] *1573*, persuasuasions *1531*   19 you.] *ed.*, you? *1531*, *1573*
23 maner] maner of *1573*   S1 Antichrist] The Pope is Antichrist. *1573*

the scripture purgatory / shrift penaunce / pardon /pena culpa / yperdulia and a thousande fayned termes moo? And as for their
marchaundice / loke whether they sell not all gods lawes and also
their awne / and all synne and all Christes merites and all that a man
can thynke. To one he selleth the faute only and to a nother the faute   5
and the payne to / and purgeth his purse of his money and his
braynes of his wittes / and maketh him so beestely / that he can
vnderstonde no godly thynge.

And Christ saith Mathew .xxiiij. their shal false anoynted arise
and shew signes and wonders: that is / they shall shew miracles and   10
so pre[H7]uayle that / if it were possible / the electe shuld be
brought out of the true waye. And these false annoynted / by the
same rule of Paul and in that christ saith also that they shal come in
his name must be in the church of christ and of them that shall call
them selves Christen / and shall shew their wonders before the electe   15
and be a sore temptacion vn to them / to bringe them out of the
waye. And the electe which are few in comparison of them that be
called and come faynedly / shall amonge that greate multitude be
kepte by the mightie hande of god agenst all naturall possibilite. So
that the church and very electe shall neuer be soch a multitude to   20
gether by them selues with out persecucion and temptacion of their
faith / as the great multitude vnder the pope is which persecute and
sofre not. And these which the pope calleth heretikes shew no miracles / by ther awne confession / nether ought they / in as moch as
they bringe no new lerninge ner ought saue the scripture which is   25
all redy receaued and confirmed with miracles. Christ also promiseth vs nought in this world saue persecucion for oure faith. And
the stories of the olde testament are also by Paulus .i. Cor. x. oure
ensamples. And there / though god at a tyme called with miracles a
greate multitude / yet the very chosen that receaued the faith in their   30
hertes / to put their trust in God alone and which endureth in temptacions were but fewe and euer oppressed of ther false brethern and
persecuted vn to the deeth and dreuen vn to corners.

---

7 [Hand]   10 Mat. 24.   27 1. Cor. 10.

---

31 alone] 1573, alowe 1531   S1 [Hand]] The Pope selleth sinne and paine & all
that can be solde. 1573

And when Paul .ij. Tessa. ij. saith that Antichristes cominge /
shalbe by the workynge of sathan with all power / signes and wonders of falshed and all disceaueablenesse for them that pe[H7v]rish /
because they conceyued not loue vn to the trouth / to besaued by /
& therfore shall god send them stronge delusion or gyle / to beleue
lies: the texte must also pertayne vn to a multitude gathered to
gether in Christes name of whych one parte & nodoute the gretter /
for lacke of loue vn to the trouth that is in Christe / to liue therafter /
shall faull in to sectes & a false faith vnder the name of Christe &
shalbe induratt and stablished therin with false miracles to perish for
their vnkyndnesse. The pope first hath no scripture that he dare a-
byde by in the light / nether careth / but blasphemith that his word is
truer then the scripture. He hath miracles with out gods worde / as
all false prophetes had. He hath lyes in all his legendes in all preach-
inges and in all bokes. They haue no loue vn to the trueth. Which
appereth by their greate synnes that they haue sett vpp aboue all the
abhominacion of all the hethen that ever were / & by their longe
continuaunce therin: not of frailte: but of malice vn to the trueth &
of obstinatt lust & selfe will to synne. Whych appereth in .ij.
thynges: the one / that they haue gotten them with wiles & falsehed
from vnder all lawes of man & even aboue kinge & emproure / that
no man shuld constrayne their bodies & brynge them vn to better
ordir / that they maye synne frely with out feare of man. And on
the other syde / they haue brought gods worde aslepe / that it shuld
not vnquiet their consciences / in so moch that if any man rebuke
them with that / they persecute him immediatly and pose him in
their false doctrine & make him an heretike and burne him and
quench it.

And Paul saith .ij. Timothe .iiij. in the later dayes there shalbe perelous times. For ther shal[H8]be men that loue them selves /
couetous / hye minded / proud / raylars / disobedient to father &
mother / vnthankfull / vngodly / churlish / promisebreakers / accusars or pickquareles / vnlouinge / dispicers of the goode / traytours /

5

10

15

20

25

30

1 2. Tessa. 2.

---

31 hye minded /] *ed.*, hye minded *1531*, high mynded, *1573*
32 promisebreakers /] promisebreakers *1531*, promisebreakers, *1573*

hedy / puffed vpp and that loue lustes moare then god / hauynge an apperaunce of godlynesse / but denienge the power therof. And by power I vnderstonde the pure faith in gods worde which is the power & pith of all godlynesse & whence all that pleaseth god springeth. And this texte pertayneth vn to them that professe Christe. And in that he saith hauinge an apperaunce of godlynesse & of that foloweth in the texte / of this sorte ar they that entre in to mens howses & lead wemen captiue laden with synne / ever axynge & neuer able to atteyne vn to the trueth (as our hearers of confessions doo) it appereth that they be soch as wilbe holier then other & teachers & leaders of the rest. And loke whether there be here any sillable that agreeth not vn to oure spiritualtie in the hiest degre. Loue they not them selues their awne decrees and ordinaunces / their awne lies and dreames and despice all lawes of god and man regarde noman but them only that be disgysed as they be? And as for their couetousenesse which all the world is not able to satisfie / tell me what it is that they make not sarue it? in so moch that if god punish the world with an evell pocke / they immediatly paynt a blocke & call it Iob to heale the disease in stede of warnynge the people to mend their lyuinge. And as for their hye minde & pride / se whether they be not aboue kynges & emproure & al the names of god / and whether any man maye come to beare rule in this world excepte he be sworn to them and come vpp vnder them.

[H8v] And as for there raylynge loke in their excomunicacion / and se whether they spare kinge or emproure or the testament of god. And as for obedience to father and mother / Nay / they be immediatly vnder god and his holy vicar the pope / he is their father and on his ceremonies they must wayte. And as for vnthankefull / they be so kynde / that if they haue receaued a thousand pound londe of a man / yet for all that they wold not receaue one of his offspringe vn to a nightes herber at his nede / for their founders sake. And

---

12–13 Loue them selves   16 Couetous   18 [Hand]
19–20 Hyemynded   21 Proude   24 Railars   25–26 Disobedient
28–29 Vnthankefull

---

5 professe] 1573, professe- 1531   S1 Loue] Loue is of 1573   S3 [Hand]] om. 1573

whether they be vngodly or no I reporte me vn to the parchment.
And as for churlishnesse / se whether they will not haue their causes
venged / though it shuld cost hole regions / ye and al christendome /
as ye shall se and as it hath cost halfe christendome all redie. And as
5   for their promise or trucebreakynge / se whether any appoyntment
maye endure for their dispensacions / be it neuer so lawfull / though
the sacrament were receaued for the confirmacion. And se whether
they haue not broken all the appoyntementes made betwene them
and their founders. And se whether they be not accusers and tray-
10   tours al so of all men / and that secretly and of their very awne
kynges and of their awne nacion. And as for their heedinesse / se
whether they be not prone / bold and runne hedelonge vn to all mischeue / with out pitie and compassion or caringe what misery and
destruccion shuld fall on other men / so they maye haue their pres-
15   ent pleasure fulfilled. And se whether they loue not their lustes / that
they will not be refrayned from them ether by any law of god or
man. And as for their apperaunce of godlynesse / se whether all be
not gods seruice that they fayne / and se whether not [I1] all most
all consciences be captiue ther to. And it foloweth in the texte / as
20   the sorserers of Egipte resisted Moses / so resisted they the trueth.
They must be therefore mightie iugulars. And to poynte the popish
with the fingre he saith / men ar they with corrupte mindes and
castawayes concerninge faith / that is they be so fleshly minded / so
croked so stoborn and so monstrouse shapen / that they can receaue
25   no facion to stonde in any buyldynge that is grounded vppon faith /
but when thou hast turned them al wayes and done thy best to hew
them and to make them frame / thou must be fayne to cast them out
with the turkes and Iewes / to serue god with the imageseruice of
their awne false werkes. Of these and like textes and of the simili-
30   tudes that christ maketh in the Gospell of the kingdome of heuen it
appereth / that though the holy gost be in the chosen and teacheth
them all trueth in Christe / to put their trust in him / so that they

1 Vngodlye   2 Churlysh   4–5 Promysebrakers   9 Accusars
11 Heedye   15–16 Louinge lustes   17–18 Apperaunce of godlinesse
29 [Hand]

29 like] such like *1573*

can not erre therin / yet while the world stondeth / God shall neuer
haue a church that shall eyther persecute or be vnpersecuted them
selues any season / aftir the fassion of the pope. But there shalbe in
the church a fleshly seed of Abraham and a spirituall / a Caim and
an Abel / an Ismaell and an Isaac / an Esau and a Iacob / as I haue   5
sayde / a worker and a beleuer / a greate multitude of them that be
called and a small flocke of them that be electe and chosen. And the
fleshlye shall persecute the spirituall / as Caim did Abel and Ismaell
Isaac & soforth / and the greate multitude the smal litle flocke and
antichrist wilbe euer the best christen man.   10

[I1v] So now the church of god is dowble / a fleshly and a spirituall: the one wilbe and is not: the other is and maye not be so called /
but must be called a lutheran / an heretike and soch like. Vnderstonde therfore / that god when he calleth a congregacion vn to his
name / sendeth forth his mesingers to cal generally. Which mesin-   15
gers bringe in a greate multitude amased & astonied with miracles
and power of the reasons which the preachers make / and ther with
be compelled to confesse that there is but one god of power and
might a boue all and that Christ is god and man and borne of a virgin
and a thousand other thinges. And then the greate multitude that is   20
called and not chosen / when they haue gotten this faith comune as
well to the deuels as them and moare strongly persuaded vnto the
deuels then vn to them / then they goo vn to their awne imaginacions sayenge: we maye no lenger serue Idoles / but god that is but
one. And the maner of seruice they fett out of their awne braynes   25
and not of the word of god / and serue god with bodily seruice as
they did in times past their Idoles / their hertes seruynge their awne
lustes still. And one will serue him in white / another in blacke / a
nother in greye and a nother in pied. And a nother to doo god a
pleasure with all / wilbe sure / that his showe shal haue .ij. or .iij.   30
good thicke soles vnder and will cut him aboue / so that in somer
while the wether is whott / thou maist se his bare fote and in winter
his socke. They wilbe shorn and shauen and Saduces: that is to saye /

11–14 This word church is taken .ij. maner wayes.   28 Frires   29 [Hand]

9 multitude] multitude shall persecute] *1573*   12 so] so be *1573*

rightewes / and phareses / that is / seperated in facions from all
wother men. Ye and they will consecrat them selues all to gether vn
to god and will annoynte their handes [I2] and halowe them as the
chalice / from all maner laye vses: so that they maye serue nether
5   father ner mother master lord or prince / for polutynge them selues /
but must wayte on god only / to gather vpp his rentes / tithes / offeringes and al other duties. And al the sacrifice that come they con-
sume in the altare of their belies and make Calil of it / that is / a
sacrifice that noman maye haueparte of. They beleue that there is a
10   god: But as they can not loue his lawes / so they haue no power to
beleue in him / But they put their trust and confidence in their awne
workes & by their awne workes they wilbe saued / as the rich of
this world / when they sue vn to greate men / hope with giftes and
presentes to obtayne their causes. Nether other seruinge of God
15   know they / saue soch as their eyes maye se and their belies feale.
And of very zele they wilbe gods vicars and prescribe a maner vn to
other and aftir what facion they shall serue god / and compell them
therto / for the avoydinge of Idolatrie / as thou seist in the phareses.
     But litle flocke / as sone as he is persuaded that there is a god / he
20   runneth not vn to his awne imaginacions / But vn to the mesinger
that called him / and of him axeth how he shall serue god. As litle
Paul acte. ix. when christ had ouer thrown him and caught him in
his nett: axed sayenge: lord what wilt thou that I doo. And as the
multitude that were conuerted actes .ij. axed of the apostles what
25   they shulde doo. And the preacher setteth the lawe of god before
them / and they offer their hertes to haue it written therin / consentinge that it is good and rightwysse.
     [I2v] And because they haue runne cleane contrary vn to that
good law they sorow and morne / and because also their bodies and
30   flesh are otherwise disposed. But the preacher comforteth them and
sheweth them the testament of Christes bloud / how that for his sake
all that is done is forgeuen / and al their wekenesse shalbe taken a

9 Calil   22 Actes .9.   24 Actes .2.

---

19 persuaded] *ed.*, perfuaded *1531*, perswaded *1573*   23 wilt] *1573*, wslt
1531   106/32–107/1 a worth] in worth *1573*   S1 Calil] Calil, is a sacrifice
that no man may haue any parte therof. *1573*

worth vn tyll they be stronger / only if they repent and will submitte
them selues to be scolars and lern to kepe this law. And litle flocke
receaueth this testament in his hert and in it walketh and serueth
God / in the spirite. And from hence forth al is christ with him / and
christ is his and he christes. Al that he receaueth / he receaueth of   5
christe / and all that he doeth / he doeth to christe. Father mother /
master / lord & prince ar christ vnto him / and as christ he serueth
them with al loue. His wife / childern / saruauntes and subiectes are
christ vn to him / and he teacheth them to serue christ and not him
selfe and his lustes. And if he receaue any good thinge of man / he   10
thanketh God in christ / which moued the mans herte. And his neyboure he serueth as Christ in all his nede / of soch thynges as god
hath lent / because that all degrees are bought as he is / with christes
bloude.

And he wil not besaued / for seruinge his brethern / nether prom-   15
iseth his brethern heuen for seruinge him. But heuen / iustifienge /
forgeuenesse / all gyftes of grace and al that is promised them they
receaue of Christ and by his merites frely. And of that which they
haue receaued of christ they serue ech other frely as one hand doeth
the other / sekinge for their seruice nomoare then one hand doeth of   20
a nother eche the others health / wealth helpe / ayde / succoure and
to assiste one a [I3] nother in the waye of christ. And god they serue
in the spirite only / in loue / hope faith and dreade.

When the greate multitude that be called and not chosen / Caim /
Ismael / Esau and carnall Israel that serue God night and daye with   25
bodyly seruice and holy workes soch as they were wont to serue
their Idoles with all / behold litle flocke that they come not forth in
the seruice of god / they rore out / where art thou? whi comest thou
not forth & takest holy watere? wherfore saith litle flocke. To put
awaye thy sinnes. Nay brethern / God forbid that ye shuld so   30
thinke / Christes bloud only washeth awaye the synnes of all that

6 [Hand]

2 litle] a little *1573*   5 he christes] he is Christes *1573*   7 ar christ] are
Christes *1573*   9 them] *1573*, then *1531*   11 thanketh] *1573*, tanketh
1531   17 forgeuenesse /] *ed.*, forgeuenesse *1531*, forgeuenes, *1573*   29 litle]
the little *1573*

repent and beleue. Fire / salt / water / bred / oyle be bodyly
thynges / geuen vn to man for his necessite and to helpe his brother
with / & god that is a spirite can not be serued therwith. Nether can
soch thinges enter in to the soule to purge hir. For gods worde only
5 is hir purgacion. No saye they / are not soch thinges halowed. And
saye we not in the halowenge of them that whosoeuer is sprinkled
with the water or eateth of the bred / shall receaue health of soule
and body? Sir the blessynges promised vnto Abraham for all nacions
are in christ / and out of his bloud we must fett them / and his word
10 is the breed / salt and water of oure soules. God hath geuen you no
power to geue thorow youre charmes soch vertue vn to vnsensible
creatures / which he hath halowed him selfe and made them all
cleane (for the bodyly vse of them that beleue) thorow his worde of
promese and permission and oure thankes geuinge. God saith / if
15 thou beleue saynt Ihons Gospell / thou shalt be saued / and not for
the beringe of it aboute the with so many crosses / [I3v] or for the
obseruinge of any soch obseruances.

God for thy bitter passion rore they out by and by / what an heretike is this? I tell the that holy church nede to allege no scripture for
20 them for they haue the holy gost which inspireth them euer secretly / so that they can not erre whatsoeuer they saye / doo or or-
dayne. Whate wilt thou despice the blessed sacramentes of holy
church wherwith god hath bene serued this .xv. hundred yere (ye
verely this .v. thousand yeres / even sens caim hithirto / and shall
25 endure vnto the worldes end / amonge them that haue no loue vn
to the trueth to be saued therby) thou art a stronge heretike and worthy to be burnt. And then he is excomunicat out of the church. If
litle flocke feare not that bogge / then they goo strayght vn to the
kinge. And it like youre grace / perelous people and sedicious / and
30 euen ynough to destroye youre realme / if ye se not to them betimes.
They be so obstinat and tough / that they will not be conuerted /
and rebellious agenst god and the ordinaunces of his holy church.
And how moch moare shall they so be agenst youre grace / if they

encrease and grow to a multitude. They wyll peruert all and suerly make new lawes and ether subdue youre grace vn to them or rise agenst you. And then goeth a parte of litle flocke to potte and the rest scatter. Thus hath it euer bene and shall euer be / lett noman therfore disceaue him selfe.

5

3 litle] the little *1573*   4 scatter] *1573*, scather *1531*

[I4] ¶An answere to Master Mores seconde boke

In the first chapter ye may not trie the doctrine of the spiritualtie
by the scripture: But what they saye / that beleue vndoutedly and
5 by that trie the scripture. And if thou finde the playne contrary in
the scripture / thou maist not beleue the scripture / but seke a glose
and an allegorie to make them agre. As when the pope saith / ye be
iustified by the workes of the ceremonies and sacramentes and so
forth / and the scripture saith / that we be iustified at the repentaunce
10 of the hert thorow Christes bloude. The first is true playne / as the
pope saith it and as it stondeth in his texte / but the second is false as
it appereth vn to thine vnderstandinge and the literall sens that kyl-
leth. Thou must therfore beleue the pope and for Christes doctrine
seke an allegorie and a misticall sens: that is / thou must leaue the
15 clere light and walke in the miste. And yet Christ and his appostles
for all their miracles required not to be beleued with out scripture /
as thou maist se Ihon .v. and Actes .xvij. and bi their diligent alleginge of scripture thorow out all the new testament.

And in the ende he saith for his pleasure / that we knowlege / that
20 noman may ministre sacraments but he that is deriuede out of the
pope. How be it this we knowlege / that noman coude ministre sacramentes with out significacion which are no sacramentes saue soch
as are of the popis generacion.

[I4v] iij.

25 In the thrid chapter and in the chapter folowynge / he vttereth
how fleshly minded he is / and how beestly he imageneth of God /
as Paule saith .1. corin. 2. the naturall man can not vnderstond the
thinges of the spirite of God. He thinketh of God / as he doeth of
his cardenall / that he is a monstre / pleased when men flater him /

---

15 [Hand]   16 Ioan .5.   27 1. Corin. 2.

20 sacraments] *ed.*, sacrament *1531*, Sacraments *1573*   23 generacion] *ed.*,
geueracion *1531*, generation *1573*   24 iij.] The iij. Chapter. *1573*

and if of whatsoeuer frailte it be / men breake his commaundementes / he is then raginge mad as the pope is and seketh to be
venged. Naye / God is euer fatherly minded toward the electe membres of his church. He loued them yer the world beganne / in Christ.
Ephe. 1. He loueth them / while they be yet evell and his enimies in   5
their hertes / yer they be come vn to the knowlege of his sone
christe / and yer his law be written in their hertes: as a father loueth
his younge sonne / whyle he is yet euell and yer it know the fathers
law to consent therto.

And aftir they be once actually of his church and the law of God   10
and faith of christ written in their hertes / their hertes neuer synne
any moare / though as Paule saith .Roman. vij. the flesh doeth in
them that the spirite wold not. And when they synne of frailte / God
ceaseth not to loue them styll / though he be angrie / to put a crosse
of tribulacions vppon their backes / to purge them and to subdue   15
the flesh vn to the spirite or to al to breake their consciences with
threateninge of the lawe and to feare them with hell. As a father
when his sonne offendeth him feareth him with the rod / but hateth
him not.

[I5] God did not hate paul / when he persecuted but had layd vpp   20
mercy for him in store / though he was angre wyth hym to scorge
hym and to teach him better. Nether were those thynges layd on his
backe which he after sofered / to make satisfaccion for his foresinnes / but only to serue hys brethern and to kepe the flesh vnder.
Nether did god hate Dauid when he had synned / though he was   25
angre with him. Nether did he after sofre to make satisfaccyon to
god for hys olde synnes / but to kepe his flesh vnder and to kepe
hym in mekenesse and to be an ensample for oure lernynge.

iiij.

In the fourth saith he if the church were an vnknowen companie /   30
how shuld the infydeles / yf they longed for the faith / come therby?

5 Roman. 5.   12 Roma. 7.   24–28 The new life doeth tame the flesh and
serue hyr neyboure.

29 iiij.] The iiij. Chapter. *1573*

O whother wandereth a fleshly minde / as though we first sought
out god. Nay / God knoweth his and seketh them out and sendeth
his mesingers vnto them and geueth them an hert to vnderstonde.
Dyd the hethen or any nacyon seke chryste? Nay / christ sought
5   them and sent hys appostles vnto them. As thou seyst in the storyes
from the begynnynge of the worlde and as the parables and simili-
tudes of the gospell declare.

And when he saith / he neuer founde ner herd of any of vs / but
that he wold forswere to saue his life. Answere / the moare wrath
10   of god will light on them / that so cruelly delite to torment them
and so craftely to begyle the weake. Neuer thelesse yet it is vntrue.
For he hath hearde of sir Thomas hitton whom the bisshopes of
Rochester and caunterbury slew at maydstone and of many that sofered in braband holland and at colen and in all [I5v] quarters of
15   douchlonde and doo dayly.

And when he saith that their church hath many marters / let him
shew me one / that died for pardons / and purgatory that the pope
hath fayned / and let hym take the mastrie.

And what a doo maketh he / that we saye / there is a church that
20   sinneth not and that there is no man but that he sinneth / which are
yet both true. We read .j. Ihon .iij. he that is born of god synneth
not. And Eph. v. men loue youre wiues as the lorde doeth the
church / and gaue him selfe for her / to santifie her and to clense hir
in the fountaine of water thorow the worde / and to make hir a glori-
25   ous church vn to him selfe / with out spott or wrincle.

And .j. Ihon .j. If we saie / we haue no sinne we disceaue oure
selues and make him a lyer and hys worde is not in vs. Master More
also wyl not vnderstond that the church ys some tyme taken for the
electe only which haue the law of god written in their hertes and
30   fayth to be saued thorow christe written there also. Whych same for
all that saye wyth paul / that good which I wold / that doo I not.
But that euell which I hate / that do I: so it is not I that doo it but
sinne that dwelleth in my flesh.

III/31–112/3 God seketh vs and we not hym.   11–12 Sir Thomas hitton
16–17 The pope hath no marters.   20 I. Ioan .3.   28–29 The church is double.

11 vntrue] *1573*, vntue *1531*

And Gala. v. the flesh lusteth contrary to the spirite and the spirite
contrary to the flesh / so that these two fightynge betwen them
selues / ye can not doo what ye wolde. For they neuer consent that
synne is good ner hate the law ner cease to fight agenst the flesh /
but assone as they be faullen / rise and fight a fresh. And that the   5
church ys some tyme taken for the commen rascall of all [I6] that
beleue / whether wyth the mouth only and carnally with out spyryte
nether louinge the law in their hertes nor fealinge the mercy that is
in christ / but ether runne all to gether at ryott or kepe the law with
cauteles and exposycions of their awne fayninge & yet not of loue   10
but for feare of hell / as the theues do for feare of the galowes / and
make recompence to god for their synnes wyth holy dedes.

He also wyll not vnderstonde / that there be twoo maner faythes:
one / that ys the faith off the electe / whych purgeth them of all their
synnes for euer. As ye se Ihon .xv. ye be cleane sayth christ / be the   15
reason of the worde: that is / thorow beleuinge christes doctryne.
And Ihon .j. he gaue them power to be the sonnes of God / thorow
beleuinge in hys name. And Ihon .iij. he that beleueth the sonne hath
euerlastynge lyfe / and a thousand like textes.

And a nother of them that be called and neuer electe. As the fayth   20
of Iudas / of symon magus / of the deuel / and of the pope. In whose
hertes the law of god ys not wrytten / as it appereth by their workes.
And therfore when they beleue many thynges of christe / yet when
they come vnto the saluacion that is in his bloude / they be but Iewes
and turkes and forsake christ and runne vn to the iustifienge of cere-   25
monies wyth the Iewes and turkes. And therfore they remayne euer
in synne within in theyr hertes.

Where the electe hauinge the law written in their brestes and louinge it in their spirites / synne there neuer / but with out in the flesh.
Agenst which sinne they fight continually & minishe it daily [I6v]   30
with the helpe of the spirite / thorow prayar / fastynge and seruinge
their neybours louingly with all maner seruice / out of the law that
is written in their hertes. And their hope of forgeuenesse is in
Christe only / thorow his bloude and not in ceremonyes.

---

1 Gala. 5.   13–14 Two maner faithes   16 Iohan .15.

28–29 louinge] *ed.*, leuinge *1531*, leuyng *1573*

v.

And vn to his .v. Chapter I answere / by the pope the scripture is
hid and brought in to ignoraunce & the true sens corrupte. And by
them that ye call heretikes we knowe the scripture and the true sens
theroff. And I saye / that the pope kepeth the scripture as did the
5   phareses / to make marchaundice of it. And agayne / that the heretikes become out of you / as out of the scribes & phareses came the
appostles and Christ him selfe and Ihon Baptiste / and that they be
plucked out of you and graffed in Christe and bilt vppon the funda-
10   cion of the appostles and prophetes.
And in the end / when he saith that the heretikes be faullen out of
Christes mistical bodi which is the pope and his. I answere that ye
be a misticall body and walke in the mist and will not come at the
light / and the heretikes be departed out of youre mist and walke in
15   the clere light of gods worde.

vj.

In the .vj. he saith that the heretikes be all nought / for they all
periure & abiure. He yet saieth vntrue. Many abyde vn to the deeth.
Many for their wekenesse ar kepte out of youre handes. Many for
20   their ouer moch boldnesse in their awne strength be deliuered in to
youre handes & fall in the flesh / their hertes abydinge still in the
trueth as Peter & thousandes did / & aftir repent [I7] & be no lesse
cristen then before though ye haue them in dirision vn to youre
awne damnacion. And many because they come to Christ for fleshly
25   liberte and not for loue of the trouth / fall as it becometh them /
vnder youre handes: as Iudas & Balam / which at the begynnynge
take christes parte / but aftirward when they finde ether losse or no
vauntage they gett them vn to the contrary part and are by profession the most cruelle ennimies & sotellest persecuters of the trouth.
30   Loke Master More and rede and marke well.

2–3 The pope hideth the scripture.   11–13 The heretikes be faulen out of the
mist.   19–20 Whi many faull

---

1 v.] The v. Chapter. *1573*   16 vj.] The vj. Chapter. *1573*

vij.

In the .vij. he saith / that he hath holy saintes and holy counsels
on his side. Name the sayntes and proue it. Name the counsells and
the holy prelates there of. Thou shalt shew me no nother popes or
cardenales / then soch as we haue now / that wyll obey nother god   5
ner man / or any law made by god or man: but compell all men to
folow them / strengthynge their kingdome with the multitude of all
misdoars.

He saith also that good and bad worshepe saintes / the good well
and the bad evell. How cometh it then / that ye shew not the differ-   10
ence & teach to doo it wel? I se but one facion amonge all the popish.

And finally he saith he is not bounde to answere vn to the reasons
and scripture that are layde agenst them. It is ynough to proue their
part / that it is a comen custume and that soch a multitude doo it /
and so by his doctrine the turkes are in the right waye.   15

viij.

[I7v] In the .viij. he saith / the saintes be moare charitable now
then when they liued. I answere / Abraham was while he liued as
charitable as the best. And yet deed / he answered him / that prayed
him / they haue Moses and the prophetes / lett them heare them.   20
And so haue we / not Moses and the prophetes only / but a moare
clere light / euen Christ and the appostles / vn to whych if we herken
we be saintes all ready.

And to proue that they in heuen be better then we in erth / he
allegeth a texte of oure sauioure Luke .vij. that the worst in heuen is   25
better then Ihon Baptist. Now the texte is / he that is lesse in the
kingdome of god is gretter then he. We that beleue are gods
kingedome. And he that is lest (in doenge seruice vn to his brythern)
is euer the grettest aftir the doctrine of Christe. Now Christ was

---

3 Counsels   13 [Hand]   17 Saintes   20 Luke .16.   26 Luke .7.

1 vij.] The vij. Chapter. *1573*   5 nother] neyther *1573*
7 strengthynge] strengthning *1573*   13 scripture] scriptures *1573*   16 viij.]
The viij. Chapter. *1573*   20 him] to hym *1573*

lesse then Ihon for he did more seruice then Iohan / and therfore
greater then he. And by their awne doctrine there was no sainte in
heuen before the resurreccion of Christe / but what care they what
they saye / blinded with their awne sophistrie.

5   Morouer cursed is he that trusteth in ought saue god saith the
texte and therfore the saintes wold haue no man to trust in them
whyle they were a liue. As Paul saith .1. Corin. iij. what is Paul saue
youre saruante to preach Christe. Did Paul die for you? were ye baptised in the name of Paul? Did I not marie you to Christ / to put
10   youre trust in him? And againe let noman reioyce or trust in man /
saith he. For all are youres whether Paul / or Appollo or Cephas:
whether the world / life / deeth / present thynges or thynges to
come: all are youres & ye are Christes / [18] and christ is gods. If
my faith be stedfast in the promises that I haue in Christes bloud / I
15   nede but to praye mi father in Christes name and he shall send me a
legion of angels to helpe me: so that my faith is lorde ouer the angels
and ouer all creatures to turne them vn to my soules health and my
fathers honoure / and maye be subiecte vn to no creature / but vn to
gods worde in oure sauioure Christe only. I may haue no trust ther-
20   fore in the saintes. If ye saye / ye put no trust in them / but only put
them in remembraunce of their dutie / as a man desyreth his neyboure to praye for him / remembring him of his dutie /and as when
we desyre our brethern to helpe vs at oure nede. That is false / for
ye put trust in all youre ceremonies and all youre holy dedes and in
25   whosoeuer disgyseth him selfe and altereth his cote from the comune facion / ye and euen in the cotes of them that be not yet saintes /
aftir youre doctrine.

Yf a prest said masse in his gowne / wold ye not rise agenst him
and slee him / and that for the false faith that ye haue in the other
30   garmentes. For what honoure can those other garmentes doo to god
moare then his gowne or profit vn to youre soules / seinge ye vnderstonde nought ther by? And therto in the collectes of saintes ye
saye / saue me God and geue me euerlastinge life for the merites of

8 1. Cor. 3.

---

1 for he did more seruice then Iohan] *om. 1573*   6 texte] *ed.,* texre *1531,* text
1573   28 gowne] *1573,* gowue *1531*

this or that saint / euery man aftir his phantasie chosynge him some one sainte singularly to be saued by. With which collectes I praye you shew me how stondeth the deeth of Christe? Paul wold saye that Christ died in vayne if that doctrine were true.

And therto in as moch as ye saye / the saintes [18v] merite or de-   5
serue not in heauen / but in this world only / it is to be feared / lest their merites besore wasted and the deseruinges of many al spent thorow oure holy fathers so greate liberaltye.

Abraham and the prophetes / and the appostles and many sens praide to no saintes & yet were holy ynough.   10

And when he saith / they coude helpe when they were aliue. That was thorow their faith in beleuinge the promise. For they had promises that they shuld doo soch miracles to stablish their doctrine and to prouoke vn to Christ / and not vn to them selues.

And when he proueth that the saintes be in heuen in glorie with   15
Christ all ready sayenge if god be their god they be in heuen / for he is not the god of the deed. There he steleth awaye Christes argument where with he proueth the resurreccion / that Abraham and all saintes shuld rise againe & not that their soules were in heuen which doctrine was not yet in the worlde. And with that doctrine he taketh   20
awaye the resurreccion quite / and maketh Christes argument of none effecte. For when Christe allegeth the scripture that god is Abrahams god / and addeth to / that god is not the god of the deed / but of the liuinge and so proueth that Abraham must rise agayne: I deny christes argument and saye with master More / that Abraham   25
is yet aliue / not because of the resurreccion / but because his soule is in heuen. And in like maner Paules argument vn to the Corrinthi-ans is nought worth. For when he saith / if there be no resurreccion / we be of all wretches the most miserablest. Here we haue no plea-sure / but sorow / care / and oppression. And therfore if we rise   30
not agayne / all our soferinge [K1] is in vayne. Nay Paul / thou art vnlerned: goo to master More and lerne a newe waye. We be not

15–17 M. More destroyeth the resurreccion.   24 Mat. 22.   28 1. Cor. 15.

---

1 some] *om.* 1573   17 the deed] *ed.*, deed 1531, the dead 1573   23 the god]
God 1573   28 resurreccion] *ed.*, refurreccion 1531, resurrection 1573
29 most] *om.* 1573   32 We be] 1573, We- be 1531

most miserable / though we rise not agayne / for oure soules goo to
heuen assone as we be deed / and are there in as greate ioye as christ
that is rysen agayne. And I maruell that Paul had not comforted the
Tessalonians with that doctrine / if he had wist it / that the soules of
5   their deed had bene in ioye / as he did with the resurreccion / that
their deed shuld rise agayne. If the soules be in heuen in as greate
glorie as the angels aftir youre doctrine / shewe me what cause
shulde be of the resurreccion.

And when he saith / whether the saintes do it them selues / or by
10   intercession made to god / it maketh no mater / so we be holpe / it
appereth bi his doctrine / that all is good that helpeth / though a man
praye vn to the deuell / by whom many be holpe. Now in Christ we
haue promises of al maner helpe & not in them. Where then is our
faith to be holpe by Christ when we hope to be holpe by the merites
15   of saintes? So it appereth that the moare trust we haue in saintes /
the lesse we haue in Christe.

And when he bringeth in a similitude that we praye phisicions /
though god can helpe vs / and therfore we must praye to saintes. It
is not like / for they haue naturall remedies for vs whych we must
20   vse & not tempte god. But the saintes haue no naturall remedies ner
promise of supernatural. And therfore it can be but a false supersticious faith. And where no natural remedie is there god hath promised to help them that beleue in him. And moreouer when I praye a
phisicion or surgion and trust to be holpe by them / I dishonoure
25   god / excepte I first praye to god and be[K1v]leue that he will worke
with their doctrine and medicines & so receaue mine health of the
hond of God. And euen so when I praye to man / to helpe me at
mine nede / I synne excepte I complayne first to god & shew him
my nede & desyre him to moue one or a nother to helpe me / and
30   then when I am holpe / thanke him and receaue it of his hande / in
as moch as he moued the herte of him that holpe me and gaue him
wherewith and a commaundement to doo it. M. More. Christ is not

---

4 1. Tessa. 4.   17 Phisicions

17 phisicions] ed., phisions 1531, Phisitions 1573   23 moreouer] 1573, moreuer
1531   24 phisicion] ed., phision 1531, Phisition 1573   32 More.] ed., More
1531, More, 1573

dishonoured because that they which here preach him truly / shall
sitte and iudge with him. Tindale. That to be true the scripture testifieth / but what is that to youre purpose that they which be deed can
heare vs and helpe vs? How be it / if master More shuld describe vs
those setes / I am sure he wold paynte them aftir the facion of my   5
lorde cardenales holy cheyar / as he doeth God aftir the similitude
of worldely tirantes and not accordinge to his awne worde. For they
that be worldely & fleshly minded can but fleshly imagen of god all
to gether like vn to the similitude of worldely thinges. Master More.
The apostles and saintes were prayd so when they were aliue and   10
god not dishonoured. Tindale. What helpeth that your carnall purpose. I haue answered you vn to that and manye thynges moo in the
obedience and other places agenst which ye replye not / but kepe
youre tune and vn to al thynge singe kokow / kokow / we be the
church and can not erre. The appostles had gods word for all that   15
they did and ye none. And yet many dishonoured god and christ for
theyr false trust and confidence which they had in the appostles as
thou maist se by paul to the corinthi.

    Then he breaketh forth in to open blasphemy [K2] and sayth that
it behoueth vs to praye vn to saintes and that god will else not heare   20
vs / for oure presumptuouse malapertenesse. So it is now presumptuous malapertenesse to trust in gods worde and to beleue that god
is true. Paul teacheth vs to bebolde to goo vn to god and sheweth vs
good cause in Christe / whi we so maye and that god wold so haue
vs. Nether is there any cause to kepe vs backe / saue that we loue   25
him not ner trust him. Yf a man saye / oure synne shuld kepe vs
backe. I saye if we repent & beleue in Christ / Christ hath taken them
awaye and therfore thorow him we maye be bolde. And Christ saide
at his last soper Ihon .xvj. I saye not that I will praye for you vnto
my father / for my father loueth you. As who shulde saye / be not   30
afrayed ner stonde with out the dores as a dastard: but be bold and
goo in to my father youre selues in my name / and shew youre com-

---

    14 1. Cor. 3.   19–20 More dryueth from god.   22 Hebr. 4.   29 Ioan
.16.

---

    9 similitude] *1573*, similitudee *1531*   21 presumptuouse] *ed.*, prefumptuouse
1531, presumptuous *1573*   31 a dastard] *1573*, dastard *1531*

playntes / for he now loueth you / because ye loue my doctrine. And
Paul sayth Ephe. ij. we haue al an open waye in thorow him / and
are now no more forennars or straungers but of the howshold of
god. Of god therfore we be bold as of a most louinge and mercifull
5 father / aboue all the mercy of fathers. And of our sauioure Iesus we
be bold / as of a thynge that is oure awne and moare oure awne then
oure awne skynnes / and a thynge that is so soft and gentle / that
lade we him neuer so moch with oure synnes / he can not be angre
ner cast them from off his backe / so we repent and wyll mend. But
10 Master More hath a nother doctrine to driue vs from god and to
make vs tremble and be afferde of him.

He likeneth god to worldly tirantes / at who[K2v]me no man
maye come / saue a few flaterars whych ministre vn to them all voluptuousnesse and sarue their lustes at all poyntes. Which flaterars
15 must first be corrupte with gyftes / yer a man may come at the
kinge. Then he saith / a man maye praye to euery deed man. That
me thinketh shuld be agenst the popes doctrine and profite also. For
he will haue no man prayed to vntyll he haue canvesed him / I wold
saye / canonised him / and tyll god or at the lest waye the deuell
20 haue shewed miracles for him.

Then he bringeth how one that was deed and in the inuisible purgatory holpe a nother that was aliue and in the visible purgatory.
This is a straunge case / that a man there maye helpe a nother and
not him selfe. And a moare straunge case that god heareth a man
25 here for him selfe / beinge in his awne purgatory and helpeth him
cleane out / or easeth him if it be to sore. But and he be in the popes
purgatory god will not heare him for him selfe / and that because
the pope might haue somewhat to deliuer him. And the straungest
case of all is that the pope is allmyghty there and god can do there
30 nought at all as the pope can not here in this purgatori. But because
this is not gods worde ner like godis doctrine / I thinke it no damnable synne to beleue it poetrie.

Then how ye maye praye for them and to them / tyll they be can-

---

1 Ephe. 2.   15–18 M. More is agenst the popes profite.   21 Purgatori

9 mend] amende *1573*   14 poyntes. Which] *ed.*, poyntes which *1531*, pointes
which *1573*

onised: and when they be canonised / but to them only / for then ye
be sure that they be in heuen. By what token? I maye be as sure by
the canonisynge / as I am that all the bisshopes which the pope con-
firmeth / be holy men / and all the doctours that he maketh wel
lerned / and that all the prestes which he annoyn[K3]teth haue the   5
holy gost. If ye saye / because of the miracles / then doo men
wronge to praye for kinge henry of windesore at cambryge and
Eton. For he / as men saye doeth miracles. And also if the miracles
certifie vs / what nedeth to by the popis canonisynge?

ix.   10

In the .ix. he putteth no ieopardy to praye to him that is damned
and to steke vpp a candle to him ner I trow vn to the deuell therto /
if he might haue a vauntage by him.

Then he maketh no ieopardie to doo and beleue whatsoeuer an
open multitude called godes church doeth and beleueth. For god   15
will haue an open church that can not erre. For saith he / when the
Israhelites fell to Idolatrie / the true church remayned in Hierusalem
amonge the Iewes. First I saye / if a man had no beter vnderstondinge then M. Mores doctrine / he coud not know whether were the
true church / the Iewes or the Israelites. For the Israelites were in   20
numbre .v. tymes moo then the Iewes and worsheped god / though
as present in the image of a calfe / as the Iewes for the most part /
present in the arcke of testimonie. And secondarily he saith false.
For the Iewes were faullen in to open Idolatrie a thousand tymes
worse then the Israelites / even in their very temple / as it appereth 25
by open stories and bi the Prophetes: so that for their open Idolatrie /
whych they wold for no preachynge of the prophetes amende / their
prestes therto resistynge the prophetes and coragynge the people in
their wekednesse / god sent them captiue out of the lande. Ye and
the people erred in folowynge the scribes and phareses and the   30
[K3v] open multitude called Gods church / at the comynge of

<hr />

120/33–121/1 Canonisynge   8–9 Kinge henrye of windsore

10 ix.] The ix. Chapter. *1573*   28 coragynge] encoragyng *1573*
S2 windsore] *ed.*, winsore *1531*, Windsore *1573*

Christ / as it is to se in the gospell / contrary vn to Master Mores
deceytfull poetrye. And againe / god reserued him a litle flocke euer
in Israel and had euer prophetes there / some tyme openly and some
tyme in persecucion / that euery man must hide him selfe and kepe
5   his faith secret: and euen in the houses of the euell kynges both of
Iewri and also of Israel he had good people / and that amonge the
hie officers / but secretly / as Nycodemus amonge the phareses. So
that the very church was euery where oftimes in captiuite and persecucion vnder their brethern / as we be vnder oures in the
10 kingedome of the pope.

Then he putteth no ieopardy to worshupe an vnconsecrated
hoste. But with what worshupe men shuld worshepe the consecrated doeth he not teach / nether the vse of that sacrament or any
other / ner how ought maie be worsheped but teacheth only that all
15 thynges maye be worsheped / and sheweth not the right worshepe
from the false.

Then he noteth Paule .1. Corin. 1. how he exhorteth vs to agre
only / but not on the trueth or on the good / but only to agre a greate
multitude to gether. O this depe blindenesse. Did not Paul first teach
20 them the true waye? And did he not instructe them anew in the true
waye and in the saide epistle rebuke the false confidence that they
had in men / the cause of all their dissension and all erroures that
were amonge them?

Then he saith / the Iewes had saintes in honoure / as the Patriarkes
25 and Prophetes. We teach to dishonoure none: But the Iewes prayd
[K4] to none.

More. Christ rebuked not the Phareses for garnishinge the sepulchres of the prophetes but for that they folowed the condicions of
them that slew them. Tindale. Yes & for their false trust in soch
30 werkes as we doo you. And ye Sir thynke that ye deserue heuen in
worshepynge the saintes bones / and be as redy to sle them that beleue / teach and liue as the saintes did / as youre fathers were to sle
them: besydes that ye worshepe saintes that folowed Christ aftir the

18 1. Cor. 1.

17 vs] *1573*, vn *1531*   21 confidence] *1573*, coufidence *1531*

ensample of youre holy cardenall / of whom I doute not but that ye
wil make a god in processe of tyme also.

Then repeteth he for forgettynge / how Eliseus bones reysed vpp
a deed body. That was to confirme his preachinge only. For the Israelites / as weked as they were / nether prayed to him / nether   5
kissed his bones / ner offered ner steked vpp candels before him.
Which thynge if they had done in the kingdome of the Iewes / I
doute not but that some good kynge wold haue burnt his bones to
asshes / as wel as the brasen serpent / that was as greate a relique as
deed bones. And Christ shewed miracles at the findynge of the   10
crosse. That was to stablish the faith of Christes deeth & that it shuld
be a memory of his deeth / and not that we shuld trust in the wod
as we doo. For whych false abuse / the hole lande where Christ did
his miracles / is destroyed.

Then he allegeth the woman that was healed / thorow twitchinge   15
of Christes cote / because we shuld worshepe it. When Christ said
hir faith hath made hir hole / not in the cote / but in Christe.

[K4v] And the miracle was shewed / to prouoke to the worshepinge of the preachynge and not of the cote. Though to kepe the cote
reuerently in the memoriall of the dede / to prouoke vn to the faith   20
of Christ were not evell of it selfe. And Paule by youre doctrine /
sent his napken to heale the seke / that men shuld shrine his sneueled
napken / and not to beleue his preachinge.

x.

The .x. chapter of sent walary is mete for the auctor and his wor-   25
sheple doctrine.

xj.

In the .xj. he iugleth with this misticall terme latria. I answere /
god is no vayne name / but signifieth one that is almightie / all mer-

4 a deed body] *ed.*, a deed *1531*, a dead body *1573*   24 x.] The x. Chapter.
1573   25–26 worsheple] worshipfull *1573*   27 xj.] The xj. Chapter. *1573*

cifull / all true and good. Which he that beleueth will goo to god /
to his promises and testament and not folow his awne imaginacions /
as Master Mores doctrine teacheth.

He saith that bodyly seruice is not latria. No but bodyly seruice
5   done and referred vn to him which is a spirite / is Idololatria.

He trusteth that men know the image from the saint. I axe M.
More whi god did hide Moyses body and diuers other. The Iewes
wold haue knowen that Moses had not bene god and that Moses
bones had not bene Moses. And they knew that the brasen serpent
10   was not god / and that the golden calues were not god / and that
wod and stone were not god. But Sir there is euer a false imaginacion by. The world because they can not worshepe god in the spirite / to repent off euell and to loue the lawe and to beleue that he
wyll helpe at all nede / therfore runne vn to theyr awne imagynacy-
15   ons [K5] and thinke that god for soch seruyce as they doo to images / will fulfill their worldly desyres: for godly can they nought
desyre. Now God is a spirite and wilbe worsheped in his worde only
which is spirituall / and wil haue no bodylye seruice. And the ceremonies of the olde law he set vpp / to signifie his worde only and to
20   kepe the people in minde of his testament. So that he which obseru-
eth any ceremonie of any other purpose is an Idolater / that is / an
imageseruer.

And when he saith / if men axe wemen whether it were oure lady
of walsingam or Ipsewich that was saluted of Gabriel or that stode
25   by Christ when he henge on the crosse / they will saye nether
nother. Then I axe him what meaneth it / that they saye oure lady
of walsynggam praye for me oure lady of Ipswich praye for me our
lady of wilsdon praye for me / in so moch that some which reken
them selues no small foles / make them roules of halfe an houre
30   longe / to praye aftir that maner. And they that so praye / thou maist
besure / meane oure lady that stode by the crosse / and hir that was
saluted therto.

Then he reherseth many abuses / and how wemen singe songes of

7 Moses

_____

8 and] *1573*, an *1531*   14 runne] runne they *1573*   25 henge] hung
1573   33 how] how that *1573*

ribaudrie in processions in cathedrall churches. Vn to which abhominacions yet our holy church that can not erre / consent with full
delectacion. For on the on syde they will not amend the abuse. And
on the other syde they haue hired M. More to proue with his sophistrie / that the thynges ought not to be put doune.   5

Then he bringeth in how the wild Irish and the welch praye /
when they goo to stele. And ax[K5v]eth whether / because they
abuse prayar / we shuld put all prayenge downe. Naye M. More / it
is not like. Prayar is gods commaundement / and where faith is /
there must prayar nedes be and can not be awaye. How be it /   10
thinges that are but mennes tradicions and all indifferent thinges
which we maye be as well with out as with / maye welbe put doune
for their dishonouringe of god / thorow the abuse. We haue turned
kissinge in the church in to the pax. We haue put done watchinge all
night in the church on saintes evens / for the abuse. And Ezechias   15
brake the brasen serpent .iiij. of kinges .xviij. for the abuse. And
euen so / soch processions and the multitude of ceremonies and of
holidayes to / might as wel be put downe. And the ceremonies that
be left wold haue their significacions put to them & the people shuld
be taught them. And on the sondayes gods word wolde be truly   20
preached. Which if his holy church wold do / nether the Irish ner
yet the welsh wold so praye. By which prayenge and other like
blindnesse / Master More maye se / that buzssynge in latine on the
holy dayes helpeth not the hertes of the people. And I wondre that
M. More can laugh at it and not rather wepe for compassion / to se   25
the soules for which christ shed his bloude / to perish. And yet I
beleue that youre holy church wil not refuse at ester to receaue the
tithes of all that soch blind people robbe / as wel as they dispence
with all false gotten good that is brought them / And will laye the
ensample of Abraham and Melchisedec for them.   30

124/33–125/1 Processions   6 Wyld irish   7 Welch men
16 Ezechias

---

15 evens] eues *1573*   16 of] *om. 1573*   28 tithes] *1573*, rithes *1531*
S1 Processions] Processions, though they be abused may not be put downe. *1573*

xij.

[K6] In the .xij. he allegeth that S. Hierom and Augustine prayed to sayntes / and concludeth / that if any secte be one better then a nother they be the beste. I answere / though he coude proue that they prayed to saintes / yet coude he not proue him selfe therby of the best secte ner that it were good therfore to praye to saintes. For first the apostles / patriarkes and prophetes were sure to befolowed / which prayed to nonne. And agayne / a good man might erre in many thynges and not be damned / so that his erroure were not directly agenst the promises that are in christes bloude / nether that he held them maliciously. As if I beleued that the soules were in heuen immediatly and that they praid for vs / as we doo one for a nother / and did beleue that they herd all that we spake or thought / and vppon that prayed to some saint / to praye for me / to put him in remembraunce only / as I praye my neyboure / and with out other trust or confidence and though al be false / yet shuld I not be damned / so longe as I had no obstinacie therin / for the faith that I haue in christes bloude shuld swalowe vp that erroure / tyll I were better taught / but master More shuld haue alleged the places where they prayed vn to sayntes.

And then he allegeth agenst him self / that the miracles were wrought by god / to confirme his doctrine and to testifie that the preacher therof was a true mesinger. But the miracles that confirme praienge to saintes / doo not confirme gods doctrine. But mannes imaginacions. For there was neuer man yet that came forth and saide / loo / the soules of the sayntes that be deed [K6v] be in heuen in ioye with christe and god wil that ye praye to them. In token wherof / I doo thys or that miracle.

And when he triumpheth a litle after / as though all were wonne saynge / if oure old holy doctoures were false and their doctrine vntrue and their miracles fayned / let them come forth and doo miracles them selues and proue oures fayned. Sir / ye haue no doctours

7 [Hand]

---

that did miracles to stablish youre worshepynge of images and so
forth. Youre doctrine is but the opinion of faithlesse people / which
to confirme the deuel hath wrought moch sotilte. And as for the
miracles done at sayntes graues and at the presens of reliques / as
longe as true miracles endured and vntyll the scripture was auten- 5
tickly reaceaued / wher done to confirme the preachinge that soch
saintes had preached / whyle they were alyue. And therto the miracles which witches doo / we confounde not with other miracles /
But with scripture we proue them not of god / but of the deuel / to
stablish a false fayth and to leade from god / as youre doctrine doeth. 10
And likewise where we can confunde youre false doctryne wyth
autenticke and manifest scripture / there nede we to doo no miracle.
We bringe gods testament confirmed wyth miracles for al that we
doo / and ye ought to require no moare of vs.

And in like maner do ye firste geue vs autenticke scripture for 15
youre doctrine. If ye haue no scripture come forth and preach youre
doctryne and confirme it wyth a myracle. And then if we brynge not
autenticke scripture agenst you or confounde youre myracle wyth a
greater as Moses dyd the sorserars of Egypte / we wyll beleue you.

[K7] And when he speaketh of tryal of miracles what doo ye to 20
trie youre miracles / whether they be true or fayned. And besydes
that / gods worde which shuld be the triall / ye refuse and do al that
ye can to falsifie it.

And when he speaketh of sectes of heretykes / I answere / that
they which ye call heretikes beleue all in one christe / as the scripture 25
teacheth / and ye in all thinge saue christe. And in youre false doctrine of youre awne fayninge with out scripture / ye haue as many
sundrie sectes as all Monkes and freres and studentes in diuinite in
all youre vniuersites. For first yer ye come to diuinite / ye be all
taught to denye the saluacion that is in christe. And none of you 30
teacheth a nother so moch as the articles of youre fayth. But folow
all most euery man a sundrie doctoure and in the scripture his awne
brayne / framinge it euer after the false opynyons whych he hath
professed yer he come at it.

8 Witches   15 [Hand]   24 Sectes

26 thinge] *om.* 1573   S3 Sectes] The sectes in the popishe church are almost
innumerable. 1573

And when he saith that god wold sone vttur fayned miracles. I
answere / God hath had at all tymes one or a nother to improue
youres wyth gods worde. And I axe whether Mahometes fayned
myracles haue not preuayled .viij. hundred yeres. And youre ab-
5 hominable dedes worse then the turkes testifye that ye loue the
trouth lesse then they. And vn to them that loue not the trueth hath
god promised by the mouth off paul .ij. Thessalo. ij. to send them
aboundaunce and strength of false miracles / to stablysh them in lies
and to dysceaue them and leade them out off the waye / so that they
10 can not but perysh / for their vnkyndnesse / that they loued not the
trueth / to lyue therafter and to honoure god in thir membres.

[K7v] And when he saith the heretykes haue no myracles. I answere / they nede not / so longe as they haue autenticke scripture.

And when he sayth God sheweth no miracles for the doctours of
15 the heretikes. No moare he nedeth not / for all they preach / ys the
scripture confirmed with miracles / and receaued many hundred
yeres agoo. And therefore God nedeth not to shew miracles for
them whyle they lyue to strength theyr preachynge. And to shew
myracles for them when they be deed / to moue the people to praye
20 to them and to put their trust in them / as ye doo in youres / were
to make them Idoles and not sayntes.

And when he speaketh of miracles done in theyr church in tyme
of persecucyon. I answere / those were not the miracles of youre
church but of them that beleued the scripture and sofered for it / as
25 the heretykes doo now. For ye had neuer persecucyon for youre false
doctrine / which ye haue brought in besides the scripture / ner any
that died for it: But ye persecute and slee / whosoeuer wyth Gods
worde doeth rebuke it. And as for youre awne myracles of whych
ye make youre boost / ye haue fayned them so grosly thorow out
30 all youre legendes of sayntes / that ye be now asshamed of them and
wold fayne be ryd of them if ye wyst how with honeste / and so
wolde ye of a thousand thynges which ye haue fayned. And the
cause why heretykes fayne no miracles as ye do / ys that they walke
puerly and entend no falshed.

6–8 The cause of false miracles

7 Thessalo.] *ed.*, Thessolo. *1531*, Thess. *1573*   22 church] churches *1573*

And whi the deuel doeth none for them / ys that they cleue fast to
gods worde whych the deuell [K8] hateth and can doo no miracles
to further it / But to hindre it / as he doeth with you. Reade the
stories of youre popis and cardenales / & se whether the deuell hath
not holpe them vn to their hie dignities. And loke whether youre 5
holy bysshopes come any other wyse vn to their promocions / then
by seruinge the deuell / in settinge all christendome at variaunce / in
sheddynge bloude / in bringynge the comen wealth to tyranny and
in teachinge christen princes to rule moare cruelly then did euer any
hethen / contrary vn to the doctrine of christe. 10

And as for the turkes and sarasenes that ye speake of / I answere
that they were christen once / at the lest waye for the most parte.
And be cause they had no loue vn to the trouth to liue ther aftir as
ye haue not / God did send them false miracles to carye them out of
the right waye as ye be. And as for the Iewes / whi they byde out / 15
is only because they haue sett vpp their awne rightewesnesse / as
ye haue / and therfore can not admitte the rightewesnesse that is in
Christes bloude / as ye can not and as ye haue for sworne it.

And when he saith / in that they haue miracles and the heretikes
none / it is a sure signe that they be the true church and the heretikes 20
not. Had ye gods word with youre miracles and the heretikes doctrine were with out / then it were true. But now because ye haue
miracles with out gods worde / to confirme youre false imaginacions / and they which ye call heretikes haue Gods word confermed
with miracles / fyve hundred yeares to gether / it is a sure [K8v] 25
signe that they be the true church and ye not / in as moch also as
christ saith / that the disceauers shall come with miracles: ye and in
his name ther to / as ye doo. For when christ sayth their shall come
in my name that shall saye he him selfe is Christe / who is that saue
youre pope / that wilbe christes vicar and yet maketh men to beleue 30
in him selfe / in his bolles and calues skinnes and in what soeuer he
listeth. And who be those false annoynted that shall come with miracles to disceaue the electe if it were possible / saue youre pope with
his gresiamus?

And when he repeteth his miracles / to proue that the old holy doc- 35

31 Mat. 24.

tours were good men in the right beleffe. I answere agayne / that the
doctours which planted gods worde watered it with miracles / while
they were aliue. And when they were deed God shewed miracles at
their graues / to confirme the same / as of Heliseus. And that continued
till the scripture was ful receaued and autenticke. But ye can not shew /
ner shall / any doctoure which beinge aliue preached youre false doctrine confirminge it with miracles / as god doeth his scripture.

Then saith he / God had in the old testament good men full of
miracles / whose liuinge a man might be bold to folow and whose
doctrine a man might be bold to beleue be reason of their miracles /
and then iugleth sayenge: if god shuld not so now in the new testament haue doctours with miracles to confirme their doctrine and liuinges / but contrary wise shuld bringe to passe or sofre to be
brought to passe with false miracles / that his church shuld take ypocrites for saintes / which expounded the scripture falsly / then shuld
he disceaue his church and not haue his [Li] spirite present in hys
church / to teach them all trouth / as he promised them. I answere /
god sofereth not his church to be disceaued: But he sofereth the
popes church because they haue no loue vnto the trouth / to liue
after the lawes of god / but consent vnto all iniquite / as he sofered
the church of Mahomete. Moare ouer the gift of miracles was not all
waye amonge the preachers in the olde testament. For Ihon baptist
dyd no miracle at all. The miracles were ceased longe yer christe.
And as for you in the popes kingdome had neuer man that ether
confirmed gods doctrine / or youre awne with myracles. All youre
sayntes be first saintes when they be deed and then doo first miracles / to confirme tithes & offerynges & the poetry which ye haue
fayned / and not true doctrine. For to confirme what preachynge
doeth Saint thomas of canterburie miracles? He preached neuer ner
liued any other life then as our cardenall / and for hys mischeue died
a mischeuous deeth. And of our cardenall / if we be not diligent /
they wyll make a sainte also and make a greater relike of his showe
then of the others.

19–20 Whi the pope fell   29–31 S. Thomas of canterbury

9–10 whose doctrine] *ed.*, whose / doctrine *1531*, whose, doctrine *1573*   10 be
bold to] *om. 1573*   12 miracles] *1573*, miraches *1531*

And of youre deed saintes lat vs take one for an ensample.
Thomas de aquino is a saynt full of miracles / as freres tell. And hys
doctrine was / that our lady was borne in originall sinne. And dunce
doynge no miracle at all / because I suppose no man wotteth where
he lieth / improueth that with his sophistrie and affirmeth the con-   5
trary. And of the contrary hath the pope / for the deuocion of that
the graye frires gaue him / ye maye well thynke / made an article of
the fayth.

And finally as for the miracles / they ar to make a man astonied
and to wonder and to dra[Liv]we him to heare the worde ernistly /   10
rather then to write it in his herte. For whosoeuer hath no nother
fealynge of the law of god that it is good / then because of miracles /
the same shall beleue in Christe / as did Simon Magus and Iudas: and
as they that came out of Egipte with Moses / and fell awaye at euery
temptacion / & shall haue good werkes like vn to our popes / bissh-   15
opes and cardenales. And therfore when the scripture is fully receaued / there is no nede of miracles. In so moch that they which
wyll not beleue Moses and the prophetes when the scripture is receaved / the same wilbe no true beleuers by the reason of miracles /
though one arose from deeth to life to preach vn to them by the testi-   20
monie of Christe.

And agayne / how doeth S. Hierom / Augustine / Bede and many
other old doctoures that were before the pope was cropt vpp in to
the consciences of men and had sent forth his damnable sectes / to
preach him vnder the name of christe / as christ prophisied it shuld   25
be / expounde this texte / thou arte Peter and vppon this rocke I wyll
byld my church / and this texte / Peter fede my shepe / and all power
is geuen me in heuen & in erth / and innumerable soch textes cleane
contrary vnto al those new old holy doctours that haue made the
pope a god? They knew of no power that man shuld haue in the   30
kyngdome of Christ / then to preach Christ truly. They knew of no
power that the pope shuld haue to send to purgatory or to deliuer
thence / nether of any pardons ner of any soch confession as they

1–2 Thomas de aquino   3 Dunce   7 [Hand]   9 Miracles
26 Mat. 16.   28 Ioan .21.

31 then] but 1573

preach & teach / nether were many that are articles with you / articles of their faith. They al preached forgeuenesse of synnes thorow
repentaunce towar[L2]de the lawe and faith in oure sauioure
Christe / as all the scripture playnly doeth and can no notherwise be
5   taken / and as al the hertes of as many as loue the law of god / doo
fele / as surely as the fingre feleth the fire hote.

¶An answere vnto Master Mores thirde boke

[L2v] In his third boke he procedith forth as before to proue that the opinions which the popish teach with out scripture are of equal auctorite with the scripture. He axeth what iff there had neuer bene scripture written? I answere / god careth for his electe and therfore hath prouided them of scripture / to trie all thynges and to defende them from all false prophetes. And I saye morouer that if there had bene no scripture written / that god for his mercy and fatherly loue and care toward his electe / must haue prouided / that there shulde neuer haue bene heresies or agenst all tymes when sectes shulde arise / haue stered vpp preachers to confunde the heresies with miracles. Take this ensample / the grekes haue the scripture and serue god therin moch moare diligently then we. Now latt vs geue that there were no scripture / but that we receaued all our faith by the auctoryte of oure elders / and the grekes by the auctorite of their elders. When I shall dispute with a greke aboute the articles of the faith which my elders taught me and his elders denye / as eareconfession / the holy pardons of the pope and all his power that he hath aboue other bisshopes & many other thynges besyde the scripture which we hold for articles of oure faith and they denye. If there be no nother proffe of ether parte / then to saye / my elders which can not erre so affirme and that he shuld answere / his elders whych can not erre so denie / what reason is it / that I shuld leaue the auctorite of my elders and goo and beleue his / or that he shuld leaue the auctorite of his elders and come and beleue myne? no[L3]ne at all verely. But the one partie must shew a miracle or else we must referre oure causes vnto autenticke scripture receaued in olde tyme & confirmed with miracles and therwith trie the controuersie of our elders.

And when he axeth whether there were no true faith from Adam to Noe. I answere / that god partely wrote their faith in their sacri-

---

5–7 What iff there had bene no scripture   13 Grekes   31 Noe

S1 bene no] *1573*, beno no *1531*   S2 Grekes] *1573*, Grekes [*first* "e" *upside down*] *1531*

fices / and partly the patriarkes were full of miracles as ye maye se
in the Bible.

And when More / to vtter his darkenesse & blinde ignorauncie
sayth / that they whych were ouerwhelmed with Noyes floude / had
5   a good faith / and bringeth for him Nicolaus de Lira. I answere /
that Nicolaus de Lira delirat. For it is impossible to haue a faith to
be saued by excepte a man consent vn to gods law with all his hert
and all his soule / that it is rightwysse / holy / good and to be kepte
of all men / and there vppon repent that he hath broken it / and
10 sorow that his flesh moueth vn to the contrary / and then come and
beleue that god for his mercy wyll forgeue him all that he hath done
agenst the lawe / and will helpe him to tame his flesh / and sofre his
weakenesse in the meane season / till he be waxed stronger: which
faith if they that perished in Noyes floud had had / they coude not
15 but haue mended their liuinges and had not hardened their hertes
thorow vnbeleffe and prouoked the wrath of god and waxed worse
and worse an hundred and .xx. yeres which god gaue them to repent / vn tyll god coude no lenger sofre them / but whashed their
filthinesses awaye with the flode (as he doeth the popes same ab-
20 hominacions with like invndacions of water) and destroyed them
vtterly.

[L3v] And when he axeth whether Abraham beleued no moare
then is written of him. I axe him how he wyll proue that there was
no writynge in Abrahams tyme and that Abraham wrot not. And
25 agayne / as for Abrahams person / he receaued his faith of god /
whych to confirme vn to other / miracles were shewed dayly.

And when he fayneth forth / that they beleued only because they
knew their olders coude not erre. How coude they know that with
out miracles or writynge confirmed with miracles / moare then the
30 turcke knoweth that his elders so many hundred yeres in so great a
multitude can not erre and teach false doctrine to damne the beleuers. And the contrary doeth Master More se in all the byble / how

5–7 What faith saueth   19 [Hand]   23 Abraham   27–28 The elders
did erre.

3 ignorauncie] ignoraunce 1573   8 holy /] ed., holy 1531, holy, 1573
19 filthinesses] filthines 1573; same] shamefull 1573   28 olders] elders 1573

aftir all was receaued in scripture confirmed with miracles and
though miracles ceased not / but were shewed dayly / yet the elders
erred and fell to Idolatrie an hundred for one that bode in the right
waye and led the younger in to erroure with them so sore / that god
to saue the yonger / was faine to destroye the elders and to begynne 5
his testament afresh with the new generacion.

He seith also that the most part were al waye Idolaters for all the
scripture and true myracles therto / and beleued the false miracles of
the deuel / because his doctrine was moare agreable vnto their carnall vnderstondynge / then the doctrine of gods spirite / as it now 10
goeth with the pope: did not the scribes / phareses / and prestes
whych were the elders erre?

And when he axeth who taught the church to know the true scripture from false bokes. I [L4] answere / true miracles that confunded
the false / gaue auctorite vn to the true scripture. And therby haue 15
we euer sens iudged al other bokes and doctrine.

And by that we know that youre legendes be corrupte with lyes.
As Erasmus hath improued many false bokes whych ye haue fayned
& put forth in the name of S. Hierom / Augustine / Ciprian / Deonise and of other / partly with auctentick stories and partely by the 20
stile and latine and like euident tokens.

And when Master More sayth vn to them that beleue nought but
the scripture / he wyll proue with the scripture / that we be bound
to beleue the church in thynges where fore they haue no scripture.
Because god hath promised in the scripture / that the holy gost shall 25
teach his church all trouth. Naye / that texte will not proue it. For
the first church taught nought but they confirmed it with miracles
which coude not be done but of god / tyll the scripture was auten-
tickly receaued. And the church folowynge teacheth nought that
they will haue beleued as an article of the faith / but that whych the 30
scripture proueth and maynteneth. As S. Augustine protesteth of his
workes that men shuld compare them vn to the scripture and therby
iudge them and cast awaye whatsoeuer the scripture dyd not alowe.

19 Erasmus

_____

19 Augustine /] *ed.*, Augustine *1531*, Augustine, *1573*

And therfore they that wilbe beleued with out scripture are false
ypocrites and not Christes church. For though I know that that mesinger whych Christe sendeth / can not lye / yet in a companye where
many lyars be / I can not know whych is he / with out a token of
5   scripture or of miracle.

[L4v] And when he saith / the scripture selfe maketh vs not to
beleue the scripture but the church teacheth vs to know the scripture: for a man might reade it and not beleue it. And so I saye / that
a man might heare you preach and yet beleue you not also. And I
10   saye therto / that youre church teacheth not to know the scripture:
but hideth it in the latine from the comen people. And from them
that vnderstond latine they hide the true sence with a thousand false
gloses.

And I saye morouer that the scripture is the cause why men beleue
15   the scripture / as well as a preacher is the cause why men beleue his
preachinge. For as he that first told in Englonde that the Rodes was
taken / was the cause whi some beleued it / euen so might writynge
sent from those parties be the cause that some men which red it beleued it. Master More wyll saye / that letter had his auctorite of the
20   man that sent it / and so hath the scripture his auctorite of the
church. Naye / the scripture hath hir auctorite of him that sent it /
that is to wete of god / which thynge the miracles did testifie / and
not of the man that brought it. He wyll saye / thou knowest the
scripture by their shewenge. I graunt at the begynnynge I doo.
25   Then wyll he saye / why shuld ye not beleue them / in all their
other doctrine besydes the scripture and in all their exposicions of
the scripture / as well as ye beleue them / when they tell you that
soch and soch bokes ar the scripture. May they not shew you a false
boke? yes / and therfore at the begynnynge I beleue all a like. Euery
30   lye that they tell out of their awne braynes we [L5] beleue to be
scripture / and so shuld I beleue them if they shewed me a false boke
but when I haue red the scripture and find not their doctrine there
ner depende therof / I doo not geue so greate credence vn to their

8–10 The pope hideth the scripture.

6 selfe] it selfe *1573*   12 hide] hid *1573*   18 men] *1573*, me *1531*
20 his] her *1573*

other doctrine as vn to the scripture. Why? For I finde moo witte-
neses vn to the scripture then vn to their other doctrine. I finde hole
nacions and contres that receaue the scripture and refuse their other
doctrine and their exposicions in many places. And I finde the scripture other wyse expounded of them of old tyme then they which   5
now wilbe the church / expounde it. Wherby their doctrine is the
moare susspecte. I finde mencion made of the scripture in stories /
that it was / when I can finde no mencion or likelyhode that their
doctrine was. I finde in all ages that men haue resisted their doctrine
with the scripture and haue sofred deeth by the hundred thousandes   10
in resistynge their doctrine. I se their doctrine brought in and
maynetened by a contrary waye to that by whych the scripture was
brought in. I finde by the selfe same scripture / when I loke diligently theron / that their other doctrine can not stonde therwith.

I finde in the scripture that they which haue not Christes spirite to   15
folow the steppes of his liuinge perteyne not vn to Christ Romano.
viij. I find in the scripture / that they whych walke in their carnall
birth aftir the maner of the childern of Adam can not vnderstonde
the thinges of the spirite of god .i. Cor. ij. I finde in the scripture
that they whych seke glorie can not beleue christ Ihon .v. I finde in   20
the scripture that they which submitte not them selues to doo the
[L5v] will of god / can not know what doctrine is of god and what
not Ihon .vij. I fynde in the scripture Hieremie .xxxj. and hebre.
viij. that all the childern of god / which only are the true members
of his church haue euery one of them the lawe of god written in their   25
hertes: so that if theyr were no law to compell / they wolde yet naturally out of their awne hertes kepe the lawe of god: ye and agenst
uiolence compellynge to the contrary. And I se that they whych
wilbe the church (and to proue it haue not so great trust in the scripture as in their sophistrie and in the swerd which they haue sett vpp   30
in all landes to kepe them with violence in the rowme) are so ferre
off from hauinge the lawes of god written in their hertes / that they

136/33–137/6 Why the pope is not to be beleued wythout scripture & whi he is not
the true church   16 Roma. 8.   19 1. Cor. 2.   21 Ioan .5.   22 Ihon
.7.   25 Hebre. 8.

29 haue] hath 1573   S3 1 Cor. 2.] appears twice in 1573

nether by gods lawe ner mans refrayne from their open outwarde weked lyuinge. Loke in the chronicles what bloud yt hath cost englond to attempte to brynge them vnder the law. Ye and se what busynes the realme hath had / to kepe the prelates wythyn the
5 realme from takinge the benefyces with them and lyenge at Rome / and yet scacely brought yt to passe / for all that the pope hath the stinte of euery bysshoperyke and of euery greate abbey therto as offt as any is voyde / yer a newe be admitted to the rowme. And I se them bonde vn to their awne wyll and both to doo and too consent
10 vn to other to doo all that God hath forboden. I se them of all people moost uaynegloryous. I se them walke after their fleshly birth. I se them so ferre off from the image of chryste / that not only they wyll not dye for their flocke after hys ensample / but also / yer they wold lose one towne / or vylage / any pollynge or pryuilege whych they
15 haue falsly gotten / bryngyn[L6]ge them selues in to good pastures wyth wyles and shuttynge their flocke without / they wold cast a waye an hundred thousande off them in one daye and begger theyr realmes / ye and interdyte them and brynge in straunge nacyons / though yt were the turke / to conquere them and sle them vppe / so
20 moch as the innocent in the cradell. And I se that there other doctrine is for their wauntage only and that therwyth they haue gotten all that they haue.

    And I fynde in the scripture that the Iewes before the cominge of christe knew that those bokes were the scripture by the scribes and
25 the phareses. And yet as many as beleued their other doctrine and many exposicions of the scripture were dysceaued / as ye se / and how chryst delyuered them out of erroure. And I se agayne (whych ys no small myracle) that the mercyfull care of god to kepe the scripture to be a testimonye vnto hys electe / ys so greate / that no men
30 be moare gelous ouer the bokes / to kepe them and shew them / and to allege / that they be the scripture of god and true / then they which when yt is reed in their eares haue no power to beleue yt / as the Iewes and the popishe. And therfore because they nether can be-

12 Ioan .10.   28 [Hand]

  6 scacely] scarsely *1573*   10 forboden] forbidden *1573*   11 fleshly] *1573*, fleshy *1531*   26 scripture] *1573*, scipture *1531*

leue yt false / nether consent that yt ys true as yt soundeth playnly
in theyr eares in that yt ys so contrary vnto their fleshly wysdome /
from whych they can not departe / they seke a thousand gloses to
turne yt in to a nother sens / to make it agre vn to theyr beestlynesse / and where yt wyll receaue no soch gloses / theyr they   5
thynke that no man vnderstondeth yt.

[L6v] Then in the end of the chapter master More cometh vn to
his wise conclusion and prouith nothinge saue sheweth his ignoraunce / as in all thynge. He saith we beleue the doctrine of the scripture without scripture / as for an ensample / the popis pardons / be-   10
cause only that the church so teacheth / though no scripture
confermeth it. Whi so? because saith he the holy gost by inspiracion / if I doo my deuoure and captiuat myne vnderstondynge /
teacheth me to beleue the church concerninge Gods word taught by
the church and grauen in mens hertes with out scripture / as wel as   15
he teacheth vs to beleue wordes written in the scripture. Marke
where he is now. Afore he saith / the scripture causeth vs not to beleue the scripture / for a man maye read it and beleue it not. And
moch more the precher maketh vs not to beleue the preacher / for a
man maye heare him and beleue him not also. As we se the appostles   20
covde not cause all men to beleue them. For though the scripture be
an outward instrument and the preacher also to moue men to beleue / yet the chefe and principall cause why a man beleueth or beleueth not is within. That is / the spirite of god teacheth hir chyldern
to beleue and the deuell blyndeth his childern and kepeth them in   25
vnbeleue and maketh them to consent vn to lies and thynke good
euell and euell good. As the actes of the appostles saye in many
places there beleued as many as were ordeyned vn to euerlastynge
life. And christ saith Ihon .viij. they that be of god heare gods
worde. And vn to the weked Iewes he saith ye can not beleue be-   30
cause ye be not of god. And in the same place saith he / ye be of
youre father the deuell and his will ye will doo / & he bode not in
the trouth / [L7] and therfore will not soffre his childern to consent

7–8 Predestinacion   24 [Hand]   28 Actes .13.   30 Ioan .8.

13 deuoure] endeuour 1573   24 hir] his 1573   S1 Predestinacion] *appears
opposite* 140/16–17 *in 1573*

to the trueth. And Ihon in the tenth saith christ / al that came before
me / be theves and murtherars / but my shepe hearde not their
voyces. That is / all that preach any saluacion saue in christ murther
the soules. How be it christes shepe coude not consent to their lies /
5   as the rest can not but beleue lies / so that there is euer a remanaunt
kepte by grace. And of this I haue sene diuers ensamples. I haue
knowen as holy men as might be / as the world counteth holinesse /
which at the houre of deeth had no trust in god at all / but cryed cast
holiwater / light the holy candell / and so forth / sore lamentynge
10 that they must dye. And I haue knowen other which were dispiced /
as men that cared not for their diuine seruice / which at deeth haue
fallen so flatt vppon the bloude of christ as is possible and haue
preached vn to other mightyly as it had bene an appostle of our sauioure and conforted them with comforte of the life to come and haue
15 died so gladly / that they wold haue receaued no worldes good / to
byde still in the flesh. And thus is M. More faulen vppon predestinacion and is compelled with violence of scripture to confesse that
which he hateth and studieth to make appere false / to stablish frewill with all not so moch of ignoraunce I feare as for lucres sake and
20 to gett honoure / promocion / dignite and money by helpe of oure
mitred monsters. Take ensample of balam the false prophete which
gaue councel and sought meanes / thorow like blind couetousnesse /
to make the trueth and prophisie which God had shewed him / false.
He had the knowlege of the trouth but with out loue therto and ther-
25 fore for vauntage became enimie vn to the trouth / [L7v] but what
came of hym?

   But M. More peperith his conclusion lest men shuld fele that taste
sayenge if we endeuoure our selues & captiue oure vnderstondinge
to beleue. O how betleblinde is fleshlye reason! the wil hath none
30 operacion at all in the workynge of faith in my soule / no more then
the child hath in the begetinge of his father. For saith paule it is the
gift of god and not of vs. My witte must conclude good or bad yer
my will can loue or hate. My witt must shew me a true cause or an

21 Balam
----

1 tenth] x. *1573*   20 helpe] *1573*,   hepe   *1531*   27 that]   the
1573   29 reason!] *ed.*, reason? *1531, 1573*

apparent cause whi / yer my will haue any workinge at all. And of
that peperinge it well appereth what the popis fayth ys: euen a blind
imaginacion of theyr natural witte / wrought with out the light of
the spirite of god / agreinge vnto their voluptious lustes in which
their bestly wil so deliteth that he wyll not lett there wittes attende   5
vnto any other lernynge for vnquiettynge hym selfe and sterynge
from his pleasure and delectacion.

And thus we be as ferre a sunder as euer we were and his mightie
argumentes proue not the value of a podynge pricke. M. More feleth
in his hert by inspiracion and with his endeuerynge him selfe and   10
captiuatynge hys vnderstondynge to beleue it / that there is a purgatory as whot as hell. Where in if a sily soule were appoynted by god /
to lye a thousand yeres / to purge him wyth all / the pope for the
value of a grote shall commaunde him thence full purged in the
twinkelinge of an eye / and by as good reason if he were goyng   15
thence / kepe him there still. He felith by inspiracion and in captiuatinge his wittes that the pope can worke wonders with a calfes skyn /
that he can commaunde one to eate fleshe though he be neuer so
lustie / and that a nother [L8] eate none in payne of damnacion /
though he shulde die for lacke of it: and that he can forgeue synne   20
and not the payne / and as moch and as litle of the payne or all yf he
luste / and yet can nether helpe hym to loue the law or to beleue or
to hate the flesh / seinge he preacheth not. And soch thynges innumerable M. More feleth true / and therfore beleueth that the pope
ys the true church.   25

And I cleane contrary fele that there ys no soch worldely and
fleshely imagined purgatory. For I fele that the soules be purged
only by the worde of god and doctrine of christe / as it is written
Ihon .xv. ye be cleane thorow the worde / saith christ to his appostles. And I fele agayne that he which is cleane thorow the doctryne /   30
nedeth not but to washe his fete only / for hys heed and handes ar
cleane al redye Ihon .xiij. that is / he must tame his flesh and kepe it
vnder for his soule is cleane all redy thorow the doctrine. I fele also

9–10 More feleth.   12–13 Purgatorye   26–27 Tyndale feleth.
27–28 Purgatorye   29 Ihon .15.   32 Ihon .13.

17 calfes] Calues 1573   19 in] on 1573

that bodyly payne doeth but purge the body only: in so moch that
the payne not only purgeth not the soule / but maketh yt moare
foule / excepte that there be kinde lerninge by / to purge the soule:
so that the moare a man beteth his sonne / the worse he is / excepte
5   he teach hym louingly and shew hym kindnesse besydes / partely to
kepe hym from desperation and partely that he fall not in to hate of
his father and of hys commaundement therto /and thynke that hys
father is a tirant and his law but tyranny.

Master More feleth with his good endeuoure and inspiracion to
10 gether / that a man may haue the best faith coupled with the worst
life and wyth consentinge to sinne. And I fele that it is impossible to
beleue truly excepte a man repent / and that yt ys [L8v] impossible
to trust in the mercy that is in christ or to fele it but that a man must
immediatly loue god and his commaundementes / and therfore disa-
15 gre and disconsent vnto the flesh and be at bate therwith and fight
agenst it. And I fele that euery soule that loueth the law and hateth
his flesh and beleueth in christes bloude / hath hys synnes which he
committed and payne whych he desarued in hatynge the law and
consentynge vnto hys flesh / forgeuen hym / by that faith. And I fele
20 that the frailtie of the flesh agenst which a beleuinge soule fighteth to
subdue yt / ys also forgeuen and not rekened or imputed for sinne
all the tyme of our curynge: as a kind father and mother rekene not
or impute the impossibilite of their younge childern to consent vnto
their law / and as when the childern be off age and consent / then
25 they reken not ner impute the impossibilite of the flesh to folowe it
immediatly / but take al a worth and loue them no lesse / but rather
moare tenderly then their old and perfecte childern that doo their
commaundementes / so longe as they goo to scole and lerne soch
thynges as their fathers & mothers set them to.

30   And I beleue that euery soule that repenteth / beleueth and loueth
the law / is thorow that fayth a membre of christes church and pure
with out spott or wrincle / as paul affirmeth. Eph. v. And yt ys an
artycle of my beleffe that chrystes electe church ys holy and pure

32 Ephe. 5.

---

9 endeuoure] *ed.*, endenoure *1531*, endeuour *1573*   23 impossibilite] *ed.*, im-
possibite *1531*, impossibilitie *1573*

with out synne and euery membir of the same / thorow faith in
christe and that they be in the full fauoure of god. And I fele that the
vnclennesse off the soule ys but the consent vnto sinne and vnto the
flesh. And therfore I fele that euery soule that beleueth and consenteth vnto the lawe and here in [M1] this life hateth his flesh and the   5
lustes therof and doeth his best to driue sinne out of his flesh and
for hate of the sinne gladly departeth from hys flesh / when he is
deed (and the lustes of the flesh slayne with deeth) nedeth not as it
were bodyly tormentynge to be purged of that wherof he is quite
all redy. And therfore if ought remayne / it is but to be taught and   10
not to be beten. And I fele that eueri soule that bereth frute in christ
shalbe purged of the father to bere moare frute daye by daye / as it
is written Ihon .xv. not in the popis purgatory where no man felith
it / but here in this life soch frute as is vn to his neyboures profitt /
so that he which hath his hope in christ purgeth him selfe here / as   15
Christ is pure .1. Ihon .iij. and that euer yet the bloud of Ihesus only
doeth purge vs of all oure synnes for the imparfectenesse of oure
workes. And I fele that the forgeuenesse of synnes is to remitte mer-
cyfully the payne that I haue deserued. And I do beleue that the
payne that I here sofre in my flesh / is to kepe the body vnder and   20
to serue my neyboure and not to make satisfaccion vn to god for the
fore synnes.

   And therfore when the pope describeth god aftir his couetous
complexion / and when Master More felith by inspiracion and capti-
uattinge his wittes vn to the pope / that god forgeueth the euerlast-   25
ynge payne and wyll yet punish me a thousand yeres in the popis
purgatory / that leuen sauereth not in my mouth. I vnderstond my
fathers wordes as they sounde and aftir the most mercifull maner
and not aftir the popes leuen & M. Mores captiuinge his wittes / to
beleue that euery poetes fabell is a true story. There is no father here   30
that punisheth his sonne to purge [M1v] him / when he is purged
all redy and hath vtterly forsaken synne and euell and hath submit-

---

11 Ioan .15.   16 1. Ioan .3.   20–21 Payne of synne   24–25 The
popes leuen   26 Purgatory

---

   17 oure synnes] ed., youre synnes 1531, our sinnes 1573   S5 Purgatory] Purgatory profitable to the Pope 1573

ted him selfe vn to his fathers doctrine. For to punish a man that hath
forsaken synne of his awne accorde / is not to purge him / but to
satisfie the lust of a tirant. Nether ought it to be called purgatory /
but a Iayle of tormentynge and a satisfactory. And when the pope
5 saith it is done to satisfye the rightewesnesse as a iudge. I saye we
that beleue haue no iudge of him / but a father / nether shall we come
in to iudgement as Christ hath promised vs / but are receaued vnder
grace mercy and forgeuenesse. Shew the pope a litle money and god
is so mercyfull that there is no purgatory. And why is not the fire
10 out as well / if I offer for me the bloud of Christe? If Christ hath
deserued al for me / who gaue the pope might to kepe parte of his
deseruynges from me & to by and sell Christes merites and to make
marchaundice ouer vs with fayned wordes. And thus as M. More
feleth that the pope is holy church / I fele that he is antichriste. And
15 as my felynge can be no proffe to him / no moare can his with all his
captiuatinge his wittes to beleue phantasyes be vn to me. Wherfore if
he haue no nother probacion to proue that the pope is holy church /
then that his hert so agreeth vn to his lernynge / he ought of no right
to compel with swerde vn to his secte. How be it there are ever .ij.
20 maner people that wil cleaue vnto god a fleshli & a spiritual. The
spiritual which be of god shal heare gods worde & the childern of
the trueth shall consent vn to the trueth. And contrary / the fleshlye
and childern of falshed and of the deuel whose hertes be full of lyes /
shall naturally consent vn to lies (as younge childern though they
25 [M2] haue eate them selfes as good as deed with frute / yet wyll not
ner can beleue him that telleth them that soch frute is nought: but
him that prayseth them wyll they heare and eate them selues starke
deed / because their hertes befull of lyes & they iudge all thynges as
they appere vn to the eyes). And the fleshly minded / assone as he
30 beleueth of god as moch as the deuel doeth / he hath ynough / and
goeth to & serueth god with bodily seruice as he before serued his
Idoles / and aftir his awne imaginacion & not in the sprite / in louinge his lawes & beleuinge his promises or longynge for them: no if

8 [Hand]

___

5 as] *1573*, is *1531*   S1 [Hand]] Money dispatcheth Purgatory. *1573*

he might euer liue in the flesh he wolde neuer desyre them. And god must doo for him agayne / not what god hath promised / but what he lusteth. And his brother that serueth god in the spirite acordynge to gods word / him wyll the carnall beest persecute. So that he whych wyll godly liue must sofre persecucion vn to the worldes 5 ende / acordynge vn to the doctrine of christe & of his apostles & acordyng vn to the ensamples that are gonne before.

And finally I haue better reasons for my felynge that the pope is antichrist then M. More hath for his endeuorynge him selfe & capti-uinge his wittes that he is the true church. For the church that was 10 the true mesinger of god / hath euer shewed a signe & a bage therof / ether a present miracle or autenticke scripture / in so moch that Mo-ses when he was sent / axed how shall they beleue me and god gaue him a signe / as euer before & sens. Nether was there any other cause of the writynge of the new and last and euerlastinge testament / then 15 that when miracles ceased / we might haue wherewith to defende oure selues agenst false doctrine and heresies. Whych we coude [M2v] not doo / if we were bounde to beleue that were no where written. And agayne / if the pope coude not erre in his doctrine / he coude not synne of purpose and profession / abhominably and 20 openly aboue the turkes and all the hethen that euer were / and de-fende it so malyciouslye as he hath .viij. hundred yeres longe and wyll not be reformed / and maketh them his saintes & his defenders that synne as he doeth. He persecuteth as the carnall church euer did. When the scripture is a waye / he proueth his doctrine with the 25 scripture and assone as the scripture cometh to light he runneth a waye vnto his sophistrie and vnto his swerde. We se also by stories how youre confession / penaunce and pardons ar vpp come and whence youre purgatory is spronge. And youre falshed in the sacra-mentes we se by open scripture. And all youre workes we rebuke 30 with the scripture and therewith proue that the false beleffe that ye couple to them / maye not stonde with the true fayth that is in oure sauioure Iesus.

---

2 god] he *1573*   28 vpp come] come vppe *1573*

ij.

In the ende of the seconde chapter he bringeth in Euticus that fell
out at a window Actes .xx. whom saith he s. Paulis merites did recouer. Verely Paule durst not so saye / but that Christes merites did
5   it. Peter sayth Actes .iij. ye men of Israel why gase ye and stare
vppon vs / as though we by our power and godlynesse had made
this man goo. Naye / the name of Iesus and fayth that is in him /
hath geuen him strength and made him sounde: And euen here / it
was the name of Iesus thorow paules faith that did that miracle and
10   not Paules merites / though he were neuer so holy.

[M3] iiij.

In the .iiij. chapter he sayth that bilneyes iudges which he yet nam-
eth not for feare of sclaunderynge them / were indifferent. Naye /
they that take rewardes be not indifferent. For rewardes and giftes
15   blynde the eyes of the seinge and peruerte the wordes of the righteous Deute. xvij. Now all that be shoren take greate rewardes to
defende pilgremages / purgatory and prayenge vn to sayntes: even
the third parte I trow of all christendome. For all they haue they haue
receaued in the name of purgatory & of saintes / and on that funda-
20   cion be all their bisshoprikes / abbeyes / coleges & cathedral
churches bylte. If they shalbe indifferent iudges / they must be made
seruauntes and doo saruice as their dutie is. And when they haue
done a quarters saruice / then geue them wages as right is / vnto
every man that laboureth in christes heruest a sufficient liuynge and
25   no moare / and that in the name of his laboure and not of sayntes
and so forth. And then they shalbe moare indifferent iudges / when
there cometh no vauntage to iudge moare on one syde then a nother.

3 Euticus   5 Actes .3.   14 Iudges   16 Deu. 17.

1 ij.] The second chapter. *1573*   4 so saye] say so *1573*   11 iiij.] The third
Chap. *1573*   20 abbeyes] *ed.*, albeyes *1531*, Abbeyes *1573*   21 shalbe] be *1573*

iiij.

In the ende of the fourth he sayth the man toke an oth secretly and was dismissed with secret penaunce. O ypocrites / why dare ye not doo it openly?

v.   5

In the . v. the mesinger axeth him whether he were present. And he denyeth and sayth euer he hearde saye. Alas sir whi take you brybes to defende that you knowe not / why suffre you not them that were present and to whom the mater perteyneth / to lye for them selues? [M3v] Then he iesteth out the mater with wilken and simken / as 10 he doeth Hunne and euery thinge / because men shuld not consydre their falshed ernestly. Wherin be hold his sotle conveyaunce. He axeth what if simken wold haue sworne that he saw men make those printes. Where vnto Master More answereth vnder the name of / quod he / that he wold swere / that besydes the losse of the wager / 15 he had lost his honestye & his soule therto. Beholde this mannes gravite / how coude you that doo when the case is possible. You shulde haue put him to his proues and bydde him brynge recorde.

Then saith he the church receaueth no man conuicte of heresie vn to mercy / but of mercy receaueth him to open shame. Of soch 20 mercy / god geue them plentye that are so mercyfull.

Then he sheweth how mercyfull they were to receaue the man to penaunce that abode styll in periury and deedly synne. O shamelesse ypocrites how can ye receaue in to the congregacion of christe an open obstinat synner that repenteth not / when ye are commaunded 25 of christ to cast all soch out? And agayne o scribes and phareses / by what ensample of christe and of his doctrine can ye put a man that repenteth vn to open shame and to that thinge where by euer aftir he is had in derision amonge his brethern of whom he ought to be loued and not mocked. Ye might enioyne honest thinges / to tame 30

19 [Hand]

---

1 iiij.] The fourth Chap. *1573*   5 v.] The fift Chapter. *1573*   6 .v.] fift *1573*

his flesh / as prayer and fastynge and not that whych shuld be to him shame euer aftir and soch as ye youre selues wold not doo.

vij.

[M4] In the .vij. chapter he maketh moch to doo aboute sweringe
5   and that for a sotle purpose. Notwithstondinge / the trueth is / that no iudge ought to make a man swere agenst his wyll for many in-conuenientes. If a man receaue an office he that putteth him in the rowme ought to charge him to doo it truly and maye & happly ought to take an othe of him. If a man offer him selfe to beare witte-
10   nesse / the iudge maye and of some haply ought to take an oth of them: but to compell a man to beare wittenesse ought he not. And Morouer if a iudge put a man to an othe that he shall answere vn to all that he shalbe demaunded off / he ought to refuse. How be it if he haue sworn / and then the weked iudge axe him of thynges hurte-
15   full vn to his neyboure and agenst the loue that is in Christe / then he must repent that he hath sworn / but not synne agayne and to fulfyll his othe. For it is agenst gods commaundement / that a man shuld hurte his neyboure that hath not deserued it.

viij.

20   Vn to church / prest / charite / grace / confession and penaunce is answered him in the begynnynge of the boke. And when he sayth Tindale was confederatt with Luther that is not trueth.

ix.

Then his .ix. chapter is there nothynge moare folishe. For if he
25   wold haue any wyse man to beleue that my translacion wold de-stroye the masse any other wyse then the latine or greke texte / he shuld haue alleged the place and howe.

---

4 Swerynge

---

3 vij.] The vij. Chapter. *1573*   16 and] *om. 1573*   19 viij.] The viij. Chap-ter. *1573*   23 ix.] The ix. Chapter. *1573*

xj.

[M4v] In the .xj. chapter Master More will not defende the liuinge of our spiritualtie / because it is so open that he can not. And as litle shuld he be able to defende their lies / iff the light were abrode that men might se. And as he can not deny them abhominable / so can 5 he not deny them obstinat and indurat therin / for they haue bene oft rebuked with gods worde / but in vayne. And of soch the texte is playne that they can not vnderstonde the scripture. And yet M. More wyll receaue rewardes to dispute agenst the heresies of some soch as be cast out of Christes church by soch holy patriarkes / 10 whose liuenges he him silfe can not prayse. As holy Iudas / though the prelates of his church that is the pharises were neuer so abhomi-nable / yet because Christes doctrine was condemned of them as of gods church that coude not erre / and all that beleued on him ex-comunicat / he was bold to saye. Quid vultis mihi dare et ego trad- 15 am eum vobis? That is / what will you geue me and I will deliuer him vn to you?

xij.

In the .xij. he hath one conclusion / that the prayars of an evel preest profite not. Which though be true / yet the contrary is beleued 20 amonge a greate mayny / in all quarters of englonde / so blynd be the people and wotte not what prayar meaneth. I haue hearde men of no small reputacion saye yer this in greate audience / that it mak-eth no mater whether the prest were good or bad so he toke money to praye as they sealden praye with out / for he coude not hurte the 25 prayer were he neuer so noughty.

And when he saith that the euell preest hurteth vs not so moch with his lyuynge / as he pro[M5]fiteth vs with ministrynge the sac-ramentes. O worldlye wisdome / if a man lead me thorow a ieoper-

---

11 Iudas   19–21 Prayars of an evell preest profite not.

---

1 xj.] The xj. Chapter. *1573*   7 rebuked] *1573*, rekuked *1531*   10 church] Churches *1573*   18 xij.] The xij. Chapter. *1573*   20 though] *1531*, though it] *1573*   21 mayny] many *1573*

dous place by daye / he can not hurte me so greatly as by night.
The turke seith that murther / thefte / extorcion / oppression / and
adultery be synne. But when he leadith me by the darkenesse of sacramentes with out significacion / I can not but ketch harme and put
5 mi trust and confidence in that which is nether god ner his worde.
As for an ensample / what trust put the people in anoylynge & how
crie they for it / with no nother knowlege then that the oyle saueth
them / vn to their damnacion and denyenge of Christes bloude?

And when he saith the preest offereth or sacrificeth Christes body.
10 I answere / Christ was offered once for all as it is to se in the epistle
to the Hebrues. As the prest sleeth Christ / breaketh his body and
shedith his bloude / so he sacrificeth him and offereth him. Now
the preest sleeth him not actually ner breaketh his body actually ner
shedith his bloude actually nether scorgeth him and so forth /
15 thorow out al his passion: but representeth his sleinge / his body
breakynge and bloudshedynge for my synnes and all the rest of his
passion and playeth it before myne eyes only. Which significacion
of the masse / because the people vnderstonde not / therfore they
receaue no forgeuenesse of their synnes therby / and therto can not
20 but ketch hurte in their soules / thorow a false faith as it well ap-
peareth / how euery man cometh therto for a sundrye imaginacion /
all ignoraunt of the true waye.

Let no man begyle you with his iuglynge sophistrie. Oure offeringe of Christ is to beleue in him / and to come with a repentinge
25 herte vn [M5v] to the remembraunce of his passion and to desyre
god the father for the breakynge of Christes body on the crosse and
shedynge of his bloude and for his deeth and all his passions / to be
mercyfull vn to vs and to forgeue vs acordynge vn to his testament
and promise. And so we receaue forgeuenesse of oure synnes. And
30 other offerynge or sacrifisinge of Christ is there now none. Walke in
the open light and felynge & lett not youre selues be led with iuglynge wordes as mules and asses in whych there is none vnderstondinge.

9 Sacrifice   11 Hebr. 10.

13 body actually] 1573, body actualy 1531   31 led] lead 1573

M. Deacons were had in price in the olde tyme. T. For the deacons then toke the care of all the pore and sofered none to goo a beg-gynge / but prouided a lyuynge for euery one of them. Where now they that shulde be deacons make them selues prestes and robbe the pore of landes / rentes / offerynges and all that was geuen them / deuourynge all them selues and the pore dienge for hongre.

M. prestes be dispised because of the multitude. T. if there were but one in the worlde as men saye of the fenix / yet if he lyued ab-hominably / he coude not but be dispised.

M. a man maye haue a good faith coupled with all maner synne. T. a good faith puteth awaye al synne / how then can alwaye synne dwell with a good faith? I dare saye / that Master More durst af-firme / that a man might loue god and hate his neyboure both at tonce / and yet S. Ihon in his epistle wyll saye that he sayeth vntru-lye. But Master More meaneth of the best fayth that euer he felte. By al lyklyhod he knoweth of no nother but soch as maye stonde with all wekednesse / nother in him selfe ner in [M6] his prelates. Wherfore in as moch as their faith maye stond with all that Christ hateth / I am sure he loketh but for small thankes of god for his de-fendynge of them. And therfore he playeth suerly to take his re-warde here of oure holy patriarkes.

M. few durst be prestes in the old tyme. T. then they knew the charge and fered god. But now they know the vauntage & dread him not.

M. if the lawes of the church were executed which tyndale and Luther wold haue burnt / it wolde be better. T. iff the testament of oure sauioure might be knowen for blinde wretches & couetous ti-rantes / it wold write the law of god in all mens hertes that beleued it / and then shuld men naturally and with out compulsion kepe all honestie. And agayne / though the popis law coude helpe / is not yet no law as good as a lawe vnexecuted?

5

10

15

20

25

30

1 More	2 Deacons	3 Tindale	7 More	8 Preestes
9 Tindale	10 More	11 Tindale	12 1. Ioan .4.	22 More
23 Tindale	24 More	25 Tindale		

---

11 alwaye] all maner of *1573*   14 Ihon] *ed.*, Ikon *1531*, Iohn *1573*
17 nother] neither *1573*   19 thankes] *1573*, thanges *1531*   29–30 is not yet] yet
is *1573*   30 vnexecuted] *1573*, vnexcuted *1531*   S5 Preestes] *ed.*, Hreestes
1531, Priestes *1573*   S9 Ioan] *ed.*, Ioau *1531*, Iohn *1573*

xiij.

In the .xiij. he rageth and fareth exceadynge foule with him selfe. There he biteth / sucketh / gnaweth / towseth / and mowseth tindale. There he weneth that he hath wonne his spores and that it is
5 not possible to answere him. And yet there / because he there most stondeth in his awne conseyte / I doute not vn to them that be lerned in Christe to proue him moste ignoraunt of all and cleane wyth out vnderstondynge of godly thynges. And I saye yet / that as no woman ought to rule a mans office / where a man is present / by the
10 ordir of nature / & as a younge man ought not to be chosen / to ministre in the church / where an olde mete for the rowme maye be had / by the ordir of nature / euen so it was Pauls meaninge / to preferre the maried before the vnma[M6v]ried / for the inconuenientes that might chaunce by the reason of vnchastite / which
15 inconuenientes Mastre More mighte se with sorow of herte (if he had as greate loue to Christ as to other thinges) to happen dayly vn to the shame of Christes doctrine / amonge prestes / freres and monkes / partly with open whores / partly with their sodomitrie wherof they cast ech other in the teeth dayly in euery abbey / for the
20 least displeasure / that one doeth to a nother. M. More might se what occasions of vnchastite begeuen vn to the curates euery where by the reason of their office and dayly conuersacion with the maried.

And when he sayth neuer man coude finde that exposicion tyll now / there he sayth vntrue. For S. Hierom him silfe saith that he
25 knew them that so expounded the texte / and rebuked them of Rome because they wold not admitte in to the clargye them that had had two wyues / the one before baptim and the other aftir sayenge: if a man had kylled .xx. men before his baptym / they wold not haue forboden him / and why then shuld that which is no synne at all be
30 a lett vn to him. But the god of Rome wold not heare him. For sathan began then to worke his misteries of wekednesse.

And when he sayth / he that hath .x. wiues hath one wife. I saye

2–3 Prestes maye haue wives.   25 S. hierome

1 xiij.] The xiij. Chapter. *1573*   13–14, 15 inconuenientes] inconueniences
1573   29 forboden] forbidden *1573*   S1 Prestes maye haue wives.] *om. 1573*

that one is taken by the vse of speakynge for one only. As when I
saye / I am content to geue the one / meanynge one only. And vnto
him that hath no helpe / is there one helpe / to loke for no helpe /
where one helpe is taken for one only / and many places else.

And when master More saith / he that hath had .ij. wiues one after   5
a nother maye not be preest / and that if a prestes wife dye he maye
not [M7] haue a nother if nede be / or that if he were made preest
hauynge no wife / he might not aftir marie iff he burnt / I desyre a
reason of him. Yf he saye / it hath bene so the vse: then saye I an
hore is better then a wife / for that hath bene the vse of oure holy   10
father many hundred yeres. But I affirme vn to Master More the
contrary. And I saye first with Paule / that the kyngdome of god is
not meate and drynke / and by the same reason nether husbonde or
wife / but the kepinge of the commaundementes and to loue euery
man his neyboure as him silfe. And therfore as meate and drynke   15
ware ordeyned for mans necessite / and as a man maye eate &
drynke at all nedes in all degrees / so ferre as it letteth him not to
kepe the commaundementes and to loue his neyboure as him selfe:
even so was the wife created for the mans necessite / and therfore
maye a man vse hir at all his nede in all degrees / as ferre as she letteth   20
him not to kepe gods law which is no thinge else by Paules lern-
ynge / then that a man loue his neyboure as him selfe. Now I desyre
a reason of master Mores doctrine / what doeth my seconde wife or
my third hinder me to loue my neyboure as mi selfe and to doo him
seruice agenst I come to be preeste? What let is youre seconde wife   25
to you to serue oure holy father the pope moare then youre first
wold haue bene? And in like maner if my first wife dye / when I am
preest / why maye I not loue my neyboure and doo him as good
seruice with the seconde as with the firste? And agayne / if I be made
prest hauinge no wife and aftir burne / & therfore marie / why maye   30
I not loue my neyboure and serue him with that wife / as well as he
that brought a wife with him?

[M7v] It was not for nought that paul prophesyed that some shuld

13 Rom. 14.

_____

7 if nede be] *om. 1573*   28 preest] a Priest *1573*

departe from the fayth / and attende vnto disceueable spirites and
deuelysh doctryne forbiddynge to mary and to eate meates which god
hath created to be receaued with thankes of them that know the trouth /
to bye dyspensacyons to vse lawfull mete and vnlawfull wyues.

5   If I axe Master More whi he that hath the seconde wife or hath had
.ij. wives may not be a prest / or whi if a prestes first wyfe die / he
maye not mary the seconde / he wyll answere be cause the prest
must represent the misteries or secret properties and vnion of christe
the only husbonde of his only wife the church or congregacion that
10 beleueth in him only. That is / as I haue in other places sayde / the
scripture describeth vs in matrimonie the misteries and secret benefites which God the father hath hyd in christ for all them that be
chosen and ordeyned to beleue & put their trustes in hym to be
saued. As when a man taketh a wife he geueth hir him selfe / his
15 honoure / hys riches and all that he hath and maketh her of equall
degre vn to him selfe: if he be kinge and she before a beggers
doughter / yet she is not the lesse quene and in honoure a boue all
other / if he be emproure she ys empresse and honoured of men as
the emproure and partetaker of all. Euen so yf a man repent and
20 come & beleue in christ to be saued from the damnacyon of the
synne of which he repenteth / christ ys hys awne good immediatly:
christes deeth / payne / prayar / passion / fastynge and all his merites
are for that mans synnes a full satisfaccyon and a sacrifice of might
and power to absolue hym a pena et a culpa: christes enheretaunce /
25 hys lo[M8]ue and fauoure that he hath with god his father are that
mans by and by / and the man by that mariage is pure as christ and
cleane wyth out synne / and honourable / glorious / well beloued
and in fauoure thorow the grace of that mariage. And because that
the prest must represent vs thys significacion / is the cause whi a
30 preest maye not haue the seconde wife saye they / whych popish

---

1 1. Timo. 4.   7–11 Apparent godlinesse whi the prest maye not haue the
seconde wyfe   12–17 Christes benefytes towardes vs are figured by matrimonye.

---

5 If] And *1573*   9 church] *1573*, crurch *1531*   13 trustes] trust *1573*
24 and] *1573*, aud *1531*   30 they / whych] *ed.*, they whych *1531*, they, which
1573   S3 towardes] toward *1573*

reason hath disceaued many wise / as who can be but disceaued in
some thinge / if he receaue all hys doctrine by the auctorite of hys
elders / excepte he haue an occasion as we haue to runne to Moses
and the prophetes and there heare and se with oure awne eyes and
beleue no lenger by the reason of oure forefathers / when we se them   5
so shamfully begild them selues and to begile vs in a thousande
thinges whych the turkes se.

Now to oure purpose / iff thys doctryne be true / then must euery
preest haue a wyfe or haue had a wife. For he that neuer had wife
can not represent vs this. And againe he that hath an hore or a nother   10
mans wyfe / hath lost this propirte and therfore ought to be put
downe.

And agayne / the seconde mariage then of no man is or can be a
sacrament by that doctryne. And yet I will describe you the mariage
off christ as well by hys mariage that hath had .ix. wiues and hath   15
now the tenth / as by his that hath now the firste.

O wil they saye / his wife was no virgin or he when they were
maried. Sir the significacyon stondeth not in the virginite but in the
actual wedlocke. We were no virgens when we came to christ but
comen hores beleuinge in a thousand Idoles.   20

[M8v] And in the seconde mariage or tenth and ye will / the man
hath but one wife and all his is hirs / and his other wiues be in a lande
where is no husbonde or wife. I saye therfore with Paul that this is
deuellish doctrine and hath a similitude of godlynesse with it but the
power is a waye. The myst of it blindeth the eyes of the simple and   25
begyleth them / that they can not se a thousande abhominacions
wrought vnder that clocke.

And therfore I saye still / that the apostles meaninge was that he
shuld haue a wife / if haply his age were not the gretter / and that by
one wife he excludeth them that had two and them that were de-   30
famed with other saue their awne wiues / and wolde haue them to
be soch as were knowen of vertuouse liuynge / for to doo reuerence
and honoure vn to the doctrine of Christe. As it appereth by the

---

6 thousande] *ed.*, thousaude *1531*, thousand *1573*   22 is] are *1573*
24 deuellish] a deuilishe *1573*   27 clocke] cloke *1573*

wedowes whych he excludeth before .lx. yeres for feare of vnchastite and admitteth yet none of that age excepte she were well knowen
of chast / honeste and godly behauoure / and that to honoure gods
worde with all / than whych the pope hath nothynge moare vile.

5   And when Master More to mocke / bringeth forth the texte of the
wedowe / that she must be the wife of one man. I answere for all his
iestynge / that Paul excludeth not hir that had .x. husbandes one aftir
a nother / but hir that had .ij. husbandes attonce. And when More
laugheth at it / as though it had neuer bene the gyse. I wold to god

10   for his mercy that it were not the gyse this daye / and then I am sure
his wrath wold not be so greate as it is. Paul meaneth only that he
wold haue no diffamed woman chosen wedowe for dishonourynge
the worde of god [N1] and the congregacion of Christ / and therfore
excludeth comen wemen and soch as were dyffamed besydes their

15   husbandes and haply the deuorced therto. And that I proue by the
same doctrine of Paule / that the kyngdome of god is no soch busynes but the kepynge of gods commandementes only and to loue one
a nother. Now loke on the thynge and on the office of the wedowe.
It was but to wayte on the sicke and pore people and to washe

20   straungers fete. Now the wedowes of .x. husbandes must haue be
founde of the cost of the congregacion / iff they were destitute of
frendes / as all other pore were / though in tyme passed they haue
bene diffamed persons.

But vnder .lx. wold Paul let none ministre for feare of occasions

25   of vnchastite / and therto none but soch as were well knowen of
honeste liuynge and of good reporte. Now in as moch as the wedow
of .x. husbandes must be founde of the comen cost at hir nede / what
vnclennesse is in hir by the reason of hir seconde husbonde / that she
is not good ynough to be a seruaunte vn to the pore people / to

30   dresse their meate / to wash their clothes / to make their beddes and
so forth and to wash straungers fete / that came out of one congregacion vn to a nother a boute busynesse / and to doo all maner seruice
of loue vn to her pore brethern and sisters. To haue had the seconde

---

1 Wedowes

10 this] at this *1573*   30 to wash] wash *1573*

husbande is no shame amonge the hethen: it is no shame amonge
the christen for when the husbonde is deed / the wife is fre to mary
to whom she wyll in the lorde / and by as good reason the husbande / and of right who moare fre then the preeste? And therfore
they shame not our doctrine ner oure congregacion / [N1v] ner dis-   5
honoure god amonge the hethen or weake Christen. Now when we
haue a playne rule that he whych loueth his neyboure as him selfe
kepeth all the lawes of god / lett him tell me for what cause of loue
towarde his neyboure / a wedowe of two lawfull husbandes maye
not doo seruice vn to the pore people.   10

Why maye not a wedowe of .l. doo seruice vn to the pore? paule
whych knitteth no snares ner leadeth vs blinde ner teacheth vs wyth
out a reason geuynge of his doctrine / answereth / for feare of occasions of euell / lest she be tempted or tempte other: And then if she
be taken in misdoenge / the doctrine of Christ be euell spoken of   15
therto and the weake offended.

And when Master More mocketh wyth my reason that I wolde
haue euery preest to haue a wife because fewe men can liue chaste /
I answere / that if he loued the honoure of Christ and his neyboure
as he doeth his awne couetousnesse / he shuld finde that a good argu- 20
mente. Paul maketh the same and moch moare sclenderly then I
after youre sophistrie. For he disputeth thus / some younge wedowes do dishonest the congregacion of Christe and his doctrine /
therfore shall no younge wedow at all ministre in the comune seruice therof: But shall all be maried and bere childern and serue their 25
husbandes. And it is a fer lesse rebuke to the doctrine of Christ and
his congregacion / that a woman shuld doo amisse / then the bisshope or preest. I am not so mad / to thinke that there coude no prest
at all liue chaste. Nether am I so folish to thynke that there be not as
many wemen that coude liue chast at .l. as prestes at .xxiiij. And yet   30
though of a thousande wedowes of .l. yere olde [N2] .ix. hundred
.xc. and .ix. coude lyue chast / Paul because he knoweth not that
one / wyll lett none at all ministre in the comen seruice amonge oc-

7 Roma. 13.

---

7 selfe] *1573*, felfe *1531*   30 prestes at] *ed.*, prestes as *1531*, Priestes as *1573*
157/33–158/1 occasion] occasions *1573*

casion of vnchastite. Christes appostles consydered all infirmities
and all that might hindre the doctrine of Christe / and therfore did
their beste to preuent all occasions. Wherfore as fish is no better then
flesh / ner flesh better then fish in the kyngdome of Christ / euen so
5   virginite wedlocke and wedowed are none better then other to be
saued by in their awne nature or to please god with all / but with
whatsoeuer I maye best serue my brethern / that is euer best acordinge vn to the tyme and facion of the worlde. In persecucion it is
good for euery man to liue chast can he / and namely for the
10   preacher. In peace when a man maye liue quietly and abyde in one
place / a wife is a sure thynge to cutt of occasions.

Then he wold make it seme that prestes wiues were the occasions
of heresies in almanye. Naye / they fell first to heresies and then toke
wiues / as ye fell first to the popis holy doctrine and then toke
15   whores.

M. the church byndeth no man to chastite. T. of a trueth / for it
geueth licence to who soeuer wyll / to kepe hores / and permitteth
to abuse mens wiues and sofereth sodomitrie / and doeth but only
forbid matrimonie.

20   And when he sayth / chastite was allmoste receaued by generall
custome / before the law was made: one lye. And good fathers did
but geue their aduise therto: a nother lye. And it was ratified and
receaued wyth the consent of all christendome: the third lye.

They dyd well to chose a poete to be their [N2v] defender. First
25   it was attempted in generall counsell and resisted by holy fathers
whych yet them selues were neuer maried / sayenge that men might
not knitte a snare for their weake brethern / agenst the doctrine of
Christ and his appostles. Nether coude it be brought to passe / vntyll
the pope had gott the emproures swerde out of his hande. The
30   grekes which were the one halfe of christendome then I suppose /
wold neuer admitte it.

Now godly loue wold neuer sofre them to consent that we shuld

---

12 More   13 [Hand]   14 Tindale   16 More   17 Tindale
20–21 Thre lyes atonce

---

6 god] *ed.*, good *1531*, God *1573*   9 can he] if he can *1573*

be bound vn to the burthen which they them selues coude not beare as M. More in a nother place affermith that they dyd. And agayne / we haue manyfest stories that it was brought in with violence of swerde and that all the prestes of germany were compelled to put awaye their wiues. And we finde that whersoeuer the pope raygn- 5 eth / he came in with disceauinge the kynge of the contre and then with his swerde compelled the reste. The pope came but now late in to wales to raygne there ouer the bisshopes and prestes / and that with the swerd of the kinge of Englonde.

And yet though all the clergie of christendome had graunted it / 10 all the church had not made it ner yet the tenth parte of the church. The laye people be as well of the church as the prestes. Nether can all the prestes in the world of ryght make any lawe wherin their parte lyeth with out their consent. Now it perteyneth vn to the comen people and most of all vn to the weakest / that their prestes 15 be endued with all vertu and honestie. And the chastite of his wife / doughter and seruaunt perteyneth vn to euery particular man / whych we se by experience defiled [N3] dayly / by the vnchaste chastite of the spiritualtye.

Wherfor if the parishes or any one parish / after they had sene the 20 experience what inconuenientes come of their chastite / wold haue no curat excepte he had a wife to cutt of occasions / as Paul when he had sene the proffe / wold haue no younge wedowes ministre / who saue a tirant / shuld be agenst them?

Morouer the generall counsels of the spiritualtye ar of no nother 25 maner sens the pope was a god then the generall parlamentes of the temperaltie. Where no man dare saye his mynde frely and liberally for feare of some one and of his flaterars.

And loke in what captiuite the parlamentes be vnder the priuatt counsels of kynges / so are the generall counsels vnder the pope and 30 his cardenales. And this is the maner of both. Some one two or three wilie foxes that haue all other in subieccion / as ye haue sene in my lorde cardenall / imagen / not what ought to be / but what they

25–26 Generall counsell   29–30 Parliament

21 inconuenientes] inconueniences *1573*; come] came *1573*   25 spiritualtye] *ed.*, spiriritualtye *1531*, spiritualtie *1573*   31 three] *1573*, there *1531*

lust to haue & conceaue in their awne braynes and goo with
child / some tyme a yere .ij. iij. iiij. v. vj. or .vij. and some
tyme .xx. and a boue / castynge / canvesynge and compasynge
for the birth agenst oportunite: openinge the mater priuely vnder
5 an oth a litle and a litle vn to certayne secretaries whose parte is
therin / as they finde men of actiuite and of corage / prepared to
sel soul and body for promocion.

And the mater in the meane tyme is turmoyled and tossed
amonge them selues: and persuacions and sotle reasons ar forged to
10 blinde the right waye and to begyle mens wittes. And [N3v] whom
they feare to haue aduersaries able to resiste them / for soch meanes
ar sought / to brynge them in vn to their partie or to conuey them
out of the waye. And when oportunite is come / they call a counsell
or parlament vnder a contrary pretence. And a masse of the holy
15 gost / whom they desyre as ferre awaye as were possible / is songe
and a goodly sermon is made / to blere mens eyes with all. And then
sodenly other men vnprouided / the mater is opened / aftir the most
sotle maner. And many are begyled with sotle argumentes and craf-
tie persuasions. And they that hold harde agenst them ar called asyde
20 and resoned with aparte and handeled aftir a facion / and partly en-
tised with fayre promises and partly feared with cruell threat-
enynges / and so some ar ouercome with syluer sylogismoses and
other for feare of threateninges are dreuen vnto silence / And if any
be founde at the last / that wyll not obeye their falshed and tiranny /
25 they rayle on him and ieste him out of countenaunce and call him
opinatiue / selfeminded and obstinat / and bere him in hand that the
deuell is in him that he so cleueth vn to his awne witte / though he
speake no sillable then gods worde / and is axed whether he wilbe
wyser then other men. And in the spiritualtye they excomunicat
30 him & make an heretike of him. And this to betrue in the clargies
chastite is as clere as the daye by manifest chronicles / in so moch
that the prelates of Rome / were a brewenge it a boue an hundred
yeres and I wott not how longe lenger / yer they coude brynge it to
passe / and yet in vayne till they had gotte the emproures swerde to

23 threateninges] threatnyng *1573*   28 then] but *1573*

proue that it was most expedient so to be. And for what entent? to brynge all vnder the pope / and [N4] that the prelates of all landes might as the olde maner was / come and wayte on the pope at Rome / where he prepared them hores ynow.

And that his sworen prelates in euery lande / might the moare   5 conueniently wayte in kynges courtes / to ministre the comen welth vn to the popis pleasure and profite. For had the clargie kepte their wiues / they coude neuer haue come vn to this aboue where they now be / and to these pluralities / vnions and totquottes. For their is no laye man though he were neuer so evell disposed / that coude for   10 his wife and childern haue leyser to contriue soch mischeue and to runne from contre to contre / to lerne falshed and sotilte / as our spiritualtye doo / which with out feare of god and shame of man / kepe whores whersoeuer they come. And thus ye se that the clargies chastite perteyneth as moch vn to the temporalte as vn to the spiri-   15 tualte.

And a nother is this / no power amonge them that professe the trouth / maye bynd where god lowseth / saue only where loue and my neybours necessite requireth it of me. Nether can any power now bynd them to come / but they may frely kepe or breake / as the   20 thynge is hurtfull or expedient. Nether can there be any bonde where loue and necessite requireth the contrary. So that this law / loue thy neyboure / to helpe him as thou woldest be holpe / must interpret all mans lawes.

As if I had sworn younge or vnwysely that I wold liue chaste and   25 all the world had bound me / if afterward I burnt and coude not ouercome the passion / I ought to mary.

For I must condicyon my vowe and shew [N4v] a cause of it therto. I maye not vow for the chastite it selfe as though it were sac-rifice to please god in it selfe / for that is the Idolatrie of hethen. I   30 must therfore vowe to doo my neyboure seruice (which in that case he maye not require) or to geue my selfe moare quietly to prayer & studie (which is not possible as longe as I burne & the mynd wyll

2–4 Why preestes maye haue no wyues   28 Vowes

4 ynow] inough 1573   8 aboue] om. 1573

not be quiet) or that I maye the better kepe the lawes of god whych
if I burne I stond thorow my chastite in moare ieoperdie to breake
and to hurte my neyboure and to shame the doctrine of christe. And
in like maner / If I had forsworen fleshe & all the world had bound
5   me / yet if necessite require it of me / to saue my life or my health /
I ought to breake it. And agayne though I had sworn chastite / and
the comen wealth or the necessite of a nother required the contrary /
I must breake it. But on the one syde / of all that euer burnt in the
popis chastite / he neuer gaue prest licence to take wife / but to kepe
10   hores only. And on the other syde / all that vow any vow / doo it
for the thynge it selfe as though it were as I said seruice or sacrifice
to god that had delite in the dede / as younge childern haue in
apples / and that for that dede they shall haue an hier rowme in heuen
then their neyboures / which is the Idolatrie of the hethen / when he
15   ought to bestow his vow vppon his neyboure to brynge him to
heuen and not to envye him and to seke therby an hier rowme not
carynge whether his neyboure come thither or no. And finally to
burne and not to wyll vse the naturall remedye that god hath made /
is but to tempte god / as in all other thynges. But and if god haue
20   brought the in to a strayte and haue therto taken the naturall remedye from [N5] the / then to resiste and to crie vn to God for helpe
and to sofre / is a signe that thou louest gods lawes. And to loue
Gods law is to besure that thou art Gods child electe to mercie. For
in all his childern only / he writeth that token.
25   And then he saith / euery man hath his choyce whether he wilbe
preest or no. But what nettes and snares doeth antichrist laye for
them? First his false doctrine / where with the elders begyled / compell their childern and sacrifice them / to burne in the popis chastite
with no nother mynde / then those old Idolaters sacrificed their
30   childern vn to the false god Moloch: so that they thinke / by the
merites of their childerns burninge / after the popes false doctrine /
to please god and to gett heuen / cleane ignoraunt of the testament
made in christes bloude.

27–28 The popes snares   29   I.

18 wyll] *om.* 1573

Then what a multitude ar blinded and drawen in to the nett / with
the bayte of promocion / honoure / dignite / pleasures / fredome
and liberte to synne and to doo al mischeue vnpunished / thinges
which all evell that feare not god doo desyre?

And what a numbre brought vpp ydely vn to .xx. and a boue /   5
then put their heedes in his halter / because they haue no nother craft
to gett their liuinges & not because they can liue chaste.

Also some liue chast at .xxiiij. which same burne at .xxx. And
that to be true dayly experience teacheth and good naturall causes
therbe.   10

And then loke on the appostles lerninge & ordinaunce. When one
or .ij. younge wedowes had broken there chastite / he wold neuer
after let any moo be chosen of the same age. How cometh it then
that the pope for so many hundred thousandes that miscary / wil
nether breake the [N5v] ordinaunce or mitigat it / or let any goo   15
backe / but if any burne / sendeth them vn to the shame of christes
doctrine and offendinge and hurte off his church and neuer vn to the
lawfull remedie of mariage.

And when Master More calleth it heresie / to thinke that the maried were as pleasant to god as the vnmaried / he is surelye an here-   20
tyke that thynketh the contrary. Christes kingdome is nether meat
ner drinke ner husband ner wife ner wedow ner virgin / but the kepynge off the commaundementes and seruinge of a mans neyboure
louingely by the doctrine of S. paule. Where not to eate helpeth me
to kepe the commaundementes better then to eate / there yt ys better   25
not to eate then to eate. And where too eate helpeth me to kepe the
commaundementes and to doo my dutie vn to my neyboure / there
it is better to eate then not to eate. And in like case where to be with
out a wife helpeth moare to kepe the commaundementes and to
serue a mans neyboure / there yt is better to be vnmaried then mar-   30
ied / and where a wife helpeth too kepe the commaundementes better then to bewith out / there it is better to haue a wife then to be
with out. That herte only whych is readye to do or lett vndone all
thynges for his neyboures sake / is a plesaunt thynge in the syght of
god.   35

1   2.   5   3.   8   4.   11   5.   33 [Hand]

And when he wyll haue the prestes to liue chaste / for reuerence
off the sacramentes yt ys deuellish doctrine hauinge the similitude
of godlynesse / but the pith and mary is awaye. If he meane water /
oyle salt and soch like / then is the [N6] wife with hir body and all
5   hir vses in the lawes of god / incomparable purer and holyer. If he
meane the sacrament of christes body / I answere / that the handes
defile not the man ner ought that goeth thorow the handes be they
neuer so vnwashe / by the testimonie of christe / and moch lesse can
they then defile christe.

10   Morouer the prest twitcheth not christes natural body with his
handes by youre awne doctrine / ner seith it with his eyes / ner
breaketh yt with his fingers ner eateth it wyth hys mouth ner chammeth yt wyth hys teeth ner drinketh his bloude with his lippes / for
christe is impassible. But he that repenteth towarde the law of god /
15   and at the sight of the sacrament or off the breakinge / felynge / eatynge / chamminge or drinkinge / calleth to remembraunce the
deeth of christe / his body breakynge and bloudshedynge for our
synnes and all hys passion / the same eateth our sauioures body and
drinketh his bloude thorow faith only and receaueth forgeuenesse of
20   all his synnes therby / and other not. And all that haue not this doctrine of the sacrament come therto in vayne. And therfore there is
no moare cause that he which sayeth the masse shuld lyue chast then
he that heareth it / or he that ministreth the sacrament / then he that
receaueth it. It is to me greate maruell that vnlawfull whoredome
25   couetousnesse and extorsion can not defyle their handes / as well as
lawfull matrimonie. Cursed therfore be their deuellish doctrine with
false apperinge godlinesse the frute and power awaye / out of the
hertes of all christen men.

And when he bringeth the ensample of the hethen / I praise him.
30   For the hethen because they [N6v] coude not vnderstond god spiritually / to serue him in the sprite to beleue in him and to loue his
lawes / therfore they turned his glorie vn to an image and sarued

---

8 Mat. 15.   14–18 The sacrament of the altare and how it must be receyved
25 [Hand]

---

8 vnwashe] vnwashed *1573*   S2 altare and] body & bloud of Christ *1573*
S3 [Hand]] *om. 1573*

him after their awne imaginacion with bodyly seruice as the hole
kingdome of the pope doeth / hauinge lesse power to serue him in
spirite than the turkes. For when the hethen made an image of the
axes or feuers and sacrificed therto / they knew that the image was
not the feuers / but vnder the similitude of the ymage / they wor-   5
sheped that power of god which plaged them with the feuers / wyth
bodyly seruice / as the pope doeth aboue al the Idolaters that euer
were in the worlde. As when we paynte saint Micael weyenge the
soules and steke vpp a candell to flater him and to make him fauour-
able vn to vs / and regarde not the testament of christ ner the lawes   10
of god / because we haue no power to beleue ner to loue the trueth.
And euen so to referre virginite vn to the person of god / to please
him therwith is false sacrifice and hethenish Idolatrie. For the onely
seruice of god is to beleue in christ and to loue the lawe. Where fore
thou must referre thi wedlocke / thi virginite and all thi wother   15
deades vn to the kepinge of the lawe and seruinge thy neyboure
only. And then when thou lokest with a louinge herte / on the law
that saith breake not wedlocke / kepe no whore and so forth / and
findest thi body weake and thine office soch that thou must haue
conuersacion with mens wiues / doughters and seruauntes / then it   20
is better to haue a wife then to bewith out. And agayne if thou se
seruice to bedone that thou canst not so wel do with a wife as with
out / then if thou haue power to bewith out it is best so to be / and
in soch like. And else the [N7] one is as good as the other and no
difference. And to take a wife for pleasure / is as good as to absteyne   25
for displeasure.

And when Mastre More seith no nother cause / why it is not best
that oure spiritualtie were all gelded / then for losse of merite in resistynge / besydes that that imaginacion is playne Idolatrie / I hold
M. More begylde / iff all we reade of gelded men be true and the   30
experience we se in other bestes. For then the gelded lust in their
flesh as moch as the vngelded. Which if be true / then the gelded /
in that he taketh soch great payne in geldynge / not to minysh his

4 [Hand]   8–10 S. Micael wayeth the soules.   30–33 Whether it were
best that prestes were gelded

6 that] the *1573*   32 if] *1531*, if it] *1573*

lustes but if lustes ouercome him / yet that he haue not were with to
hurte his neyboure / deserueth moare then the vngelded. And then
it were best that we ate and dronke and made oure flesh stronge that
we burned / to deserue in resistynge / as some of youre holy sayntes
haue layd virgens in their beddes / to kendle their corage / that they
might after quench their hete in colde water / to deserue the merite
of holy marters.

And when he saith / the prestes of the olde law absteyned from
their wiues when they serued in the temple. Many thynges were forboden them / to kepe them in bonde and seruile feare and for other
purposes. And yet I trow he findeth it not in the texte that they were
forboden their wiues. And when he imageneth so be cause zacha-
rias / when his course was out / gatt him whom to his howse I
thynke it was better for him to go to his howse / then to send for his
howse to him he was also olde and his wife to. But and if they were
forboden / it was but for a tyme / to geue them to prayar / as we
might doo right well and as well as they. But I read that [N7v] they
were forboden to drinke wine & stronge drinke / when they ministred: of which oures powre in with out measure.

M. More christ liued chast and exhorteth vn to chastite. Tindale.
we be not al of christes complexion / nether exhorteth he to other
chastite then wedlocke / saue at a tyme to serue oure neyboures.
Now the popis chastite is not to serue a mans neyboure / but to
runne to riotte and to carie a waye with him the liuynge of the pore
and of the true preacher / even the tythes of .v. or .vj. parishes and
to go and ether dwell by a stues or to carye a stewes with him / or
to corrupte other mennes wiues.

Pannutius a man that neuer proued mariage is praysed in the stories / for resistynge soch doctrine with gods worde in a generall
counsel before the pope was a god. And now M. More a man that
hath proued it twise is magnified for defendynge it with sophistrie.
And ageyne me semeth that it is agreate ouer sight of M. More to

5 [Hand]   18 Leuit. x.   20 More   21 Tyndale   28 Panutius

3 ate and dronke and made] did eate and drinke & make *1573*   9 temple] *1573,*
themple *1531*   9–10, 12, 16, 18 forboden] forbidden *1573*   28 Pannutius]
Paphnutius *1573*   S5 Panutius] Paphnutius *1573*

thinke that christ though he were neuer maried wold not moare accepte the seruice of a maried man that wold moare saye trouth for
him then they that abhorre wedlocke: in as moch as the spiritualte
accepte his humble saruyce & rewarde his merites with so hye honoure / because he can better fayne for them / then any of their   5
vnchaste / I wold saye awne chast people / though he be bigamus
and past the grace of his necke verse.

And finally / if M. More loke so moch on the pleasure that is in
mariage / why setteth he not his eyes on the thankes geuynge for
that pleasure and on the pacience of other displeasures.   10

xiiij.

[N8] M. Wicleffe was the occasion of the vttur subuersion of the
realme of Bohem / both in faith and good liuynge and of the losse of
many a thousand liues. T. the rule of their faith ar christes promises /
and the rule of their liuynge gods lawe. And as for losse of liues / it is   15
trouth that the pope slew I thynke an hundred thousande of them because of their faith and that they wold no lenger serue him. As he slew
in englonde many a thousande / and slew the true kynge and sett vpp
a false vn to the effusion of all the noble bloude and murtherynge vpp
of the cominaltie / because he shulde be his defender.   20

M. The constitucion of the bisshopes is not that the scripture shall
not be in englysh / but that no man maye translate it by his awne
auctorite or reade it / vntill they had approued it. T. if no translation
shalbe had vntill they geue licence or till they approue it / it shall
neuer be had. And so it is al one in effecte to saye there shalbe none   25
at all in englysh / and to saye / tyl we admitte it / seinge they be so
maliciouse that they wil none admitte / but fayne al the cauellacions
they can / to proue it were not expedient. So that if it be not had
spite of their hertes it shal neuer be had. And therto / they haue done
their best to haue had it enacted by parlament / that it shuld not be   30
in englysh.

12 M. More   14 Tyndale   21 M. More   23 Tyndale

11 xiiij.] The xiiij. Chapter. *1573*   25 neuer] *1573*, ueuer *1531*   S1, S3 M.]
om. 1573

XV.

He iesteth out hunnes deeth with his poetrie where with he bylte vtopia. Many greate lordes came to baynardes castell (but all name-lesse) to examen the cause (as the [N8v] credible prelates so wel

5   lerned / so holy and so indifferent which examined bilney and Ar-ture / be also all namelesse).

M. Horsey toke his pardon / because yt is not good / to refuse gods pardon and the kynges. T. Gods pardon can no man haue ex-cepte he knowlege him selfe a synner. And euen so he that receaueth

10   the kynges yeldeth him selfe giltie / And morouer it is not possible that he which putteth his trust in god / shulde for feare off the xij. men or of his iudges / receaue pardon for that he neuer was fautie vn to the dishonouringe of our sauioure Iesus / but wold haue denied it rather vn to the deeth.

15   And therto / iff the mater were so clere as ye iest it out / then I am sure the kynges graces both curtesie and wysdome / wolde have charged the iudges to haue examined the euidence layed agenst him diligently and so to haue quitte him with moare honestie then to geue him pardon of that he neuer treaspased in / and to haue rid the

20   spiritualtye out of hate and all suspycion.

Then saith he hunne was sore susspecte of heresie and conuicte. And after he saith hunne was an heretike in dede and in perell so to be proued. And then how was he conuicte? I herde saye / that he was first conuicte / when he was deed and then they did wronge to

25   burne him / til they had spoken with him / to wete wether he wolde abiure or no.

M. the bisshope of london / was wyse / vertuous and conynge. T. For all those .iij. yet he wold haue made the old deane Colet of paules an heretyke / for translatynge the Pater noster in englyshe /

30   had not the bysshope of canterbury holpe the deane.

---

    2 Hunne   6 M. More   7 Horsey   8 Tyndale
    21 Hunne   23 [Hand]   27 M. More   28 Tyndale
    29 Doctoure Colet

---

    1 xv.] The xv. Chapter. *1573*   10 yeldeth] *1573*, yeldelth *1531*   S2, S7 M.] *om. 1573*

[O1] xvj.

The messinger axeth hym / if there be an olde lawfull translacion before wicleffes / how happeneth it that it is in so few mens handes / seinge so many desyre it? He answereth the printer dare not print it and then hange on a doutful triall / whether it were translated sens 5 or before. For if it were translated sens / it must be first approued.

What maye not Master More saye by auctorite of his poetrie? there is a lawfull translacion that noman knoweth which is as moch as no lawfull translacion. Whi mighte not the bisshopes shew which were that lawful translacion and lat it be printed? Naye if that might 10 haue bene obteyned of them with large money it had be printed ye maye besure longe yer this. But sir answere me here vn to / how happeneth that ye defendars translate not one youre selues / to cease the murmoure of the people / and put to youre awne gloses / to pre- uent heretikes? ye wold nodoute haue done it longe sens / if ye coude 15 haue made youre gloses agre with the texte in euery place. And what can you saye to this / how that besydes they haue done their best to disanull all translatynge by parlament / they haue disputed before the kinges grace / that is it perelous and not mete and so concluded that it shal not be / vnder a pretence of deferrynge it of certayne 20 yeres. Where Master More was their speciall orator / to fayne lyes for their purpose.

M. nothinge discorageth the clergie so moch as that they of the worst sorte most calleth after it. T. it might wel be / phareses full of holynesse longe not after it / but publicans that hongre after mercie 25 myght sore desyre it. How be it / it is [O1v] in very dede a suspecte thinge and a greate signe of an heretike to require it.

Then he iugleth wyth allegories. Syr / Moses deliuered them al that he had receaued of god and that in the mother tonge / in which all that had the hert therto studied & not the prestes only as thou 30 mayst se in the scripture. And the apostles kepte nothinge behinde / as paul testified actes .xx. how he had shewed them all the counsell

---

1–2 Old translation   23 More   24 Tindale

1 xvj.] The xvj. Chapter. *1573*

of god and had kepte nought backe. Shuld the laye people lesse herken vnto the exposicions of the prelates in doutfull places / if the
texte were in their handes when they preached?

M. the Iewes geue greate reuerence vnto the bible & we sit on it.
5   T. the pope putteth it vnder his fete & treadeth on it / in token that
he is lorde ouer it that it shulde sarue him / & he not it. M. God
hath ordeyned the ordinaries for chefe phisicions. T. they be lawiers
ordeined of the pope / & can no moare skill of the scripture than
they that neuer sawe it: ye and haue professed a contrary doctrine.
10 They be right hangemen to murther whosoeuer desireth for the
doctrine that god hath geuen to be the ordinary of our faith and liuinge.

And when he maketh so greate difficulte and hardnesse in paules
pistles. I saie / it is impossyble to vnderstond ether peter or paul or
15 ought at al in the scripture / for him that denieth the iustifienge of
faith in christes bloude. And agayne it is impossible to vnderstonde
in the scripture moare then a turke for whosoeuer hath not the law
of god written in his herte to fulfil it. Of which pointe and of true
faith to / I feare me that you are voyde and empte with all youre
20 spiritualtie / whose defender ye haue taken vppon you to be / for to
mocke out the trouth for lucre and vauntage.

4 M. More   5 Tindale   6 M. More   7 Tindale

14 pistles] Epistles *1573*   S1, S3 M.] *om. 1573*

[O2] ¶An answere vnto Master Mores fourth boke

Christes church hath the true doctrine all redy / and the selfe same that S. Paul wold not geue an angel audience vn to the contrary. T. but the popis church wil not heare that doctrine. M. confirmed with soch a multitude of miracles and so moch bloud of marters / & comen consent of al christendome. T. who shewed a miracle to confirme his preachynge of eareconfession & pardons with like pedelery? or who shed his bloude for them? I can shew you many thousandes that ye haue slayne for preachynge the contrary. And againe grecia the one halfe of christendome consenteth not vn to them / which grekes if soch thinges had come from the apostles shulde haue had them ere ye. M. the spiritualte be not so tender eared / but that they maye heare their sinnes rebuked. T. they consent not vn to the waye of trueth / but sinne of malice & of profession. And therfore as they haue no power to repent / euen so can they not but persecute both him that rebuketh them & his doctrine to / after the ensamples of the phareses & al tirantes that begonne before / namely if that preacher twich any grounde wherby they shuldbe reformed or by what meanes they maynetene their misheue.

5

10

15

20

ij. chapter

M. A freres liuinge that hath maried a nunne maketh it easye to know that his doctrine is not good. T. that profession of etherother is playne idolatrie / & disceauinge of a mans soule & robbynge him of his good / & taken vppon them ignorauntly therto. Wherfore when they become vn to the knowlege of the trouth / they ought no lenger therin to abide. But the popis forbiddinge matrimonie & to

25

---

3 M. More   4 Tindale   5 More   7 Tindale   13 More
14 Tindale   22 M. More   23 Tindale   26 Pope

1–2 ¶] ed., An answere vnto Master Mores fourth boke] *running title 1531*, An aunswere to M. . . . booke *1573*   18–19 that preacher] the preacher *1573*
20 misheue] mischief *1573*   21 ij. chapter] The second Chapter. *1573*   S1,
S7 M.] *om. 1573*   S9 Pope] Pope forbiddeth matrimony & the eatyng of meates.
1573

eate of meates created of god for mannes vse which is deuellish doctrine by paulis prophesie / his geuenge licence to hold whores / his
continuall occupienge of pri[O2v]nces in shedynge of christen
bloude / his robbynge of the pore thorow out christendom of al that
was geuen to mayntene them / his settynge vpp in rome a stues not
of wemen only / but of the male kynd also agenst nature and a
thousand abhominacions to grosse for a turke / are tokens good
ynough that he is the right antichrist and his doctrine spronge of the
devell.

M. in penaunce marten saith there neadeth no contricion ner satisfaccion. T. call it repentaunce and then it is contricion of it selfe.
And as for mendesmakynge with worldely thinges / that doo to thi
brother whom thou hast offended / & vn to god offer the repentaunce of thine herte and the satisfaccion of christes bloude.

M. tyndale saith that the confessoure vttureth the confessions of
them that be rich. But yet we se that both rich and pore kepe hores
openly with out payenge peny. T. if they be very rich they be sofered / because they maye be good defenders of the spiritualtie / and
if they be very pore / because they haue no money to paye or else
they fine with one or other secretly.

M. vppon that lye tindale bildeth the destruction of the sacrament
of penaunce. T. sacrament is a signe signifienge what I shuld doo or
beleue or both. As baptim is the signe of repentaunce signifienge
that I must repent of euel and beleue to be saued therfrom by the
bloude of christe. Now Sir in youre penaunce describe vs which is
the signe and the outwarde sacrament & what is the thynge that I
must do or beleue. And then we will enserch whether it maye be a
sacrament or no.

M. tindale sayth that confession is the worst inuencion that euer
was. T. as ye facion it me[O3]ane I / & of that filthy priapish confession which ye spew in the eare wherwithe ye exclude the forgeuenesse that is in christes bloude for al that repent and beleue therin /

10 M. More   11 Tindale   15 M. More   16 Tindale   21 M.
More   22 Tindale   29 More   30 Tindale   172/30–173/2 Eare
confession destroyeth the benefite of Christes bloud.

5 stues] *1573*, stuees *1531*   S1, S3, S5 M.] *om. 1573*

and make the people beleue that their sinnes be neuer forgeuen vntyll they be schryuen vn to the preste / and then for no nother cause saue that they haue there told them and for the holy dedes to come which the confessoure hath enioyned them moare profitable ofte tymes for him selfe then any man else. 5

M. neuer man had grace to spie that before tyndale. T. yes very many. For many nacions neuer receaued it. And the grekes when they had proued it and sawe the bawdery that folowed of it / put it downe agayne. For which cause and to know al secretes and to leade the consciences captiue / the pope falsly maynteneth it. 10

M. what frute wold then come of penaunce? T. of youre iugglynge terme penaunce I can not affirme. But of repentaunce wold come this frute / that noman that had it / shuld synne willyngely / but euery man shuld continually fight agenst his fleshe.

M. He teacheth that the sacrament hath no vertu at all / but the 15 faith only. T. the faith of a repentynge soule in Christes bloude doeth iustifie only. And the sacrament stondeth in as good sted as a lyuely preacher. And as the preacher iustifyeth me not / but my fayth in the doctryne: euen so the signe iustifieth not / but the faith in the promise which the sacrament signifieth and preacheth. And to 20 preach is al the vertue of the sacrament. And where the sacramentes preach not / there they haue no vertue at all. And sir we teach not as ye doo / to beleue in the sacrament or in holy church / but to beleue the sacrament [O3v] and holy church.

M. He teacheth that fayth sufficeth vn to saluacion with out good 25 werkes. T. the scripture sayth / that assone as a man repenteth of evel and beleueth in Christes bloude / he obteyneth mercye imediatly / because he shuld loue god and of that loue doo good werkes / & that he tarieth not in synne styll tyll he haue done good werkes / & then is first forgeuen for his werkessake / as the pope beareth his 30

---

5 More   6 Tindale   10 More   11 Tindale
12 Repentance   15 More   16 Tindale   17 Sacrament
25 More   26 Fayth   27 Tindale

---

6 tyndale.] *ed.*, tyndale *1531*, Tyndall. *1573*   11 penaunce?] *1573*, penaunce *1531*   15 but the] but by *1573*   16 repentynge] *ed.*, repentyuge *1531*, repenting *1573*   29 good] *1573*, god *1531*

in hande / excludynge the vertue of christes bloude. For a man must
be first reconsyled vn to god by Christ and in gods fauoure / yer his
werkes can be good & pleasaunt in the sight of god. But we saye not
as some damnablye lye on vs / that we shuld doo euell to be iustified
5 by fayth / as thou maist se in the third of the romanes how they said
of the appostles for like preachinge.

   M. He calleth it sacrilege to please god with good werkes. T. to
refer the werke vn to the person of god to by out thy synne therwith / is to make an Idole of god or a creature. But if thou referre
10 thy werke vn to thy neyboures profitt or tamynge of thine awne
flesh / then thou pleasest god therwith.

   M. Item that a man can doo no good werke. T. it is false. But he
sayth a man can doo no good werke tyll he beleue that his synnes be
forgeuen him in Christe and tyll he loue gods law and haue obtayned
15 grace to worke with. And then saith he that we can not doo oure
werkes so perfectely / by the reason of our corrupte flesh but that
there is some imperfectenesse therin / as in the werkes of them that
be not their craftes master. Whych is yet not rekened / because they
doo their good willes and be scolars and [O4] goo to scole to lerne
20 to doo better.

   M. Item that the good and rightewesse man synneth all waye in
doynge well. T. in all his werkes there lacketh some what and is a
faute vntyll he doo them wyth as greate loue vn to his neyboure as
Christ did for him and as longe as there is moare resistence in his
25 flesh then was in Christes / or lesse hope in god: and then no lenger.

   M. Item that no synne damneth a man saue vnbeleffe. T. whatsoeuer a man hath done / if he repent and beleue in Christe / it is
him forgeuen. And so it foloweth that no synne damneth saue there
where there is no beleffe.

30 M. Item that we haue no frewyll to doo ought therwith / though
the grace of god be ioyned therto / and that god doeth all in vs both

7 More	8 Workes	9 Tindale	12 More	13 Tindale
21 More	22 Synne	23 Tindale	26 More	27 Vnbeleffe
28 Tindale	30 More	31 Frewyll		

5 in the third of the romanes] Rom. iij. *1573*   28 him forgeuen] forgeuen
him *1573*

good and bad and we doo but sofre as waxe doeth of the werke man.
T. first when he affermeth that we saye / our wyll is not fre to doo
good and to helpe to compell the membres / when god hath geuen
vs grace to loue his lawes / is false. But we saye that we haue no
frewyll to captiuat oure wittes and vnderstondynge / for to beleue   5
the pope in what soeuer he saith with out reason geuinge / when we
find in the scripture contrary testimonie / and se in him so greate
falshed and dedes so abhominable and therto all the signes by whych
the scripture teacheth vs to know antichriste.

And we affirme that we haue no frewyll to preuent god & his   10
grace & before grace prepare oure selues therto / nether can we consent vn to god before grace become. For vntill god haue preuented
vs & powred the spirite of his grace in to our [O4v] soules / to loue
his lawes / and hath grauen them in oure hertes by the outwarde
mynistracyon of his true preacher and inwarde workynge off his   15
spirite or by insperacion only / we know not god as he is to be
knowen ner fele the goodnesse or any swetnesse in his law. How
then can we consent therto? Saith not the texte / that we can doo no
good while we be euell and they which seke glorie and to clime in
honoure a boue theyr brethern can not beleue the trueth / and that   20
hores theues murtherars extorcionars and such like haue no parte in
the kyngdome of god and christe ner any felynge therof? And who
shall take those diseases from them? God only thorow his mercie /
for they can not put of that complexion of them selues / vntyll they
be taught to beleue and to fele that yt ys damnable and to consent   25
vnto the contrary liuynge.

And vnto the seconde part I answere / that in respecte of god we
doo but sofre only and receaue power to doo all oure dedes whether
we doo good or bad / as christ answered Pilat / that he coude haue
no power agenst him except it were geuen him from a boue and no   30
moare coude Iudas nether. But in respecte of the thinge wherin or
wherwith we worke and sheade out agayne the power that we haue
receaued / we worke actually. As the axe doeth nothinge in respecte

1 Tindale   10–13 We haue no frewyl to preuent grace and prepare oure
selues.   19 Mat. 12.   21 Ioan .5.   22 1. Cor. 6.   27 Ioan .19.

2 when] where *1573*

of the hand that heweth / saue receaue: but in respecte of the tre that
is cutte / it worketh actually and powreth out againe the power that
it hath receaued.

M. Item that god is auctor of good & euell: as wel of the euel will
5 of Iudas in betrayenge christe / as of the goodwill of christ in sofer-
ynge his passion. T. the power where wyth we doo [O5] good and
euell is of god and the will is of god. As the power which the mur-
therar abvseth and wherwith he killeth a man vnrightwesly is off
God and the will where with he willeth it. But the wekednesse of
10 his will and crokednesse or frowardnesse where with he sleeth
vnrightwesly / to auenge him selfe and to satisfie his awne lustes /
and the cause whi he knoweth not the law of god and consenteth
not to it / which law shuld haue informed his will and corrected the
crokednesse therof and haue taught hym to vse hys will and his
15 power right / is his blindnesses faute only and not gods. Which blindnesse the deuell hath poysoned him with.

M. Item matrimonie is no sacrament. T. Matrimonie is a similitude of the kyngdome of heuen / as are many thynges mo / like as
it appereth by christ in the gospell. But who institute it to be a sacra-
20 ment? Or who at hys mariage was taught the sygnificacion of it?
Who was euer bounde to receaue yt in the name of a sacrament. I
wold to christes bloude that ye wold make a sacrament of yt vn to
all men and wemen that be maried and vn to all other / and wold at
euery mariage teach the people to know the benefyte off christ
25 thorow the similitude off matrimonye. And I affirme that in the
popis church there ys no sacrament. For where no significacion is /
there ys no sacrament. A signe ys no sygne vn to him that vnderstondeth nought therby: as a speche is no speche vn to hym that
vnderstondeth it not. I wold too christes passyon that ye wold let
30 them be sacramentes whych christ institute and ordeyned for sacramentes. And then yff ye make of youre awne braynes .v. hundred
therto I wolde not [O5v] be so greatly greued / though I wold not
geue my consent vnto so great a multitude / partely for the bondage / and specially lest we shuld in time to come / the significacions

of them lost / fall in to Idolatrie agayne and make holy werkes of
them / after the ensample off the blyndnesse wherin we be nowe /
but I wold haue the worde euer liuely preached out of the playne
texte.

M. Item that all holy orders be but mennes inuencion. T. the office   5
of an apostle / bisshope / prest / deacon / and wedowe / are of god:
But as concerninge the shauinge / the oylenge and dyuersite of rayment and many degrees sens added therto / proue that they be not
mens tradycions. But and ye wyll make sacramentes of the oyl-
ynge / shauynge / sherynge / and garmentes / put theyr significa-   10
cions vn to them and let the kynges grace compell them to kepe
them and I admitte them for sacramentes / and vntyll that tyme I
hold them for the false signes of ypocrites.

M. Item that euery man and woman is a prest and maye consecrat
the body of christe. T. in bodyly seruice if the officer appoynted be   15
awaye / euery other person not only maye / but also is bounde to
helpe at nede / euen so moch as his neyboures dogge. How moch
moare then ought men to assiste one a nother in the health of their
soules / at all tymes of nede? yf the man be awaye / the woman maye
and is bounde to baptise in tyme of nede / by the lawe of loue /   20
which offyce perteyneth vnto the prest only. Yf she be lady ouer the
greatest ordeined by god / that she maie baptise / why shulde she
not haue power also ouer the lesse / to ministre the ceremonies
which the po[O6]pe hath added to / as his oyle / his salt / his spitell /
his candel and cresomcloth? And whi might she not praye all the   25
prayars / except that Idole the pope be greater then the very god? yf
wemen had brought a child to church and while the prest and other
men taried the childe were in ieoperdy / might they not baptise him
in the font / if there were no nother water by? And if other water
were by / yet if that holpe better one mite / loue requireth to baptise   30
him therein. And then why might not wemen twich all their other
oyle? If a woman lerned in christe were dreuen vn to an Ile where

---

5 More   6 Orders   7 Tindale   14 More   15 Tindale

16 Consecrat

---

8 not] but *1573*   24 spitell /] *ed.*, spitell *1531*, spitell, *1573*   S5, S6 *reversed*
in 1573

christ was neuer preached / might she not there preach and teach to
ministre the sacramentes and make officers? The case is possible /
shew then what shuld let that she might not? loue thy neyboure as
thy selfe doeth compel. Nay / she maye not consecrat. Whi? If the
5   pope loued vs as well as christ / he wold finde no faulte therwyth /
though a woman at nede ministred that sacrament yf yt be so necessary as ye make it. In bodily welth / he that wold haue me one ace
lesse then hym selfe / loueth me not as wel as him selfe how moch
moare ought we to loue one another in thynges pertaynynge vn to
10 the soule?

M. Item that the host ys no sacryfyce. T. christ is no moare
kylled. It is therfore the sacrament signe and memoriall of that sacrifice where wyth chryste offered hys body for oure synnes and commaunded saynge / thys doo in the remembraunce off me. We be not
15 holpe with any visible dede that the prest there doeth / saue in that
it putteth vs in remembraunce of christes deeth [O6v] and passion
for oure synnes. As the garmentes and straunge holy gestures / helpe
vs not / but in that they putt vs in remembraunce of thinges that
Christ sofered for vs in his passion. Euen so the shewenge
20 breakynge and eatynge of the host / the shewenge and drinkynge of
the cuppe of Christes bloude / and the wordes and the consecracion /
helpe vs not a pinne ner ar gods serues / saue only in that they stere
op oure repentynge faith to call to mynde the deeth and passion of
christ for our synnes. And therfore to call it a sacrifice / is but abused
25 speach / as when we call one that is new come home to breakefast
& sett a capon before him and saye / this is youre wellcome home /
meanynge yet by that speach / that it is but a signe of the loue of
mine herte which reioyseth and is glad that he is come home saffe
and sounde. And euen so is this but the memoriall of the very sacri-
30 fice of christ once done for all. And if ye wold no nother wyse
meane / ye shall haue my good wyll to call it so styll / or iff ye can
shewe me a reason of some other meaninge. And therfore I wold
that it had bene called (as it in dede is and as it was commaunded to
be) Christes memoriall / though that I doute not but that it was

---

11 More   12 Sacrifice   13 Tindale   24–25 An ensample
33–34 Christes memoriall

called masse of this Ebrue worde Misach / whych signifieth a pensiongeuynge / because that at euery masse men gaue euery man a
porcion accordynge vn to his power vn to the sustentacion of the
pore. Which offerynge yet remayneth. But to a false vse and profyt
of them that haue to moch / as all other thynges are peruerted.   5

Fynally it is the same thynge that it was when Christ institute it /
at his last soper. If it were then the very sacrificinge of Christes
bo[O7]dy / and had that same vertue and power wyth it that his
very passion after wrought / whi was he sacrificed so cruelly on the
morow and not hold excused therwith / seinge he was there verely   10
sacrificed?

M. Item that there remayneth bred and wine in the sacrament. T.
improue it. What is that that is broken and that the prest eateth with
his teth / ayre only? if a child were fed with no nother fode he shuld
wax haply as longe as his father. Where of then shuld his body / his 15
flesh and bones growe? where of shuld that come (wyth reuerence I
speake it) that he pisseth and soforth? all by miracle wyll they saye.
O what wonderfull miracles must we fayne to saue antichristes doctrine / I might with as good reason saye that the hoste is nether
rounde ner white / But that as my mouth is disceaued in the tast of   20
bred / euen so myne eyes ar in the syght of roundnesse and so is
there nothynge at all. Whych all are but the disputacions of men
with corrupte myndes with out spirite to iudge. Neuer the later
when the prest hath once rehersed the testament of our sauioure
theron / I loke not on bred and wine / but on the body of Christ   25
broken and bloud shed for my synnes / and by that fayth am I saued
from the damnacion of my synnes. Nether come I to masse for any
other purpose then to fett forgeuenesse for Christes deethes sake /
ner for any other purpose saye I confiteor and knowlege my synnes
at the begynnynge of masse. And iff ye haue other doctrine teach vs 30
a reason & lead vs in light and we wyll folowe. Christ sayth Ihon
.vj. it is the spirite that quikeneth / the flesh profiteth nothynge at
all / the wordes whych I speake sayth he / ar spirite and life. That

is / the [O7v] fleshly eatynge and drinkynge of Christes body and
bloud profit not / as his carnall presens profited not / by the reason
of his presens only as ye se by Iudas and the phareses and the sow-
diours that twiched him / and how his bodyly presens did lett the dis-
5   ciples to vnderstonde spiritually. But to eate and drinke in the spirite / that is / to herken vn to his wordes and with a repentynge hert
to beleue in his deeth / bryngeth vs all that Christ can doo for vs.

    M. Item that the masse auayleth no man but the preest. T. if ye
speake of the prayars / his prayars helpe vs as moch as oures him. If
10   ye speake of the sacrament / it helpeth as many as be present as moch
as him / if moued therby they beleue in Christes deeth as well as he.
If they be absent / the sacrament profiteth them as moch as a sermon
made in the church helpeth them that be in the feldes. And how profiteth it the soules of the deed tell me vn to whom it is no signe?
15   If ye meane the carnall eatynge and drinkynge / then it profiteth
the prest only / for he eateth and drinketh vpp all allone and geueth
no man parte with him.

    M. Item that a man shuld not be howseled tyll he laye a dyenge.
T. That is to shamelesse a lye.
20   M. Item that men and wemen shuld not spare to twich it. T. a
perelous case. Why? because the pope hath not oyled them. Never-
thelesse Christ hath annoynted them with his spirite & with his
bloude. But wot ye why? The pope thynketh if they shuld be to
busy in handelynge it / they wold beleue that there were bred /and
25   for that cause to strength their feythes / he hath imagened lytle pretty
thinne manchetes that shynne [O8] thorowe and seme moare like to
be made of paper or fine parchement then of wheten floure. Aboute
which was no smal question in oxforde of late dayes / whether it
were bred or none: some affirminge that the floure with longe ly-
30   enge in water was turned to starch & had lost his nature. M. Item
that the sacrament shuld not be worsheped. T. It is the sacrament of
Christes body & bloud. And Christ calleth it the new & euer last-

8 More	9 Masse	10 Tindale	18 More	19 Tindale
20 More	21 Twich	22 Tindale	30 More	31 Worshepe
32 Tindale				

27 wheten] wheate 1573   31 worsheped] ed., worspeped 1531, worshipped 1573

ynge testament in his bloude & commaunded that we shuld so doo
in the remembraunce of him / that his body was broken & his bloud
shed for our synnes. And Paule commaundeth therby to shew or
preach the lordes deeth. They saye not praye to it / nether put any
fayth therin. For I maye not beleue in the sacrament / but I must   5
beleue the sacrament / that it is a true signe and it true that is signified
therby (which is the onlye worshuppynge of the sacrament / if ye
geue it other worshuppe ye playnlye dishonoure it). As I maye not
beleue in Christes church / but beleue christes church / that the doctrine which they preach of christe is true. If ye haue any other doc-   10
trine / teach vs a reason and lead vs in light / and we wyll folow.

M. Item that a christen is not bounde to kepe any lawe made by
man or any at all. T. you saye vntrulye: a Christen man is bounde
to obey tiranny / if it be not agenst his faith ner the lawe of god /
vntyll god delyuer him therof. But he is no christen man that bynd-   15
eth hym to any thynge saue that whych loue and his neyboures necessite requireth of them.

And when a law made / is no lenger profitable / christen rulars
ought to breake it. But now adayes when tyrantes haue gotten the
[O8v] simpell people vnder / they compell them to serue their lustes   20
and wily tiranny / with out respecte of any comen welth. Whych
wily tiranny / because the trueth rebuketh it / is the cause why they
persecute it / lest the comen people seynge how good they shulde be
and felynge how weked they are / shuld wythdraw their neckes
from their vnrightwesse yocke. As ye haue ensample in Herode / in   25
the scribes and Phareses and in many other.

M. Item that there is no purgatory. T. beleue in Christ and thou
shalt shortely finde purgatoryes ynow / as ye now make other fele.

M. Item that all soules lye and slepe tyll domes daye. T. and ye in
puttynge them in heuen hell and purgatory / destroye the argu-   30
mentes wherewith Christ and paule proue the resurreccion. What
god doeth with them / that shall we know when we come to them.

---

12 More   13 Tindale   26 More   27–28 Purgatorie
28 Tindale   29 More   30–31 Soules slepe   32 Tindale

---

7 worshuppynge] *ed.*, worshuppnge *1531*, worshippyng *1573*   20 people]
1573, pleople *1531*

The true fayth putteth the resurreccion which we be warned to loke-
fore euery houre. The hethen philosophoures denyenge that / did
put that the soules did euer liue. And the pope ioyneth the spirituall
doctrine of christe and the fleshly doctrine of philosophers to
5 gether / thynges so contrary that they can not agre / no moare then
the spirite and the flesh do in a Christen man. And because the
fleshly mynded pope consenteth vn to hethen doctrine / ther fore he
corrupteth the scripture to stablish it. Moses sayth in Deute. / the
secret thynges perteyne vn to the lorde / and the thynges that be
10 opened pertayne vn to vs / that we doo all that is written in the boke.
Wherfore Sir if we loued the lawes of god and wold occupye our
selues to fulfill them / and wolde on the other syde be meke and lett
god alone with his secretes and [P1] sofre him to be wiser then we /
we shuld make none article of the faith of this or that. And agayne /
15 if the soules be in heuen / tell me whi they be not in as good case as
the angelles be? And then what cause is there of the resurreccion?

M. Item no man shall praye to sayntes. T. when ye speake with
saintes that be departed / it is not euell to put them in remembraunce
to praye for you. M. whi doo they not heare vs? T. if they loue you
20 so feruently and be so greate with god / whi certifie they you not /
that they so doo? M. so they doo in that we fele oure peticions
graunted. T. God saued the old Idolatres with worldly saluacion and
gaue them their peticions / which they yet axed of their Idoles / as ye
se thorow out al the old testament. God heareth the crowes / foules /
25 beestes and wormes of the erth / as the texte saith / men and beestes
doeth god saue / which bestes yet praye not to god. The Iewes and
turkes doeth god saue in this worlde and geueth them their worldly
peticions. Which yet worshepe not god / as his godly nature is to be
worsheped but aftir their awne imaginacion: not in the spirite with
30 faith hope and loue / but with bodyly seruice as the pope doeth. As
the popish serue S. Appoline for the toth ache and ar healed: euen so
the Iewes and turkes be healed and pray not to hir / but serue god
aftir a nother maner for the same disease. So that God doeth saue in
this worlde all that kepe the worldely lawes worldly / that is to

wite / outwarde in the body for bodyly rewarde and not in the herte
of loue that springeth out of the mercy that God hath geuen vs in
christe which same / though they be turkes / if they breake the
worldly lawes / he rebuketh them / as the ni[P1v]niuites and punisheth them diuersly. And if they knowlege their synne and mende /   5
he healeth them agayne. But and if they harden and synne as beestes
and will not amend / he destroyeth them vtterly / as the sodomites.
And yet all soch haue no parte in the life to come.

But with his childern in whose hertes he writeth the faith of his
sonne Iesus & the loue of his lawes / he goeth other wise to werke   10
his lawes in their wil: & their peticions are his honoure and their neyboures welth: and that he will prouide them of al thinges necessarie
vn to this life and gouern them that their hertes be not ouercome of
euell. And he heareth them vnto his honoure and their euerlastynge
saluacion / and purgeth them and teacheth them thinges wherof the   15
popish and all they whose hertes the god of this world hath blynded
to serue god with workes haue no fealynge.

And when he saith that the emproure and that counsell which decreed that images for the abuse shuld be put out of the church / were
heretikes / it is moch easier so to saye than so to proue. Vnderstond   20
there fore / that images were not yet receaued in the church in the
tyme of S. Hierom / at the least waye generally / whether in some
one place or no I can not tell. For .s. Hierome reherseth of one Epiphanius a bisshope in the contre of Cipirce and that the most perfecte of al the bisshopes of his tyme / how that the sayd Epiphanius   25
and the bisshope of Ierusalem went to gether to bethel / and by the
waye they entred [P2] in to a church for to praye and there found a
vayle hangynge before the dore and an image paynted theron / as it
had bene of christ or some saint. For the bisshope was so moued
therwith / because saith Saint Hierom / that it was contrary to the   30
scripture / that he cutte it and counseled to bury some dede therin
and sent a nother cloth to hange in the sted. And aftirward when

18 Images   22 Hierome   30–32 Epiphanius cutte the image.

11 in] *1573*, is *1531*   17 haue] hath *1573*   25 bisshopes] *ed.*, bissopes *1531*,
Byshops *1573*   26 bisshope] *ed.*, bissope *1531*, Byshop *1573*   28 image] *ed.*,
image: *1531, 1573*   31 cutte it] cut *1573*

they ware crepte in a litle and litle: there was no worshepynge of
them / at the least waye generally vntyll the tyme of S. Gregory.

    In so moch that when Cirenus the bisshope of Masilia offended
with the supersticiousnesse of the people burnt them / Saynt Gregory wrote that he shuld not destroy the images / but teach only that
the people shuld not worshepe them. But when it was so ferre come
that the people worsheped them with a false faith (as we now know
no nother vse) and were no longer memorials only / then the bisshopes of grece and the emproure gathered them to gether / to prouide a remedye agenst that misheue and concluded that they shuld
be put doune for the abuse / thinkynge it so most expedient / hauinge for them / first the ensample of God whom a man maye boldely
folowe / which commaunded in the beginnynge of all his preceptes /
that there shuld be no image vsed to worshepe or pray before / not
for the image it selfe / but for the wekenesse of his people: and hauinge agayne before theyr eyes / that the people were fallen vn to Idolatrie and imageseruinge by the reason of them.

    Now answere me / by what reason canst thou [P2v] make an her-
etike of him / that concludeth nought agenst god / but worketh with
god and putteth that blocke out of the waye / where at his brother
the price of christes bloud stombleth and loseth his soule. They put
not doune the images for hate of god and of his saintes / no moare
then Ezechias brake the brasen serpent for enuye of the greate miracle that was wrought by it / or in spite of god that commaunded it
to be kepte for a memoriall. But to kepe the people in the true faith
only. Now seinge we maye be all with out images and to put them
doune is not agenst Gods commaundement but with it / namely if
they be abused / to the dishonoure of god and hurt of oure neybours / where is charite / if thou which knowest the trouth and canst
vse thine image well / wilt not yet forbere thine image and sofre it
to be put out of the waye / for thy weake brothers sake whom thou
seist perish therthorow? ye and what thynge maketh both the turke
and the Iew abhorre our faith so moch as our imageseruice? But the

4 Gregorye   5 Cirenus   9–12 A councell gathered in grecia did put
doune all images.   23 Ezechias

10 misheue] mischief 1573

pope was then glad to fynde an occasion to picke a quarell with the
emproure / to gett the empire in to his awne handes which thynge
he brought to passe with the swerd of fraunce and clame so hye that
euersens he hath put his awne auctorite in stede of gods worde in
euery generall counsell & hath concluded what him liste / as agenst   5
al gods worde and agenst al charite he condemned that blessed dede
of that counsell and emproure.

M. they blaspheme our lady and all saintes. T. that is vntrue. We
honoure our blessed lady and all holy saintes and folow their faith
and liuynge vn to the vttemost of oure power and [P3] submitte our   10
selues to be scolars of the same scole.

M. they maye not abyde salue regina. T. for therin is moch blas-
phemie vnto our blessed lady / because christ is our hope and life
only and not she. And ye in asscribynge vn to hir that she is not /
dishonoure god and worshepe hir not.   15

M. they saye if a woman beinge aliue beleue in god and loue him
as moch as our lady / she maye helpe with hir prayars as moch as
our lady. T. tel whi not. Christ when it was told him that his mother
and his brethern sought him / answered / that his mother / his sisters
and his brethern were al they that did his fathers wyll. And vn to the   20
woman that saide to christ / blessed be the wombe that bare the and
pappes that gaue the sucke / christ answered / Naye blessed are they
that heare the worde of god and kepe it. As paul saith .i. Corin. ix.
I haue nought to reioyse though I preach / for necessite lieth vppon
me / and wo is me / if I preach not. If I doo it vnwillyngly / an office   25
is committed vn to me / but and if I do it with a good wil / then I
haue a rewarde. So now carnall bearynge of christ and carnall geuynge him sucke make not our lady great. But our blessed ladies
greatnesse is hir faith and loue wherin she exceaded other. Wherefore if God gaue his mercy that a nother woman were in those .ij.   30
poyntes equall with hir / whi were she not like greate and hir prayers
as moch herde.

[P3v] M. Item that men shuld not worshepe the holy crosse. T.

8 More   9 Oure lady   10 Tindale   12 More   13–14 Salue regina   15 Tindale   16 More   18 Tindale   19 Mat. 12.
22 Luce .11.   33 More

10 vttemost] vttermost *1573*

wyth no false worshepe and supersticious fayth / but as I haue said /
to haue it in reuerence for the memoriall of him that died theron.

　　M. Item Luther hateth the festes of the crosse and of corpus
Christi. T. not for enuy of the crosse whych synned not in the deeth
5　of Christ ner of malice towarde the blessed body of christ but for
the ydolatrye vsed in those festes.

　　M. Item that no man or woman is bounde to kepe any vowe. T.
lawfull vowes ar to be kepte vntyll necessite breake them. But
vnlawfull vowes ar to be broken immediatly.

10　　M. Marten appelled vn to the nexte generall counsell that shuld
be gathered in the holy gost / to seke a longe delaye. T. of a trouth
that were a longe delaye. For shuld Marten liue / tyll the pope wold
gather a counsell in the holy gost or for any godly purpose / he were
like to be for euery here of his heed a thousand yeres olde.

15　　Then bryngeth he in the inconstauncie of Marten / because he
saith in his later boke / how that he seith further then in his firste.
Paraduenture / he is kynne to oure doctours whych when with
preachynge agenst pluralities they haue gotte them .iij. or .iiij. benefices / allege the same excuse. But yet to saye the truth the very
20　appostles of Christ lerned not all trouth in one daye. For longe after
the ascencion they wist not that the hethen shuld be receaued vn to
the faith. How then coude Marten (brought vppe in the blyndnesse
of youre secte aboue .xl. yeres) spie out all youre falshed in one
daye.

25　　M. Marten offered at wormes before the emproure and all the
lordes of germanye / to aby[P4]de by his boke & to dispute / which
he might well doo / sith he had his safe conducte that he shuld haue
no bodyly harme. T. o mercifull god / how fome ye out youre awne
shame? ye can not dispute excepte ye haue a man in youre awne
30　daunger to doo him bodyly harme / to diote him aftir youre facion /
to tormente him and to murther him. Yf ye might haue had him at
youre pleasure / ye wold haue disputed wyth him: first wyth soph-

1 Crosse	2 Tindale	3 More	4 Tindale	7 More
8 Vowe	9 Tindale	10 More	11 Marten	12 Tindale
15 Marten	25 More	28 Tindale		

27 sith] sithens 1573　　　28 fome] come 1573

istrie and corruptynge the scripture: then with offerynge him promocions: then with the swerde. So that ye wold haue bene sure / to
haue ouercome him with one argument or other.

M. He wold agre on no Iudges. T. What iudges offered ye him /
saue blynde bisshopes & cardenales / enimies of all trouth / whose   5
promocions and dignites they feare to be plucked from them / if the
trouth came to light / or soch Iudases as they had corrupte with
money to mayntene their secte? The appostles might haue admitted
as well the hethen bisshopes of Idoles to haue bene their iudges as he
them. But he offered you autenticke scripture and the hertes of the   10
whole worlde. Whych .ij. iudges / iff ye had good consciences and
trust in god / ye wold not haue refused.

iiij.

The fourth chapter is not the first poetrie that he hath fayned.

v.   15

In the ende of the fifte he vntrulye reporteth / that Marten saith /
no man is bound to kepe any vowe. Lawfull promises are to be kepte
and vnlawfull broken.

vj.

[P4v] In the beginnenge of the .vj. he discrybeth marten aftir the   20
ensample of his awne nature / as in other places he discribeth god
aftir the complexion of popes cardenals and worldly tirantes.

M. Marten will abyde but by the scripture only. T. and ye will
come at no scripture only: And as for the old doctours ye wyll heare

---

 1 [Hand]   4 More   5 Marten   6 Tindale   22 More
23 Marten   24 Tindale

   4 Iudges] 1573, Iugdes 1531   13 iiij.] The iiij. Chapter. 1573   15 v.] The v.
Chapter. 1573   17 are] 1573, arte 1531   18 vnlawfull] 1573, vnlawfulll 1531;
broken] to be broken 1573   19 vj.] The vj. Chapter. 1573   21 awne] ed., a
awne 1531, own 1573

as litle / saue where it pleaseth you / for all youre crienge / old holy
fathers. For tel me this / whi haue ye in englonde condemned the
vnion of doctours but because ye wold not haue youre falshed dis-
closed by the doctrine of them.

5   M. they saye / that a christen man is discharged of al lawes spirituall and temperall saue the gospell. T. ye iugle / we saye that no christen man ought to bynde his brother violently / vn to any lawe wher
of he coude not geue a reason out of christes doctrine and out of the
lawe of loue. And on the other syde we saye / that a christen man is
10   called to sofre wronge and tiranny (though no man ought to bynde
him) vntill god rid vs therof: so fer yet as the tiranny is not directly
agenst the law of god and faith of Christe / and no further.

M. marten was the cause of the destruccion of the vplondish people of germanie. T. that is false for then he coude not haue escaped
15   him selfe. Marten was as moch the cause of their confusion / as
Christ of the destruccion of Ierusalem. The duke elector of saxon
cam from the warre of those vplondish people and other dukes with
him / in to Wittenberge where Marten is / with .xv. hundred men
of armes / so that Marten if he had bene gyltie / coude not [P5] haue
20   gonne quite. And therto all the dukes and lordes that cleaue vn to
the worde of god thys daye / were no lesse combred with their
comen people then other men.

Then after the lowdest maner he setteth out the cruelnesse of the
emproures soudioures whych they vsed at Rome: but he maketh no
25   mencion of the treason which holy church wrought secretly / were
with the men off warre were so set on fire.

viij.

M. what good dede will he do / that beleueth marten / how that
we haue no frewill to do any good with the helpe of grace? T. O
30   poete with out shame.

---

3 Vnion   5 More   6 Tindale   8–11 How ferre a christen man is
bounde to suffre   13 More   14 Tindale   28 M. More   29 Tyndale

16 destruccion] *ed.*, destrucciou *1531*, destruction *1573*   19 haue] *1573*, ha-
haue *1531*   27 viij.] The viij. Chapter. *1573*   S7 M.] *om. 1573*

M. what harme shal he care to forbere / that beleueth luther / how god alone / with out oure will worketh all the misheue that they doo. T. O naturall sonne of the father of all lies.

M. what shall he care / how longe he liue in synne that beleueth luther / that he shall after thys life / fele nether good ner evell in   5 bodye ner soule vntyll the daye of dome? T. Christ and hys appostles taught no nother / but warned to loke for christes cominge agayne euery houre. Which cominge agayne / because ye beleue will neuer be therfore haue ye fained that other marchaundice.

M. Martens bokes be open / if ye will not beleue vs. T. Naye / ye   10 haue shutt them vpp and therfore be bold to saie what ye liste.

M. they liue as they teach and teach as they liue. T. but nether teach ner liue as other lye on them.

ix.

M. though the turke offer pleasures vn to the receauers and deeth   15 vn to the refusers of his [P5v] secte (as the pope doeth) yet he sofereth none to breake their promises of chastite dedicat to god (though haply they vse no soch vowes / and as the pope wyll not excepte it be for monye) but luther teacheth to breake holy vowes. T. luther teacheth that vnlawfull vowes grounded on a false fayth vnto the   20 dyshonourynge of god are to be broken and no nother. And agayne constrayned seruice pleaseth not God. And thridly youre pope geueth licence and his blessynge to breake all lawfull vowes / but with the most vnlawfull of all will ye not dispence.

Then he bringeth forth the ensample of the hethen / to confirme   25 the popis chastite. And no wronge / for the same false imaginacion that the hethen had in theirs / hath the pope in hys. Vnderstonde therfore / If thou vow ane indifferent thynge / to please god in hys awne person / he receaueth not thyne Idolatrie: for hys pleasure and

1 M. More   3 Tyndale   4 More   6 Tyndale   10 M. More
11 Tindale   12 M. More   13 Tindale   15 M. More   19 Tyndale
28 Vowes

2 misheue] mischiefe 1573   11 liste] luste 1573   14 ix.] The ix. Chapter.
1573   S1, 5, 7, 9 M.] om. 1573

honoure is / that thou shuldest be as he hath made the / and shulde
receaue all soch thynges of hys hand and vse them as ferforth as they
were nedfull and geue him thankes and be bounde to him: and not
that thou shuldest be as thou haddest made thy selfe / and that he
5   shulde receaue soch thynges off the to be bounde to the / to thanke
the and rewarde the. And agayne / thou must geue me a reason of
thy vow out off the worde of God. Morouer when thou vowest lawfully thou maist not do it precyselye / but all waye excepte / yf thyne
awne or thy neyboures necessite required the contrary. As yf thou
10 haddest vowed neuer to eate flesh or drinke wine or stronge drinke /
to tame thi flesh / and thou after warde fellest in disease so that thy
body in that behalfe were to tame or that there coud no no[P6]ther
sustinaunce be gotten. Then thou must interpret soch cases excepte /
though thou madest no mencion of them / at the makinge of thi
15 vow. Some man wold saye / other shifte might be made: what then?
If other drinke as whote as wine & of the same operacion / and other
meate of the same power and vertue as flesh is / must be had / whi
shuldest thou forswere wine or fleshe / seinge it is now no lenger for
the taminge of thy bodi. And so forth of al wother / as I haue aboue
20 declared.

And when he bringeth in the apostles / marters / confessoures and
.xv. hundred yeres / it is cleane contrary. For they had no soch false
imaginacion of chastite or of any other worke: but they vsed it to
serue their neyboure and to avoyde trouble in time of persecucion
25 and to be eased of that burthen that was to heuy for their weake
shulders and not to compell god to thanke them for the liberte for
which they be bound to thanke him.

X.

In the tenth he inveyeth and rayleth agenst that which nether he
30 ner any fleshly mynded papiste can vnderstonde / as they haue no

---

28 Frewyll

1 shulde] shouldest 1573   2 as ferforth] so farforth 1573   4 selfe /] ed.,
selfe. 1531, selfe, 1573   19 thy] 1573, they 1531   28 x.] The tenth Chapter.
1573

power to consent vnto the lawes of god. Which herein appereth /
that they compell their brethern which be as good as they to do &
beleue what they lust and not what god commaundeth. He affirmeth that marten saith how that we do no synne oure selues wyth
oure awne wylle / but that god synneth in vs and vseth vs as a deed   5
instrument and forseth vs ther vn to and damneth vs / not for oure
awne deedes but for hys / and for hys awne pleasure / as he compelleth vn to synne for hys pleasure or rather he for hys pleasure
synneth in vs. I saye / that a man synneth voluntaryly. [P6v] But
the power of the will and of the dede is off god and euery will and   10
deed are good in the nature of the dede and the euelnesse is a lacke
that there is / as the eye / though it be blinde is good in nature in
that it is soch a member created for soch a good vse: but it is called
euell for lacke of sighte. And so are oure dedes euell because we
lacke knowlege and loue to referre them vn to the glorie of God.   15
Which lacke cometh of the deuell that blyndeth vs with lustes and
occasions that we can not se the goodnesse and rightwysnesse of the
law of god and the meanes how to fulfill it. For coud we se it and the
waye to doo it we shuld loue it naturally as a chyld doeth a fayre
apple. For as a child when a man sheweth him a fayre apple and wyll   20
not geue it hym wepeth / so shuld we naturaly morne when the
members wold not come forwarde to fulfyll the law acordynge to
the desyre of oure hertes. For paule saith .ij. Cor. iiij. if our gospell
be hid / it is hyd vnto them that perish / amonge which the God of
this world hath blinded the wittes of the vnbeleuers / that the light   25
of the glorious gospell of christ shuld not shyne to them. And christ
saith that the briddes eate vpp the seed sowen vppon the waye and
interpreteth by the seed the worde / and by the foules / the deuell. So
that the deuel blindeth vs with falshed and lies which ys our worldly
wisdome / and therwith stoppethout the true light of gods wis-   30
dome / which blindnes is the euellnesse of all our dedes.

  And on the other syde / that a nother man loueth the lawes of God
and vseth the power that he hath of God well / and referreth his wyll

23 2. Cor. 4.

---

1 the] *1573*, that *1531*   2 do] *1573*, de ["e" *upside down and reversed*] *1531*
20 as] *om. 1573*

and hys dedes vn to the honoure off God / cometh off the mercy off
God which hath oppened hys [P7] wittes and shewed him light to
se the goodnesse and rightwysnesse of the law of god and the waye
that is in Christ to fulfill it. Wherby he loueth it naturally & trusteth
5   to doo it. Why doeth god open one mans eyes and not a nothers?
Paul Roma. ix. forbiddeth to aske that why. For it is to depe for
mans capacite. God we se is honoured therby and his mercy sette
out & the moare sene in the vesels of mercy. But the popish can sofre
god to haue no secret hid to him selfe. They haue serched to come
10   to the botome of his botomlesse wisdome / and because they can
not attayne to that secrete and be to proude to let it alone / and to
graunt them selues ignoraunt with the appostle that knew no nother
then Gods glorye in the electe / they goo and sett vpp frewyll with
the hethen philosophers & saye that a mans frewyll is the cause why
15   god choseth one & not a nother / contrary vn to all the scripture.
Paul saith it cometh not of the will ner of the dede / but of the mercy
of god. And they saye that euery man hath at the least waye power
in his frewyll / to deserue that power shuld be geuen him of god to
kepe the lawe. But the scripture testifieth that Christ hath deserued
20   for the electe euen then when they hated god / that there eyes shuld
be opened to se the goodnesse of the lawe of God and the waye to
fulfill it / and forgeuenesse of al that is passed where by they be
drawen to loue it and to hate synne.

I axe the popish one question whether the wyll can preuent a mans
25   wytte and make the witt se the rightwesnesse of the law and the
waye to fulfil it in christ? If I must first se the reason why yer I can
loue how shall I wyth my wyll doo that good thynge that I know
not of? how [P7v] shall I thanke god for the mercy that is layed vpp
for me in christ / yer I beleue it? For I must beleue the mercy yer I
30   can loue the worke. Now faith cometh not of oure frewyl / but is
the gyft of god geuen vs by grace yer therbe any wyl in our hertes
to doo the lawe of god. And whi god geueth it not euery man I can
geue no rekeninge of his iudgementes. But well I wott / I neuer de-

---

30 Faith

6 that] *om. 1573*   31 gyft] grace *1573*   S1 Faith] Faith is the gift of God &
commeth not by free wil. *1573*

serued it ner prepared my selfe vn to it / but ran a nother waye cleane
contrary in my blyndenesse / and sought not that waye / but he
sought me and found me out and shewed it me and therwith drew
me to him. And I bow the knees of myne herte vn to god nyght and
daye / that he wyll shew it all other men. And I sofre all that I can   5
to be a seruant to open theyr eyes.

For well I wott they can not se of them selues before God haue
preuented them wyth his grace. For Paul sayth Philip. i. he that began a good werke in you shall continue or bringe it vn to a full ende /
so that God must begynne to worke in vs. And Philip. ij. God it is   10
that worketh both the willynge and also bryngynge to passe. And it
must nedes be / for god must open mine eyes & shew me some what
& make me se the goodnesse of it / to draw me to him / yer I can
loue / consent or haue any actuall wyll to come. And when I am
willynge / he must assiste me and helpe to tame my flesh / & to   15
ouercome the occasions of the worlde & the power of the fendes.
God therfore hath a speciall care for his electe / in so moch that he
wyll shorten the weked dayes for their sakes in which no man / if
they shuld continue / might endure. And Paul sofereth all for the
electe .ij. Timothe .ij. And gods sure fundacion stondeth sayth   20
Paul / god knoweth his. So [P8] that refuse the trouth who shall /
god wyll kepe a numbre of his mercye / & call them out of blyndnesse / to testifie the trueth vn to the rest / that their damnacion
maye be with out excuse.

The turcke / the Iew and the popish bild vppon frewyll and as-   25
scribe their iustifienge vn to their workes. The turke when he hath
synned / runeth to the purifienges or ceremonies of Mahomete / and
the Iew to the ceremonies of Moses / and the pope vn to his awne
ceremonies / to fette forgeuenesse of their synnes. And the christen
goeth thorow repentaunce towarde the lawe / vn to the faith that is   30
in Christes bloude.

And the pope saith that the ceremonies of Moyses iustified not /
compelled with the wordes of Paul. And how then shuld his iustifie?
Moses sacramentes were but signes of promises of fayth / by whych
fayth the beleuers ar iustified / and euen so be Christes also. And   35

8 Philip. 1.   9 Phil. 2.   17 Mat. 24.

now because the Iewes haue put out the significacions of their sacramentes and put their trust in the workes of them / therfore they be
Idolaters / and so is the pope for like purpose. The pope sayth that
Christ dyed not for vs but for the sacramentes / to geue them power
5   to iustifie. O Antichriste.

xj.

His .xj. chapter is as true as his storie of vtopia and all his other
poetrie. He meaneth doctoure Ferman person of hony lane. Whom
after they had handelled after their secret maner and disputed wyth
10   secretly and had made him swere that he shuld not vtter how he was
dealte wyth / as they haue made many other / then they contriued a
maner of dispicions had [P8v] with him / with soch opposicions /
answerynges & argumentes as shuld serue only to sett forth their
purpose. As master More thorow out all his boke maketh / quod
15   he / to dispute and moue questions after soch a maner as he can soyle
them or make them appere soyled / and maketh him graunte where
he listeth and at the last to be concluded and led wother Master More
wyll haue him. Wherfore I wyll not reherse all the argumentes / for
it were to longe / and is also not to be beleued that he so made them
20   or so disputed with them / but that they added and pulled awaye and
fayned as they liste as their gise is. But I wyll declare in light that
which Master More ruffeleth vpp in darkenesse / that ye maye se
their falshed.

First if ye were not false ypocrites / why had ye not disputed
25   openly with him / that the world might haue hearde and born recorde / that that whych ye now saye of him were true? what cause
is there that the laye people might not as well haue hearde his wordes
of his awne mouth / as reade them of youre wrytynge / excepte ye
were iuglynge spirites that walke in darkenesse?
30   When Master More saith the church teacheth that men shuld not
trust in their workes / it is false if he mene the popis church. For they

7–8 Doctor ferman

6 xj.] The xj. Chapter. *1573*   12 dispicions] disputations *1573*   14 quod]
quoth *1573*   24 ypocrites] *ed.*, ypocrires *1531*, hypocrites *1573*

teach a man to trust in domme ceremonyes and sacramentes / in penaunce and all maner workes that come them to profite / whych yet helpe not vnto repentaunce ner to fayth ner to loue a mans neyboure.

Master More declareth the meaninge of no sentence he describeth the propir significacion of no worde ner the difference of the significa[Q1]cions of any terme / but runneth forth confusedly in vnknowen wordes and general termes. And were one worde hath many significacions he maketh a man some time beleue that manye thinges are but one thynge / and some time he leadeth from one significacion vn to a nother and mocketh a mans wittes. As he iugleth with thys terme church / makynge vs in the begynnynge vnderstonde all that beleue and in the conclusyon the prestes only. He telleth not the office of the lawe / he describeth not his penaunce ner the vertue therof or vse / he declareth no sacrament / ner what they meane ner the vse ner wherin the frute off confession stondeth / ner whence the power of the absolucion cometh / ner wherein it resteth / ner what iustifienge meaneth / ner the ordir ner sheweth any diuersite of faithes / as though all faithes were one faith and one thinge.

Marke therfore / the waye towarde iustifienge or forgeuenesse of sinne / is the lawe. God causeth the lawe to be preached vn to vs and wryteth yt in oure hertes and maketh vs by good reasons fele that the lawe is good and ought to be kept and that they which kepe it not are worthy to be damned. And on the other syde I fele that there ys no power in me / to kepe the lawe where vppon it wold shortly folow that I shud dyspeare / if I were not shortly holpe.

But God which hath begon to cure me and hath layde that corosy vn to my sores / goeth forth in hys cure / and setteth hys sonne Iesus before me and all hys passyons and deeth / and saith to me: thys is my dere sonne / and he hath prayed for the and hath sofred all thys for the / and for hys sake I wil forgeue the al that thou hast done agenst thys good lawe / and I wyll heale [Q1v] thy flesh and teach

5

10

15

20

25

30

21–23 The order of iustifienge

the to kepe thys lawe / if thou wilt lerne. And wyll beare wyth the
and take al a worth that thou doest / tyll thou canst doo better. And
in the meane season / not wythstondynge thy wekenesse / I wyll yet
loue the no lesse then I doo the angels in heauen / so thou wylt be
5   delygent to lerne. And I wyll assiste the and kepe the and defende
the and be thy shilde and care for the.

And the herte here begynneth to mollyfye and wax softe and to
receaue health and beleueth the mercy of God and in beleuynge is
saued from feare of euerlastynge deeth and made sure off euerlast-
10   ynge lyfe / and then beinge ouercome wyth thys kindnesse / begynneth too loue agayne and to submitte hyr selfe vn to the lawe of God
to lerne them and to walke in them.

Note now the ordyr / first God geueth me light to se the goodnesse and ryghtwysnesse off the lawe and mine awne synne and
15   vnryghtwesnesse. Out of whych knowlege springeth repentaunce.
Now repentaunce teacheth me not that the law ys good / and I euell /
but a lyght that the spyryte off God hath geuen me / out off whych
lyght repentaunce springeth.

Then the same spirite worketh in myne herte trust and confidence
20   to beleue the mercye of God and hys trueth / that he wyll doo as he
hath promised. Whych beleffe saueth me. And immediatly out of
that trust springeth loue towarde the lawe of god agayne. And what
soeuer a man werketh of any other loue then thys it pleaseth not
God / ner is that loue Godly. Now loue doeth not receaue thys
25   mercy but [Q2] fayth only / out of which fayth loue springeth / by
which loue I power out agayne vppon my neyboure that goodnesse
wych I haue receaued of God by fayth. Here of ye se that I can not
be iustified wyth out repentaunce and yet repentaunce iustyfieth me
not. And here of ye se that I can not haue a faith to be iustified and
30   saued / excepte loue springe therof immediatly / and yet loue iustifieth me not before God. For my naturall loue to god agayne doeth
not make me first se and fele the kyndnesse of God in christ / but
fayth thorow preachinge. For we loue not God first / to compel him

1 And] And I *1573*   9 feare] the feare *1573*

to loue agayne: but he loued vs first and gaue hys sonne for vs / that
we might se loue and loue agayne / sayth sent Ihon in hys first epistle. Whych loue of God to vs warde we receaue by Christ thorow
fayth saith Paule. And thys ensample haue I sett out for them in dyuers places / but their blinde popysh eyes haue no power too se it /   5
couetousnesse hath so blinded them. And when we saye fayth only
iustifyeth vs / that ys to saye / receaueth the mercye wherewyth God
iustifyeth vs and forgeueth vs / we meane not fayth whych hath noo
repentaunce and fayth whych hath no loue vn to the lawes off God
agayne and vn to good werkes / as wyked ypocrytes falsly belie vs.   10

For how then shulde we sofre as we doo all mysery / too call the
blynde and ygnoraunte vn to repentaunce and good werkes / whych
now doo but consent vn to all euell and studye mischeue all daye
longe / for al theyr preachynge their iustifyenge of good workes.
Let Master Moore ymproue thys wyth hys sophystrye and sett forth   15
hys awne doctryne that we maye [Q2v] se the reason of yt and
walke in light.

Herof ye se what faith it is that iustifyeth vs. The faith in christes
bloude of a repentinge herte towarde the lawe doeth iustifie vs onli
and not all maner faythes. Ye must vnderstond therfore / that ye   20
maye se to come out of Mores blinde mase / how that there be many
faithes and that all faythes be not one fayth / though they be all called
with on generall name. There is a story fayth with out felynge in the
herte / where with I maye beleue the hole story of the bybble and yet
not sett myne herte ernestly therto / takynge yt for the fode of my   25
soule / too lerne to beleue and trust God / to loue him / dreade him
and feare him by the doctrine and ensamples therof / but to seme
lerned and to know the story / to dispute and make marchaundice /
after as we haue ensamples ynowe. And the faith wherwith a man
doeth miracles / is a nother gyft then the fayth of a repentinge herte   30
to be saued thorow christes bloude / and the one no kynne too the
other though Master More wold haue them so appere. Nether is the

---

1 1. Ioan .4.   18–20 What fayth iustifyeth

5 popysh eyes] *ed.*, popysheyes *1531*, Popish eyes *1573*   10 vs.] *1573*, vs?
1531   15 sophystrye] *ed.*, sopystrye *1531*, sophistrie *1573*   29 ynowe] ynough
1573

deuels fayth and popis faith (where wyth they beleue that there ys a
god and that chryst ys and all the story off the byble and maye yet
stonde wyth all wekednesse and full consent too euell) kynne vnto
the fayth of them that hate evell and repent off their mysdedes and
5   knowlege their synnes and be fled with ful hope and truste off mercye vn to the bloude off Christ.

And when he sayth / yf fayth certyfye oure hertes that we be in
the fauoure off God and oure synnes forgeuen and become good yer
we doo good werkes / as the tre must be first good [Q3] yer it
10   bringe forth good frute / by christes doctrine then we make good
workes but a shadowe where with a man is neuer the better. Naie
Sir we make good werkes / frutes where by oure neyboure is the
better and wherby God is honoured and oure flesh tamed. And we
make of them sure tokens where by we know that our faith is no
15   fayned imaginacion and deed opinion made with captiuynge oure
wyttes after the popis tradicions / but a lyuely thinge wrought by
the holygoste.

And when he disputeth / if they that haue faith / haue loue vn to
the law and purpose to fulfill it / then fayth alone iustifieth not / how
20   will he proue that argument? he iugleth with this worde alone: and
wold make the people beleue that we said / how a bare faith that is
with out all other companye / of repentaunce / loue and other
vertues / ye and with out gods spirite to / did iustifie vs / so that we
shuld not care to doo good. But the scripture so taketh not alone ner
25   we so meane / as Master More knoweth well ynough. When an
horse bereth a sadell and a man therin / we maye well saye / that the
horse only and alone bereth the sadell / and is not holpe of the man
in beringe therof. But he wold make men vnderstonde that we
ment / the horse bare the sadell emptie and no man therin: let him
30   marke this to se his ignoraunce / which wold god were not coupled
with malice. Euery man that hath witte / hath a will to and then by
master mores argument / witte only geueth not the light of vnderstondynge. Now the conclusion is false and the contrary true. For

7 Workes   18 Alone   25 Similitude

10 christes] ed., cbristes 1531, Christes 1573   13 God] 1573, Gos 1531
S2 Alone] Fayth alone iustifieth. 1573   S3 Similitude] A similitude 1573

the witte with out helpe of the will geueth the light of the
vnderstondynge / nether doeth the will worke [Q3v] at all / vntyll
the wytt haue determined thys or that to be good or bad. Now what
is faith saue a spirituall lyght of vnderstondinge and an inwarde
knowlege or felynge of marcie. Out of whych knowlege loue doeth   5
springe. But loue brought me not that knowlege / for I knew yt yer
I loued. So that loue in the processe off nature to dyspute from the
cause to the effecte helpeth not at all to the felynge that God is mercifull to me no moare than the louynge herte and kynd behavoure of
an obedyent wyfe to hir husbonde / maketh hyr se hys loue and   10
kyndenesse to hir / for many soch haue vnkynde husbandes. But by
hys kynde dedes to hir doeth she se his loue. Euen so my loue &
dedes make me not se Gods loue to me in the processe of nature: but
hys kynde dedes to me / in that he gaue his sonne for me maketh me
se his loue and to loue agayne.   15

Oure loue and good werkes make not god first loue vs / and
chaunge hym from hate to loue / as the Turke / Iew and vayne popish meane but hys loue and dedes make vs loue and chaunge vs from
hate to loue. For he loued vs when we were euell and hys enimies as
testifieth Paul in dyuers places and chose vs to make vs good and to   20
shew vs loue and to draw vs to hym / that we shuld loue agayne.

The father loueth hys chyld / when yt hath no power to doo good
and when yt must be sofered to runne after the awne lustes wyth out
lawe / and neuer loueth yt better then then / to make yt better and
too shewe yt loue / to loue agayne. Yf he coude se what ys wrytten   25
in the fyrst pistle of Ihon / though al the other scripture were layed
aparte / he shuld se all thys.

[Q4] And ye must vnderstonde / that we some tyme dispute
forwarde / from the cause to the effecte and some tyme backwarde
from the effecte to the cause / and must beware that we be not ther-   30
with begyled / we saye somer is come and therfore all is grene / and
dispute forwarde. For somer is the cause of the grenesse. We saye
the trees be grene / and therfore somer is come / and dispute back-

---

19 Roma. 5.   32 [Hand]

26 pistle] epistle *1573*

warde from the effecte to the cause / For the grenetrees make not
somer / but maketh somer knowen. So we dispute backwarde / the
man doeth good dedes and profitable vn to his neyboure / he must
therfore loue god: he loueth god / he must therfore haue a true fayth
5   and se mercye.

     And yet my workes make not my loue ner my loue my fayth ner
my fayth Gods mercye: But contrary / Gods mercye maketh my
fayth and my fayth my loue and my loue my workes. And if the
pope coude se mercy and worke of loue to his neyboure and not sell
10 his workes to god for heuen after Master Mores doctrine / we neded
not so sotle disputynge of fayth.

     And when Master More allegeth Paul to the Corinthians / to
proue that fayth maye be wyth out loue / he proueth nothynge / but
iugleth only. He sayth it is euident by the wordes of Paul / that a
15 man maye haue a fayth to doo miracles wyth out loue and maye
geue all his good in almes with out loue / and geue his body to burne
for the name of Christe / and all with out charite. Well I wyll not
stycke wyth him: he maye so doo wyth out charite and wyth out
fayth therto. Then a man maye haue fayth wyth out fayth. Ye verely
20 because there be many differences of fayth / as I haue sayde / [Q4v]
and not all faythes one faith / as master More iugleth. We read in the
workes of S. Cipriane / that there were marters that sofred marterdom for the name of christ al the yere longe / and were tormented
and healed agayne and then brought forth afreshe. Which marters
25 beleued / as ye doo / that the payne of their marterdome shuld be a
deseruinge and merite ynough / not only to deserue heuen for them
selues / but to make satisfaccion for the synnes of other men therto /
and gaue pardons of their merites after the ensample of the popis
doctrine and forgaue the synnes of other men which had openly de-
30 nyed christe / and wrote vn to Cipriane / that he shuld receaue those
men that had denied christe in to the congregacion agayne / at the
satisfaccion of their merites. For which pride Cipriane wrote to
them & called them the deuels marters and not Gods. Those marters

---

22 Cipriane   24–27 Marters that sofered al a yere longe

3–4 neyboure / . . . must] *ed.*, neyboure . . . m/st *1531*, neyghbour, . . . must
1573   25 the] *1573*, he *1531*

had a faith without faith. For had they beleued that all mercy is
geuen for christes bloudeshedynge / they whold haue sent other
men thither / and wold haue sofered their awne marterdom for loue
of their neyboures only / to sarue them and to testifie the trueth of
god in oure sauioure Iesu / vnto the worlde / to saue at the least waye   5
some / that is to wete / the electe / for whose sake Paule sofereth al
thinge and not to winne heuen. Yf I worke for a worldely purpose /
I get no rewarde in heuen: euen so if I worke for heuen or an hier
place in heuen I gett there no rewarde. But I must doo my worke
for the loue of my neyboure / because he is my brother and the price   10
of Christes bloude and because christe hath deserued it and dysyreth
it of me / and then my rewarde is greate in heuen.

[Q5] And all they whych beleue that their synnes be forgeuen
them and they receaued as the scripture testifieth / vn to the enheri-
taunce of heuen for Christes merites / the same loue christ & their   15
brethern for his sake and doo all thynge for their sakes only / not
once thynkinge of heuen / when they worke / but on their bretherns
neade. When they sofre them selues aboue might / then they comforte their soule with the remembraunce of heuen / that this wrech-
ednesse shall haue an ende and we shall haue a thousandfold plea-   20
sures and rewardes in heuen / not for the merites of oure
deseruynges but geuen vs frely for Christes. And he that hath that
loue hath the right faith. And he that hath that faith hath the right
loue. For I can not loue my neyboure for Christes sake / excepte I
first beleue that I haue receaued soch mercy of Christe. Ner can I   25
beleue that I haue receaued soch mercy of Christ / but that I must
loue my neyboure for his sake / seinge that he so instantly desyreth
me.

And when he allegeth S. Iames / it is answered him in the mammon / and S. Augustine answereth him. And saynt Iames expound-   30
eth him selfe. For he saith in the first chapter / God whych begatt vs
of his awne wyll with the worde of trueth / which worde of trueth is
his promises of mercye and forgeuenesse in oure sauioure Iesus / by

29 Iames .2.

1 without] ed., withont 1531, without 1573   32 trueth / . . . trueth] ed., trueth
. . . trueth / 1531, truth, . . . truth, 1573

whych he begatt vs / gaue vs life & made vs a new creature thorow
a fast fayth. And Iames goeth and rebuketh the opinion & false fayth
of them that thynke it ynough to be saued by / iff they beleue that
there is but one god and that Christ was borne of a virgen and a
5   thousand thynges whych a man may beleue. And yet not beleue in
Christe / to be saued from [Q5v] sinne thorow him. And that Iames
speaketh of a nother fayth then at the begynnynge appereth by his
ensample. The deuelles haue fayth saith he: ye but the deuels haue
no fayth that can repent of euell or to beleue in Christ / to be saued
10   thorow him / or that can loue god and worke his will of loue. Now
Paul speaketh of a faith that is in Christes bloude to be saued therby /
which worketh immediatly thorow loue of the benefite receaued.
And Iames at the beginninge speaketh of a faith that bydeth trienge
sayenge / the trienge of youre fayth worketh or causeth paciens. But
15   the faith of the deuels wyll byde no trienge / for they wyll not worke
gods wyll because they loue him not. And in like maner is it of the
fayth of them that repent not or that thynke them selues with out
synne. For except a man fele out of what daunger Christ hath delyuered him / he can not loue the worke. And therfore Iames saith
20   right / that no soch faith that wyll not worke can iustifie a man.

And when Paul saith faith only iustifieth: and Iames / that a man is
iustified by werkes and not by fayth only / there is greate difference
betwene Pauls only and Iameses only. For Paules only is to be vnderstonde / that fayth iustifieth in the hert and before god / wyth out
25   helpe of werkes / ye and yer I can worke. For I must receaue life
thorow fayth to worke wyth / yer I can worke. But Iames only is
this wise to be vnderstonde / that faith doeth not so iustifie / that no
thynge iustifieth saue fayth / For dedes doo iustifie also. But fayth
iustifieth in the herte and before god / and the dedes before the world
30   only and maketh the other sene as ye maye se by the scripture.

[Q6] For Paul saith Roma. iiij. if Abraham haue workes / he hath
wherof to reioce / but not before god. For if Abraham had receaued
those promises of deseruynge / then had it bene Abrahams prayse

27–29 How workes iustefye   33 Roma. 4.

---

23 Iameses] Iames *1573*

and not gods / as thou maist se in the texte: nether had god shewed Abraham mercy and grace / but had only geuen him his dutie and deseruinge. But in that Abraham receaued all the mercie that was shewed him / frely thorow fayth / out of the deseruinges of the seed that was promised him / as thou maist se by Genesis and by the gos- 5 pell of Ihon / where Christ testifieth that Abraham saw his daye and reioysed / and of that ioye nodoute wrought / it is gods prayse / and the glory of his mercye. And the same maist thou se by Iames / when he saith Abraham offered his sonne / and so was the scripture fulfilled / that Abraham beleued / and it was rekened him for right- 10 wysnesse and he was therby made gods frende.

How was it fulfilled? before god? Naye / it was fulfilled before god manye yeres before / & he was gods frende many yeres before / euen from the first appoynttment that was made betwene god and him. Abraham receaued promises of all mercie and beleued and 15 trusted god & went & wrought out of that faith. But it was fulfilled before vs which can not se the herte / as Iames sayth / I wyll shew the my fayth out of my workes / and as the angell said to Abraham / now I know that thou dreadest god. Not but that he knew it before / but for vs spake he that / whych can se nought in Abraham moare 20 then in other men / saue by his workes.

And what workes ment Iames? verely the wor[Q6v]kes of mer- cye. As if a brother or a sister lacke rayment or sustinaunce and ye be not moued to compassion ner fele their diseases / whate fayth haue ye then? No faith (be sure) that feleth the mercye that is in 25 Christe. For they that fele that / be mercifull ageyne and thankefull. But loke on the werkes of oure spiritualtie which wyll not only be iustified with werkes before the world / but also before god. They haue had all christendome to rule this .viij. hundred yeres / and as they only be annoynted in the heed / so haue they only bene kynge 30 and emproure and haue had al power in their handes and haue bene the doers only and the leders of those shadowes that haue had the name of princes / and haue led them whother they wolde and haue brethed in to their braynes what they listed. And they haue wrought the world out of peace and vnite and euery man out of his wellfare 35

6 Ioan .8.

and are become alone well at ease / only fre / only at liberte / only
haue all thynge and only do nought therfore / only laye on other
mennes backes and beare nought them selues. And the good werkes
of them that wrought out of faith and gaue their goodes and landes
5   to finde the pore / them deuoure they also alone. And what workes
preach they? Only that ar to them profitable and wherby they raigne
in mens consciences as god: to offer / to geue to be prayed for and
to be deliuered out of purgatory and to redeme youre synne of
them / and to worshepe ceremonies and to be shryuen and so forth.
10   And when Master More is come to him selfe & sayth the first fayth
and the first iustifienge is geuen vs with out oure deseruinge. God
be thanked / and I wold fayne that he wold de[Q7]scribe me what
he meaneth by the seconde iustifienge. I know no moare to doo /
then when I haue receaued all mercy and all forgeuenesse of Christ
15   frely / to goo and powre out the same vppon my neyghboure.
      M. Dauid lost not his faith / when he committed adultery. T. No /
and therfore he coude not continue in synne / but repented assone
as his faulte was told him. But was he not reconsyled by fayth only /
and not by dedes? sayd he not haue mercy on me lorde for thy greate
20   mercye and for the multitude of thy mercies put awaye my synne.
And agayne / make me heare ioye & gladnesse / that the bones
which thou hast broken maye reioyse. That is latt me heare thy
voyce that my synne is forgeuen and then I am saffe and wyll reioyse. And afterward he knowlegeth that god delyteth not in sacri-
25   fices for synnes / but that a troubled spirite and a broken herte is that
whych god requireth. And when the peace was made / he prayeth
boldly and familiarly to god / that he wold be good to Sion and Ierusalem / and sayth that then last of all when god hath forgeuen vs
of mercy / and hath done vs good for our euell / we shall offer sacri-
30   fice of thankes to him agayne. So that our dedes are but thankesgeu-
ynge. When we haue sinned / we goo with a repentynge herte vn to
Christes bloude / and there wash it of thorow faith. And oure dedes
are but thankes geuenge to god to helpe oure neyboures at their

---

16 More   17 David   18 Tindale   20 Psal. 51.

---

5 pore /] *ed.*, pore *1531*, poore, *1573*   8 purgatory] *ed.*, purgarory *1531*, Purgatory *1573*

nede / for which oure neyboures and ech of them owe vs as moch
agayne at oure nede. So that the testament of forgeuenesse of
synnes / is bylt vppon faith in christes bloude and not on workes.
Master More wyll runne to the pope for forgeuenesse a pena & culpa.
[Q7v] By what merites doeth the pope that? by Christes. And
Christ hath promised all his merites to them that repent & beleue
and not geuen them vn to the pope to sell. And in youre absolucions
ye oft absolue wyth out ioynynge of penaunce. He must haue a purpose to doo good werkes wyll ye saye. That condicion is sett before
him to doo / out of the mercy that he hath receaued & not to receaue
mercie out of them. But the popish can not repent out of the hert.
And therfore can not fele the mercie that faith bryngeth / & therfore
can not be mercifull to their neyboures to doo their werkes for their
sakes. But they fayne them a sorow for their synne in whych they
euer continue and so morne for them in the mornynge that they
laugh in them yer middaye agayne. And then they imagen them
popish dedes / to make satisfaccion to God and make an Idole of
him.

And fynally that good workes / as to geue almes and soch like /
iustifie not of them selues / is manifeste. For as the good which are
taught of god doo them well / of very loue to god and Christ and of
their neybours for Christes sake / even so the euell doo them of
vayne glorie and a false faith wykedly / as we haue ensamples in the
phareses / so that a man must be good yer he can doo good. And so
is it of the purpose to doo them: Ones purpose is good and a nothers
evell: so that we must be good yer a good purpose come. How then /
to loue the law of god and to consent therto and to haue it written
in thine hert and to professe it / so that thou art ready of thyne awne
accorde to doo it and wyth out compultion / is to be righteous: that I
graunt and that loue maye be called rightwysnesse before God [Q8]
passiue and the life and quickenesse of the soule passiue. And sofer-
forth as a man loueth the law of god / so forforth he is righteous /
and so moch as he lacketh of loue toward his neiboure after the en-

---

3–4 Pena culpa   19–22 Workes of them selues iustefye not.

2 testament of] Testament or 1573   17 Idole] 1573, Iodole 1531

sample of Christe / so moch he lacketh of rightwysnesse. And that
thynge whych maketh a man loue the lawe of god / doth make a
man righteous and iustifieth him effectiuely and actually and maketh
him alyue as a worke man & cause efficient. Now what is it that
5   maketh a man to love? verely not the dedes / for they folow and
springe of loue / if they be good. Nether the preachynge of the law /
for that quickeneth not the herte Gala. iij. but causeth wrath Rom.
iiij. and vttereth the synne only Romanorum .iij. And therfore sayth
Paule that rightewysnesse spryngeth not out of the dedes of the law
10   in to the herte / as the Iewes and the pope meane: but contrary the
dedes of the law sprynge out of the rightwysnesse of the hert if they
be good. As when a father pronounceth the law / that the child shall
goo to scole / it saith naye. For that killeth his hert and all his lustes /
so that he hath no power to loue it. But what maketh his herte aliue
15   to loue it? verely fayre promises of loue and kindnesse / that it shall
haue a gentle scolemaster and shall playe ynough and shall haue
many gaye thynges and so forth. Even so the preachynge of fayth
doth worke loue in oure soules and make them aliue and draw our
hertes to God. The mercye that we haue in Christ doeth make vs
20   loue only and only bryngeth the spirite of life in to our soules.

And therfore saith Paul / we be iustified by fayth and by grace
with out dedes: that is / yer [Q8v] the dedes come. For faith only
bringeth / the spirite of life and deliuereth our soules from feare of
damnacion / which is in the law and euer maketh peace betwene god
25   and vs / as oft as there is any variaunce betwene vs. And finally when
the peace is made betwene god and vs and all forgeuen thorow faith
in Christes bloude / and we begynne to loue the lawe / we were
neuer the nere excepte faith went with vs / to supplye out the lacke
of full loue / in that we haue promises / that that litle we haue is take
30   aworth & accepted tyll moare come. And agayne when our frailtie
hath ouerthrowen vs and feare of damnacion invadeth our consciences / we were vtterly lost / if fayth were not bye to helpe vs vpp
agayne / in that we are promised that when soeuer we repent of euell
and come to the right waye agayne / it shalbe forgeuen for Christes

sake. For when we be fallen / there is no testament made in werkes
to come / that they shal saue vs. And therfore the werkes of repentaunce or of the sacramentes can neuer quiet our consciences and
deliuer vs from feare of damnacion. And last of all in temptacions
tribulacion and aduersites / we perished dayly excepte fayth went   5
with vs to deliuer vs / in that we haue promises / that god wyll assiste us / cloth vs / fede vs and fight for vs and rid vs out of the
handes of oure enimies. And thus the rightewysse liueth euer bye
faith / even from faith to faith / that is / as sone as he is deliuered out
of one temptacion a nother is sett before him to feighte agenst and   10
to ouercome thorow fayth. The scripture sayth / blessed is the man
whose transgression is forgeuen & his synnes hid / and vn to whom
the lorde rekeneth not vnrightwysnesse. So that the only right-
[R1]wysnesse of him that can but synne and hath nought of hym
selfe to make amendes / is the forgeuenesse of sinne / which faith   15
only bringeth. And as forforth as we be vnryghtwese / faith only
iustifieth vs actiuely and else nothinge on our partie. And as ferforth
as we haue synned / be in sinne or do synne or shall synne / so ferforth must fayth in christes bloud iustifie vs only and else nothynge.
To loue / is to be rightwesse so ferforth as thou louest / but not to   20
make rightwesse / ner to make peace. To beleue in christes bloud
with a repentinge hert is to make rightwesse and the only makynge
of peace and satisfaccion to godwarde. And thus because termes be
darke to them that be not experte and excercysed / we all waye sett
out our meanynge wyth clere ensamples / reportynge our selues vn   25
to the hertes and consciences of all men.

   M. the blasphemous wordes of luther seme to signifie / that both
saynt Ihon baptiste & oure ladie were synners. T. Ihon baptiste sayde
too christ .Mat .iij. I had nede to be baptised of the and comest thou
to me? wherof did Ihon confesse that he had nede to be washed and   30
purged by chryste / off hys holynesse and good dedes? when Ihon
sayd / behold the lambe off god that taketh a waye the synne of the
worlde / he was not off that sorte ner had any synnes to be taken

---

8 [Hand]   26 More   27 Tyndale

4 temptacions] temptation *1573*   16 vnryghtwese] *ed.*, vnryghwese *1531*,
vnrighteous *1573*

awaie at any time / ner any parte in christes bloude whych dyed for
synners only. Ihon came too restore all thynge sayth christ. That is /
he came to enterpret the law of God truly and to proue all flesh synners / too send them to Christe / as paul doeth in the begynnynge
5   off the Romans. Whych law if Master More coude vnderstonde how
spirituall yt ys and what yt requireth off [R1v] vs / he wolde not so
dyspute. And yf there were no imperfectenesse in oure ladies dedes /
whi did christ rebuke hyr Ihon .ij. when he ought rather to haue
honoured hys mother / and why did he make hir seke him .iij.
10 dayes. Chrisostimus dare saye / that our lady was now & then taken
wyth a litle vayne glorie. She loked for the promises off hym that
shulde come and blesse hyr / from what? She beleued to be saued by
christ / from what? Thys I graunt / that our lady / Ihon baptiste /
Isaac / Iacob / Ioseph / Moses and many lyke / dyd neuer consent
15 too synne / to folow it: But had the holy gost from the bygynnynge.
Neuer the later whyle they folowed the spirite and wrought theyr
best / yet chaunces met them by the waye and temptacyons / that
made theyr werkes come some tymes vnperfectely too passe / as a
potter that hath hys craft neuer so well / meteth a chaunce now and
20 then / that maketh hym facyon a pott amisse. So that I thinke the
perfectest of them all as we haue ensamples off some / were compelled to saye wyth Paull / that good that I wold / I doo not and that
euell that I wolde nott / that I doo. I wolde not sweere on a boke
that yf our lady had bene let slipp as woother were and as harde ap-
25 posed wyth as present deeth before hyr eyes / that she wolde not
haue denyed some thynges that she knewe true. Ye but she was preserved by grace that she was not. No but though she were kepte by
grace from the outwarde dede / yet yf theyr were soch wekenesse
in hyr flesh / she had synne. And the grace was / that she knew it
30 and was meke too beleue in chryst / too haue yt forgeuen hyr and
too be preserued that yt shulde not bud forth. Ihon the euangelyst /
when he was as [R2] holy as euer was Ihon the baptyst said / yf we
saye we haue no synne / we dysceaue oure selues.

9–10 Chrisostymus   32 1. Ioan .1.

24 woother] we other 1573   28 wekenesse] wickednes 1573   29 it] 1573,
yet 1531

Then he compareth faith and dedes too gether and wyll that fayth shulde stonde in no beter seruice off ryght then dedes. Yes / for the dedes be examined by the law / and therfore yt ys not ynough too doo them only / or to doo them wyth loue: but I must doo them wyth as greate loue as christ dyd for me / and as I receaue a good dede at my nede. But fayth ys vnder no lawe / and therfore be she neuer so feble / she shal receaue acordynge too the trueth off the promyser.

M. what thynge coude we axe god of ryght because we beleue hym? T. verely all that he promyseth / maye we be bold to axe of right and dutye and by good obligation.

M. Ferman said that all workes be good ynough in them that god hath chosen. T. I am sure yt ys vntrue / for their best be not good ynough / though God forgeueth them their euell of hys mercye / at the repentaunce of theyr hertes.

Then he endeth in hys scole doctryne contrary vn to all the scripture / that god remitteth not the synne of his chosen people / because that he hath chosen them or of hys mercye / but off a towardnesse that ys moare in one then in another sayenge God sawe before that Peter shuld repent and Iudas wolde dyspeare / and therfore chose Peter. If God chose Peter because he dyd repent / why chose he not Iudas to / which repented as moch as he and knowleged hys synne and brought the money agayne? O thys [R2v] blyndenesse / as god had wrought nothynge in the repentaunce of peter. Sayd not christ before / that peter shuld faull. And sayd he not that he had prayed for hym that he shulde be holpe vpp agayne? Christ prayed a stronge prayer for peter to helpe hym vpp agayne and sofred a stronge deeth therto. And before his deeth he committed them vn to hys father saynge I haue kepte them in thy name & I departe / kepe them now from euell. Peter had a good hert too god and loued his lawe and beleued in christe and had the spirite of god in him which neuer left him for all his faull. Peter sinned of no malice / but of frailtie & so-

5

10

15

20

25

30

1–3 Workes are vnder the lawe.   4–6 Faith ys vnder no lawe.
9 More   10 Tyndale   11 More   12 Tindale   24 Luce .22.
28 Ioan .17.

---

18 or] not 1573

den feare of deeth. And the goodnesse of God wrought hys repentaunce and all the meanes by whych he was brought vpp agayne
at christes requeste. And Iudas was neuer good ner came to christ
for loue of his doctrine / but of couetousnesse / ner dyd euer beleue
5 in christe.

Iudas was by nature and birth (as we all be) heyre of the wrath of
god / in whom the deuel wrought hys will and blynded hys hert
with ignoraunce. In which ignoraunce and blyndnesse he grue / as
he grue in age and fell deper and deper therin / and therby wrought
10 all hys wekednesse and the deuels wyll and perished therin. From
whych ygnoraunce god purged peter off hys mercye and gaue hym
light and hys spirite too gouern hym / and not of any towardnesse
that was in peter off his awne byrth: but for the mercy that we haue
in the birth of chrystes deeth.

15 And how wil M. More proue that god choseth not off hys goodnesse but off oure towardnesse? [R3] what good towardnesse can he
haue and endeuoure that is all to gether blynde and caried awaye at
the wyll of the deuell / tyll the deuell be cast out? Ar we not robbed
of all towardnesse in Adam and be by nature made the childern of
20 synne / so that we synne naturally and to synne is our nature? So
that as now / though we wold doo well / the flesh yet synneth naturally nether ceaseth to synne / but so ferforth as it is kepte vnder
with violence: euen so once our hertes synned as naturally wyth full
lust and consent vn to the flesh / the deuel possessynge our hertes
25 and kepynge out the light of grace. What good towardnesse and endeuoure can we haue to hate synne / as longe as we loue it? what
good towardnesse can we haue vnto the wyll of god / whyle we hate
it and be ignoraunte therof. Can the wyll desyre that the witte seith
not? Can the will longe for and sigh for that the wytt knoweth not
30 of? Can a man take thought for that losse that he wotteth not of?
what good endeuoure can the turkes childern / the Iewes childern
and the popis infantes haue / when they be taught all falshed only
wyth lyke persuasions of worldly reason / to be all iustified with

6 Iudas

12 gouern] *ed.*, geuern *1531*, gouerne *1573*

werkes? It is not therfore as Paul sayth / of the runnynge or willynge
but of the mercye of god / that a man is called and chosen to grace.

The first grace / the first fayth and the first iustifienge is geuen vs
frely sayth Master More. Whych I wold fayne wete how it wyll
stond with his other doctrine / and whether he meane any other   5
thynge by chosynge then to haue gods spirite geuen me and fayth
to se the mercie that is layd vpp for me and to haue my synnes
forgeuen with out all deseruynge and preparynge [R3v] of my selfe
God did not se only that the thefe that was saued at christes deeth /
shuld come thither / but god chose him to shew his mercie vn to vs   10
that shuld aftir beleue / and prouided actually and wrought for the
bringynge of him thither that daye / to make him se and to receaue
the mercie that was layed vpp for him in store / before the world
was made.

<h1 style="text-align:center">xïj.   15</h1>

In the .xij. in chafinge him selfe to hepe lye vppon lye / he vttereth
his feleable blindnesse. For he haxeth this question wherefore serueth exhortacions vn to fayth / if the hearers haue not libertye of their
frewyll / by which to gether with gods grace a man may laboure
to submitte the rebellion of reason vn to the obedience of faith and 20
credence of the worde of God. Whereof ye se / that besydes his
graunt that reason rebelleth agenst faith / contrary to the doctrine of
his first boke / he will that the will shall compell the witte to beleue.
Which is as moch to saye that the carte must draw the horses and
the sonne begett the father / and the auctorite of the church is greater 25
then gods worde. For the will can not teach the witt ner leade hir /
but foloweth naturally: so that what soeuer the witt iudgeth good
or euell / that the wyll loueth or hateth. If the witte se and leade
streight / the will foloweth. If the witt be blinde and lead amisse /
the will foloweth cleane out of the waye. I can not loue gods worde 30
before I beleue it / ner hate it / before I iudge it false and vanite.

---

1 Roma. 9.   20 Frewill   29–31 The witte leadeth the will.

6 then] them *1573*   15 xij.] The xij. Chapter. *1573*   24 that] as *1573*
25 greater] *1573*, greather *1531*

He might haue wiselier spoken on this maner / where fore serueth
the preachynge of faith / if the witt haue no power to draw the will
to loue that which the witte iudgeth true and good. If [R4] the will
be nought / teach the witt better and the will shall alter and turne to
5   good immediatly. Blindnesse is the cause of all euel and light the
cause of al good: so that where the faith is right there the herte can
not consent vnto euell / to folowe the lustes of the fleshe / as the
popes faith doeth. And this conclusion hath he halfe a dosen tymes
in his boke / that the will maye compell the witt and captiuate it / to
10   beleue what a man lusteth. Verelye it is like that his wittes be in captiuite and for vauntage tangled with oure holy fathers sophistrie.

His doctrine is aftir his awne felynge and as the profession of his
herte is. For the popish haue yelded them selues / to folowe the lustes
of their fleshe / and compell their witte to absteyne from lokynge
15   on the trouth lest she shuld vnquiet them and draw them out of the
podell of their filthie voluptuousnesse. As a carte that is ouer laden
goinge vp an hill draweth the horses backe / and in a tough mire
maketh them stonde styll. And then the carter the deuel which driueth
them is euer by and whistelleth vn to them and biddeth them capti-
20   uatt their vnderstondynge vn to profitable doctrine for which they
shall haue no persecucion but shall raigne and be kynges and enioye
the pleasures of the worlde at their awne will.

xiij.

In the .xiij. he saith that the clergie burneth no man. As though
25   the pope had not first found the lawe / & as though al his preachers
babled not that in euery sermon / burne these heretikes burn them
[R4v] for we haue no nother argument too conuince them and as
though they comppelled not both kinge and emproure to swere that
they shall so doo / yer they croune them.
30   Then he bryngeth in prouisions of Kynge Henry the .v. Of whom
I axe M. More whether he were ryght heyre vn to englonde or held

---

16 [Hand]   30–31 Kinge Henry the .v.

11 oure] out *1573*   23 xiij.] The xiij. Chapter. *1573*

he the lande wyth the swerde as an hethen tyraunte / agenst all
ryght. Whom the prelates / lest he shulde haue had leyser too herken
vn to the trouth / sent in to fraunce / too occupie hys mynde in
warre / and led him at their wil. And I axe whether his father slew
not his lege kinge and true enheretoure vnto the croune and was ther-   5
fore set vpp of the bisshops a false kinge to maynetene theyr
falsehed? And I axe whether after that weked dede / folowed not
the destruccion of the comenaltie and quenchynge of all the noble
bloude.

xiiij.   10

In the .xiiij. he affirmeth that Marten luther saieth it is not lawfull
to resiste the turke. I wondre that he shameth not so to lye seynge
that marten hath written a singular tretice for the contrarye / besydes that in many other workes he proueth it laufull / if he invade
vs.   15

xvj.

In the .xvj. he allegeth counsels. I axe whether counsels haue auctorite to make articles of the faith with out gods worde / ye and of
thynges improued by gods worde?

He allegeth Augustine / Hierom and Cipriane. Let him put their   20
workes in english and S. prosperus with them. Whi damned they
the vnion of doctoures / but be cause the doctours are agenst them.

[R5] And when he allegeth marters / lett him shew one and take
the calfe for his laboure.

And in the end he biddeth bewarre of them that liue well in any   25
wise. As though they whych liue euell can not teach amisse. And if
that be true then they be of the surest syde.

M. when Tindale was apposed of his doctrine / yer he went ouer

---

12 [Hand]   27 [Hand]   28 More

8 the noble] noble *1573*   10 xiiij.] The xiiij. Chapter. *1573*   12 turke.] *ed.*,
turke *1531*, Turke. *1573*   13 contrarye /] *ed.*, contrary. *1531, 1573*   16 xvj.]
The xvj. Chapter. *1573*

se/ he said and sware / he ment no harme. T. he sware not nether
was there any man that required an oth of him: but he now swereth
by him whom he trusteth to be saued by / that he neuer ment or yet
meaneth any other harme then to sofre all that god hath prepared to
be leyd on his backe / for to brynge his brothern vn to the light of
our sauiour Ihesus which the pope thorow falshed and corruptynge
soch poetes as ye are (ready vn to all thynge for vauntage) leadeth in
the darkenesse of deeth.

M. Tyndale doeth know how that S. Augustine & S. Hierom doo
proue with holy scripture that confession is of necessite vn to saluacion. T. that is false if ye meane eareconfession. Whi allege ye not
the places where? But ye knowe by S. Hierom and other stories and
by the conuersation with Erasmus / how it come vpp and that the
vse was once ferre other then now.

M. I meruell that Tyndale denieth purgatory / excepte he entende
to goo too hell. T. he entendeth to purge here vn to the vttermost
of his power and hopeth that deeth wyll ende and fynish his purgacion. And if there be any other purgynge / he wyll committe it to
god and take it as he findeth it / when he cometh at it / & in the
meane tyme take no thought therfore / but for this that is present
where with all sayntes were purged & were taught so to be. And
Tyndale [R5v] maruelith what secret pilles they take to purge them
selues which not only wil not purge here with the crosse of christe /
but also bye out their purgatory there of the pope / for a grote or
.vj. pens.

xviij.

M. the clergie doeth nothynge vn to the heretikes but as the holy
doctours did. T. yes ye put them in youre presones and diote them
and handle them after youre facion as temporall tirauntes / and dispute with them secretly & wil not come at light. And ye sle them

| 1–2 Tindale | swereth. | 9 More | 11 Tindale | 15 More |
| 16 Purgatori | 17 Tyndale | 27 More | 28 Clargye | 29 Tyndale |

1 and sware] and sweare *1573*   13 come] came *1573*   26 xviij.] The xviij.
Chapter. *1573*

for rebukynge you with Gods worde / and so did not the old holy
doctours. If a man sle his father / ye care not. But if any man twich
one of you though he haue neuer so greate an occasyon geuen hym /
ye curse him / and yf he wyll not submitte him selfe vn to youre
punishement / ye leaue him vn to the temporall power whom ye   5
haue hyred with the spoyle of his goodes to be youre hangman / so
that he must lose hys lyfe / for geuinge one of you but a blow on the
cheke.

   M. Saynt paul gaue .ij. heretikes vn to the deuell whych tormented their flesh which was no small punishment and haply he   10
slew them. T. O expounder of the scripture like hugo charensys
which expoundeth hereticum hominem deuita / take the heretike
out of his life. We reade of no payne that he had whom the Corinthians excomunicat and gaue to sathan / to sle hys flesh / saue that he
was asshamed of hym selfe and repented / when he saw hys offence   15
so ernistly taken and so abhorred. But ye because ye haue no power
to delyuer them to sathan to blynde theyr myndes / ye deliuer them
to the fyre to destroy their flesh / that no moare is sene of them after
then the asshes.

---

2 Note   9 More   11 Tindale

14 excomunicat] excommunicated 1573

[R6] The table of the boke

A.

B.

---

1 The table of the boke] *ed., running title 1531*

23 doctryne] *ed.*, doctyne *1531*

D.

E.   25

21 H.] ed., om. 1531

15, 16 Images /] *ed.*, Images *1531*   29 Knowlege /] *ed.*, Knowlege *1531*

L.

M.

N.

O.

P.

10 to gyther /] *ed.*, to gyther *1531*   19 wyues /] *ed.*, wyues *1531*

R.

[S2v] S.

---

14 touchynge] *ed.*, thouchynge *1531*

T.

V.

W.

---

4 Teynterden steple] *ed.*, Teynterdensteple *1531*

Finis

COMMENTARY

As a reformer, Tyndale argues most forcefully *sola scriptura*. Every octavo page of *Answer to More* has three or four biblical references, totalling nearly a thousand. Direct quotations from Tyndale's NT are cited by reference to the old-spelling edition of Wallis and the modern-spelling edition of Daniell. Direct quotations from Tyndale's OT are cited by reference to the old-spelling edition of Mombert for the Pentateuch and the modern-spelling edition of Daniell from Genesis through 2 Chronicles plus Jonas. Other OT references are based on the King James Version. Since there are no verse numbers in Tyndale's biblical translations, we use those of the KJV.

In arguing against More, Tyndale appeals to non-scriptural authors, especially to the Fathers of the Church. Within the Commentary, references are made to editions first in the original language, then in a translation. Following the example of Tyndale in promoting the vernacular, we usually give titles in English when there is a published translation; we keep *Moriae encomium* because of the pun on More's name. References to Greek and Roman literature are based on the Loeb Classical Library. For the Fathers, we use Corpus Christianorum, Series Latina or "CCL" when available; otherwise "CSEL" and "PL." Where the Toronto edition of Erasmus is still in progress, we say "not yet in CWE." When the American edition of Luther does not give an English translation, we say "not in LW." Proper names appear in various forms because they are spelled as found in the source indicated; e.g., "Maarten van Dorp" from CWE and "Martin Dorp" from CWM (14/28n). Abbreviations in *Answer* and other 16c books have been expanded except for the ampersand (&). Exact quotations from the Bible, *Dialogue Concerning Heresies* (CWM 6), and *Confutation of Tyndale* (CWM 8) are cited by the reference; allusions are introduced by "cf." For other works, the reader can tell from the context the difference between direct and indirect quotes.

George Joye clouded the issue of authorship by attributing Tyndale's *Answer to More* to John Frith. To avoid a like confusion, we state that, in general, annotations were made by: Anne O'Donnell for the Bible, *Unio Dissidentium,* Erasmus, More, and the English setting; by Jared Wicks (JW) for Luther, Zwingli, and the Continental setting. After she completed her doctoral studies, Jennifer Bess (JB) turned the cross-references to the other independent works of Tyndale into short essays. Although the Commentary has been severely pruned, it is still full because its roots reach down to the Scriptures and the Fathers and its branches spread out to the humanists and the reformers.

3/11–16 **Awake . . . light.** Eph. 5.14. This same epigraph is found on the title page of John Frith, *An other boke against Rastel* (c1537), STC 11385: "¶ Awake thou that slepeste and | stonde vppe from deeth / and | Chryste shall geue the | lyght. Ephesians. v."

5/1–6 **The grace . . . Amen.** CWM 8/1.41/5–10. Ten Pauline epistles greet the reader with prayers for "grace and peace" (Romans, 1 and 2 Corinthians, Galatians, Ephesians, Philippians, Colossians, 1 and 2 Thessalonians, Philemon). Three open with "grace, mercy and peace" (1 and 2 Timothy, Titus). *Answer* outdoes Paul by praying for "grace," "light," "repentaunce," "faith," and "loue."

5/7–18 **Oure . . . kepe it.** CWM 8/1.44/7–20.

5/9–10 **holye gost . . . iudgement.** Cf. John 16.8, 11.

5/20–24 **the naturall . . . god.** Cf. 1 Cor. 2.14.

5/22 **sore.** Used as adjective or adverb, one of Tyndale's favorite words.

5/25–26 **the spirituall . . . secretes of god.** Cf. 1 Cor. 2.15, 10.

5/27–28 **serchinge . . . why.** Cf. CWM 8/1.261/12–13, 196/7–12, 197/1, 199/13–15; *Mammon* C1.

5/29–32 **Take . . . herte.** CWM 8/1.49/18–20, slightly paraphrased at CWM 8/1.51/22–24.

5/30 **loue god with all thyne herte.** Cf. Deut. 6.5, Matt. 22.37, Mark 12.30, Luke 10.27. Altogether, the First Great Commandment occurs five times in *Answer.*

5/32–6/2 **And when . . . gladlye.** CWM 8/1.55/30–32.

5/32–6/1 **obeye . . . worlde.** Cf. Rom. 13.1–7.

6/2–5 **And when . . . forth.** CWM 8/1.56/36–38.

6/3 **loue his neyghboure as him silfe.** Cf. Lev. 19.18, Matt. 19.19, Matt. 22.39, Mark 12.31, Luke 10.27, Rom. 13.9, Gal. 5.14, Jas. 2.8. Altogether, the Second Great Commandment occurs eighteen times in *Answer.*

6/5–14 **and therfore . . . tirannie.** CWM 8/1.57/12–22.

6/12–14 **iudgeth . . . tirannie.** Repeated at CWM 8/1.60/21–23.

6/14 **right.** This adjective is another one of Tyndale's characteristic words.

6/15–32 **If god . . . in vs.** CWM 8/1.60/32–61/10.

6/15 **drinke no wyne.** Cf. Lev. 10.9, Ezek. 44.21.

6/17 **forbade diverse meates.** Cf. Ezek. 44.31.

6/18–19 **man . . . creatures.** Cf. Gen. 1.28.

6/25–26 **David . . . breed.** Cf. 1 Sam. 21.3–6.

6/26–27 **Moses . . . yeares.** Cf. Josh. 5.2–7.

6/31–32 **ensamples . . . in vs.** Repeated at CWM 8/1.73/26–27.

6/32–7/5 **And likewyse . . . church.** CWM 8/1.74/14–20.

6/32–33 **the daye . . . man.** Cf. Mark 2.27.

7/5–14 **and so . . . forth.** CWM 8/1.76/10–18.

7/8–13 **the preast . . . oyle.** Cf. CWM 8/1.58/31–33.

7/11–13 **holysalt . . . oyle.** Used in the sacrament of Baptism, cf. 19/3. For material objects used in religious rites, cf. 70/23–24n.

7/15–17 **But . . . hed.** CWM 8/1.121/11–14.

7/15 **captyvateth his witte.** Cf. 2 Cor. 10.5. Tyndale taunts More with this clause fourteen times.

7/18–22 **He beleveth . . . lyves.** CWM 8/1.123/26–29. Cf. CWM 8/2.810/17–24.

7/18 **turcke.** Tyndale associates Turks with papists in their erroneous belief in justification by works, not faith. Thus, *Answer* has more references to the Turks than any other of the independent works. Cf. *Mammon* I1; *Obedience* C7v, D2v, I3v; *Prelates* B5; *Matthew* a3v, f3v, o2, o6.

By opposing killing Turks in the name of Christianity, Tyndale echoes the final section of Erasmus' 1515 account of the adage *Dulce bellum inexpertis;* "Wars are sweet to them who know them not," Tilley W58. Cf. *Adagia* 4.1.1 (LB 2.966D–970A; not yet in ASD or CWE); Margaret Mann Phillips, *The 'Adages' of Erasmus* (Cambridge UP, 1964) 344–52. Rather than arms or scholastic philosophy, Erasmus offers the *philosophia Christi* as a better way to overcome the Turks in the preface to a new edition of the *Enchiridion.* Cf. Ep. 858, To Paul Volz, Basel, 14 August 1518 (Allen 3.364/78–366/154; CWE 6.75/85–77/165; also found in Holborn 5/14–7/20; CWE 66.10–12). Because of the moral failures of Christendom, Erasmus was pessimistic about a victory over the Turks in his 1530 "consultation," *De bello Turcis inferendo.* See the introduction to *De bello* by A.G. Weiler (ASD 5/3.20–27; not yet in CWE).

Early in his career, Luther had denounced collecting indulgence money, not only for the supposed release of the souls in purgatory, e.g. Thesis 27, but also for a crusade against the Turks, *Resolutions* of 1518 (WA 1.535/29–39; LW 31.91–92). Gradually his position became more nuanced. In his *On War Against the Turk,* 1529 (WA 30/2.107–48; LW 46.161–205), and again in *Eine Heerpredigt wider den Türken,* 1529 (WA 30/2.160–97; not in LW), Luther affirmed the right of the emperor to make a military defense against the Turks. (JW)

Writing in the Tower of London in 1534–35, More sets his *Dialogue of Comfort* (CWM 12) in Hungary between the Muslim victory at Mohács (August 1526) and the unsuccessful siege of Vienna (October 1529). The Great Turk is at once Suleiman the Magnificent and Henry VIII. See Brandon H. Beck, *From the Rising of the Sun: English Images of the Ottoman Empire to 1715,* American University Studies, Series IX, History 20 (New York: Peter Lang, 1987).

7/19–20 **whom . . . loue.** Cf. Matt. 5.44, Luke 6.35.

7/22–34 **He supposeth . . . blinde.** CWM 8/1.124/36–125/11. Tyndale opposes the legalistic definition of charity as the mere absence of irate feeling and ill-will. Such teaching is exemplified by Silvester Prierias in his treatment of love of enemies in the frequently reprinted *Summa summarum de casibus conscientiae* (Bologna, 1514), s.v. *charitas.* Luther had rejected a similar reduction of charity to an obligation to give help only in cases of dire necessity, in the earliest extant disputation that he chaired in Wittenberg, September 1516 (WA 1.149; not in LW). (JW)

7/23 **angrye with him.** Cf. Matt. 5.22.

7/25 **wordlie purposse.** Tyndale frequently makes a pun on "wordly" and "worldly": e.g., 48/6n, 63/23, 72/31; *Mammon* A6v etc., *Obedience* A7 etc., *1 John* F4v etc.

7/32–33 **writen in his harte.** Cf. Jer. 31.33, Heb. 8.10, Heb. 10.16. This is the most frequently quoted biblical text in *Answer,* twenty-three times in all. For an examination of this text in relation to Tyndale's emphasis on justification by faith and as a foreshadowing of covenant theology, cf. O'Donnell, "Scripture versus Church," *Moreana* 106–7, "Biblical Interpretation in the Age of Thomas More: Numéro spécial William Tyndale" (July 1991) 119–30, esp. 120 and n7.

Marc'hadour discusses Jer. 31.33 (cf. *Bible* 3.194–96), quoted in Heb. 8.10 and Heb.10.16, as one of seven major biblical texts frequently used by More. His other key texts are Matt. 16.18, Matt. 18.20, Matt. 28.20, John 16.13, John 20.30, and Ps. 67.7 in Vulgate (Ps. 68.6 in KJV) (cf. *Bible* 4.117). Following the Hebrew text, the numbers of the psalms in the KJV are usually one digit higher than the Septuagint and the Vulgate after Ps. 8 and before Ps. 148 (NCE 11.935). Since the KJV does not count the heading as a verse, within individual psalms its numbers are often one digit behind the Vulgate.

7/34 **betell blinde.** Cf. 140/29 and Tilley B219.

7/34–8/5 **If . . . forth.** CWM 8/1.125/35–126/3.

8/1–2 **charter house monkes.** The Carthusians were founded in the French Alps by St. Bruno in 1084. They never eat meat (*Obedience* O4v), and keep silence except for a period on Sundays and major feasts (NCE 3.162–67; OER 1.266–69). Tyndale satirically advises the husband of a garrulous wife to buy silence from the Charterhouse (*Obedience* Q8v). Erasmus contrasts a veteran with a monk who meditates on the Bible and Fathers in "The Soldier and the Carthusian," August 1523, *Colloquies* (ASD 1/3.314–19; CWE 39.328–43).

According to his son-in-law, More lived without vows in the London Charterhouse before finally deciding to marry (Roper 6/9–11). On 4 May 1535, two months before his own death, More and his daughter Margaret watched three Carthusian priors leave the Tower on their way to execution (Roper 80/9ff).

Among the fifty persons who died under Henry VIII for rejecting the royal supremacy, the Carthusians were the largest group with a total of eighteen, followed by eleven diocesan priests including Fisher, seven laypeople including More, seven Benedictines, five Franciscans, one Austin friar and the Bridgittine Richard Reynolds (NCE 9.318–32, 17.36).

8/5–8 **And the holidaye . . . lawes.** CWM 8/1.126/16–19.

8/8–12 **And in ceremonyes . . . out.** CWM 8/1.127/17–21.

8/13–17 **For . . . myte.** CWM 8/1.128/4–8.

8/17–19 **He . . . forth.** CWM 8/1.128/18–19.

8/19–28 **Wherfore . . . vnderstondinge.** CWM 8/1.130/16–24.

8/20–21 **holye gost . . . iudgement.** Cf. John 16.8, 11.

8/22–23 **if . . . se.** Cf. Mark 8.18.

8/24–25 **the spirituall . . . secretes.** Cf. 1 Cor. 2.15, 10. In Luther's *To the Christian Nobility,* 1520, the spiritual foundation for critical discernment (cf. 1 Cor 2.15) was pivotal in calling believers to test Roman practices by the norm of the common faith (WA 6.411/8–412/38; LW 44.133–36, esp. 135). (JW)

8/27–28 **oxe . . . vnderstondinge.** Cf. Ps. 32.9.

8/29 **Iudge . . . church.** Cf. CWM 8/1.131/18–19.

8/30–32 **whether . . . can.** CWM 8/1.132/23–25.

8/30 **whether their auctorite be aboue the scripture.** Later (188/3n, 213/22), Tyndale refers to *Unio Dissidentium,* a patristic anthology on Reformation topics. The handbook (UD 1.X2) contains an excerpt from Ep. 82, Augustine to Jerome (AD 405) on the supremacy of Scripture, 1.3 (PL 33.277; CSEL 34/2.354; Parsons 1.392). For further statements on this theme by Augustine, cf. 135/31–33n.

8/32–9/1 **And agenst . . . yies.** CWM 8/1.134/28–30.

9/1–8 **Iudge . . . thinges.** CWM 8/1.135/21–28.

9/2 **domme ceremonies.** Cf. CWM 8/2.638/27–31.

9/3 **purgatorye.** Tyndale refers to purgatory in his other major works: as an invention of the pope to gain money (*Obedience* K2v, L2, N5v, T1), as an extension of papal power (*Prelates* E5), as lasting as long as hell (*1 John* C1v), as no more real than Utopia (*Matthew* k1).

Early in 1529 the lawyer Simon Fish produced a pamphlet against financial exactions by the church entitled *A Supplicacyon for the Beggers* (Appendix B, CWM 7.412–22). Later that same year, More published two editions of *The Supplication of Souls,* a dramatic monologue spoken by the souls in purgatory "To all good Crysten people" (CWM 7.111–228). Still later, John Frith published *A disputacion of purgatorye* (Antwerp, 1531) STC 11386.5, a well-organized attack against the arguments of Rastell from reason, More from Scripture, and Fisher from the Fathers.

9/4 **prayinge to postes.** Veneration of relics of the true cross on Good Friday originated in Jerusalem, and was introduced at Rome by the mid-7c. The custom is still observed by Roman

Catholics. The presider and two attendants hold a replica of the cross for the faithful to honor by genuflecting before it and kissing it (NCE 6.621–24, esp. 622–23). More calls the procession "creeping to the cross" (CWM 8/1.150/5–6). For the wooden statue of Our Lady of Willesden, cf. 124/27–28n.

9/8–13 **Marke . . . swerde.** CWM 8/1.136/4–8.

9/10 **aboue .viij. hundred yeares.** Cf. CWM 8/1.152/9–10, 368/24–25. This is the first reference in *Answer* to Tyndale's position that the fall of the church, the beginning of papal and hierarchical misrule with the ascendancy of error on faith and good works, began eight hundred years before. Although this period coincides with the rise of Islam, Tyndale refers particularly to the anointing of Pepin III, the father of Charlemagne, by Stephen II (pope, 752–57) in 754 (*Prelates* D7r–v), which signified the alliance with the Franks that was basic to papal claims to territories in Italy. (JW)

9/13–17 **Haue . . . inspire them.** CWM 8/1.137/7–10.

9/16 **samsumims.** The Zamzummims supposedly were giants who lived in a region later claimed by the Ammonites, cf. Deut. 2.20.

9/17–21 **Marke . . . theirs.** CWM 8/1.137/26–29.

9/18 **scribes / pharises.** For the opposition of scribes and Pharisees to Christ as anticipating persecution by Catholics of reformers, cf. Matt. 23.13–29. **Pilate.** Cf. Matt. 27.17–26, Mark 15.1–15, Luke 23.1–25, John 18.29–19.16. **Herode.** Cf. Luke 23.7–12. **Caiphas & Anna.** Cf. John 18.13–14, 19–24.

9/18–19 **gathered to gether agenst God & Christ.** Ps. 2.2.

9/20 **achitophell.** Cf. 2 Sam. 16.20–23.

9/21–26 **Marke . . . darkenesse.** CWM 8/1.139/9–14.

9/26–31 **Wherfore . . . Amen.** CWM 8/1.139/31–36.

9/26–27 **it is tyme to awake.** Cf. Rom. 13.11.

9/27–28 **if . . . iudge.** Cf. 2 Tim. 4.1.

9/30 **spirite.** Divine power or influence. Tyndale uses "holy gost" for the third person of the Trinity.

10/2 **Thys . . . significacions.** CWM 8/1.145/18.

10/2–7 **it . . . goodly.** Quoted almost verbatim at CWM 8/1.148/15–18.

10/2–6 **signifyeth . . . praye.** Summarized at CWM 8/1.145/20–23.

10/7–8 **the officers . . . vnderstode.** Cf. CWM 8/1.150/13–14, 161/14–15.

10/11 **instructe . . . howsholde.** Cf. 1 Tim. 3.4.

10/12–14 **buzsinges . . . beres.** Cf. CWM 8/1.150/10–12.

10/16–18 **we . . . all.** Cf. CWM 8/1.148/21–22.

10/17 **promyses . . . christe.** Cf. 2 Cor. 1.20.

10/19–21 **And of the lawe . . . power.** Cf. CWM 8/1.149/15–17. Tyndale attacks Catholic works-righteousness by likening it to Turkish, i.e. Muslim, and pagan beliefs in the natural power of free will to obey God's will, supposedly without the intervention of God's grace and help. For an account of Luther's critique of works-righteousness, cf. Wicks, *Luther's Reform* 7–9, 16–21, 30–33, and 63–70. (JW)

10/20 **olde hethen people.** Tyndale names Aristotle the chief of philosophers because of his great learning (*Obedience* H6v). Tyndale rejects as works-righteousness Aristotle's definition of virtue as the habit of performing good acts, the foundational principle of the *Ethics* (*Mammon* G5r–v, *Obedience* B8v–C1), as well as Aristotle's position on the eternal existence of the world (*On the Heavens* 1.3; *Obedience* B8v). Tyndale also makes general references to Aristotle's *Logic* (*Obedience* C2v) and *Metaphysics* (152/32n, *Mammon* G5, *Obedience* C2v). A sidenote to Deut. 4 urges subordinating Aristotle to Scripture and not vice versa (Mombert 536; TOT 262). Tyndale alludes to Socrates and Plato (*Mammon* G4v), reduces Plato and Aristotle to the same level as Robin Hood (*Obedience* H8v), and notes with approval that Augustine corrected his early attachment to Plato by diligent study of Scripture (*Obedience* B8v).

10/24–26 **neyther . . . god.** Cf. CWM 8/1.149/31–32, 159/32–33.

10/27–30 **we . . . imagininge.** Cf. CWM 8/1.149/28–31.

10/32–11/22 **In . . . disgysinges.** *Answer* objects to the misapplication of the term "church" to the hierarchy and clergy alone. *Dialogue* had already made the same point, "The chyrche therfore must nedys be the comen knowen multytude of crysten men good and bad togyther / whyle the chyrche is here in erth" (CWM 6/1.205/4–7). (JW)

11/2 **Kinge wyllyam.** By presenting himself as a defender of the church, the Duke of Normandy won support for invading England from Alexander II (pope, 1061–73) (*Prelates* F2v) (NCE 14.918–19). As William I (king, 1066–87), he confiscated gold and silver from monasteries. Cf. Bk. 7, Ch. 1 of *Polychronicon Ranulphi Hidgen Monachi Cestrensis together with the English Translations of John Trevisa and of an Unknown Writer of the Fifteenth Century,* ed. Joseph Rawson Lumby (London, 1879) 7.256–57. William also placed bishoprics and abbeys holding baronies under military rule, conscripted soldiers from dependents of religious houses, and exiled many ecclesiastics who resisted his decrees. Cf. Roger of Wendover, *Flowers of History,* 2 vols., tr. J.A. Giles (London, 1849) 1.338.

11/4 **Kinge Iohan.** Omitting references to the contract with the barons in Magna Carta (1215), Tyndale notes the struggles of John (king, 1199–1216) with the church: the contested election of Stephen Langton as Archbishop of Canterbury (*Prelates* F3v), his prohibition of appeals to Rome (*Matthew* b7), and the papal interdiction of England (*Mammon* H5v; *Obedience* L6,V5v). In 1209 Innocent III (pope, 1198–1216) excommunicated John, and later ordered Philip II Augustus of France (king, 1180–1223) to depose John and ascend his throne. In response, John promised to accept Langton and restore confiscated church property. In May 1213 he surrendered the kingdoms of England and Ireland to the legate Pandulph and received them back as papal fiefdoms with the obligation to pay a yearly tribute to Rome (NCE 7.1023–24).

By the end of the 13c, the custom of paying feudal dues to the pope was dying out; it was paid only once in the 14c: by Edward III (king, 1327–77) in 1333. In 1366 Parliament repudiated John's offer of tribute because it had been given without its consent, a decision accepted by Urban V (pope, 1362–70), cf. Lunt, *Papacy* 66–70. In *The Supplication of Souls,* 1529, More denied King John had the power to surrender sovereignty to the pope (CWM 7.129/1–7).

The Folger copy of *Answer to More* was once owned and autographed by "Iohan bale." Tyndale's anti-papal feeling thus influenced Bale's proto-history play *King Johan* (c1540–63), and indirectly Shakespeare's *King John* (performed 1596, published 1623).

11/9 **Thomas bekett.** Becket (archbishop, 1162–70) was murdered in Canterbury Cathedral at the wish of Henry II (king, 1154–89) (NCE 2.212–14). In *Prelates* Tyndale depicts Becket as a corrupt role model for Wolsey (D3, F1v–F2). Tyndale disapproved of clerical exemption from civil law, a cause for which Becket died (G3v).

Fifty years after Becket's death, his relics were transferred from the crypt to the Trinity Chapel above it on 7 July 1220. Cf. John Butler, *The Quest for Becket's Bones* (New Haven: Yale UP, 1995) 20, 45. In his last letter More comments on 6 July, the day set for his execution: ". . . it is S. Thomas evin, and the vtas [octave] of Sainte Peter and therefore to morowe longe I to goe to God. . . ." From Ep. 218, To Margaret Roper, Tower of London, 5 July 1535 (More, *Correspondence* 564/19–21).

In *Colloquies,* Erasmus describes a visit to Canterbury c1512, in which Colet contrasts Becket's alms to the poor with the bejewelled shrine, "A Pilgrimage for Religion's Sake," February 1526 (ASD 1/3.470–94; CWE 40.644/1–23). The spoliation of this shrine in September 1538 prompted the long-delayed excommunication of Henry VIII in December. See J.J. Scarisbrick, "Fisher, Henry VIII and the Reformation crisis," in Bradshaw and Duffy 155–68.

11/20 **monkes / freres / blacke / whit / pied / grey.** Cf. 105/28–29. In England and Wales at the end of the period between 1500 and 1534, there were approximately 254 communities of monks, 286 of canons regular, 183 of friars, totaling 723 male religious houses. These contained approximately 3699 monks, 2874 canons, and 2596 friars totaling 9169 male religious. Cf. David Knowles and R. Neville Hadcock, *Medieval Religious Houses: England and Wales,* 2d ed. (New York: St. Martin's, 1971) Appendix II, 494. For

Haigh's approximate estimate of 10,000 priests in religious communities in the early 1530s, cf. 75/19–20n. For negative critics, the
garb and tonsure of monks and friars exemplified self-invented
and external ways of serving God, cf. *Moriae,* 1511, 1514 (ASD
4/3.160/538–52; CWE 27.131). In his Paradise of Fools, Milton
will reprise Tyndale's satiric theme when he mocks "Embryo's and
Idiots, Eremits and Friers / White, Black and Grey, with all thir
trumperie" (*Paradise Lost* 3.474–75).

Benedictines (founded between c530 and 540) were called "Black
Monks" (NCE 2.283–85), and Cistercians (1098) were called
"White Monks" (NCE 3.885–89) because of the color of their respective habits. A sidenote to 4 Kings 23 from Matthew's Bible
(1537) makes a witty reference to the "black monks of Baal"
(TOT 537). Similarly, Augustinians were called "Black Canons"
(see below) from their black capes. Premonstratensians (1120)
were called "White Canons" from their white habits. Cf. J.C.
Dickinson, *The Origins of the Austin Canons and Their Introduction
into England* (London: SPCK, 1950) 185; H.M. Colvin, *The White
Canons in England* (Oxford: Clarendon, 1951) 3–4.

Dominicans (1216) or "Blackfriars" wore black cloaks over white tunics; Carmelites (1226) or "Whitefriars" wore white cloaks over
brown tunics. Franciscans or Minorites (1223) were called "graye
frires" (131/7) from the color of their undyed habits (NCE 6.198).

Augustinian canons evolved from diocesan priests living in community who adopted the rule of St. Augustine (1139). Erasmus joined
the Austin Canons c1487, but lived outside his monastery for
twenty-five years: from his ordination in 1492 until a papal dispensation in 1517 gave him the status of a secular priest of the
Diocese of Utrecht. After he left the Canons Regular, Erasmus
called them amphibians because of their position between monks
and diocesan canons. Cf. "A Pilgrimage for Religion's Sake," February 1526, *Colloquies* (ASD 1/3.475/157–60; CWE 40.629/7–10).

Augustinian friars were formed by the consolidation of groups of
hermits (1256) (OER 1.100–1). Luther entered the Observant
Augustinians in 1505, living as an exemplary religious at Erfurt
and Wittenberg until he was dispensed from his vows by his
provincial superior, Johann von Staupitz (OER 4.109–11).

Since Tyndale opposed the creation of fictions, we should not be surprised to learn that the Pied Friars were an actual order. The Friars of the Blessed Mary began in Marseilles in mid-13c, founded houses in London, Norwich, and Cambridge, but died out after small mendicant orders were suppressed by Lyons II (1274). Their black scapular, white mantle, and black hood made them resemble magpies. See Richard W. Emery, "The Friars of the Blessed Mary and the Pied Friars," *Speculum* 24 (1949) 228–38. Later, Tyndale will dismiss the multiplicity of religious orders because they are "as pied in their consciences as in their cotes" (100/22–23).

When the mendicant orders declined from the ideals of their founders, they were given the name of "CAIM" or "Cain," an acronym for Carmelites, Augustinians, Jacobites (from the Dominican house of St. Jacques in Paris), and Minorites. Cf. John Wyclif, *Trialogus,* Bk. 4, Ch. 25, p. 200, "A Treatise . . . against Orders of Friars," 217–56, in *Tracts and Treatises,* tr. Robert Vaughan (London, 1845). Chaucer's friar outdoes all other members of "the ordres foure" in "daliaunce and fair langage" ("General Prologue," *Canterbury Tales,* I [A] 210–11).

Continuing this negative criticism of the friars, Tyndale asserts that those who serve their bellies before God should not be trusted with preaching to the parish (*Obedience* Q6v–Q7). Friars in general are guilty of gluttony and greed, but the Austin friars in London supposedly murdered one of their brethren (*Matthew* o7v). In the *Obedience* (Q8r–v), Tyndale singles out the Franciscan Observants, who falsely portray themselves as strict adherents of the rule of poverty. In *Prelates* (G2), he cites Friar Bungay's encouragement of Edward IV to marry Elizabeth Grey instead of Isabel of Castile. For the hearing of confessions by priests in religious orders, cf. 21/4–5n.

The Franciscans, the largest order in the medieval church, are overly devoted to saints, especially their founder, who sits highest in heaven under Christ (*Matthew* a3v). In *Matthew* (i3v, o7v) Tyndale's image of rich and fat friars is a synecdoche for those who place the rules of their orders above the laws of God. Thus, Tyndale laments the daily increase in the number of monks, canons, friars, nuns (*Obedience* R1), who falsely invoke the name of Christ to preach only their own traditions (*Obedience* I5v). Trust in ceremonies and monastic vows (*1 John* F3v), wearing a Franciscan or a Dominican habit to the grave (*Mammon* A8, I1v; *Matthew* d4v, k8), all seem to overshadow faith in Christ's sacrifice. For burial in the Franciscan habit, cf. "The Funeral," February 1526, *Colloquies* (ASD 1/3.546/328 to 547/366; CWE 40.774/27 to 775/27); "The Seraphic Funeral," September 1531 (ASD 1/3.687/40 to 688/61; CWE 40.1000/36 to 1001/18). Tyndale's mockery of the orders is explained not only by their moral corruption, but by their theological error in emphasizing works over faith. (JB)

Some friars became notable reformers, e.g.: from the Observant Franciscans William Roye (d. c1531), Tyndale's assistant on the first edition of the NT; from the Dominicans Martin Bucer (1491–1551), Regius Professor of Divinity at Cambridge (OER 1.221–24); from the Carmelites John Bale (1495–1563), dramatist and historian (OER 1.113–14); from the Augustinians Miles Coverdale (1488–1568), editor of the first complete Bible printed in English (1535) (OER 1.445–46), cf. 167/30–31n.

Wearing habits similar to the men of the First Orders with black veils instead of cowls were cloistered women of the Second Orders: Benedictine, Cistercian, Augustinian, Franciscan, Dominican and Bridgittine. In England and Wales at the end of the period between 1500 and 1534, there were 142 communities of nuns and canonesses, containing approximately 1966 members (Knowles and Hadcock, Appendix II, 494). Although some women entered convents without a true vocation, perhaps only five percent of English nuns broke their vow of chastity. Cf. Eileen Power, *Medieval English Nunneries, c. 1275 to 1535* (Cambridge UP, 1922) 461.

Of special interest is the Dominican convent of Dartford in the Diocese of Rochester. Among its members were Bridget Plantagenet (d. c1517), youngest daughter of Edward IV, and Elizabeth White, half-sister of the local bishop John Fisher (CWM 2.158–59). The "Rufull Lamentation" (1503) that More composed in the voice of Elizabeth of York bids a special farewell to her Dominican sister (CWM 1.12/74–78). After the nuns were pensioned off in 1539, the monastery became the residence of Anne of Cleves from the annulment of her marriage to Henry VIII until her death (1540–57). Cf. David Knowles OSB, *The Religious Orders in England* (Cambridge UP, 1959) 3.440.

12/6–7 **I . . . measure.** Gal. 1.13. Cf. Erasmus' annotation on *Et expugnabam.*) 1516 NT, *Caeterum ecclesiam uocat congregatiunculam illam Christianorum* (Reeve 3.567). "Otherwise he calls the church 'that little congregation of Christians.'"

12/8–10 **I . . . wemen.** Acts 22.4.

12/10–12 **I . . . chryste.** Gal. 1.22.

12/12–13 **I . . . cenchris.** Cf. Rom. 16.1 in which *Answer* has "the deaconysse of the church" and NT has "a minister of the congregacion" (Wallis 342/5–6; TNT 241A). Referring to the Greek *diakonos,* Morna D. Hooker judges that "minister" is the better translation. Cf. "Tyndale's 'Heretical' Translation" in *Reformation* 2 (1997) 127–42, esp. 139.

12/13–14 **churches . . . you.** 1 Cor. 16.19.

12/15–16 **yf . . . God.** 1 Tim. 3.5. Cf. Erasmus' annotation on *Ecclesiae dei.*), 1522 NT, *Nam ecclesia opponitur domo.* 1527, *Et ecclesia magna domus est* (Reeve 3.671). "For 'church' is opposed to 'house.' And yet a church is a great house."

12/16–18 **yf . . . charged.** 1 Tim. 5.16.

12/18–19 **if . . . church or congregacion.** Cf. Matt. 18.16–17.

12/24–29 **Notwithstondinge . . . lorde.** CWM 8/1.146/4–9. This faith worth "nought" (12/25), opposed to "no fayth at all" (12/26), is "historicall faith" (48/27), which Tyndale usually contrasts with "felinge faith" (12/28).

12/24–27 **all . . . electe.** Cf. CWM 8/1.108/1–4. Tyndale's definition of "church" as the elect will recur at 28/15–25, 112/27–30, 142/30–143/2. (JW)

13/1–2 **congregacion rather then church.** Cf. CWM 6/1.286/26–34.

13/4–13 **Wherfore . . . congregacion.** Cf. CWM 8/1.164/16–21. More omits Tyndale's invective against the clergy as "hard & indurat adamandstones" (13/4–5) and "shauenflocke" (13/10).

13/21–23 **congregacion . . . ment.** Cf. CWM 8/1.165/31–33.

13/22–28 **For . . . therto.** CWM 8/1.167/8–11.

13/29–14/5 **M. More . . . ymages.** Cf. CWM 8/1.168/38–169/7.

13/31 **greke worde.** Heinz Holeczek studies the clash between

More and Tyndale over translating key NT terms in *Humanistische Bibelphilologie als Reformproblem bei Erasmus von Rotterdam, Thomas More und William Tyndale,* Studies in the History of Christian Thought 9 (Leiden: Brill, 1975) 310–58. (JW)

14/5 **companie.** Cf. Acts 19.24–41. Paul uses *ekklesia* for a secular assembly in vv. 32, 39, 41. Thus Erasmus prefers *concio* to *ecclesia;* 1516 NT (Reeve 2.316); cf. Aldridge 117.

14/6–11 **M. More ... espye them.** Cf. CWM 8/1.176/8–13 and 8/2. 938/30–33. Tyndale usually calls More's religious polemic as unreal as Utopia, whether he is defending the heresy trials of Richard Hunne (168/21n) and Robert Forman (194/8n) or the existence of purgatory (*Matthew* k1) and the validity of oral tradition (*Matthew* l6v).

A brief portrait of More (1477/78–1535) as author emerges from Tyndale's scattered allusions. Tyndale emphasizes the irony that the English hierarchy chose the twice-married More to write in behalf of clerical celibacy (166/30–31n). Outside of *Answer,* Tyndale refers to More most often in *Prelates:* once as the successor to Wolsey as Lord Chancellor (K2r–v), usually as the author of polemic against Luther (K2v), Tyndale's *Obedience* and *Mammon* (*Prelates* K2v), and Simon Fish's *Supplication of Beggars* (F5, K2v). In *Prelates* (F5, K2v) Tyndale twice calls More "the proctor of purgatory," i.e., "advocate" (OED 5.) because of his defense of purgatory in the *Supplication of Souls* of 1529 (CWM 7). In Tyndale's view, More sold his pen to the Roman cause because he was blinded by covetousness (*Matthew* l6v).

Erasmus describes More's humanistic writings in Ep. 999, To Ulrich von Hutten, Antwerp, 23 July 1519 (Allen 4.12–23; CWE 7.15–25). More's last surviving letter to Erasmus defends his polemical writings, especially against the "heretic Tyndale, a fellow Englishman, who is nowhere and yet everywhere an exile. . . ." From Ep. 2831, From Thomas More, Chelsea, [June 1533] (Allen 10.259/22; More, *Selected Letters* 179).

14/9 **daunce naked in nettes.** To act openly, believing one will escape notice. The first recorded use is from *Obedience* L4v; the second from *Confutation* (CWM 8/1.177/5), where More refers to this passage from *Answer.* Cf. ODEP 166 and Tilley N130, "You dance in a Net and think nobody sees you."

14/14 **Iudas.** Cf. Matt. 27.3–5, Acts 1.16–18.

14/15 **Balam.** Cf. Num. 22–24, and 31.8; 2 Pet. 2.15–16. Since *Prelates* had written earlier about More (F5, and a cluster on K2r–v), there may be a covert reference to More in the citation of Judas and Balaam (K8v). Only after *Dialogue Concerning Heresies* attacked Tyndale, did he openly link More to these biblical examples of greed. More alludes to this passage (14/13–23) at CWM 8/1.180/7–13 and to a later passage (22/14–23/6) at CWM 8/1.221/21–22.

14/24–28 **contended . . . housse.** Cf. CWM 8/1.177/10–14.

14/25 **Erasmus.** This is the first reference in *Answer* to Erasmus (1466/9–1536), the foremost Greek and Latin scholar in the first third of the 16c. For his life and works, see the entry by O'Donnell in *Tudor England*.

For other works of Erasmus, Tyndale makes direct reference to the *Paraclesis* (1516) and the Preface to the Paraphrase of Matthew (March 1522) in *Obedience* (C4). For Mary's supposed personal sins, Tyndale specifically cites the Annotations on Matt. 12, Luke 2, John 2 (*Obedience* S4v). In explicating the Beatitudes, Tyndale follows the NT versions of Erasmus and Luther in putting "Blessed are they that mourn" before "Blessed are the meek" (*Matthew* b6). Having translated the *Enchiridion* (1503) with the prefatory Ep. 858 (1518), Tyndale would readily recall its basic metaphor of the armor of God (*1 John* G7v), and its explanation in Ch. 7 of the tripartite division of flesh, soul, and spirit (*Matthew* p3). Tyndale's allusions to Julius II's struggle against the emperor (*Obedience* E6v) and to the pope's diplomatic alliances with Henry VIII (*Obedience* E6v; *Prelates* F8, G7) recall the *Julius Exclusus* (c1513) attributed to Erasmus (CWE 27). Tyndale perhaps echoes the *Colloquies:* "The Funeral" (1526) in *Mammon* (A8, G2), *Obedience* (L7), *1 John* (F3v); "A Pilgrimage for Religion's Sake" (1526) from *Colloquies* in the Prologue to Numbers (Mombert 393/14–15; TOT 196). Tyndale refers to Erasmus in the prefaces to his New and Old Testaments. Erasmus translates Greek *metanoeo*, not with *peniteo* for "repent," but with Latin *resipisco* for "come to myselfe or to my ryght mynde agayne" (Wallis 10/31–32; TNT 9). Erasmus praises Cuthbert Tunstall (Mombert 5/1–6; TOT 4) in the "Capita Argumentorum" of the 1527 NT (Foxe 5.811n).

14/26 **ecclesia in to congregacyon.** Erasmus' Latin version of the NT left the term *ecclesia* as the translation of the Greek *ekklesia* in the great majority of cases. But in his annotations on Rom 16.5, *Et domesticam ecclesiam.*), 1516 NT (Reeve 2.434) and 1 Cor. 16.19, *Cum domestica sua ecclesia.*), 1519 NT (Reeve 2.522), Erasmus expresses a preference for *congregatio,* to show how the Greek *ekklesia* refers to the *familia Christiana.* He translates *ekklesia* as *congregatio* at Acts 5.11, 7.38, 11.22 and 26, 14.27, also at Rom. 16.5, 2 Cor. 1.1, Philemon 1.2, and 3 John 1.10, cf. Aldridge 117.

In the Large Catechism, Luther explains why he prefers to translate *ekklesia* as *gemeyne* rather than *versammlung.* He approves the ancient interpretation of "church" as "communion of saints" because those gathered (*versammelt*) constitute a body holding in common (*als gemeinsam*) the gifts of Christ. He could say *eine Christiche gemeine oder samlung,* but prefers the former term because it indicates that those gathered hold spiritual gifts in common. He thinks the term *Gemeinschaft* is not apt because it connotates a social organization. Cf. Heinz Bluhm, *Martin Luther Creative Translator* (St. Louis: Concordia, 1965) 173f. Luther's practice may have suggested to Tyndale the making of a change, but Luther's own substitution did not give Tyndale the new term, "congregacyon," that he introduced. (JW)

Tyndale translates *ekklesia* as "congregation" here, *1 John* C2, *Matthew* d5v. *Dialogue* rejects Tyndale's translation of *ekklesia* as "congregation" in Bk. 1, Ch. 18 (CWM 6/1.107/23–24) and in Bk. 3, Ch. 8 (CWM 6/1.286/26–34).

14/28 **Moria.** Punning on the name of his host, Erasmus wrote *Moriae encomium* (1511) at More's home. Cf. Ep. 337 to Maarten van Dorp, Antwerp, [end of May] 1515 (Allen 2.90–114; CWE 3.111–39). More defends the philology, theology, and hermeneutics of *Moriae* in Ep. 15, To Martin Dorp, Bruges, 21 October <1515> (CWM 15.2–127). Besides this direct reference to *Moriae,* there are many indirect allusions in Tyndale's works: Philautia (*Obedience* B8v), scholastic terminology (*Obedience* C2v), the variety of religious rules (*Matthew* e3), fat monks (*Matthew* i3v), quick Masses (*Matthew* i5), long hours in choir (*Matthew* i6).

14/28–30 **Which . . . writeth.** Cf. CWM 8/1.178/9–10.

14/30–15/5 **Iudas . . . choked.** Cf. CWM 8/1.179/20–26.

15/1–3 **wrote . . . defendeth.** Cf. CWM 8/1.179/35–36.

15/5–6 **repent . . . worlde.** Cf. CWM 8/1.180/14–15; **resyst . . . god.** Cf. Acts 7.51.

15/7 **elder and not prest.** Cf. CWM 6/1.285/36–286/25. Tyndale translates *presbyteros* as "seniour" in *Mammon* A4 and as "senior" or "elder" in *Obedience* D1v ff, M3v.

15/8–13 **Another . . . elder.** CWM 8/1.182/8–14.

15/14–17 **And in that . . . lykewyse.** CWM 8/1.183/12–15.

15/17–22 **In . . . elder.** CWM 8/1.184/11–15.

15/19–20 **Seniores qui in vobis sunt / obsecro ego consenior / pascite qui in vobis est gregem christi.** Tyndale's quotation of 1 Pet. 5.1–2 is close to the Vulgate, which adds *ergo* after *Seniores,* omits *ego,* and uses *dei* instead of *christi.* Tyndale could have made a stronger argument against More by quoting Erasmus' 1522 NT, *Presbyteros qui inter uos sunt, obsecro, qui sum & ipse presbyter.* Out of the five Latin quotations in this section, two follow the Vulgate (15/19–20, 16/1) and three Erasmus' 1522 NT (15/26, 15/27–28, 16/4).

15/20–25 **The elders . . . persones.** CWM 8/1.186/18–22.

15/22–16/13 **And in that . . . offices.** Cf. CWM 8/1.188/21ff.

15/26 **senior electe domine et filijs eius.** Tyndale's quotation of 2 John 1.1 follows Erasmus' *filijs* (1522 NT) rather than Vulgate's *natis.*

15/27–28 **Senior Gaio dilecto.** Tyndale's quotation of 3 John 1.1 follows *dilecto* of Erasmus' 1522 NT rather than *charissimo* of the Vulgate and Erasmus' 1516 NT.

16/1–2 **paule . . . church.** Cf. Acts 20.17. Tyndale's *maiores natu* (16/1) follows the Vulgate, not *seniores* of 1516 NT, nor *presbyteros* of 1522 NT.

16/2–5 **take . . . god.** Acts 20.28.

16/4 **episcopos ad regendum ecclesiam dei.** Tyndale's quotation of Acts 20.28 follows *ad regendum* of Erasmus' 1522 NT rather than *regere* of the Vulgate.

16/12 **bisshopes or ouersears.** Cf. Acts 20.28. Tyndale translates *episkopos* as "bishop" or "overseer" elsewhere (*Obedience* I7, *1 John* E1). Tyndale explains that in the NT the names of "bishop," "priest," and "elder" referred to the same office (*Prelates* B4). For the qualities of a good bishop, cf. 1 Tim. 3.1–2 and Tit. 1.7. A side-note on the last verse equates episcopal and presbyterian forms of government (Wallis 459; TNT 320). *Unio Dissidentium* (2.K5v) quotes Jerome to Evangelus, Ep. 146, n.d., Par. 2, "[T]he fact is that the word bishops includes presbyters also" (PL 22.1195; CSEL 56.311; 2NPNF 6.289).

16/17–18 **Timothe . . . younge.** Cf. 1 Tim. 4.12.

16/20 **presbiteros / preast or elder.** For the ordaining of elders by Paul and Barnabas to serve the communities of Lystra, Iconium, and Antioch, cf. Acts 14.23. For Paul's commission to Titus to ordain elders in Crete, cf. Tit. 1.5. For the coupling of the offices of "apostles and elders," cf. Acts 15.2, 4, 6, 22, 23; 16.4. The apostle Peter calls himself an elder in 1 Pet. 5.1.

16/23–24 **Paul . . . agayne.** Cf. 1 Tim. 3.14.

16/29–30 **wemen . . . preach.** Cf. 1 Cor. 11.3, 9–10. A sidenote explains that woman's head-covering is a sign that she is subjected to man (Wallis 360; TNT 253). In spite of the prohibition against women's preaching in 1 Tim. 2.11–12, Tyndale affirms that love of one's neighbor allows women to preach and rule in cases of necessity, cf. 17/7–10, 178/1.

17/2–5 **wemen . . . new testament.** Tyndale does not name specific OT women leaders but for Deborah, cf. Judg. 4–5; for Huldah, cf. 2 Kings 22.14, 2 Chron. 34.22. An outstanding example of female preaching in the NT is Mary Magdalene's proclamation of Christ's resurrection to the apostles, cf. Mark 16.11, John 20.18.

17/7 **baptim.** Tyndale discusses the ceremonies connected with Baptism (19/3), and Baptism as a sign of repentance (172/23–25). He gave a full exposition of the traditional seven sacraments in *Obedience;* see esp. "Baptim" (M1v–M2) and "Anoylynge" (O3–O4). He treats Baptism as a promise to obey the Two Great Commandments (*1 John* A2), and as inward washing (*Matthew* b1, b2, k6v). Baptism also appears in *A Brief Declaration of the Sacraments* (A5v, B5–B6v). For Baptism administered by women, cf. 17/10, 27/28–32, 96/13–17.

17/7–12 **preach . . . Christe.** Cf. CWM 8/1.190/31–36.

17/11–12 **ministre . . . body & bloude.** Based on the needs of the neighbor, Tyndale argues that women can celebrate the Eucharist in an emergency, cf. 178/4. For More's disagreement, cf. CWM 8/1.92/17–18 and 8/2.807/32–33. For a study of Tyndale's proto-feminism, see Donald Dean Smeeton, "Marriage, Motherhood and Ministry: Women in the Dispute between Thomas More and William Tyndale," *Churchman* 108.3 (1994) 197–212.

17/13–15 **O pore . . . wife.** Cf. CWM 8/1.191/25–27. More renders *Answer's* "honeste wife" (17/15) as "good woman" (8/1.191/27). In 16c English the two phrases are synonymous, but Tyndale's connotes a married clergy.

17/15–17 **If . . . ceremonyes.** Cf. CWM 8/1.193/29–32.

17/28–29 **as . . . child.** Cf. 1 Thess. 2.7.

17/31–18/13 **bewise . . . affeccion.** Tyndale asserts that the major orders from subdeacon to pope are offices, not sacraments (*Obedience* M3). The following citations from the Epistles to Timothy discuss pastoral leadership, not priesthood.

17/31–32 **bewise . . . meke.** Cf. 1 Tim. 6.11.

17/32–34 **these . . . congregacion.** 1 Tim. 3.14–15.

17/34 **Avoyde lustes of youth.** 2 Tim. 2.22.

17/34–18/1 **beware . . . tales.** 1 Tim. 4.7.

18/1–2 **men of corrupte myndes.** 1 Tim. 6.5.

18/2 **wast . . . questions.** Cf. 1 Tim. 6.4.

18/2–3 **Let . . . youth.** 1 Tim. 4.12.

18/7–10 **rebuke . . . sisters.** 1 Tim. 5.1–2.

18/10–11 **Admitte . . . wittenesses.** 1 Tim. 5.19. More ironically rebukes Tyndale for omitting 1 Tim. 4.14 and 2 Tim. 1.6 because for More these two verses on the laying on of hands "clerely proue the holy order of presthed a sacrament" (CWM 8/1.193/2).

18/11–13 **Paul . . . affeccion.** Cf. 1 Tim. 5.21–22.

18/21–23 **And when . . . yet.** CWM 8/1.196/27–29.

18/23–32 **And when . . . consequens.** Cf. CWM 8/1.197/2–10. Tyndale makes More's frequently repeated phrase an ironic proper name for the Messenger. *Confutation* renders *Answer's* "quod youre frend" (18/28) as "quoth your frende" (CWM 8/1.197/7). Later, *Answer* calls the Messenger "quod he" (147/15, 194/14–15).

18/31–32 **concedo consequenciam et consequens.** "I concede the consequence and whatever is deducible" (tr. PS 3.20n2). Tyndale treats the rites of ordination as a hypothetical cause, "*If* these rites confer priesthood, then these men are ordained." But Tyndale denies that the rites *do* confer priesthood. More cites scriptural warrant for the laying on of hands in ordination and thus denies Tyndale's "consequency" and "consequente" (CWM 8/1.199/2–3, 4, 13).

Tyndale refers satirically to logic elsewhere: to the major and minor premise (79/17–18), to the syllogism (98/24, 160/22; *Matthew* e1r–v, g3v, o8v). Sometimes Tyndale argues from an effect, which he names a "cause declarative" backwards to the cause. Thus greenery declares that summer is here (199/31); a lunar eclipse indicates that the earth has come between the sun and the moon (*Mammon* B8v). Thanks to Prudence Allen RSM for advice on Tyndale's use of logic.

18/32–33 **annoyntynge . . . Iewes.** Cf. Lev. 8.12.

19/3 **chresom cloth.** A month after childbirth, the mother offered the chrisom-cloth or its cash equivalent to the minister. If the child died within this month, the white cloth used to wrap it at Baptism became its shroud. Cf. David Cressy, "Purification, Thanksgiving and the Churching of Women," in *Birth, Marriage, and Death: Ritual, Religon, and the Life-Cycle in Tudor and Stuart England* (Oxford UP, 1997) 197–229, esp. 210–11.

19/7–9 **And seinge . . . other.** CWM 8/1.195/4–11.

19/15–18 **whi . . . elder.** Cf. CWM 8/1.188/1–4.

19/15–16 **hiereus . . . sacerdos.** Tyndale had already discussed these words, together with the Hebrew *cohan* in *Obedience* (M3). The New Testament uses these words only for the Jewish clergy, Jesus, and Christians collectively. Of the many possible references to Christ as High Priest, Tyndale cites Heb. 6.19–20, *Obedience* M3v. For "priestly people," cf. 1 Pet. 2.5, 9; Rev. 1.6, 5.10, 20.6.

19/19 **hebrues . . . elderly.** Cf. Exod. 3.16.

19/21 **scrybes / pharises and the elders.** Cf. Matt. 26.3 etc.

19/24 **loue rather then cheryte.** Cf. CWM 6/1.286/35–288/6 and 1 Cor. 13 passim.

20/3–9 **pacyence . . . loue.** Cf. CWM 8/1.199/24–25.

20/10–15 **agape . . . loues.** *Confutation* resumes the discussion of "love" versus "charity," cf. CWM 8/1.200/4–5, and then quotes the full passage, cf. CWM 8/1.201/5–10.

20/18 **ner euery hope chrysten hope.** Cf. CWM 8/1.200/19.

20/18–19 **nor . . . beleffe.** Cf. CWM 8/1.200/12–13.

20/20–21 **vse . . . at all.** Cf. CWM 8/1.200/19–22.

20/23–24 **finally . . . neyboure.** CWM 8/1.202/17–18.

20/25–27 **though . . . doughter.** Cf. CWM 8/1.203/2–5.

20/28 **fauoure and not grace.** Cf. CWM 6/1.290/18–19.

20/29–21/3 **And wyth . . . goten.** Cf. CWM 8/1.203/22–27.

21/2 **my ladis grace.** Cf. Thomas W. Ross, *Chaucer's Bawdy* (New York: Dutton, 1972) 96–98. Variations on the phrase, "to stand in his lady's grace," occur in *Troilus and Criseyde* (cf. 3.472, 5.171), as well as in *The Canterbury Tales:* the description of the Squire ("General Prologue," I [A] 88) and "Merchant's Tale" (IV [E] 2018).

21/3 **vniuersities . . . graces.** More studied only two years at Oxford c1492–94 (Marius 25–28), while Tyndale spent a dozen years there, earning his BA in 1512 and his MA in 1515 (Mozley 12, 17).

21/4–5 **knowlege and not confessyon / repentaunce and not penaunce.** Cf. CWM 6/1.19–20. From the 2c to the mid-5c, public penance after private confession was performed for major sins: unchastity, murder, and apostasy. After Leo I (pope, 440–61) decreed in 459 that private confession was sufficent for secret sins, public penance began to decline. Cf. Ep. 168, To the Bishops of Campania, Samnium and Picenum, Ch. 2 (PL 54.1211; synopsis at 2NPNF 12.112). Lateran IV (1215), in the decree *Omnis utriusque sexus,* required all Christians, upon reaching the age of discretion, to confess their serious sins privately at least once a year to their parish priest. Aquinas taught that confession, contrition and satisfaction were the material of the sacrament of Penance (*Summa* III, Q. 84, Art. 2, *Sed contra*), and absolution by the priest was the form (*Summa* III, Q. 84, Art. 3). In 1439 the Council of Florence formally declared that God forgives mortal sin through the absolution of the priest. The Council of Trent, Session 14, 25 November 1551, *On Penance,* canon 6, declared that sacramental confession is prescribed by divine law; those who deny this are anathema. Cf. *Canons and Decrees of the Council of Trent,* tr. H.J. Schroeder OP (St. Louis: Herder, 1941) 102–3. During the Middle Ages, the penitent knelt before or at the side of the priest under the safety of public observation (Duffy, Plates 19–20). For greater privacy, the confessional box began to be used c1565.

The classic study of the sacrament of Penance is by Henry C. Lea, *History of Auricular Confession and Indulgences in the Latin Church,* 3 vols. (1896; New York: Greenwood, 1968), supplemented by Watkins (1920), and updated by Thomas N. Tentler, *Sin and Confession on the Eve of the Reformation* (Princeton UP, 1977).

Eramus noted the change from public to private confession in an annotation on Acts 19.18; 1516, 1519 NT (Reeve 2.315). His *Ratio verae theologiae* (1518) affirmed that one should certainly practice the developed form of individual confession as required by the church under the guidance of the Holy Spirit. But a theologian should not make it an article of faith that Jesus himself instituted the practice, cf. Holborn 205f, 210. In the 1520s after Edward Lee and Jacobus Stunica attacked Erasmus on this point, he defended his view, with nuances, in lengthy apologetic works. Cf. Payne 181–91, 319–22; Erika Rummel, *Erasmus' Annotations on the New Testament* (U of Toronto P, 1986) 152–56. (JW)

See Erasmus on Jas. 5.16, the clearest NT reference to confessing one's sins, not only to God, but to another human. *Peccata uestra.*) . . . 1516 NT, *Sentit enim de quotidianis offensis Christianorum inter ipsos, quos continuo uult reconciliari. Alioqui si de confessione sensisset, quam dicimus partem sacramenti poenitentiae, non addidisset "allelois," id est, uobis inuicem, sed sacerdotibus* (Reeve 3.744). "Your sins.) . . . For he is thinking about the daily offenses of Christians among themselves, whom he wishes to be reconciled immediately. If he were thinking about confession, which we call a part of the sacrament of Penance, he would not have added *allelois* that is, 'to you reciprocally,' but 'to the priests.'"

See also Erasmus' long note on Matt. 3.2, *Poenitentiam agite.*). Two sidenotes crystallize his position (Reeve 1.18): 1519 NT, *"metanoein" mutatam mentem sonat, non afflictionem corporis, "metanoein* means 'changing the mind' not 'afflicting the body'"; 1516 NT, *Resipiscere, pro poenitentiam agere,* "'To look back' for 'to do penance.'"

Referring to Tertullian, Erasmus asserts that this verse does not allude to the sacrament of Penance, 1527 NT, *Nam & in Graeco, inquit, sono poenitentiae nomen non ex delicti confessione, sed ex animi de-*

mutatione compositum est (Reeve 1.18). "He also says that the name for penance in the Greek language is constructed [from *meta* and *noeia*], not with respect to the confession of a fault, but to the alteration of the soul." Thanks to Germain Marc'hadour for help with the translation. KJV uses "repentance" but never "penance." Tyndale discusses the same crux, *metanoein* for "repente" or "forthynke" instead of "do penance" (22/3) in *Obedience* M6v. Wyclif frequently translated *metanoein* as "forthink," as in Luke 17.4 (cf. PS 1.260n2).

Tyndale shows little affinity with Luther's defense of himself on the issue of contrition as he responded to papal censure in *Exsurge Domine,* Art. 6 (DS 1456; Neuner-Dupuis 1614/6), e.g., in *Defense and Explanation of All the Articles,* December 1520 (WA 7.114–16; LW 32.34–38). On penitential satisfaction, Luther's responses were more developed (ibid., WA 7.112–13; LW 32.32–35), but he too said that God's visitation in grace leads spontaneously to love of righteousness and good works (ibid., WA 7.116–17; LW 32.38–42). However, Tyndale does not follow Luther's emphatic teaching on faith in the absolution that is given in virtue of Christ's mandate of binding and loosing (cf. Matt. 16.19). This we find in the response to *Exsurge*'s censure of Arts. 10–12 (ibid., WA 7.119–20; LW 32.45–50). (JW)

In 1528 Tyndale gives an extended discussion of penance, confession, contrition, satisfaction, and absolution in *Obedience* (M6v–O1). He deplores the burden to scrupulous consciences (L3), and asserts that the seal of confession is frequently broken for political advantage (V3v–V4). In *Prelates* (G2v) Tyndale condemns the Observant Franciscans of Greenwich, along with the Carthusians and Bridgittines, for passing political information learned from auricular confession through Cardinal Morton and Bishop Fox of Winchester to Henry VII. Tyndale might have known the case of the third Duke of Buckingham (1478–1521), a descendant of Edward III, who listened approvingly to prophecies that he would become king. His confessor John Delacourt testified against him at his treason trial despite being sworn to "keep it secret under the seal of confession" (LP 3/1, no. 1284). See Barbara J. Harris, *Edward Stafford: Third Duke of Buckingham, 1478–1521* (Stanford UP, 1986).

Tyndale approves the public penances enjoined in the early church as a means to tame the flesh (*1 John* H3v), but he decries the teachings on good works, purgatory, and indulgences as abuses of episcopal power (C2–C3v). He could accept auricular confession restored to right use (B3v).

21/6–8 **And that . . . worde.** Cf. CWM 8/1.204/26–28.

21/8–15 **But . . . subsequens.** Cf. CWM 8/1.205/7–13.

21/15–20 **wyth . . . priapus.** CWM 8/1.207/10–14. See More's earlier discussion, "Of confessyon" (CWM 8/1.89/7–8), where he quotes Tyndale's *Obedience* M8v. Probably through inadvertence, Tyndale does not give the Greek *exhomologesis* for "knowledge" instead of "confession" (21/6), but More supplies the missing word (CWM 8/1.208/4). In 1524, Erasmus published *Exomologesis sive modus confitendi* (LB 5.145A–170D). This was later translated as *A lytle treatise of the maner and forme of confession* (1535?), STC 10498. This work develops nine advantages, nine evils, and nine remedies for confession, an examination of conscience for many social roles, and types of penances. Under the first advantage, it describes public penance as required in the early church but now mitigated (LB 5.149D–F; C5r–v). Under the ninth evil, it explains that the sinner was admitted to public penance only once in the early church (LB 5.157A; G6v). Under the first evil, it complains that some priests repeat sins confessed to them, sometimes even mentioning the names of penitents (LB 5.153E; E7). In the *Colloquies,* young Gaspar doubts that auricular confession was instituted by Christ, but, nevertheless, he makes a brief confession of serious sins to a prudent priest in "The Whole Duty of Youth," March 1522 (ASD 1/3.177/1724 to 179/1760; CWE 39.96/1–97/39).

21/23–25 **And in lyke maner . . . synnes.** Cf. CWM 8/1.209/12–16.

21/26–27 **christ . . . synnes.** Cf. Eph. 1.7 and Heb. 9.14.

21/27–29 **and we . . . backe.** CWM 8/1.209/26–28.

21/30–22/2 **And if . . . of.** Cf. CWM 8/1.211/21–24.

22/2–6 **And as . . . dyd yt.** Cf. CWM 8/1.211/35–38.

22/6–9 **So . . . lyfe.** Cf. CWM 8/1.213/2–4. Note Tyndale's use of doublets: "repent or let yt forthynke you" (22/6), "gospell or glad tydynges" (22/7).

22/6–7 **repent . . . tydynges.** Cf. Mark 1.15, Rom. 10.15.

22/8–9 **lyue a new lyfe.** Cf. Rom. 6.4.

22/9–10 **And yt . . . purpose.** CWM 8/1.215/26–27.

22/10–12 **And yf . . . commaundementes.** Cf. CWM 8/1.218/22–24.

22/13–14 **These . . . yer I.** Cf. CWM 8/1.219/16–19. More began the study of Greek with William Grocyn. Cf. Ep. 2, To John Holt, <London, cNovember 1501> (More, *Correspondence* 4/14; *Selected Letters* 2). More studied Aristotle with Thomas Linacre. Cf. Ep. 15, To Martin Dorp, Bruges, 21 October <1515> (CWM 15.102/11–12). Erasmus later repeats this information. Cf. Ep. 1117, To Germain de Brie, Antwerp, 25 June 1520 (Allen 4.294/93–94; CWE 7.321/101–2).

22/14–15 **so blinde is couetousenesse.** Since Tyndale believes that More has been corrupted by avarice, *Answer* contains many references to spiritual darkness. The Foundational Essay, e.g., deplores willful blindness in religious leaders (5/13f, 7/29f, 10/30, 14/18, 22/16, 31/31, 41/32) or ignorance in their followers (34/24, 55/13, 72/26, 74/20f).

22/15–17 **Giftes . . . righteous.** Deut. 16.19. The opening verses of Tyndale's Deut. 17 (22/17; Mombert 577; TOT 280) equal the Vulgate's and KJV's Deut. 16.18–22. (The Pentateuch in TOT lacks page divisions into ABC etc.)

22/32–23/1 **sinne . . . come.** Cf. Matt. 12.31–32.

23/4–5 **Iudas . . . Pharao . . . Balam.** Cf. CWM 8/1.221/33–34. For Judas and Balaam, cf. 14/14–18n; for Pharaoh, cf. Exod. 9–14.

23/10–11 **make marchaundice of the people.** Cf. 2 Pet. 2.3.

23/12–13 **¶ Whether . . . church.** The title of this section is given at CWM 8/1.223/11–12 and repeated at CWM 8/1.225/2–4.

23/14–27 **Another . . . congregacion.** CWM 8/1.225/2–18.

23/18 **we are begotten thorow the worde.** Cf. 1 Pet. 1.3.

23/21–22 **how . . . preacher.** Rom. 10.14. O'Donnell corrected the sidenote from Rom. 9 to Rom. 10.

23/27–30 **And agayne . . . therto.** CWM 8/1.227/34–37.

24/2–6 **lienge . . . word.** Cf. CWM 8/1.242/6–10.

24/6 **Ihon .xv. . . . word.** John 15.3.

24/9–10 **Ihon .xvij. . . . thy trueth.** Cf. John 17.17.

24/9–12 **Ihon .xvij. . . . for true.** CWM 8/1.229/13–16.

24/12–13 **But . . . true.** CWM 8/1.229/20–21.

24/13–16 **And Christ . . . Christes.** CWM 8/1.229/34–36.

24/14 **Ihon .v. . . . man.** John 5.34.

24/17 **vnwritten.** *Dialogue* Bk. 1, Ch. 25, asserts that, in addition to Scripture, truths necessary to salvation are found in tradition (CWM 6/1.137–53).

24/17–18 ¶ **Whether . . . beleued.** CWM 8/1.254/1–2. For brief objections to the principle of *sola scriptura,* cf. CWM 8/1.134/7–8, 156/36–157/1.

24/19–24 **But . . . written.** CWM 8/1.255/18–23.

24/22–24 **therfore . . . written.** Cf. John 21.25. Tyndale claims that Christ and the apostles performed a miracle to validate each point of doctrine, but More denies this position (CWM 8/1.247/29–30).

24/25–30 **the pith . . . written.** Cf. CWM 8/1.258/12–14.

24/28–30 **So . . . written.** CWM 8/1.258/14–16.

24/31–25/1 **For if . . . that is written.** Cf. CWM 8/1.263/11–13.

25/2–7 **in as moch . . . people.** CWM 8/1.264/28–33.

25/2–4 **false . . . possible.** Cf. Matt. 24.24, Mark 13.22.

25/8–12 **Some man . . . sonne.** Cf. CWM 8/1.271/34–272/3.

25/12–13 **God . . . write.** CWM 8/1.273/36.

25/13–14 **And that . . . testifie.** CWM 8/1.274/8–9.

25/15–17 **Notwithstondinge . . . preachynge.** CWM 8/1.274/22–24.

25/17–22 **And beyonde . . . bokes.** Cf. CWM 8/1.276/35–277/3, 300/12–13.

25/20 **popetrie.** Cf. *Obedience* G5v, *Matthew* k2v. Tyndale refers to religious ceremonies and scriptural glosses as other examples of false "poetry" (*1 John* A6v). Tyndale rebuked his former assistant William Roye for discrediting the reformers' cause by using "raylinge rymes" (*Mammon* A3) against Wolsey in Barlowe and Roye. A sidenote on Gen. 47 views poetry as the ivy that strangles the tree of truth (Mombert 143; TOT 76). Cf. Peter C. Herman, *Squitter-Wits and Muse-Haters: Sidney, Spenser, Milton and Antipoetic Sentiment* (Detroit: Wayne State UP, 1996) 34–43, esp. 41.

25/23–25 **if . . . scripture.** Cf. CWM 8/1.279/14–16.

25/25–32 **The testament . . . declared.** CWM 8/1.277/10–17.

25/25–27 **The testament . . . raynebowe.** Cf. Gen. 9.12–17.

25/27–28 **And the appoyntement . . . circumcision.** Gen. 17.9–14.

25/29 **Actes .vij. . . . circumcision.** Acts 7.8.

25/33–26/2 **But . . . scripture.** CWM 8/1.280/11–13 and referred to at CWM 8/1.280/19–20.

26/2–4 **then all . . . miracles.** Cf. CWM 8/1.280/31–33.

26/4–14 **Wherfore . . . eyes.** Cf. CWM 8/1.282/18–27.

26/10–11 **angels . . . preached.** Cf. Gal. 1.8.

26/12–13 **How . . . scripture.** Cf. CWM 8/1.284/15–17.

26/13–14 **profitable . . . eyes.** Cf. CWM 8/1.290/21–22 and repeated at CWM 8/1.290/32.

26/14–15 **What . . . heuen.** For Mary's Assumption, cf. CWM 8/1.285/2, 290/24.

26/15–16 **what . . . purgatorye.** Cf. CWM 8/1.288/27, 290/24.

26/16 **to feare men thou wilt saye.** Cf. CWM 8/1.288/33.

26/16–20 **Christ . . . halfe pence.** CWM 8/1.289/24–27.

26/21–22 **And that . . . purpose.** Cf. CWM 8/1.290/37–38.

26/22–27/3 **because . . . mocked them.** Cf. CWM 8/1.291/27–292/4.

26/24–25 **mocked . . . resurreccion.** Cf. Acts 17.32.

26/25–26 **Christ was god and man.** Cf. John 1.14.

26/26 **died betwene .ij. theves.** Cf. Matt. 27.38, Mark 15.27, and esp. Luke 23.39–43 for the story of the Good Thief.

26/28–31 **Ye . . . wrote.** Repeated at CWM 8/1.293/34–37.

26/29–30 **bred . . . bloude.** For the institution of the Eucharist, cf. Matt. 26.26–28, Mark 14.22–24, Luke 22.19–20, 1 Cor. 11.23–26. *Dialogue* makes a dozen scattered references to the Eucharist; *Answer* clusters a dozen references to the Eucharist in Tyndale's discussion of More's Bk. 4. In both works, the sacrament is a topic less frequently examined than Scripture.

27/4–21 **Morouer . . . ypocrites.** CWM 8/1.295/2–19.

27/5 **baptim.** Cf. Rom. 6.3–4.

27/7–9 **all . . . testament.** Repeated at CWM 8/1.302/24–26.

27/7–8 **sacramentes . . . significacions.** For Tyndale's theology of sacrament as sign only, cf. *Obedience* M1–M2v, and More's critique: *Supplication of Souls,* 1529 (CWM 7.162/1–4), *Confutation,* 1532–33 (CWM 8/1.302/15–17), *Answer to a Poisoned Book,* December 1533 (CWM 11.xxx–xxxi). *Unio Dissidentium* (1.S2) quotes Augustine's praise of Baptism and the Eucharist as intelligible signs in *Christian Doctrine* (AD c396–97) 3.9.13 (CCL 32.86; 1NPNF 2.560).

27/9–21 **Wherfore ... ypocrites.** Repeated at CWM 8/1.304/2–13.

27/20–21 **false marchaundice.** 2 Pet. 2.3.

27/21–23 **And therto ... worlde.** CWM 8/1.305/20–22. Tyndale agrees with Luther's position that Orders is not a sacrament in *Contra Henricum Regem Angliae,* 1522 (cf. CWM 8/1.220/10–12; WA 10/2.220–21; not in LW).

27/23–27 **And agayne ... nature.** CWM 8/1.306/6–9.

27/28–32 **They ... them.** Cf. CWM 8/1.260/2–6.

28/1–4 **yet ... downe.** Cf. CWM 8/1.83/7–10.

28/4–6 **For ... damnacion.** Cf. CWM 8/1.309/17.

28/10 ¶ **Whether the church can erre.** Here Tyndale answers the church's claim of inerrancy on essential matters of belief as set forth in *Dialogue,* Bk. 1, Ch. 18–21 (CWM 6/1.101–21).

28/10–15 ¶ **Whether ... halt.** Cf. CWM 8/1.387/3–9. This is the first reference from *Confutation,* Part II, 1533. With regrettable fulness, More devotes three out of nine books of *Confutation* to attacking a third of *Answer*'s introductory essay.

28/15–25 **I said ... sworne.** Cf. CWM 8/1.391/9–18. Here Tyndale uses the narrow definition of "church," in which the specific mark of its members is living trust in God's merciful promises. Cf. 12/26–29, 112/26–30, 142/30–143/2. (JW)

28/22–25 **this faith ... sworne.** Paraphrased at CWM 8/1.400/30–32.

28/26–29/4 **And this ... congregacion.** CWM 8/1.403/19–28.

29/1–3 **fundacion ... household of god.** For *Answer* the foundation is faith (29/1), cf. Eph. 2.19–20. Paul holds that the Christian community is "bilt apon the foundacion of the apostles and prophetes" (Wallis 403/17–18; TNT 283D). NT sidenote has "Foundacion is the worde of God."

29/3–4 **faith ... congregacion.** Cf. Matt. 16.18. In *Answer* Tyndale interprets "the rocke" as "faith." *Unio Dissidentium* gives two passages (both 2.D3v), where Augustine interprets the "rock" as Christ, not as Peter or the Bishop of Rome: *Tractates on the Gospel* *of John* (AD 406–7, 419–24), Tr. 124, Par. 5 (CCL 36.684–85; 1NPNF 7.450); and Sermon 76 on Matt. 14.24–33 (AD 410–12), Par. 2 (PL 38.479–80; Rotelle 3/3.312). Erasmus refers to Augustine's sermon in his annotation on Matt. 16.18, *Quia tu es.*) 1516 NT (Reeve 1.70–71). More echoes Augustine in *Confutation,* where "the rokke [is] our sauyour Cryste hym selfe" (CWM 8/1.226/34). Matt. 16.18 is one of the most frequently quoted proof-texts of More, cf. Marc'hadour, *Bible* 4.117. He uses it to argue, not papal infallibility, but the church's infallibility in tradition and consensus (CWM 8/3.1549).

29/4–11 **Christ axed . . . bloude.** Cf. CWM 8/1.330/16–22. More repeats this same passage at CWM 8/1.405/2–8.

29/5 **whom they toke him for.** Cf. Matt. 16.15, Mark 8.29, Luke 9.20.

29/6–7 **thou . . . god.** Matt. 16.16.

29/7 **that art . . . worlde.** John 11.27.

29/8 **he that . . . Abraham.** Cf. Gen. 17.7, Gen. 22.18.

29/11–14 **That offeringe . . . moare.** Cf. CWM 8/1.409/30–32.

29/14–24 **And Christ . . . church.** Cf. CWM 8/1.410/35–411/9.

29/15–18 **And agenst . . . saffe.** Repeated at CWM 8/1.411/15–17.

29/18–24 **that . . . church.** Repeated at CWM 8/1.414/22–28.

29/22–24 **who soever . . . church.** Cf. CWM 8/1.417/4–6. Here and in the Prologue to Hebrews (Wallis 502/4–6; TNT 347), Tyndale accuses Roman Catholics of an unspecified heresy, namely Pelagianism. Pelagius (c354–c419) taught that Adam's sin affected only himself, that all humans are born in a state of grace and that Christ functions only as model. Later, Semi-Pelagianism taught that humans could make an initial act of faith without the help of grace. Both heresies were opposed by numerous writings of Augustine. Pelagianism was condemned by the ecumenical Council of Ephesus in 431; Semi-Pelagianism, by the provincial Council of Orange II in 529 (NCE 11.58–60; OER 3.238–41).

29/25–30 **And the church . . . church.** Cf. CWM 8/1.418/2–6.

29/25–26 **the church is christes body.** Cf. Col. 1.18.

29/26–27 **every . . . christ.** Eph. 5.29–30.

29/27–28 **Now . . . in it.** Cf. Rom. 8.9.

30/1–2 ¶ **How . . . synner.** Cf. CWM 8/1.419/17–18.

30/3–33 **Furthermoare . . . batayle.** Cf. CWM 8/1.419/31–420/27. After quoting a page and a half of *Answer, Confutation* subdivides this long quotation and deals with it in smaller portions over the next forty-some pages. Cf. nn for 30/3–4, 30/4–11, 30/8–11, 30/12–19, 30/19–33, 30/20–29, 30/27–29 and 32–33, 30/31–33.

30/3–4 **Furthermoare . . . erroures.** Cf. CWM 8/1.421/2–3.

30/4–11 **For . . . synne.** Cf. CWM 8/1.421/12–18. *Confutation* quotes *Answer*'s older verb form "kepith" (30/8) at CWM 8/1.420/3 but gives the newer form "kepys" at CWM 8/1.421/15.

30/5–7 **Now . . . God.** 1 John 3.9.

30/8–11 **And therfore . . . synne.** Cf. CWM 8/1.459/27–29.

30/12–19 **And yet . . . in me.** Cf. CWM 8/1.444/19–25.

30/14–15 **if . . . in vs.** 1 John 1.8.

30/15–16 **iff . . . in vs.** 1 John 1.10.

30/17–19 **that good . . . in me.** Rom. 7.19–20.

30/19 **Thus are we synners and no synners.** Tyndale works with Luther's thesis that the believer is *simul iustus et peccator.* But Tyndale gives a broader basis for the righteousness opposed to sin, grounding it in the promise laid hold of in trust, like Luther, but also in assent to the law as good and regret over not observing it (30/20–24). On Luther's doctrine of the *simul* a basic study is Rudolph Hermann, *Luthers These "Gerecht und Sünder zugleich"* (Gütersloh: Mohn, 1930). Also, Wicks, "Living and Praying as *simul iustus et peccator:* a Chapter in Luther's Spiritual Teaching," *Gregorianum* 70 (1989) 521–48, rpt. in *Luther's Reform.* For Luther, as for Tyndale, the condition of the one who is *simul iustus et peccator* is not static, for the Holy Spirit is actively opposing the flesh's endemic sinful seeking. (JW)

30/19–33 **Thus . . . batayle.** Cf. CWM 8/1.445/33–446/8.

30/20–29 **No . . . out.** Cf. CWM 8/1.446/24–30.

30/27–29 and 30/32–33 **when . . . out, yeld . . . serue it.** Paraphrased at CWM 8/1.455/11–13.

30/31–33 **we . . . batayle.** Cf. CWM 8/1. 448/6–8.

30/31–32 **yocke of God.** Cf. Matt. 11.29–30.

30/32 **nether . . . synne.** Cf. Rom. 6.13.

31/1–2 **How . . . erre.** CWM 8/1.461/5–6.

31/3–13 **And as . . . maliciously.** CWM 8/1.461/8–18. *Confutation* refers to part of *Answer*'s contrast between sins of malice and sins of weakness (31/5–6) at CWM 8/1.217/23–25, cf. *1 John* B4v.

31/11–27 **in other . . . resiste.** Cf. CWM 8/1.467/28–468/8.

31/13–21 **if some . . . bloude.** Repeated at CWM 8/1.472/28–36.

31/13–25 **some . . . gospel.** This passage begins in paraphrase, "some . . . bloude" (31/13–21; CWM 8/1.406/11–16), and ends in nearly verbatim quotation, "For . . . gospel" (31/21–25; CWM 8/1.406 /16–20).

31/14 **Christes brethern.** Cf. Matt. 12.46–47, Mark 3.31–32, Luke 8.19–20. Jerome defended the perpetual virginity of Mary in *Against Helvidius* (AD c383) by explaining that in Hebrew culture "brethren" meant, not only siblings, but kindred (Par. 15 in PL 23.198–99; Par. 17 in 2NPNF 6.342–43) and by referring to the writings of Ignatius, Polycarp, Irenaeus, and Justin Martyr (Par. 17 in PL 23.201; Par. 19 in 2NPNF 6.343). Cf. 95/4–5, 166/20nn. (JW)

31/28–29 **But . . . scripture.** CWM 8/1.481/20.

31/29–30 **or soch . . . scripture.** Cf. CWM 8/1.481/28–29.

31/30–31 **and saluacion . . . or noo.** Cf. CWM 8/1.481/36–37.

31/31–32/5 **and for . . . brethern.** Cf. CWM 8/1.482/7–14.

32/4 **the vnite of faith.** Cf. Eph. 4.13.

32/5–6 **Now . . . workes.** CWM 8/1.484/20–21.

32/6–9 **and they . . . faith.** Cf. CWM 8/1.484/26–29.

32/10 **Faith.** *Dialogue,* Bk. 1 argues for the inerrancy of the church: Ch. 18 on Matt. 23.2–3 as a foundational text; Ch. 20, against false interpretations of Scripture by the church; Ch. 21, for true interpretations; Ch. 24, on the Apostles' Creed; Ch. 25, on the Ten Commandments; Ch. 25–26, on condemnations of heresies (CWM 6/1.101–62 passim).

32/10–26 **Faith . . . deed.** Cf. CWM 8/1.486/1–18.

32/26–33/29 **As . . . forgeuen.** CWM 8/1.489/30–490/28.

33/27–29 **The old . . . forgeuen.** The conclusion of the previous passage is paraphrased in CWM 8/1.496/15–19. Compare Tyndale's truant schoolboy with the prodigal son of Luke 15.11–24.

33/30 **election.** In *Dialogue* Bk. 2, Ch. 3–4, the Messenger defends an invisible church composed of those predestined to heaven (CWM

6/1.195–206). In Bk. 4, Ch. 10–12 (CWM 6/1.376–405), More as Mentor attacks Lutheran teaching on predestination, which he believes will lead to moral chaos.

33/30–34/11 ¶ **The maner . . . liuynge.** CWM 8/1.497/11–25.

33/31 **Even . . . electe.** CWM 8/1.498/4.

33/31–32 **God . . . god.** Cf. John 15.16.

33/32–34/2 **sendeth . . . vn to them.** Cf. CWM 8/1.500/6–7.

34/2–4 **maketh . . . doo.** Cf. CWM 8/1.500/22–24.

34/4–11 **And then . . . liuynge.** Cf. CWM 8/1.502/13–19. The first sentence (34/4–6) is repeated almost verbatim at CWM 8/1.511/30–31, and the next three sentences (34/6–11) at CWM 8/1.512/14–18.

34/6–11 **For when . . . liuynge.** Basic to Tyndale's view of human action is the priority of wit over will. This tenet accords with the high esteem of many humanists and reformers for the inculcation of true doctrine as the essential step in reform. More, on the other hand (cf. 211/21–212/11), ascribes power to the will to compel belief. (JW)

34/11–13 **How be it . . . teth.** CWM 8/1.515/22–23.

34/13–15 **And there . . . Christe.** CWM 8/1.516/30–31.

34/13–14 **ryghtewesnes . . . god.** Cf. Rom. 10.3.

34/15–24 **And there . . . wittes.** Cf. CWM 8/1.517/32–39.

34/25–32 **And though . . . resistaunce.** CWM 8/1.519/5–12.

34/32–34 **God . . . only.** Cf. Ps. 30.7.

34/32–35 **God . . . theirs.** CWM 8/1.523/10–13.

34/35–35/27 **God . . . eateth.** Cf. CWM 8/1.529/25–530/15 and nn to 35/15–17, 35/19–22, 35/24–26.

35/1–5 **Dauids . . . Saull.** Cf. 1 Sam. 18–31.

35/3 **liued . . . vaine.** Cf. Ps. 73.13.

35/3–5 **For . . . enemie.** Ps. 73.3. This psalm is attributed to Asaph, not David. References to David's conflict with Saul occur in the headings of Pss. 18, 52, 54, 57, 59.

35/11–15 **Was . . . Abegall.** Cf. 1 Sam. 25.10–35. Because all forms of "churlish" in the OED contain a final "h," O'Donnell has emended "churlysse" (35/12) and noted the variant in the critical apparatus.

35/15–17 **How . . . Vriah.** CWM 8/1.533/38–39.

35/16–19 **adulterye . . . mekely.** Cf. 2 Sam. 11–12. David exemplifies the sins of the elect who nevertheless do not "malycyously cast of the yocke of gods commaundementes" (35/23). (JW)

35/19–22 **Now . . . a slepe.** CWM 8/1.534/18–21.

35/24–26 **There . . . meate.** CWM 8/1.538/36–539/2.

35/28–36/24 **And in lyke maner . . . faythes.** Cf. CWM 8/1.541/ 32–542/24.

35/28–29 **apostles . . . amased.** Cf. Matt. 26.56, Mark 14.50.

35/31–33 **all the wordes . . . deeth.** Cf. Matt. 16.21, Mark 8.31, Luke 9.22.

35/33–36/2 **Morouer . . . thoughtes.** Cf. Luke 18.34.

36/14 **miracles . . . doo.** For Jairus' daughter, cf. Matt. 9.18–19, 23–26, Mark 5.21–24, 35–43, Luke 8.40–42, 49–56; for the son of the widow of Nain, cf. Luke 7.12–15; for Lazarus, cf. John 11.11– 44.

36/16–17 **women . . . rysen.** Cf. Matt. 28.8, Mark 16.10–11, Luke 24.8–11.

36/20–24 **ye . . . faythes.** Cf. Luke 24.36–43. Disconsolate and doubting after the crucifixion, the apostles exemplify error but "none of them . . . was fallen in hys hert from chryste" (36/25–26). (JW)

36/25–26 **How . . . chryste.** CWM 8/1.545/30–31.

36/26–28 **Peter . . . hym.** Cf. John 20.3–9.

36/28–30 **But . . . miracle.** Cf. John 20.1–2.

36/31 **Ioseph of Arimathea.** Cf. Matt. 27.57–60, Mark 15.43, Luke 23.50–53, John 19.38. **Nicodemus.** Cf. John 19.39.

37/1–2 **And the wemen . . . annoyntmentes.** Cf. Mark 16.1–2, Luke 24.1. *Answer* has "annoyntmentes," while NT has "odures," i.e., "odours" (Wallis 120/22; TNT 86A).

37/2–4 **And the hertes . . . hym.** Cf. Luke 24.32.

37/5–7 **And thomas . . . god.** John 20.24–29.

37/7–14 **There . . . tyme.** Cf. CWM 8/1.548/19–25.

37/15–18 **Yee . . . tyme.** Cf. CWM 8/1.551/12–14.

37/15–16 **peter . . . bytterly.** Cf. Matt. 26.75, Mark 14.72, Luke 22.61–62.

37/18–32 **so that . . . expositoures.** Cf. CWM 8/1.554/8–22.

37/20 **reserued in our ladye.** Cf. CWM 6/1.108/1–21. The Sicilian canonist Panormitanus (1386–1445) had claimed that, in certain situations, a simple believer rather than the pope or bishops might possess the authentic message of Christ, as Luther adduced in his *Resolutiones* of the theses of the Leipzig Disputation, 1519 (WA 2.404/26–31; not in LW) and in responding to *Exsurge Domine* in *Defense and Explanation of All the Articles,* December 1520 (WA 7.430/9–12; LW 32.81). Luther believed that, amid widespread error, he himself preserved the true faith, *Resolutiones* of the Leipzig theses (ibid.) and a later lecture on Genesis (WA 42.334/30; LW 2.102). (JW)

Panormitanus also held that Mary had preserved the faith of the church when Peter fell. Cf. *Commentaria in libros decretalium* (Lyons, 1524) 1, *de electione,* 122r, cited by Gogan 345n156. More's interpretation, that the one candle still shining at the end of Tenebrae is a symbol of Mary, may have come from *The Life of Christ* by the 14c Carthusian Ludolf of Saxony, cited by James Monti, *The King's Good Servant but God's First* (San Francisco: Ignatius, 1997) 225 and n209.

Probably because written against More, *Answer* discusses the role of Mary more than any other of Tyndale's works. Cf. 95/4–5, 124/23f, 185/13f, 208/7f. Tyndale also alludes to her Conception free from original sin and Assumption into heaven (*Obedience* C3, S2); he accuses Mary of minor personal sins (*Obedience* S4v); he grieves that ignorant Christians rely on Marian devotions, such as the Little Office of the Blessed Virgin Mary (*Obedience* I8v, *1 John* A5) and the fast between 8 December and 2 February (*Mammon* F1v). Thanks to Stephen J. Mayer for the following interpretation: when Tyndale writes that Jesus emerged from Mary's armpit (*Matthew* p1v), he may be mocking the legend which claimed that Jesus passed through Mary's side. John of Damascus (c645–c750) (NCE 7.1047–49) rejects this idea in *Exposition of the Orthodox Faith* 4.14 (PG 94.1161–62; 2NPNF 9.86); cited by E.P. Nugent CMF, "The Closed Womb of the Blessed Mother of God," *Ephemerides Mariologicae* 8 (1958) 266 and n109.

37/22–25 **Simon ... brethern.** Cf. Luke 22.31–32. *Answer* has "come vn to thy selfe" (37/24), while NT has "converted" (Wallis 179/15; TNT 127C).

37/32 **mad colens.** Foxe (5.251) relates how Collins, crazed by his wife's infidelity, held up a dog when the priest elevated the host at

Mass. Although *non compos mentis,* Collins was burnt as a heretic at Smithfield in 1538, cf. PS 3.39. Since "dog" is "God" spelled backwards, his action might indicate a disbelief in Christ's Real Presence in the Eucharist.

38/1–2 **¶ Whether . . . or no.** CWM 8/2.576/21. Tyndale's rejection of the medieval church as the true church of Christ is addressed in *Confutation,* Bk. 5, 6, 7 (cf. CWM 8/1.134/13–14).

38/2 **Christes church.** In *Dialogue* Bk. 2, Ch. 1–2, 5, More as Mentor defends the known Catholic Church as the visible church composed of saints and sinners (CWM 6/1.187–95, 206–7).

38/3–4 **That . . . proued.** Cf. CWM 8/2.577/33–34. Repeated at CWM 8/2.579/19–20.

38/3–17 **That . . . bloud.** CWM 8/2.579/19–33.

38/18–39/4 **A nother . . . secret.** Cf. CWM 8/1.584/12–29.

38/18–19 **consenteth.** Tyndale regularly features active consent to the law of God in his accounts of repentance and justification, thus diverging in one aspect from Luther's account of justification, where the will's passivity under grace is central, while the law functions prior to justification by heightening guilt. (JW)

38/20 **forboden lawfull wedlocke.** The imposition of mandatory celibacy angers Tyndale because Scripture assumes the clergy will be married. In *Obedience* (I7, K1), Tyndale twice quotes 1 Tim. 3.2 on the wives of bishops. For Tyndale, fines for concubinage are a license to keep whores (50/29, 158/17, 172/2; *Obedience* K1, *1 John* E6). In Tyndale's view, the Church of Rome prefers whores and sodomites to an honest wife (*Matthew* o3). Tyndale's extended case against compulsory celibacy occurs at 152/2–167/10.

From the time of Gregory I (pope, 590–604) until the early 10c, most diocesan clergy were married men. Nicholas II (pope, 1058–61), along with the Lateran synod of 1059, forbad priests with a wife or concubine to say Mass and deprived them of their benefice. Gregory VII (pope, 1073–85) rigorously enforced these decrees on clerical celibacy (NCE 3.369–74). Lanfranc, Archbishop of Canterbury, was able to modify Gregory's policy by letting married clergy keep their wives and ordaining celibate priests henceforward. Cf. Charles A. Frazee, "The Origins of Clerical Celibacy in the Western Church," *Church History* 41 (1972) 149–67, esp. 166.

Lateran II (1139) declared that major orders were an impediment to valid marriage, canons 6–7 in *Conciliorum Oecumenicorum Decreta,* ed. J. Alberigo et al., 3d ed. (Bologna: Istituto per le scienze religiose, 1973) 198. Nevertheless, from the Gregorian Reform to the Reformation, the diocesan clergy, from bishop to parish priest, and even heads of monasteries frequently entered into *de facto* marriages and by papal dispensation passed their benefices onto their sons. (JW)

The Diocese of Constance had a schedule of fines to be paid to the diocesan administration by priests living in concubinage or otherwise guilty of sexual misconduct. Also a set payment had to be made for each child fathered by a priest living in concubinage. Cf. O. Vasella, *Reform und Reformation in der Schweiz* (Münster: Aschendorff, 1958) 26–36. Zwingli attacked this practice in *Eine freundliche Bitte und Ermahnung* of July 1522, cf. *Sämtliche Werke* 1.225. The fines were fees paid for suspension of the canonical punishments, such as the loss of one's benefice, by the concubinate clergy. The payment for a child was for the lifting of the impediment of illegitimacy and in some cases for securing an inheritance for children of such unions. The Council of Basel had condemned these practices in 1435, as had Lateran V in 1514 (*Concilium Oecumenicorum Decreta* 487, 623). (JW)

38/24 **doucheland.** In 15c and early 16c Germany, failures against celibacy seem high although records are incomplete for *Hurenzins* (whore tax) and *Wigenzins* (cradle tax). Cf. Joel F. Harrington, *Reordering marriage and society in Reformation Germany* (Cambridge UP, 1995) 34 and n28.

38/27 **wales.** Illegal clerical unions and their offspring were satirized by poets and censured, among others, by Gerald of Wales (c1146–c1220) and two Archbishops of Canterbury: John Pecham in 1284 and William Warham in 1504. Cf. Glanmor Williams 339–46, 401–2.

38/27 **yerland.** In Pre-Norman Ireland (before 1171–72), monasteries were frequently headed by lay abbots, who were usually married. Cf. Friedrich Kempf in Jedin and Dolan 3.223. Clerical marriage continued in Gaelic Ireland throughout the late medieval period. Bishops and abbots obtained papal dispensations for their sons to succeed them. Cf. Colm Lennon, *Sixteenth-Century Ireland: The Incomplete Conquest* (New York: St. Martin's, 1995) 126. Higher standards obtained among the friars, especially the Observant Franciscans, cf. Lennon 119. See Aubrey Gwynn and R. Neville Hadcock, *Medieval Religious Houses: Ireland* (Blackrock, Co. Dublin: Irish Academic, 1970) and, more recently, Steven G. Ellis, Ch. 8, "The Late Medieval Church and the Origins of Tudor Reform," *Ireland in the Age of the Tudors 1447–1603: English Expansion and the End of Gaelic Rule* (New York: Longman, 1998) 190–217.

38/27 **Scotland.** Sir David Lyndesay (c1486–1555) satirized the immorality of the diocesan clergy in his verse drama on *The Thrie Estatis* (1540). As a separate kingdom, Scotland implemented the Reformation at a later period than England. In 1560 the Scottish Parliament abrogated papal authority in Scotland and forbad the Latin Mass, but not until 1573 were the clergy required by statute to join the Reformation or be deprived of their benefices. (Mary Stuart returned to Scotland from France in 1561 and abdicated in 1567.) Cf. Gordon Donaldson, "The Parish Clergy and the Reformation," *Scottish Church History* (Edinburgh: Scottish Academic, 1985) 73, 88. See Ian B. Cowan and David E. Easson, *Medieval Religious Houses: Scotland,* 2d ed. (London: Longman, 1976); Gordon Donaldson, *The Scottish Reformation* (Cambridge UP, 1960).

38/27 **Fraunce.** Repeated invasions during the Hundred Years War (1337–1453) undermined the physical fabric and the spiritual life of the church in France. Cf. A. Latreille et al., *Histoire du Catholicisme en France;* Vol. 2, *Sous les rois très chrétiens* (Paris: Editions Spes, 1960) 71. In spite of efforts at reform, concubinage among the diocesan clergy continued into the 17c (OER 1.397–99).

38/27 **Spayne.** Because too many people were affected, in 1251 Innocent IV (pope, 1243–54) revoked sentences of excommunication placed by a papal legate on clerics in major orders and their mistresses, but the fines he imposed instead had little effect. Living in a pluralistic society until 1492, some clergy formed sexual relationships with Jewish or Muslim women. In 1321–22, a council in Castile decreed that such priests were to be imprisoned for two years by the bishop. Cf. J.N. Hillgarth, *The Spanish Kingdoms,*

1250–1516; Vol. I, *1250–1410, "Precarious Balance"* (Oxford: Clarendon, 1976) 111–12. Fernando (king, 1474–1516) and Isabel (queen, 1474–1504) tried to reform the diocesan clergy by nominating exemplary bishops, but their efforts did not bear much fruit until the Counter-Reformation. Cf. Vol. II, *1410–1516, "Castilian Hegemony"* (Oxford: Clarendon, 1978) 405–10. Rejecting the reforms of the Observant Franciscan Cardinal Ximenes, a thousand Conventual Franciscans converted to Islam, married their Muslim concubines and resettled in North Africa. Cf. Karl J. von Hefele, *The Life and Times of Cardinal Ximenez,* 2d ed. (London, 1885) 215–17 cited by Monti 111–12 and n51.

38/27 **Englond.** After examining visitation records in Winchester, Kent, Suffolk, Norwich, and Lincoln, Peter Marshall (144–51) concluded that fewer than five percent of these clerics were suspected of breaking their promise of celibacy. The situation was probably worse in London on account of the larger numbers of unbeneficed clergy taking advantage of the anonymity of the city. Tyndale claims that, because of the preaching of Wyclif against unchastity, priests prefer liaisons with married women to open concubinage. Thus, English bishops collect fewer fines than on the Continent. But some of the English hierarchy were themselves offenders: Bishop James Stanley of Ely with three illegitimate children, Cardinal Wolsey with two, and perhaps Archbishop Warham with a son. For Stanley, cf. Haigh 10. For Wolsey, cf. Jasper Ridley, *Statesman and Saint: Cardinal Wolsey, Sir Thomas More, and the Politics of Henry VIII* (New York: Viking, 1982) 171–72. For Warham, cf. MacCulloch, *Cranmer* 108.

The reinstitution of clerical marriage did not proceed smoothly in the English Reformation. Although Henry VIII expelled monks, friars, and nuns from their properties in 1536 and 1539, he expected them to keep their vows of celibacy, as is indicated in the Six Articles of 1539, 31 Henry VIII, Ch. 14 (*Statutes* 3.739). Men could join the ranks of the diocesan clergy; women could return to their families or live together in non-canonical communities. Most men and women religious received government pensions. In 1549 and 1551–52 priests were permitted to marry, 2 & 3 Edward VI, Ch. 21; 5 & 6 Edward, Ch. 12 (*Statutes* 4/1.67, 146–47). However, in 1553 priests were required to dismiss their wives or lose their benefices, 1 Mary, St. 2, Ch. 2 (*Statutes* 4/1.202). In 1559 priests were again allowed to marry by Injunction 29 issued by Elizabeth I in her capacity as Supreme Governor of the Church of England, cf. Bray 342–43. Marriage of the clergy was confirmed in 1604, 1 James, Ch. 25 (*Statutes* 4/2.1052).

39/2 **wicleffe.** John Wyclif (c1330–84) taught that rulers in mortal sin, especially the clergy, forfeited the right to the obedience of their subjects. He also claimed that bread and wine remained after the consecration and that Christ is present only figuratively. After his death, his teachings were condemned by the Council of Constance (1414–18) in 1417; his books were burnt and his body exhumed from consecrated ground in 1428. See Anthony Kenny, *Wyclif,* Past Masters Series (Oxford UP, 1985). Followers of Wyclif were originally called "Lollards" (OED 1.) or "mumblers" for their supposed piety. Like "Quaker," the name "Lollard" no longer expresses contempt but merely denotes a religious group.

In *De Libero Arbitrio* (1524) Erasmus recites a litany of patristic and medieval theologians who uphold free will as opposed to Manichaeus and Wyclif, who deny it. Later, Erasmus disapprovingly quotes Luther's *Assertio,* Art. 36, which embraces the position of Wyclif, "'For no one has it in his own power to think a good or bad thought, but everything (as Wyclif's article condemned at Constance rightly teaches) happens by absolute necessity.'" From Erasmus, *On the Freedom of the Will,* citing *Assertio omnium articulorum,* 1520 (WA 7.146/6–8; not in LW) in *Luther and Erasmus: Free Will and Salvation,* ed. E. Gordon Rupp and Philip S. Watson, LCC 17 (Philadephia: Westminster, 1969) 13, 13n1, 64. Cf. also 174/30n.

Tyndale denies that Wyclif caused insurrection (*1 John* H7); in fact, the Peasants' Revolt in 1381 arose from economic, not theological, reasons. In the Prologue to Jonas, Tyndale asserts that the rejection of Wyclif's call to repentance resulted in the assassination of Richard II, the usurpation of the crown by Henry IV, Henry V, and Henry VI, the invasion of France, and the civil wars in England (TOT 634–35). (The Book of Jonas in TOT lacks page divisions into ABC etc.) For pastoral care from evil clergy, cf. 149/

19–20n; for Wyclif's supposed influence in Bohemia, cf. 167/12–14n; for the kings, cf. 167/18–19; for a brief history of the Bible in English, cf. 167/21–22n; for the order of justification, cf. 195/22n.

Donald Dean Smeeton examines similarities between Tyndale and Lollards on the necessity of a vernacular Bible, the rejection of transubstantiation, and the reform of a corrupt clergy by the king in *Lollard Themes in the Reformation Theology of William Tyndale,* Sixteenth Century Essays & Studies 6 (Kirksville, MO: Sixteenth Century Journal, 1986).

39/5–14 **Ther to . . . papa.** CWM 8/1.587/23–32. The second half of this passage (39/9–14) is repeated at CWM 8/1.590/8–12. A sign of the absence of faith within the papal hierarchy is its suppression of those who would admonish its faults. In the medieval canonical tradition, a lively discussion centered on the problem in Gratian, *Decretum,* Part 1, Dist. 40, Ch. 6 (CIC 1.146). For Gratian, cf. 151/24n. The text stated that the pope was subject to no one's judgment, but it went on to make an exception, *nisi deprehendatur a fide deuius,* "unless he is found to have deviated from the faith." The commentators expanded considerably the meaning of "deviated from the faith" and thereby listed numerous cases of papal malfeasance that would be subject to judgment. Many came to designate a general council, representing the whole church, as the proper forum of such correction, even to the measure of deposing a recalcitrant pope. Cf. Brian Tierney, *Foundations of the Conciliar Theory* (Cambridge UP, 1955) 56–67. (JW)

39/15–17 **And Paul . . . of his.** CWM 8/1.594/3–5; Rom. 13.1, 4. Luther had attacked the claim of clerical immunity from prosecution for crime in his first broadside against "the three walls of the Romanists." He also declared perverse the canon forbidding the temporal power to punish "the spiritual estate" and appealed to Rom. 13.1 and 4, along with 1 Pet. 2.13–14, to justify the intervention of rulers to reform clerical abuses. Cf. *To the Christian Nobility,* 1520 (WA 6.407/9–411/7; LW 44.127–33). (JW)

39/18–27 **And Paul . . . doctrine.** CWM 8/1.595/35–596/8.

39/18–21 **if he . . . companie.** Cf. 1 Cor. 5.11. *Answer* has the Anglo-Saxon "horekeper"; NT has the Latinate "fornicator" (Wallis 352/23; TNT 248C).

39/22–27 **to receaue the sacramentes of them . . . doctrine.** During the persecution by Diocletian (AD 303–5), several bishops in North Africa pretended to comply with the imperial decrees by handing over heretical books instead of the Scriptures to be burned. The ordinations performed by these bishops were contested, especially by Donatus, schismatic Bishop of Carthage (AD 313–47). Believing that they alone were the true church, the Donatists also required rebaptism of those who had received the rite from one outside their sect (NCE 4.1001–1003).

39/28–29 ¶ **The argumentes . . . solued.** Cf. CWM 8/1.599/5–6.

39/30–40/5 **Notwithstondinge . . . this.** Cf. CWM 8/1.599/30–36.

40/7 **lutherans.** For heretics, cf. 43/16–17, 212/26. Whereas for More, Roman Catholics belong to the true church and Lutherans are heretics, for Tyndale, Catholics belong to a fleshly church but Lutherans to a spiritual one (105/13). To illustrate his point, Tyndale scoffs that Catholic priests take whores, but Lutheran ministers marry wives (158/12–15, *Matthew* 03). (JB)

40/4–18 **One . . . thynge.** Cf. CWM 8/1.601/17–31.

40/10–11 **Moses . . . phareses.** Cf. Exod. 4.29–31, Matt. 23.2.

40/19–21 **But . . . passe.** CWM 8/1.608/2–4; 1 Cor. 4.20.

40/21–41/22 **Vnder Abraham . . . worke.** Cf. CWM 8/1.609/9–610/5.

40/25 **them.** *Confutation* (CWM 8/2.609/12) and *1573* correct *1531*'s erroneous "then."

40/26 **glorious church.** Cf. Eph. 5.27.

40/27 **Iosuah.** For appointment as Moses' successor, cf. Num. 27.18–23; for exploring Canaan, cf. Num. 14.8; for surviving the Exodus, cf. Num. 15.38; for crossing the Jordan, cf. Josh. 3. **Eleazar.** For the son and successor of Aaron, cf. Num. 20.25–29. **Phineas.** For the son of Eleazar and grandson of Aaron, cf. Num. 25.6–15. **Caleb.** For exploring Canaan, cf. Num. 13.30–31; for surviving the Exodus, cf. Num. 14.24.

40/28–29 **But . . . immediatly.** Cf. Judg. 2.10–13.

40/30–32 **And god . . . agayne.** Cf. Jer. 25.1–13.

41/2–3 **scribes . . . Moses.** Cf. Matt. 23.2.

41/5 **make marchaundice.** Cf. 2 Pet. 2.3; "abvse it vn to their awne glorie & profitt" (41/5–6) is a doublet for the preceding phrase.

41/14 **leuen of the phareses.** Matt. 16.6.

41/16–17 **taken . . . knowlege.** Cf. Luke 11.52.

41/17–19 **shutt . . . wolde.** Cf. Matt. 23.13.

41/23–31 **And oure ypocrites . . . trouth.** Cf. CWM 8/2.613/35–614/6.

41/25 **lucre.** Cf. 1 Pet. 5.2.

41/27–28 **make . . . wordes.** Cf. 2 Pet. 2.3.

41/32–42/4 **And in like maner . . . aftirwarde.** Cf. CWM 8/2.630/35–631/3.

42/4–10 **and with false gloses . . . behynde the.** Cf. CWM 8/2.634/21–26. The *Glossa ordinaria* was an integral component of most Bibles produced in medieval *scriptoria* and by pre-Reformation printing presses. The biblical text occupied the center of the page, while the ample margins contained explanatory passages or "glosses" taken from patristic and early medieval commentators. The most common set of the glosses to the whole Bible stems from the circle around Anselm of Laon (d. 1117), cf. Smalley 46–66. Other attacks on glosses occur at 136/12–13, 139/3. (JW)

42/9 **thy fall.** *Confutation* glosses *Answer's* "fall" as "fatte" (CWM 8/2.634/26) as in the "fatted caulfe" of Luke 15.23 (Wallis 164/28; TNT 117E). *1573* emends "thy fall" to "that fall," thus transforming the noun into a verb; PS 3.44 follows *1573*. Cf. Glossary.

42/11–16 **And soch . . . in him.** Cf. CWM 8/2.641/28–33.

42/12 **Abraham is our father.** Matt. 3.9, John 8.39.

42/12–13 **we be Moses disciples.** John 9.28.

42/13–14 **how . . . lerned.** John 7.15, Acts 4.13.

42/14–15 **only . . . in him.** John 7.49.

42/15–16 **Loke . . . in him.** John 7.48.

42/17–20 **Wherfore . . . church.** Cf. CWM 8/2.644/27–30.

42/20–43/20 **Though . . . god.** Cf. CWM 8/2.648/5–39. With minor variations *Confutation* repeats parts of this long passage; cf. nn to 43/13–15, 43/14–15, 43/15–17, 43/16–17.

42/26 **ypocrites.** Cf. Matt. 23.13, 14, 15, 23, 25, 27, 29.

42/27 **blynd gydes.** Matt. 23.16, 24; **paynted sepulchres.** Matt. 23.27.

42/28 **generacion of vipers.** Matt. 3.7.

42/29–30 **he shall . . . god.** Luke 1.16.

42/31–32 **And he . . . childerne.** Cf. Luke 1.17.

43/1 **a spirituall hert.** Cf. Ezek. 18.31.

43/1–2 **fathers . . . Iacob.** Cf. Exod. 3.15–16.

43/2–3 **And he . . . people.** Cf. Luke 1.17. *Answer* has "the disobedient vn to the obedience of the rightteouse"; NT has "the vnbelevers to the wysdom of the iuste men" (Wallis 124/1–2; TNT 88B); KJV combines elements of both translations: "the disobedient to the wisedome of the iust . . . ."

43/4 **sett vpp . . . awne.** Cf. Rom. 10.3.

43/5 **righteewysnesse of faith.** Cf. Rom. 3.22 and 10.6.

43/10–20 **And aftir . . . god.** The commentary on CWM 8/1.143 /15–17 quotes this passage verbatim (CWM 8/3.1512) and refers to *1 John* (A7r–v) for further accusations that the medieval church corrupted the Scripture with heresies.

43/13–15 **we departe . . . rebuke them.** Cf. CWM 8/2.651/ 28–29.

43/14–15 **rebuke them in like maner.** CWM 8/2.652/26.

43/15–17 **And as . . . church.** CWM 8/2.654/9–11, 660/23–25.

43/16–17 **they that departe . . . church.** Cf. CWM 8/2.667/5–7, 817/8–11, repeated almost verbatim at 667/23–25 and 668/3–5. Augustine addresses the issue of the unity of the church in the third of his ten *Homilies on the First Epistle of John* (AD 406–7), quoted in *Unio Dissidentium* (2.Q6v). More would agree with the first part of the passage, "Certainly all who go out from the Church, and are cut off from the unity of the Church, are antichrists . . . ," Par. 7 (PL 35.2000–2001; 1NPNF 7.478). Tyndale might counter with the second part, "[W]hosoever in his deeds denies Christ, is an antichrist," Par. 8 (PL 35.2002; 1NPNF 7.479).

43/18–20 **which . . . god.** Cf. CWM 8/2.663/5–7.

43/22–44/4 **Another . . . yeres.** Cf. CWM 8/2.675/12–26.

44/1–4 **This . . . yeres.** Repeated in slightly abbreviated form at CWM 8/2.679/5–8.

44/4–6 **And this . . . obstinacie.** CWM 8/2.681/4–5.

44/4 **Iewes.** The Jews are an important topic to Tyndale as a translator of the Pentateuch through 2 Chronicles from the Hebrew Bible (Mozley 173–86; Daniell 283–315, 333–57). In *Prelates* Tyndale assigns guilt for Christ's death to the leaders of the Jews (A2r–v), but in *Obedience* he rejects the legitimacy of killing religious opponents, whether Jews, Turks, or heretics (C7v). His chief objection to the Jews is that they, like Turks and papists, supposedly believe in justification by works. Tyndale repeats this charge numerous times in *Answer* and once in *Matthew* (06). Jews openly profess their faith although they are outnumbered by Christians in contemporary Europe (*Matthew* 02). For the expulsion of the Jews from England, cf. 68/11n.

Tyndale and Erasmus both oppose the Jews for "works-righteousness"; Tyndale focuses on their lack of faith in Christ and Erasmus on their supposed trust in religious ceremonies. In the pivotal Fifth Rule of the *Enchiridion* (1503), Erasmus warns Christians "that we do not attempt to win God's favour like the Jews through certain observances as if they were magic rites . . ." (Holborn 80/3–5; CWE 66.76). In the Afterword to Markish (152), Cohen summarizes Erasmus' position on the Jews: "His is always an anti-Semitism of letters and literatures, of sources and origins, of languages and texts, and never an anti-Semitism of policy." Although More was proud of his prosecution of heretics, Marius (8) notes that "we find no hostile remark or metaphor about contemporary Jews in all the works of Thomas More."

Confident that the Jews would be converted to a reformed Christianity, Luther first showed a positive attitude toward them in *That Jesus Christ was born a Jew,* 1523 (WA 11.314–36; LW 45.199–229). After the Jews themselves began to proselytize, his attitude began to change as seen in *Against the Sabbatarians,* 1538 (WA 50.312–37; LW 47.65–98). The comparatively moderate tract *Von den letzten Worten Davids,* 1543 (WA 54.28–100; not in LW), was followed by the harsh *On the Jews and their Lies,* 1543 (WA 53.417–552; LW 47.137–306) and *Vom Schem Hamphoras,* 1543 (WA 53.579–648; not in LW). On 15 February 1547, three days before his death, Luther added an admonition, *"Eine vermanung wider die Juden,"* to his last sermon (WA 51.195–96; not in LW). Cf. Oberman, *Luther* 350n73, 292–97. (JW)

44/7–13 **And when . . . scripture.** CWM 8/2.685/31–37.

44/10–11 **their auctorite is greater then the scripture.** In 1525 Johann Eck (1486–1543) compiled a handbook against Lutheran teachings which went through more than a hundred editions (OER 2.17–19). In Ch. 1 of his *Enchiridion,* "On the Church and

Her Authority," Eck states the priority of the church over Scripture and argues that consequently the church authenticates Scripture (Fraenkel 27; Battles 12–13). Thus, one taking up the arms of biblical argument against ecclesiastical institutions gets entangled in an implicit acknowledgment of the church as the guarantor of the books he wants to cite. (JW)

44/14–15 **Notwithstondinge . . . spirite.** Cf. CWM 8/2.690/ 23–24.

44/15–46/8 **And therfore . . . good.** Cf. CWM 8/2.691/9– 692/28. With minor variations *Confutation* repeats parts of this long passage below (45/8–10, 46/5–8).

44/24–25 **Ihon . . . thynge.** Cf. Matt. 17.11 and 13, quoting Mal. 4.5–6.

44/27 **phareses . . . leuen.** Cf. Matt. 16.6 and 11, Mark 8.15, Luke 12.1.

44/28–29 **He . . . smoth.** Cf. Luke 3.5, quoting Isa. 40.4.

44/31 **weked gloses.** For John the Baptist's mission to remove false glosses from Scripture, cf. *Mammon* G2v–G3.

44/32–45/1 **honoure . . . mother.** Exod. 20.12, Deut. 5.16.

45/3–8 **God . . . they.** Cf. Matt. 15.3–6, Mark 7.9–13.

45/8–10 **As . . . saintes.** Cf. CWM 8/2.697/36–37.

45/26–27 **toke . . . knowlege.** Cf. Luke 11.52.

45/27–28 **stopped . . . in.** Cf. Matt. 23.13.

46/5–8 **Now . . . good.** Cf. CWM 8/2.705/23–26.

46/8–47/5 **Therfore . . . determined.** CWM 8/2.706/21– 707/13.

46/11 **lucre.** Cf. 1 Pet. 5.2.

46/12 **had they coude.** *Confutation* (CWM 8/2.706/24) keeps *1531*'s form, but *1573* emends it to "if they coulde." Cf. "can he" (158/9), meaning "if he can."

46/17 **leuen.** Cf. Matt. 16.6 and 11, Mark 8.15, Luke 12.1.

46/24–25 **legend . . . sayntes.** Tyndale probably refers to the *Golden Legend* by Jacobus de Voragine OP (c1230–98), who compiled his commentaries on the feasts of Christ and the saints c1260. Second in popularity only to the Bible, it was widely translated. William Caxton made and published an English version in 1483 (GL 1.xiii–iv).

46/25 **false bokes.** In his edition of Jerome (1516), Erasmus names many false attributions among Greek and Latin classics, books of the Bible, and Christian authors, e.g.: *The Battle of the Frogs and Mice* by Pseudo-Homer, *Rhetorica ad Herennium* by Pseudo-Cicero, the supposed correspondence between Paul and Seneca, Ezra 3 and 4, the Apocalypse of John, and the *Hierarchies* of Pseudo-Dionysius (not in LB; CWE 61.71–73).

46/26 **S. Hierome.** Jerome (c345–c420) is the greatest Scripture scholar among the Western Fathers (NCE 7.872–74; OER 1.163–67). He corrected the Old Latin version of the NT according to the Greek (AD 382–85), but he did not make a new translation, as Erasmus correctly notes in the preface to Valla's *Annotations.* Cf. Ep. 182, To Christopher Fisher, Paris, [about March] 1505 (Allen 1.410/149–50; CWE 2.94/168–70). Both Erasmus and Tyndale assert that Jerome was not the author of the Vulgate. Cf. Ep. 337, To Maarten Van Dorp, Antwerp, [end of May] 1515 (Allen 2.110/773–74; CWE 3.135/811–12) and Tyndale's preface to the New Testament (Wallis 10/24; TNT 9).

Erasmus dedicated his edition of Jerome to William Warham, Primate of England. See Ep. 396, Basel, 1 April 1516 (Allen 2.210–21; CWE 3.252–66; also CWE 61.3–14). After Augustine, Jerome is the Father most frequently represented in *Unio Dissidentium,* with about eighty passages (14%), most from his exegetical works. G. Lloyd Jones ranks Jerome first "among the Christian Hebraists of the Early Church" (7). Eugene Rice further claims that Jerome had better knowledge of Hebrew than any Christian until the 17c. Cf. *Saint Jerome in the Renaissance* (Baltimore: Johns Hopkins UP, 1985) 10. Jerome had a working knowledge of the whole Hebrew Bible, but Tyndale was executed after translating only half. See also Jerry H. Bentley, *Humanists and Holy Writ: NT Scholarship in the Renaissance* (Princeton UP, 1983). In his Prologue to Numbers, Tyndale objects to Jerome's "vngodly perswasions" to celibacy (Mombert 395/26; TOT 197).

46/26–27 **saynt Augustine.** For his many theological works, at once passionate and profound, Augustine (354–430) is the greatest Father of the Western Church (NCE 1.1041–58; OER 1.98–100). He was converted to Christianity through the decisive experience of reading Rom. 13.13–14, "Let vs walke honestly as it were in the daye lyght: not in eatynge and drinkynge: nether in chamburynge and wantannes: nether in stryfe and envyinge: but put ye on the Lorde Iesus Christ. And make not provision for the flesshe, to ful-fyll the lustes of it" (Wallis 338/24–28; TNT 239D). From *Confessions* (AD 397–401) 8.12.29 (PL 32.762; CSEL 33.195; 1NPNF 1.127). As Bishop of Hippo (395–430), Augustine wrote against Donatists (39/21–27n), Pelagians, and Semi-Pelagians (29/22–24n). Tyndale beats More to the punch by offering his own inter-pretation of Augustine's famous dictum on the relation between the Gospel and the church (47/31–32n).

Erasmus contributed a preface to Juan Luis Vives' edition of *The City of God*. See Ep. 1309, To the Reader, [Basel, c August 1522] (Allen 5.117–21; CWE 9.168–73). He dedicated the complete edition of Augustine to Alfonso Fonseca, Primate of Spain. See Ep. 2157, Freiburg, <May> 1529 (Allen 8.145–61; not yet in CWE). Augus-tine's *De cura agenda pro mortuis* (AD 421) is cited by name in *Testament of Tracy* (A3v). (Day reproduces Tracy's will in WCS 182.) Sidenotes on 1 Sam., Ch. 18 and Ch. 28 refer to Augustine (TOT 405, 419). The latter may have been supplied by John Rogers, who published Judges through 2 Chronicles in Matthew's Bible (1537), the year after Tyndale's execution. *Unio Dissidentium* contains about 250 passages (43%) from Augustine, especially from his anti-Pelagian writings, such as *On the Spirit and the Letter* (AD 412) (PL 44.199–216; CSEL 60.155–229; 1NPNF 5.83–114). Augustine is represented more frequently than any other Father in *Unio*. See O'Donnell, "Augustine in *Unio Dissidentium* and Tyndale's *Answer to More*," *Reformation* 2 (1997) 241–60.

46/27 **S. Cyprian.** Bishop of Carthage, Cyprian went into hiding during the persecution of Decius (AD 250–51) and was beheaded during the persecution of Valerian (AD 258) (NCE 3.564–66), cf. 200/33n. In the preface to his edition, Erasmus praises Cyprian for not excommunicating those who accepted the validity of Baptism administered by schismatics and heretics. Cf. Ep. 1000, To Cardinal Lorenzo Pucci, Louvain, 31 July 1519 (Allen 4.28/132–34; CWE 7.30/136–37). *Unio Dissidentium* contains seventeen passages (3%) from Cyprian, most from his letters, one selection from *On the Lapsed* (AD 251) (CCL 3.221–42; ANF 5.437–47) and none from *On the Unity of the Church* (AD 251) (CCL 3.249–68; ANF 5.421–

436) on the collegiality of bishops. Since Cyprian opposed Stephen I (pope, 254–57) on the question of rebaptism, Tyndale believes Cyprian would resist the contemporary monarchical papacy (*Obedience* T3v). In *To Demetrianus* (AD 252), Cyprian denied that rejection of the ancient gods by Christians was causing the decline of the Roman Empire (CCL 3A.33–51; ANF 5.457–65). Tyndale denies that the Reformation prompts its adherents to disobey civil authority (*Obedience* C6).

46/27 **S. Deonise.** Cf. Acts 17.22–34. This 5c or early 6c author assumed the name of the Athenian converted by Paul's sermon on the Areopagus (NCE 11.943–44). Lorenzo Valla denied that Dionysius belonged to the apostolic era chiefly because he was not mentioned before the time of Gregory I (pope, 590–604). In 1505 Erasmus was the first to publish Valla's *Annotations on the NT* (1453–57). He quotes the annotation on Acts 17 in his 1516 NT and later explains, "Dionysius, who in his second Hierarchy [*Ecclesiastical Hierarchy* of deacons, priests, and bishops], gives a fairly full description of the early rites of the church, is thought by the learned to be someone more recent than the celebrated member of the Areopagus who was a disciple of Paul." From Ep. 916, To Erard de la Marck, Louvain, 5 February 1519 (Allen 3.482/50–52; CWE 6.238/56–59). Cf. Karlfried Froehlich, "Pseudo-Dionysius and the Reformation of the Sixteenth Century," in Pseudo-Dionysius, *The Complete Works,* tr. Colm Luibheid et al., Classics of Western Spirituality (Mahwah, NY: Paulist, 1987) 33–46.

In 1501, William Grocyn changed his mind about the authorship of the *Ecclesiastical Hierarchy* during the course of a lecture series which he gave in London. Cf. Ep. 2, To John Holt, <London, cNovember 1501> (More, *Correspondence* 4/14n); Ep. 118, To Robert Fisher, London, 5 December [1499] (Allen 1.273n22; CWE 1.236n26).

Although a Londoner by birth, John Colet was a resident of Oxford (1496–1505) when Grocyn gave his lectures at St. Paul's. Perhaps for this reason, Colet held that Dionysius was the disciple of Paul when he later (1512–16) wrote on the *Celestial Hierarchy* and *Ecclesiastical Hierarchy,* cf. Gleason 92, 200–1. For the texts, see *Two Treatises,* ed. and tr. J.H. Lupton (1869; Ridgewood, NJ: Gregg, 1966) 19. For Colet's PN, cf. 168/28n.

When Luther rejected Dionysius as the sole patristic witness for Orders as a sacrament, Henry VIII defended him as an ancient authority and a saint in Ch. 12 on Orders (*Assertio,* CC 43.212). Familiar with the humanist position on Dionysius as a later Father, More mentions him only three times: "Saint Dionysius, who [Luther] does not deny is very ancient," *Responsio ad Lutherum,* 1523 (CWM 5/1.69/19–20); "Dyonise the fyrste chapyter of *Ecclesiasticae hierarchiae,* of the leders and maysters of the crysten fayth, sayth that they delyuered vs many thynges to be kepte, partely by wrytynge and partely by theyr instytucyons vnwryten," *Confutation,* 1532–33 (CWM 8/1.369/23–26); "Saynt Denise also in his booke *de Ecclesiastica Hierarchia,* sayth that the apostles taught the maner of consecrating in the masse by mouth" *Treatise upon the Passion,* 1534–35 (CWM 13.152/1–3).

46/27–28 **other holy men.** For a survey of Erasmus' patristic editions, see John Olin, "Erasmus and the Church Fathers," in *Six Essays on Erasmus* (New York: Fordham UP, 1979) 33–47. (JW) The four great Latin Fathers are: Ambrose, Jerome, Augustine, and Gregory. For the four major Greek Fathers, cf. 208/10n.

As Bishop of Milan, Ambrose (c339–97) baptized Augustine at Easter 387. Influenced by Philo and Origen, Ambrose practiced allegorical interpretation of Scripture (NCE 1.372–75). Erasmus dedicated his edition of Ambrose to John Lasky, Primate of Poland. See Ep. 1855, Basle, 13 August 1527 (Allen 7.118–26; not yet in CWE). Tyndale does not mention Ambrose by name, but he probably read the thirty-some passages from his biblical commentaries, letters, and treatises in *Unio Dissidentium.*

46/30 **talmud.** The authoritative body of post-biblical Jewish law. In the Talmud the base-text is the Mishnah (compiled AD c200) while the Gemara compiles the extensive elaborations of the rabbis down to the seventh Christian century. The first printed edition came out in Venice in 1520. The complete Talmud profoundly influenced classical, medieval, and modern Judaism. See R. Goldenberg, "Talmud," in *Encyclopedia of Religion,* ed. Mircea Eliade, 16 vols. including Index (New York: Macmillan, 1987) 14.256–60. (JW)

46/33 **dunce.** Cf. *Mammon* (G5) and *Obedience* (B8). The Franciscan John Duns Scotus (c1266–1308) taught the superiority of will to intellect in God and in humans, and consequently emphasized love and freedom (NCE 4.1102–6). Cf. 75/9–11n for opposition of the Scotists to humanism and 131/3n for Scotus' teaching in behalf of the Immaculate Conception.

46/33 **Thomas.** The Dominican Thomas Aquinas (c1225–74) wrote biblical commentaries, notably on the Gospel of John (NCE 14.102–15), cf. 131/2n. Tyndale spurned his *Summa Theologica* because it used the categories of Aristotelian philosophy to explain the Gospel.

Tyndale compares biblical exegeses by Scotus and Aquinas with the Talmud to emphasize how inferior the scholastics are to the Bible itself. In *Mammon* (G5) Tyndale assures his readers that it is not through the reading of the *Summa* that one comes to know God. In *Obedience* (B8) Tyndale cites followers of Aquinas among a list of debaters, and in *Prelates* (F1) he mocks the universities for emphasizing disputation over interpretation of Scripture. In the same place he opposes Aquinas for making the pope into a god, and claims the pope returned the compliment by making Aquinas a saint. Tyndale admires Aquinas for questioning the Immaculate Conception (131/3) but opposes him by allowing an equitable amount of interest in *Matthew* (h2v–h3). (JB)

47/6–30 **Now ... knowe.** Cf. CWM 8/2.717/29–718/17. Parts of this long passage are repeated below: 47/12 **euen ... father** at 8/2.724/34–35; 47/12–15 **and Christes ... foote** at 8/2.725/8–11; 47/16–19 **his electe ... not** at 8/2.726/10–13; 47/19–30 **Christes ... knowe** at 8/2.726/29–727/3; 47/26–30 **geuen ... knowe** at 8/2.728/23–25.

47/9–11 **Did ... erre.** Cf. Matt. 3.9–10.

47/11 **egles.** Cf. CWM 8/1.176/22. In place of Tyndale's eagle, More will later scoff at a "worshyppefull wyld gose" (CWM 8/2.680/23). Germain Marc'hadour sees here an allusion to the name "Hus" meaning "goose." For Jan Hus, cf. 167/12–14n. Later More says that, if the reformers are eagles, Augustine (8/2.723/24–25) and the faithful are "the pore chykens of his mother thys knowen catholyke chyrche" (8/2.724/9–10).

47/14–15 **ye ... steppe.** Cf. Matt. 14.25–32.

47/16 **the world knoweth him not.** Cf. John 1.10.

47/19 **Christes . . . Christ.** Cf. John 10.4.

47/22–23 **excepte . . . Gommor.** Isa. 1.9.

47/25–26 **the lord . . . seed.** Rom. 9.29, quoting Isa. 1.9.

47/26 **gathered him a flocke.** Cf. Ezek. 34.12.

47/27–28 **eares to heare . . . can not se.** Cf. Mark 8.18.

47/28 **blynde leadars of the blynd.** Matt. 15.14.

47/28–29 **hert to vnderstonde.** Cf. Jer. 24.7.

47/29 **generacion of poysoned vipers.** Cf. Matt. 12.34.

47/31–48/22 **If they . . . vnbeleffe.** This long passage is quoted almost verbatim at CWM 8/2.730/9–32.

47/31–32 **I had not beleued the gospell / excepte the auctorite of the church had moved me.** *Against the Epistle of Manichaeus called Fundamental* (AD c397) 1.5 (PL 42.176; CSEL 25/1.197; 1NPNF 4.131). When his Manichaean opponents used the Gospels to confirm the authority of their teacher Mani, Augustine replied that the Gospels are given to us by the same Catholic Church that has condemned Mani's teaching. In *Christian Doctrine* (AD c396–97) 2.8.12 (CCL 32.39; 1NPNF 2.538), Augustine describes the formation of the canon, not by decree, but by consensus. *Unio Dissidentium* quotes neither of these two passages on the church's validation of the books of the Bible.

In arguing for the authenticity of the seven sacraments, Henry VIII appeals twice to this famous proof-text: Ch. 10 on Confirmation (*Assertio,* CC 43.189); Ch. 12 on Orders (*Assertio,* CC 43.208). For More, the saying expressed well the priority of the church, with its instinct for the true books, over Scripture: CWM 6/1.181/11–12, 249/21–22; 6/2.526, 655–56. (The reference on 6/1.181/10–12n should be to *Responsio ad Lutherum,* 1523 [CWM 5/2.735f], cf. 5/2.742–43). Cf. also More's *Supplication of Souls,* 1529 (CWM 7.182/14–23) and *Confutation,* 1532–33 (CWM 8/2.676/20–22, 736/25–738/18). This text is More's most frequently quoted passage from Augustine (CWM 8/3.1634), cf. Marc'hadour, *Bible* 4.201–6. On the importance of Augustine's saying for More, cf. Gogan 74, 95, 146, 198–99, and 295–96. Eck, like many Catholic opponents of the Reformation, cited Augustine's text in his argument that Scripture is authenticated by ecclesiastical authority (Fraenkel 28; Battles 13). (JW)

Tyndale maintains that Augustine was not referring to hierarchical authority as the authenticator of Scripture but to the "ernest liuinge" (48/7) of the Christian people, which persuaded Augustine to take up the Christian Scriptures for personal examination. *Confutation* explicitly rejects Tyndale's interpretation of "authority" as "vertuouse lyuynge" (8/2.734/13) because Augustine saw that the church was a "company of both good and badde" (8/2.734/17). Later (8/2.796/10–12), More argues that, if Augustine accepted the Scripture because of the good example of Christians, he would be moved by historical not feeling faith.

48/4–5 **preachinge . . . folishnesse.** Cf. 1 Cor. 1.23.

48/6 **wordly wisdome.** 1 Cor. 1.17, cf. "wysdome of wordes" (Wallis 348/2; TNT 244C; KJV), cf. 7/25n.

48/13–16 **Peter . . . conuersacion.** Cf. 1 Pet. 3.1–2.

48/16–17 **how . . . husbande.** Cf. 1 Cor. 7.16.

48/23–28 **And when . . . faith.** Cf. CWM 8/2.741/12–17.

48/27–28 **historicall faith . . . felynge faith.** More claims that Tyndale's twofold division of "historical faith" and "feeling faith" is a "dystynccyon made by Melancthon [sic]" (CWM 8/2.741/35). Cf. *Loci Communes* in *Werke in Auswahl,* ed. Robert Stupperich (Gütersloh: Mohn, 1951–75) 2/1.13–16; *Loci Communes* of 1521, in *Melanchthon and Bucer,* ed. Wilhelm Pauck, tr. Lowell J. Satre, LCC 19 (Philadelphia: Westminster, 1969) 27–29. In December 1521, Philip Melanchthon (1497–1560) coined the phrase "historical faith": "For pedagogical reasons I used to call that which was acquired and incomplete, 'historical faith'; now I do not call it faith at all, but merely 'opinion.'" In the next paragraph Melanchthon describes the sinner's response to justification by faith, "This trust in the goodwill or mercy of God first calms our hearts and then inflames us to give thanks to God for his mercy so that we keep the law gladly and willingly." From *Werke in Auswahl* 2/1.92/4–6, 27–30; *Melanchthon and Bucer* 91–92.

Like Melanchthon, Tyndale defines "historicall faith" (48/27) or "story fayth" (197/23) as "imagination or opinion" (*Mammon* B3v). He reminds us throughout his corpus that not all faith is the same, citing examples of historical faith in biblical events or miracles (197/24f; *Mammon* B3v–B4; *1 John* A8v, B6, F7). In contrast,

"felynge faith" (48/27–28) or "lively faith" (*1 John* B6) is characterized by an immutable trust that one has been saved by Christ.
Works performed out of love for humanity are the visible tokens
of feeling faith (cf. *1 John* G1, *Matthew* p2r–v). Neither reception
of the sacraments nor the performance of good works alone justifies the soul (173/16–24, 197/18–198/17; *1 John* G1; *Matthew*
k5v–k7, p2r–v). When Tyndale writes that "faith justifieth"
(*Matthew* k5v), he emphasizes how God's grace, not human will,
delivers us from sin (192/16–23). God alone justifies us "as cause
efficient or workman" of our salvation (*Matthew* k6v) through
grace (192/31). Tyndale's concept of faith emphasizes the law of
God as good and right. (JB)

48/28–50/15 **The historical . . . worlde.** Cf. CWM 8/2.742/4–
743/18. Parts of this long passage are repeated below: 49/18–27
But . . . therin at 8/2.752/5–14; 50/6–9 **For . . . mad men** is
paraphrased at 8/2.760/29–32; 50/10–15 **saith . . . worlde** at
8/2.763/ 6–11.

49/14 **roben hode.** There are at least a hundred references to this
chameleon figure between a record of a murder by a servant of
the Abbot of Cirencester (1213) and the allusions in More's *Dialogue* (CWM 6/1.335/31) and in Tyndale's *Obedience* (both 1528).
Cf. Lucy Sussex, "Appendix, References to Robin Hood up to
1600," in Stephen Knight, *Robin Hood: A Complete Study of the
English Outlaw* (Oxford: Blackwell, 1994) 262–88. The earliest allusion to Robin Hood in English literature occurs in *Piers Plowman* (c1377), where Sloth confesses, "I kan noght parfitly my Pa-
ternoster as the preest it syngeth, / But I kan rymes of Robyn
hood and Randolf Erl of Chestre," Passus V, lines 394–95.

Tyndale often cites the legend of Robin Hood as an example of a
foolish but widely held belief. Furthering his attack on non-bibli-
cal authorities, he insists that Fisher lists so many, he may as well
include Robin Hood with Plato, Aristotle, and Origen (*Obedience*
H8v). Compared to the eternal word of God and the inspiration
of the Holy Spirit, the authority of the Fathers is as unreliable as
this legend (*Mammon* D8v, *Obedience* T4). Tyndale also wonders
why the pope permits the laity to read stories of Robin Hood,
Bevis of Hampton, Hercules, Hector, and Troilus but not the

Bible (*Obedience* C4). Although Tyndale concedes that allegorical interpretations of the Bible, like tales of Robin Hood, may serve to illustrate a point, he insists that they be used sparingly, since they prove nothing themselves and require a foundation in the Scripture (*Obedience* R4). References to Robin Hood also occur in the prologues to Genesis (Mombert 11/10; TOT 8) and Jonas (TOT 629) and in a sidenote to Deut. 11 (Mombert 561; TOT 273). (JB)

49/18–19 **They . . . of God.** John 6.45 quoting Isa. 54.13.

49/20–21 **the spirite . . . God.** Rom. 8.16.

49/28–33 **Samaritanish . . . come in.** Cf. John 4.28–29, 39–40.

50/3–6 **the woman . . . worlde.** Cf. John 4.42.

50/10–11 **cursed . . . arme.** Jer. 17.5.

50/16–17 **The faith . . . weke.** CWM 8/2.764/23–24.

50/18–25 **If . . . nature.** Cf. CWM 8/2.765/2–8n and 172/16. Ulrich von Hutten rejects Cisalpine sexual mores with righteous indignation: "Am I to cringe to these epicene priestlings? Must I keep my hands off these mincing sodomites and worship these lecherous popes . . . ?" From Ep. 1161, To Erasmus, Ebernburg, 13 November 1520 (Allen 4.382/56–58; CWE 8.89/61–63).

Tyndale's charge that Roman prostitutes numbered some 30,000 agrees with the report given by Francesco Delicado of Cordova, a resident of Rome after 1523. But a more careful analysis, based on the census of 1526–27, arrived at the number of 1,550 prostitutes, which was 3% of the population of Rome. Cf. Pio Pecchiai, *Roma nel cinquecento* (Bologna: Cappelli, 1984) 304. The bath-houses listed by Pecchiai (312ff) do not mention any that offered the service of "younge boyes agenst nature" (50/25), although the same author has evidence that the "vice of the Greeks" had made inroads in Renaissance Rome (317). Here Tyndale may be under the influence of the stereotypical charge of pederasty in the anti-Italian polemics of northern humanists. See Ingrid G. Rowland, "Revenge of the Regensburg Humanists, 1493," *Sixteenth Century Journal* 24 (1994) 307–22. (JW)

50/19–52/2 **For if . . . can runne.** To exemplify the two kinds of faith, Tyndale alleges the empty teaching by pope and hierarchy on the sinfulness of lechery and avarice. Papal connivance in sex-

ual immorality is shown by the Roman bordello established under Sixtus IV (pope, 1471–84), from which annual taxes were said
to bring in some 80,000 ducats for the papal treasury. Cf. G. Denzler, *Das Papstum und der Amtszölibat,* 2 vols. (Stuttgart: Hiersemann, 1973–76) 1.134. On the "licence to kepe euery man his
whore" (50/29), cf. 38/20n. (JW)

50/25–27 **stues . . . lawe.** Cf. Lev. 20.13. The type of death penalty
for sodomy is not specified; burning is the death penalty for marriage first to a mother and then to her daughter (verse 14).

50/28 **.xl. or .l. hundred thousand.** Tyndale claims that in his day
there were four or five million clergy bound to celibacy in the
Roman Church. This number, equaling 9% or 11% of the population of Western Europe, is much too high. In England about 2%
of the population were ordained priests, cf. 75/19–20n.

In 1500, one estimate would total 45.3 million Latin-rite Christians:
British Isles (4), Iberia (8.3), France and the Low Countries (16),
Italy (5.5) Germany (7), Scandinavia (.5), Poland (2), and Hungary
(2); 8.25 million Orthodox Christians: Greece (.75), the Balkans
(1.5), and Russia (6); 16.25 million Muslims in the Ottoman Empire: Greece (.75), the Balkans (1.5), Asia Minor (6), Syria (2),
Egypt (2.5), and North Africa (3.5). Cf. Glenn T. Trewartha, *A Ge-
ography of Population: World Patterns* (New York: John Wiley &
Sons, 1969) 21, Table 1.3. This table does not include Jews in Italy,
Germany, Poland, and Russia. For a discussion of the proportion
of Christians to Muslims, cf. 52/3n.

51/14–15 **vnions and tot quottes.** Cf. *Obedience* K3v; *1 John* D2v,
D5v, E6, F4v. For the phrase "pluralities of benefices," cf. *Prelates*
K2v–K3.

51/18 **couetousnesse.** Because prelates do not practice what they
preach about the sin of avarice, More does not defend them
against Tyndale's accusation of covetousness. William E. Lunt gives
the essential background in *Papal Revenues in the Middle Ages,* 2
vols. (New York: Columbia UP, 1934), while Barbara M. Hallman
treats the abusive practices that lived on through most of the 16c,
in *Italian Cardinals, Reform, and the Church as Property* (Berkeley: U
of California P, 1985). Luther gave extensive coverage to Roman
financial exploitation of Germany in his reform tract, *To the*

Christian Nobility, 1520 (WA 6.407/9–411/7; LW 44.142–68), where he mentions the same canonical measures named by Tyndale (51/14–15) by which high clerics circumvented the sanctions against pluralism of pastoral benefices and offices. (JW)

51/19 **lecherye.** In the preface to a new edition of *Enchiridion,* Erasmus cites a patristic criticism of poor moral judgment on the clergy: "Augustine complains in his letters that lechery is the one offence imputed to the clergy in Africa, while the vices of avarice and drunkenness are almost counted to their credit." Cf. Ep. 22, Augustine to Bp. Valerius (AD c392) 1.3 (PL 33.91; CSEL 34/1.56–57; Parsons 1.53), cited by Erasmus, Ep. 858, To Paul Volz, Basel, 14 August 1518 (Allen 3.372/417–20; CWE 6.85/441–44; also Holborn 15/15–17; CWE 66.18). In his memorial of Colet, Erasmus praises the better judgment of his friend: "He used to say that avarice and pride were much more to be abhorred in a priest than if he had a hundred concubines." From Ep. 1211, To Justus Jonas, Anderlecht, 13 June 1521 (Allen 4.521/467–68; CWE 8.239/508–10).

51/25–26 **bilt . . . sonde.** Cf. Matt. 7.26.

52/3–17 **The turkes . . . waye.** CWM 8/2.767/15–29.

52/3 **.v. tymes mo then we.** Based on the estimates for 1500 given at 50/28n, 45.3 million Catholic plus 8.25 million Orthodox would give a total of 53.55 million Christians compared to 16.25 million Muslims in the Ottoman Empire (i.e., excluding Northern India and Indonesia). Thus Christians could outnumber Muslims about three to one. The number of sixteen million approximates the ten to fifteen million people in the Ottoman Empire suggested for the beginning of the 16c by Albert Hourani, *A History of the Arab Peoples,* Belknap (Cambridge: Harvard UP, 1991) 232. Perhaps Tyndale's sense of Christians as a minority beseiged by Muslims stems from the conquests in the Middle East and North Africa in the 7c and 8c and in Greece and the Balkans in the 15c and 16c. *Confutation* accepts *Answer's* ratio of five Muslims to one Christian (CWM 8/2.770/35–771/1).

52/10–11 **beynge . . . made.** Cf. Rom. 9.7–8.

52/10 **Abrahams seed.** Cf. John 8.33.

52/12–14 **And we . . . multytude.** Cf. CWM 8/1.252/9–10.

52/16 **litle flocke.** Cf. Jer. 23.3 KJV, "the renmant [sic] of my flocke," paraphrased by Luke 12.32. Tyndale echoes Luther in the latter's

Responsio of 1521 to Ambrosius Catharinus: *indicat paucos servare ab eorum perditione* (WA 7.727/6; not in LW). Tyndale uses variations on this name in *Obedience* C6v and eleven times in *Answer.* (JW)

52/18–54/12 ¶ **How . . . trueth.** CWM 8/2.773/13–774/37.

52/20–22 **not . . . chyldren.** Rom. 9.6–7.

52/23–28 **Euen . . . church.** Cf. CWM 8/2.777/30–35.

52/25–26 **Master Mores fayth / the popes fayth and the deuels fayth.** For this infernal triad, cf. CWM 8/2.773/20–23, 787/ 25–26.

52/31–53/3 **There is . . . brethern.** Cf. CWM 8/2.788/27–31.

52/31–53/1 **Isaac and Ismael.** Cf. Gen. 21.9–13; cf. 105/5, 8–9.

53/1 **Iacob and Esau.** Cf. Gen. 27.1–45, cf. 105/5.

53/1–2 **And Ismael . . . spiritual.** Cf. Gal. 4.21–31.

53/2–3 **paul . . . brethern.** Cf. Gal. 2.4.

53/3–4 **as we . . . ende.** Cf. CWM 8/2.788/33–34.

53/4–5 **What . . . Moses.** According to Exod. 12.37, about 600,000 men left Egypt, not counting women and children.

53/6–7 **Simon magus . . . miracles.** Cf. Acts 8.13.

53/8–11 **.vj. . . . them.** According to Num. 14.29 and 26.63–65, all of the adult males who left Egypt died in the forty-year trek through the desert except Joshua and Caleb.

53/31–32 **Samaritanes . . . woman.** Cf. John 4.39, 42.

54/6 **laytyne tongue agayne.** Cf. 75/12n.

54/13–29 **It hath . . . seruice.** Here Tyndale supplies a key component of his didactic conception of rites and sacraments. Only feeling faith allows the elect to approach sacraments and ceremonies not as good works but as instructional reminders about God's grace and human duty. Cf. the passages indicated in 7/11–13n. (JW)

54/13–14 **God . . . christ.** Cf. Eph. 2.4.

54/14 **before the world was made.** Cf. Eph. 1.4.

54/14–15 **when wee were deed in synne.** Cf. Eph. 2.5.

54/15 **and his enemies.** Cf. Rom. 5.10.

54/21–25 **how . . . memorials.** *Confutation* paraphrases Tyndale's definition of true worship, cf. CWM 8/2.775/9–12.

54/31–55/1 **can iudge . . . person.** *Confutation* quotes Tyndale's discussion of true love of neighbor nearly verbatim, cf. CWM 8/2.775/15–18.

55/6–78/13 ¶ **Of worshepinge . . . workes.** *Confutation* dismisses the sixth and last topic of Tyndale's Foundational Essay, a critique of false ceremonies, as either "comenly knowen allredy" or "false and blasphemouse" (CWM 8/2.775/29, 31).

55/11 **dulia / yperdulia and latria.** For Aquinas, *dulia* is rendered to a human being who participates in some limited way in God's power and dignity; *hyperdulia* is the highest species of *dulia,* being the veneration of Mary in virtue of the special affinity to God that is her divine motherhood; *latria* is the veneration due to God in virtue of his supreme dominion (*Summa* II–II, Q. 103, Art. 3–4). This systematic analysis was cited by 15c English defenders of devotional images and the veneration of the saints against Lollard attacks. Cf. W.R. Jones, "Lollards and Images: the Defense of Religious Art in Later Medieval England," *Journal of the History of Ideas* 34 (1973) 27–50, esp. 44f. More defines these three grades of worship by giving *dulia* to living superiors, *hyperdulia* to angels and saints as well as to Mary, and *latria* to God alone (CWM 6/1.97/ 28–33). He brands the charge that people mistakenly offer *latria* to saints as a cloak for the heresy of refusing any role to the saints in Christian devotion (CWM 6/1.230/1–232/36). For More's comment on the rejection of scholastic distinctions by Luther and Tyndale, cf. CWM 8/2.741/32–34, 91/31, 123/28, 124/4. (JW)

55/16 **the cardinalles hatte.** The son of a butcher, Thomas Wolsey (c1473–1530) exercized powers in England second only to the king and the pope. In tracing Wolsey's secular career, Tyndale refers to his brisk management of the French campaign in 1513 (*Prelates* D3), which earned his appointment as Lord Chancellor, December 1515; his meetings with Charles V (emperor, 1519–55/ 56) in May 1520 and July 1521 (*Prelates* H1v); his efforts to raise money from Parliament for the invasion of France in 1523 (*Obedience* E7); his treaty with France in 1527 (*Prelates* H6). Although Wolsey was forced to resign the office of Lord Chancellor, Tyndale mistakenly asserts that he continued his policies through More, his preferred successor (*Prelates* K2). Tyndale sneers at Wolsey's death from intestinal disease (*1 John* D3, D5v), which saved him from trial and execution for treason.

Tyndale attacks Wolsey's pluralism in the pun "Wolfsee" (*Prelates* G4r–v, G6r–v, G7, G8v, H1; *1 John* D5v) and calls him "Cayphas"

(*Prelates* H7). Tyndale mocks Wolsey's successively richer ecclesiastical offices (*1 John* D5v), chief of which were Archbishop of York (September 1514) and Cardinal (September 1515). He became papal legate *a latere* for a limited term in 1518 and for life in 1524 (*Obedience* L4, L8v; *1 John* D5v). His supposed papal ambitions, however, were frustrated (*Prelates* H6).

Tyndale scorns the elaborate ceremonies associated with Wolsey's reception of the red hat (*Prelates* K5, *1 John* D3). His gentleman usher George Cavendish describes Wolsey's weekday processions to Westminster Hall and Sunday processions to Greenwich, cf. Cavendish 22/32–24/33. Tyndale ironically anticipates Wolsey's canonization (123/1–2, 130/31–33; *Obedience* P7). Then, his personal belongings would be venerated as relics: red hat, (55/16, 91/32), ceremonial pillars and pole-axes (81/32–33n, 99/32), ornate chair (119/6).

Tyndale does not comment on Wolsey's efforts between 1517 and 1526 to protect tenant farmers and laborers against unlawful land enclosures. Cf. Peter Gwyn, *The King's Cardinal: The Rise and Fall of Thomas Wolsey* (London: Barrie and Jenkins, 1990) 411–35. Nor does Tyndale mention Wolsey's grandiose projects, Hampton Court and Cardinal College. See *Cardinal Wolsey: Church, state and art,* ed. S.J. Gunn and P.G. Lindley (Cambridge UP, 1991).

Tyndale's older contemporary John Skelton (c1460–1529) targets Wolsey's virtual usurpation of royal power in his verse satires of 1521–22: "Speke, Parott," "Collyn Clout," and "Why Come Ye Nat to Courte?" See *John Skelton: The Complete English Poems,* ed. John Scattergood (New York: Penguin, 1983). Later in the century, Foxe summarizes Wolsey's career (4.587–617).

55/26 **vnto his awne likenes.** Cf. Gen. 1.27, repeated at 56/11, 58/9.

55/27 **christ . . . bloude.** Cf. 1 Pet. 1.18–19.

55/32–56/1 **loue his lawe.** Cf. Ps. 119.97.

56/3–4 **father / mother.** Cf. *Obedience* F8v–G1v; **master.** Cf. *Obedience* G2r–v; **husband.** Cf. *Obedience* G1v–G2; **lorde and prince.** Cf. *Obedience* G3v–G7. Tyndale here alludes to the duties of those in temporal authority, treated more fully in the earlier book.

56/9 **helpe him at all his nede.** Cf. 1 John 3.17, repeated at 56/20–21, 56/29–30.

56/10 **as thou woldest be holpe.** Cf. Matt. 7.12, Luke 6.31.

56/23 **saruant.** For the believer as a servant of Christ, cf. Eph. 6.6.

57/18 **saruauntes to other.** For those in authority as servants to their subjects, cf. Matt. 20.27, Matt. 23.11.

57/19 **hand . . . a nother.** Cf. 1 Cor. 12.15, 25.

57/23 **man is lorde ouer them.** Tyndale appears to be the only Reformation critic of images who argued from the place of human beings in the hierarchy of being and ordered service. His norm is the human lordship over images and pious objects, which are subordinate creatures: "[W]e be lordes ouer all soch thynges and they our seruauntes" (88/12–13). The varieties of early 16c argument are treated by Eire passim. (JW)

57/23–24 **man . . . sarue him.** Cf. Ps. 8.6.

57/27 **ceremonies / images / reliques.** In *Dialogue* Bk. 1, Ch. 3, the Messenger opposes these sacramentals (CWM 6/1.51–60), but More as Mentor defends them in Bk. 2, Ch. 9–10 (CWM 6/1.217–29). Cf. the opening chapters of Keith Thomas, esp. p. 27, where saints' images are treated with apposite citations of More and Tyndale. Delumeau surveys the use of protective blessings, objects, and processions in Part I (33–176) and the aid sought from saints in Part II (179–289). (JW)

58/1–2 **werkmansheppe . . . man.** Cf. Ps. 115.4.

58/6 **the holy daye . . . man.** Cf. Mark 2.27.

58/10 **naked.** Cf. Jas. 2.15–16.

58/19–59/3 **If . . . the churches.** In *Obedience* O4v, Tyndale comments wittily on fraudulent relics, e.g., Christ's robe: "For that is here yet / I wott not in how many places." This passage of *Answer* describes uses of the cross that promote the essentials of piety, contrasting with abusive practices attacked as idolatrous at 59/21–60/18. Cf. 85/17–26, 123/10–14, 185/33–186/6. More incorrectly asserts that Tyndale rejects all devotion to the cross (CWM 8/1.129/1–5). (JW)

58/33–59/1 **whosoeuer . . . persecucion.** Cf. Matt. 16.24.

59/7 **the true life of a saynt.** More as Mentor defends praying to saints in *Dialogue,* Bk. 2, Ch. 8 and 11 (CWM 6/1.210–17, 229–37). The right use of their images will promote imitation of their faith, love, and patient suffering. Displacement of right use will be mentioned at 61/13–27 and will recur frequently, cf. 83/13–18n. (JW)

59/29 **God . . . pacyence.** Cf. 1 Thess. 2.4.

60/2 **serue God only.** Cf. Deut. 11.13.

60/3 **promyses of mercye.** Cf. Luke 1.72.

60/4 **Saynt Ihons Gospell.** CWM 7.181/2 and n. The Prologue on the incarnation of the Word (John 1.1–14) was a favorite medieval locus of God's power to save. It was at times recited over the sick before the Last Rites and was read as a blessing for good weather. In the late Middle Ages its recital became associated with the final blessing at Mass, as the "Last Gospel," being seen as protection against the devil's attacks which would recommence when Mass-goers left the consecrated building, cf. Jungmann 2.543–46. (JW)

60/6–7 **and wythe reuerence on the very arses.** Henry Walter, the Victorian editor, bowdlerized this passage but uncannily pre-served the offensive word "arse" in "coarse": "A coarse expression is here omitted" (PS 3.61n2). Keith Thomas (36) and Brigden (16n48) both cite the PS version, but Duffy (215) quotes the orig-inal. Walter also omitted references to sexual organs, *Obedience* P2v (PS 1.285n1); to marital relations, *Matthew* o5 (PS 2.125n2); to ex-cretory functions, *Prelates* F7 (PS 2.300n1), *1 John* D3, D5v (PS 2.174n2, 2.177n3), but Walter did not omit references to ex-cretory functions in *Mammon* F7v (PS 1.100). Walter castrated the text of *Obedience* by omitting "the privey membre of God which ys" (R8v) before the phrase "the word of promise" (PS 1.311 without note). For another unmarked emendation, cf. 179/16–17n.

60/19 **S. Agathes letter.** After Agatha was martyred in Sicily (c251), Mt. Etna stopped erupting when prayers were offered through her intercession (NCE 1.196–97). In *Dialogue,* the Messenger in-directly refers to Agatha (CWM 6/1.227/8) among the many saints who are the object of superstitious devotion.

Tyndale repeatedly cautions against praying to saints for assistance, associating such practices with idolatry. Examples include using "S. Agathes letter" as a charm against the burning of houses (cf. PS 3.61n3), ascribing healing powers to Apollonia (182/31n), fearing the vengeance of Laurence (d. 258) and Anthony of Egypt (251–356) (*1 John* C4v), and believing the visions of Bridget of Sweden (1303–73) (*Obedience* B8). Duffy gives illustrations of Agatha (Plate 69) and Bridget of Sweden (Plates 61–62) among others. (JB)

The Temptation of St. Anthony was painted by Hieronymus Bosch (c1505–10) in Antwerp (Ill. 200–2) and by Mathias Grünewald in 1515 for the Isenheim Altarpiece (Colorplate 55) at Colmar. Although the innermost level of the altarpiece features St. Anthony, the middle level highlights the Annunciation and Resurrection, and the outermost the Crucifixion. See James Synder, *Northern Renaissance Art* (Englewood Cliffs, NJ: Prentice-Hall, 1985).

60/25 **limeteriers.** Tyndale's friars, licensed to beg within certain limits (here and *Obedience* H3v), are brothers of Chaucer's "lymytour" ("General Prologue," *Canterbury Tales,* I [A] 209).

60/25–26 **in principio erat verbum.** John 1.1. The opening words of the Gospel of John were used to drive demons away; cf. the Friar's greeting ("General Prologue," *Canterbury Tales,* I [A] 254). Duffy (216) adds, "Inscribed on parchment, it was frequently worn round the neck to cure disease, and lay people also hung it on the necks or horns of ailing cattle." In the preface to his Paraphrase on John, Erasmus tries to spiritualize this custom: "Surely it is the teaching of that gospel that we ought to wear next our hearts to be our shield against all the sickness of sin." From Ep. 1333, To Ferdinand of Austria, Basel, 5 January 1523 (Allen 5.169/255–57; CWE 9.239/272–73).

60/27 **corne in the feld.** On Rogation Days, the three days before Ascension Thursday, the clergy and people walked in a procession around the boundaries of the parish. The priest read passages from the Gospels at station-points in lanes and fields to drive out evil spirits and to insure the fertility of the crops. Duffy (279) cites this passage from *Answer.*

For the reformers, however, popular ceremonies based on pagan customs corrupt God's truth. These include reciting the Gospels during the Rogation procession (also *Obedience* K2v) or celebrating the Feast of Asses with a procession of a girl and child on an ass (*Mammon* F1v, cf. PS 1.91–92n3). The first is a Christian version of the pagan observance of Robigalia, and the second is part of Saturnalia. God is a spirit, but images, relics, ceremonies, pilgrimages, and fasts only reveal a lack of faith through a dependence on fleshly memorials (*1 John* H1v). Even the use of rosary beads reveals a false understanding of God (*Matthew* n2). Since a person is saved by faith, a pilgrimage will not secure the forgiveness of sins (*Obedience* O6v). (JB)

61/3 **the riches that is bestowed on images.** Tyndale argues that prelates are wrongly diverting contributions meant for the poor into supplying precious ornaments for statues. Lollard polemics against images had argued in this manner, cf. Hudson 83/1–86/121. Such a critique of images of the saints had also been sounded by Erasmus, Andreas Karlstadt, and Martin Bucer, cf. Eire 44f, 90f. (JW)

61/14 **ensample of the saint.** The biography of the Roman deacon and martyr Laurence (d. AD 258) and the West Saxon (?) Witta, who shared wealth, food, and clothing with the poor, served to celebrate the charity of the early church in implicit contrast to the greed of the contemporary church (*Prelates* B5, *1 John* H2r–v). While rejecting the intercession of the saints, Tyndale does agree that their lives provide examples of righteousness. The collects of Stephen and Laurence, for example, recall their enduring faith and love (*Obedience* I8v, cf. PS 1.231n3). For an illustration of the shrine of St. Candida or Witta, Whitchurch Canonicorum, Dorset, see Duffy (Plate 78). Cf. 59/7, 83/13–18, 116/32 nn. (JB)

61/19–20 **Idolater . . . serueimage.** Tyndale gives similar translations in *1 John* G8v: "Idolatre" as "imageseruice," "Idolater" as "imageseruaunt."

61/25 **promises . . . sonne.** Cf. Eph. 3.6.

62/1 ¶ **Pilgrimages.** A major theme of *Dialogue* Bk. 1, Ch. 2–17 (CWM 6/1.5–101). An ample account of the background is found in Jonathan Sumption, *Pilgrimage: An Image of Medieval Religion* (London: Faber, 1975), in which Ch. 14–15 treat the late-medieval increase of pilgrimages, both to long-revered sanctuaries like Walsingham and Mont-Saint-Michel and to new centers of enthusiastic devotion like Wilsnak, near Wittenberg, with its bleeding host. Lollards attacked pilgrimages as wasteful of time and money, as occasions of lechery, gluttony, and drunkenness away from home and neighbors, and as wrong in localizing Christ or Mary at one place, cf. Hudson 86/122–87/167. Luther's *To the Christian Nobility,* 1520 (WA 6.447/17–450/21; LW 44.185–89), called for the suppression of pilgrim shrines with their many abuses so people could seek Christ's word and sacrament in their parish churches. Cf. later passages on pilgrimages: 80/13, 84/4–12, 87/16–88/3, 146/17. (JW)

The most engaging literary treatment of the theme occurs in Chaucer's *Canterbury Tales* (c1387–c1400), where the thirty-odd pilgrims to the shrine of Becket represent every class of feudal society. Margery Kempe (c1373–c1439), who dictated the earliest surviving autobiography in English, left a vivid narrative of her three major pilgrimages: to Jerusalem, Assisi, and Rome; to Santiago; to Wilsnak and Aachen. See *The Book of Margery Kempe,* ed. Sanford Brown Meech and Hope Emily Allen, EETS 212 (London: Oxford UP, 1940).

62/5–6 **viset . . . presoner.** Cf. Matt. 25.36.

62/19–20 **gods . . . mouth.** Cf. Rom. 10.8.

62/29–30 **god . . . handes.** Cf. Acts 17.24.

62/30–31 **steuen . . . prophetes.** Acts 7.48–49, quoting Isa. 66.1–2.

62/32 **thirde of the kinges.** The Vulgate designates 1 and 2 Samuel as "1 and 2 Kings," 1 and 2 Kings as "3 and 4 Kings." We follow the titles used in the KJV because it is based on the Hebrew.

63/1–3 **he had . . . there.** Cf. 1 Kings 8.27, 30.

63/4–5 **false . . . their.** Cf. Jer. 7.4.

63/7–9 **psalme .xlix. . . . glorifie me.** Ps. 50.15; *Answer* gives the Vulgate number **Psal. 49.** (63/S1), cf. 67/12–15n.

63/10–11 **Iob . . . dongehyll.** Cf. Job. 2.8. KJV has "among the ashes." David Daniell noted in a letter that "dunghill" comes from the Septuagint and the Vulgate, but "ashes" is found in Luther and Geneva.

63/11 **Poules [prayer] in the temple.** Cf. Acts 22.17.

63/12–13 **Whatsoeuer . . . you.** John 16.23.

63/15–16 **God . . . spirite.** Cf. John 4.24.

63/30 **ceremonies . . . of the olde testament.** In Israel sacraments instituted to preach and instruct degenerated into good works to gain God's favor. Illustrations are circumcision (64/1–21), the paschal lamb (64/22–23), sacrifices (64/24–65/5, 65/27–66/13), the sabbath (66/14–28), the brazen serpent (66/29–67/3), and the Temple (67/4–10). The present section sets the stage for Tyndale's account of an analogous loss in Christianity of the original didactic purpose of rites, ceremonies, and sacraments (68/6–78/13). The fall into idolatry, in fact, marks humanity universally outside the ambit of the elect who are inwardly taught by the Holy Spirit (cf. 54/13–29). (JW)

63/31 **sacramentes.** Tyndale's emphasis on the didactic function of ceremonies in general contrasts with the concern of medieval scholasticism to explain how the seven sacraments are both signs and causes of sanctifying grace in those receiving them devoutly. Peter Lombard's mid-12c formulation contrasted OT rites, which only signify, with the Christian sacraments that also cause the sanctification they signify (*Sentences* Bk. 4, Dist. 1, Ch. 4). The Franciscan tradition of St. Bonaventure and Duns Scotus understood sacramental causality broadly, emphasizing God's decree or *pactum* to give grace upon performance of the Christian rites. Aquinas founded an opposing tradition that insisted on the true instrumentality of the sacramental means of grace, but he also broadened the notion of signification by elaborating a threefold reference of the sacramental sign: to Christ's passion, the principal cause of sanctification, as *signum rememorativum;* to the grace now given, as *signum demonstrativum,* e.g. of rebirth, nourishment, etc.; and to future glory, as *signum prognosticum* (*Summa* III, Q. 60, Art. 3, *Sed contra*). Aquinas' sacramental doctrine received official sanction at the Council of Florence (1439), where his work *De articulis fidei et ecclesiae sacramentis* was incorporated into the Decree of Union with the Armenians, cf. 193/34n. Erasmus could cite Lombard's formula on sacraments as causes and made reference to the Franciscan notion of God's *pactum,* but Erasmus was more influential as a critic of externalized ritual practice that neglected the inner meaning, for sacraments represent divine archetypes and exhort to virtuous behavior, cf. Payne 97–103.

Luther's early works on sacraments single out the promissory word of God that every sacrament contains and corroborates by its outward rite. The chief concern, however, is faith by which recipients pass over from doubt and anguish of conscience to lay hold of the mercy that Christ's promise conveys, e.g., *Sacrament of Penance,* 1519 (WA 2.719–20; LW 35.17f); *Holy Sacrament of Baptism,* 1519 (WA 2.732; LW 35.35f); *Babylonian Captivity,* 1520 (WA 6.516–18;

LW 36.42–44). In *Obedience* (October 1528) Tyndale was strongly influenced by Luther's emphasis on rightly using the true sacraments, Baptism and the Eucharist, in faith.

However, Luther signalled a transition in 1526 in the opening lines of *The Sacrament of the Body and Blood of Christ* (WA 19.482f; LW 36.335) for the external means instituted by Christ had come under fire from Karlstadt and Zwingli. In a new emphasis not influencing Tyndale, Luther asserts emphatically the priority of the outward means over the inward spiritual result: "God has determined to give the inward to no one except through the outward. For he wants to give no one the Spirit or faith outside the outward Word and sign instituted by him." From *Against the Heavenly Prophets,* 1525 (WA 18.136; LW 40.146).

Emblematic of this second concern are Luther's lengthy polemics against Zwingli's spiritualizing of the Lord's Supper. Luther defended the true presence and reception of the body and blood of Christ under the outer forms of bread and wine, e.g.: *That These Words of Christ, "This is My Body," etc. Still Stand Firm Against the Fanatics,* 1527 (WA 23.64–283; LW 37.13–150); *Confession concerning Christ's Supper,* 1528 (WA 26.261–509; LW 37.161–372). Parallel expressions of Tyndale's sacramental doctrine in *Answer* are 7/6–14, 38/5–13, 45/29–33, 54/13–29, 74/7–13. At 173/16–24, he echoes Luther's teaching on faith in the promise announced in the sacrament.

An influence on Tyndale may have come from Zwingli's works of the 1520s, which attack a causal view of the sacraments, for no external thing may justify a human being or confirm faith. The sacraments for Zwingli do evoke the commemoration of a past event, but more emphatic is the renewed declaration of believers' fidelity to Christ by their devout participation in the rites. Cf. J. Pollet, "Zwinglianisme," *Dictionnaire de Théologie catholique* 15/2.3811–18. (JW)

63/31 **signes preachinge.** For the sacraments as signs, cf. *Obedience* M1, M7; CWM 8/1.84/2. For the preaching implied by the water of Baptism, cf. *Obedience* M2. For the necessity of preaching the signification of the Eucharist, cf. *Obedience* M2; CWM 8/1.96/1–2, 17–26.

Tyndale's Eucharistic theology is similar to that of Zwingli and

Oecolampadius. Huldrych Zwingli (1484–1531) was leader of the Reformation in Zurich. At the Marburg Colloquy in October 1529, he argued against Melanchthon that the Eucharist remained bread and wine (OER 2.320–23). Through independent study, Johannes Oecolampadius (1482–1531) came to agree with Zwingli that the Lord's Supper memorialized only the spiritual presence of Christ. He defended this position against Luther at Marburg (OER 3.169–71). For Fisher's *De veritate corporis et sanguine Christi* (1527), see Surtz, Ch. 18, "Answering Oecolampadius on the Real Presence," 337–50.

64/3–4 **encrease . . . erth.** Cf. Deut. 6.3.

64/18–19 **circumcision . . . not.** Cf. Rom. 2.25.

64/20–21 **god . . . not.** Cf. Rom. 3.30.

64/22 **paschall lambe.** Cf. Exod. 12.21–28.

64/24 **first frutes.** Cf. Exod. 34.22–26.

64/33 **doues / turtles.** For turtledoves as burnt offerings, cf. Lev. 1.14–17.

65/1 **lambes.** For the sacrifice of a lamb each morning and evening, cf. Exod. 29.39–42; for the sin offering of a private person, cf. Lev. 4.32–35. **kyddes.** For sin offerings, cf. Lev. 4.22–26. **shepe.** For peace offerings, cf. Lev. 22.21. **calues / gottes and oxen.** For male goats as sin offerings, calves and lambs as burnt offerings, oxen and rams as peace offerings, cf. Lev. 9.3.

65/1–5 **no . . . them.** Cf. Lev. 9.7. Moses tells Aaron to sacrifice a calf to "make an attonement for the[e] and for the people" (Mombert 322; TOT 161).

65/4 **seedes . . . Abraham.** Cf. Gen. 22.18 and 26.4, Gal. 3.16.

65/10 ¶ **False worshepynge.** In terminology Tyndale may be echoing Lutheran usage in indicting the pre-Reformation church, especially in numerous position papers drawn up in preparation for the Diet of Augsburg. Cf. Wicks, "Abuses" 257–63 and 274 in reference to Luther's *Exhortation to all the Clergy Assembled at Augsburg,* 1530 (WA 30/2.345–52; LW 34.52–59). (JW)

65/14–15 **workes . . . iustified.** For Tyndale Turks, Jews, and papists believe in justification by works and are not counted among the elect because ceremonies alone cannot purge sin from the heart (10/19–26, 65/10, 104/21–29, 113/20–27, 129/11–18). In *Matthew* (06) he notes how Turks and Jews give alms, but cannot gain salvation because they lack saving faith. For believing that good works make a person righteous, the pope joins the company of the heretical Pelagius (*1 John* E3v, D8v; *Matthew* m1v). Tyndale thus contrasts the works of Turks, Jews, and papists with the faith of the elect, who trust in the promise of Christ's blood (193/25–31, *Matthew* o6); their good works are the fruit of faith and love of God (173/28–174/3, 197–207) (JB)

65/16 **parable of the pharesey and publican.** Cf. Luke 18.9–14.

65/23 **man . . . shepe.** Cf. Matt. 12.12.

65/24–25 **For . . . calues.** Cf. Isa. 1.11.

65/31 **oxe . . . shepe.** Cf. Exod. 20.24.

66/3 **doue.** Cf. Lev. 12.8, Luke 2.24. The poor may substitute a pair of doves for a lamb.

66/6–7 **they offered . . . images.** Cf., e.g., Lev. 18.21, Deut. 18.10.

66/10–12 **Abraham . . . blessed.** Cf. Gen. 22.9–18.

66/14 **sabbath.** Cf. Exod. 31.12–17. The sidenote links sabbath observance to justification by faith (Mombert 258–59; TOT 131).

66/18–19 **holy daye . . . sanctified.** For listening to preaching as the purpose of the sabbath, cf. CWM 8/1.76/1–2.

66/27–28 **the ruler . . . holy daye.** Cf. Luke 13.14.

66/29 **brasen serpent.** Made by Moses, cf. Num. 21.9. Destroyed by Hezekiah after it became an object of idolatry, cf. 2 Kings 18.4.

67/4 **temple . . . there.** Cf. Jer. 7.9–15.

67/7 **prayar.** Prayer is the longing of the believer for the effects of God's promises (*Mammon* F2v, *Obedience* Q7, *Introduction to Romans* a4v). It consists of praise, thanksgiving, and petitions for defense against temptation (*Matthew* i4, n4v–n6v). It is not the empty pattering of longer hours in choir and more numerous Masses for the Dead (*Obedience* Q3v–R1). For Tyndale, the believing heart is a true temple because the word dwells there as source of prayer (67/6–8). (JB)

67/12–15 **.xlix. psalme . . . gottes.** Ps. 50.9, 13. *Answer* gives the Vulgate number, cf. 63/7–9n.

67/15–18 **what . . . gottes.** Isa. 1.11.

67/22–23 **referrynge theyr fast . . . spirite.** Cf. CWM 8/1.64/2–3. Tyndale accepts fasting only as a means of taming the flesh, cf. 1 Cor. 9.27, Col. 3.5, but he rejects it as a form of works-righteousness. He discusses the proper methods and motives for fasting in

Mammon (F1r–v). In commenting on Matt. 6.16–18, he will discuss fasting extensively in *Matthew,* e.g., in Advent and Lent (k8v) and on the seasonal Ember Days and fasts in honor of Mary (l5); cf. Duffy (41). Relying solely on the merits of Christ, Tyndale would reject the idea of fasting as satisfaction for sin, as defended by the *dramatis persona* of Antony in *Dialogue of Comfort,* 1534–35 (CWM 12.95/10–96/11).

67/24–26 **how . . . know it.** Isa. 58.3.

67/27–33 **behold . . . naked.** Isa. 58.3–7.

68/2–3 **What . . . fote stole.** Isa. 66.1. *Answer* reverses the order of the OT, putting the rhetorical question before the answer.

68/4 **steuen.** cf. Acts 7.49–50, quoting Isa. 6.1–2.

68/5 **paul.** cf. Acts 17.24.

68/8–9 **Israelites . . . world.** Cf. Jer. 9.16, Ezek. 12.13–15. After Samaria was conquered by Assyria in 721 BC, its leading citizens were deported to various parts of the empire. Nebuchadrezzar deported Judeans in several waves to Babylon after he conquered Jerusalem in 587 BC.

68/11 **how Englonde was once full.** Tyndale notes the expulsion of the Jews from England in 1290, but not from Spain in 1492. Cf. John Edwards, *The Jews in Christian Europe 1400–1700* (London: Routledge, 1988) 11.

68/17–18 **haply . . . aboute.** Three thousand were converted on Pentecost, cf. Acts 2.41; the converts in Jerusalem later increased to five thousand, cf. Acts 4.4.

68/21–24 **For . . . myracles.** Cf. Acts 8, the Ethiopian eunuch.

68/25–26 **we hethen . . . after.** Cf. Acts 10, Cornelius the centurion.

69/6–8 **not al that . . . seed.** Rom. 9.6–7.

69/9–11 **not all they . . . garment.** Cf. Matt. 22.1–14.

69/15–17 **kyngdome . . . bad.** Cf. Matt. 13.47–48.

69/31–33 **not as God . . . dedes.** Cf. Gal. 3.22.

69/32 **faith / so beleuinge in christ.** Cf. Rom. 3.22.

70/1 **As oure papistes beleue.** Tyndale attacks "popish faith" for relying on the common consent of many (cf. 48/24–49/27, 79/11n) and for the claim that faith, as acceptance of revelation, may coexist with sinful consent to evil. Scholastic teaching distinguished "unformed faith," the mind's assent to God's word as true, from "formed faith," where one's will and practice correspond to what one believes. On the basis of this distinction, those guilty of serious sin can still be considered true members of the church if they profess the truth of revelation mediated by the church, even if they fail to practice justice, temperance, and love. This theology lay behind More's position that the church is "the comen known multytude of crysten men good and bad togyther" (CWM 6/1.205/5) and grounds his argument against the Lutheran tenet that faith alone justifies (CWM 6/1.376–402, esp. 383/18–34, 384/31, 385/28–34). (JW)

70/10–11 **their father the deuell.** Cf. John 8.44.

70/17–21 **because . . . Moses.** Cf. CWM 8/1.194/17–19.

70/23–24 **holy water . . . holy salt.** Background on the liturgical and devotional use of such blessed objects is given in the respective entries, "Wasser," "Feuer," "Brot. Religiöse Volkskunde," "Brotschutzen," and "Salz," in LThK. Delumeau treats them among the *rites rassurants* (37–50). Authors dealing with this theme draw heavily on Adolph Franz, *Die kirchlichen Benediktionen im Mittelalter,* 2 vol. (Freiburg: Herder, 1909). For other references to sacramentals, cf. nn on 7/11–13, 17/6–7, 74/1, 108/1. (JW)

70/29 **kyssynge of the pax.** The ceremony may have been a substitute for the Eucharist (Duffy 125) or for the kiss of peace (OED 3.). Agreeing with the latter, Tyndale explains how kissing the pax symbolizes forgiveness and love (*Obedience* O5v). Yet, trusting in ritual can lead to the neglect of true Christian love (*1 John* F1v). For the use of the pax at the Field of the Cloth of Gold, cf. 104/5n.

70/31 **loue . . . ensample.** Cf. John 13.15.

71/1 **confirmacion.** Confirmation had evolved as a distinct rite in the early medieval West through the gradual dismemberment of the ancient church's complex rite of baptismal initiation. Theologically, it is the imparting of the Holy Spirit to strengthen a maturing Christian as he or she advances to active membership in the church. Luther saw Confirmation as an ecclesiastical rite of blessing, but that it was a sacrament based on a sure promise of grace he denied in *Babylonian Captivity,* 1520 (WA 6.549–50; LW 36.91–92). Erasmus may have influenced Tyndale's view (72/5–6) of the desirability of climaxing the catechizing of youth with a rite of public profession of the signification of one's baptism. Cf. *Pio lectori*, Preface to Paraphrase of Matthew, 1522 (LB 7.★★3v). Tyndale's protest at the loss of the original didactic purpose of Confirmation (*Obedience* O1–O3) anticipates his criticisms in *Answer*. At the same time, Martin Bucer spoke of the need of such a rite, which he then introduced in the churches of Hesse and Strasbourg, René Bornert, *La réforme protestante du culte à Strasbourg* (Leiden: Brill, 1981) 362–66. The best brief overview on Confirmation is Georg Kretschmar's entry "Firmung" (TRE 11.192–204). (JW)

72/2–3 **the deuell / the world and the flesh.** Patristic and medieval exegetes paired the three temptations of Christ (bread into stones, kingdoms of the earth, pinnacle of the Temple in Luke 4 and *Paradise Regained*) with *concupiscientia carnis, et concupiscientia oculorum, et superbia vitae* of the Vulgate (1 John 2.16). Cf. Gregory's homily on Matt. 4.1–11 against gluttony, avarice and vainglory (PL 76.1136); the three winds of the World, the Flesh, and the Fiend which buffet the Tree of Charity in *Piers Plowman* (Passus XVI, line 48). See Patrick Cullen, *Infernal Triad: The Flesh, the World, and the Devil in Spenser and Milton* (Princeton UP, 1974).

In his 1516 NT, Erasmus renders *he epithumia tes sarkos, kai he epithumia ton ophthalmon, kai he alazoneia tou biou* as *concupiscentia carnis . . . , & concupiscentia oculorum, fastus facultatum* [pride of resources]. Following Erasmus' Latin, Tyndale translates the Greek as "the lust of the flesshe, the lust of the eyes, and the pryde of goodes" (Wallis 488/23–24; TNT 339C), cf. 193/15–16n.

72/18 **a monstrous laten.** For other references in *Answer* to Latin as an obstacle to religious understanding, cf. 75/19–20, 129/34, and 136/10–13. Tyndale interprets *sacerdos* as sacrificer and mediator (*Obedience* M3). Because the baptized share in the eternal priesthood of Christ, a separate priestly caste is unnecessary. He does accept *Sanctus* or "holy" as one of the true names for Christ (*1 John* E1). (JB)

72/18–19 **pater noster.** After the emergence of Lollardy (39/2n), knowledge of the basic prayers in English was used as evidence of heresy. Anne Hudson cites cases from Norwich in 1426, Coventry in 1485, and the Chilterns between 1518 and 1521, in "Lollardy:

The English Heresy?" *Lollards and Their Books* (London: Hambledon, 1985) 161–62. Bale recalled that in 1506 as a boy of eleven he watched the burning of a young man in Norwich for possessing the Lord's Prayer in English. Cf. Preface to *A treatyse made by Johan Lambert* . . . (Wesel, 1548?) STC 15180, fol. 3v in *The Complete Plays of John Bale* 1, ed. Peter Happé (Cambridge: D.S. Brewer, 1985) 2n10. Foxe (4.557) reports that in 1519 seven Lollards were burnt at Coventry for teaching their children the Pater Noster in English.

In the early 16c a few texts scrupulously follow the prohibition in the Constitutions of Oxford (1409) by omitting the PN in English. Although Duffy devotes a whole chapter (53–87) to explaining . . . *[H]ow the plowman lerned his pater noster* (1510) STC 20034, this poem fails to give a translation or even a paraphrase. Margaret Roper translates Erasmus' commentary on the *Precatio Dominica* (1523), LB 5.1219A–1228C, as *A deuout treatise vpon the Pater noster* . . . (1526?) STC 10477, but she leaves the actual prayer in Latin.

On the other hand, English versions of the Lord's Prayer were published by authors of proven orthodoxy, such as the Austin canon John Mirk in *Instructions for Parish Priests* (c1450), rev. ed. Edward Peacock and F.J. Furnivall, EETS Original Series 31 (1902; New York: Greenwood, 1969); and the Bridgittine monks Thomas Betson in . . . *[A] ryght profytable treatyse* (1500), STC 1978; and Richard Whitford in *A werke for housholders* . . . (1530?), STC 25421.8. For a translation of the PN in English by John Colet, cf. 168/28n.

Tyndale published a preface and a paraphrase of the PN as an appendix to *A Compendious Introduccion unto the Pistle to the Romayns,* facsimile of STC 24438 (Worms, 1526), The English Experience 767 (Norwood, NJ: Johnson, 1975). The prayer-dialogue is a translation and expansion of Luther's *Auslegung deutsch des Vaterunser für die einfältigen Laien,* 1519 (WA 2.80–130; LW 42.15–81) (Daniell 150 and n21). This same work, now called *The pater noster spoken of the sinner: God answerynge him at euery peticyon,* was published separately (c1535) STC 16818, as well as jointly with Savonarola, *An exposition . . . vpon the .li. psalme* . . . (Antwerp, 1536) STC 21789.5. Tyndale might well have read other commentaries by Luther on the

Lord's Prayer in *Personal Prayer Book,* 1522 (WA 10/2.375–406; LW 43.11–45); *Large Catechism,* 1529 (WA 30/1.125–238; *The Book of Concord* 358–461); *Small Catechism,* 1529 (WA 30/1.243–425; *The Book of Concord* 338–56). Luther's *Wochenpredigten über Matth. 5–7,* 1532 (WA 32.299–544; LW 21.3–294), a sermon series given in Wittenberg on Wednesdays between October 1530 and April 1532, is the basis of Tyndale's *[E]xposicion vppon the. v. vi. vii. chapters of Mathew* (Antwerp, 1533) STC 24440. In this translation, paraphrase and expansion of Luther, the explanation of the PN is Tyndale's own (*Matthew* i5v–k4). In spite of the self-effacing tone, these few pages tersely reveal the conflict Tyndale faced between obedience to king or conscience.

Allusions to the Lord's Prayer occur in Tyndale's other independent works. Christians should do everything out of love for God's glory (*Mammon* G6v). Although Christians sin daily against God and their neighbors, God forgives them so that they might forgive others (*1 John* B4). The faithful pray continually for God to sanctify his name, fulfill his will, keep them from temptation, and deliver them from evil (*Mammon* F2v). (JB)

73/13–27 **amice . . . handes.** The use of allegory in explaining the vestments and gestures of the celebrant of the Mass goes back to the Carolingian epoch, especially to Amalar of Metz, *De ecclesiasticis officiis* (PL 105.985–1242). Rupert of Deutz (d. 1135) set the pattern for connecting each vestment with an event of Jesus' passion. William Durandus' *Rationale divinorum officiorum* (late 13c) was the source for numerous popularizations. Cf. Jungmann 1.87–91, 107–18, 177f. More claims that Durandus was Tyndale's source (cf. CWM 8/1.111/7 and n).

Gabriel Biel devotes one preliminary chapter to relating the vestments allegorically to events in the passion of Jesus and another to a tropological account connecting the vestments to the virtues of Jesus set forth for imitation. Cf. *Canonis Missae expositio* (Reutlingen, 1488; seven further printings before 1530), ed. H.A. Oberman and W. J. Courtenay, 1 (Wiesbaden: Steiner, 1963) 86–99. The earliest German explanation of the whole Mass (c1480) offers a lengthy table of the different allegorical meanings ascribed by the author to the parts of the Mass. Cf. *Die älteste deutsche Gesamtausle-*

gung der Messe, ed. F.A. Reichert, CC 29 (Münster: Aschendorff, 1967) XCIII–CVII. (JW)

73/13–15 **kercheue . . . smote the.** Cf. Matt. 26.67–68, Luke 22.64.

73/18 **croune of thorne.** Cf. Matt. 27.29, John 19.2.

73/19 **white garment.** Cf. Luke 23.11.

73/22 **.iiij. nayles.** Cf. John 20.25.

73/23 **cord . . . bound with.** Cf. Matt. 27.2, Mark 15.1, John 18.12.

73/24–25 **bounde . . . scorged.** Cf. Matt. 27.26, Mark 15.15, John 19.1.

73/25–26 **sindon . . . buryed.** Cf. Matt. 27.59.

73/27–28 **splayenge . . . crosse.** Cf. Matt. 27.35, Mark 15.24, Luke 23.33, John 19.18.

73/30–74/1 **ye . . . heven.** Matt. 5.14 and 16.

74/1 **salt.** Cf. Matt. 5.13, Mark 9.50, Luke 14.34.

74/13 **S. Augustine.** *Unio Dissidentium* (1.T5) gives a long excerpt on religious practices made obligatory without the warrant of Scripture, a council, or universal custom from Ep. 55, Augustine to Januarius (AD c400) 19.35 (PL 33.221–22; CSEL 34/2.209–10; Parsons 1.290–91).

Erasmus cites this passage from Augustine in his annotation on Matt. 11.30, *Iugum meum suaue.*) 1519 NT (Reeve 1.54), an essay sharply critical of sacramental practice, fasting laws, marriage legislation, use of excommunication, dispensations, etc. For Erasmus it is high time to reclaim the evangelical freedom preached by St. Paul. (JW)

75/5 **Greke.** Reciprocal excommunications (1054), the First Crusade (1095–99), and the conquest of Constantinople by the Latins (1204) violated the relationship between the Western and Eastern Churches. In *Prelates* (B8) Tyndale blames the Eastern Schism on the excessive claims of the Roman Church. Greek presence at the Councils of Constance (1414–18), Basel (1431–37), and Ferrara-Florence (1438–39) helped renew cultural ties with the West, see Berschin passim. For the scholars who left Greece before, during, and after the conquest of Constantinople by the Turks (1453), see John Edwin Sandys, *A History of Classical Scholarship,* Vol. 2, *From the Revival of Learning to the End of the Eighteenth Century* (1908; New York: Hafner, 1967) passim.

Knowledge of Greek was acquired through private tuition and in collegiate settings. In Paris, George Hermonymus of Sparta taught Greek to Johann Reuchlin, Guillaume Budé, and Erasmus (Sandys 2.169, 256). During his stay in Italy (1506–9), Erasmus perfected his Greek on his own in Bologna and with Girolamo Aleandro and Arsenius in Venice. Cf. Léon-E. Halkin, *Erasmus: A Critical Biography,* tr. John Tonkin (1987; Oxford: Blackwell, 1993) 65–72. For More's knowledge of Greek, cf. 22/13–14n. Luther learned the fundamentals of Greek from the Augustinian Johann Lang at Wittenberg about 1511. Cf. Maria Grossmann, *Humanism in Wittenberg, 1485–1517* (Nieuwkoop: De Graaf, 1975) 77. Tyndale probably studied Greek at Magdalen Hall, Oxford (afterwards Hertford College) (Daniell 23, 30). Later, he translated an oration by Isocrates, characterized by periodic sentences and eloquent tropes, to prove his ability to translate the NT (Daniell 87–90). As further witness to the vivid diction and compelling syntax of Tyndale, 84% of his 1534 NT was adopted by the KJV. Cf. Jon Nielson and Royal Skousen, "How Much of the King James Bible Is William Tyndale's: An Estimation Based on Sampling," *Reformation* 3 (1998) 49–74.

75/5 **specially of the Hebrue.** Smalley (passim) examines the preservation of the knowledge of Hebrew in NW Europe from the 8c to 12c. From the 13c to 15c Jews were expelled from England, France, Germany, and Spain, "and in those places where they remained they were not always willing to teach Hebrew" (Friedman 19).

Although he successfully taught himself Greek, Erasmus failed to learn Hebrew. He does not mention Hebrew in *On the Method of Study,* 1511 (ASD 1/2.111–51; CWE 24.665–91) for boys, but he recommends it for mature students in many works from *Ratio verae theologiae,* 1518 (Holborn 177–305; not yet in CWE) to *Ecclesiastes,* 1535 (ASD 5/4–5; not yet in CWE), cf. Markish 113. Henry VIII needed to consult some scholar for his brief observation in Ch. 6 that the Hebrew language lacks neuter gender (*Assertio,* CC 43.140). Fisher studied the works of the Hebraist Johann Reuchlin and was tutored by Robert Wakefield c1516 (Surtz 143, 148). In a letter Germain Marc'hadour observed that, while More never learned Hebrew, he may have met Jews in Antwerp or Paris.

After receiving his doctorate from the University of Erfurt in 1512,

Luther was appointed to the chair of biblical theology in Wittenberg. From 1511 to 1513, Luther began the study of Hebrew, using
Jerome, Lyra, and Paul of Burgos. His *Dictata super Psalterium,*
1513–16 (WA 4.1–462; not in LW) was based on the Vulgate as
found in Lefèvre's *Psalterium quincuplex* (1509), but his *Operationes
in Psalmos,* 1519–21 (WA 5; not in LW) shows a good knowledge
of Hebrew. The Jewish convert Matthaeus Adrianus taught at Wittenberg from Fall 1519 to February 1521 (CWE 5.155n7; CWE
10.191n5). Between 1522 and 1534, Luther translated the OT, using Rashi (1040–1105), David Kimchi (1160–1235), Sanctes Pagninus OP (1470–1536), and Sebastian Münster (1489–1552) (G.
Lloyd Jones 59).

Robert Wakefield was appointed the first official university lecturer
in Hebrew at Cambridge in 1524, the same year that Tyndale left
England for Germany. Tyndale could have begun Hebrew under
Matthew Aurogallus at Wittenberg and continued his studies at
Worms, an important center for German Jews since the 11c. In
translating the Hebrew Bible, Tyndale could have used the edition
published by Gershom Soncino (Venice, 1488) or by Daniel
Bomberg (Venice, 1517) or the Complutensian Polyglot printed in
1514–17 and released in 1522. He used Münster's *Dictionarium Hebraicum* (Basel, 1525) and Pagninus' *Thesaurus linguae sanctae seu lexicon hebraicum* (Lyons, 1529). In Winter 1535, Tyndale wrote to the
governor of the castle of Vilvoorde, "But above all, I beg and en-
treat your clemency earnestly to intercede with the lord commis-
sary, that he would deign to allow me the use of my Hebrew
Bible, Hebrew Grammar, and Hebrew Lexicon, and that I may
employ my time with that study." English translation with the
Latin original in Mombert li–ii; for the Latin with a slightly different translation, cf. Mozley 333–35. Cf. G. Lloyd Jones on Tyndale as "the father of English Hebraists" (115–23, esp. 122).

Apart from the prefaces to his biblical translations, Tyndale makes
scattered comments on specific Hebrew words and phrases
throughout his independent works. The pamphlet *Sacraments*
quotes twenty-six words or phrases from the Hebrew to argue
that OT names and NT sacraments are signs of divine activity.

75/9–11 **dunces disciples . . . raged in euery pulpyt.** Cf. 46/33n.

For More's defense of the New Learning against conservative clerics, see his four letters, actually treatises: Ep. 15, To Martin Dorp, Bruges, 21 October <1515> (CWM 15.2–127); Ep. 60, To the University of Oxford, Abingdon, 29 March <1518> (CWM 15.130–49); Ep. 75, To Edward Lee, n.p., 1 May 1519 (CWM 15.152–95); Ep. 83, To a Monk, n.p., <March–September 1519> (CWM 15.198–311). Tyndale twice uses the phrase "new learning" (*Obedience* C5v, *1 John* D3) to refer to a revival of the primitive meaning of Scripture.

75/12 **the true Latine tonge.** Throughout the medieval period, certain Latin authors were known continuously. Chaucer (c1343–1400) read Ovid, Virgil, Statius, Juvenal, and some Cicero and Seneca (Sandys 2.219). But between 1333 and 1433, major Latin works were recovered by humanists searching through monastery libraries. For example, Poggio Bracciolini (1380–1459) discovered several orations of Cicero and a complete copy of Quintilian's *Institutio Oratoria* in Transalpine monasteries during recesses of the Council of Constance (1414–18). (Sandys 2.25–27). Whereas Virgil had been the favored classical author of the Middle Ages, e.g. of Dante (1265–1321), Cicero had more influence on the Renaissance. Tyndale praises Virgil as chief of poets, "Tully" as chief of orators (*Obedience* H6v).

75/15 **tirens or virgill.** In all his writings, Tyndale mentions only three classical poets: Terence (195/85 to 159 BC); Virgil (70–19 BC), and Ovid (43 BC to AD 18). There are general references to Virgil here and in *Obedience* H6v, to the Trojan Horse from *Aeneid* 2.58–259 in *Prelates* G4v, to a proverb from *Aeneid* 2.354 in *Answer* 153/3, to avarice from *Aeneid* 3.56–57 in *Testament of Tracy* (B2). There is a general reference to Ovid in *Obedience* R5, to *Remedia Amoris* in Prologue to Numbers (Mombert 395/27–28; TOT 197), to the mother of Meleager (*Metamorphoses* 8.451–525) in the Prologue to Jonas (TOT 633). Sidenotes in Matthew's Bible, probably not by Tyndale, contain a reference to Pliny the Elder (AD 23/4–79), *Natural History* 13.7 *pace* Judges 9 (TOT 357), to Josephus (AD 37–c100), *Jewish Antiquities* 7.12 *pace* 2 Sam. 23 (TOT 456), and a general reference to Josephus *pace* 2 Kings 8 (TOT 514).

75/19–20 **.xx. thousand prestes curattes.** Haigh (5) estimates that
there were 2.5 million people in England and Wales in the early
1530s. Of these, 50,000 or 2% of the population were ordained,
with 40,000 diocesan priests and 10,000 monks and friars.
(Haigh's estimate of 10,000 priests in religious communities is
close to another tally of 9169 at the end of the period between
1500 and 1534, cf. 11/20n). Tyndale's figure of 20,000 curates who
could not translate the PN into English would equal 40% of the
clergy.

75/21–22 **fiat . . . terra.** Matt. 6.10, Luke 11.2.

75/29 **bosh at the tauern dore.** A branch or bunch of ivy (perhaps
as a plant sacred to Bacchus) was hung up as a sign of a tavern or
the sign-board itself. Cf. *Obedience* M1v, *1 John* E2, and *Confutation*'s "tauerners busshe" (CWM 8/2.633/27–28).

76/8–21 **Yee . . . holy water.** Stinginess with the poor who must
beg contrasts with largess in support of devotional religion as
preached by the mendicants. The number of poor people was in
fact increasing in the England of Tyndale's time because produc-
tivity could not keep pace with demographic growth, as is shown
in John Pound, *Poverty and Vagrancy in Tudor England* (London:
Longman, 1971). The continental reformers did not treat begging
by the poor with the detached acceptance implied by Tyndale.
One issue of reform in *To the Christian Nobility,* 1520 (WA 6.450/
22–451/6; LW 44.189f), is for every city to organize a fund for the
relief of its own poor and then to allow no beggars from elsewhere even to enter the city. This measure was implemented in
Augsburg and Nuremberg in 1522 and in Strassburg in 1523 and
was found in Tudor poor law. Luther denounced begging in early
sermons and treatises, e.g. *Trade and Usury,* 1524 (WA 6.41/
33–42/13; LW 45.281f, 286f). (JW)

76/34–77/1 **so tenderly . . . sonne.** Cf. John 3.16.

77/13 **the true . . . spirite.** Cf. John 4.23.

77/22 **teynterden steple.** Good works connected with ceremonies,
such as contributing to building funds for church steeples, divert-
ed resources from the upkeep of English harbors. Tenterden is a
village fifty-three miles SE of London. Five of its inhabitants were
burnt for heresy during Warham's term as Archbishop of Canter-

bury. Cf. Samuel Lewis, *A Topographical Dictionary of England* (1831; Baltimore: Genealogical Publishing Co., 1996) 4.278. The folk wisdom of More's Kentish man became current as the proverb, "Tenterden Steeple was the cause of Goodwin Sands," Tilley T91. Cf. CWM 6/1.413/10, 6/2.720, 8/2.775/35f. Antonio's ship is wrecked on "the Goodwins" in *The Merchant of Venice* 3.1.2–4 (performed 1596–97, published 1600).

79/5 **a letter sent from no man.** "The letter of credence" (CWM 6/1.24/4–26/7) was supposedly sent from More's "ryght worshypfull frende" (CWM 6/1.21/7) to introduce the Messenger. As More once fashioned "Utopia" or "no place," he now creates "no man." Ch. 1 also contains "The letter of the author sent with the boke" (CWM 6/1.26/8–27/27). More as Author sends his fictional friend a transcription of the four sessions between himself as Mentor and the Messenger. So in *Tusculan Disputations* (45–44 BC), Cicero sent Brutus a transcription of five days of supposed dialogue between "M." and "A.": "Magister" and "Adolescens" or "Marcus" and "Auditor." These speakers offer a model for Anthony and his nephew Vincent in More's *Dialogue of Comfort* (1534–35). See O'Donnell, "Three Dialogues of Comfort."

79/9 **worsheping . . . images.** In the second edition of *Dialogue* (May 1531), More added a long passage to Bk. 1, Ch. 2 defending religious images (CWM 6/1.39/26–47/22, 6/2.556–57). For other long additions to *Dialogue,* cf. 184/2n on images and 201/29n on faith.

79/11 **in comune.** Cf. 70/1n, and "the comen fayth" (CWM 6/1.37/34, 38/1), "comen report" (CWM 6/1.38/4), "commonly condempned" (CWM 6/1.38/9).

79/17–18 **maior . . . minor.** Tyndale accuses More of the fallacy of the "undistributed middle," of using the words "common," "church," "faith," and "good" in one sense in his major premise and another sense in his minor premise and thus drawing a false conclusion.

79/19–26 **seruaunt . . . images.** Cf. CWM 6/1.48/27–49/12.

79/19–20 **seruaunt . . . sake.** Cf. Matt. 10.40, Mark 9.37, Luke 9.47, John 13.20.

79/20–21 **what . . . Christ.** Cf. Matt. 25.40.

79/22–23 **.xij. . . . christe.** Cf. Matt. 19.28, Luke 22.30.

79/24–25 **Mary . . . passion.** Cf. Matt. 26.7, Mark 14.3, CWM 6/1.49/13–16, *Answer* 83/6–7n.

80/3–4 **God . . . only.** Cf. John 4.23–24.

80/4 **Faith to his promises.** Cf. Gal. 3.22, Heb. 6.12.

80/12–13 **Fastynge . . . goinge.** Cf. CWM 6/1.44/14–19.

80/13 **pilgrimage.** More defends pilgrimages in Bk. 1, Ch. 4 and 16, cf. 62/1n. The Messenger describes the shrine of St. Valery in Bk. 2, Ch. 10, cf. 123/25n.

80/14–15 **god . . . drinke.** Cf. Ps. 50.13.

80/30–31 **yet . . . only.** Cf. 2 Cor. 12.14.

81/1 **The deuel . . . god.** Cf. Lev. 20.2–5.

81/5 **wenisdaye . . . S. katerine.** Some fasted on Wednesdays in honor of John the Baptist, Catherine of Alexandria, Christopher, or Margaret of Antioch for the grace to receive the last sacraments before they died. See *Here begynneth a lytel treatyse that sheweth how every mon & woman ought to fast and absteyne them from flesshe on the Wednesday* (1500), STC 24224 (Duffy 319–20 and n48).

81/6 **fast sayntes euens.** Medieval Christians were required to fast on the day before the following feasts: Christmas, Pentecost, Birth of John the Baptist, Laurence, Assumption, All Saints; also on the vigils of the Apostles except Philip and James in the Easter season and John the Evangelist during Christmas week (Duffy 41). Tyndale mocks this heavy discipline by extending it to the vigils of lesser saints: Anthony the Hermit, Patrick, and Brendan (*Matthew* l5).

81/17–18 **promises . . . mercy.** Cf. Luke 1.72.

81/20 **gaye cote.** Cf. Gen. 37.23, 32. Tyndale describes Joseph's cloak as a "gay coote," i.e., "gay coat" (Mombert 113–14; TOT 61). Tyndale in Gen. 37.3 (Mombert 112; TOT 60) and KJV in all three verses use "coat of many colours." Tyndale refers to Tamar's "gay kirtle" (2 Sam. 13.19; TOT 439E); KJV to her "garment of diuers colours." Tyndale lists among David's gifts to the future temple "gay stones" (1 Chron. 29.2; TOT 578A); KJV, "glistering stones, and of diuers colours." Tyndale and KJV both describe the rich as wearing 'gaye clothynge' in Jas. 2.3 (Wallis 524/20; TNT 364A). In his Prologue to Jonas, Tyndale describes a conversion based on works-righteousness: "[T]hey had made their souls gay against the receiving again of the wicked spirit" (TOT 634). He alludes here to Matt. 12.44, where Tyndale (Wallis 47/21; TNT 36D) and KJV both describe the soul as "garnisshed." More uses the phrase "gay sworde" in *Dialogue* (CWM 6/1.254/39).

81/32–33 **pilars / polaxes . . . hattes.** Two silver-gilt pillars (OED 5.) were carried before Wolsey as sign of his office as cardinal. Before his cardinal's hat, Wolsey's body-guard also carried gilt pole-axes (OED 2.), cf. Cavendish 24/3. More as Speaker of the House of Commons in 1523 thought it prudent to allow Wolsey to appear there accompanied "with his maces, his pillars, his pollaxes, his crosses, his hat, and great seale too" (Roper 17/13–14). For Wolsey, cf. 55/16n.

82/10 **sacrifices of the old law.** Cf. CWM 6/1.50/2–3.

82/14–18 **And when . . . old testament.** Cf. Isa. 58.3–7, Joel 2.13, Hos. 6.6.

82/19–20 **Rom. xiiij. . . . abounde.** Cf. Rom. 14.5. *Answer* translates the Vulgate, *unusquisque in suo sensu abundet.* Tyndale's 1526 NT gives "Se that no man waver in hys awne mynde"; 1534 NT has "in his awne meanynge" (Wallis 339/9; TNT 239B). KJV has, "Let euery man bee fully perswaded [fully assured] in his owne minde." The 1557 edition of *Dialogue* (CWM 6/1.50/14) identifies this quote as 1 Thess. 4.[10]. Cf. "We beseche you brethren that ye encreace more and more" (Wallis 430/15–16; TNT 302B).

82/26–27 **Luther . . . immediatly.** Luther's sermon on 14 September 1522, feast of the Exaltation of the Cross, attacked giving contributions of silver and gold for reliquaries holding fragments of the true cross, while at the same time paying no heed to God's mandate to help the poor (WA 10/3.332–34; not in LW). This sermon also circulated in Latin in a collection published in Strassburg in 1526 (WA 10/3.xxi). (JW)

82/26–30 **Luther . . . ferthynge.** Cf. CWM 6/1.51/10–17.

82/31–33 **the poore . . . them.** Cf. Matt. 25.35–40.

82/33–34 **almes . . . commaundement.** Cf. Luke 12.33.

83/6–7 **we . . . heed.** Cf. CWM 6/1.49/21–22. **powringe . . . heed.** Cf. Matt. 26.7, Mark 14.3.

83/12–13 **S. Steuens tombe.** After Stephen's tomb was discovered near Jerusalem in 415, his relics were widely distributed (Rotelle 3/9.125n). Cf. Augustine's Sermon 318 (AD 425) preached at the installation of some of these relics at Hippo, Par. 1 (PL 38.1437–38;

Rotelle 3/9.147). The *Golden Legend* quotes *The City of God* 22.8 (AD 413–27) (CCL 48.821–24; 1NPNF 2.488–90), on miracles that occurred when sufferers came into contact with the relics of Stephen (GL 1.48–49).

83/13–18 **the miracles . . . preachinge.** Tyndale's emphasis on the saints as transmitters of doctrine is a creative variation on the Reformation argument over their role. In early works Luther associated Christ and the saints as helpers of all who by faith are in communion with them, *The Blessed Sacrament and the Brotherhoods,* 1519 (WA 2.744–45, 748; LW 35.52–54, 58). Luther could observe critically that feast days in honor of the saints have multiplied excessively and are not celebrated religiously, cf. *Treatise on Good Works,* 1520 (WA 6.229/32–230/6; LW 44.55). Later, Luther's paramount concern is the lack of any warrant from Scripture for prayer invoking the saints' aid, leaving it among the abusive human inventions of the church: *Confession concerning Christ's Supper,* 1528 (WA 26.508; LW 37.370); *On Translating, An Open Letter,* 1530 (WA 30/2.643–45; LW 35.198–200). The Augsburg Confession of 1530 affirms the commemoration of the saints as models of faith and good works in their calling, but holds that praying to them for help is ruled out by Jesus' sole mediatorship, Art. 21, cf. *The Book of Concord* 46f. Melanchthon's *Apologia* for the Confession fleshes out commemoration into thanksgiving for gifts given the saints, encouragement from their experiences of grace, and imitation. But there is no scriptural ground for invoking them, even if we believe they continue to pray for the church on earth (ibid., 229–36). Upper German reformers, such as Martin Bucer in Strassburg, took more radical action in eliminating both prayer to the saints and their commemoration.

Catholic controversialists went to the defense of venerating and invoking the saints, as in Josse Clichtove's *De veneratione sanctorum* (Paris, 1523) and Jacob van Hoogstraten's *Dialogus de veneratione et invocatione sanctorum contra perfidiam Lutheranam* (Cologne, 1524). Johann Eck systematized the Catholic case in Ch. 15 of his *Enchiridion,* "Concerning the Veneration of the Saints" (Fraenkel 173–90; Battles 110–21), arguing from foreshadowings in Scripture, from reason, the Fathers, and longstanding custom in the church. Eck wards off Reformation arguments from the exclusive mediatorship of Christ as wrongly dissociating Christ from those who are, in him and with him, mediators of intercession. The imperial response to the Augsburg Confession digested Eck's arguments, while highlighting how the Lutherans, by denying invocation of the saints, associated themselves with a line of medieval heretics whom the church had already condemned. Cf. *Die Confutatio der Confessio Augustana,* ed. Herbert Immenkötter, CC 33 (Münster: Aschendorff, 1979) 124–31, esp. 125. Johann Dietenberger, writing in Augsburg in October 1530, argued that it is permissible to invoke the saints because the church defines for belief and practice only what is obscure and implicit in Scripture. Cf. *Phimostomos scripturariorum,* ed. Erwin Iserloh et al., CC 38 (Münster: Aschendorff, 1985) 114–56. The title, "A Muzzle for Those Gone Mad Over Scripture," polemically implies that the reformers are rabid dogs. Underlying the biblical and theological argument for praying to the saints were the fears and anxieties of believers, for whom the saints were "friends in high places" and influential protectors. Cf. Delumeau, Part II, "Nous ne sommes pas seuls," 177–289. (JW)

83/16–17 **As . . . seke.** Cf. Acts 19.12.

83/19–20 **Eliseus . . . Iordayne.** Cf. 2 Kings 5:10, 14.

83/22–23 **bones . . . a deed man.** Cf. 2 Kings 13.21.

83/26–28 **whosoeuer . . . him selfe.** Cf. Num. 19.16–19.

83/28–30 **place . . . poluted.** Cf. 2 Kings 23.14, 16, 20.

84/1 **miracles done at the holy crosse.** When Helena, mother of Constantine, discovered three crosses under the temple of Venus built by Hadrian in Jerusalem, the cross of Christ was identified by miracles. Socrates Scholasticus (c380–c450) (NCE 13.408–9) relates that the Bishop of Jerusalem cured a dying woman with a piece of the true cross. Cf. his *Ecclesiastical History* [on AD 305–439], 1.17 (PG 67.117–22; 2NPNF 2.21–22). Sozomen (c400–c450) (NCE 13.489) repeats this story and briefly alludes to the raising of a dead youth. Cf. his parallel *Ecclesiastical History* [on AD 323–425], 2.1 (PG 67.929–34; 2NPNF 2.258–59). The *Golden Legend* gives both incidents but greatly enlarges the latter with details taken from Luke 7.11 on the son of the widow of Nain (GL 1.280–82).

84/4–5 **pilgrimes . . . circles.** Cf. CWM 6/1.55/21–23.

84/6 **prayenge in the spirite.** Cf. John 4.24 and CWM 6/1.58/ 12–15.

84/7–8 **we . . . a nother.** Cf. CWM 6/1.59/30–31.

84/19 **tabernacle.** Cf. Lev. 17.8–9. **temple.** Cf. Ezra 6.13–18.

84/33–85/1 **we . . . the paschall lambe.** Cf. CWM 6/1.55/33–56/3.

85/1–2 **Christ . . . for vs.** Cf. Exod. 12.1–13 and 1 Cor. 5.7. *Answer* has "paschall lambe" (85/1); NT has "esterlambe" (Wallis 352/15; TNT 248C); KJV has "Passeouer."

85/3–4 **Morouer . . . Egypte.** Cf. Exod. 12.40–42. Tyndale treats the Exodus as a literal escape from Egypt, not as an allegorical escape from sin.

85/7 **holy straunge gestures.** CWM 6/1.56/4.

85/11 **left . . . tyme.** Cf. CWM 6/1.56/6–7. Tyndale omits More's qualifying phrase, "greate parte wherof" (CWM 6/1.56/6).

85/12 **For . . . did.** Cf. 1 Cor. 11.23–26.

85/14–15 **Paule . . . nothinge.** Cf. Acts 20.27.

85/17–18 **moare . . . with out it.** Cf. CWM 6/1.56/23–24.

85/20–22 **And at the sight . . . deed.** Tyndale voices a common 16c critique of the emphasis on compassion with the suffering Christ in late medieval piety. Erasmus had warned against a merely natural pity for Christ's sufferings in the Seventeenth Rule of the *Enchiridion,* 1503 (Holborn 117/12–13; CWE 66.110). Luther was also critical of this form of affective participation in the passion of Jesus in *Freedom of a Christian,* 1520 (WA 7.29/11–13; LW 31.357). Cf. "Passion (mystique de la)" in *Dictionnaire de Spiritualité,* ed. Marcel Viller SJ et al., 17 vols. including Index (Paris: Beauchesne, 1937–95) 12.329–32; F. Vandenbroucke, "La devotion au Crucifié à la fin du moyen âge," *Maison Dieu,* no. 75 (1963) 133–43. (JW)

85/27 **prayenge at church.** Cf. CWM 6/1.57/34–36.

86/1 **presence . . . temple.** Cf. CWM 6/1.57/19–20.

86/2 **prophetes . . . there.** Cf. Isa. 66.1.

86/3 **Paul.** Cf. Acts 17.24. **Steuen.** Cf. Acts 7.48–50.

86/4 **Salomon.** Cf. 1 Kings 8.27, 30.

86/7–8 **false . . . destroyed it.** Cf. Matt. 24.2

86/11 **piler of fire & cloude.** Cf. Exod. 13.21, CWM 6/1.57/12.

86/14–15 **eyes . . . se.** Cf. Matt. 11.5, Luke 7.22.

86/19–20 **seke . . . verite.** Cf. John 4.21–24.

86/28–33 **And so longe . . . the temple.** Cf. Jer. 7.4.

87/2–3 **god . . . a nother.** Cf. CWM 6/1.60/9.

87/7 **Nether . . . there.** Cf. Matt. 24.23.

87/7–8 **in oure hertes . . . dwelleth.** Cf. 1 John 4.12–13.

87/10–11 **god . . . a nother.** Cf. CWM 6/1.61/15–16.

87/16 **miracles done in Egipte.** Aaron's rod, cf. Exod. 7.8–12; the ten plagues, cf. Exod. 7–12. **red se.** cf. Exod. 14.21–29.

87/16–17 **mount Sinay.** Cf. Exod. 24.16–17.

87/23–25 **Siloe . . . sight.** Tyndale remembers the blind man told to wash in the pool of Siloam, cf. John 9.7. More refers to the paralytic who sat by the pool of Bethesda, cf. John 5.2–9, CWM 6/1.60/30ff. O'Donnell has corrected the erroneous gloss of *1531* and *1573* from "Ioan 4" to "Ioan 5."

87/31 **lazarus.** Cf. John 11.1–44, CWM 6/1.61/18.

88/7–8 **god which is a spirite.** Cf. John 4.24.

88/22–23 **God . . . christ.** Cf. Luke 15.7, 10.

88/25–27 **vntyll . . . christ.** Eph. 4.13.

88/27–28 **misteries . . . christ.** Cf. Col. 2.2–3. *Answer* has "misteries and secretes"; NT has only "mistery" (Wallis 421/1; TNT 296A).

88/28–31 **that . . . begile vs.** Cf. Eph. 4.14. *Answer* has "sotiltie and wilinesse"; NT has only "wylyness" (Wallis 405/13; TNT 285A).

88/31–32 **So . . . images.** Cf. Gal. 3.2–3.

88/32–33 **is a spirite.** Cf. John 4.24.

88/33 **angeles of heuen.** Cf. Gal. 1.8.

89/1–2 **testament . . . sauyoure.** Cf. Heb. 10.29, 13.20.

89/7–8 **beleueth . . . beleue.** Cf. CWM 6/1.62/13–19.

89/8 **comen consent.** CWM 6/1.62/18. Cf. Gogan 96–107, 160–63, 211–13, 217, 298–302. (JW)

89/13 **Elias . . . Samary.** Cf. 1 Kings 18.22. Tyndale finds the opposition between Catholics and reformers foreshadowed in Israel's widespread consent to the prophets of Baal, against whom Elijah stood alone as prophet of the Lord. (JW)

89/15–17 **he proueth . . . done.** For *Dialogue* Bk. 1, Ch. 6 thru 18, cf. CWM 6/1.63/4–110/23. More relies on human prudence to recognize false miracles, e.g., by Humphrey Duke of Gloucester (CWM 6/1.86/18ff) and "the kynges moder," either Lady Margaret Beaufort for Henry VII or Elizabeth of York for Henry VIII (CWM 6/1.87/26ff).

89/21 **xvj.** Tyndale skips nine chapters on miracles, Bk. 1, Ch. 7– 15.

89/22 **mayde of Ipswich.** Cf. CWM 6/1.93/13–94/5. Supposedly, the Maid of Ipswich was possessed by the devil and the Maid of Kent (90/12n) was inspired by the Holy Spirit, but both experienced the same trances and disfigurements, proving the difficulty of distinguishing between true and false visionaries (*Obedience* T3v–T4). The authenticity of St. Peter's apparition at Westminster was also doubtful (*Obedience* T3v, PS 1.326n1; cf. *Richard III, CWM* 2.27/32–28/6 and n). (JB)

More's description of the twelve-year-old daughter of Sir Roger Wentworth contains symptoms of an epileptic seizure. Cf. R.E. Hemphill, "Historical Witchcraft and Psychiatric Illness in Western Europe," *Proceedings of the Royal Society of Medicine* 59 (1966) 891–902; rpt. in Articles on Witchcraft, Magic and Demonology 3, ed. Brian P. Levack, *Witch-Hunting in Early Modern Europe: General Studies* (New York: Garland, 1992) 314. Diarmaid MacCulloch considers the Maid of Ipswich "a classic case of child hysteria and manipulation," *Suffolk under the Tudors* (Oxford: Clarendon, 1986) 145. After a cure attributed to Our Lady of Ipswich, Anne Wentworth became a Franciscan nun in London until the closing of the monasteries.

89/23–24 **Moses . . . lorde.** Cf. Deut. 13.1–3.

89/25–26 **lienge . . . possyble.** Cf. Matt. 24.24, Mark 13.22.

90/9 **the testament . . . bloude.** Cf. Heb. 10.29, 13.20.

90/12 **maide of kent.** Prudently, More never mentions the Maid of Kent in *Dialogue* or *Confutation*. Here and in *Obedience* (T4), Tyndale refers to this politically dangerous case. After a cure in 1526 attributed to Mary, Elizabeth Barton became a Benedictine nun in Canterbury. Her pious visions turned political when she declared that Henry VIII would die seven months after he married Anne Boleyn. Fisher believed her revelations, but More counselled her not to meddle in public affairs. See Ep. 192, To Elizabeth Barton, Chelsea, Tuesday <1533?> (More, *Correspondence* 464–66). For his connection with Barton, Fisher was fined 300 pounds, one year's revenue from his diocese, but More's caution won him exemption from penalty. See Alan Neame, *The Holy Maid of Kent: The Life of Elizabeth Barton, 1506–1534* (London: Hodder and Stoughton, 1971). Barton was executed, together with five priests,

on 20 April 1534, the day that the guildsmen of London were
called upon to take the oath of succession. Cf. Richard Rex, "The
Execution of the Holy Maid of Kent," *Historical Research* 64 (1991)
216–20, esp. 219. Three days earlier, Fisher and More had gone to
the Tower because they refused to take the oath which implicitly
rejected papal authority.

In her trances, locutions and fasts the Maid of Kent showed some of
the characteristics of hysteria. Cf. Nicholas P. Sanos, "Witchcraft
in Histories of Psychiatry," *Psychological Bulletin* 85 (1978) 417–39;
rpt. in Articles on Witchcraft, Magic and Demonology 3.212. In
her defense, see Diane Watt, "Reconstructing the Word: the Political Prophecies of Elizabeth Barton (1506–1534)," *Renaissance
Quarterly* 50.1 (Spring 1997) 136–63.

91/7 **those possessed.** Cf. Matt. 17.14–18, Mark 9.17–29.

91/11–20 **the deuell . . . diseases.** Cf. CWM 8/1.245/27–29. For
examples of false miracles by witches, cf. 127/8; by Mohammed,
cf. 128/3–4n; by Roman Catholics, cf. 128/28. See also *Obedience*
P3v–Q3, "Of miracles and worsheppinge of sayntes."

91/16 **legend of S. Bartholomewe.** According to the *Golden Legend,*
when Bartholomew preached the gospel in India, he saw an idol
inhabited by a demon, who supposedly cured the sick. Bartholomew bound the demon, cured a young woman, and converted her father the king and his people to Christianity (GL 2.110–
12).

91/28 **ioyes of Orestes.** The Furies drove Orestes mad after he killed
his mother Clytemnesta for murdering his father Agamemnon; cf.
Euripides, *Orestes* (408 BC). Erasmus calls the conservative Catholic Edward Lee "raving mad, like Orestes in the play." From Ep.
1113, To Philippus Melanchthon, Louvain, [before 21 June 1520]
(Allen 4.287/12; CWE 7.313/11–12). More quotes Persius (*Satires*
3.118) on "mad Orestes": Ep. 15, To Martin Dorp, Bruges, 21 October <1515> (CWM 15.32/28); Ep. 86, To Germanus Brixius,
n.p., 1520 (CWM 3/2.604/24); *Responsio ad Lutherum,* 1523
(CWM 5/1.252/31).

92/6–7 **false . . . agayne.** Cf. CWM 6/1.104/18–24. For the Good
Samaritan, cf. Luke 10.35.

92/8–9 **allegories . . . can proue nothynge.** Cf. CWM 8/1.81/2–3.

It was a scholastic principle that allegorical interpretations of biblical passages had no probative value in theology (*Summa* I, Q. 1, Art. 10, Reply to Obj. 1). (JW)

In the *Enchiridion* (1503), Erasmus frequently allegorizes classical literature; e.g, he compares the creation of humans out of clay by Yahweh and Prometheus (Gen. 2.7; Plato, *Protagoras* 320D–322A): "if you read the poetic fable in an allegorical sense, it will be more profitable than the scriptural account if you do not penetrate the outer covering" (Holborn 70/29–30; CWE 66.68). In his Annotations on the NT, Erasmus repeatedly analyzes the literal meaning of the Greek; in the Paraphrases he draws pastoral applications from NT events for the individual reader. See Manfred Hoffmann, Part Three, "The Allegorical Nature of Scripture," *Rhetoric and Theology: The Hermeneutic of Erasmus* (U of Toronto P, 1994) 95–133.

Tyndale refers contemptuously to the practice of quoting "a fabell of Ovide," rather than the Scriptures to support a "poynte of fayth" (*Obedience* R5). In his preface to the Pentateuch (1530), Tyndale scoffs at the distrust of the literal meaning of Scripture shown by Erasmus but without naming him, "[S]ome which seme to them selves great clarkes saye: they wott not what moare profite is in many gestes of the scripture if they be read with out an allegorye, then in a tale of robenhode" (Mombert 11/7–10; TOT 8).

92/9–11 **Chryst . . . neyboure.** Cf. Luke 10.36–37.

92/22–23 **scribes . . . Moses sete.** Cf. Matt. 23.2, which More discusses at CWM 6/1.101/10–11, 104/25–33.

92/22–31 **scribes . . . tradycyons.** Cf. CWM 8/1.355/5–12, 356/7–9.

92/25–26 **bewarre . . . doctrine.** Matt. 16.6, 11; Mark 8.15, Luke 12.1.

92/26–28 **rebuked . . . them.** Cf. Matt. 12.1–8, Mark 2.23–28, Luke 6.1–5.

92/28–29 **what soeuer . . . rotes.** Cf. Matt. 15.13.

93/1–3 **Oure prelates . . . awne.** Cf. Luke 22.25–26.

93/3–5 **Peter . . . required.** Cf. Acts 15.10.

93/5–6 **paul . . . obedience.** Cf. 2 Cor. 11.4.

93/6–7 **galathyans . . . bondage.** Cf. Gal. 5.1.

93/8–9 **peter . . . superioures.** Cf. CWM 6/1.106/30–33.

93/9–10 **obey . . . swerde.** For temporal rulers, cf. Eph. 6.5–7, Tit. 2.9, Tit. 3.1, Heb. 13.17, 1 Pet. 2.13–14, 18.

93/11–12 **obey . . . awne.** For spiritual leaders, cf. 2 Pet. 2.1, Gal. 1.8.

93/14–19 **Of tradicions . . . vnite.** Erasmus had lamented that the life of Christians is burdened by "human constitutions" that impose ceremonial practices. Still, liturgical ceremonies, with due moderation, add proper solemnity to divine worship. Cf. *Ratio verae theologiae* (1518) in Holborn 238–39, 252.

Luther formulated his protest against obligatory ecclesiastical traditions in *Avoiding the Doctrines of Men,* a short tract of 1522 that also circulated in a 1525 Latin version. Luther stressed that two Pauline texts, 1 Tim. 4.1–4 and Col. 2.16–23, foresaw and condemned such attempts to ensnare Christian consciences regarding fasts and feasts (WA 10/2.72–92; LW 35.131–47). Here Christian freedom rests on ten biblical texts that undercut any ecclesiastical authority to lay down binding obligations. The observance of fasts and feasts is not evil in itself, but making them obligatory is, according to Luther, to add to God's commandments in contravention of Deut. 4.2 and to make God's good creatures defiling, against Matt. 15.11.

Johann Eck dedicated Ch. 13 of his *Enchiridion,* "On Human Constitutions" (Fraenkel 146–57; Battles 93–99), to demonstrating from other biblical texts that church authorities are empowered to enact laws concerning matters that are coherent with Scripture and that promote discipline and communal activity. Eck also took up eight texts cited by reformers and argued that each of them was wrongly used in the polemic against "traditions." In 1530 the same argument unfolded between Articles 15 and 26 of the Augsburg Confession (cf. *The Book of Concord* 36f and 63–70) and the corresponding articles of the imperial *Die Confutatio der Confessio Augustana* (112–15 and 176–85). The 1530 argument is treated in Wicks, "Abuses" 280–85 (Augsburg Confession) and 297–300 (*Confutatio*). For fasting, cf. nn on 67/22–23, 81/5, 81/6. (JW)

93/22–24 **For . . . trulye.** Cf. Matt. 5.17–19.

93/27 **ye be the salt of the erth.** Matt. 5.13. The rest of the verse is paraphrased below, "vnsauerye . . . vnderfote" (94/4–5). "The notion that this verse applies only to priests and bishops is probably taken from the *Glossa ordinaria* (PL 114.91)" (CWM 6/2.635).

94/6–7 **a man . . . liuinge.** Cf. CWM 6/1.109/26–28; CWM 8/ 1.396/10–11 and 8/3.1591.

94/7 **I haue proued it a lie in a nother place.** Against More, Tyndale asserts that true faith will bear fruit in good works, cf. *Mammon* B2, *Obedience* F3v.

94/7–9 **fayth . . . two.** Cf. 1 Cor. 13.8–13.

94/7–11 **fayth . . . worke.** Cf. CWM 8/2.780/20–21.

94/13–14 **prayinge . . . erre.** Cf. CWM 6/1.112/13–24.

94/16 **it is sinne to beleue to moch.** Cf. CWM 6/1.111/17–18.

94/19–20 **god . . . sake.** Cf. CWM 6/1.112/21–22.

94/22–23 **all . . . god.** Unlike Tyndale, More separates faith from hope (cf. CWM 8/1.54/28) and from charity (cf. CWM 8/1.54/33).

94/25–26 **promyses . . . Iesu.** For intercession to God by the Suffering Servant, cf. Isa. 53.12; by prophets, cf. Jer. 28.18; by the Holy Spirit, cf. Rom. 8.27; by the risen Christ, Rom. 8.34, Heb. 7.25.

94/27 **xxv.** Tyndale makes no comment here on five chapters of *Dialogue* Bk. 1, Ch. 20–24. In the section on "Whether the church can erre" (28/10–29/30), Tyndale answers in a general way the church's claim of inerrancy as set forth in Bk. 1, Ch. 18, 20–21, 24–26 (CWM 6/1.101–62 passim), cf. 32/10n. *Dialogue* Bk. 1, Ch. 22 upholds the value of the liberal arts, philosophy, and patristics as aids to the study of Scripture. For Tyndale's negative evaluation of Aristotle and Plato, cf. 10/20n; for his minimal use of Latin poets such as Terence and Virgil, cf. 75/15n; for his qualified approval of the Fathers, cf. Cyprian (46/27n), Jerome (46/26n), Augustine (46/26–27n), and Gregory (184/2n). *Dialogue* Bk. 1, Ch. 23 gives a positive role to reason in explaining Scripture. Tyndale holds that the will follows reason (34/8–9), but he emphasizes that carnal reason is blind; e.g., 40/17, 65/27–28, 66/12–13, 76/27 and esp. 140/29, "O how betleblinde is fleshlye reason!"

94/28 **how iugleth he.** Cf. CWM 8/1.311/11.

94/28–95/1 **al . . . written.** Cf. CWM 6/1.144/8–12 and John 21.25.

94/29 **not written.** In response to More's position "that many thynges haue bene taught by god without wrytynge" (CWM 6/1.137/27), *Answer* passes over More's account of the Holy Spirit's inscription of the faith upon believing hearts (e.g. CWM 6/1.143/4–144/7) to concentrate instead on More's argument that Christ's apostles gave oral instructions on some essential doctrines that were not set down in the NT (CWM 6/1.144/8–146/13, 147/31–148/32).

Yves Congar treats the background of More's position in medieval theology in *Traditions and Tradition* (London: Burns & Oates, 1966) 87–101, citing William of Occam's influential classification of the different types of "Catholic truths" on p. 95. Occam's scheme recurred in numerous late medieval works, such as John Brevicoxa's treatise (c1375), where we read, "The second category consists of those [truths of faith] which have come down to us from the Apostles by a handing down of revelation or by writings of the faithful but which are not found in Scripture nor are deducible from it." From *A Treatise on Faith, the Church, the Roman Pontiff, and the General Council,* in Oberman, *Forerunners* 72. Wyclif and Hus mounted a protest against this view, while asserting, in effect if not in exact terms, the complete sufficiency of Scripture for faith. Their 15c opponents, like the English Carmelite Thomas Netter of Walden, made "unwritten traditions" fundamental to their theological accounts of beliefs about the saints and the origins of the sacraments that lack a NT institution-narrative. Henry VIII's *Assertio* appealed to divinely grounded unwritten traditions of faith as vehicles of transmission of the church's faith regarding certain sacraments, cf. 99/16–18n. Tyndale has already affirmed the sufficiency of Scripture at 24/17–28/9 and will re-state it at 98/5–19 and 99/7–15. (JW)

95/2–3 **Ihon ... faith.** Cf. CWM 8/1.311/11–12, repeated at 311/38–39.

95/4–5 **perpetuall ... faith.** Cf. CWM 6/1.150/1–151/23, CWM 8/1.287/5–15 and CWM 8/1.406/3–5. The perpetual virginity of Mary was defined by Constantinople II (AD 553), the fifth ecumenical council, as a corollary to the definition of two natures in Christ (DS 214; 2NPNF 14.312); cf. also 31/14, 166/20nn. It was restated by a synod at the Lateran (AD 649), called by Martin I (pope, 649–53) (DS 256). While they accept this belief, Luther and Tyndale do not consider it an essential article of faith. For Luther, cf. *Vom Schem Hamphoras,* 1543 (WA 53.640; not in LW). More argues that, following their principle of *sola scriptura,* the reformers ought to reject whatever is not stated explicitly in the Bible, cf. CWM 8/2.809/1–4. (JW)

95/8–9 **many . . . antichriste.** Cf. CWM 6/1.146/14–15. In 95/S1 *1531*'s "Pope" becomes *1573*'s "Antichrist is knowen." Below, Tyndale will set forth, on the basis of NT passages, his case for identifying the papacy as the foretold Antichrist, cf. 100/6n and 145/8–27. (JW)

95/12 **Paules tradicions.** Cf. CWM 6/1.148/3–6. In 2 Thess. 2.15 More finds two distinct sources of revelation, oral tradition and scripture: *siue per sermonem siue per epistolam nostram.* Tyndale affirms that Paul preached the same doctrine, whether in oral or written form (*Obedience* H7). See Ch. 11, "Holy Writ and Holy Church," in Oberman, *Harvest* 361–422.

95/13–14 **I haue . . . preached.** Cf. CWM 8/1.324/20–21.

95/13 **I haue answered rochester in the obedience.** John Fisher (1469–1535) was Bishop of Rochester and Chancellor of Cambridge University from 1504 until his death. In *Obedience* (E8v, G8v, H4v, H5v, H6, H7–I2v, V7r–v), Tyndale attacks the sermon preached at the burning of Lutheran books on 12 May 1521 (Fisher 311–48). For Fisher's exegesis of Gal. 5.6 in this sermon, cf. 196/25n. Tyndale does not mention the sermon preached at the abjuration of Robert Barnes on 11 February 1526 (Fisher 429–76). Fisher was considered the best preacher of his generation in England. Cf. Marc'hadour, "Fisher and More: a note," in Bradshaw and Duffy 103. For his life and works, see the entry by O'-Donnell in *Tudor England.*

95/15–19 **And when . . . Masse.** Cf. CWM 6/1.148/8–11; quoted exactly by CWM 8/1.315/29–33.

95/19 **christes soper.** Cf. 1 Cor. 11.20. Tyndale debates the more appropriate name of the Eucharistic celebration here and at 179/1–2n. For Tyndale's rejection of the Mass as a sacrifice, cf. 150/9n, 178/11n. For his rejection of transubstantiation, cf. 164/10n, 180/27–30n; of consubstantiation, cf. 179/12n.

95/20–21 **A greate . . . do it.** CWM 8/1.317/10–11.

95/22 **water . . . wine.** Cf. CWM 6/1.148/19–28.

95/22–32 **A greate . . . haue.** Cf. CWM 8/1.318/11–20.

95/28–29 **For . . . 1 corin. xiiij.** Cf. 1 Cor. 14.2–3, CWM 8/1.161/29–30.

95/30–31 **sheperdes . . . shere.** Cf. Ezek. 34.2–3.

96/1–2 **Iames . . . workes.** Cf. Jas. 2.24 and CWM 6/1.149/7.

96/2 **Mammon.** Tyndale assumed public responsibility for his writings when he put his name at the head of the preface of *Mammon* (May 1528). He refers to *Mammon* in *Obedience* (I2v, Q3v), the afterword to Genesis (TOT 82) and *Answer* (here and 201/29–30). For Tyndale's gradual acknowledgment of authorship, see O'Donnell, "Editing the Independent Works of William Tyndale," in *Editing Texts From the Age of Erasmus* (U of Toronto P, 1996) 49–70.

96/4–12 **And as for . . . with out it.** Cf. CWM 6/1.149/21–28; quoted exactly by CWM 8/1.321/6–14. In the OT the Sabbath is characterized by abstention from work (Exod. 20.8), a festive spirit (Isa. 58.13), and religious instruction (Lev. 23.3). The early church moved the Sabbath from Saturday to Sunday to commemorate Christ's Resurrection. Tyndale's freedom regarding which day to observe the Sabbath is based on Col. 2.16, Rom. 14.5 (NCE 12.778–82; OER 3.459–60). Between 1527 and c1540, Anabaptists in Silesia and Moravia celebrated the Lord's Day on Saturday. This development prompted Luther to write *Against the Sabbatarians* in 1538 (WA 50.312–37; LW 47.65–98).

96/6 **holy daye.** *1531*'s "dage" could be a mispelling by the Flemish compositor.

96/13–14 **by . . . christen.** For baptism by women, cf. CWM 6/1.149/28–30, 8/1.307/31–32.

96/18–19 **likelyhode . . . now.** Cf. CWM 6/1.151/32–35.

96/22 **iustifienge of faith . . . Paule and Ihon.** Cf. Rom. 3.28 and 1 John 5.4. For other references to Rom. 3.28, cf. nn to 170/15–16, 173/25–26, 197/6–7, 197/18, 201/30, 202/21, 206/21–22. In Luther's practice, the key to all the biblical books is to grasp Christ's utterly gratuitous work and gift of salvation as this is formulated in texts like Rom. 1.16–17, 3.21–26, 5.6–11, or John 1.14–17, 3.16–17. Statements and illustrations of this conviction are found in Luther's *Brief Instruction on What to Look for and Expect in the Gospels,* 1521 (WA 10/1/1.8–18; LW 35.117–24) and his

1522 Preface to the NT, cf. 148/22n. The principle of justification by faith is central to *Mammon, Obedience,* and Tyndale's testimony at his trial. (JW)

96/25 **the scripture wolde be easye.** Cf. CWM 8/1.337/15. For another assertion that a proper explanation of Baptism would make Scripture clear to the believer, cf. *1 John* A5v. To claim that Scripture is easily understood if one only grasps the central truth of its message is to voice a fundamental Reformation conviction. In Luther's concise phrasing, Scripture should be *sui ipsius interpres,* in *Assertio omnium articulorum,* 1520 (WA 7.97/23; not in LW). (JW)

97/1–2 **neuer . . . faith.** Cf. CWM 6/1.152/33–35.

97/3 **christ . . . scripture.** Cf. John 5.39.

97/4–5 **Paules . . . no.** Cf. Acts 17.11.

97/9 **xxvij.** Tyndale makes no comment here on *Dialogue* Bk. 1, Ch. 26, with its message, "In all doubtes beleue the church" (CWM 6/1.162/2–3 Gloss). In the Foundational Essay, however, he deals with this topic under "Another Argument against the Pope" (43/21–50/15), cf. 44/9–10, 47/31–32nn.

97/10–12 **Paul . . . a nother.** Cf. CWM 6/1.163/34–164/3 citing 1 Cor. 1.10.

97/17 **power of the resurreccion of christ.** Cf. Phil. 3.10. Tyndale's NT has "the vertue of his resurreccion" (Wallis 414/22; TNT 291C); KJV has "power."

97/26 **generall counsell.** Louis XII of France (king, 1498–1515) and Maximilian I (emperor, 1493–1519) convened the Council of Pisa (1511–12), attended mostly by French prelates. Julius II (pope, 1503–13) condemned this potentially schismatic council and convoked his own, Lateran V (1512–17). Dominated by Julius, the first five sessions repudiated conciliarism, the theory that a council is superior to the pope. The later sessions under Leo X (pope, 1513–21) approved minor reforms of canon law, the Curia, the episcopacy and the religious orders. Historians note that this ineffectual council ended in March 1517, seven months before Luther circulated his 95 Theses (NCE 8.409; OER 2.397–99). Cf. Richard Marius, *Martin Luther: The Christian between God and Death,* Belknap (Cambridge: Harvard UP, 1999) 137–39. For Luther's appeal to a general council, cf. 186/10n.

98/5–10 **Now . . . endure.** Cf. CWM 8/1.336/27–32, 339/4–8.

98/5 **last and euerlastinge testament.** Cf. Heb. 8.6, 13.20.

98/9–10 **all . . . scripture.** Cf. John 20.31.

98/10–13 **By . . . mencion.** CWM 8/1.340/28–30.

98/13–14 **And by . . . false.** Cf. CWM 8/1.342/5–6.

98/14–19 **And by . . . scripture.** Cf. CWM 8/1.343/8–12.

98/16–17 **they haue . . . heare them.** Cf. Luke 16.29.

98/20–24 **And when . . . made.** Cf. CWM 8/1.345/9–13.

98/20 **he that heareth you heareth me.** Cf. Luke 10.16.

98/20–21 **he that . . . hethen.** Cf. CWM 6/1.165/2–4. **if . . . he-then.** Cf. Matt. 18.17.

98/23 **figure.** More describes his syllogism as arranged in the first figure, the third mode (CWM 8/1.346/19–20, 8/3.1578–80n).

98/24–28 **Christes disciples . . . miracles.** Cf. CWM 8/1.346/27–31.

98/30–99/1 **In . . . writer.** Cf. CWM 8/1.331/36–38.

98/30–31 **christ . . . teach.** Cf. CWM 6/1.178/23–29. **holy gost . . . teach.** Cf. John 14.26.

99/1–4 **I . . . write.** CWM 8/1.333/17–19.

99/3 **goo and teach all nacions.** Among More's brethren who cited Matt. 28.19, and underscored that Jesus did not mandate writing, was Johann Eck in his *Enchiridion,* Ch. 1, "On the Church and Her Authority" (Fraenkel 26; Battles 12). (JW)

99/4–15 **I answere . . . the soule.** Cf. CWM 8/1.334/2–13. Where More appeals to teaching by means other than writing, both by the Holy Spirit and by the apostles, Tyndale responds that the more fundamental commandment of love prompted the apostles to leave a clear and definite expression of the faith that would stand against heresies unto the end of time. (JW)

99/10–11 **these . . . life.** Cf. John 20.31.

99/11–12 **these . . . deceaue you.** Cf. 1 John 2.26.

99/12–13 **Paul and Peter . . . places.** Cf. 1 Cor. 4.14, 2 Pet. 3.1.

99/16–18 **kinges . . . not erre.** Cf. CWM 6/1.183/31–184/19. Henry VIII's *Assertio septem sacramentorum* (1521) met Luther's claims that the sacrament of Holy Orders is not found in Scripture by constructing an argument for God's teaching the church not only by Scripture but also by apostolic oral traditions. The starting point was Luther's own statement that the church is endowed with the power rightly to discern God's word from human words, as in its delimitation of the biblical canon, *Babylonian Captivity,* 1520 (WA 6.561; LW 36.107). If this be the case, the royal *Assertio* argues, then the church must also be able to discern the "divine sense" of Scripture from human glosses and comments; otherwise having the Scriptures would not suffice for the transmission of true teaching. Then Henry goes a step further by claiming that the same reason, the avoidance of error, grounds a power by which the church discerns God's teachings *et in his quae non scribuntur* ("also in these things that are not written"). This third point is especially relevant regarding the sacraments, so that the church would not err by placing its trust in spurious signs that do not mediate God's grace (*Assertio,* CC 43.208–9).

The king's book against Luther has long been considered to be the work of royal theological advisors, but the identity of those who shaped the arguments has eluded scholars. David Daniell (252) acknowledges that "Thomas More himself claimed only a minor role" in Henry VIII's book. Yet Daniell finds in the *Assertio* the bitter attack on Luther's character and the cautious approach to papal primacy found in More's known writings. At his trial More stated that he was "only a sorter out and placer of the principall maters therin contayned" (Roper 67/18–19), a claim that would have been foolish if at odds with Henry's own recollections, cf. Alistair Fox, *Thomas More: History and Providence* (New Haven: Yale UP, 1983) 128.

In his critical edition, Pierre Fraenkel sees More contributing only minimally to the content of the *Assertio,* less than John Longland, Bishop of Lincoln, and Edward Lee, later Wolsey's successor as Archbishop of York (1531–44). Fraenkel also holds that John Fisher's role was greater than is ordinarily thought (*Assertio,* CC 43.20–21). But Henry's three-step argument for ecclesial inerrancy in discerning non-written traditions, as related above, has no echo in the "ten truths" of Fisher's criteria of doctrinal validity, as set forth in the *Prooemium* of his 1523 *Assertionis Lutherianae confutatio,* now in Fisher's *Opera omnia* (Würzburg: Fleischmann, 1597) 277–96. (JW)

99/20 **his grace.** Henry VIII's *Assertio* was placed first in Fisher's *Opera omnia* (6–79), followed by a treatise that Fisher certainly wrote, *Assertionum defensio* (81–100, misnumbered 110). Thanks to Nelson H. Minnich for these references from the reprint (Farnborough, Hants.: Gregg, 1967). There is an English translation, not easily accessible: *Assertion of the Seven Sacraments,* ed. Louis O'Donovan, tr. anon. (New York: Benziger, 1908).

Tyndale discussed the traditional seven sacraments in *Obedience* (M1–P3v). Elsewhere (in *Prelates* C3r–v, K4v and *Obedience* E6v) Tyndale writes scornfully of opposing the authority of the king's book to the authority of Scripture. He also mocks the title "Defender of the Faith," which Leo X gave Henry VIII in 1521 as a reward for writing the *Assertio.*

Tyndale reviews the major events of the reign of Henry VIII (king, 1509–47) from his accession to the dismissal of Wolsey in 1529 (*Prelates* G4–K4v). These include the shifts of alliance among England, France, and the Empire, the marriage in 1514 of Henry's sister Mary to Louis XII of France. For further references to Henry VIII's military and diplomatic moves against France, cf. *Prelates* F8v; *Obedience* V2v, V4v. Unlike the other English reformers, Tyndale upheld the validity of Henry's marriage to Catherine of Aragon (1485–1536) (*Prelates* H4v–K1v). His defense was omitted from the 1548 and 1549 editions of *Prelates,* as well as from the 1573 *Whole Works,* but was restored in the 1831 edition by Thomas Russell and the 1849 edition by Henry Walter (PS 2.319–34).

99/23–25 **whatsoeuer . . . liuinge.** Cf. CWM 6/1.185/1–3. More does not limit the church to "the pope and his brode" (99/23), but includes the Fathers (e.g., CWM 6/1.38/22), general councils (CWM 6/1.62/24, 125/12), and "the hole congregacyon of crysten people" (CWM 6/1.107/23). In *Dialogue* More does not deny the witness power of miracles, which he examines in Bk. 1, Ch. 4–17. In Bk. 2, Ch. 11, More discusses various saints honored for their martyrdom or good works; he also acknowledges the existence of superstitious devotions to the saints.

99/27 **though one pope condemne a nother.** Tyndale refers to Honorius I (pope, 625–38), whose utterances about Christ's having a single will and operation were condemned by his successors and then by the sixth ecumenical council Constantinople III in 680–81. The last judgment, by Leo II (pope, elected 681, reigned 682–83), mentions Honorius by name (DS 510–22, 544, 556, 566; 2NPNF 14.351). See Georg Schwaiger, "Honorius I," TRE 15.566–68. (JW)

99/30–32 **layde . . . polaxes.** Cf. Matt. 27.60, 66, Mark 15.46, Luke 23.53, John 19.40.

100/6 **antichriste.** This section on the recognizable signs of Antichrist expounds four NT texts foretelling the rise of a vicious and powerful opponent of Christ and his elect. The term "Antichrist" occurs in 1 John 2.18, 2.22, 4.7, and 2 John 7. But Tyndale's proofs that the papacy is the foreseen antagonist use other passages with different vocabularies. They are 2 Pet. 2.1–3 (100/ 15–19), Matt. 24.24 (101/9–12), 2 Thess. 2.9–11 (102/1–6), and, climactically, 2 Tim. 3.1–9 (102/29–104/29).

During the first millennium, unformulated opinions about the Antichrist were held by various Christian thinkers. These beliefs then came together in a widely accepted scenario about the role of the great persecutor to appear shortly before the end of the world. Amid papal-imperial struggles from Gregory VII (pope, 1073–85) to the Concordat of Worms (1122), the term "Antichrist" was first used as a polemical epithet hurled against an opponent now living in this world. The radical Franciscans of the early 14c branded John XXII (pope, 1316–34) "Antichrist" for his rejection of the spiritual church. The background of this theme is treated, with abundant bibliography, in the multi-authored entry "Antichrist," TRE 3.20–50. See Bernard McGinn, *Antichrist, Two Thousand Years of Human Fascination with Evil* (San Francisco: Harper, 1994).

Wyclif's late writings list numerous signs that the papal, hierarchical church is Antichrist, now in conflict with Christ and the predestined elect. Cf. *De postestate papae,* ed. Johann Loserth (London: Wyclif Society, 1907) 118–26, 148–50, 185–90, and 322–30. The Lollards transmitted this fragment of Wyclif's polemic: the pope is Antichrist (Hudson 122/7, 126/159, 126/164, and 126/172); prelates will be damned (Hudson 122/13, 125/128). Tyndale is in all likelihood an eventual recipient of and further spokesman for this conviction. Responding to *Exsurge Domine,* Leo X's bull of censure, Luther first targeted the papal Antichrist in two works of late 1520: *Adversus execrabilem Antichristi bullam* (WA 6.597–612; not in LW) and *Wider die Bulle des Endchrists* (WA 6.614–29; not in LW). Luther restated this theme in his pamphlet following the burning of *Exsurge* in Wittenberg on 10 December 1520 (WA 7.176–80; LW 31.392–94). Tyndale almost certainly knew Luther's expanded case for the pope as Antichrist, given in an exposition of Dan. 8.23–25, published in 1521 in the *Responsio* to an attack by the Dominican Ambrosius Catharinus (WA 7.705–78; not in LW), interpreting Daniel on 722–77. But this exegetical treatment starts with a prologue expounding 2 Pet. 2.1–3 (ibid., WA 7.725–28; not in LW), upon which Tyndale draws below. In 1524 this work came out in German under the title *Offenbarung des Endchrists aus dem propheten Daniel,* which John Frith translated as . . . *The reuelation of Antichrist* (Antwerp, 1529) STC 11394, and which was banned in 1530. Cf. TRP 1, no. 129, p. 194.

Luther argues that the pope is the *rex potens faciebus* of Dan. 8.23 because of the massive edifice of external forms (*facies*), such as rank, riches, garb, buildings, rites, and allied institutions, which in the papal church overlay God's fundamental ordinances. Then Luther expounds how the papacy is *intelligens propositionum* (Dan. 8.23) through the plethora of enactments and doctrines (*propositiones*) raised by popes to greater binding power than God's word itself. On Luther's Antichrist argument, see John M. Headley, *Luther's View of Church History* (New Haven: Yale UP, 1963); Scott H. Hendrix, *Luther and the Papacy: Stages in a Reformation Conflict* (Philadelphia: Fortress, 1981); Konrad Hammann, *Ecclesia spiritualis: Luthers Kirchenverständnis in den Kontroversen mit Augustin von Alveld und Ambrosius Catharinus* (Göttingen: Vandenhoeck & Ruprecht, 1989) 162–219 (text), 294–314 (notes), on Luther's interpretation of Dan. 8 in 1521.

Tyndale's first independent work, *Mammon,* is partly a translation of Luther's sermon for the Ninth Sunday after Trinity, 1522 (WA 10/2.283–92; not in LW). In the preface (A3v–A4v), the English reformer asserts that Antichrist is a stealthy spiritual force present throughout history, which has emerged in the pope and his prelates and which is now raging because those versed in Scripture have begun to unmask him. Tyndale developed the Antichrist motif in an extended passage of *Obedience* (I8v–L8v), less in order to prove its realization in the papacy than to unmask the practices of pope and prelates as fulfilling what Jesus had foretold about Antichrist's ways in Matt. 24.24 and Mark 13.6. Special emphasis fell on their craft against kings and their laws (K3), leading to Tyndale's outcry for monarchs to arraign prelates, judge them by Scripture, and regain their rightful authority (K6–L8v). Other references show Antichrist opposing key Reformation doctrines by giving false interpretations of Scripture (B6) and teaching that good deeds earn God's love (Q3r–v). Both *Obedience* (I8v–L8v) and *Answer* (100/6–109/5) devote a whole section to Antichrist. Other references in *Answer* assert that Antichrist has already appeared (95/9–11) in the person of the pope (144/14–145/9, 175/5–9); the imposition of clerical celibacy is one of his works (162/26–33). In *1 John* (D7r–v, D8v), Tyndale recognizes the presence of Antichrist in the apostolic era and in the Docetist heresy (F3), which denies the true humanity of Jesus. (JW)

100/15–19 **there . . . ouer you.** 2 Pet. 2.1–3. Tyndale's Prologue to 2 Peter concludes with a brief outline of the epistle taken from Luther's 1530 revised preface. The whole second chapter is accordingly Peter's prophetic description of conditions in the era of papal rule and the dominance of human, not godly, doctrine (WA/DB 7.315; not in LW). (JW)

100/20–21 **law . . . law.** Rom. 3.19.

100/22–24 **Now . . . Christe.** Tyndale follows Luther's *proemium* to his exegesis of Dan. 8.23–25 in the *Responsio* to Ambrosius Catharinus, 1521 (WA 7.726f; not in LW), where the "sectes" are identified as the religious orders, each of which has a different garb and a rule prescribing certain works as a way to salvation. For the clothing of the various orders, cf. 11/20n. (JW)

100/26 **they . . . trueth.** Cf. 2 Pet. 2.2.

101/1 **pena culpa.** This Latin term meaning absolution "from punishment and guilt" was coined by Peter Lombard and adopted by Aquinas (*Summa* I, Q. 48, Art. 5). God discharges the guilt in view of the penitent's contrition and faith; the priest remits the punishment of eternal damnation upon the penitent's confession and satisfaction. Tyndale asserts that Christ's satisfaction for sin cancels out these legalistic measures. Cf. 154/24, 205/4; *Obedience* N7, V8; *1 John* A2v, A3v, B6. (JW)

101/9–12 **their shal . . . true waye.** Matt. 24.24, which is also paraphrased in 101/15–17. Matt. 24.24 is cited by a Lollard text against the papacy, cf. Hudson 126/150–53. Luther cited or referred to Matt. 24.24 four times in his treatment of Dan. 8, taking the Gospel text as prophetic of the papacy and helpful in elucidating Dan. 8.25, *Et prosperatur dolus in manu eius.* This is the papal deception (*dolus*) by which otherwise good Christians, like Bernard, Dominic, Francis and Bonaventure, were deceived into acknowledging papal supremacy, cf. *Responsio* to Ambrosius Catharinus, 1521 (WA 7.744; not in LW). But Tyndale's interpretation develops instead an aspect of the condition of the remnant of tempted and persecuted elect persons who rely only on canonical Scripture. (JW)

101/12 **false annoynted.** Cf. 2 Cor. 11.13.

101/13–14 **they shal come in his name.** Cf. Matt. 7.22, Mark 13.6, Luke 21.8.

101/17–18 **the electe . . . called.** Cf. Matt. 20.16, 22.14.

101/26–27 **Christ . . . faith.** Cf. Mark 10.30, John 16.33.

101/27–29 **And the stories . . . ensamples.** Cf. 1 Cor. 10.11.

101/29 **miracles.** Irenaeus of Lyons (c130–200) describes miracles performed by post-apostolic Christians in *Against Heresies* 2.32.4 (PG 7.828–30; ANF 1.409). For miracles after the discovery of Stephen's relics in 415, cf. 83/12–13n.

102/1–6 **Antichristes . . . lies.** 2 Thess. 2.9–11. *Answer* has "conceyued" (102/4), while NT has "receaved" (Wallis 436/17; TNT 306C). *Answer* has "stronge delusion or gyle" (102/5); NT has only "stronge delusion" (Wallis 436/18; TNT 306C).

The Lollard text critical of the papacy cites part of 2 Thess. 2.9–11, cf. Hudson 126/156–59. Although the term "Antichrist" does not occur in these verses, Luther's 1522 preface to the epistle says that Ch. 2 shows that the Antichrist will establish himself in Rome, a point included in Tyndale's prologue to the epistle (WA/DB 7.251; not in LW). Luther cited 2 Thess. 2.9–11 five times in his 1521 treatment of Daniel's prophecy, but he did not emphasize, as

Tyndale does, its foretelling of papal wiles, obduracy, and persecution of critics. (JW)

102/13–14 **miracles . . . prophetes.** Cf. Matt. 7.22.

102/24–28 **they haue . . . quench it.** In Tyndale's prophetic view of salvation history, prosecution for alleged heresy is recurrently the fate of those who, like Wyclif and Hus, admonish the higher clergy on the basis of God's word. Cf. 128/27, 171/13–20, 214/30–215/8. (JW)

102/29–103/2 **in the later dayes . . . therof.** 2 Tim. 3.1–4. Tyndale follows Luther in finding here a prophetic account already fulfilled by the depravity of "oure spiritualtie" (103/12). Luther's 1522 preface to 2 Timothy, freely translated in Tyndale's NT, summarized Ch. 3 and 4 of the epistle as an announcement of the dangers of the end-time, in which outward splendor will cloak the corruptions of the higher clergy (WA/DB 7.273; LW 35.389). However, Tyndale's itemized account of the specific vices and practices is his own work. (JW)

103/7–9 **of this sorte . . . trueth.** 2 Tim. 3.6–7.

103/18–19 **paynt a blocke & call it Iob.** A popular cult of Saint Job flourished in late medieval Europe, with Job serving as patron and helper of syphilitics. Cf. Lawrence L. Bessermann, *The Legend of Job in the Middle Ages* (Cambridge: Harvard UP, 1979) 2, 64, 131. (JW)

103/26–28 **And as for . . . wayte.** Cf. Mark 7.10–13.

104/2–3 **causes venged.** An example of vindictive conquest by the higher clergy was the series of campaigns mounted by northwest German bishops, led by Archbishop Gerhard II of Bremen, against the recalcitrant peasants of the lower Weser in 1232–34. Gregory IX (pope, 1227–41) issued a crusade-bull in support. Cf. Konrad Algermissen, "Stedinger," LThK 9.1027–28. Other examples of use of the crusade for political causes are given by Hans Wolter in Jedin and Dolan 4.284f. (JW)

104/5 **trucebreakynge.** During the summit meeting at the Field of the Cloth of Gold, Wolsey celebrated Solemn High Mass for Henry VIII and Francis I (king, 1515–47) on Saturday, 23 June 1520. The kings did not receive the Eucharist, but both kissed the pax (LP 3/1, no. 870). In spite of this pledge of peace, England de-

clared war against France on 29 May 1522 (LP 3/2, no. 2292).
English troops then undertook a campaign of burnings in northern France in September 1522 (LP 3/2, no. 2530). For the pax, cf.
70/29n.

104/5–9 **whether . . . founders.** Dispensations (cf. 154/4n) also
served to remove legal impediments to the rise of ecclesiastics
from lower-paying dioceses, offices, and benefices to more lucra-
tive ones. One could be dispensed from the prohibition against
holding a plurality of beneficed positions, and dispensations from
higher authorities could allow the diversion of bequests to ends
other than those stipulated by the original donors, cf. 51/14–15n.
(JW)

104/20 **the sorserers of Egipte resisted Moses.** Cf. Exod. 7.11–12,
22.

104/22–23 **men . . . faith.** Cf. 2 Tim. 3.8. Their names are not given
in Exodus, but according to Paul they were called Jannes and Jam-
bres.

104/27–29 **cast . . . false werkes.** Cf. 2 Tim. 3.9.

104/31–32 **holy gost . . . trueth.** Cf. John 16.13.

105/4 **fleshly seed of Abraham.** Cf. Rom. 4.1. **spirituall.** Cf. Gal.
3.7.

105/5 **Ismaell . . . Isaac.** Cf. Gen. 21.9–13.

105/6–7 **greate multitude . . . chosen.** Cf. Matt. 22.14.

105/10 **antichrist.** Cf. 1 John 2.22 and 100/6n.

105/21–22 **faith comune as well to the deuels.** Cf. Jas. 2.19.

105/33 **Saduces.** From Zadoc ("righteous"), high priest in the time
of Solomon, cf. 1 Kings 1.39, or from *Tzaddikim* ("righteous
men"). They denied the resurrection of the dead, the existence of
angels and spirits, and the obligation of the unwritten law allegedly handed down from Moses.

106/1 **phareses / that is / seperated.** From *perushim* ("those who
are separated") or *perishut* ("those who sanctify"). They were distinguished by their strict observance of the traditional and written
law and by their claims to superior sanctity. For "Sadducees" and
"Pharisees," cf. *Illustrated Dictionary and Concordance of the Bible*,
gen. ed. Geoffrey Wigoder (New York: Macmillan, 1986).

106/4–7 **so that . . . duties.** Cf. Mark 7.10–13.

106/8–9 **Calil . . . haueparte of.** The Hebrew word *Calil* refers particularly to a "whole burnt offering." Cf. Deut. 33.10, Ps. 51.19, Mark 12.33.

106/16–18 **zele . . . phareses.** Cf. Matt. 23.13–33, Luke 11.42–44.

106/19–107/23 **But . . . dreade.** The role ascribed to the law sharply distinguishes Tyndale's account of justification from that of Luther, for whom saving faith is exclusively focused on God's redemptive mercy in Christ toward those whom the law has prepared by convicting them of sin. In justification, for Luther, God relates to a believer who has been carried beyond the demands of the law. (JW)

106/21–22 **litle Paul.** Cf. Erasmus' annotation on Rom. 1.1, *PAVLVS*.), 1516 NT, *Paulus autem Graecis sonat quietum, . . . Romanis pusillum sonat* (Reeve 2.334). "'Paul' means 'calm' among the Greeks, . . . 'very small' among the Romans."

106/23 **lord . . . doo.** Acts 9.6, 22.10.

106/24–25 **what . . . doo.** Acts 2.37.

106/31 **testament of Christes bloud.** Cf. Heb. 13.20.

107/2–14 **litle flocke . . . bloude.** This is a passage of lyrical beauty, such as is seldom met in controversial writing of the period. On the same topic, cf. 201/13–28. (JW)

107/5 **christ . . . christes.** Cf. 1 Cor. 3.23.

107/6 **and all . . . christe.** Cf. Matt. 25.40.

107/15–23 **And he . . . dreade.** Compare Luther's account of the believer's willing service of others without thought of recompense: "to serve, help, and deal with the neighbor as he sees that God through Christ has dealt with him and still deals with him," *Freedom of a Christian*, 1520 (WA 7.35/25–27; LW 31.366). (JW)

107/18–19 **And of that . . . frely.** Cf. Matt. 10.8.

107/24–109/3 **When . . . agenst you.** The account of the inner-ecclesial dualism ends with the two parties in dialogue. Carnal multitude interrogates and indicts (107/28–30, 108/5–8, 108/17–27), while Little Flock defends itself doctrinally (107/30–108/5, 108/8–17). Carnal multitude then turns to warn the king of the subversion likely to follow from Little Flock's obstinacy against traditions and ecclesial sacraments (108/29–109/3). (JW)

107/24 **greate . . . chosen.** Cf. Matt. 22.14.

108/1 **Fire / salt / water / bred / oyle.** Little Flock opposes the multitude's claim that objects have spiritual potency by appealing to the sole saving power of Christ's blood laid hold of by faith in his word. The beliefs of the multitude rest on the church's myriad prayers of blessing over objects, which are studied panoramically in A. Franz, *Die kirchlichen Benediktionen im Mittlealter,* 2 vol. (Freiburg: Herder, 1909). (JW)

108/3 **god . . . therwith.** Cf. John 4.24.

108/8 **blessynges . . . nacions.** Cf. Gen. 18.18, Gal. 3.16.

110/3–7 **In . . . agre.** Cf. *Dialogue* where in Bk. 2, Ch. 1 (CWM 6/1.187/19–29), the Messenger recapitulates the arguments of Bk. 1, Ch. 28, on the teaching authority of the church, a section on which Tyndale did not comment, cf. 97/9n.

110/9–10 **we . . . bloude.** Cf. Rom. 5.9.

110/14–15 **thou . . . miste.** Cf. John 3.20. Tyndale makes a pun on "misticall sens" of Scripture and "miste." For a pun on "Mystical Body of Christ," cf. 114/13n.

110/16 **required . . . scripture.** Cf. John 5.39 and Acts 17.11.

110/19–21 **we . . . pope.** Cf. CWM 6/1.192/20–23. Tyndale here makes no comment on the theme of *Dialogue* Bk. 2, Ch. 2, the departure of the reformers from the Church of Rome. He discusses this topic in the Foundational Essay (40/5–9) and again under Bk. 2, Ch. 5 (114/6–8).

110/26 **how beestly he imageneth of God.** More holds that some of the reprobate can be found inside the visible church and that some of the elect can be found outside it, "and bothe the one and the other without reason or good cause why" (CWM 6/1.197/33–34). Perhaps for this statement, Tyndale thinks that *Dialogue* Bk. 2, Ch. 3–4 presents God as a monster (cf. 110/29). Later, Tyndale claims that the doctrine of purgatory makes God into a tyrant for punishing a soul already forgiven (143/30–144/3). *Dialogue* claims (6/1.403/1) that Lutheran teaching on predestination casts God as a tyrant (187/21–22n). For God as an unapproachable monarch, cf. 119/6–7n and 120/12.

110/27–28 **naturall man . . . spirite of God.** Cf. 1 Cor. 2.14.

111/1–3 **if . . . venged.** Because Tyndale believes that salvation depends on absolute trust in Christ's merits, he excuses the temporary "frailte" (111/1) of the elect. Because More believes in the cooperation of divine grace and human action, he emphasizes "malycyous wyll" in sinners, cf. CWM 6/1.197/30.

111/4 **yer . . . Christ.** Cf. Eph. 1.4.

111/5 **He . . . enimies.** Cf. Rom. 5.8.

111/12–13 **flesh . . . not.** Cf. Rom. 7.19.

111/20–22 **when . . . better.** Cf. Acts 9.1–18, Gal. 1.13–16.

111/24 **serue hys brethern.** Cf. Col. 1.24; **kepe the flesh vnder.** Cf. 2 Cor. 12.7.

111/25 **Dauid . . . synned.** Cf. 2 Sam. 11–12.1–25.

111/30–31 **if . . . therby.** Cf. CWM 6/1.200/29–34.

112/1–2 **as . . . god.** Cf. 1 John 4.10.

112/4–5 **christ . . . vnto them.** Cf. Matt. 28.19, Mark 16.15, Luke 24.47.

112/5–7 **storyes . . . declare.** For God's mercy to Adam and Eve after the Fall, cf. Gen. 3.9–24. For the liberation of a remnant from the Babylonian captivity, cf. Ezek. 34.11. For the extension of Yahweh's favor to the Gentiles, cf. the three foreign women in the genealogy of Jesus: the Canaanite Rahab, cf. Josh. 2.1–21; the Moabite Ruth, cf. Ruth 1.4; the Hittite Bathsheba, cf. 2 Sam. 11.3. God's quest for the lost soul is depicted in the parables of the lost sheep and the lost coin, cf. Luke 15.4–6, 8–9.

112/8–9 **he neuer . . . life.** Cf. CWM 6/1.201/21–22.

112/12 **sir Thomas hitton.** To counter *Dialogue*'s claim that reformers would not die for their beliefs (cf. CWM 6/1.201/20–22), Tyndale asserts Hitton's perseverance unto death (*Prelates* K6). *Confutation* calls Hitton "the dyuyls stynkyng martyr" (CWM 8/1.17/1), and *Apology* opposes Hitton's execution near Canterbury to Becket's martyrdom in Canterbury (CWM 9.355). Foxe briefly summarizes Hitton's imprisonment and death at Maidstone in 1530 (4.619) and his interrogations by Warham and Fisher (8.712–15). Cf. nn to 114/17–18, 148/6–7, 215/17–19.

112/13 **caunterbury.** William Warham (c1456–1532) was Lord Chancellor (1504–15) until he was replaced by Wolsey, and Archbishop of Canterbury (1503–32) until his death. On 15 May 1532, the higher clergy of the Archdiocese of Canterbury accepted the king's authority to license the legislative acts of the English Church, and the next day, Warham as Primate presented the document of submission to Henry. Later the same day, More resigned from the Chancellorship (NCE 14.811; OER 4.257–58). In the *Obedience,* Tyndale accuses Warham of wanting to keep the NT as the secret of priests and a mystery to layfolk (K2v). Here, Tyndale condemns Warham and Fisher for their part in burning Thomas Hitton alive for importing a Tyndale NT in 1529. (JB)

112/14 **in braband.** A reference to the vigorous imperial prosecution of Lutherans in the Spanish Netherlands. The first victims were two Antwerp Augustinian friars, Heinrich Voes and Johann van Esch, who were burned in the Great Square of Brussels on 1 July 1523. Luther was deeply moved by news of their deaths and composed both an open letter of encouragement to the surviving reformers in the Low Countries, *Ein Brief an die Christen im Niederland* (WA 12.77–80; not in LW), and a ballad (WA 35.411–15; not in LW). (JW)

Erasmus comments on this event in Ep. 1384, To Huldrych Zwingli, Basel, 31 August [1523] (Allen 5.327/4–6; CWE 10.81/5–7). He refers to the execution of these two friars and of Louis de Berquin in April 1529 in Ep. 2188, To Charles Utenhove, Freiburg, 1 July 1529 (Allen 8.210/11–211/31; not yet in CWE).

112/14 **at colen.** The Cologne faculty of theology had condemned numerous propositions found in Luther's works even before the papal bull *Exsurge Domine.* In 1529 a quickly conducted heresy trial resulted in the burning of the Lutherans Adolph Clarenbach and Peter Fliesteden. (JW)

112/14–15 **in all . . . douchlonde.** Ten Germans were executed between the Brussels and Cologne burnings. Heinrich von Zütphen, the first Lutheran preacher in Bremen, was executed at Heide in December 1524, and Wolfgang Schuch and six others died in Alsace in 1526 and 1527. The Bavarian authorities executed Georg Wagner at Munich and Leonhard Kaiser at Schärding in 1527. Cf. "Märtyrer," *Religion in Geschichte und Gegenwart,* ed. Hans Frhr. v. Campenhausen et al., 3d ed., 7 vols. including Index (Tübingen: Mohr/Siebeck, 1957–65) 4.590. (JW)

112/16 **their . . . marters.** Cf. CWM 6/1.201/26–30.

112/19–20 **we . . . he sinneth.** Cf. CWM 6/1.203/18–204/28.

112/19–113/34 **And what . . . ceremonyes.** More calls Luther a "mad man" (CWM 6/1.203/25) for putting forth "a very frantyke argument" (CWM 6/1.204/17), namely, that the true church is without sin but composed of those in whom sin is still a pervasive presence. Tyndale accounts for the paradox first by appealing to the NT warrants for both tenets (112/21–113/19). (JW)

112/21–22 **he that . . . not.** 1 John 3.9.

112/22–25 **men . . . wrincle.** Eph. 5.25–27.

112/26–27 **If . . . in vs.** 1 John 1.8. *Answer* has "hys worde" (112/27), while NT and KJV have "trueth" (Wallis 487/14; TNT 338B).

112/28–29 **church . . . only.** Cf. CWM 6/1.196/28–29. More is willing to find a sinless church in heaven (CWM 6/1.206/1), but not on earth (CWM 6/1.196/30).

112/31–33 **that good . . . flesh.** Rom. 7.19–20.

113/1–3 **the flesh . . . wolde.** Gal. 5.17.

113/13 **twoo maner faythes.** For "historical faith" and "feeling faith," cf. 48/27–28n. Since *Dialogue* addresses primarily Catholic readers, More does not use these names in Bk. 2, Ch. 4 or any-where else in *Dialogue*. Only in Bk. 4, Ch. 11, does More examine an affective approach to faith as "truste / confidence / & hope" (CWM 6/1.388/14). *Confutation* briefly alludes to historical faith versus feeling faith in Bk. 4 (CWM 8/1.448/15–19). Then More gives a fuller treatment of the topic in the second half of Bk. 7 (CWM 8/2.741–849).

113/15–16 **ye . . . worde.** John 15.3.

113/17–18 **he gaue . . . name.** Cf. John 1.12.

113/18–19 **he that . . . lyfe.** Cf. John 3.16.

113/21 **symon magus.** Cf. Acts 8.9–13, 18–24. **the deuel.** Cf. Jas. 2.19.

113/25–26 **iustifienge of ceremonies.** Cf. Gal. 2.16.

113/33–34 **forgeuenesse . . . bloude.** Cf. Eph. 1.7.

114/2–3 **the pope . . . corrupte.** Cf. CWM 6/1.206/28 where More says that the Scriptures are "delyuered / kept and conserued" in the church.

114/9 **plucked . . . Christe.** Cf. Rom. 11.17.

114/9–10 **bilt . . . prophetes.** Eph. 2.20.

114/11–12 **the heretikes . . . mistical bodi.** Cf. CWM 6/1.207/11–12. Cf. other early uses of this name for the church: "crystys mystycall body" in *Supplication of Souls,* 1529 (CWM 7.202/17); "the mystycall body of our mother holy chirche," in "Sermon against Luther, 1521" (Fisher 322/8–9).

114/13 **misticall body . . . mist.** For a pun on the "misticall sens" of Scripture, cf. 110/14–15n.

114/13–14 **will not . . . light.** Cf. John 3.20.

114/17–18 **heretikes . . . abiure.** Cf. CWM 6/1.208/31–33. Tyndale

responds to More's generalization on inconstancy among reformers with a fourfold classification. Exemplars of the first, steadfast,
type would be the priests Thomas Hitton, Thomas Benet or Dusgate, and the Benedictine monk and book smuggler Richard Bayfield. The second class, providentially saved from arrest, would not
have any notoriety. Third, those who once recanted under judicial
pressure but returned to their new faith and then suffered martyrdom, would include the lawyer Thomas Bilney, the leather-seller
John Tewksbury, and the lawyer James Bainham. In the fourth
class, those who rejected the Reformation, would be Thomas
Arthur and Edward Crome (CWM 8/3.1170, 1251). For Hitton,
cf. 112/12n; for Bilney, cf. 146/12–13n, for all the heretics who
were executed during More's chancellorship, cf. 215/17–19n.
(JW)

114/22 **Peter.** Cf. Matt. 26.69–75, Mark 14.66–72, Luke 22.55–62,
John 18.17, 25–27.

114/24–25 **fleshly liberte.** Cf. Gal. 5.13, 1 Pet. 2.16.

115/2 **In the .vij.** Refutation of More's specific arguments on the
role of the saints is the principal topic of the rest of Tyndale's response to *Dialogue* Bk. 2. Tyndale's constructive views on the saints
are treated above in 59/7–16, 83/13–18 nn. (JW)

115/2 **saintes . . . counsels.** Cf. CWM 6/1.209/25, 29.

115/9–10 **good and bad . . . evell.** Cf. CWM 6/1.210/8–10.

115/12–14 **not . . . doo it.** Cf. CWM 6/1.210/13–16.

115/17–18 **the saintes . . . liued.** Cf. CWM 6/1.211/30–31. More argues that the saints will not have less charity in heaven than they
had on earth (cf. CWM 6/1.211/23–25).

115/20 **they haue . . . heare them.** Luke 16.29.

115/25–27 **Luke .vij. . . . then he.** Cf. CWM 6/1.211/27–30. *Confutation's* sidenote of 1557 identifies this text as Matt. 11.[11] while
Tyndale cites the cognate verse, Luke 7.28. More misinterprets
"the kingdom of heaven" as those that were "all redy in heuyn"
(CWM 6/1.211/29), whereas Tyndale correctly refers to believers
(115/27) in the New Dispensation.

115/28–29 **And he . . . grettest.** Cf. Mark 9.35.

116/5 **cursed . . . god.** Cf. Jer. 17.5.

116/7–8 **what . . . Christe.** Cf. 1 Cor. 3.5.

116/8–9 **Did . . . Paul.** Cf. 1 Cor. 1.13.

116/9 **Did . . . Christ.** Cf. 2 Cor. 11.2.

116/10–13 **let . . . gods.** 1 Cor. 3.21–23.

116/15–16 **praye . . . legion of angels.** Cf. Matt. 26.53.

116/20–22 **put . . . for him.** Cf. CWM 6/1.215/22–25.

116/26 **euen . . . saintes.** Cf. CWM 6/1.215/29–31 and n. More alluded to a miracle in which a man was cured by touching a coat which had belonged to someone then in purgatory. Cf. Gregory the Great, *Dialogues,* Bk. 4 (Ch. 40 in PL 77.396–97; Ch. 42 in FOTC 39.249–50).

116/28 **said masse in his gowne.** While Luther was in hiding at the Wartburg, his associate Andreas Karlstadt (1486–1541), wearing his professor's gown instead of liturgical vestments, publicly celebrated a simplified Lord's Supper in Wittenberg at Christmas 1521. He recited the words of consecration in German without reference to sacrifice and urged the people to take the bread and cup in their own hands (OER 1.178–80). Even though Karlstadt was largely implementing Luther's position in *Babylonian Captivity,* 1520 (WA 6.512/26–35; LW 36.36), the latter charged his colleague with rushing things, before the people were well-instructed and able personally to grasp and appropriate the changes. At this time, Luther published a tract against coercive and violent reforming actions, *A Sincere Admonition to All Christians to Guard against Insurrection and Rebellion* (WA 8.676–87; LW 45.57–74). (JW)

116/32 **the collectes of saintes.** The collect is the prayer of petition said by the celebrant to close the opening rites of Mass. Many saints' days have their own collect, which is also said at the close of each hour of the divine office. Tyndale's general assertion about the prominence of the merits of the saints is, however, not borne out by the collects of the *Missale* of 1508 enshrining the form used in the Roman curia. Of some ninety collects for saints, from Andrew the Apostle (30 November) through the Beheading of John the Baptist (29 August), only six appeal to God with reference to the merits of the saint. More frequently, the collects pray for God to be gracious and bless by the intercession, *patrocinium* or *suffragia* of the saint of the day. (JW)

117/4 **Christ . . . true.** Cf. Gal. 2.21.

117/5–6 **saintes . . . only.** In *Dialogue* More does not discuss the saints' merits or the possibility of sharing in them in Bk. 2, Ch. 8, but he claims in Bk. 3, Ch. 2 that Eutyches, the sleeping youth who fell out the upper-story window, was raised from the dead by the "merites of saynt Powle" (cf. Acts 20.9–12) (CWM 6/1.259/ 19).

117/11 **they coude . . . aliue.** Cf. CWM 6/1.212/19.

117/15–19 **the saintes . . . againe.** Cf. CWM 6/1.212/9–16. More's belief that the souls of the saints pass immediately upon death into the beatitude of heaven, formulated here and at 117/32–118/3 and 118/6–7, accords with the dogmatic constitution *Benedictus Deus* which Benedict XII (pope, 1334–42) issued in 1336 to counteract the opinion of his predecessor John XXII (pope, 1316–34) that the departed souls remain "beneath the altar" until the final resurrection on the last day. *Benedictus Deus* is found in DS 1000–1001; in English in Neuner-Dupuis 2305–6. The doctrine was briefly restated by the Council of Florence in *Laetentur coeli,* the bull of reunion between the Latin and Greek churches, in 1439 (DS 1305; Neuner-Dupuis 2308–9), and was indirectly confirmed in 1513 by Lateran V's declaration against Paduan Averroism, *Apostolici regiminis* (DS 1440–41), which affirms the natural immortality of the human soul. Cf. 182/2–8n, where Tyndale characterizes this doctrine as an unsalutary amalgam of pagan philosophy with biblical faith. (JW)

117/17, 117/23 **not the god of the dead.** Cf. Matt. 22.32, Mark 12.27, Luke 20.38.

117/17–118/8 **he steleth . . . resurreccion.** Tyndale's rebuttal here rests on the primacy in NT eschatology of belief in final resurrection, which he believes an immediate passage to glory would render meaningless. (JW)

117/28–29 **if . . . most miserablest.** 1 Cor. 15.13, 19. Tyndale suggests that More might have used this text to argue for the existence of the soul between death and the general resurrection. For the double superlative, cf. "most highest", Deut. 32.8 (Mombert 625; TOT 300); "This was the most unkindest cut of all," *Julius Caesar* 3.2.177 (performed 1599, published 1623).

118/3–6 **I maruell . . . agayne.** Cf. 1 Thess. 4.14–15. While More understands the sleep of death figuratively, Tyndale (here and *1 John* E3) follows Luther in taking it literally. Tyndale very likely knew Luther's 1522 sermon on the rich man and Lazarus (Luke 16.19–31), which circulated widely in German and came out in Latin in 1526. Luther explains that the soul of the departed believer rests in the word of God, as represented first by "Abraham's bosom" (Luke 16.22) and then by Christ's bosom, until the last day (WA 10/3.176–200; not in LW). Luther's postil for the fifth Sunday of Lent, published in 1525, gives a model homily on John 8.46–59. Regarding John 8.52, "yf a man kepe my sayinge, he shall never taste of deeth" (Wallis 206/15–16; TNT 146G), he explains that the believer does not feel death but instead sleeps in peace until being awakened in resurrection (WA 17/2.231–37; not in LW). Paul Althaus sets forth Luther's teaching on death and resurrection in *The Theology of Martin Luther* (Philadelphia: Fortress, 1966) 410–16. Gerhard Ebeling discusses Luther's views of the soul and human mortality, offering comparisons with Aristotle, Aquinas, Gabriel Biel, Lateran V, and Johann Eck. Cf. *Lutherstudien 2/2, Disputatio de homine: Die philosophische Definition des Menschen* (Tübingen: Mohr/Siebeck, 1982) 60–186.

Heinrich Bullinger (1504–75), reformed pastor of Zurich, attacked the doctrine of the soul's sleep in 1531 and John Calvin (1509–64) wrote against it in his first Reformation writing, *Psychopannychia* (composed 1534, published 1542), which ascribes the belief to certain unnamed Anabaptists. Calvin holds that the immortality of the soul rests on a densely woven complex of biblical and patristic texts. This work of Calvin has been edited by Walter Zimmerli (Leipzig: Deichert, 1927). An abridged version in English appeared in 1549 and a full translation in 1581. See the modern edition in Calvin's *Tracts* 3, ed. Henry Beveridge (Edinburgh, 1851), rpt. as *Tracts and Treatises: In Defense of the Reformed Faith* (Grand Rapids, MI: Eerdmans, 1958) 413–90.

The course of early-modern English opinion on the soul's condition after death has been charted in Norman T. Burns, *Christian Mortalism from Tyndale to Milton* (Cambridge: Harvard UP, 1972), beginning with the More-Tyndale argument (98–116). The doctrine of soul-sleep, seen as heretical by the established church, was transmitted in 16c radical conventicles. In the 17c the soul's annihilation between death and the Second Coming was held as Christian doctrine by the young Sir Thomas Browne (149–54), John Milton (164–83), and Thomas Hobbes (183–87), a tradition continued in present-day Jehovah's Witnesses and Seventh-day Adventists. (JW)

118/5–6 **resurreccion . . . agayne.** Cf. 1 Thess. 4.16.

118/9–10 **whether . . . holpe.** Cf. CWM 6/1.212/24–28.

118/12 **praye vn to the deuell.** In *Dialogue* Bk. 2, Ch. 11, the Messenger, not More as Mentor, tells a merry tale of a Lombard who prayed to God, Mary and all angels and saints for his gout, but without relief. He then horrified his wife and friends by praying to the devil (CWM 6/1.233/31–234/4).

118/17–18 **we praye . . . helpe vs.** Cf. CWM 6/1.214/14–19.

118/22–23 **And where . . . in him.** Cf. 1 Cor. 10.13.

118/32–119/2 **Christ . . . with him.** Cf. CWM 6/1.214/30–33.

119/1–2 **they which . . . with him.** Cf. Matt. 19.28. Instead of using NT's "which folowe me" (Wallis 61/24; TNT 46D), *Answer* gives "they which here preach him truly" (119/1).

119/6–7 **aftir the similitude of worldely tirantes.** Here and at 120/12, Tyndale declares that More regards God as an inaccessible monarch and the saints as friends at court who intercede for us, cf. 110/26n.

119/10–11 **The apostles . . . dishonoured.** Cf. CWM 6/1.214/35–215/2.

119/17 **false . . . apostles.** Cf. 1 Cor. 1.12–13, 3.3–4.

119/20–21 **it behoueth . . . malapertenesse.** Cf. CWM 6/1.215/19–22.

119/23 **bebolde to goo vn to god.** Cf. Heb. 4.16, Eph. 3.12.

119/29–30 **I saye not . . . loueth you.** John 16.26–27.

119/31–32 **be bold and goo in to my father.** Cf. Heb. 4.16, Eph. 3.12.

120/2–4 **we haue . . . howshold of god.** Cf. Eph. 2.18–19.

120/16 **a man . . . deed man.** Cf. CWM 6/1.215/28–29. Tyndale quotes the Messenger; More as *dramatis persona* adds the qualification that one may pray to any deceased person who was good.

120/18–19 **canvesed him . . . canonised him.** Tyndale pretends to make a verbal slip.

120/21–22 **one that . . . purgatory.** Cf. CWM 6/1.215/30–31.

120/33–121/2 **Then . . . heuen.** Cf. CWM 6/1.216/27–31.

121/7–8 **kinge henry . . . Eton.** Henry VI (king, 1422–61) founded Eton College and King's College, Cambridge. The last Lancastrian king, he was defeated at Tewkesbury by the Yorkist Edward IV (king, 1461–83), murdered in the Tower, and buried in St. George's Chapel, Windsor Castle. After Richard III (king, 1483–85) was overthrown by Henry VII (king, 1485–1509), the latter promoted the cult of Henry VI. As steps to canonization, Alexander VI (pope, 1492–1503) and Julius II (pope, 1503–13) authorized inquiries into the sanctity and alleged miracles of "Blessed Henry." The process continued until the late 1520s when the matrimonial troubles of Henry VIII foreshadowed his break with Rome. Cf. John W. McKenna, "Piety and Propaganda: The Cult of King Henry VI," in *Chaucer and Middle English Studies in honour of Rossell Hope Robbins* (Kent State UP, 1974), 72–88. In *Historia Richardi Tertii* (c1513), though not in the English version, More judges Henry VI to be more innocent than wise: *Rex innocentior esset quam sapientior* (CWM 2.6/12–13).

Prelates notes the influence of good Duke Humphrey (F5) and crafty Cardinal Beaufort (G1v), and laments the unprofitable marriage to Margaret of Anjou (G2). Cf. *The Brut of The Chronicles of England,* ed. Friedrich W.D. Brie, EETS Original Series 136 (London: Kegan Paul, 1908) 511–12.

121/11 **no ieopardy . . . damned.** Cf. CWM 6/1.223/10–12.

121/14–16 **no ieopardie . . . erre.** Cf. CWM 6/1.224/11–14. More argues that the Holy Spirit guarantees the validity of this consensus (CWM 6/1.224/15–17).

121/16–18 **when . . . Iewes.** Cf. CWM 6/1.220/13–15.

121/17–18 **Israhelites . . . Iewes.** Cf. 1 Kings 12.21. The Southern kingdom of Judea was formed by the tribes of Judah and Benjamin; the Northern kingdom of Israel by the other ten tribes.

121/22 **image of a calfe.** Cf. 1 Kings 12.28–30.

121/23 **arcke of testimonie.** Cf. 1 Kings 8.1–9.

121/24–25 **Iewes . . . temple.** Cf. 2 Kings 21.

121/24–26 **Iewes . . . Prophetes.** Cf. CWM 6/1, 220/10–12. More comments briefly on the punishment of the Jews for idolatry.

121/29 **captiue out of the lande.** The Assyrians conquered Samaria and deported Israelites in 721 BC (cf. 2 Kings 18.11–12). The

Chaldeans captured Jerusalem and deported the leading citizens of Judea in three stages: 598 BC (cf. 2 Kings 24.12–16), 587/6 BC (cf. 2 Kings 25.8–21; Jer. 39.8–10, 52.12–34) and 582–81 BC.

121/31 **open multitude called Gods church.** For the wheat and tares, cf. Matt. 13.24–30; for the dragnet, cf. Matt. 13.47–50.

122/5–7 **houses . . . secretly.** The master of the palace hid one hundred prophets of Yahweh from Jezebel, cf. 1 Kings 18.3–4. The wife of a priest in Jerusalem saved the young Joash from Athalia, cf. 2 Kings 11.

122/7 **Nycodemus amonge the phareses.** Cf. John 3.1–2.

122/11–12 **no ieopardy . . . hoste.** Cf. CWM 6/1.223/12–13.

122/17–19 **Paule . . . to gether.** Cf. 1 Cor. 1.10. Cf. CWM 6/1.223/31–224/10. Tyndale omits More's argument that the Holy Spirit would never allow the church to believe what was "dampnable false and fayned" (CWM 6/1.224/20).

122/24–25 **the Iewes . . . Prophetes.** Cf. CWM 6/1.224/25–26.

122/27–29 **Christ . . . slew them.** Cf. Matt. 23.29–31. Cf. CWM 6/1.225/11–14.

123/3–4 **Eliseus . . . a deed body.** Cf. 2 Kings 13.21; CWM 6/1.225/8–9, 17–18. In adding a noun to the article and adjective, *1573* agrees with CWM 6/1.225/9. After the text and variants were set in type, with *1573*'s "a dead body" substituted for *1531*'s "a deed" (and the emendation noted), O'Donnell discovered analogous forms without a noun: "a righteous" and "a wicked" occur in Ezek. 18.24, 26, 27, Tyndale's translation of an OT reading used in the Sarum Rite (TNT 397). For another example of the construction of article plus adjective without noun, cf. 144/4n.

123/10–11 **Christ . . . crosse.** Cf. CWM 6/1.225/20–22.

123/15–16 **woman . . . Christes cote.** Cf. Matt. 9.20–22, Mark 5.27–28, Luke 8.43–44. Cf. CWM 6/1.225/31.

123/17 **hir faith hath made hir hole.** Cf. Matt. 9.22, Mark 5.34, Luke 8.48.

123/21–22 **Paule . . . the seke.** Cf. Acts 19.12.

123/25 **sent walary.** In *Dialogue* Bk. 2, Ch. 10, the Messenger, not More as Mentor, describes phallic votive offerings at the shrine of St. Valery in Picardy. Duffy (197) observes that this incident parodies the more usual offering of a crutch or the model of a foot.

124/4 **bodyly seruice is not latria.** Cf. CWM 6/1.230/19–20.

124/6 **He trusteth . . . saint.** Cf. CWM 6/1.231/2–3.

124/7 **Moyses body.** Cf. Deut. 34.5–6; **diuers other.** For example, Elias, cf. 2 Kings 2.11.

124/10 **golden calues.** Cf. Exod. 32.1–8.

124/11 **wod.** Cf. 1 Kings 14.15. Wooden poles, "asherim," were symbols of the Canaanite fertility goddess. **stone.** Cf. Lev. 26.1.

124/17–18 **God . . . spirituall.** Cf. John 4.24. Tyndale glosses spiritual worship as focussed on "his worde only" (124/19).

124/23–26 **if . . . nother.** Cf. CWM 6/1.232/12–16.

124/26–27 **oure lady of walsynggam.** Walsingham is located a few miles from the coast of Norfolk, 117 miles NE of London. Early in his reign, Henry VIII walked the last mile of pilgrimage barefoot; he visited the shrine again in January 1511 to give thanks for the birth of a son. Catherine of Aragon prayed there after the victory at Flodden Field in 1513. Recalling his own visit in 1512, Erasmus satirized the shrine's claim to possess milk of the Virgin. Cf. "A Pilgrimage for Religion's Sake," February 1526, *Colloquies* (ASD 1/3.478/277 to 482/434; CWE 40.632/13 to 636/21). The shrine was suppressed in 1538. Cf. J.C. Dickinson, *The Shrine of Our Lady of Walsingham* (Cambridge UP, 1956) 141–44.

124/27 **oure lady of Ipswich.** The statue in the Lady Chapel in the parish church of St. Matthew was greatly venerated. In 1525 Wolsey received a grant of a papal indulgence for those who on specified days prayed for him and his parents and gave alms at this chapel in his native city, cf. Lunt, *Papacy* 503.

124/27–28 **our lady of wilsdon.** The pilgrimage church of Willesden northwest of London in Middlesex County contained a wooden statue of Mary, which had been partly burnt. In 1508 the accused Lollard Elizabeth Sampson declared that "if [Mary] might have holpen men and women who go to her on pilgrimage, she would not have suffered her tail to have been burnt" (Foxe 4.126). See Margaret Aston, "Lollards and Images," in *Lollards and Reformers* (London: Hambledon, 1984) 135–92. A certain Edmund Peerson accused Thomas Bilney of preaching that the crown, rings, and beads offered to this madonna "were bestowed amongst harlots, by the ministers of Christ's church" (Foxe 5.43). More may have visited the shrine while visiting his stepdaughter, Alice Alington, in the months before his arrest. Cf. Ep. 192★, To John Harris, Willesden, Sunday <January–April 1534> (More, *Selected Letters* 185–88 and n33).

124/33–125/1 **wemen . . . churches.** Cf. CWM 6/1.235/37–236/ 5.

125/3 **will not amend the abuse.** On 1 September 1523, Cuthbert Tunstall as the new bishop of London decreed that all the churches of his diocese should celebrate on 3 October the anniversary of their dedication to reduce the occasions for drinking and dancing, cf. Wilkins 3.701–2.

125/6 **the wild Irish and the welch.** Cf. CWM 6/1.236/33–237/ 2. The Norman-Welsh churchman Gerald of Wales (c1146–c1220) visited Ireland with Prince John in 1185, and Wales with the Archbishop of Canterbury in 1188. Gerald does not comment on theft among the Irish, but he observes of the Welsh, "This nation conceives it right to commit acts of plunder, theft, and robbery, not only against foreigners and hostile nations, but even against their own countrymen." Cf. *History of the Conquest of Ireland,* tr. Thomas Forester, and *Description of Wales,* tr. Richard Colt Hoare (p. 509) in *The Historical Works of Giraldus Cambrensis,* ed. Thomas Wright (London: Bell, 1892). Because they had been guilty of theft and arson, the Irish, Scots, and Welsh were not admitted to Cambridge in 1429 without providing sureties against disorderly conduct, cf. Williams 243. Keith Thomas (115 and n3) cites no other source for the "widely inappropriate" prayers of the Irish and Welsh than this passage from More. Falstaff would later justify his foray into highway robbery: "Why, Hal, 'tis my vocation, Hal. 'Tis no sin for a man to labour in his vocation," *1 Henry IV* 1.2.92–93 (performed 1596–97, published 1598). Tyndale was born near the marches of Wales, where thieves were formally cursed by the locate curates (*Obedience* N8v). Glanmor Williams (334, 496, 497) notes the powerful curses of the clergy at the shrines of St. David in Pembrokeshire and St. Derfel in Merionethshire.

125/9–10 **Prayar . . . awaye.** Cf. Mark 13.33, Luke 18.1.

125/26 **the soules . . . to perish.** Cf. 1 Cor. 8.11.

125/30 **Abraham and Melchisedec.** Cf. Gen. 14.16, 20, Heb. 7.2.

126/2–4 **S. Hierom and Augustine . . . beste.** Cf. CWM 6/1.238/ 2–7. At the conclusion of his eulogy of the widow Paula

(347–404), Jerome asks prayers of his deceased friend. Cf. Ep. 108, To Eustochium, (AD 404) (Par. 34 in PL 22.906; Par. 33 in CSEL 55.350–51; Par. 34 in 2NPNF 6.212). *Unio Dissidentium* (2.N8v) cites a passage where Augustine urges restraint in honoring saints. Cf. *On True Religion* (AD 390) 55.108 (CCL 32.256); in *Augustine: Earlier Writings,* tr. John H.S. Burleigh, LCC 6 (Philadelphia: West-minster, 1953) 280. Henry Walter (PS 3.126–27n2) cites a more af-firmative passage from Augustine, not included in *Unio,* approving prayers to saints. Cf. *On the Care to Be Had for the Dead* (AD c421) 4.6 (PL 40.596; 1NPNF 3.542).

Testimonies from Ambrose, Jerome, and Augustine on prayer to the saints are given by P. Séjourné, "Saints (culte des)," *Dictionnaire de Théologie catholique,* 14 (1939) 905–15. Recent expositions are found in Peter Brown, *The Cult of the Saints: Its Rise and Function in Latin Christianity* (U of Chicago P, 1982); Karl Hausberger, "Heilige/Heiligenverehrung, III, Anfänge," TRE 14 (1985) 646–51. (JW)

126/10 **promises . . . christes bloude.** For a covenant in the blood of animals, cf. Gen. 15.9–21; for a new covenant in the blood of Christ, cf. Heb. 9.13–15.

126/13 **spake.** Tyndale's Antwerp compositor may have been influ-enced by Low German "spreken" to give *1531*'s "sprake."

126/17–18 **faith . . . in christes bloude.** Cf. Rom. 3.25.

126/21–23 **miracles . . . mesinger.** Cf. CWM 6/1.239/26–29.

126/30–32 **if . . . fayned.** Cf. CWM 6/1.241/8–14.

127/7–8 **miracles which witches doo.** Witchcraft usually means the employment of occult means to cause physical harm, even death, to humans and animals. It is assigned the death penalty by the He-brew Bible (Exod. 22.18) and condemned by Paul (Gal. 5.20). In the late Middle Ages the idea began to emerge that the witch gained her power through a pact with the devil. Keith Thomas (439) cites the treatise *Dives and Pauper* (c1410), Commandment 1, Ch. 39, "What is wychecraft," ed. Priscilla Heath Barnum, EETS 275 (Oxford UP, 1976) 167–69; the bull against witches of Inno-cent VIII, *Summis desiderantes affectibus* (1484); the "summa" (1486) of court procedures by two Dominican Inquisitors. See *The Malleus Maleficarum of Heinrich Kramer and James Sprenger,* tr. Montague Summers (1928, 1948; New York: Dover, 1971). H.A. Kelly cites sixteen cases brought before the court of the Bishop of London between 1475 and 1528. See "English Kings and the Fear of Sorcery," *Mediaeval Studies* 39 (1977) 206–38, rpt. in Witchcraft, Magic and Demonology 2, *Witchcraft in the Ancient World and the Middle Ages,* ed. Brian P. Levack (New York: Garland, 1992) 211–12n16.

Early in his career, Erasmus described a case of witchcraft punished by imprisonment. Cf. Ep. 143, To Antoon van Bergen, Paris, 14 January 1501 (Allen 1.336/68–340/232; CWE 2.5/74–11/255); Ep. 149, To Antoon van Bergen, [Paris?, 16 March? 1501] (Allen 1.353/69–76; CWE 2.27/80–89). In 1532, the *Constitutio criminalis Carolina* transferred cases of witchcraft from ecclesiastical to secular courts and imposed the death penalty for harmful magic. Cf. Christina Larner, *Witchcraft and Religion,* ed. Alan Macfarlane (Oxford: Blackwell, 1984) 59. The next year Erasmus described two cases of women who were burnt to death for witchcraft. Cf. Ep. 2846, To Damian a Goes, Freiburg, 25 July 1533 (Allen 10.275/124–52; not yet in CWE); Ep. 2880, To Peter Richardot, Freiburg, 19 November 1533 (Allen 10.324/29–36; not yet in CWE). The increased severity in penalty foreshadows the mass executions of 1560 to 1630. Cf. Brian P. Levack, *The Witch-Hunt in Early Modern Europe,* 2d ed. (New York: Longman, 1995) 185–232.

127/11–12 **And likewise . . . miracle.** Cf. CWM 8/1.251/13.

127/19 **Moses . . . Egypte.** Cf. CWM 8/1.271/5. For Aaron's rod, cf. Exod. 7.8–12; for the ten plagues, cf. Exod. 7–12.

127/20 **tryal of miracles.** Cf. CWM 6/1.241/21.

127/24 **sectes of heretykes.** Cf. CWM 6/1.241/31, 8/2.611/23– 24. In classical Greek, *hairesis* meant first "a taking," then "taking for oneself", i.e., "a course of action or thought." In Hellenistic Greek, the word *hairesis,* meaning "teaching or school," was used to translate the Hebrew *minim,* eventually in a negative sense. This development affected NT Greek, where *hairesis* occurs in the singular or plural eight times. Tyndale translates with "sect/s" all but once (Acts 5.17, 15.5, 24.5, 26.5; 1 Cor. 11.19, Gal. 5.20, 2 Pet. 2.1). He uses "heresy" when Paul explains his religious position to the Gentile judge Felix in Acts 24.14: "But this I confesse vnto the, that after that waye (which they call heresy) so worshippe I the God of my fathers" (Wallis 283/11–12; TNT 200C). Jerome explains the etymology of *hairesis:* "It is so called from the word 'choice' because each one chooses for himself that teaching which he prefers," *Commentariorum in Epistolam ad Galatas,* 3.5.507–8 (PL 26.417). Jerome addressed this commentary to his friends Paula and Eustochium in AD 387 (2NPNF 6.496, note to Jerome's preface). Augustine's handbook *On Heresies* (AD c428–29), not quoted in *Unio,* briefly summarizes and refutes the teachings of eighty-eight groups from the apostolic era to his own. Cf. CCL 46.273–345; Liguori G. Mueller OFM, "Introduction," *The De Haeresibus of Saint Augustine* (Washington, DC: Catholic University of America P, 1956). For a survey of the word "heresy" in OT and NT, cf. Mueller 38–42; for the quotation from Jerome, cf. Mueller 43 and n41.

127/25 **one christe.** Cf. Eph. 4.5.

127/28–29 **sundrie sectes . . . in all youre vniuersites.** These are the different religious orders and the *viae* of late medieval scholasticism, such as the *via antiqua* (Thomism), the *via Scoti,* and the *via moderna* (Occamism). Tyndale's accusations of their neglect of Scripture rest on the lengthy prolegomena on method and science found at the beginning of many scholastic commentaries on Lombard's *Sentences.* Also, much speculation occurred on aspects of the relation between the First Cause and creatures. Little intellectual energy was expended on the doctrine of human redemption by Christ. (JW)

127/30 **saluacion . . . in christe.** Duffy (234–56) describes numerous devotions to Christ's Passion: general meditations by Bernard (c1090–1153), Richard Rolle (c1300–49), and Nicholas Love (fl. 1410), and specific meditations on the Five Wounds and the Seven Last Words.

128/1 **god . . .miracles.** Cf. CWM 6/1.242/24–25.

128/3–4 **Mahometes . . . yeres.** Cf. CWM 8/1.252/31–32, 253/16. For the miracles of Islam, cf. *Prelates* B8v.

128/7–11 **send . . . trueth.** Cf. 2 Thess. 2.11–12. *Answer* has the triplets: "to stablysh them in lies," "to dysceaue them," "leade them out off the waye" (128/8–9). NT has "that they shuld beleve lyes" (Wallis 436/18; TNT 306C)

128/12 **heretykes haue no myracles.** This theme pervades *Dialogue* Bk. 2, Ch. 12, but is sharply asserted at CWM 6/1.244/2.

128/14–15 **God . . . heretikes.** Cf. CWM 6/1.242/35–36.

128/22–23 **miracles . . . persecucyon.** Cf. CWM 6/1.243/1–4.

129/1 **the deuel doeth none for them.** Cf. CWM 8/1.382/15. For miracles performed by the devil or Antichrist, cf. *Obedience* F5v, P3v, P4v, T3v.

129/11 **turkes and sarasenes.** Cf. CWM 6/1.243/29–32.

129/15 **the Iewes.** Cf. CWM 6/1.243/32–35.

129/16–18 **they haue . . . Christes bloude.** Cf. Rom. 10.3.

129/19–21 **they haue . . . not.** Cf. CWM 6/1.243/35–244/6.

129/27 **disceauers . . . miracles.** Cf. Matt. 24.24.

129/28–29 **their shall come . . . Christe.** Cf. Matt. 24.5.

129/34 **gresiamus.** With his mock Latin for "we anoint" (cf. PS 3.130n1), Tyndale rejects both the pope's claim to be "christes vicar" (129/30) and the ordination ritual. (JB)

129/35–130/1 **miracles . . . beleffe.** Cf. CWM 6/1.244/12–13.

130/3–4 **And when . . . Heliseus.** Cf. CWM 8/1.271/5. Cf. 2 Kings 13.21.

130/8–10 **God . . . miracles.** Cf. CWM 6/1.244/19–24. More avoids the repetition of "bold" (130/9, 10) by substituting "surely": "whose doctryne they myght boldely byleue / and whose lyuyng they myght surely folowe" (CWM 6/1.244/22–24).

130/11–17 **if . . . promised them.** Cf. CWM 6/1.244/25–35.

130/16–17 **spirite . . . trouth.** Cf. John 14.26.

130/24–25 **And as . . . myracles.** Cf. CWM 8/1.247/36–37.

131/1–6 **deed saintes . . . affirmeth the contrary.** Cf. CWM 8/1.268/5 and CWM 8/2.248/8–10.

131/2 **Thomas . . . full of miracles.** The biography of Thomas Aquinas by Bernard Gui OP (1324) dedicated its third part to the recital of 102 miracles through Thomas's intercession that occurred between his death in 1274 and his canonization in 1323. Bonino Mombrizio's *Sanctuarium seu vitae sanctorum* (1477; critical edition in 2 vols., Paris: Fontemoing, 1910) offered a selection from Gui's life (2.565–88), but gave only the introduction to the third part and related just one of the miracles, cf. 46/33n. (JW)

131/3 **our lady . . . originall sinne.** Aquinas held that Mary was conceived but not born in original sin (*Summa* III, Q. 27, Art. 1).

The feast of Mary's Conception was allowed at that time, but was not extended to the universal church. Thomas took it as the celebration of Mary's sanctification in her mother's womb.

The English Franciscan William of Ware taught that Mary was conceived immaculately, following a preference for attributing the highest prerogatives to her. Duns Scotus took up this principle and argued that Christ, as the most perfect mediator, found the more perfect way to save his mother by preserving her from original sin. Scotus admitted this teaching was not stated in Scripture, but held it was enough that Scripture and the Fathers did not rule it out, cf. *Quaestiones in tertium Librum Sententiarum,* Dist. 3, Q. 1 (*Opera Omnia* 14.157).

Dominican theologians argued against Scotus, but even the canonization of Thomas in 1323 could not stem the tide of popular devotion in favor of the Immaculate Conception. In 1438 it was taught by the Council of Basel but after Eugenius IV (pope, 1431–47) had withdrawn his legate. Tyndale alludes to Sixtus IV (pope, 1471–84), a Franciscan who favored the Immaculate Conception and decreed in 1483 that it is safe to preach but wrong for holders of either view to charge the other side with heresy. Among his condemnations of scholastic disputations (*Obedience* B7v–B8, R5), Tyndale cites this controversy over the Immaculate Conception (*Obedience* C3). (JW)

In a letter written to a Dominican, Erasmus takes the Franciscan position that Mary is free of original as well as personal sin. Cf. Ep. 1196, To [Vincentius Theoderici], [Louvain, c. middle of March, 1521] (Allen 4.465/58–59; CWE 8.178/66–67). In 1509 four Dominicans were burnt at the stake in Bern for faking apparitions in which Mary voiced her opposition to the teaching of the Immaculate Conception. Cf. "The Seraphic Funeral," 1531, *Colloquies* (ASD 1/3.693/233–43; CWE 40.1007/10–21). More attributed the discovery of this fraud to divine providence (CWM 6/1.88/32–35).

131/14–15 **they that . . . temptacion.** The Israelites succumbed to various temptations: complaining about lack of food (cf. Exod. 16.2–3) and water (cf. Exod. 17.2–3), worshipping the golden calf (cf. Exod. 32), wanting to return to Egypt because of fear of giants in the land of Canaan (cf. Num. 14.1–4).

131/17–20 **In so moch . . . deeth.** Cf. Luke 16.31.

131/22 **S. Hierom / Augustine.** Four texts of Jerome relating to the Roman primacy are given in Carl Mirbt and Kurt Aland, eds., *Quellen zur Geschichte des Papstums und des römischen Katholizismus* 1, 6th ed. (Tübingen: Mohr, 1967) 163–65, followed by four excerpts from Augustine referring to Peter and his successor on 169, 171f, and 172f. The early development of the primacy is treated by Karl Baus in Jedin and Dolan 1.355–65, 2.245–69. Augustine explains *petra* as Christ; Origen explains it as all Christians. Both are cited by Erasmus' annotation on Matthew 16.18, *Quia tu es.*). The sidenote has *Ecclesia non est fundata super Petrum* (Reeve 1.71). (JW)

Where Fisher counts Jerome and Bede among those who interpret Matthew 16.18 as a justification for papal primacy, Tyndale contends that the Fathers knew no such authority of one bishop over another and would not have made the pope a god (131/29–30; *Obedience* H6v, H7, T3v). Tyndale argues that when Jerome said that OT priests could make a leper clean or unclean (cf. Luke 17.4), he did not imply that NT priests could bind and loose sins, because only God can do so (*Obedience* N6r–v). Tyndale uses Bede's interpretation of the same incident to argue that only followers of false doctrine must show their sins to the priests (*Obedience* N2). (JB)

131/22 **Bede.** The Anglo-Saxon monk Bede (c673–c735) is best known today for his *Ecclesiastical History* (see 131/32n), but he produced a notable body of scriptural exegesis: e.g., on Genesis (CCL 118A), 1 Samuel (CCL 119), Mark and Luke (CCL 120), Acts and the Catholic Epistles (CCL 121). Bede used Greek in his second commentary on Acts, cf. Berschin 101. Bede had a rudimentary knowledge of Hebrew, cf. G. Lloyd Jones 8. He was a major source of the 12c *Glossa ordinaria,* cf. CWE 11.100n12. In dedicating his *Paraphrases of 1 and 2 Peter and Jude* to Cardinal Wolsey, Ep. 1112, Louvain, [c June 1520], Erasmus praises Bede, "a man who lacked neither learning nor industry by the standards of his time" (Allen 4.284/30–31; CWE 7.311/37–38; also CWE 44.77). *Unio Dissidentium* offers five passages of NT exegesis by Bede.

131/26–27 **thou . . . church.** Matt. 16.18.

131/27 **fede my shepe.** John 21.16–17.

131/27–28 **all . . . erth.** Matt. 28.18.

131/32 **purgatory.** Tyndale is correct in asserting that the Fathers did not credit the pope with power over purgatory, but they did begin to formulate an argument for its existence. Jerome asserts, "[W]e believe that the judgment of Christian sinners, whose works will be tried and purged in fire[,] will be moderate and mixed with clemency," *In Isaiam* 66.24 (AD 408–10) (tr. LeGoff 61; he erroneously gives XLVI for LXVI; CCL 73A.799). Naming Augustine "The True Father of Purgatory," Le Goff (61–85) cites the *Confessions* (AD 397–401) 9.13.34–37 (PL 32.778–79; CSEL 33.223–26; 1NPNF 1.139–41) on prayers for Monica; *On the Care to Be Had for the Dead* (AD c421) (PL 40.591–610; 1 NPNF 3.539–51); *City of God* (AD 413–27) 21.26 (CCL 48.796–99; 1NPNF 2.473–75). He finds "explicit mention of purgatorial fire" in Bede's homily (PL 94.30; Le Goff 102, 386n8) and in Drythelm's vision of purgatory (Le Goff 113–16) in 5.12 of *Bede's Ecclesiastical History of the English People,* ed. Bertram Colgrae and R.A.B. Mynors, Oxford Medieval Texts (Oxford: Clarendon, 1969) 488–502. See Jacques Le Goff, *The Birth of Purgatory,* tr. Arthur Goldhammer (U of Chicago P, 1981); Marc'hadour, "The Dogma of Purgatory," *Supplication of Souls,* CWM 7.lxxxvii–cxvii. (JW)

Unio Dissidentium does not quote passages from Augustine that foreshadow the development of a doctrine of purgatory, e.g., *Enchiridion* (AD 422–23), Ch. 109–10 (CCL 46.108–9; 1NPNF 3.272–73).

132/2–3 **They . . . repentaunce.** Cf. Acts 5.31.

133/4–5 **the opinions . . . scripture.** Cf. CWM 6/1.247/6–8.

133/5–6 **He axeth . . . written.** Cf. CWM 6/1.252/7–8.

133/17–19 **greke . . . eareconfession.** In *Obedience* (N1), Tyndale claims that auricular confession was abolished in Constantinople after a deacon sexually assaulted a woman. Socrates Scholasticus reports in his *Ecclesiastical History* 5.19 (PG 67.613–20; 2NPNF 2.128) that the woman told the priest penitentiary of her adultery with a deacon, who was then excommunicated. In his parallel *Ecclesiastical History* 7.16 (PG 67.1457–64; 2NPNF 2.386–87), Sozomen gives another version: the deacon raped the woman, whom he found alone in church offering penitential prayers. Both Socrates and Sozomen correctly state that the office of priest penitentiary was then abolished. One could mistakenly conclude that Eastern Christians afterwards confessed their sins only to God. However, Nectarius, Patriarch of Constantinople, did not abolish private confession in 391 but an office established to reconcile the many Christians who had apostasized during the Decian persecution (AD 250–51), cf. Watkins 1.477–78. St. Nicephorus I, Patriarch of Constantinople from 806 to 815 (NCE 10.438–39), affirmed the bishop's right to delegate authority to hear confessions (Canon 88) (FJO 183). Auricular confession in the Eastern Church was recognized at the first reunion council, Lyons II (1274), and continues to the present day. Cf. Alexander P. Kazhdan, "Confession," 1.493; Robert F. Taft SJ et al, "Penance," 3.1622–23 in *The Oxford Dictionary of Byzantium,* ed. Alexander P. Kazhdan, 3 vols. (New York: Oxford UP, 1991).

133/30–31 **whether . . . Noe.** Cf. CWM 6/1.252/11–12. For the genealogy of believers between Adam and Noah, cf. Gen. 5.

134/1 **patriarkes were full of miracles.** Cf. the aged Abraham's begetting of Isaac, (cf. Gen. 21.1–5, Rom. 4.19) and Isaac's rescue from death as a human sacrifice (cf. Gen. 22.9–14).

134/4–5 **they whych . . . Lira.** Cf. Gen. 7.21–24 and CWM 6/1.252/20–35. The Yale editors quote Nicholas of Lyra's comment on 1 Pet. 3.20: "One can probably say that, seeing the flood increase as Noah had predicted, many believed who formerly had not believed and repented of their sins. And thus they descended into limbo with the other patriarchs" (CWM 6/2.674, tr. O'Donnell).

134/6 **Nicolaus de Lira delirat.** The Franciscan Nicholas of Lyra (c1270–1349) was the author of the widely used *Postillae perpetuae,* also known as the *Postilla litteralis,* that commented concisely on the whole of the Bible. This was the first biblical commentary to be printed. Because he had mastered Hebrew, Lyra was mistakenly thought to be Jewish, cf. Friedman 16. Lyra was especially esteemed for his knowledge of Hebrew, extensive use of Jewish exegesis, and consistent attention to the literal sense of the text. Cf. Ceslaus Spicq, *Esquisse d'une histoire de l'exégèse latine au moyen âge* (Paris: Vrin, 1944), 335–42. (JW)

Preferring moral allegory to Lyra's literal interpretation of the Hebrew Bible, Erasmus mocks him with the proverb, "an ass with a lyre," *Moriae encomium,* 1514 ed. (ASD 4/3.100/515; CWE 27.145). See also *Adagia* no. 335, *Asinus ad lyram* (ASD 2/1.434–36; CWE 31.344–45); "To see an Ass play on a harp," Tilley A366. There is a satirical portrait of Lyra playing a hurdy-gurdy (or *lyra rustica*) by Hans Holbein the Younger in a copy of Froben's 1518 ed. of *Moriae encomium* in the Kupferstichkabinett, Basel (CWE 5.364). More defends the virtue and learning of Lyra but notes the pun on his name: *delirasse Lyranum,* "delirium in Nicolas de Lyra," in Ep. 83, To a Monk, n.p., <March–September 1519> (CWM 15.216/10); *lyra delirat* in *Confutation,* 1532–33 (CWM 8/1.233/18, 273/8). Tyndale includes Lyra in the mob of contentious medieval scholars (*Obedience* B8).

In his earliest lectures on Scripture, the *Dictata super Psalterium,* 1513–16 (cf. 75/5n), Luther promoted a Christological interpretation of the Psalms and so opposed Lyra's attempts to illumine the text from Israelite history and worship. The older Luther criticized Lyra when he followed the medieval Jewish commentator Rashi (G. Lloyd Jones 60). (JW)

134/7–8 **consent . . . soule.** Cf. Matt. 22.37, Mark 12.30, Luke 10.27. A concise statement on justification, with Tyndale's characteristic emphasis on consent to the law as an intrinsic component along with the laying hold of God's mercy. Cf. nn for 38/18–19, 106/19–107/23, 195/22. (JW)

134/14 **Noyes floud.** Cf. CWM 8/1.273/5–7.

134/17–18 **hundred and .xx. yeres . . . repent.** Cf. Gen. 6.3.

134/19–20 **popes . . . invndacions of water.** The Tiber flooded in AD 589, causing the plague that killed Pelagius II (pope, 579–90) and making way for the election of Gregory I (pope, 590–604). For the flood, cf. *Dialogues* 3.19 (PL 77.268; FOTC 39.149–50). For the plague, cf. *Dialogues* (4.18 in PL 77.349; 4.19 in FOTC 39.213). Cf. also Grégoire le Grand, *Dialogues,* 3 vols., ed. Adalbert de Vogüé, tr. Paul Antin (Paris: Les Editions du Cerf, 1978–80) 2.347n2 for the flood, 3.73n2 for the plague.

134/22–23 **Abraham . . . of him.** Cf. CWM 6/1.253/4–6.

134/25 **Abrahams . . . god.** Cf. Gen. 15.1–6.

134/27–28 **they beleued . . . not erre.** Cf. CWM 6/1.253/16–17.

135/4–6 **god . . . generacion.** Cf. Jer. 31.31–33.

135/7–8 **the most part . . . scripture.** Cf. CWM 6/1.253/11–15.

135/13–14 **who . . . false bokes.** Cf. CWM 6/1.253/21–23. In his *Ecclesiastical History* [on AD 1–324] 3.25.1–3 (PG 20.267–70; 2NPNF 1.155–56), Eusebius distinguishes between the accepted, the disputed, and the rejected books of the NT. The first include: the four Gospels, Acts, the epistles of Paul, 1 John, 1 Peter, and probably the Apocalypse. The second include: the epistles of James, Jude, 2 Peter, 2 and 3 John. The *Shepherd of Hermas* (AD c140–55) is an example of a book ultimately judged to be non-canonical (NCE 6.1074). Eusebius states the opinion that Clement of Rome translated Paul's Epistle to the Hebrews from Hebrew into Greek in 3.38.2–3 (PG 20.294; 2NPNF 1.169). In Matthew's Bible (1537) a sidenote on 2 Sam. 23 (TOT 456) refers to Eusebius.

135/22–24 **vn to them . . . no scripture.** Cf. CWM 6/1.253/33–254/1.

135/25–26 **Because . . . trouth.** Cf. CWM 6/1.244/34–35. Tyndale here quotes one of More's favorite prooftexts (John 16.13): "the holy gost shall teach his church all trouth." Cf. Marc'hadour, *Bible* 4.117.

135/31–33 **S. Augustine . . . not alowe.** Augustine said that the canonical books of Scripture have such singular authority that all other books are to be tested by them. Cf. *Reply to Faustus the Manichaean* (AD c400) 11.5 (PL 42.248–49; CSEL 25/1.320–21; 1NPNF 4.180). He applied this test to his own teaching in Ep. 147, to Paulina (AD 413), *The Book on the Vision of God,* Prologue, Par. 4 (PL 33.598; CSEL 44.278; Parsons 3.173). Erasmus repeated this principle in his *Ratio verae theologiae,* saying that Augustine would have his own works read *non cum necessitate credendi, sed cum libertate iudicandi* (Holborn 205/8–9). (JW)

Unio Dissidentium offers further proofs of Augustine's submission to Scripture: Ep. 82, cf. 8/30n; Ep. 148, To Fortunatianus, Bishop of Sicca (AD 413) 4.15 (UD 1.X2, PL 33.628–29; CSEL 44.344–45; Parsons 3.235–36); *On the Holy Trinity* (AD 399–422) Prologue to 3.2 (UD 1.X3; CCL 50.128; 1NPNF 3.56).

136/6–8 **the scripture . . . know the scripture.** Cf. CWM 6/1.254/5–7, 9–10.

136/8 **for . . . beleue it.** Cf. CWM 6/1.254/10–13.

136/16 **Rodes.** More refers to the fall of Rhodes to Suleiman in December 1522 in *Dialogue Concerning Heresies,* 1529, 1531 (CWM 6/1.84/22, 6/2.625) and in *Dialogue of Comfort,* 1534–35 (CWM 12.8/5). For the Turks, cf. 7/18n.

137/4–6 **the scripture . . . expounde it.** Cf. CWM 8/1.249/5–8.

137/15–16 **they which . . . Christ.** Cf. Rom. 8.9.

137/17–19 **they whych . . . spirite of god.** Cf. 1 Cor. 2.14.

137/20 **they whych . . . christ.** Cf. John 5.44.

137/21–23 **they which . . . not.** Cf. John 7.17.

138/7 **stinte.** Tyndale refers to "annates," or "a portion of the first year's income paid to the papacy by the new incumbent of a benefice . . ." (Lunt, *Papacy* 307). This exaction was first levied on England in 1306 (ibid.). In 1332 a papal decree defined annates as a tenth of the assessed value of a benefice. If the benefice was not assessed, annates would equal half of the income of the first year (ibid. 308). Later, certain statutes required a royal license to apply for a papal provision to an English benefice, permission being granted mainly to archbishops, bishops, and abbots (ibid. 408): in 1351, 25 Edward III, St. 4 (*Statutes* 1.316–18); in 1390, 13 Richard

II, St. 2, Ch. 2 (*Statutes* 2.69–74). Before 1534 the pope collected annates from the more important and affluent offices, but after 1534 the monarch (except for Mary I, queen, 1553–58) collected annates from all benefices. The largest recorded sum paid to Rome in the 16c was about 211 pounds in 1505, whereas the king received 14,034 pounds in 1535 (Lunt, *Papacy* 444–45). Under Anne (queen, 1702–14) annates were put in a fund to increase poor clerical livings; this fund was reorganized in 1947, cf. Bray 88. For legislation severing ties with Rome, cf. 159/29n.

138/11 **walke . . . birth.** Cf. 1 Cor. 3.3.

138/13 **dye . . . ensample.** Cf. John 10.11, 15.

138/23–25 **the Iewes . . . the phareses.** Cf. Neh. 8 and 9. Eusebius quotes Josephus, *Against Apion* (1.8), on the canon of the Hebrew Bible: five books of Moses, thirteen books of history and prophecy (Joshua, Judges and Ruth, Samuel, Kings, Chronicles, Ezra and Nehemiah, Esther, Isaiah, Jeremiah and Lamentations, Ezekiel, Daniel, Twelve Minor Prophets, Job), four books of hymns and precepts (Psalms, Proverbs, Ecclesiastes, Song of Songs). This total of twenty-two sacred books equals the number of letters in the Hebrew alphabet. Cf. *Ecclesiastical History* 3.10.1–3 (PG 20.241–44; 2NPNF 1.144–45 and n1).

138/25–27 **And yet . . . erroure.** Cf. Matt. 23.23, Luke 11.42.

138/32–33 **when . . . the Iewes.** Cf. 2 Cor. 3.14–15.

139/7–9 **Then . . . all thynge.** Tyndale attacks the conclusion of *Dialogue* Bk. 3, Ch. 1, probably because More asserts that we should use the interpretation of the church against *sola fide* and *sola scriptura*. More calls these two principles the sword and buckler of the Reformation (cf. CWM 6/1.254/39–255/3).

139/8–9 **saue sheweth his ignoraunce.** In this instance the OED criticizes Tyndale's "confused use" of the verb after the conjunction (*save,* 2.β.).

139/9–16 **we beleue . . . scripture.** Cf. CWM 6/1.254/5–7.

139/12–13 **by inspiracion . . . vnderstondynge.** Because More believes that the will can compel the intellect, Tyndale parodies More's words: first, "inspyracyon" (CWM 6/1.254/22) at 141/10, 141/16, 143/24; second, "endeuour" (CWM 6/1.254/28) at 140/28, 141/10, 145/9; third, "captiue and subdew our vnderstand-ynge" (CWM 6/1.254/28–29) at 140/28, 141/11, 141/16–17, 143/24–25, 143/29, 144/16, 145/9–10, 175/5. For Tyndale's positon on wit over will, cf. 34/6–11n.

139/12–16 **the holy gost . . . scripture.** Cf. CWM 6/1.254/13–18.

139/17–18 **the scripture . . . beleue it not.** Cf. CWM 6/1.254/9–13.

139/20–21 **the appostles . . . beleue them.** Cf. Acts 4.1–12, 17.32.

139/24–25 **the spirite of god . . . to beleue.** Cf. CWM 6/1.254/13–15, 22–24.

139/28–29 **beleued . . . life.** Acts 13.48.

139/29–31 **they that . . . god.** Cf. John 8.47.

139/31–32 **ye be of . . . ye will doo.** John 8.44.

140/5–6 **remanaunt kepte by grace.** Cf. Rom. 11.5. For a remnant's return from the Babylonian captivity, cf. Isa. 10.20–22, Mic. 2.12, Zech. 8.6, 12.

140/16–17 **predestinacion.** Cf. CWM 6/1.254/30–35. More does not use the term "predestination" but describes a synergistic co-operation between divine grace and human choice.

140/21–23 **balam . . . false.** Cf. CWM 8/1.180/7–15 and 8/1.221/27.

140/29–141/1 **O how . . . at all.** Cf. CWM 8/1.501/29–33. Probably because it is repetitious, More omits the sentence, "My witte must conclude good or bad yer my will can loue or hate" (140/32–33). The last sentence of this passage, "My witt . . . at all" (140/33–141/1), is quoted again at CWM 8/1.507/30–31.

140/29–31 **the wil . . . his father.** Cf. CWM 8/2.785/24–27. For the blindness of reason, cf. *Obedience* E3v. For other references to free will, cf. 39/2n, 174/30n.

140/32 **gift of god and not of vs.** Cf. Eph. 2.8–9.

141/9 **proue not the value of a podynge pricke.** Slender wooden skewer with which the ends of a sausage or pudding were fastened. This example is the first use of the proverb recorded in ODEP 653; cf. Tilley P626, "Not worth a Pudding."

141/9 **M. More feleth.** Cf. 141/24, 142/9, and 144/13–14, where Tyndale effectively uses this satirical refrain. Tyndale buffets More for putting equal trust in Scripture and church in *Dialogue* Bk. 3, Ch. 1. The Parker Society edition joins these pairs: 141/S1–2 as

"More feeleth Purgatory." and 141/S3–4 as "Tyndale feeleth Purgatory."

141/11–16 **purgatory . . . still.** Cf. CWM 8/1.156/27–28.

141/29 **ye be . . . worde.** John 15.3.

141/30–32 **cleane . . . al redye.** John 13.9–10.

142/6 **kepe hym from desperation.** Cf. Col. 3.21.

142/19–22 **And I fele . . . curynge.** Cf. CWM 8/2.787/31–32.

142/20–22 **frailtie . . . curynge.** Cf. CWM 8/2.787/31–32.

142/31–32 **pure . . . wrincle.** Eph. 5.27.

143/11–12 **eueri soule . . . moare frute.** Cf. John 15.2.

143/15–16 **he which . . . pure.** Cf. 1 John 3.3.

143/27 **leuen.** For the leaven of the Pharisees, cf. Matt. 16.6 and 11, Mark 8.15, Luke 12.1. For "the old leaven," cf. 1 Cor. 5.7.

144/4 **a satisfactory.** For another example of the construction of article plus adjective without noun, cf. 123/3–4n.

144/6–8 **nether . . . forgeuenesse.** Cf. Rom. 8.33–34.

144/8–9 **Shew . . . purgatory.** Cf. CWM 8/1.374/34–35 and *1 John* C3.

144/20 **a fleshli & a spiritual.** Cf. Rom. 8.5.

144/30 **beleueth . . . deuel.** Cf. Jas. 2.19.

145/3 **serueth god in the spirite.** Cf. Rom. 7.6.

145/4–5 **So that . . . persecucion.** Cf. 2 Tim. 3.12.

145/12–14 **Moses . . . a signe.** Cf. Exod. 4.1–9.

145/15 **euerlastinge testament.** Heb. 13.20.

145/18–19 **that were no where written.** As the subject of "were," supply "the necessary poyntes of the faith" (CWM 6/1.247/6) from the heading of *Dialogue,* Bk. 3, Ch. 1, to which this section responds.

146/2–3 **Euticus . . . window.** Cf. Acts 20.9–12.

146/2–4 **Euticus . . . recouer.** Cf. CWM 6/1.259/14–19.

146/5–8 **ye men . . . sounde.** Cf. Acts 3.12, 16.

146/12–13 **bilneyes . . . indifferent.** Cf. CWM 6/1.260/14–15. John Skelton wrote a verse satire against Thomas Arthur and Thomas Bilney, "A Replycacion Agaynst Certayne Yong Scolers Abjured of Late" (c1528), linking them to Wyclif (line 166) and Luther (lines 167, 266). The same poem names the four great Latin Fathers (lines 275–77) and defines *latria, hyperdulia,* and *dulia* (lines

282–91). For Skelton's attacks on Wolsey, cf. 55/16n. Tyndale makes passing references to their examination for heresy (168/ 5–6; *Prelates* H5). *Confutation* declares that Bilney made a last-minute recantation (CWM 8/1.518/26–36). More's *Apology,* published about Easter 1533, refers briefly to Bilney (CWM 9.93/39). Foxe (4.619–56) gives a long account of the career of Thomas Bilney, rejecting, as a Utopian fiction, More's assertion that Bilney abjured a second time before his death in August 1531. Foxe (4.621–23) briefly relates Arthur's examination for heresy and his recantation (OER 1.173–74).

146/14–16 **rewardes . . . righteous.** Cf. Deut. 16.19. Both 22/S1 and 146/S4 refer to Deut. 17. (TOT puts Deut. 16.18–22 at the beginning of Deut. Ch. 17.)

147/2–3 **the man . . . penaunce.** Cf. CWM 6/1.270/4–6.

147/6–7 **the mesinger . . . saye.** Cf. CWM 6/1.272/33–36.

147/10 **wilken and simken.** Cf. CWM 6/1.274/11–275/18. More as Mentor tells the Messenger a merry tale about a wager between Wilkin and Simkin. Like Tyndale, the Messenger scoffs at Simkin's sophistry, "Tut quod he this were a wyse inuencyon" (CWM 6/1.275/9). For another dialogue-within-a-dialogue, cf. 194/7–8n.

147/11 **Hunne.** For a fuller entry, cf. 168/21n.

147/13–14 **what . . . printes.** Cf. CWM 6/1.275/5–8.

147/15–16 **quod he . . . therto.** Cf. CWM 6/1.276/3–5. Tyndale does not observe that the flippant remark on the loss of Simkin's soul is spoken not by More as Mentor but by the Messenger.

147/19–20 **the church . . . open shame.** Cf. CWM 6/1.277/33–37.

147/22–23 **how . . . deedly synne.** Cf. CWM 6/1.279/8–10.

147/25–26 **open . . . out.** Cf. Matt. 18.17.

148/1 **prayer and fastynge.** Cf. Matt. 17.21.

148/4 **sweringe.** Cf. CWM 6/1.281/21ff. Tyndale makes no comment on *Dialogue* Bk. 3, Ch. 6 where More inveighs against the "proude periury and hye malycyous mynde" (CWM 6/1.280/12) of the heretic who refuses to abjure.

148/6–7 **no iudge . . . inconuenientes.** Cf. CWM 6/1.282/19– 26. More follows the norm of conciliar justice, where the accused must answer questions about an open crime probably committed.

For Tyndale's opposition to obliging the accused to testify against himself, cf. *Obedience* G4r–v. Thomas Hitton (112/12n) also made a case against self-incrimination: "It is against God's laws and good conscience, for any man to swear to shed his own blood, for so he should be a murderer of himself, and become guilty of his own death" (Foxe 8.713). Cf. Anne Richardson, "William Tyndale and the Bill of Rights," *William Tyndale and the Law,* Sixteenth Century Essays & Studies 25, ed. John A.R. Dick and Anne Richardson (Kirksville, MO: Sixteenth Century Journal, 1994) esp. 17–29.

148/22 **Tindale was confederatt with Luther.** Cf. CWM 6/1.288/ 20–21. Cf. Paul's protest that the newly baptized were not followers of Paul, Apollos, or Cephas but of Christ (1 Cor. 1.12–13, 3.4–7). In accusing him of being confederate with Luther, More twice calls Tyndale by his alias "Hychens" (CWM 6/1.288/13, 15), to suggest that Tyndale needs two names because he is two-faced. Tyndale's allusions in *Answer* highlight critical events from the middle years of Martin Luther (1483–1546). On 28 November 1518, Luther registered a notarized appeal from the pope to a general council (186/10 and n). Luther's books were banned (189/11) by *Exsurge Domine* on 5 June 1520 threatening excommunication, and by *Decet Romanum* on 3 January 1521 actually excommunicating him. From 6 March to 4 May 1521, Luther appeared at the Diet of Worms, relying on a safe-conduct pass (186/25–28, 187/ 14n). His speech before this assembly on 18 April 1521 was a notable occasion for proclaming the principle of *sola scriptura* (187/ 23). He distinguished between unlawful and lawful vows in the treatise *Judgment . . . concerning Monastic Vows* (1521–22), a position which foreshadowed his marriage in 1525 (189/19n). In keeping with his emphasis on human sinfulness, he declared in a sermon of 1524 that even Mary was a sinner (207/27–28n). In spring 1525, he wrote two treatises on the Peasants' Rebellion, *An Admonition to Peace* and *Against the Robbing and Murdering Hordes of Peasants* (188/13–22n). In December 1525, he answered Erasmus with *On the Bondage of the Will,* denying that free will can do anything of its own power to earn salvation (174/30n). In 1529 he revised his opposition of 1518 to a crusade against the Turks by approving a defensive war against them, *On War Against the Turk* (213/11–15n).

Cf. "Chronology" in Bainton 12–14; "Chronological Outline" in Oberman, *Luther* 355–63.

Although Tyndale denies More's charges of confederacy with Luther, he kept similarities of format between his NT and Luther's by putting Hebrews, James, Jude, and Revelation last (Daniell 110). Tyndale translated and expanded several works of Luther: preface to the 1522 NT (WA/DB 6.2–11; LW 35.357–62) as Prologue to the incomplete NT (Cologne, 1525) STC 2823, revised as *A path way into the holy scripture* (1536?) STC 24462; preface to the 1522 Epistle to the Romans (WA/DB 7.2–27; LW 35.365–80) as *A compendious introduccion, prologe or preface vn to the pistle off Paul to the Romayns* (Worms, 1526) STC 24438; sermon for the Ninth Sunday after Trinity, 1522 (WA 10/2.283–92; not in LW) as *The parable of the wicked mammon* (Antwerp, May 1528) STC 24454. For Tyndale's use of Luther's commentaries on the Lord's Prayer, cf. 72/18–19n.

Tyndale prefers Luther's devotion to the Bible to the actions of Fisher and Henry VIII. If Luther's burning of canon law amounts to the murder of the pope, then Fisher's burning of the NT amounts to the murder of Christ (*Obedience* I1). Tyndale even mocks the king's pride in his title of "Defender of the Faith" and criticizes his *Assertio* against Luther for subordinating Scripture to the pope (*Prelates* K4v–K5v). (JB)

Tyndale was not a minister or member of one of the Lutheran territorial churches, as these, for example, were represented at the imperial Diet of Augsburg in 1530. In at least two points of doctrine, Tyndale differs notably from Luther: on the role of consent to the law in justification; on the process by which the believer receives the benefit of the Lord's Supper, cf. 150/9n. Further, Tyndale did not espouse the great concern of Luther in his works of 1525–30 directed against Zwingli and others who denied the Real Presence of the body and blood of Christ in and with the elements of bread and wine in the Lord's Supper (179/12n). (JW)

148/25–26 **my translacion . . . the masse.** Cf. CWM 6/1.291/13–14. More refers to the poem of Barlowe and Roye (lines 710–18): Wolsey and Tunstall burnt Tyndale's NT (1526) because it destroyed the Mass. Later, writing to Erasmus, Ep. 2831, Chelsea, [June 1533], More associates Tyndale with Wyclif, who opposed transubstantiation, and contrasts him with Melanchthon, who taught consubstantiation (Allen 10.259/22–27; More, *Selected Letters* 179 and n5). Elizabeth McCutcheon is the first to realize that More here quotes Tyndale's letter to Frith in the Tower of London, which the authorities must have intercepted. Cf. "Prison Letters of More and Tyndale," WCS 244 and n6.

149/1 **xj.** Tyndale makes no comment on *Dialogue* Bk. 3, Ch. 10 (CWM 6/1.293/1–11), which claims that his NT has so many mistakes it would need to be retranslated in order to correct it.

149/2–3 **not defende . . . spiritualtie.** Cf. CWM 6/1.295/1–6. As in *Utopia* (CWM 4.229/34–231/4), More recommends ordaining fewer and better candidates (CWM 6/1.295/27–29).

149/4–5 **iff . . . might se.** Cf. John 4.20.

149/15–17 **Quid . . . I will deliuer him vn to you.** Matt. 26.15. Vulgate and Erasmus' 1516 NT both have *vobis eum tradam,* but Tyndale gives *tradam eum vobis.*

149/19–20 **the prayars of an evel preest profite not.** Cf. CWM 6/1.299/13–17. Tyndale agrees with this statement, which is reminiscent of the Wycliffite principle: "The prayer of a reprobate availeth no man" (Foxe 3.61). In his biographical portrait, Erasmus cautiously suggests that Colet agreed with "those who doubted whether a priest who was an open and notorious evil-liver can accomplish anything by his sacramental function." From Ep. 1211, To Justus Jonas, Anderlecht, 13 June 1521 (Allen 4.522/480–81; CWE 8.240/523–24). Cf. *Erasme: Vies de Jean Vitrier et de John Colet,* tr. André Godin (Angers: Editions Moreana, 1982) 69n462. Tyndale, who was ordained deacon at St. Paul's in 1515, may have heard Dean Colet preach there (1505–19), cf. 153/29–30n.

149/27–29 **the euell preest . . . the sacramentes.** Cf. CWM 6/1.299/9–13. Tyndale rejects More's defense of religious services from a corrupt clergy but would agree with another Lollard tenet: "That if a bishop or a priest be in mortal sin, he doth not ordain, consecrate, nor baptize" (Foxe 3.21).

150/9 **sacrificeth Christes body.** Here and at 178/11, Tyndale agrees with the rejection of Eucharistic sacrifice that Luther inaugurated in 1520 with his *Treatise on the New Testament* (WA 6.364–70; LW 35.93–100) and the section on the Lord's Supper in *Babylonian Captivity,* 1520 (WA 6.523–26; LW 36.51–57). In *The Misuse of the*

Mass, 1521 (WA 8.506–37; LW 36.162–98), Luther added to his arsenal of attack the Epistle to the Hebrews, to which Tyndale refers at 150/10. Where Luther emphasized hearing the testamentary words of Christ repeated by the celebrant, Tyndale stresses the visual impact of the gestures. (JW)

150/10 **Christ was offered once for all.** Cf. Heb. 10.12, 14.

150/12–17 **Now . . . only.** Cf. CWM 8/1.115/2–4.

150/32–33 **mules . . . vnderstondinge.** Cf. Ps. 32.9.

151/1 **Deacons . . . tyme.** Cf. CWM 6/1.300/29–31.

151/1–2 **For . . . the pore.** Cf. Acts 6.1–3. Tyndale explains the function of the *diakonos* in the early church here, cf. *Obedience* I8, *Prelates* B4v.

151/7 **prestes . . . multitude.** Cf. CWM 6/1.301/1–2.

151/10 **a man . . . synne.** More does not examine the coexistence of intellectual consent to the truth of faith with a life of sin in *Dialogue* Bk. 3, Ch. 12, but in Bk. 3, Ch. 1 he discusses Noah's contemporaries and his own, who had faith but lacked charity, cf. 70/1n and CWM 6/1.252/22–24 on unformed and formed faith.

151/14–15 **S. Ihon . . . vntrulye.** Cf. 1 John 4.20.

151/22 **few . . . tyme.** Cf. CWM 6/1.301/17–19.

151/24 **the lawes of the church.** The proliferation of laws by local churches, regional and ecumenical councils, and the papacy led to successive codifications. The collection by Gratian, *Concordia discordantium canonum* (c1140), had wide influence in the Western Church and was supplemented by further collections before the Reformation (NCE 4.348).

Luther's colleagues organized a ceremonial burning of canon law books at the Elster Gate of Wittenberg on 10 December 1520. Luther tossed into the flames the copy of the papal bull *Exsurge Domine* that he had received on 10 October and that gave him sixty days to recant the erroneous teachings listed therein. Cf. Luther's account in *Why the Books of the Popes and his Disciples Were Burned* (WA 7.162–82; LW 31.383–95). (JW)

For the medieval British church, William Lyndwood (1375?–1446), Bishop of St. David's in Wales, compiled *Provinciale, (seu Constitutiones Angliae),* a digest with gloss of the constitutions of the province of Canterbury from 1207 to 1443, first printed at Oxford in 1483 (cf. CWM 6/2.691). More as Mentor to the Messenger

cites from this collection the constitution of 1409 requiring episcopal permission to translate the Bible into English (cf. 167/21–
22n; CWM 6/1.316/16–17).

151/24–25 **if . . . better.** Cf. CWM 6/1.302/4–7. Tyndale changes
More's clause "Luther & Tyndall wolde haue all broken" (6/1.302/
4–5) into "Luther wold haue burnt" (151/25).

152/2–4 **rageth . . . tindale.** Cf. CWM 6/1.303/14–19. More calls
Tyndale's *Obedience* a "frantyke boke" (6/1.303/18). Specifically
scoffing at Tyndale's moral integrity and literary ability, More
claims that Tyndale's books "be nothyng ellys in effecte but the
worst heresyes pycked out of Luthers workes and Luthers worst
wordys translated by Tyndall and put forth in Tyndalls owne
name" (6/1.303/15–18).

152/10–12 **a younge man . . . had.** Cf. 1 Tim. 4.12.

152/13 **preferre the maried.** Cf. 1 Tim. 3.2, 12. Paul assumes that
bishops and deacons will be married, although he himself was
called to celibacy, cf. 1 Cor. 7.7.

152/23–24 **neuer . . . now.** For More's satiric reference to a newly
discovered commandment for priests to marry, cf. CWM
6/1.304/3–7.

152/24 **S. Hierom.** Jerome admonished Oceanus for interpreting 1
Tim. 3.2 in a restrictive manner, i.e., as excluding from ordination
those who had been married before Baptism and then, after Baptism and as widowers, married once more. Against this exclusion,
Jerome appeals to the widespread practice of admitting such remarried men to orders. For Jerome, to take account of their first
marriage is tantamount to questioning the baptismal re-creation
of the person. Cf. Ep. 69, To Oceanus (AD 397), Par. 2–5 (PL
22.654–59; CSEL 54.680–89; 2NPNF 6.142–45). Tyndale takes
Oceanus as representing a Roman practice of excluding the remarried, which More had claimed was universal, based on the patristic interpretation of 1 Tim. 3.2 (CWM 6/1.304/13–305/30).
The facts pointed out by Jerome undercut More's case for an early Christian preference for a celibate clergy. (JW)

152/26–27 **clargye . . . two wyues.** Cf. 1 Tim. 3.2.

152/31 **misteries of wekednesse.** Translation of *mysterium iniquitatis,*
2 Thess. 2.7.

152/32 **he that hath .x. wiues hath one wife.** Cf. CWM 6/1.305/

23–26. More's quibble recalls Aristotle's teaching that one is not a number but the basis of number in *Metaphysics,* Bk. 14, 1088a. Thanks to William A. Wallace OP for this reference. Cf. Tilley O54: "One is no number, mayds are nothing then, / Without the sweet societie of men," *Hero and Leander,* Bk. 1, lines 255–56, spelling as in Gill (Vol. 1, 1987). Cf. also "Thou single wilt prove none," Sonnet 8, line 14; "Among a number one is reckoned none," Sonnet 136, line 8, in *Shakespeare's Sonnets,* ed. Katherine Duncan-Jones, Arden Shakespeare, Third Series (London: Nelson, 1997).

153/2–3 **vnto him that hath no helpe / is there one helpe / to loke for no helpe.** This is Tyndale's version of *Una salus victis nullam sperare salutem,* "The one safety of the conquered is to hope for no safety" (*Aeneid* 2.354); John Bartlett, *Familiar Quotations,* 15th ed. (Boston: Little, Brown, 1980) p. 105, no. 2. Elizabeth McCutcheon calls attention to the quotation and gloss on Virgil in Tyndale's second letter to Frith in the Tower (cMay 1533): "[T]o look for no man's help, bringeth the help of God to them that seem to be overcome in the eyes of the hypocrites" (Foxe 5.132) in "Prison Letters of More and Tyndale," WCS 248 and n12.

153/5–6 **he that . . . preest.** Cf. CWM 6/1.305/7–9.

153/7–8 **if . . . aftir marie.** Cf. CWM 6/1.310/8–9. More does not mention that Greek canon law forbids a priest to remarry after his wife dies, but he does acknowledge that Greek tradition prohibits an unmarried man from marrying once he has been ordained. In 692 the provincial council of Trullo affirmed that married deacons and priests could keep their wives (Canon 13) (FJO 159, 163; 2NPNF 14.371), but that the wife of one chosen to become a bishop must retire to a monastery (Canon 48) (FJO 160; 2NPNF 14.388). The Latin Church recognizes the customs of the Oriental Churches regarding a married clergy, cf. Gratian, *Decretum,* Part 1, Dist. 31, Ch. 14 (CIC 1.115).

153/8 **iff he burnt.** Cf. 1 Cor. 7.9.

153/12–13 **kyngdome . . . drynke.** Rom. 14.17.

153/14 **kepinge of the commaundementes.** Cf. Matt. 19.17.

153/15–17 **as meate . . . degrees.** Cf. CWM 8/1.74/11–12.

153/21–22 **Paules lernynge . . . loue his neyboure as him selfe.** Cf. Rom. 13.9–10, Gal. 5.14.

153/29–30 **if I be made prest.** Perhaps because he was a fugitive in a foreign country, Tyndale himself never married, although More taunts him with such an intention, cf. CWM 8/1.191/28–33. Mozley (21n) discovered the record of Tyndale's ordination as a subdeacon on 10 June 1514 in Hereford. Andrew J. Brown discovered the records of Tyndale's ordination as a deacon on 24 March 1515 in St. Paul's, London, and as a priest on Holy Saturday, 7 April 1515, in the hospital of St. Thomas Acon, London. Cf. *William Tyndale on Priests and Preachers* (London: Inscriptor Imprints, 1996) 16–17.

153/30 **aftir burne.** Cf. 1 Cor. 7.9.

153/33–154/3 **some shuld . . . thankes.** Cf. 1 Tim. 4.1, 3.

154/4 **dyspensacyons.** In canon law, a dispensation is an administrative act suspending an obligation or prohibition laid down by church law. The law is not revoked, but for the good of the subject permission is given to act contrary to the law, cf. 38/20n. Late medieval church authorities, both in Rome and in many dioceses, gained part of their income from fees for the dispensations they gave. The most widely discussed dispensation in Tyndale's day had been granted in 1509 when Julius II (pope, 1503–13) suspended the marriage impediment existing between Prince Henry and Catherine, the widow of Henry's brother Arthur. (JW)

154/8–9 **misteries . . . congregacion.** Cf. Eph. 5.32. *Answer* has "misteries or secret properties" (154/8); NT has "great secrete" (Wallis 407/21; TNT 286G).

154/10–28 **That is . . . mariage.** Luther had described the union realized in justification between Christ and the believer as the mutual sharing, by exchanging title, goods, and possessions, much as in matrimony, *Sermo de duplici iustitia,* 1519 (WA 2.145; not in LW); *Freedom of a Christian,* 1520 (WA 7.25f; LW 31.351f). (JW)

154/11–12 **misteries . . . christ.** Cf. Col. 2.2–3. *Answer* has "misteries and secrete benefites"; NT has "mistery" (Wallis 421/1; TNT 296A).

154/29 **represent vs thys significacion.** Cf. "represent vs this" (155/10). In both cases, "vs" is indirect object.

155/8–11 **then . . . mans wyfe.** Cf. CWM 8/1.87/25. In this section on Matrimony in *Confutation,* More addresses *Obedience* (I7v) on a married clergy.

155/20 **common hores . . . Idoles.** Cf. Jer. 3.1, Ezek. 16.15–35, Hos. 4.15.

155/22–23 **lande . . . wife.** Cf. Matt. 22.30, Mark 12.25, Luke 20.35.

155/24–25 **hath . . . a waye.** Cf. 2 Tim. 3.5.

155/28–33 **And therfore . . . of Christe.** Tyndale interprets "the husband of one wyfe" (1 Tim. 3.2; Wallis 443/6; TNT 310A) as St. Paul's positive prescription for those selected for the office of bishop or priest. More had taken the text as a temporary concession amid the circumstances of the nascent church and as excluding those who had remarried as widowers (CWM 6/1.303/24–308/20). But Tyndale follows Luther and Zwingli in their prescriptive interpretation. For Luther, cf. *To the Christian Nobility,* 1520 (WA 6.440–43; LW 44.175–79) and *Babylonian Captivity,* 1520 (WA 6.557; LW 36.101f). Zwingli cited 1 Tim. 3.2 in 1522 as an apostolic text that stands in the way of compulsory celibacy, both in his *Supplicatio* to Bishop Hugo of Constance and in his *Freundliche Bitte* to the confederates of Zürich. Cf. *Sämtliche Werke* 1.205, 231f; Huldreich Zwingli, *Selected Works,* ed. Samuel Macauley Jackson (Philadelphia: U of Pennsylvania P, 1901) 35. (JW)

155/30–32 **one wife . . . liuynge.** Cf. 1 Tim. 3.2.

156/1–3 **wedowes . . . behauoure.** Cf. 1 Tim. 5.9–10. Tyndale discusses the services performed by sixty–year old widows in the early church (*Prelates* B4v). After Louis II of Hungary (king, 1516–26) died fleeing from the Turks at Mohács, his twenty-year-old widow Mary of Austria declined to remarry, contrary to the counsel of Erasmus in *On the Christian Widow,* 1529 (LB 5.723C–766E; CWE 66.184–257). Instead, from 1531 to 1555 she served as Regent of the Netherlands for her brother Charles V. Tyndale was executed under her adminstration by a decree that Foxe (5.127) alleged had been enacted at the Diet of Augsburg.

156/5–6 **mocke . . . one man.** Cf. CWM 6/1.306/32–307/4.

156/6 **wedowe . . . one man.** Cf. 1 Tim. 5.9.

156/19–20 **It was . . . fete.** Cf. 1 Tim. 5.10.

156/21 **founde . . . congregacion.** 1 Tim. 5.16.

156/21–22 **destitute of frendes.** Cf. 1 Tim. 5.5.

156/24–25 **But . . . vnchastite.** Cf. 1 Tim. 5.11–12.

156/29–31 **seruaunte . . . fete.** Cf. 1 Tim. 5.10.

157/2–3 **when . . . wyll.** Cf. Rom. 7.3.

157/6 **weake Christen.** Cf. Rom. 14.1–2.

157/7–8 **he . . . god.** Cf. Rom. 13.8–9.

157/13–15 **feare . . . spoken of.** Cf. 1 Tim. 5.11–12.

157/17–18 **More . . . chaste.** Cf. CWM 6/1.308/21–24.

157/22–23 **some . . . doctrine** Cf. 1 Tim. 5.11–12.

157/25–26 **But . . . husbandes.** Cf. 1 Tim. 5.14.

157/30 **prests at .xxiiij.** Thanks to Germain Marc'hadour for pointing out that twenty-four was the minimum age for ordination to the priesthood with its obligation of celibacy, cf. 163/8.

158/8–9 **In persecucion . . . chast.** Cf. 1 Cor. 7.26.

158/12–13 **prestes wiues . . . almanye.** Cf. CWM 6/1.311/10–11.

158/16 **the church . . . chastite.** Cf. CWM 6/1.311/23–24, 312/35–37.

158/20–21 **chastite . . . made.** Cf. CWM 6/1.311/13–16.

158/26–27 **men . . . brethern.** Cf. Rom. 14.13.

158/29 **the pope had gott the emproures swerde.** In *Prelates* (B7v), Tyndale mistakenly asserts that Boniface III (pope, 607) backed by the Byzantine Emperor Phocas ordered German priests to put away their wives. Concern for the alienation of church property and a renewal of the monastic spirit by the Cluniac reform (910) led in the later 10c and 11c to a renewed effort to enforce celibacy by popes and regional councils. For example, Nicholas II (pope, 1058–61) at a Lateran synod (1059) decreed priestly celibacy but shifted the papal alliance from the emperor to the Normans in Southern Italy. Gregory VII (pope, 1073–85) at Roman synods (1074, 1075) repeated these decrees but relied on papal legates to enforce them. He is noted also for his conflict with Emperor Henry IV over lay nomination of bishops.

158/32–159/1 **we shuld . . . beare.** Cf. Acts 15.10.

159/2 **M. More . . . dyd.** Cf. CWM 6/1.105/4–7.

159/7–8 **The pope . . . wales.** During the first half of the 12c, the four Welsh sees (Llandaff, St. David's, Bangor, and St. Asaph) pledged their obedience to Canterbury. After the last Celtic Prince of Wales was killed in 1283, both Edward I (king, 1272–1307) and the Archbishop of Canterbury visited the country the next year. During the first decade of the 15c, a Welsh rebellion against Henry IV (king, 1399–1413) was led by Owen Glendower, who offered to recognize the anti-pope in return for establishing Wales as an independent ecclesiastical province with St. David's as its metropolitan see. The Lancastrians harshly repressed this revolt, thus further alienating Tyndale, who already blamed them for the murder of Richard II (king, 1377–99) and the persecution of the Lollards. See Glanmor Williams 2–3, 41–44, 225–28.

159/10–19 **And yet . . . spiritualtye.** Tyndale argues that the laity should have given their consent to the imposition of celibacy because of their rightful concern for the virtue of their priests and the chastity of their womenfolk. He argues in a manner akin to the well-known procedural rule of medieval canon law that what affects all should be discussed and approved by all. Yves Congar showed the broad span of applications made of this norm adopted from the Code of Justinian (2d ed., AD 531) even by popes as conscious of their own authority as Innocent III (pope, 1198–1216) and Boniface VIII (pope, 1294–1303). See "Quod omnes tangit, ab omnibus tractari et approbari debet," *Revue historique de droit français* 36 (1958) 210–59; rpt. as Study III in *Droit ancien et structures ecclésiales* (London: Variorum, 1982). More recently, Constantin Fasolt has treated William Durant the Younger's appeal to the principle in his *Tractatus de modo generalis concilii celebrandi* (1311), as requiring consultation with those who would be affected by innovations changing the already existing laws governing their lives and action. See "*Quod omnes tangit, ab omnibus approbari debet:* the Words and the Meaning," in *In Iure Veritas,* Festschrift Schafer Williams, ed. Steven Bowman (U of Cincinnati School of Law, 1991). (JW)

159/22–23 **Paul . . . ministre.** Cf. 1 Tim. 5.11–12.

159/29 **parlamentes.** Henry VIII summoned nine parliaments during his reign. As Lord Chancellor, Archbishop Warham successfully persuaded the Commons in 1512 to grant Henry 127,000 pounds for the invasion of France. His successor Cardinal Wolsey asked the Commons in 1523 for 800,000 pounds for the invasion of Scotland and France but settled for 136,256 pounds. More as Speaker of the House assisted in the bargaining process and re-

ceived a bonus of 100 pounds from a grateful Wolsey. More himself served as Lord Chancellor during the first three sessions of the
Reformation Parliament, furthering much secular business but remaining aloof from the king's marital problems. Cf. Jennifer
Loach, *Parliament under the Tudors* (Oxford: Clarendon, 1991) x,
58–61. In *Supplication of Souls* (1529), More complains that the
king intimidates both Lords and Commons (CWM 7.140/6–
141/21 and nn).

A member of the king's council since 1531, and as rising minister
from 1532, Thomas Cromwell (c1485–1540) drafted bills and lob-
bied Parliament to approve major legislation affecting the church
in England, e.g.: Act for the Conditional Restraint of Annates,
March 1532, 23 Henry VIII, Ch. 20 (*Statutes* 3.385–88); Act in Restraint of Appeals to Rome, April 1533, 24 Henry VIII, Ch. 12
(*Statutes* 3.427–29); Act Confirming the Submission of the Clergy,
March 1534, 25 Henry VIII, Ch. 19 (*Statutes* 3.460–61); Act Re-
straining the Payment of Annates, March 1534, 25 Henry VIII, Ch.
20 (*Statutes* 3.462–64); Act of Succession, March 1534, 25 Henry
VIII, Ch. 22 (*Statutes* 3.471–74); Act of Supremacy, November
1534, 26 Henry VIII, Ch. 1 (*Statutes* 3.492); Oath of Succession
denying papal primacy, November 1534, 26 Henry VIII, Ch. 2
(*Statutes* 3.492–93). For the early history of annates in England, cf.
138/7n. Cromwell was not named vicegerent for spiritual affairs
until cJanuary 1535. See G.R. Elton, *Reform and Reformation: England, 1509–1558* (Cambridge: Harvard UP, 1977). Regarding the
Act of Succession of March 1534, which rejected papal validation
of Henry's marriage to Catherine, More explains that he came to
believe that papal primacy was instituted by God after reading the
king's *Assertio.* Cf. Ep. 199, To Thomas Cromwell, Chelsea, 5
March <1534> (More, *Correspondence* 498/200–499/247).

Tyndale disapproved of Wolsey's successful efforts in 1523 to move
Parliament to levy high taxes (cf. *Obedience* E7). As an opponent of
Antichrist, he must have applauded the acts severing financial and
legal ties with the papacy. Tyndale was guilty of treason, however,
for rejecting Henry's marriage with Anne Boleyn, until it was an-
nulled on 17 May 1536, two days before her execution; cf. Mac-
Culloch, *Cranmer* 158–59.

159/30 **generall counsels.** For Julius II at Lateran V, cf. 97/26n.

160/1–2 **conceaue . . . child.** Cf. Jas. 1.15.

160/22 **syluer sylogismoses.** Good alliteration but not a figure of logic.

161/18 **bynd where god lowseth.** Cf. Matt. 16.19, 18.18.

161/23 **helpe . . . holpe.** Cf. Matt. 7.12, Luke 6.31.

161/25–162/8 **As if . . . breake it.** As the laws of the church are limited, so also is the binding power of vows, especially that of celibacy, as Luther had stated in *To the Christian Nobility,* 1520 (WA 6.441–43; LW 44.177f). For further discussion of the vow of chastity, cf. 189/19n. (JW)

161/29–30 **I maye not . . . it selfe.** Cf. CWM 6/1.312/21–29.

162/19–22 **But . . . lawes.** Cf. 1 Cor. 10.13. This promise of God's help, when the remedy of marriage was not available, must have consoled Tyndale in exile.

162/22–23 **to loue Gods law.** Cf. Ps. 119.97.

162/23 **electe.** Cf. Rom. 8.33. NT uses "chosen" instead of "electe" (Wallis 331/13; TNT 233F).

162/25–26 **euery man . . . or no.** Cf. CWM 6/1.311/21–22.

162/29–30 **those . . . Moloch.** For the prohibition of human sacrifice, cf. Jer. 32.35. For the offering of children by Ahaz, cf. 2 Kings 16.3, and by Manasseh, cf. 2 Kings 21.6.

162/32–33 **testament . . . bloude.** Cf. Heb. 9.14–16, 10.29, 13.20–21. Aquinas expounds the idea of "testament" (*Summa* III, Q. 78, Art. 3, Reply to Obj. 3–4).

163/11–13 **When . . . age.** Cf. 1 Tim. 5.11–15.

163/19–20 **More . . . vnmaried.** Cf. CWM 6/1.311/32–34.

163/21–22 **Christes . . . ner drinke.** Cf. Rom. 14.17.

163/23–26 **seruinge . . . then to eate.** Cf. Rom. 14.15, 20.

163/28–29 **with out . . . commaundementes.** Cf. 1 Cor. 7.2.

163/30 **serue a mans neyboure.** Cf. 1 Cor. 7.32–34. Tyndale's NT relates both celibacy and marriage to service of the neighbor in the sidenote to 1 Cor. 7.26 (Wallis 355; TNT 250).

164/1 **prestes to liue chaste.** Tyndale corrects the multiple misunderstandings underlying More's claim that continence befits a sacramental minister (CWM 6/1.311/34–312/1, 312/26–29). Marital sex is more holy than numerous ritual objects. Matt. 15.17–20 gives a new basis for defilement in the disposition of the heart. Regarding the Eucharist, it is traditional doctrine that the hands and teeth do not affect Christ, whose natural body can no longer suffer. In any case, the law of celibacy occasions sins that More should see as more defiling than marital sexuality. (JW)

The laity were expected to abstain from sexual intercourse for three days before receiving Communion. Because of the emphasis on the transcendence of the sacrament, as well as the practical implications for their marital relationship, most received only on Easter, cf. Marshall 159–63, 185.

164/1–2 **prestes ... sacramentes.** Cf. CWM 6/1.311/35–312/1 and 6/1.312/26–29.

164/6–8 **handes ... vnwashe.** Cf. Matt. 15.17–20.

164/10 **christes natural body.** Tyndale rejects an excessively materialistic understanding of the Eucharist, such as Berengar of Tours (c999–1088) was made to affirm in 1059, "I believe that the bread and wine which are laid on the altar are after the consecration not only a sacrament but also the true body and blood of our Lord Jesus Christ, and they are physically taken up and broken in the hands of the priest and crushed by the teeth of the faithful, not only sacramentally, but in truth" (quoted by Lanfranc, *Liber de corpore et sanguine domini,* (c1059–62) (PL 150.410–11, tr. by Rubin 19–20; Latin in 20n49). The crude philosophical realism of this formula was modified by a Lateran synod of 1079, which introduced the term "substance" into the account of the Eucharistic presence (Neuner-Dupuis 1501). Aquinas quotes the earlier statement and comments, "[T]he breaking and the crushing with the teeth is to be referred to the sacramental species, under which the body of Christ truly is" (*Summa* III, Q. 77, Art. 7, Reply to Obj. 3). (JW)

164/29. **ensample of the hethen.** Cf. CWM 6/1.312/1–7.

164/32 **turned ... image.** Cf. Rom. 1.23.

165/8–9 **saint Micael weyenge the soules.** Late medieval English churches were frequently decorated with paintings of the Archangel Michael holding the scale of justice with devils in one pan and souls in the other. The latter are helped by Mary, who adds her rosary beads for good measure. Tyndale would probably object to this image for depicting justification by works and the intercession of the saints. Cf. Duffy 319 and Plate 122 and Brigden 21n73. In Duffy Plate 121, a devil pulls on one pan while Mary weighs down the other.

165/17–18 **law . . . whore.** Cf. Exod. 20.14, Deut. 5.18, Heb. 13.4.

165/25–26 **And to . . . for displeasure.** Cf. CWM 6/1.311/32–34.

165/30 **gelded men.** Although found in *1531* and *1573,* Walter omits 165/S3: "Whether it were best that prestes were gelded."

166/5 **haue layd virgens in their beddes.** Leaders in the early church denounced the custom of "syneisakitism" or the cohabitation of a celibate man and woman. Some indeed slept together, ideally only in the literal sense. If they would not separate, Cyprian ordered them excommunicated. Cf. To Pomponius, Bishop of Dionysiana [sic] (AD c249) (Ep. 62 in PL 4.364–72; Ep. 4 in CSEL 3B.17–26; Ep. 61 in ANF 5.356–58). In Canon 3, Nicea I in 325 prohibited clerics from living with women who were not close female relatives, but its decree was not everywhere obeyed. Cf. Gratian, *Decretum,* Part 1, Dist. 32, Ch. 16 (CIC 1.121; 2NPNF 14.11). Jerome deplores the practice in his famous letter describing corrupt Roman society, To Eustochium, Ep. 22 (AD 384), Par. 14: "One house holds them and one chamber. They often occupy the same bed, and yet they call us suspicious if we fancy anything amiss." (PL 22.403; CSEL 54.162; 2NPNF 6.27). Also in the late 4c, John Chrysostom wrote two treatises against *mulieres subintroductae: Against Those Men Cohabiting with Virgins* and *On the Necessity of Guarding Virginity* (PG 47.495–532), in *Jerome, Chrysostom, and Friends: Essays and Translations,* tr. Elizabeth A. Clark, Studies in Women and Religion 1 (New York: Mellen, 1979) 164–246.

Robert of Arbrissel (c1055–1117), a wandering preacher, slept among his female followers, for which he was rebuked by Marbod, Bishop of Rennes, Ep. 6 (PL 171.1481) and Geoffrey, Abbot at Vendome, Bk. 4, Ep. 47 (PL 157.182). Cf. Dyan Elliott, *Spiritual Marriage: Sexual Abstinence in Medieval Wedlock* (Princeton UP, 1993) 111n68. In 1100 Robert founded the abbey of Fontevrault on the Loire, where Eleanor of Aquitaine was later confined after she supported the revolt of her sons against Henry II. Separate houses for men and for women on the same land were jointly ruled by an abbess, as were Bridgittine monasteries such as Syon. Robert was beatified but never canonized. Cf. NCE 12.528–29; Jacqueline Smith, "Robert of Arbrissel: *Procurator Mulierum,*" in *Medieval Women,* ed. Derek Baker (Oxford: Blackwell for the Ecclesiastical Historical Society, 1978) 175–84; D.D.R. Owen, *Eleanor of Aquitaine: Queen and Legend* (Oxford: Blackwell, 1993) 9.

166/8–19 **And when . . . measure.** More claimed an OT precedent for celibacy in the temporary continence of Temple priests (cf. CWM 6/1.312/12–17). Lev. 22.4 forbade the sons of Aaron to serve in the tabernacle if they had a skin disease, touched a corpse or had a nocturnal emission. Tyndale answers that the code of ritual purity laid down in Lev. 21–22 makes no mention of marital continence. Further, Zechariah may have been away from his wife during his Temple duty (Luke 1.23), but the reason was simply that their home was not in Jerusalem. (JW)

166/15–16 **But . . . prayar.** Cf. 1 Cor. 7.5.

166/18–19 **forboden . . . ministred.** Cf. Lev. 10.9.

166/20 **christ . . . chastite.** Cf. CWM 6/1.312/21–29. Tyndale omits More's clause, "whiche was . . . borne of a vyrgyn" (CWM 6/1.312/22), but he affirms Mary's perpetual virginity although he does not believe that this doctrine is necessary for salvation, cf. 31/14, 95/4–5nn. (JW)

166/21–22 **other . . . neyboures.** Cf. 1 Cor. 7.5.

166/28–30 **Pannutius . . . generall counsel.** Socrates Scholasticus reported that Paphnutius, a celibate bishop of Upper Thebes, persuaded members of Nicea I to allow bishops, presbyters, and deacons who were already married to keep their wives; those unmarried at ordination should remain so. Cf. his *Ecclesiastical History* 1.11 (PG 67.101–4; 2NPNF 2.18). Sozomen added subdeacons to this list. Cf. his parallel *Ecclesiastical History* 1.23 (PG 67. 925–26; 2NPNF 2.256). Socrates' account is now seen as legendary. Cf. E. Jombart and E. Herman, "Célebat des clercs," *Dictionnaire de Droit canonique,* 3 (1942) 134, 147f; Georg Denzler, *Das Papstum und der Amtszölibat,* 2 vols. (Stuttgart: Hiersemann, 1973–76), 1.9–11. (JW)

166/30–31 **M. More . . . twise.** Tyndale comments on the irony that the English bishops commissioned More, a twice-married layman, to defend the clergy. While More addressed the laity in English, Fisher wrote in Latin, *Sacri sacerdotii defensio contra Lutherum* of 1525 (Surtz xvii, 329–30). More himself acknowledged, "I am all redy marryed twyse / & therfore neuer can be preste" (CWM 6/1.53/10–12). Tyndale would prefer that each person serve Christ as he can, married or celibate (cf. PS 3.165n2).

In the *Obedience,* Tyndale pursues the complications imposed by canon law on marriage. He criticizes its rules governing marriage among those related by spiritual kindred (L3) and the entrance of a married man into a religious order (D3v, cf. PS 1.171n2). As such decretals complicate marriage, they also muddle pastoral affairs. Since God gave temporal kings the swords necessary to punish all evil-doers equally, the clergy ought to set an example for the laity by subjecting themselves to the king's governance and ought not to desire their sins to go unpunished (*Obedience* E1, cf. PS 1.178n1). Tyndale also confronts the issues of taxation of the clergy (*Obedience* E1, cf. PS 1.179n2), the sacraments (*Obedience* M5), and ordination (*Obedience* M5). Finally, calling into question popish authority and the body of canon law simultaneously, Tyndale criticizes the papal office for writing its laws to stand above all others (*Obedience* T4v). (JB)

167/6 **vnchaste . . . awne chast.** Tyndale pretends to make a verbal slip from "unchaste" to "own chaste" here and in *Matthew* 03.

167/7 **necke verse.** The ability to read a passage in Latin, usually the first verse of the *Miserere* (Ps. 51.1 in KJV), enabled a man to claim trial in an ecclesiastical court. There, the accused faced harsh confinement in a bishop's prison instead of death by hanging. To curb multiple appeals to clerical privilege, a statute of 1488–89 decreed that a literate man who was a first-time offender should suffer branding on the left thumb: "M" for murder or "T" for theft, 4 Henry VII, Ch. 13 (*Statutes* 2.538). In 1598 Ben Jonson escaped hanging for killing a fellow actor, Gabriel Spencer, in a duel. Cf. David Riggs, *Ben Jonson: A Life* (Cambridge: Harvard UP, 1989) 49–53. Benefit of clergy was finally abolished in 1827. Cf. Leona C. Gabel, *Benefit of Clergy in England in the Later Middle Ages,* Smith College Studies in History 14.1–4 (1928–29; New York: Octagon, 1969) 124.

167/8–10 **And finally . . . displeasures.** *Dialogue* Bk. 3, Ch. 13, with its exaltation of celibacy, provoked Tyndale to many pages of rebuttal (152/1–167/10).

167/12–14 **Wicleffe . . . liues.** Cf. CWM 6/1.315/6–8. The argument turns to Wyclif's influence on Jan Hus (c1372–1415), whose treatise *De ecclesia* (c1413) emphasized the spiritual rather than the juridical nature of the church. Notwithstanding a safe-conduct pass, he was condemned and burnt at the stake by the Council of Constance. Papally sanctioned "crusades" against the Hussites by Emperor Sigismund met one defeat after another between 1420 and 1434. Cf. Karl August Fink in Jedin and Dolan 4.447–48, 457–59, 476. (JW)

167/18–19 **the true kynge . . . a false.** Without naming him, Tyndale describes Richard II as "A kinge that is soft as sylke and effeminate . . ." (*Obedience* E1v). Thanks to David Daniell for this identification. Tyndale upholds the legitimacy of Richard II (king, 1377–99) and opposes the Lancastrian kings Henry IV (king, 1399–1413), Henry V (king, 1413–22) and Henry VI (king, 1422–61). According to Tyndale, orthodox prelates opposed Richard and supported Henry (*Prelates* F3v–F4v). Here the reformer claims that Richard was slain because he supported the Wycliffites and Henry was crowned because he resisted them. Later, Tyndale repeats his assertion that Richard was the rightful king (213/4–7; *Matthew* f4v), whose murder prepared the way for three illegitimate rulers (*1 John* H7).

167/21–22 **scripture . . . in englysh.** An outline history of the translation of the Vulgate into English begins in the 8c with Bede, who translated probably only the first six chapters of the Gospel of John. Alfred the Great (king, 871–99) is traditionally associated with a prose translation of Psalms 1–50; a later author made a verse translation of the remaining psalms. In the mid-10c a gloss in the Northumbrian dialect was added to the Lindisfarne Gospels and another in the Mercian dialect to the Rushworth Gospels. In the early 11c, Aelfric, Abbot of Eynsham near Oxford, made abridged translations of the Pentateuch and other books of the Old Testament. In the same era, the anonymous *West-Saxon Gospels* appeared. After the Norman Conquest, the literate laity

were mainly French-speaking for the next three hundred years.
But by the mid-14c Richard Rolle translated the whole Psalter
into Middle English. Cf. Geoffrey Shepherd, "English Versions of
the Scriptures before Wyclif," in *Cambridge History of the Bible,* Vol.
2, *The West from the Fathers to the Reformation,* ed. G.W.H. Lampe
(Cambridge UP, 1969) 362–87.

167/21–23 **The constitucion of the bisshopes . . . approued it.** Cf.
CWM 6/1.315/27–35. In the late 14c, the followers of John Wyclif
twice translated the whole Vulgate into English: "Wyclif A," a literal translation after 1382, and "Wyclif B," a more idiomatic one
after 1387. In response, Thomas Arundel, Archbishop of Canterbury, and his clergy promulgated the Constitutions of Oxford, of
which the seventh forbad unauthorized translations of the Bible
into English, *Ne quis texta S. scripturae transferrat in linguam Angli-
canum,* 14 January 1409 [New Style], 10 Henry IV (Wilkins
3.317). Nevertheless, many manuscripts circulated, cf. Foxe 3.245
and CWM 6/2.684. Cf. Henry Hargreaves, "The Wycliffite Versions," in *Cambridge History of the Bible,* 2.387–415, esp. 392, 399,
409; CWM 6/2.684. In 1517 Lady Alice Danvers gave a copy of
the first version to the Bridgittine monastery at Syon. Earlier,
Henry VI had presented a copy of the second version, without
heretical prologues or glosses, to the Carthusian monastery at
Sheen. More might have seen both.

Although his greatest work was a new Latin translation of the NT
from the original Greek, Erasmus vigorously defended vernacular
translations of Scripture to be read by all, even uneducated men,
women, and non-Christians. Cf. "Paraclesis," Holborn 142/10–19;
Desiderius Erasmus: Christian Humanism and the Reformation, tr.
John C. Olin (New York: Harper & Row, 1965) 96–97. This passage contains the wish of the Latin scholar carried out by the
English translator: *Utinam hinc ad stivam aliquid decantet agricola
. . . ;* "Would that, as a result, the farmer sing some portion of
them at the plow . . ." (Holborn 142/21; Olin 97). Tyndale later
declared, "If God spare my life, ere many years I will cause a boy
that driveth the plough shall know more of the scripture than
thou dost" (Mozley 34, paraphrasing the indirect discourse in
Foxe 5.117). In *1 John* (A7r–v), Tyndale defends the fidelity of his

translations and offers as authentic interpretations his *Introduction to Romans, Pathway, Exposition of 1 John.*

On 24 October 1526, Cuthbert Tunstall, Bishop of London, ordered the confiscation of Tyndale's unauthorized NT (Foxe 4.667). Several days later he preached at St. Paul's while some copies were burned. Tyndale deplores the Constitutions of Oxford, which bar the laity from the vernacular Scripture (*Obedience* A2v), but he promotes their access to it (*Obedience* B4). Cf. Deanesly passim; S.L. Greenslade, "English Versions of the Bible, A.D. 1525–1611," in *Cambridge History of the Bible,* Vol. 3, *The West from the Reformation to the Present Day,* ed. S.L. Greenslade (Cambridge UP, 1963) 141–70.

167/30–31 **parlament . . . not be in englysh.** On 22 June 1530, Tyndale's NT (1526) and Pentateuch (1530) were banned because they were supposedly "corruptly translated." After consulting with prelates and theologians, the king decided to continue to rely on preachers to explain the Scriptures to the common people, and to postpone the making of a vernacular translation: "[H]is highness intendeth to provide that the Holy Scripture shall by great, learned and Catholic persons [be] translated into the English tongue, if it shall then seem to his grace convenient so to be" (TRP no. 129, 1.196). In 1531 a bill was drafted "for appointing certain lords to hear opinions of those who wish to have the NT in the mother tongue" (LP 5, no. 50), but it was not passed. Cf. Stanford E. Lehmberg, *The Reformation Parliament: 1529–1536* (Cambridge UP, 1970) 120–23.

Miles Coverdale published the *editio princeps* of the English Bible. Although unauthorized, it depicted Henry VIII at the bottom of the title-page and was dedicated to the king. Cf. reproductions of the title-page (Antwerp, 1535) STC 2063 and (Southwark, 1535) STC 2063.3 (Plates 2 and 3) in Henry Guppy, "Miles Coverdale and the English Bible, 1488–1568." Rpt. from *Bulletin of the John Rylands Lbrary* 19.2 (1935). See Guido Latré, "The Place of Printing of the Coverdale Bible," *Tyndale Society Journal* 8 (November 1997) 5–18.

To Tyndale's Pentateuch, Jonah and NT, Coverdale added his own translations of the rest of the Hebrew Bible and Apocrypha based on the Latin of the Vulgate and Sanctes Pagninus OP, and the

German of Luther and the Zurich Bible. Coverdale did not use Tyndale's translation of Joshua through 2 Chronicles, which was first printed in Matthew's Bible of 1537. Cf. F.F. Bruce, *The English Bible* (London: Lutterworth, 1961) 55, 58–59, 65. See also J.F. Mozley, *Coverdale and His Bibles* (London: Lutterworth, 1953).

Implementing Cromwell's injunction of 1538, Coverdale supervised the publication of the Great Bible (1539) to be set up in every church for the parishioners to read. This order was confirmed by a royal proclamation of April 1539, limiting explanation of the Bible to university graduates or licensed teachers, and requesting the laity to read the Bible quietly, especially during church services (TRP no. 191, 1.285). In 1543, the Act for the Advancement of True Religion permitted Bible reading to nobles, gentry, and merchants but forbad it to the lower classes until the king decided otherwise. Cf. 34 & 35 Henry VIII, Ch. 1 (*Statutes* 3.896). This act also banned by name the biblical translations of Tyndale as "craftye false and untrue" (*Statutes* 3.894), although Tyndale's Pentateuch, Joshua through 2 Chronicles, and NT had already appeared in Matthew's Bible (1537), licensed by the king, cf. Daniell 334–38.

168/3–4 **Many . . . cause.** Cf. CWM 6/1.318/27–32.

168/7–8 **Horsey . . . kynges.** Cf. CWM 6/1.325/19–20.

168/8–9 **Gods . . . synner.** Cf. Luke 18.13–14.

168/21 **hunne . . . conuicte.** Cf. CWM 6/1.327/11–12. *Dialogue,* Bk. 3, Ch. 15 (CWM 6/1.316–30) deals with the case of Richard Hunne. Cf. also *Supplication of Souls* (CWM 7.116/31–117/10, 132/21–136/19), *Apology* (CWM 9.126/26). In December 1514, Hunne was found hanged in the Lollards' Tower at St. Paul's under suspicious circumstances. Posthumously, Hunne was convicted of heresy, his body burnt at Smithfield, and his goods confiscated by the crown. In 1515 at the king's intervention, the bishop's chancellor William Horsey was tried in the secular Court of King's Bench and acquitted of murder. Nevertheless, he was ordered to pay the equivalent of Hunne's goods to his children in 1523. After a parliamentary act of 1529 limited the payment of mortuary fees, many stopped paying them, cf. Marshall 220–22.

W.R. Cooper retrieved the report of the inquest on Hunne's death from the Public Record Office in 1988 and read it with infra-red light. He discovered a deposition from the maidservant of Charles Joseph, who told her how he tried to kill Hunne by thrusting a wire up his nose into the brain. From the state of Hunne's body and clothes, the jury concluded that he was dead before he was hanged. For Cooper's report and analysis, see "Richard Hunne," *Reformation* 1 (1996) 221–51.

In *Obedience,* Tyndale accuses the bishops of burning Hunne's body after they themselves have murdered him (I1). Hunne's case illustrates the greed of churchmen who demand mortuaries from the dead in addition to tithes from the living (*Obedience* K2v, *Matthew* e3v). The poor especially cannot afford to pay this substitute for forgotten tithes (*Obedience* K4v). (JB)

168/22–23 **hunne . . . be proued.** Cf. CWM 6/1.327/17.

168/27 **the bisshope . . . conynge.** Cf. CWM 6/1.327/29–30.

168/28 **old deane Colet.** In Oxford John Colet (1467–1519) gave free public lectures on all the epistles of Paul, according to Erasmus. Cf. Ep. 1211, To Justus Jonas, Anderlecht, 13 June 1521 (Allen 4.515/282; CWE 8.233/311–12). Written versions survive on Romans, Ch. 1–16 (Oxford, c1499–1505); Romans, Ch. 1–5 (London, c1505–11); 1 Corinthians, Ch. 1–5 (London, c1505–11) and Ch. 6–16 (London, c1512–16). For the places and dates, cf. Gleason 92. For the texts, see J.H. Lupton, ed. and tr., *Exposition of . . . Romans,* Ch. 1–16 (1873); *Exposition of . . . Romans,* Ch. 1–5 (1876); *Exposition of . . . First . . . Corinthians* (1874) (Ridgewood, NJ: Gregg, 1965–66). See also *John Colet's Commentary on First Corinthians,* tr. Bernard O'Kelly, ed. Catherine A.L. Jarrott (Binghamton, NY: MRTS, 1985). For Colet's writings on Dionysius the Areopagite, cf. 46/27n. In a brief letter to Erasmus, Colet confided unnamed difficulties with his local bishop: "[H]e of London [Fitzjames] still plagues me." From Ep. 314, From John Colet, London, 20 October [1514] (Allen 2.37/9; CWE 3.48/11). Erasmus eulogized Colet as a reformer who remained within the Roman communion in Ep. 1211, To Justus Jonas, Anderlecht, 13 June 1521 (Allen 4.514/245–527/633; CWE 8.232/274–244/692).

While Dean of St. Paul's (1505–19), Colet was accused of heresy, but not for translating the Pater Noster, cf. Gleason 236–37. Colet had inferred "that the pope's unique status depended on his conformity to ecclesiastical and, *a fortiori,* divine law," Gleason 252. His stray remarks could be used by enemies to present him as a Lollard sympathizer. But in 1511–12 he worked on a trial commission that examined and condemned heretics of Lollard persuasion, cf. Gleason 239–40. (JW)

Tyndale is Foxe's only source (4.247) for a charge against Colet on the Lord's Prayer. In fact, Colet's English translation of the Pater, Ave and Credo appeared posthumously in . . . *[M]yrrour or lokynge glasse of lyfe . . . ,* written by J. Goodale or J. Gowghe (1532?), STC 11499, d3r–v. For checking their copies of *[M]yrrour,* special thanks to Nicholas Smith, Cambridge University Library (Syn. 8.53.108) and Aude Fitzsimmons, Pepys Library, Magdalene College, Cambridge. The following is a transcription from the copy in the Bodleian Library, Oxford (Crynes 846):

[d3] ¶ The Pater noster by Iohnn colet Dean of Paules in englysshe. The .iiii. Chapytre.

O Father that art in heuen / halowed be thy name / amonge men in erth / as it is with the[e] in heuen amonge thyne aungels. O father thy kyngdom come and rayne amonge men in erthe / as thou raynest amonge thy aungels in heuen[.] O father gyue to vs thy chyldren our dayly sustynaunce. And helpe vs (as we gyue & helpe them that haue nede of vs.) O father forgyue vs our synnes done to the[e] / as [d3v] we do forgyue them that trespas agaynst vs. O father let not vs be ouercome with euyll temptacion. But o father delyuer vs from all euyll. Amen.

169/2–4 **The messinger . . . desyre it.** Cf. CWM 6/1.331/9–15.

169/4–6 **the printer . . . approued.** Cf. CWM 6/1.331/22–27.

169/23–24 **nothinge . . . after it.** Cf. CWM 6/1.332/1–5.

169/24–25 **phareses . . . mercie.** Cf. Luke 18.10–14.

169/28 **Then . . . allegories.** Cf. CWM 6/1.333/27–334/8.

169/28–29 **Moses . . . tonge.** Cf. Deut. 31.9–13. From Moses, who probably lived in the 13c BC, arose oral traditions which were written down, combined, and edited from the 10c to 6c BC to form the Pentateuch. Cf. *New Jerome Biblical Commentary,* ed. Raymond E. Brown SS, Joseph A. Fitzmyer SJ, and Roland E. Murphy O. Carm. (Englewood Cliffs, NJ: Prentice Hall, 1990) 4–5, 1226.

169/31–170/1 **And the apostles . . . backe.** Cf. Acts 20.27.

170/4 **the Iewes . . . on it.** Cf. CWM 6/1.342/21–28.

170/6–7 **God . . . phisicions.** Cf. CWM 6/1.343/19–20.

170/13–14 **so greate ... pistles.** Cf. CWM 6/1.343/32–35. Cf. 2 Pet. 3.16.

170/14–18 **it is impossyble ... to fulfil it.** Jacobus Latomus (c1475–1544) was one of the three theologians who debated with Tyndale at his trial (Mozley 324–33), where the primary issue was the key to Scripture: *de clave scientiae salutaris ipsius scripturae.* In his position paper, Latomus noted seven points of agreement on justification, but argued against Tyndale that the person who is justified without merit can then perform good works that merit God's reward. Cf. *Confutationum* in *Opera* 183r–v, 186v; tr. Willis 346–48, 354–55. See Robert J. Wilkinson, "Reconstructing Tyndale in Latomus: William Tyndale's last, lost, book," *Reformation* 1 (1996) 252–85. For justification by faith, cf. 96/22n; for Latomus, cf. 209/1n. See also Jos E. Vercruysse SJ, "Latomus and Tyndale's Trial," WCS 197–214. (JW)

170/15–16 **iustifienge of faith in christes bloude.** Tyndale conflates Rom. 3.28 and 5.9.

171/3–4 **Christes church . . . contrary.** Cf. CWM 6/1.346/6–9, referring to Gal. 1.8.

171/5–7 **confirmed . . . christendome.** Cf. CWM 6/1.346/26– 31.

171/13–14 **the spiritualte . . . rebuked.** Cf. CWM 6/1.346/35– 347/2.

171/22–23 **A freres . . . good.** Cf. CWM 6/1.349/2–4 and CWM 8/2.804/26–28.

171/27–172/2 **forbiddinge . . . doctrine.** Cf. 1 Tim. 4.1, 3.

172/10–11 **in penaunce . . . satisfaccion.** Cf. CWM 6/1.349/19– 20; *Babylonian Captivity,* 1520 (WA 6.544–49; LW 36.84–90).

172/13–14 **vn to god . . . herte.** Cf. Acts 26.20.

172/14 **satisfaccion of christes bloude.** Cf. Heb. 9.12.

172/15–16 **tyndale . . . rich.** Cf. CWM 6/1.349/36–350/2 and CWM 8/1.180/25.

172/16–17 **But . . . peny.** Cf. CWM 6/1.350/8–10.

172/21–22 **vppon that lye. . . penaunce.** Cf. CWM 6/1.350/16–18 and CWM 8/1.41/21–22.

172/25–28 **penaunce . . . sacrament or no.** The implication that Penance is not a sacrament, because it lacks a sign-action like immersion in water or eating and drinking, goes back to the concluding remarks of Luther's *Babylonian Captivity,* 1520 (WA 6.572; LW 36.124), a work however that had treated Penance among the authentic sacraments (ibid., WA 6.543–49; LW 36.81–91). Notwithstanding abuses, Luther gave hearty approval of private confession with absolution (ibid., WA 6.546/10–17; LW 36.86). Also the Augsburg Confession of 1530 treats confession with absolution as part of the sacramental instruction of the Lutheran churches, cf. *The Book of Concord* 34f. Tyndale accepts Luther's critical views but does not follow the constructive side of Lutheran teaching. (JW)

172/29–30 **tindale . . . was.** Cf. CWM 6/1.350/19–20.

172/31–32 **forgeuenesse . . . bloude.** Cf. Eph. 1.7.

173/6 **neuer . . . tyndale.** Cf. CWM 6/1.351/35–352/1.

173/11 **what . . . penaunce.** Cf. CWM 6/1.352/4–5.

173/15–16 **He teacheth . . . faith only.** Cf. CWM 6/1.352/25–26.

173/15–17 **sacrament . . . iustifie only.** Cf. CWM 8/1.309/25–27.
From CWM 6/1.352/27–355/1 More gives an itemized list of
Lutheran heresies, which Tyndale addresses from 173/15 to
182/17.

173/16–24 **the faith . . . holy church.** Tyndale expresses Luther's
doctrine of the primacy of the word of promise and of faith in
sacraments. But specific themes of Luther's sacramental instruction of 1519–24 are missing, such as the testamentary character of
the promise in the Lord's Supper, the content as forgiveness of
sins, and the addressee as the troubled and terrified conscience, cf.
63/31n. (JW)

173/17–22 **And the sacrament . . . at all.** Cf. CWM 8/1.95/23–26.

173/25–26 **He teacheth . . . werkes.** Cf. CWM 6/1.352/27–28 and
Rom. 3.28. Cf. CWM 6/2.700 for references to Luther's sources.

173/26–174/29 **the scripture . . . no beleffe.** Here Tyndale explains
Luther's teaching on how good works are consequent upon the
forgiveness of sins, for example, as expounded in *The Freedom of a
Christian,* 1520 (WA 7.25/26–26/31, 29/31–34/22; LW 31.351–53,
358–65). Later, in the Augsburg Confession of 1530, in a passage
Tyndale apparently did not know, Lutherans claimed to be untir-
ing teachers of good works, as evidenced by Luther's *Treatise on
Good Works,* 1520 (WA 6.202–76; LW 44.21–114) and his catechet-
ical expositions of the commandments. Cf. Art. 20 of the Confession, *The Book of Concord* 41–46. (JW)

173/26–28 **assone . . . imediatly.** Cf. Rom. 3.23–25.

174/1–3 **For . . . god.** Cf. CWM 8/1.326/14–16, 402/12–14. Tyndale refers to Bk. 4, not Bk. 3 as More mistakenly says.

174/3–5 **But . . . by fayth.** Cf. Rom. 3.8.

174/7 **He calleth . . . werkes.** Cf. CWM 6/1.352/28–29.

174/12 **no good werke.** Cf. CWM 6/1.352/30.

174/15–25 **And then . . . no lenger.** Tyndale states Luther's doctrine
of *simul iustus et peccator,* cf. 30/19n. For Tyndale the non-imputa-
tion of sin rests on the believer's fundamental good will and readiness to improve, while for Luther it is based solely on the righteousness of Christ, with whom one is united by faith in the

promises. Also, Tyndale introduces a reason for ongoing sinfulness that Luther did not feature, namely, that one is at fault to the extent that one's love is less than Christ's love. Luther defended the *simul,* e.g., in response to the censure of Art. 31 of *Exsurge* (*In omne opere bono iustus peccat;* DS 1481; Neuner Dupuis 1923/31) in *Defense and Explanation of All the Articles,* December 1520 (WA 7.136–38; LW 32.83–86). Here he writes that there is sin whenever one falls short of the command to love God with all one's heart and strength, and that the *simul* has backing in Isaiah, Paul, Augustine, and Gregory the Great. (JW)

174/21–22 **good . . . doynge well.** Cf. CWM 6/1.352/31–32.

174/26 **no synne . . . vnbeleffe.** Cf. CWM 6/1.352/33–34. Cf. Matt. 12.31–32, Luke 12.10. In *The Supplication of Souls* (1529), More discusses blasphemy against the Holy Spirit as the unforgivable sin (CWM 7.191/11–192/14). In his prologue to the Book of Numbers, Tyndale claims that malicious persecution of the clear truth is the sin against the Holy Spirit (Mombert 388/29–32; TOT 193).

174/30–175/1 **no frewyll . . . the werke man.** Cf. CWM 6/1.352/36–353/5. Where More saw error in Luther's doctrine of the bondage of the will, Tyndale offers a key distinction. Humans have no power to overcome darkness and sin until God frees the will to do good voluntarily. But the will itself is the creator's gift, which sinful human beings misuse because of the blindness inflicted by the devil (176/9–16). Luther had developed his doctrine in 1520 and 1521 in response to censure in *Exsurge,* Art. 36 (DS 1486; Neuner-Dupuis 1923/36), e.g., in *Defense and Explanation* (WA 7.142–49; LW 32.92–94). The culmination then came in Luther's broadside against Erasmus, *On the Bondage of the Will,* 1525 (WA 18.600–787; LW 33). Cf. also 39/2n. Tyndale further discusses other difficulties concerning free will raised by More: God's initiative in justification (175/10–12, 211/3–4), the effect on morality of lack of belief in free will (188/28–29, 189/1–6), the dilemma of God's causality and responsibility for evil (191/4–9). (JW)

175/10–18 **we affirme . . . therto.** A concise account of God's justifying grace according to Tyndale. It is the impression upon the heart of love for God's law, now known in its "swetnesse" and so affirmed as good and consented to. This differs from Luther, for whom grace is the saving verdict of forgiveness *propter Christum* ("for Christ's sake"), a verdict that delivers a person from the law's condemnation. (JW)

175/13 **powred . . . soules.** Cf. Gal. 4.6.

175/17 **swetnesse in his law.** Cf. Ps. 119.103.

175/18–19 **we can doo . . . euell.** Cf. Matt. 12.35, Luke 6.45.

175/19–20 **seke . . . trueth.** Cf. John 5.44.

175/21–22 **hores . . . god.** Cf. 1 Cor. 6.9–10.

175/29–30 **Pilat . . . a boue.** Cf. John 19.11.

175/33–176/3 **As . . . receaued.** Cf. CWM 8/2.786/20–25.

176/4–6 **god is auctor . . . passion.** Cf. CWM 6/1.353/6–8.

176/9–16 **But . . . poysoned him with.** Cf. CWM 8/2.787/15–18. Contrary to More's accusation, Tyndale attributes the corruption in human will to the devil, not to God.

176/17–177/4 **Matrimonie . . . playne texte.** Rejecting the declaration of the Council of Florence in 1439, Luther had contested the sacramental nature of Christian marriage in *Babylonian Captivity,* 1520 (WA 6.550–53; LW 36.92–96). He granted, however, that it is a figure of Christ's union with the church, according to Eph. 5.31–32. Here Tyndale speaks more generally of a likeness between marriage and the kingdom of heaven (176/17, but cf. 154/10–28n). However, Luther's main point is that a sacrament is a NT rite accompanied by a promise of salvation which evokes faith. Tyndale, too, denies that Matrimony is a sacrament (*Obedience* M2v). For More's response, cf. CWM 6/1.353/9. (JW)

176/17–19 **Matrimonie . . . gospell.** Cf. CWM 8/1.86/2–5. More gives a precis of *Obedience* M2r–v. Among parables drawn from marriage are the wedding garment, cf. Matt. 22.1–14 and the ten bridesmaids, cf. Matt. 25.1–13.

176/26–28 **For where . . . therby.** Cf. CWM 8/1.84/3–4.

177/5 **all holy orders . . . inuencion.** For More's response to the rejection of Orders as a sacrament, cf. CWM 6/1.353/20–21, 8/1.186/30. Tyndale has in mind the five church offices or orders warranted by the NT, cf. 177/6n. In *Obedience* M3–M6 (1528), Tyndale asserts that the offices of subdeacon, deacon, priest, bishop, cardinal, and pope are not sacraments because not linked to Christ's promise of salvation. Rites, garb, and other offices, such as the "minor orders" of acolyte, exorcist, lector, and porter, are merely human traditions, cf. 93/14–19n. Tyndale, surprisingly, opens the door to accepting these as sacraments if royal authority were to insist (177/9–12). This view sharply contrasts with Luther's arguments for explicit sacramental institution by Christ. On the universal priesthood, Tyndale does not argue from its basis in Baptism and faith, as Luther commonly did, but instead from the needs of others, whom one is obliged by the commandment of love (177/20, 177/30, 178/3–4) to assist especially in spiritual matters. (JW)

177/6 **apostle.** Cf. Matt. 10.2–4, Luke 6.13–16, Gal. 1.1 etc. **bisshope.** Cf. 1 Tim. 3.1–7. **prest.** Cf. 16/20n. **deacon.** Cf. Acts 6.2–3, 1 Tim. 3.8–12. **wedowe.** Cf. 1 Tim. 5.9–10.

177/14–15 **euery . . . christe.** Cf. CWM 6/1.353/22–24, 289/20–22.

178/11 **the host ys no sacryfyce.** Cf. CWM 6/1.353/30. Tyndale contests the idea of Eucharist as sacrifice and proposes a "representative" view of the Lord's Supper for stirring memory and inciting repentant faith. For other references to sacraments, esp. the Eucharist, cf. 63/31, 150/9nn. (JW)

178/12 **signe and memoriall.** For More's opposition to Tyndale's sacramentarianism, cf. CWM 8/1.301/24–25.

178/20 **eatynge of the host.** Frequency of reception of the Eucharist by the laity had diminished to the minimal communion at Easter as legislated by Lateran IV in 1215 or at Christmas, Easter, and Pentecost as encouraged by local synods. Aquinas argues that, although the paschal lamb was eaten once a year, manna had been eaten daily (*Summa* III, Q. 80, Art. 10, Reply to Obj. 2).

178/20–21 **drinkynge of the cuppe.** Perhaps in compensation for the withdrawal of the cup from the laity during the 12c, the host and chalice were elevated after the consecration for all to see from the late 12c (Rubin 70–72, 55). The followers of Jan Hus urged the restoration of the cup to the laity, but this practice was rejected by the Council of Constance in 1415, considered but not accepted by the Council of Basel in 1433, requested again at the Diet of Augsburg in 1530 and 1548, and at the Council of Trent in 1562. Reception from the cup was allowed in certain Roman dioceses of Central Europe in 1564 and to the whole Roman Church after Vatican II. For Constance and Basel, cf. Karl August Fink in

Jedin and Dolan 4.456, 476; for Augsburg, cf. Erwin Iserloh in Jedin and Dolan 5.262, 291; for Trent, cf. Hubert Jedin in Jedin and Dolan 5.491, 497.

The policy of extending the communion cup to the laity was begun by Karlstadt and continued by Luther; it was adopted wherever the Reformation was established. In England, the laity were prohibited from receiving the cup by the second of the conservative Six Articles, 1539, 31 Henry VIII, Ch. 14 (*Statutes* 3.739). The practice of communion under both kinds was reinstated in 1547, 1 Edward VI, Ch. 1 (*Statutes* 4/1.3). It was promoted by a royal proclamation of 8 March 1548 (TRP no. 300, 1.417–18) and affirmed by the Prayer Books of 1549 and 1552. Cf. *The Two Liturgies . . . of King Edward VI,* ed. Joseph Ketley, Parker Society 29 (Cambridge UP, 1844) 92, 279. The statute of Edward VI was repealed in 1553 by 1 Mary, St. 2, Ch. 2 (*Statutes* 4/1.202), and restored in 1559 by 1 Elizabeth, Ch. 1 (*Statutes* 4/1.351) for the Prayer Book of 1559.

178/26 **capon.** Tyndale's image of the dish of capon as a sign of welcome home is developed by Frith into an analogy of the Eucharist eaten by both faithful and unfaithful Christians (Wright 432).

179/1–2 **Misach . . . pensiongeuynge.** For the Lord's Supper Tyndale would use the term "Christes memoriall" (178/34), from Jesus' command (e.g. 1 Cor. 11.24) because the biblical name focusses on the essential content of the rite. Tyndale mistakenly derives the word "Mass" from the Hebrew *misach* for gifts to the poor rather than from the dismissal at the end of the Latin rite, *Ite, missa est.* Cf. Joseph A. Jungmann SJ, "Messe," LThK 7.321; 95/19 n. (JW)

179/12 **there remayneth bred and wine.** Cf. CWM 6/1.353/37–354/2. More discusses here, not Tyndale on sacramentarianism, but Luther on consubstantiation. In his anonymous pamphlet *Maynung vom Nachtmal* (1526), the Swiss reformer Leo Jud tried to show a similarity between Luther and Erasmus on the Eucharist, but the latter protested in Ep. 1708, To the Swiss Confederacy, Basle, 15 May 1526 (Allen 6.337–42; not yet in CWE); Ep. 1737, To Conrad Pellican, <Basle>, <c. 27 August 1526> (Allen 6.382–84, esp. nn 1, 5; not yet in CWE).

Tyndale does not enter into exegetical debate over the literal or fig-

urative meaning of "is" in the words of institution, and he does
not argue from Christ's Ascension as definitively placing his body
in heaven. Both of these are of major importance in documents of
Zwinglian provenance, such as Cornelisz Hoen, "A Most Christian Letter," published by Zwingli in 1525, now in Oberman, *Forerunners* 268–76. Zwingli's section on the Eucharist is found in
Commentary on True and False Religion (1525), ed. Samuel Macauley
Jackson and Clarence Nevin Heller (Durham, NC: Labyrinth,
1981), 198–253, esp. 206–16. See also Zwingli's *On the Lord's Supper*
(1526), in *Zwingli and Bullinger,* ed. G.W. Bromily, LCC 24
(Philadelphia: Westminster, 1953) 185–238. A concise secondary
presentation is Gottfried W. Locher, *Zwingli's Thought,* Studies in
the History of Christian Thought 25 (Leiden: Brill, 1981) 220–28.
For Luther's main responses to Zwingli and his allies, cf. 63/31n.
(JW)

Although he assigns the Eucharist first place among the traditional
seven sacraments in *Obedience,* Tyndale gives only one paragraph
to "The sacrament of the body and bloud of Christe" while he
devotes five sections to Penance (M6v–O1v). For Tyndale, the Eucharist reminds the faithful of the promise of forgiveness (*Obedience* M1v); it is a sign of Christ's last will and testament (*1 John*
H3). Tyndale asserts that the chalice was removed from the laity
because the taste of wine would make it harder for them to believe in transubstantiation. For the same reason, the communion
wafer is made as unlike ordinary bread as possible (180/25–27; *1
John* H5v). Tyndale repeats that "the fyue wittes" prove that bread
and wine remain after consecration (*Matthew* p1v). This passage
was omitted from the posthumous edition of 1537 because it was
contrary to the Ten Articles of 1536. Finally, Tyndale outlines three
positions on the Eucharist: Catholic transubstantiation, Lutheran
consubstantiation, and, his own preference, Zwinglian memorial
(*Sacraments* C6v–C8). For denying transubstantiation, Anne Askew
was burnt at the stake under Henry VIII in 1546 (Foxe 5.537–50).

179/13–14 **What . . . only.** Cf. CWM 8/1.117/6–7. Aquinas asserts
that the consecrated bread and wine can physically nourish the
recipient: "Although the sacramental species are not a substance,
still they have the virtue of a substance" (*Summa* III, Q. 77, Art. 6,
Reply to Obj. 3).

179/16–17 **where of . . . soforth.** The Victorian editor silently omits
Tyndale's reference to excretory functions (PS 3.178). For other
examples of bowdlerization, cf. 60/6–7n.

179/32–33 **it is . . . life.** John 6.63, cf. CWM 8/1.313/12–13.

180/4–5 **how . . . spiritually.** Cf. John 16.7, 12–13.

180/8 **the masse . . . preest.** Cf. CWM 6/1.354/14–15 and CWM
8/1.317/19–20.

180/18 **howseled . . . dyenge.** Cf. CWM 6/1.354/19–20. Tyndale
wastes no energy on More's erroneous charge that reformers re-
serve communion to one's deathbed. In 1521, the king had made
the same charge in Ch. 5, his defense of giving communion to the
laity only in the form of bread (*Assertio,* CC 43.137). The idea was
lifted out of context from Luther's conclusion to *Babylonian Captivity,* 1520, where he spoke of Baptism as a new birth and the
Lord's Supper as both the memorial of Christ's death and the as-
similation of communicants to that death (WA 6.572/23–34; LW
36.124f). Luther said, however, that one exercises both aspects of
the Eucharist throughout life and earlier had given good reasons
for regular communion (ibid., WA 6.526/23–33; LW 36.57). (JW)

180/20 **not spare to twich it.** Cf. CWM 6/1.354/22–23.

180/21 **perelous . . . oyled them.** Cf. CWM 8/1.117/12–13.

180/22 **Christ . . . spirite.** Cf. 2 Cor. 1.21–22.

180/22–23 **with his bloude.** 1 Pet. 1.2.

180/27–30 **Aboute . . . starch.** Cf. CWM 8/1.117/14–16. In pon-
dering how long flour preserves its nature, Aquinas takes no firm
stand: "And because starch comes of corrupted wheat, it does not
seem as if the body of Christ could be made of the bread there-
from, although some hold the contrary" (*Summa* III, Q. 74, Art. 3,
Reply to Obj. 4). According to Tyndale, Oxford theologians were
still debating the topic.

180/31 **sacrament shuld not be worsheped.** Cf. CWM 6/1.354/
23–25.

180/31–181/11 **It is . . . wyll folow.** Cf. CWM 8/1.117/27–118/3.

181/4–5 **They saye . . . fayth therin.** Cf. CWM 8/1.367/22–24.

181/5–10 **For . . . is true.** Tyndale applies to the relation of faith and
the sacrament the medieval commonplace of faith's different relations to its object. Based on Augustine (see below), it was held
that *credere Deo* means accepting what God says, and *credere Deum*

is believing that God exists, while *credere in Deum* is to give oneself over lovingly to God. Peter Lombard cited Augustine on this distinction (*Sentences*, Bk. 3, Dist. 23, Ch. 4), and thereby transmitted a textbook theme to later medieval theologians, e.g. Aquinas (*Summa* II–II, Q. 2, Art. 2). For Tyndale, the sacrament is believed as valid testimony (*credere sacramento*), but one does not give oneself in loving trust to the sacrament itself (not *credere in sacramentum*), which is analogous to what Augustine had said about believing Paul and Peter, but not believing *in* them. Cf. *Tractates on the Gospel of John* (AD 406–7, 419–24) Tr. 29, Par. 6 (CCL 36.287; 1NPNF 7.185). Tyndale goes on, as above at 173/16–24, to apply this distinction to the church by admitting that one believes the church, but not *in* the church, which agrees with the Nicene Creed's distinction in wording between *Credo in Deum Patrem . . . in unum Dominum . . . in Spiritum Sanctum* and *Credo unam, sanctam, . . . ecclesiam*. The Creed thus expresses self-donation in faith to the triune God but only ascertains in faith the existence of the one, holy church. (JW)

181/7 **the onlye worshuppynge of the sacrament.** Luther actually taught that adoration of the Eucharist, although not commanded, cannot in fact be withheld. Cf. *The Adoration of the Sacrament,* 1523 (WA 11.432–56, esp. 445–49; LW 36.275–305, esp. 293–96). Tyndale argues against such adoration, from biblical arguments (180/32–181/4) and by analyzing belief (181/5–10n). (JW)

181/12–13 **a christen . . . any at all.** Cf. CWM 6/1.354/29–31. More cites Luther's declaration of Christian freedom from human laws, especially in the church, probably taken from the chapter on Baptism in *Babylonian Captivity,* 1520 (WA 5.535/27–538/3; LW 36.70–73), which the Sorbonne had censured as subversive and erroneous in 1521. Cf. C.E. Du Boulay, *Historia Universitatis Parisiensis* 6 (Paris, 1683; Frankfurt/M.: Minerva, 1966) 120. Tyndale affirms the duty of civil obedience in a response akin to Luther's treatise, *Temporal Authority, To What Extent It Should Be Obeyed,* 1523, which both grounded Christian observance of civil rulers and delineated a sphere of faith that such rulers may not enter (WA 11.245–80; LW 45.81–129). Tyndale, however, is more outspoken on present-day "wily tiranny" (181/22). (JW)

181/25 **Herode.** Cf. Luke 2.7–8.

181/26 **scribes and Phareses.** Cf. Matt. 23.2–3.

181/27 **no purgatory.** Cf. CWM 6/1.354/32.

181/29 **slepe tyll domes daye.** Cf. CWM 6/1.354/33, CWM 8/1.288/9–10, 8/2.702/34–36. See 118/3–6n. (JW)

182/2–8 **The hethen . . . stablish it.** A current of Christian patristic thought culminating in Augustine gladly absorbed the Platonic and Neoplatonic doctrine of the soul's natural immortality, even to the point of finding here the attribute by which the human person most resembles God's image and likeness (Gen. 1.26–27). Medieval scholastic thought offered a cluster of philosophical arguments for individual immortality, especially in response to the 13c Parisian Averroist doctrine of a collective immortality. The Italian Renaissance celebration of human dignity climaxed in Marsilio Ficino's *Theologia platonica, sive de immortalitate animorum* (1483), which provided a remote backdrop for Lateran V's doctrinal affirmation of the soul's immortality in *Apostolici regiminis* (DS 1440–41; Neuner-Dupuis 410), promulgated in 1513 against Averroists at Padua such as Nicoletto Vernia and Pietro Pomponazzi. Tyndale represents a resolute return to the NT doctrine of the resurrection of the whole person (e.g. John 5.25–28, 1 Thess. 4.15–17, 1 Cor. 15.12–56). (JW)

182/17 **no man . . . sayntes.** Cf. CWM 6/1.355/1.

182/22–24 **God . . . old testament.** Here Tyndale offers the opinion that the prayers pagans addressed to their idols were answered by Yahweh. The general attitude of the Old Testament towards idol worship is negative. Cf. "They that make them [idols] are like vnto them [i.e., dumb, blind, deaf etc.]: *so* is euery one that trusteth in them" (Ps. 115.8). However, Yahweh is dramatized as addressing Cyrus the Persian, who in 538 BC allowed the Jews to leave Babylon and return to Palestine to rebuild the Temple: "For Jacob my seruants sake, and Israel mine elect, I have euen called thee by thy name: I have surnamed thee, though thou hast not knowen me" (Isa. 45.4 KJV).

182/25–26 **men . . . saue.** Cf. Ps. 36.6 in KJV.

182/28–29 **Which . . . spirite.** Cf. John 4.22–24.

182/31 **S. Appoline.** During the persecution of Decius (AD 250–51), executioners knocked out the teeth of Apollonia (GL 1.268–69). Erasmus' *Enchiridion* of 1503 mocks the quasi-pagan custom of assigning particular functions to particular saints, such as Apollonia's power to relieve toothaches (Holborn 66/10–11; CWE 66.64). For illustrations of Apollonia, cf. Duffy (Plates 60, 73).

183/2–3 **mercy . . . christe.** Cf. 1 Cor. 1.4.

183/7 **he destroyeth . . . sodomites.** Cf. Gen. 19.24–28.

183/18–20 **the emproure . . . heretikes.** Cf. CWM 6/1.355/8–10.

183/23–32 **s. Hierome . . . in the sted.** Actually the narrative is by the protagonist himself, the heresy-hunting bishop Epiphanius, whose letter to Bishop John of Jerusalem Jerome translated from Greek into Latin. Cf. Jerome, Ep. 51 (AD 394) Par. 9 (PL 22.526–27; CSEL 54.411; 2NPNF 6.88–89). (JW)

183/30–31 **contrary to the scripture.** For prohibition of graven images, cf. Exod. 20.4–5, Deut. 5.8–10.

184/2 **S. Gregory.** Gregory the Great (pope, 590–604) sent forty Benedictine monks under Augustine of Canterbury to evangelize the Anglo-Saxon invaders of Britain (597). Gregory's *Pastoral Rule* (AD 590) (PL 77.13–128; 2NPNF 12.1–72) was translated into Old English (AD 901). See *King Alfred's West-Saxon Version of Gregory's Pastoral Care,* ed. Henry Sweet, EETS 45, 50 (London, 1871). In Gregory's *Dialogues* (AD 593–94) (PL 77.149–430; FOTC 39), the pope and his deacon Peter offer a model for Anthony and his nephew Vincent in More's *Dialogue of Comfort* (1534–35). See O'Donnell, "Three Dialogues of Comfort." *Unio Dissidentium* contains thirteen passages (2%) from Gregory: from his exegesis of Ezekiel (CCL 142), Job (CCL 143, 143 A, 143 B), and the Canticle (CCL 144). For an illustration of the Four Latin Fathers with Gregory's papal tiara scraped out, cf. Duffy (Plate 33).

In the second edition of *Dialogue Concerning Heresies* (May 1531), More added a long passage to Bk. 4, Ch. 2 on Gregory's defense of images (CWM 6/1.355/28–359/31, 6/2.557). For other long additions to More's *Dialogue,* cf. 79/9n on images and 201/29n on faith. For the role of Stephen Vaughan in sending a partial manuscript of Tyndale's *Answer* to Cromwell, cf. Daniell 209–17. Vaughan's daughter was later a Marian exile and the author of the first known sonnet-sequence in English (1560): "A Paraphrase upon the 51. Psalme of David." See *The Collected Works of Anne Vaughan*

Lock, ed. Susan M. Felch, MRTS 185 (Tempe, AZ: Arizona Center for Medieval and Renaissance Studies, 1999) 62–71.

184/3–6 **Cirenus . . . worshepe them.** More discusses Gregory the Great's teaching on the proper use of images as found in his two letters to Serenus, Bishop of Marseilles: Bk. 9, Ep. 105, n.d. (PL 77.1027–28; 2 NPNF 13.23); Bk. 11, Ep. 13, n.d., To Serenus (PL 77.1128–30; 2NPNF 13.53–54). Gregory is much more admonitory of Serenus than Tyndale allows to appear. In the *Obedience* (H6v), Tyndale praises Gregory's reluctance to embrace the papal office when it was offered to him, citing Bk. 8, Ep. 30, To Eulogius, n.d. (PL 77.933; 2NPNF 12.241). (JW)

184/5 **images.** The provincial council of Hieria, convened by Emperor Constantine V, condemned the use of images in 754, the same year as the Donation of Pepin. Nicea II, the seventh ecumenical council, decreed the use of images in 787, making a distinction between worship (*latreian*) of God and "honourable reverence" (*timetiken proskunesin*) of the saints (2NPNF 14.550). A succinct account of the controversy over religious images is given by Hans-Georg Beck in Jedin and Dolan 3.26–36. (JW)

In *1 John* (D6v) Tyndale affirms that general councils could correct the clergy, but in *Prelates* (E6v–E8) he claims that general councils appeal to tradition over Scripture. Below (213/17–19), he protests that councils cannot define articles of faith against God's word. He probably believes that Nicea II defended the veneration of images contrary to the Second Commandment (Exod. 20.4–5) (NCE 7.327–29; OER 2.303–306). In 1563, the year that the Council of Trent ended, the Church of England declared in no. 21 of the Thirty-Nine Articles that General Councils may err.

184/16–17 **people . . . imageseruinge.** Exod. 32.1–24.

184/20–21 **putteth . . . soule.** Cf. 1 Cor. 8.9–11.

185/2–3 **empire . . . fraunce.** In the 8c when a weakened Byzantium could not send military aid, popes appealed to Frankish rulers for assistance against Lombard kings. In Tyndale's opinion, this era marks the definitive fall of the church "eight hundred years ago."

185/8 **blaspheme . . . saintes.** Cf. CWM 6/1.359/31–33, 8/1.314/15–16.

185/12 **they . . . salue regina.** Cf. CWM 6/1.359/34–35, 8/1.314/

12–13. Erasmus agrees with the executed heretic Louis de Berquin that the title, *spes et vita nostra* or "our hope and life," belongs properly to Christ not Mary. Cf. Ep. 2188, To Charles Utenhove, Freiburg, 1 July 1529 (Allen 8.212/103–5; not yet in CWE). After his resignation from the chancellorship, More teased his family that, as a last resort, they could support themselves on alms by stopping "at euery mans doore to singe *salue Regina*" (Roper 54/11). In Ch. 9 of his biography, Thomas Stapleton relates that More's household customarily recited Pss. 50/51, 24/25, 66/67, 129/130, and the *Salve Regina* as part of their evening prayers. Cf. *The Life and Illustrious Martyrdom of Sir Thomas More,* tr. Philip E. Hallett, ed. E.E. Reynolds (New York: Fordham UP, 1966) 88–89.

185/13 **christ is our hope and life.** For "hope," 1 Tim. 1.1; for "life," cf. John 14.6.

185/16–18 **they saye . . . our lady.** Cf. CWM 6/1.360/1–3.

185/18–20 **his mother . . . wyll.** Cf. Matt. 12.50, Mark 3.35.

185/21–23 **blessed . . . kepe it.** Luke 11.27–28. *Answer* has "Naye" (185/22), while NT has "Ye[a]" (Wallis 154/29; TNT 110D).

185/24–27 **I haue . . . rewarde.** 1 Cor. 9.16–17. The two clauses of v. 17 are given in reverse order.

185/33 **not worshepe . . . crosse.** Cf. CWM 6/1.360/4.

186/3 **festes of the crosse.** Cf. CWM 6/1.360/8–9. Roman Catholics celebrated "The Finding of the Cross" on 3 May (dropped from the liturgical calendar in 1969) and "The Exaltation of the Cross" on 14 September.

186/3–4 **corpus Christi.** Inspired in part by the formulation of transubstantiation by Lateran IV in 1215, the Eucharist is especially honored on the Thursday after Trinity Sunday. This commemoration was extended to the Western Church in 1264 by Urban IV (pope, 1261–64), who requested Aquinas to compose a Mass and Office. Celebrated in late spring, the feast is characterized by an outdoor Eucharistic procession and mystery plays. In England, complete cycles survive from York, Chester, Wakefield, and N-town, with the Chester cycle incorporating Aquinas' hymn *Lauda Sion.* For an comprehensive study of the theological and devotional texts, see Rubin passim.

186/7 **no man . . . vowe.** Cf. CWM 6/1.360/10–11, 8/1.42/24–25.

On vows, Tyndale concisely states at 196/8–9 what is set forth more diffusely at 161/17–162/24 and 189/18–190/7. (JW)

186/10 **Marten . . . nexte generall counsell.** Cf. WA 2.36; WA 7.76. In *Prelates* (D2), Tyndale discusses in general terms power struggles between pope and emperor over calling a council. During his brief pontificate, Adrian VI (pope, 1522–23) was requested by the Diet of Nuremberg to call a council in a German city within a year. In 1524, 1526, 1530, and 1532 Charles V formally requested Clement VII (pope, 1523–34) to convene a general council. In 1526 Charles even threatened to ask the cardinals to convoke it. But Clement feared conciliarism and the power of the Empire as demonstrated in the Sack of Rome (6–15 May 1527) by mutinous troops. Cf. Olivier de la Brosse et al., *Latran V et Trente,* Histoire des Conciles Oecuméniques 10 (Paris: Editions de l'Orante, 1975) 165–84.

186/12–13 **the pope . . . a counsell.** On 2 June 1536, Paul III (pope, 1534–49) summoned a council to be held at Mantua. Circumstances prevented this from taking place, but a second bull of convocation specified Trent as the venue in 1542. Finally, the bull of 30 November 1544 was effective, and the Council of Trent opened 13 December 1545, two months before Luther died on 18 February 1546. (JW)

186/15 **inconstauncie of Marten.** Cf. CWM 6/1.362/14–16.

186/16 **his later boke . . . his firste.** Cf. CWM 6/1.362/2–6. As a respectful subject whose theological views differed from his sovereign's, Tyndale avoids naming Henry VIII's *Assertio* (1521), which attacked Luther's *Babylonian Captivity* (1520) and evoked his *Contra Henricum Regem Angliae* (1522) (WA 10/2.180–222; not in LW).

186/20 **lerned not all trouth in one daye.** Tyndale has no further information to offer concerning Luther's development in the years from 1517 to 1522, and so he parries More's charges with ironical observations on the delay in convening a council (186/11–14), on "disputations" staged by inquisitors with their prisoners (186/28–187/3), and on the corrupt judges appointed to the Luther case (187/4–10). Luther advanced gradually, much like Jesus' apostles, to his grasp of biblical truth and ecclesiastical falsehood, but then he showed biblical grounds and had the backing of Christians everywhere (186/19–24, 187/10–12). (JW)

186/21 **the hethen.** For the conversion of the Roman centurion Cornelius, cf. Acts 11.1–18.

186/25–28 **Marten . . . harme.** Cf. CWM 6/1.362/29–35.

187/4 **He . . . Iudges.** Cf. CWM 6/1.363/4–5.

187/14 **not . . . fayned.** The new fiction that More supposedly created in Bk. 4, Ch. 4 is that Luther wrote his own version of events at the Diet of Worms in the third person but dropped his mask when he inadvertently slipped into the first person. Cf. "Luther at the Diet of Worms," 1521 (WA 7.825–57; LW 32.105–31), and CWM 6/2.709–10. (JW)

187/16–17 **Marten . . . vowe.** Cf. CWM 6/1.366/9–10. On vows, cf. 161/17–162/24 and 189/19n.

187/21–22 **god . . . tirantes.** Cf. CWM 6/1.402/32–403/2. More believes that Lutheran teaching on predestination casts God in the role of a tyrant (6/1.403/1) for not imputing guilt to the elect for their sins nor merit to the reprobate for their good deeds (6/1.400/7–9).

187/23 **Marten . . . only.** Cf. CWM 6/1.367/11.

187/23–190/27 **Marten . . . thanke him.** Tyndale takes up a series of allegations from *Dialogue,* Bk. 4, Ch. 7–9, which have little thematic unity. (JW)

188/3 **vnion of doctours.** See also 213/22. This handbook in Latin contains brief biblical quotations in roman type which introduce longer passages from the Fathers in italic. *Unio* gives passages on the main topics of early Reformation controversy: original sin, infant baptism, justification, the law, grace, faith and works, confession, fasting, indulgences, the Eucharist, venerating saints, and the Antichrist. *Unio* quotes approximately 570 passages from Christian authors from the 2c to 12c. Nine Fathers cited by Tyndale, most in *Answer* and a few in *Obedience,* are found in *Unio:* Augustine (42%), Jerome (14%), Chrysostom (10%), Origen (6%), Ambrose (5%), Cyprian (3%), Prosper of Aquitaine (3%), Gregory the Great (2%), Bede (1%), and the church historians Eusebius, Socrates Scholasticus, and Sozomen (1%). *Unio* quotes other theologians (13%) whom Tyndale never names: Clement of Rome, Tertullian, Athanasius, Hilary, Cyril of Alexandria, Lactantius, Fulgentius, Theophylactus, and Bernard.

The editor of the two-part *Unio Dissidentium* gives his name as Hermannus Bodius, probably a pseudonym. The earliest surviving edition (in two parts) was printed supposedly at Cologne but actually at Antwerp by Martin de Keyser, March and July 1527. In the Folger copy, both parts were supposedly printed at Cologne with Part 1 dated "1527, Decimo Kalendas Decembris" [22 November] and Part 2, "1527, X. Kalen. Augusti" [23 July]. Cf. J.M. De Bujanda et al., *Index de l'Université de Paris: 1544, 1545, 1547, 1549, 1551, 1556*, Index des Livres Interdits 1 (Sherbrooke, Québec: Editions de l'Université de Sherbrooke, 1994) 144–46.

After examining twenty-four editions of *Unio Dissidentium,* Robert Peters reports that editions published in and after 1531 contain material from Pseudo-Augustine, *De Essentia Divinitatis* (PL 42.1199–1206). Since the Folger copy includes extracts from this short work (UD 2.S3r–S8v), the ascribed date of 1527 cannot be correct. Cf. "Who Compiled the Sixteenth-Century Patristic Handbook *Unio Dissidentium?*" *Studies in Church History* 2, ed. G.J. Cuming (London: Nelson, 1965) 237–50, esp. 237, 239. Robert Peters tentatively identified the anthologist as the Strassburg reformer Martin Bucer because of *Unio*'s emphasis on church discipline administered in a loving spirit. Cf. ibid., esp. 245. Later, Peters suggested that the compiler is the Basel reformer Johannes Oecolampadius because of *Unio*'s choice of texts on the Eucharist as a mere sign of Christ's presence. Cf. "The Enigmatic *Unio Dissidentium:* Tyndale's 'Heretical' Companion?" *Reformation* 2 (1997) 233–40, esp. 237.

On 24 October 1526 Cuthbert Tunstall, Bishop of London, promulgated an order for confiscating dangerous books, including *Unio Dissidentium* (Foxe 4.667). Other prohibitions followed in the Netherlands, France, Spain, and Rome. Tyndale must have used other patristic sources besides *Unio,* but it would have given him an extensive though partisan survey of the Fathers. As editor of *Whole Works,* John Foxe added the marginal note in 1573, "The union of doctors a good booke" (338b).

188/5–26 **they saye . . . set on fire.** In answering *Dialogue*'s Bk. 4, Ch. 7, Tyndale inadvertently omits the heading "vij."

188/5–6 **they saye . . . gospell.** Tyndale quotes CWM 6/1.368/

29–31 nearly verbatim and CWM 6/1.354/28–31 more freely. More refers to Luther's *Freedom of a Christian*, 1520 (WA 7.49–73; LW 31.333–77) and works in German which he could not read (cf. CWM 6/2.702).

188/13–22 **marten . . . other men.** Cf. CWM 6/1.369/6–30. It was common among Catholics to charge that Luther's writings caused the peasant uprisings in Germany in 1525. Cf. Mark U. Edwards, "*Lutherschmäung?* Catholics on Luther's Responsibility for the Peasants' War," *Catholic Historical Review* 76 (1990) 461–80; *Printing, Propaganda, and Martin Luther* (Berkeley: U of California P, 1994) 149–62, 209–13. Tyndale had already denied Luther's responsibility in *Obedience* (C5). Tyndale's ingenious rebuttal seems to rest on his memories of Wittenberg just after the princes crushed the peasant bands at Frankenhausen on 15 May 1525. Later that month, the new Saxon Elector, Duke Johann, visited Wittenberg with his retinue. On 1 June, Johann had seventeen peasant rebel leaders beheaded at Eisleben (WA *Briefwechsel* 3.520n1; not in LW). Other princes of Lutheran persuasion who put down the rebellion were Philip of Hesse and the Counts of Mansfeld. (JW)
At first, Luther was sympathetic to the peasants' cause, in *Admonition to Peace: a Reply to the Twelve Articles of the Peasants in Swabia* (WA 18.291–334; LW 46.17–43), but later he condemned their violence in *Against the Robbing and Murdering Hordes of Peasants* (WA 18.357–61; LW 46.49–55). Erasmus comments on the great loss of life, "[T]his bloody crisis . . . sent about 100,000 peasants into the world of Orcus." From Ep. 1633, To Daniel Mauch, Basel, 10 October 1525 (Allen 6.199/17–18; CWE 11.325/20–326/21). Modern historians estimate that "between 70,000 and 100,000 peasants were killed in Germany in 1525." Cf. Steven Ozment, *The Age of Reform, 1250–1550: An Intellectual and Religious History of Late Medieval and Reformation Europe* (New Haven: Yale UP, 1980) 284. Erasmus gives a partial justification for the Peasants' War. Cf. Ep. 2328, To <Lorenzo Campegio>, Freiburg, 24 June 1530 (Allen 8.447–51; not yet in CWE).

188/13–14 **vplondish people.** Cf. "comen vplandysh people," CWM 6/1.369/7.

188/16 **destruccion of Ierusalem.** Cf. Matt. 24.2, Mark 13.2, Luke 21.6.

188/23–26 **Then . . . set on fire.** More attributes the 1527 Sack of Rome to Lutheran soldiers, cf. CWM 6/1.370/28–372/20 and Appendix C, 773–77. Tyndale retorts that Clement VII brought the disaster upon himself by treacherously entering alliances against Emperor Charles V. On these, cf. Judith Hook, *The Sack of Rome 1527* (London: Macmillan, 1972) 43, 51–61. Charles V had also charged papal culpability, and his Latin secretary Alfonso de Valdés formulated it in his 1529 "Dialogue of Lactancio and an Archdeacon," ed. and tr. John E. Longhurst, *Alfonso de Valdés and the Sack of Rome* (Albuquerque: U of New Mexico P, 1952). (JW)

188/28–29 **what good dede . . . grace.** Cf. CWM 6/1.373/18– 20, 8/3.1315–35. On our inability to do good, *Unio Dissidentium* (1.K4v) quotes Augustine, Sermon 156, Rom. 8.12–17, Against the Pelagians (AD 419) Par. 12 (PL 38.856; Rotelle 3/5.103–4).

189/1–3 **what harme . . . doo.** Cf. CWM 6/1.373/23–24.

189/4–6 **what shall . . . daye of dome.** Cf. CWM 6/1.373/26–28. For soul sleep, cf. 177/15–19, 182/2–8 nn. (JW)

189/7–8 **warned . . . houre.** Cf. Matt. 24.44, Mark 13.33, Luke 21.36.

189/10 **Martens bokes . . . beleue vs.** Cf. CWM 6/1.373/32–33.

189/12 **they liue as they teach and teach as they liue.** Cf. CWM 6/1.374/5. Tyndale reverses the order of More's antithetical clauses.

189/15–16 **pleasures . . . refusers.** Cf. CWM 6/1.374/20–21.

189/16–19 **yet . . . vowes.** Cf. CWM 6/1.375/4–7. Tyndale interpolates two asides into these paraphrases of More: "(as the pope doeth)" (189/16) and "(though . . . monye)" (189/17–19).

189/19 **luther . . . vowes.** After giving a postive account of vowed chastity in *The Holy Sacrament of Baptism,* 1519 (WA 2.735f; LW 35.41f), Luther attacked "that most widespread delusion of vows" as derogatory of Baptism and contrary to Christian freedom in the Baptism section of *Babylonian Captivity,* 1520 (WA 6.538/26– 542/38; LW 36.74–81). In November 1521 he composed his wide-ranging *Judgment . . . concerning Monastic Vows* (printed 1522) (WA 8.573–669; LW 44.251–400), which argues that vows rest on an erroneous basis, namely, the distinction between universally binding precepts and special evangelical counsels, and that they are contrary to the true nature of faith, Christian freedom, the com-

mandments, and natural reason. Tyndale's account of the case
against vows refers to faith and freedom, but argues more point-
edly than Luther that vows should give way to the primary precepts of self-maintenance and service to one's neighbor (190/7–15
and above, 161/25–162/8 with n). (JW)

On 13 June 1525 Luther married Catherine von Bora, a former Cistercian nun who had been sent to the convent while still a child
(NCE 8.1090). Their happy union of twenty years produced six
children and a new appreciation of conjugal spirituality. See Ch.
17, "The School for Character," Bainton 223–37. More obsessively
returns to the theme of their marriage about ten times in *Dialogue*
and over twenty times in *Confutation*. Although More knows the
popular belief that "Antecryste sholde be borne betwene a frere
and a nunne . . ." (CWM 8/1.51/3–4), he holds that Luther is not
Antichrist but his forerunner (8/1.271/11–13).

189/19–21 **luther . . . no nother.** Cf. CWM 8/1.135/17–18.

189/25 **ensample of the hethen.** For the Vestal Virgins, cf. CWM
6/1.375/16–28.

190/21–22 **apostles . . . yeres.** Cf. CWM 6/1.376/1–3.

190/24 **avoyde . . . persecucion.** Cf. 1 Cor. 7.26–27.

190/29 **he inveyeth and rayleth.** More does indeed use vehement
language against Luther's teaching that God's universal causality
includes even sin: "And thus these wretched heretyques wyth this
blasphemouse heresye alone / lay more vylaynous rebuke to the
greate maieste of god / than euer eny one rybaulde layed vnto a
nother" (CWM 6/1.377/6–9). Fisher also defends free will vigorously, especially in Art. 36 of his *Assertionis Lutheranae confutatio,*
1522, cf. Surtz 227–34.

191/4–5 **how . . . synneth in vs.** Cf. CWM 6/1.377/3–6.

191/5–8 **vseth . . . synne for hys pleasure.** Cf. CWM 6/1.377/
24–28.

191/14–18 **And so . . . fulfill it.** Cf. 34/6–11n.

191/23–26 **if . . to them.** 2 Cor. 4.3–4.

191/27–28 **briddes . . . the deuell.** Cf. Matt. 13.4, 19, Mark 4.4,
Mark 4.15, Luke 8.5, 12.

192/6 **Paul . . . why.** Cf. Rom. 9.20.

192/8 **vesels of mercy.** Rom. 9.23.

192/13 **Gods glorye in the electe.** Cf. Rom. 9.23–24.

192/16–17 **cometh . . . god.** Cf. Rom. 9.16.

192/19–20 **Christ . . . god.** Cf. Rom. 5.8.

192/28–29 **mercy . . . christ.** Cf. 2 Tim. 4.8, where a "croune of rightewesnes," the result of Christ's mercy, is laid up (Wallis 454/27; TNT 317C).

192/31 **gyft . . . grace.** Cf. Rom. 5.15.

193/5–6 **And I . . . seruant.** For the apostles as servants of God and Jesus Christ, cf. the first verse of the following epistles: Rom., Phil., Tit., 2 Pet., Jas., Jude. Cf. also John 13.1–17 for Jesus' washing of the apostles' feet as a symbol of the service they should give others.

193/12–14 **god . . . come.** Cf. CWM 8/2.798/12–14 and "blinde . . . blinded them" (197/5–6).

193/15–16 **flesh . . . worlde . . . fendes.** For "the world, the flesh and the devil," cf. 72/2–3n.

193/19–20 **Paul . . . electe.** Cf. 2 Tim. 2.10.

193/22 **god . . . mercye.** Cf. Rom. 11.5.

193/34 **Moses sacramentes.** Tyndale considers circumcision analogous to Baptism. Cf. Rom. 2.29 "circumcision of the herte" (Wallis 322/17; TNT 227D).

193/34 **signes of promises of fayth.** Where the scholastic tradition distinguished sharply between OT rites, such as circumcision and the paschal supper, and the NT sacraments, Tyndale holds a basic similarity, for in both cases justifying faith is to be elicited. The scholastic distinction became papal doctrine at the Council of Florence, in the Decree of Union with the Armenians, cf. p. 297. This document incorporated passages from Aquinas, including the affirmation that while OT sacraments were mere signs of grace to come, the NT sacraments are both signs and causes of that grace in those who receive them worthily (DS 1310; Neuner-Dupuis 1310). (JW)

194/3–5 **The pope . . . to iustifie.** Commonly, medieval theologians derived the efficacy of the Christian sacraments from the death of Christ, with the water and blood that flowed from his side (John 19.34) signifying Baptism and the Eucharist and signalling the transcending of circumcision and the paschal meal. Cf. Peter Lombard, *Sentences,* Bk. 2, Dist. 18, Ch. 3; Bk. 4, Dist. 8, Ch. 2. (JW)

194/7–8 **chapter . . . poetrie.** Cf. CWM 6/1.379/17–383/34. *Dialogue* Bk. 4, Ch. 11 presents the cross-examination of a preacher with Lutheran leanings within the dialogue between More and the Messenger. For another dialogue-within-a-dialogue, cf. 147/10n.

194/8 **doctoure Ferman person of hony lane.** *Dialogue* does not name Dr. Forman as the pastor of All Hallows, Honey Lane, Cheapside, but More hints at his identity when he exclaims "what poyson [Lutheran preachers] put forth vnder the cloke of hony" (CWM 6/1.399/31). Cuthbert Tunstall disputed with Forman on 19 March 1528, then forbad him to celebrate Mass and preach publicly under pain of law (Brigden 113n156 citing LP 4/2, no. 4175). Forman also directed a contraband trade in heretical books between London and Oxford. Writing in August 1528, Anne Boleyn asked Wolsey, "I beseech your grace with all mine heart to remember the parson of Honey Lane for my sake shortly" (Brigden 128n225 quoting BL, Cotton MS Vespasian F iii, fo. 15v, paraphrased in LP 4/3, Appendix 197). Through the influence of Anne and Wolsey, the parson was not tried for heresy but let off with a secret penance (Brigden 161). Foxe (4.769, 5.416) names the rector "Robert." He seems to be a separate person from Thomas Forman of Norfolk, who received his BA from Queens' College, Cambridge (1512) and later became its Master. There he protected Lutheran undergraduates and hid Lutheran books from confiscation. Cf. H.C. Porter, *Reformation and Reaction in Tudor Cambridge* (1958; Hamden, CT: Archon, 1972) 42–43, 46.

194/21–22 **But . . . darkenesse.** Cf. John 3.20–21.

194/29 **walke in darkenesse.** Cf. John 12.35.

194/30–31 **the church . . . workes.** Cf. CWM 6/1. 380/13–19. Tyndale omits More's admonition to put one's trust "in goddys goodnes" (6/1.380/19).

195/22 **the lawe.** Tyndale makes the law of God an intrinsic factor in justification, cf. nn to 38/18–19, 106/19–107/23, and 134/7–8. The law is not just preparatory, as in Luther, for whom the law brings a salutary despair over ever fulfilling God's precepts with the love he requires. Tyndale sees the law preceding the announcement of Jesus, but the latter effects loving submission to the law

(195/21–196/12), closely linked with trust in God's mercy (196/ 19–22). This emphasis in Tyndale may well derive from the understanding of Scripture itself as the communication of "Goddis lawe" as this was emphatically stated in the *General Prologue* (1395) of the Wycliffite vernacular Bible. Translation into English is to serve the instruction of every person in this saving law in an accurate and understandable form, cf. Deansley 255f. (JW)

195/22 **God . . . vn to vs.** Cf. Rom. 10.14–17.

195/25–26 **I fele . . . lawe.** Cf. Rom. 7.18.

196/7 **mollyfye and wax softe.** Example of doublet.

196/24–25 **Now . . . springeth.** Cf. CWM 8/1.43/9–10. Cf. *Pathway* B3v, *Mammon* A7–B7.

196/25 **out of which fayth loue springeth.** Cf. Gal. 5.6. NT has "faith which by love is mighty in operacion" (Wallis 397/6; TNT 279A). Sidenote has "Fayth which- [sic] worketh thorow loue is the true fayth and all god requireth of vs." In "Sermon against Luther, 1521," Fisher (331/2–3) translated the Vulgate's *fides qu[a]e per dilectionem operatur* as "Faythe whiche is wrought by loue." As Tyndale scornfully notes in 1528, Fisher thus "maketh a verbe passive of a verbe deponente" (*Obedience* I1v). In attacking Fisher, Tyndale cites Erasmus' 1516 NT for Gal. 5.6, *fides per dilectionem operans,* with the present participle. For further analysis, cf. Marc'hadour, "Tyndale and Fisher's 1521 Sermon," WCS 150–53. In classical Latin, *operor* is a deponent verb, passive in form but active in meaning. However, Lewis and Short in *A Latin Dictionary* (Oxford: Clarendon, 1955) list *opero* as an active verb in ecclesiastical Latin, meaning "produce by working." Both forms are found in the scholastic description of the sacraments by which they give grace *ex opere operato* (passive) "from the work performed" (e.g., the consecration of the bread and wine by the priest) and *ex opere operantis* (active) "from the work of the worker" (e.g., the devout reception by the communicant).

196/26 **power . . . neyboure.** Cf. 1 John 4.11.

196/31–32 **For . . . christ.** Cf. 1 John 4.10.

196/33 **fayth thorow preachinge.** Cf. Rom. 10.17.

197/3 **loue of God to vs warde.** Cf. Eph. 2.4.

197/3–4 **we receaue . . . fayth.** Cf. Eph. 2.8–9.

197/6–7 **fayth only iustifyeth vs.** Cf. Rom. 3.28.

197/8–10 **we meane . . . belie vs.** Cf. CWM 8/1.52/16–17.

197/13–14 **studye . . . longe.** Cf. Ps. 38.12.

197/18–198/1 **what faith . . . deuels fayth.** Tyndale contrasts saving faith with other dispositions: 197/18 **what faith it is that iusti-fyeth vs.** Cf. Rom. 3.28. 197/23–31 **story fayth . . . bloude.** Cf. CWM 8/1.315/19–21. 197/29–30 **And the faith . . . miracles.** Cf. 1 Cor. 13.2. 198/1 **deuels fayth.** Cf. Jas. 2.19.

198/7–10 **yf fayth . . . doctrine.** Cf. CWM 6/1.381/22–28, 8/1.401/26–31.

198/9–10 **as the tre . . . frute.** Cf. Matt. 7.17, Luke 6.43.

198/10–11 **then . . . better.** Cf. CWM 6/1.382/3–6. This objection was raised by Dr. Forman's inquisitors.

198/12–13 **good werkes . . . tamed.** Cf. CWM 8/1.401/26–31.

198/18–19 **if . . . iustifieth not.** Cf. CWM 6/1.382/12–14.

198/19 **fayth alone.** Cf. Jas. 2.22.

199/4–5 **inwarde . . . marcie.** Cf. CWM 8/1.90/29–31.

199/14 **he gaue his sonne for me.** Cf. Rom. 8.32.

199/16 **Oure . . . loue vs.** Cf. 1 John 4.19.

199/19 **he loued . . . enimies.** Cf. Rom. 5.8.

199/22 **The father loueth hys chyld.** Cf. 1 John 3.1.

200/2–4 **the man . . . loue god.** Cf. 1 John 4.20.

200/12–13 **Paul . . . loue.** Cf. CWM 6/1.385/28–29. As in his NT, Tyndale substitutes "loue" (200/13) for More's "cheryte" (CWM 6/1.385/29).

200/14–17 **a man . . . charite.** Cf. CWM 6/1.383/30–34, 385/17–20. More quotes 1 Cor. 13.2–3 twice in Bk. 4, Ch. 11. Whereas More's *Dialogue* uses "charite" (6/1.383/33) and "cheryte" (6/1.385/20) in both paraphrases, Tyndale's *Answer* uses "loue" twice (200/15–16) but "charite" (200/17) once.

200/33 **deuels marters and not Gods.** Cyprian, Bishop of Carth-age, had to deal with Christians who had fallen away during the persecution of Decius (AD 250–51). Some were then seeking im-mediate reconciliation with the church on the basis of "letters of peace" issued to them by those who had suffered for the faith. In a letter of AD 250 Cyprian admonishes the clergy of Carthage to observe the law and discipline of the church, Par. 3 (Ep. 10 in PL

4.255; Ep. 15 in CSEL 3/2.515; Ep. 10 in ANF 5.291). In his treatise *On the Unity of the Church* (AD 251), Cyprian explains that even those who have confessed the faith in time of persecution can later become ensnared by the devil, Ch. 20–22 (PL 4.482–84; CSEL 3/1.227–30; ANF 5.427–28). Tyndale finds these martyrs presuming on their own merits as able to atone for the sins of others. The right attitude would have been to refer the lapsed to the passion of Christ, the sole ground of mercy, and to bear their own suffering as a witness beneficial to their fellow Christians. (JW)

201/1–2 **all . . . bloudeshedynge.** Cf. Eph. 1.7.

201/5–6 **saue . . . some.** Cf. 1 Cor. 9.22.

201/6–7 **for . . . al thinge.** 1 Cor. 9.19, 2 Cor. 1.6–7.

201/7 **not to winne heuen.** But Paul in 1 Cor. 9.24–25 urges the Corinthians to "runne" for "an vncorruptible croune" (Wallis 358/20–22; TNT 252E).

201/10–11 **brother . . . bloude.** Cf. 1 Cor. 8.11.

201/12 **rewarde is greate in heaven.** Cf. Matt. 5.12, Luke 6.23.

201/13–28 **And all . . . desyreth me.** A passage recalling 107/2–14 on the freedom from spiritual self-interest that flows from justification, a centerpiece of Reformation piety. (JW)

201/13–15 **And all . . . heuen.** Cf. Acts 13.38–39, Heb. 9.15.

201/24–25 **For . . . Christe.** Cf. Matt. 25.40, 1 John 4.11.

201/29 **S. Iames.** Cf. Jas. 2.19–20 quoted by CWM 6/1.386/9–17. In the second edition of *Dialogue* (May 1531), More added to Bk. 4, Ch. 11 a further explanation of the relationship between faith and works (CWM 6/1.386/18–388/34, 6/2.557). For other long additions to *Dialogue,* cf. 79/9 and 184/2nn on images.

201/30 **S. Augustine answereth.** *Unio Dissidentium* (1.Q4v) quotes Augustine on the reconciliation of Paul and James: "For the former [Rom. 3.28] is speaking of the works which precede faith, whereas the latter [Jas. 2.20], of those which follow on faith." From CCL 44A.221; *Eighty-Three Different Questions* (AD c395–96), end of Ch. 76, tr. David L. Mosher, FOTC 70 (Washington, DC: Catholic University of America P, 1977) 196. In *On Faith and Works* (AD 412–13), Augustine explains that when Paul taught justification by faith, not by the works of the law, he did not mean to denigrate the good works that follow faith and the Spirit's gift of love. James, then, is one of the apostles who make it clear that faith without works of love is of no avail. *De fide et operibus,* not cited in *Unio,* was in vol. 6 of the Amerbach edition of Augustine (Basel, 1506) and was printed separately at Cologne in 1527 (PL 40.197–230; CSEL 41.35–97; ACW 48). (JW)

201/31–32 **begatt . . . trueth.** Cf. Jas. 1.18.

202/1 **a new creature.** Cf. 2 Cor. 5.17.

202/8 **deuelles haue fayth.** Cf. Jas. 2.19. In Sermon 158, Rom. 8.30–31, Against the Pelagians (AD 417), not cited in *Unio Dissidentium,* Augustine urges his congregation to have a better faith than the demons do, Par. 6 (PL 38.865; Rotelle 3/5.117).

202/14 **trienge . . . paciens.** Cf. Jas. 1.3.

202/17–18 **thynke . . . synne.** Cf. 1 John 1.8.

202/20 **no such faith . . . a man.** Cf. Jas. 2.14.

202/21 **faith only iustifieth.** Cf. Rom. 3.28.

202/21–22 **a man . . . fayth only.** Jas. 2.24.

202/26–30 **Iames . . . sene.** Cf. CWM 8/2.688/2–7.

202/31–32 **if . . . god.** Rom. 4.2.

203/3–5 **But . . . promised him.** Cf. Gen. 15.4–6.

203/6–7 **Abraham . . . reioysed.** Cf. John 8.56.

203/9 **Abraham offered his sonne.** Jas. 2.21.

203/9–10 **scripture fulfilled.** Jas. 2.23.

203/10–11 **Abraham . . . frende.** Jas. 2.23 quoting Gen. 15.6.

203/13–15 **he was . . . and him.** Cf. Gen. 15.4–18.

203/17–18 **I wyll shew . . . workes.** Jas. 2.18.

203/19 **now . . . god.** Gen. 22.12.

203/23–25 **As if . . . then.** Cf. Jas. 2.15–16.

204/2–3 **laye . . . them selues.** Cf. Matt. 23.4, Luke 11.46.

204/11–13 **first iustifienge . . . seconde iustifienge.** Cf. CWM 6/1.391/20–27. More agrees that humans cannot merit the grace of Baptism but asserts that after Baptism they must perform good works. Tyndale rejects the logic of this second step, for what can supplement the one gift of God's mercy and forgiveness? (JB)

However, More anticipates the position of Richard Hooker (?1554–1600), who distinguishes between the righteousness of justification and the righteousness of sanctification, cf. PS 3.203n1. Cf. "A Learned Discourse of Justification," in *The Folger Library Edition of the Works of Richard Hooker* 5, gen. ed. W. Speed Hill, Belknap (Cambridge: Harvard UP, 1990) 113/16–114/4.

204/16–17 **Dauid . . . repented.** Cf. 2 Sam. 11–12.1–25. In a passage not found in *Unio Dissidentium,* Augustine contrasts David's single lapse into adultery with Solomon's continued submission to his idolatrous wives. Cf. *Christian Doctrine* (AD c396–97) 3.21.31 (CCL 32.96; 1NPNF 2.565).

204/S4 **Psal. 51.** The Hebrew number. In the two other instances where a psalm is identified, *Answer* follows the Vulgate number, cf. 63/7–9, 67/12–15nn. 204/19–20 **haue mercy . . . my synne.** Ps. 51.1. 204/21–22 **make . . . reioyse.** Ps. 51.8. 204/24–26 **god . . . requireth.** Cf. Ps. 51.16–17. 204/27–28 **he wold . . . Ierusalem.** Cf. Ps. 51.18. 204/29–30 **we shall . . . agayne.** Cf. Ps. 51.19.

204/31–32 **sinned . . . wash it of.** Cf. Rev. 1.5.

205/6 **Christ . . . beleue.** Cf. Rom. 3.24.

205/19–24 **geue almes . . . phareses.** Cf. Matt. 6.2.

206/6–7 **preachynge . . . herte.** Cf. Gal. 3.21.

206/7 **causeth wrath.** Cf. Rom. 4.15.

206/8 **vttereth the synne only.** Cf. Rom. 3.20.

206/9–10 **righteweysnesse . . . meane.** Cf. Rom. 9.31–32.

206/21–22 **we . . . dedes.** Cf. Rom. 3.28. Tyndale makes "fayth" and "grace" (206/21) synonymous as the source of justification.

206/24–25 **maketh . . . and vs.** Cf. Eph. 2.14. *Answer* says "faith" (206/22) makes us one with God; NT says "he," i.e. "Christ" (Wallis 403/8; TNT 283C).

206/34–207/1 **forgeuen . . . sake.** Cf. 1 John 2.12.

207/5–6 **we perished . . . deliuer vs.** Cf. Ps. 56.1, 2, 13.

207/6–7 **god wyll assiste us.** Cf. Isa. 41.14.

207/7 **cloth vs.** Cf. Matt. 6.30, Luke 12.28. **fede vs.** Cf. Matt. 6.26, Luke 12.24. **fight for vs.** Cf. Exod. 14.14.

207/7–8 **rid vs . . . enimies.** Cf. Ps. 31.15.

207/8–9 **the righteweysse lieueth euer bye faith.** Cf. Hab. 2.4 quoted in Rom. 1.17, Gal. 3.11, Heb. 10.38.

207/11–14 **blessed . . . vnrightweysnesse.** Cf. Ps. 32.1–2.

207/19 **fayth . . . only.** Cf. Rom. 3.24–25.

207/21 **To beleue in christes bloud.** Cf. Rom. 3.25.

207/22–23 **makynge . . . godwarde.** Cf. Eph. 2.15–16.

207/27–28 **blasphemous wordes . . . synners.** Cf. CWM 6/1.396
/2–4. The pervasive influence of sin, even in the righteous, was
defended by Luther in his 1521 works against the papal bull *Exsurge Domine.* See his *Defense and Explanation of All the Articles,* December 1520 (e.g., WA 7.328–45; LW 32.19–29) and his response
to a doctrinal attack by Jacobus Latomus (e.g., WA 8.63–73,
88–99; LW 32.172–81, 202–17), cf. 30/19n. Later, in his sermon on
10 January 1524, Luther claimed that Mary sinned to some extent
in losing the child Jesus in Luke 2.43–45 (WA 15.414–17; not in
LW). Tyndale suggests the same idea in *Obedience* (S4v) and at
208/7–10. This sermon did not circulate in printed form in the
16c, but Tyndale could have heard about it during the months
when he probably visited Wittenberg in 1524–25. (JW)

207/28 **Ihon baptiste.** What More drew out of Luther's doctrine is
correct in its application to John the Baptist, as Scripture shows,
both in gospel passages concerning John (207/29–208/2) and in
Romans, chapters 1–3. (JW)

207/29–30 **I had nede . . . to me.** Matt. 3.14.

207/32–33 **behold . . . worlde.** John 1.29.

208/2 **Ihon . . . thynge.** Cf. Matt. 17.11, Mark 9.12.

208/3–4 **proue all flesh synners.** Cf. Rom. 3.20.

208/4 **send them to Christe.** Cf. Rom. 1.5.

208/8 **whi did christ rebuke hyr.** John Chrysostom attributed some
vainglory to Mary in Homily 27 on Matt. 8.14–15 (Ch. 3 in PG
57.347, Ch. 5 in 1NPNF 10.187), Homily 44 on Matt. 12.46–49,
Ch. 1 (PG 57.463–65; 1NPNF 10.278–80), and Homily 21, Ch. 2
on John 2.4 (PG 59.130; 1NPNF 14.74). His opinion was cited in
Erasmus' annotation on Matt. 12.47, *Quarentes te.*) 1519 NT
(Reeve 1.58). These sermons are not quoted in *Unio Dissidentium.*
Tyndale holds that Mary, like other biblical saints, did not consent
to sinful flesh. (JW)

208/9–10 **seke him .iij. dayes.** Cf. Luke 2.45–48.

208/10 **Chrisostimus.** John (c349–407) served as Patriarch of Constantinople (398–404), where his eloquence earned him the title
"Golden-Mouthed" (NCE 7.1041–44). Along with Athanasius
(c296–373), Basil (c330–79), and Gregory Nazianzen (329–89),
John Chrysostom is one of the four great Eastern Fathers. Eras-

mus dedicated his Latin translation of Chrysostom to the Catholic Bishop of Augsburg soon after the Augsburg Confession was proclaimed on 25 June 1530. Cf. Ep. 2359, To Christopher of Stadion, Freiburg, 5 August 1530 (Allen 9.3–6; not yet in CWE). After Augustine and Jerome, *Unio Dissidentium* quotes most frequently from Chrysostom (c7%), with forty-two passages from his homilies, not counting thirteen selections from the *Opus imperfectum in Matthaeum* (c2%), a 5c Arian commentary wrongly attributed to Chrysostom (PG 56.611–946).

208/11–12 **She loked . . . blesse hyr.** Cf. Luke 1.49, 55.

208/19–20 **potter . . . amisse.** Cf. Jer. 18.4.

208/22–23 **good . . . doo.** Rom. 7.19.

208/32–33 **yf . . . oure selues.** 1 John 1.8. More makes a Latin paraphrase of the biblical verse at his trial (Roper 89/18–20). Dr. Faustus gives a Latin paraphrase of 1 John 1.8 with translation, [Scene 1], lines 41–43, in Gill (Vol. 2, 1990).

209/1 **faith and dedes.** In a dialogue-within-a-dialogue, the Catholic inquisitor affirms against the Lutheran sympathizer Dr. Forman that there is a certain parity between faith and good works in justification (CWM 6/1.397/20–22). Tyndale, however, asserts the radical deficiency of works when measured by their norm, namely, Christ's love for humankind. But faith has value from outside itself, namely, from God who utters the word that faith lays hold of. In his refutation of the points Tyndale set forth as a prisoner at Vilvoorde, Jacobus Latomus singled out his finding sinful those deeds that lack Christ's fulness of charity. For Latomus, those whom God justifies receive a measure of the Spirit that elicits in them sufficient love to fulfil God's law. Cf. *Confutationum* in *Opera* 188r, 190r; tr. Willis 357, 362; cf. also 170/14–18n. (JW)

209/16 **schole doctryne.** Scotus emphasizes God's freedom in choosing humans for heaven apart from foreknowledge of their merits, *ante praevisa merita*. Occam and Biel attribute election to God's foreknowledge of human merits, *post praevisa merita*. Cf. Oberman, *Harvest* 187, 205, 211, 473. Tyndale rejects the notion that predestination has any foundation in human actions.

209/17–18 **god . . . chosen them.** Cf. CWM 6/1.401/16–20.

209/19–21 **God sawe before . . . chose Peter.** Cf. CWM

6/1.401/34–402/3. For Peter's repentance, cf. Matt. 26.75, Mark 14.72, Luke 22.61–62. For Judas' remorse, cf. Matt. 27.3–5. Tyndale interprets Judas' return of the thirty pieces of silver as a sign of contrition, but More interprets his suicide as an act of despair. More could have found this theory of predestination based on God's foreknowledge of a person's faith in Proposition 60 (PL 35.2078–79) of an early work (AD 394–95), *Augustine on Romans: Propositions from the Epistle to the Romans,* tr. Paula Fredriksen Landes, Texts and Translations 23, Early Christian Literature Series 6 (Chico, CA: Scholars, 1982) 30–33. This paragraph is not found in *Unio Dissidentium,* which quotes heavily from Augustine's later anti-Pelagian works. More's contemporary Eck in 1514 wrote *Chrysopassus,* "a treatise on predestination in which he argues that God predestines to rewards and punishments on the basis of fore-knowledge of human merits and demerits" (OER 2.17).

209/25 **peter shuld faull.** Cf. Matt. 26.34, Mark 14.30, Luke 22.34, John 13.38.

209/25–26 **prayed . . . agayne.** Cf. Luke 22.32.

209/29–30 **I haue kepte . . . from euell.** John 17.12, 13, 15.

210/3–4 **Iudas . . . couetousnesse.** Cf. John 12.6.

210/6–7 **by nature . . . god.** Cf. Eph. 2.3.

210/18–19 **Ar we not . . . Adam.** Cf. Rom. 5.12.

211/1–2 **It is not . . . god.** Rom. 9.16. *Answer* and KJV give "run-nynge" (211/1) but NT gives "cunnynge" (Wallis 332/19; TNT 234D). The Greek *trechontos* from *trecho* means "run" literally but "exert oneself to the limit" figuratively. See *A Greek-English Lexicon of the NT,* ed. William F. Arndt and F. Wilbur Gingrich (U of Chicago P, 1957).

211/3–4 **The first grace . . . frely.** *Unio Dissidentium* (1.K1) quotes Augustine on the gratuity of initial justification, Sermon 169, Phil. 3.3–16, Against the Pelagians (AD 416), Par. 3 (PL 38.916–17; Rotelle 3/5.223–24).

211/9 **thefe . . . deeth.** Cf. Luke 23.43.

211/13–14 **the mercie . . . was made.** Cf. Eph. 1.4.

211/17–19 **wherefore . . . frewyll.** *Unio Dissidentium* quotes the anti-Pelagian treatise, *On Grace and Free Will* (AD c426–27), in which Augustine explains that God gives us commandments to teach us our inability to keep them without grace (UD 1.K3; PL

44.900–1; INPNF 5.457). Upholding *sola gratia,* Tyndale refers to More's synergistic position in the phrase "to gether with gods grace" (211/19).

211/17–18 **wherefore . . . fayth.** Cf. CWM 6/1.403/12–13. Tyndale substitutes "fayth" (211/18) for More's "good workes" (CWM 6/1.403/13).

211/18–21 **if . . . God.** Cf. CWM 6/1.403/17–20.

211/23–25 **the will . . . the father.** Cf. CWM 8/1.503/26–27. More never wrote the refutation of Tyndale's Answer to Bk. 3 and 4, promised at CWM 8/1.503/6–8. But *Confutation* responds to Tyndale's essential arguments by addressing all of the major topics in the Foundational Essay except religious ceremonies, which *Dialogue* had treated so fully.

211/24 **the carte must draw the horses.** Tilley C103.

212/5–6 **Blindnesse . . . good.** Cf. Matt. 6.22–23, Luke 11.34.

212/13–14 **lustes of their fleshe.** Cf. Gal. 5.16, 1 John 2.16.

212/24 **the clergie burneth no man.** Cf. CWM 6/1.410/7–8.

212/28–29 **kinge . . . croune them.** The following list summarizes the Acts of Parliament dealing with heresy:

1382, 5 Richard II, St. 2, Ch. 5, ordered the arrest of preachers of heretical sermons (*Statutes* 2.25–26).

1401, 2 Henry IV, Ch. 15, *De heretico comburendo,* popularly known as *Ex officio,* ordered burning of an unrepentant or lapsed heretic by the secular government (*Statutes* 2.125–28, also in Foxe 3.239–40).

1414, 2 Henry V, St. 1, Ch. 7, linked heresy to sedition and treason (*Statutes* 2.181–84, also in Foxe 3.353–55).

1533–34, 25 Henry VIII, Ch. 14, replaced the statute of 1401 applying papal laws against heresy by its own: accusations were not accepted in private but from grand juries; two lawful witnesses were necessary; trials must be open; the monarch's writ was necessary to burn a heretic; denial of papal supremacy was not heresy; bail was allowed (*Statutes* 3.454–55).

1539, 31 Henry VIII, Ch. 14, Six Articles of Religion. The First Article defined denial of transubstantiation as heresy punishable by death (*Statutes* 3.739–40). Because of its severity, this act was popularly called the "Bloody Statute" (OED 2.c.).

1543–44, 35 Henry VIII, Ch. 5, confirmed the Six Articles of Religion but required accusations of heresy to be brought by twelve men or more (*Statutes* 3.960–62).

1547, 1 Edward VI, Ch. 12, repealed the statutes of 1382, 1414, 1533–34, 1539 and 1543–44 (*Statutes* 4/1.19).

1554, 1 & 2 Mary & Philip, Ch. 6, revived the statutes of 1382, 1401 and 1414 (*Statutes* 4/1.244).

1559, 1 Elizabeth, Ch. 1 (*Statutes* 4/1.351–52), repealed the statutes of 1382, 1401, 1414 and 1554.

1677, 29 Charles II, Ch. 9, abrogated the writ *De heretico cumburendo* and substituted ecclesiastical penalties such as excommunication for the death penalty in punishing heresy (*Statutes* 5.850). In the British Isles a statute is a formal Act of Parliament (OED 2.). A writ is a legal document issued by king, bishop etc. (OED 3.a.) or by a court in the name of a competent legal authority directing a person to do or refrain from doing a specified act (OED 3.b.).

212/30 **Henry the .v.** Cf. CWM 6/1.409/24–410/6 and CWM 6/2.720. Because he rejected papal supremacy, Lord Cobham (c1378–1418) was executed for treason and heresy by being hanged in chains over fire (Foxe 3.320–402, 541–45). In an earlier draft of *1 Henry IV,* Shakespeare used Cobham's given name, Sir John Oldcastle, cf. "my old lad of the castle" (1.2.37). Shakespeare changed the name to "Falstaff" after Cobham's descendant, lord chamberlain in charge of licensing plays (1596–97), censored the depiction of the Lollard martyr as a tippler, *Norton Shakespeare* 1152–54. Tyndale refers again to the unlawful succession of the House of Lancaster to the throne of Richard II (*1 John* H7). He affirms that Henry V was misled by the higher clergy (*Prelates* F4v), especially into invading France (*Obedience* V4v, *Prelates* G1v). For chanting the divine office in relays (*Matthew* i6v), Tyndale mocks Henry V's foundations, the Bridgittine monastery of Syon and the Charterhouse at Sheen.

213/8–9 **noble bloude.** Tyndale refers to the 15c civil war between the White Rose of York and the Red Rose of Lancaster. In *1 Henry IV* (performed 1596–97, published 1598) and *2 Henry IV* (performed 1597–98, published 1600), the name of "Poins," Prince

Hal's companion, may be derived from the Poyntz family of Gloucestershire. Cf. Giorgio Melchiori, *Shakespeare's Garter Plays: Edward III to Merry Wives of Windsor* (Newark: U of Delaware P, 1994) 136n12. Tyndale tutored the two sons of Sir John and Lady Anne (née Poyntz) Walsh at Little Sodbury. Later, Tyndale lived in the English House at Antwerp with her distant relative, the merchant Thomas Poyntz, who tried unsuccessfully to obtain Tyndale's release from prison at Vilvoorde (Mozley 23ff, 264ff, 302ff).

213/11–12 **Marten . . . turke.** Cf. CWM 6/1.411/21–24, 32/15–16.

213/11–15 **Marten . . . invade vs.** Cf. CWM 8/1.123/31–35. In his 1518 *Explanations of the Ninety-Five Theses* (cf. WA 1.535; LW 31.91f), Luther spoke of the Turks as God's rod of punishment against sinful Christians and suggested that to war against the Turks was to oppose God. This opinion was censured in Leo X's *Exsurge Domine* in 1520 (DS 1484) and by the Sorbonne in 1521. Cf. C.E. Du Boulay, *Historia Universitatis Parisiensis* 6 (Paris, 1683; Frankfurt/M.: Minerva, 1966) 126. Luther's remark was a standard object of Catholic attack, e.g., by Eck in Ch. 22 of his *Enchiridion,* "Concerning the War against the Turks" (Fraenkel 241–46; Battles 155–58). After the Turkish victory at Mohács in 1526, Luther wrote the work to which Tyndale refers here, *On War Against the Turk,* 1529, that set forth the Emperor's secular duty to defend his realm and subjects against Turkish incursions (WA 30/2.107–48; LW 46.161–205, esp. 184–92). (JW)

213/16 **xvj.** Tyndale makes no comment on Bk. 4, Ch. 15 where More argues for the rigorous treatment of Luther's followers.

213/17 **he allegeth counsels.** Cf. CWM 6/1.423/23–25. In Bk. 4, Ch. 17 (not 16), More refers to three heretics who had been condemned by unnamed councils and synods: Arius by Nicea I in 325 (NCE 1.814–15), Pelagius by the Council of Ephesus in 431 (29/22–24n), and the Manichaean Faustus by Leo I (pope, 440–61) at a Roman synod in 444 (NCE 9.153–60). Earlier, in Bk. 4, Ch. 2, More refers to the provincial Council of Hiereia, which condemned icons in 754, and to the ecumenical Council of Nicea II, which approved them in 787, cf. CWM 6/1.355/8–10.

213/20 **Augustine / Hierom and Cipriane.** Cf. CWM 6/1.420/13–14.

213/21 **S. prosperus.** A layman like More, Prosper of Aquitaine (c390–c455) defended Augustine's doctrine of grace and predestination against the dissenting views of the monks of southern Gaul (NCE 11.878). Prosper's *Adversus inimicos gratiae libellus,* against John Cassian, came out in Mainz in 1524 and was part of Johann Sichardus' *Antidotum contra diversas hereses* (Basel, 1528). (JW)

Tyndale sees need of Prosper's witness against More's doctrine of free choice. In denying that we can prepare ourselves for grace, Tyndale invokes Prosper in his Prologue to the Epistle to the Romans (Wallis 296/25; TNT 209). *Unio Dissidentium* quotes once from Prosper's *Liber Sententiarum* (CCL 68A) and fourteen times from *Call of the Nations* (PL 51.647–722, ACW 14), which it attributes to Ambrose.

213/22 **the vnion of doctoures.** Cf. 188/3n.

213/23 **marters.** Cf. CWM 6/1.421/32–33.

213/23–24 **take the calfe.** Tyndale challenges More to find even one early martyr who died for the faith that More holds. Tyndale could be referring to Erasmus, *Adagia* no. 151, *Taurum tollet, qui vitulum sustulerit* (ASD 2/1.266–68; CWE 31.192–93); "He may bear (carry) a Bull that hath borne (carried) a calf," Tilley B711.

213/25 **bewarre . . . liue well.** Cf. CWM 6/1.421/15–18, 22–24. When the Messenger describes the fasting and almsgiving of the reformers, More as Mentor tells him to beware of false prophets.

213/28–214/25 **Tindale . . . .vj. pens.** In responding to *Dialogue's* Bk. 4, Ch. 17, Tyndale inadvertently omits the heading "xvij."

213/28–214/1 **Tindale . . . harme.** Cf. CWM 6/1.424/10–16.

214/1 **he sware not.** When unnamed persons brought accusations of heresy against Tyndale, he was interrogated by John Bell, chancellor and archdeacon of the diocese of Gloucester from 1518 to 1527 (Mozley 31n). Contradicting More, Tyndale declares in the Preface to his Pentateuch of 1530 (Mombert 4/34–41; TOT 4) that he was not required to forswear his beliefs, but was verbally abused and dismissed (Daniell 75–76). The process for investigating a charge of heresy was reformed by statute in 1533–34, cf. 212/28–29n.

214/3 **by him . . . saued by.** Cf. 1 Tim. 4.10.

214/5–6 **light . . . Ihesus.** Cf. John 8.12.

214/8 **darkenesse of deeth.** The pope leads souls here, contrary to Christ, who will give light to those who sit "in shadowe of deth," Luke 1.79 (Wallis 127/5; TNT 91G).

214/9–11 **S. Augustine & S. Hierome . . . saluacion.** Cf. CWM 6/1.425/16, 24–26. In quoting Ep. 265, To Seleuciana, n.d., *Unio Dissidentium* omits Augustine's reference to public penance for serious sins in Par. 7 (PL 33.1088; CSEL 57.645; Parsons 5.280). *Unio* (2.C6) quotes the same letter on private confession to God for lesser sins in Par. 8 (PL 33.1089; CSEL 57.646; Parsons 5.281). In his eulogy of Fabiola, Jerome describes how this noble Roman matron took her place in sackcloth among the public penitents because she remarried after divorce. Cf. Ep. 77, To Oceanus (AD 399), Par. 4–5 (PL 22.692–93; 2NPNF 6.159–60). Jerome's comment on Jesus' conferral of the power of binding and loosing (cf. Matt. 16.19) accused the bishops and presbyters of his time of wrongly understanding the text as giving them authority to condemn the innocent or remit the sins of the guilty (PL 26.118). Jerome wrote his Commentary on Matthew in AD 398 (2 NPNF 6.495, note to Jerome's preface). (JW)

214/14 **ferre other then now.** Tyndale asks why More does not state that annual confession of serious sin to the parish priest was not imposed on all Christians until Lateran IV in 1215.

214/15–16 **I meruell . . . hell.** Cf. CWM 6/1.425/31–33.

214/27–28 **the clergie . . . doctours did.** Cf. CWM 6/1.428/26–28. *Unio Dissidentium* (2.E6) quotes Augustine's description of the verbal persuasion which the clergy addressed to the schismatic Donatists. The laity, however, reacted with violence to Donatist assaults on persons and property. Cf. Ep. 88, Catholic Clergy of Hippo to Januarius, Donatist bishop and primate (AD 406), Par. 8–9 (PL 33.307–8; CSEL 34/2.414–16; Parsons 3.29–31). *Unio* does not quote Ep. 185, To Boniface, tribune and count in Africa (AD 417), *On the Treatment of the Donatists.* Here Augustine approves physical coercion in 6.21 (PL 33.802; CSEL 57.19–20; Parsons 4.161–63) plus fines and exile but not the death penalty in 7.26 (PL 33.805; CSEL 57.25; Parsons 4.167–68).

214/30 **wil . . . light.** Cf. John 3.20.

215/5–6 **ye leaue . . . hangman.** Tyndale does not comment on

More's assertion of the prince's duty to persecute heretics in *Dialogue,* Bk. 4, Ch. 15 (CWM 6/1.415–18).

215/9–11 **Saynt paul . . . slew them.** CWM 6/1.429/23–28. The two heretics rejected by Paul were Hymenaeus and Alexander, cf. 1 Tim. 1.20.

215/11–13 **O expounder . . . out of his life.** Tyndale remembers having read this odd interpretation of the precept to shun a heretic after two admonitions. But he mistakenly thought it was in Hugh of St. Cher's *Postillae,* which surrounded the Vulgate text in the Amerbach *Biblia latina cum postillis Hugonis de s. Charo,* 7 vols. (Basel, 1498–1502). The interpretation comes instead from a story told by John Colet repeated by Erasmus in his annotation on *Deuita.*) 1519, 1522 NT (Reeve 3.701). At a meeting of "the Council" (probably the commission of 1511–12 that convicted some Lollards), someone asked what biblical basis there was for inflicting capital punishment on heretics. An elderly theologian offered Titus 3.10, which says, *"devita,"* using the imperative of *devitare* ("to avoid") to mean "to take someone *de vita*" ("out of life"). Erasmus concludes with a warning about the danger of mistaking the meanings of words, as when doctors give as a remedy what they should recognize from the label as poison. Erasmus had also included this incident in Folly's narrative of what she heard on one of her frequent visits to theological disputations (*Moriae encomium,* ASD 4/3.186/53–54; CWE 27.146). (JW)

215/11 **hugo charensys.** The Dominican Hugh of St. Cher (c1200–1263) compiled a Latin Concordance of the Bible (1240), wrote *Postillae* or exegetical notes on the whole Bible, and attempted textual emendation of the Vulgate (NCE 7.193–94). Although he defends Hugh of St. Cher, More plays with consonance on his name: *vel Carrensem conuincat errasse,* Ep. 83, To a Monk, n.p., <March–September 1519> (CWM 15.216/9–10).

215/13–14 **whome . . . flesh.** Cf. 1 Cor. 5.1–5.

215/15 **asshamed . . . repented.** Cf. 2 Cor. 7.9.

215/17–19 **ye deliuer . . . asshes.** King Utopus, who ruled by reason alone, granted religious toleration to all except those who denied the immortality of the soul and divine providence (CWM 4.221/27–32). In his *Apology,* More denies beating heretics except for those whose reason was underdeveloped: a child and a former inmate of Bedlam (CWM 9.117–18). He specifically denies mistreating George Constantine, a distributor of contraband books (CWM 9.118/33–37), and Segar Nicholson, a Cambridge bookseller (CWM 9.119/18–26). During More's term as Lord Chancellor, 25 October 1529 to 16 May 1532, six men were executed for heresy by the secular government with his approval: Thomas Hitton (d. Maidstone, February 1530), Thomas Benet or Dusgate (d. Exeter, January 1531), Thomas Bilney (d. Norwich, August 1531), Richard Bayfield and John Tewkesbury (d. London, December 1531), and James Bainham (d. London, April 1532) (CWM 8/3.1207, 1247, 1645), cf. 114/17–18n. More mentions Hitton (112/12n) and Bilney (146/12–13n) by name; perhaps More was unaware of Benet in the West Country; More directed the search for Bayfield and Tewkesbury and interrogated Bainham at Chelsea, cf. Ackroyd 292–99. Thanks to Andrew Hope for the reference to Benet (Foxe 5.18–26). Bainham's public affirmation of Reformation belief ritually undid his public abjuration. Cf. Stephen Greenblatt, *Renaissance Self-Fashioning: From More to Shakespeare* (U of Chicago P, 1980) 74–84. In his *Apology,* published about Easter 1533 (CWM 9.xc), More protests "that men shold causelesse vppon such surmysed and vnproued crueltye, chaunge the good lawis byfore made agaynste heretyques" (CWM 9.167/8–10). He declares ironically that he is "but a playne soule and can inuent no neweltyes, but [is] content to stande to the olde order and lawes . . ." (CWM 9.168/17–18). A few months later, More sent Erasmus a copy of the inscription on the tomb he hoped to occupy in Chelsea, describing himself as "a source of trouble to thieves, murderers, and heretics." From Ep. 2831, Chelsea <June? 1533> (Allen 10.261/93–95; More, *Selected Letters* 181).

Tyndale deplores the violence of churchmen who urge their followers to win salvation by killing Turks, Jews, and heretics (*Obedience* C7v). Whereas More defends such a policy, Tyndale repeatedly condemns those who advocate the burning of heretics (212/26). Curates who make secret accusations of heresy against their parishioners resemble the wolves who attack the flock in Acts 20

(*Obedience* K5r–v). Clerics accused of heresy are questioned in secret, constrained in prison, and degraded from office before being burnt (*Obedience* K1v). Like Pilate, papists in heresy trials condemn the innocent to death (*Mammon* A4v). Tyndale hopes that a true Christian would help the weak, not threaten them with literal fire (*Matthew* a6). Through Christ's favor, even those who built their hopes on their own imagination could repent, suffer the spiritual fire of tribulation, and obtain mercy (*Mammon* H4). Tyndale returns the word "heresy" to the original meaning of *hairesis,* a "choosing" (OED), in this case, to accept the gift of faith, cf. 127/24n. Tyndale would agree with John Milton, who argued throughout his long career that freedom, not force, enables the faithful to serve God, e.g.: *Of Reformation Touching Church-Discipline* (1641), *A Treatise of Civil Power in Ecclesiastical Causes* (1659), and *Of True Religion* (1673). (JB)

APPENDIX, GLOSSARY, INDICES

APPENDIX: SIDENOTES FOUND ONLY IN
WHOLE WORKS, 1573

This appendix records the sidenotes found only in *1573*, which John Foxe added to those in *1531*. The numbers refer to the lines in this edition that contain the initial and final words of the passage where a sidenote is found in *1573*. Because *1573* adds a period to most sidenotes, the editor has supplied a period where one is missing. Although Foxe uses both lower-case and capital "W" at the beginning of sidenotes, capitals have been used throughout this transcription.

Preface

5/9–13 The holy ghost shall rebuke the world for lacke of true iudgement.

5/24–26 The spiritual iudgeth all thynges spiritually.

6/4–9 The spirituall man searcheth out the cause why hee ought to loue hys neighbour.

6/17–20 Man is Lord ouer all the creatures of the earth.

6/27–29 Circumcision not frequented in xl. yeares.

6/32–7/2 Holy dayes are ordeined for man, and not man for the holy dayes.

7/6–10 The signification of thynges are to be sought and not to serue the visible signes.

7/11–14 Ceremonies without some good doctrine are to be reiected.

7/17–25 Turkes are rather to be lamented for their ignoraunce and to be wonne with good doctrine & example of good lyfe, then to be hated and murthered.

7/29–32 We do nothyng well except we do it of loue from a pure hart.

8/2–7 Superstitious obseruations are rather the breakyng of the law then the kepyng of the same.

8/20–23 The world is to be rebuked for lacke of iudgement.

8/29–31 Iudge by these things whether the Pope haue erred or not.

9/1–4 Iudge what baggage is in the Popes doctrine and of his making.

9/9–11 Note the practise of our fleshly spiritualtie.

9/13–20 The Papistes are gathered together agaynst Christ.

9/21–23 Our sinne is the cause that hypocrites reigne.

9/24–25 The practice of prelates.

Foundational Essay

10/2–3 Significations of the woorde church are diuers.

10/7–13 The ministers of the church are appointed to preach to the people surely the worde of God, & to pray in a toung that all men vnderstand.

10/19–22 The lawe cannot be fulfilled with workes, be they neuer so holy.

10/27–28 A great abuse in prayer.

10/32–11/2 The church taken for the spiritualty.

11/11–14 Holy Church hath borne a great swinge.

11/16–18 The Pope and his rable taken for the church.

11/25–28 The church is a congregation of people of all sortes gathered together.

12/3–5 The church of God how it is taken in Scripture.

12/19–23 The church is a multitude of all them that beleue in Christ wheresoeuer they be gathered together.

13/5–9 The cause why Tyndall translated the word church into this worde congregation.

13/21–24 Congregation is vnderstand by the circumstaunce.

13/31–14/1 Ecclesia is a greke worde, and signifieth a congregation.

14/6–8 M. More was skilful in Poetry.

14/18–20 A good admonition to M. More.

14/25–26 M. More did greatly fauour Erasmus.

15/1–2 M. More was a depe dissembler.

15/8–10 M. More is captious.

16/3–4 Byshops are ordeyned to be ouerseers and gouernours of the Church.

16/9–13 The ministers of the church why they were called Elders.

16/21–23 Byshops ought to be byders in one place.

17/6 God poureth hys holy spirite & endoweth wyth wisdome & learning aswell [sic] wemen as men.

17/18–20 God is vnder no law, necessitie lawlesse.

17/23–26 The cause why young Timothy was preferred by Paul to be a Byshop.

17/32–34 Paul was a fatherly instructer to Timothy.

18/5–8 S. Paule was a worthy & most reuered father & instructour.

18/16–20 A great difference betwene teaching of the people, and teaching of a preacher.

18/21–24 Oylyng, nor shauing is any thing or any part of priesthode.

19/2–3 Oile, salt, & spittle are no parts of Baptisme.

19/9–12 Oyle hath in it no vertue at all, though the Byshop halow it.

19/18–21 The ministers among the Iewes were named Elders, because of their age.

19/25–27 Why Tyndall useth this worde loue rather than charitie.

20/1–3 Charitie hath diuers significations.

20/8–9 Loue also is diuersly vnderstand.

20/16–18 Euery loue is not charitie nor euery charitie is not loue.

20/29–30 Why Tyndall sayth fauour and not grace.

21/6–8 Knowledge and not confession, repentaunce and not penaunce.

21/15–19 The Papistes may not forbeare to haue their iugglyng termes.

21/24–26 Penaunce was profitable to the Papistes.

21/29–31 True penaunce what it is.

22/9–11 Fayth in Christ bringeth true repentaunce.

23/14–17 The chu[r]ch before the gospell, or the Gospell before the church.

23/25–27 The word which is the Gospell was before the church.

24/14–15 Note well thys.

24/19–21 Whether the Apostles taught any thing that they did not write.

24/27–30 So much is written as is necessary for our saluation.

25/1–4 The scripture written must confounde the unwritten verities.

25/11–12 Writing hath bene from the beginning.

25/15–18 God from the beginning hath written his will in the hartes of his elect.

25/23–25 The Pope hath taken from vs the significations of the Sacramentes.

26/4–7 There can no more be taught vs then is conteyned in the scriptures.

26/29–33 The Heathen thoght nothing more madder then the doctrine of the resurrection.

27/4–7 The Apostles taught nothing that they were afrayde to write.

27/15–19 All the Sacramentes taught eyther in the olde testament or new, haue significations.

27/26 The Popish Sacramentes striue one agaynste an other.

27/32–28/2 Sacraments with out significations are not to be receaued.

28/11 Whether the Church can erre or not.

28/26–28 By fayth we are made the sonnes of God.

29/10–13 The offeryng of Christes body and bloud is the onely satisfaction for our sinnes.

29/21–24 There is no way to saluation, but by Christes death and passion.

30/13–14 1. John. 1.

30/23–24 All fleshe doth sinne.

31/8–10 We sinne of frailtie & weakenes.

31/22–24 We may erre[,] & yet be saued.

31/33–32/2 Who they be that erre from the way of fayth.

32/11–13 Faith is euer assailed with desperation.

32/23–25 All power & readines to do good commeth of God & not of our selues.

32/27–28 A very good example.

33/11–13 The faythfull though they slip, yet they fall not.

33/22–24 Faith in the goodnes of God is our staye.

34/4–9 If we consider how mercifull god is vnto vs, we cannot chuse but submit our selues vnto hys lawes.

34/18–19 Christian men must be patient.

35/7–9 The elect of God must haue patience & be long sufferers.

35/14–17 God trieth his elect by suffering them to fall into temptation.

35/24–26 We may commit sinne and yet not forget God.

35/28–32 The Apostles beyng amased with temptations forgat all Christes myracles.

36/5–7 A great temptation layd vpon the Apostles.

36/20–22 The Apostles were very doubtfull.

37/1–2 Christ hys resurrection.

37/7–11 The Disciples were not without fayth but yet the same was very doubtfull.

37/25–23 A foolish glose made by M. More.

38/5–7 The Pope & his sect are not the Church of Christ.

38/20–23 The Pope in forbyddyng mariage to Priestes, doth not consent that the lawe of god is good.

38/26–29 The Pope licenceth whordome whiche God forbiddeth.

39/6–7 The Popish Clergy are persecutours.

39/11–13 An abhominable, wicked & deuilish decree.

39/21–22 The Pope is vtterly against the doctrine of Christ.

40/12–14 One Argument confuted with an other of like nature.

40/33–41/2 The right fayth dyd neuer long continue in the greater nomber of the Church.

41/23–27 Hypocrites are crept vp in to the seate of Christ & his Apostles.

41/32–42/3 The Pope and hys Clergye haue corrupted the Scriptures of God with their traditions.

42/17–19 The scriptures beare witnes who are the right Church.

43/2–5 The doctrine of Iohn brought the hart of the Iewes into the right way.

43/10–13 Our Popish hypocrites haue nede of a Iohn Baptist to conuert them.

43/16–19 Those which depart from the fayth of hypocrites are the true Church.

43/27–29 Note here this Popish Argument.

44/6–9 The Pope and his sect say they are the church and can not erre.

44/18–20 Iohn Baptist was a true expositor of the law.

44/32–45/2 The Phariseis added false gloses to the Scripture.

45/16–17 The Papisticall doctrine.

45/29–32 The Phariseis and papistes agree in the false interpreting of the scriptures.

46/2–3 The sacramentes are signes to fayth.

46/6–9 The Pope will by his reason make Christ and all his Apostles heretiques.

46/19–25 The Pope and his sect would (if they could) destroy the scripture as well as they destroy the preachers thereof.

47/7–9 A good answere to be made to the Papistes.

47/32–48/3 The true meaning of the wordes of S. Augustine.

48/26–27 There are two maner of faithes.

48/28–29 An historicall fayth.

49/9–10 A feeling fayth.

49/22–23 The true & sure feeling fayth.

50/5–7 The feling fayth doeth farre excell the historicall fayth.

50/11–12 Cursed is he that trusteth in man.

50/24–26 The abhomination of the Romish Church.

50/27–29 Mariage forbidden & whoredom allowed.

51/21–25 The Papistes thinke lechery nor couetousnes to be any sinne.

51/28–33 As the Pope teacheth with the mouth onely, so the Papistes beleue with theyr mouth onely.

52/8–13 The Turkes and Iewes beleue that they can not erre because they beleue as their Elders dyd.

52/16–17 God reserued a little flocke.

52/27–30 Who they be that are of Gods true Church.

53/1–3 The fleshly persecute the spirituall.

53/11–14 The children of this world are the Papistes.

53/24–25 Aunsweres to be made to captious Papistes.

54/3–6 Teachers of Grammer vnderstode not the Latine toung.

54/16–20 The fayth in Christ, & loue of our neyghbors is all that is required of a Christian man.

55/8–10 Worshipping and honouring are both one.

55/21–24 The true wordes that expresse the honour of God.

55/32–56/1 The true honour of God.

56/20–23 To deny to helpe my neighbour is to dishonour hym.

57/1–3 To do that God forbiddeth is to dishonour God.

57/22–24 All creatures are ordeyned to serue man.

58/3–6 Images are seruauntes to man, and not man to images.

58/23–24 How a man may vse Images well.

59/15–19 Images & reliques at the first were well used but now shamefully abused.

59/24–25 The abuse of Images.

59/33–60/3 My body must serue the Prince & my neighbour, but my soule must serue God onely.

60/11–13 This is the true crossing that we should vse.

61/17–19 To worshyp Images is Idolatry.

62/2–6 True Pilgrimage is to walke from place to place the better to serue God & to helpe my neighbour.

64/3–7 All the ceremonies of the olde lawe were preachers to the people.

64/11–14 The Iewes by fayth were iustified, & not by the deedes of the lawe.

65/8–9 Workes must serue vs, and not we the workes.

65/21–24 The Iewes became seruauntes & captiues to theyr workes.

65/27–28 The blind reason of hipocrites.

66/5–6 O blinde & folishe imagination.

65/18–20 The Saboth day must serue vs, and not we the Saboth day.

66/22–25 How the Saboth day should be occupyed.

67/7–9 Prayer without fayth is no prayer.

67/13–15 God despised the sacrifices of the unfaithfull Iewes.

67/23–24 Supersti[ti]ous fasting doth God abhorre.

67/31–32 True fasting, what it is.

68/24–27 Many Iewes were conuerted to the faith of Christ.

69/6–8 All that came of Israell are not Israelites.

69/19–23 The Iewes came not to vnderstanding of Christ of loue, but were enforced therunto by the scriptures.

70/5–7 The Turkes are a farre greater number then the Papistes.

70/19–21 Ceremonies set vp in the newe testament.

71/3–6 Confirmation how it came first vnto the church.

71/20–22 The maner of confirming of children.

71/29–30 This is a right confirmation.

72/11–12 The abuse of confirmation.

72/18–19 The frut[e]s of ignoraunce.

72/25–28 Confirmation is made now a confirmyng in all superstition, ignoraunce and popery.

73/1–2 The Papisticall tyranny.

73/8–13 How the ceremonies about the ministration of the Lordes Supper came first into the Church.

74/7–9 All ceremonyes at the begynnyng had significations.

74/14–17 The state of the Iewes more easie then the Christians vnder traditions.

74/28–30 The multitude of ceremonies put away preachyng.

75/2–4 Ceremonies are the chief cause of ignoraunce.

75/8–9 The doctrine of Dunce aduaunced.

75/11–14 The blynd Papistes are enemyes to all good learnyng and knowledge.

75/19–20 Ignoraunt Priestes.

75/27–29 Ignoraunce made vs seruauntes to ceremonies.

76/9–11 The idle Papistes are preferred by ceremonyes.

76/21–28 As long as we had the signification of the ceremonies, so long they were sufferable, but the signification [corrected] beyng gone, the ceremony is mere superstition.

77/3–8 When the people by ignoraunce waxed superstitious then the clergie holpe them forward with falsifiyng the scripture.

77/10–12 Christes death purchased grace for mans soule.

77/31–78/3 The building of Abbeies, cloysters & religious houses haue bene a great decay to the good state of this realme.

Answers to the First Book

79/13–15 Subtile iuggling with wordes.

80/24–28 They that are in heauen do chiefly desire that we harken to God & do hys wyll.

81/3–5 All popishe imaginations are Idolatry.

81/17–22 We receaue all thinges of God our father for Iesus Christes sake hys sonne and our onely Sauiour.

81/33–82/1 We must doe all thynges of loue.

82/19 Rom. 14.

83/6–9 A difference betwene Christes naturall body, and a paynted Image.

83/13–15 Miracles were done by the saints to confirme theyr doctrine.

83/25–27 Dead bones may not be worshypped.

84/9–11 More reasoneth vntowardly.

84/13–14 God is like good in euery place.

84/20–27 The people were specially called to the Temple to behold the monuments there, wherby they might the better learne the mighty power of God.

85/20–22 The true beholdyng of the signe of the crosse.

85/27–29 The Church is a place of prayer.

85/30–31 God heareth our prayer in all places.

86/6–8 Ierusalem and the temple is destroyed.

86/16–18 God is present in all places alike.

86/27–30 All places are to be preferred where we may worship God most quietly.

87/11–13 Miracles were not done for the place but for the people.

87/28–31 Miracles done to draw the people to heare the worde of God.

88/5–7 All places must serue man, & not man bound to serue any place.

88/15–18 God is worshipped in our hartes, & not in any other place.

88/31–33 God cannot be serued with bodely seruice.

89/7–9 Our fayth may be grounded vpon men.

89/17–20 Al true miracles prouoke vs to fayth and trust in God.

90/16–19 The mayde of Ipswich & the maide of Kent were both false dissembling harlotes.

91/7–9 Such as were possessed with deuils fled from Christ.

91/13–15 A false delusion to bryng vs to Idolatry.

91/22–24 Our Lady dyd the mayde of Kent small pleasure.

92/16–18 A true exposition of the parable of the Samaritan.

92/24–27 All that God hath not planted shalbe plucked vp by the rootes.

93/1–3 Byshops should be seruauntes and not Lordes.

93/8–12 The Pope will not obey princes though God haue commaunded hym so to do.

93/20–22 Christes burthen is easie and gentle.

94/2–4 The salt of our Prelates is vnsauery.

94/15–17 We must beleue neither to much nor yet litle.

94/21–25 We are promised all thinges for our Sauiour Christes sake & not for the Saintes.

95/4–5 The virginite of our Lady.

96/12–14 Paules traditions were the doctrine of the Gospel.

95/20 The consecration.

96/1–3 Iustification of workes.

96/6–8 The Saboth day & holy dayes are made for vs & not we for them.

96/32–97/2 A good tale if it were long enough.

97/14–17 All beleue in God that haue the law written in their harts.

97/31–98/3 Popes may not be beleued without Scripture.

98/11–13 Counsailes ought to conclude accordyng to the Scriptures.

99/4–7 The cause why the Apostles wrote the Gospels.

99/17–19 The Pope and hys Cardinals erred in K. Henry the eights case.

99/22–23 M. Mores conclusion.

99/33–100/3 The surest way to oppresse true doctrine, is to lay the preachers fast.

100/22–24 A swarme of sectes set vp by the Pope.

100/30–101/2 The Pope by setting vp of false workes denieth the truth of gods word.

101/19–22 The popish church are persecutors but no suffere[r]s.

101/29–31 The chur[c]h of Christ is euer persecuted.

102/6–9 The church of Antichrist is the false church and euer the greater number.

102/11–13 The Pope is a deuelishe blasphemer of God.

102/21–23 The Pope is aboue kyng and Emperor.

102/25–27 The Pope persecuteth the word of God.

102/30–32 S. Paule describeth the Pope & his in their coulers.

103/5–7 Gods worde is the power and pith of all goodnes.

103/9 Confession.

104/20–22 The Pope and his are mighty iugglers.

105/4–6 In the Churche shall there be for euer, both good and euill.

105/13–16 The spirituall Churche of God are called Lutherans and heretickes.

105/24–27 The fleshly Churche serue God with workes of their owne.

105/30–32 The blasing of hypocrites.

106/19–22 The small flocke of Christ cometh to the word and promises of God.

106/30–107/1 Christ onely is the perfect comforter of the Christian.

107/9–12 The Christian man in all thinges seketh the honour of Christ.

107/16–18 The Christian seketh his saluation onely in Christ.

107/24–27 A pretye Antithesis betwen the Popes Churche & Christes litle flocke.

108/5–7 The Popish church aunswereth.

108/7–8 The litle flocke.

108/18–19 The Popes church.

108/29–30 The maner of the Popes cleargie.

109/3–4 Little flock goeth euer to wracke.

Answers to the Second Book

110/5–8 The Pope will not be tryed by scripture but the scripture must be iudged by hym.

110/19–23 None can minister the Sacramentes supersticiously but the Popes generation.

110/28–111/3 The naturall & carnall man sauoreth not the things that be of God.

111/5–7 God is fatherly to his elect members.

111/12–16 If we sinne of frailtie God is mercifull & ready to forgeue.

112/8–9 More a lying papist.

112/23–25 There is a church that sinneth not.

113/7–8 The carnall church sinneth.

113/20–22 The faith of them that be called, but not elect.

115/29–116/4 Christ dyd such seruice as all the Saintes could not do.

116/19–20 We may not trust to Saintes.

117/1–3 Prayer to Saintes is a great superstition.

117/10–12 Before Christ we vsed not to pray to Saintes.

118/12–15 The more trust we haue in Saintes, the lesse we haue in Christ.

118/28–31 We must first call vppon God, & then send for the phisition.

119/7–9 The fleshly mynded cannot iudge the thinges that be of God.

120/4–6 We may be bolde to resort to god, for he willeth vs so to do.

120/24–26 A purgatory visible, and a purgatory inuisible.

121/3–5 How you may know who be Saintes in heauen.

121/11–13 A straunge doctrine to pray to him for helpe that is dead & damned.

121/20–22 The Israelites were mo in number then the Iewes.

121/26–28 The Iewes committed Idolatry.

122/2–4 God euer reserueth a litle flocke.

122/11–13 More feareth not to worship an vnconsecrated hoste.

122/18–21 We must first know the true way & then agree in the same.

122/28–31 Christ rebuked the false trust the Iewes had in their wil works.

123/5–9 The myracles done by the prophetes and Apostles, was to confirme their doctrine.

123/15–17 Christ made the woman whole and not hys coate.

123/20–23 Miracles were done for the confirmation of doctrine.

123/25 A filthy chapter.

124/8–9 Moses bones.

124/9–10 The brasen Serpent.

124/17–19 God is a spirite and wilbe worshipped spiritually.

124/27–30 The Idolatrous person worshippeth the Image for the Saint.

125/8–10 Many thinges are altered for the abuses sake.

125/20–24 The true preaching of Gods worde remoueth theft and all other wickednes.

126/9–11 A good man may erre & yet not be dampned.

126/23–26 The myracles of Saintes confirme mans imaginations.

127/6 There were no doctours neither Apostles that did myracles to establishe the worshipping of Images.

127/11–14 Where true doctrine is set forth, there needeth no myracle.

127/16–18 Let the Papistes for lacke of scriptures come forth and do miracles.

127/20–21 Gods word is the touchstone to trie myracles.

128//1–3 Mahomets doctrine hath preuailed these viij. hundred yeares.

128/12–14 Where the Scripture is, there nedeth no miracles.

128/17–20 The preachers of the worde of God nede no miracles.

128/25–27 False doctrine was neuer persecuted.

128/29–31 The Papistes are ashamed of their Legend of lyes.

129/3–5 The deuill hath holpen Popes to their dignities.

129/13–16 The cause why the Turkes & Iewes can not come to the truth.

129/19–26 Popish doctrine nedeth miracles but Christes doctrine nedeth not now of miracles, for it was confirmed by Christ with myracles.

129/30–33 The Pope commeth in Christes name with false miracles.

130/3–7 The preachers of gods word confirmed the same with miracles whyle they were alyue.

130/10–14 God suffereth such as haue no loue to hys truth, to be deceaued with lying miracles.

30/22–25 In the Popish church all miracles are wrought by dead Saintes.

131/13–17 Our fayth may not be grounded onely vpon miracles, but vpon the worde of God.

131/31–132/2 The Apostles of Christe knew no such authoritie as the Pope now vsurpeth.

Answers to the Third Book

133/16–19 God to avoide heresies caused the scriptures to be written.

134/12–15 Where true faith is, there is repentaunce and amendment of life.

134/32–135/2 The elders in the time of the Iewes did erre.

135/7–9 The Scribes, Phariseis and Elders did erre.

135/14–16 The scripture was aucthorised by true myracles.

135/17–19 False bookes set forth by the Papistes.

135/29–33 The true church teacheth nothing but that which the scripture proueth and mainteineth.

136/9–10 The Papistes hide the scripture.

136/14–16 The scripture is the cause why men beleue the scripture.

136/25–28 The Papistes doctrine is not to be beleued without scripture.

137/2–6 The doctrine of the Papistes hath bene many times resisted by the scripture.

137/15–17 What thinges we finde in scripture.

137/32–138/4 The Papistes will neither by Gods lawe nor mans refraine from their wicked liuyng.

138/15–18 The Papistes will lose nothing that belongeth to them.

138/25–27 Christ deliuered the Iewes out of errour.

138/33–139/4 None have more care of the scripture, then those that beleue it not.

139/17–19 M. More reasoneth agaynst him selfe.

140/1–3 They that preach not Christ truly are murtherers.

140/10–11 The end of hipocrites.

140/33–141/2 Wit must first shew a cause, and then will is sturred to worke.

141/13–15 Popish doctrine concernyng Purgatory.

141/19–21 The pope, how he can both forgeue and reteine sinne.

142/1–3 Bodyly payne purgeth the body and not the soule.

142/9–11 M. More is of an euil opinion.

142/19–22 Faith in Christes bloud purchaseth forgeuenes of sinne.

142/33–143/3 There is no purgatory for hym that dyeth repentaunt & beleueth.

144/4–5 Purgatory is a tormenting Iayle as the Pope maketh it.

144/14–15 The Pope is Antichrist.

144/22–24 The fleshly children do naturally consent vnto lyes.

144/30–32 The fleshly mynded can never consent vnto Gods law.

145/2–3 The fleshly persecute them of the spirite.

145/9–12 The true church is not with out a signe or a miracle to proue that it is Gods church.

145/18–22 The popes life & doctrine is more wicked then the Turkes & all the heathen that euer were.

146/7–10 All glory and honour is to be geuen to the name of Iesu.

146/18–20 Purgatory is the foundation of Abbeyes, Colledges. &c.

147/10–11 M. More is a common iester and a scoffer.

147/26–28 The Papistes are cruell and vnmercyfull.

148/9–13 The oth of a witnes may be taken, but no man may be compelled to sweare & be a witnes.

148/15–16 A godly lesson.

148/20–21 M. More is a lyer.

149/5–7 The Papistes are obstinate & will not repent.

149/22–23 A fond saying.

150/3–6 To minister Sacraments with out signification is to be lead in darkenesse.

150/11–14 Christes body in the Sacrament is not carnall, but spirituall.

150/26–28 Christe was sacrificed on the crosse once for all.

151/3–5 Christes Deacons and the popes Deacons differ much.

151/14–16 M. Mores fayth was a common fayth.

151/29–30 As good no lawe, as a law not executed.

152/9–10 Age is to be preferred before youth.

152/15–18 The chast vnchastitie of the Papistes is abhominable both to God and man.

152/29–31 The Pope iudgeth no sinne to bee sinne, and sinne to be no sinne.

153/8–11 A Priest by the Popes order may haue a whore, but not a wife.

153/23–25 Mores doctrine is superstitious.

154/1–2 The Pope forbiddeth mariage.

155/17–19 We were Idolaters when we came to Christ.

155/28–30 S. Paules doctrine is that priests shuld haue wiues.

156/9–10 More is a scoffer.

156/30–32 The office of the widdowes in the primatiue church.

157/22–25 Young widowes were forbidden to minister in the common seruice.

158/2–6 Fishe no better then fleshe, nor fleshe no better then fishe in the kingd[o]me of Christ.

159/3–6 Priestes compelled to put away their wiues.

159/14–16 Priestes must be endued wyth vertue and honesty.

159/32–160/2 The maner vsed both in generall counsailes, and also in parliamentes.

160/19–21 A practise vsed in all counsayles and Parlamentes.

160/29–33 The spiritualtie make heretickes of them that resist theyr power and will.

161/13–18 The chastitie of the Clergy perteineth to the temporalitie, as much as to the spiritualtie.

162/2–5 No oth is to be kept that is agaynst charitie or necessitie.

163/19–21 Tyndall doth here playnly proue More an hereticke.

163/26–30 That is euer best, that moueth man to the kepyng of Gods commaundementes.

164/1–2 Deuilish doctrine.

164/10–12 Christes natural body is not in the Sacrament.

165/13–15 The true seruice of God, what it is.

166/32–167/1 More had two wiues & therefore was Bigamus.

167/15–16 The Pope a cruell tyraunt.

167/25–28 The spiritualtie would not haue the scripture in Englishe.

168/10–12 If we be not giltie, we neede no pardon.

168/16–19 More woulde excuse the murther of Hunne.

169/7–8 More was a subtill Poet.

169/15–19 The hauyng of the Scripture in English is vtterly agaynst the myndes of the Popish Clergie.

169/28–31 The scripture was first deliuered to the people in their vulgare toung.

170/9–14 The ordinaries are hangmen to such as desire the knowledge of the scripture.

170/16–19 None can vnderstand the Scripture except he knewe Christ to be his iustification.

Answers to the Fourth Book

171/8–11 Eare confession and pardons were neuer confirmed by miracle.

171/15–18 The Popish spiritualitie are tyraunts & persecutors.

172/5–7 The wicked & monstrous doynges of the Pope.

172/23–26 All Sacramentes teach vs what to do, or what to beleue.

174/1–3 The Papistes are slaundrers of the Gospell.

174/15–19 We can do no good worke except we beleue that our sinnes are forgeuen in Christ.

175/23–25 The hearing of gods worde causeth repentaunce.

175/30–176/1 There can be no repentaunce in vs but god doth first worke in vs by hys grace.

176/7–14 All power that we haue to good or euil is of God: But the croked and naughty vsage of the same is of our owne cankerd & corrupt nature.

176/21–27 Matrimony can be no Sacrament except a doctrine be added therunto that the people may know the benefite of Christ that we haue by matrimony.

177/9–10 No Sacrament is without signification.

177/21–27 Women that are vertuous and discrete may in cases of necessitie minister the Sacramentes as well as the Priest.

178/27–31 The supper of the Lord is geuen vs to be a memoriall of his death once offered for all.

179/18–22 The corrupt and vayne disputations of men to proue christ to be really in the Sacrament.

180/9–14 The Sacrament of Christes body when it is faithfully ministred doth profite as many as do beleue in Christes death.

181/5–10 The true worshipping of the Sacrament, is to beleue that it is a true signe that Christ suffered death for vs.

181/32–182/2 The soules departed rest at Gods will & pleasure.

182/28–33 Saintes are not to be called vpon, for we haue no promise nor assuraunce that either they heare vs or can profite vs.

183/9–11 The children of god are obedient to hys lawes.

183/25–27 Images were not allowed in the primitiue church.

184/26–27 Images are not to be had in Churches.

185/25–29 The prayers of all good women are aswell accepted of God as the prayers of our Lady.

186/17–19 All falsehode is not espyed out in one day.

189/20–22 Vnlawfull vowes are not to be obserued.

190/7–9 All vowes are to be made wyth great aduisement.

190/15–17 We must vse Gods creatures for our necessitie.

190/23–27 All our abstinence & chastising of our selues, is to our owne profite.

191/4–5 More blasphemeth God.

191/14–18 Our dedes are euill, because we lacke knowledge to referre them vnto the glory of God.

191/26–29 The deuill is the blinder &/and keper of vs from the vnderstanding of gods/Gods wyll/wil. (In *1573* the same note is found at the bottom of Oo6v, p. 328 and the top of Pp1r, p. 329.)

192/6–8 We may not be curious to search gods secretes.

192/12–13 A Papisticall opinion.

192/24–26 Witte, reason, & iudgement goeth before will.

193/11–14 God is the first worker & bringger to passe of our well doynges.

193/29–31 The Christians seeke helpe of Christ.

194/3–4 O abhominable blasphemy.

194/14–16 Master doctour Ferman was a vertuous godly and learned man.

194/24–25 A true note to know hypocrites.

195/11–13 M. More is a iuggler with termes.

195/21–22 A lyuely description of our iustification.

196/9–12 The great mercy and kindenes of God moueth man to repentaunce.

196/14–16 The right order of our iustification.

197/4–5 Faith only apprehendeth our iustification.

197/23–26 There are diuersities of faith, and but one faith that iustifieth vs.

198/12–14 Out of a liuely and iustifiyng faith springeth good workes.

198/31–32 More is maliciously blynde.

199/7–9 An apt and proper exsample of loue.

199/19–21 God loued vs first, that we should loue him againe.

200/2–4 He that loueth God loueth hys neighbour.

200/7–8 Note here the mercy & goodnes of God.

200/13–16 Faith may be had without loue, but it is a barreine & naked faith.

200/32–201/1 The deuils Martyrs.

201/7–10 We must doe good workes of loue, and not for reward.

201/21–24 Our doynges can deserue nothyng, but Christe hath deserued for vs.

202/2–5 Iames reproueth false frutes and not a true and liuely fayth.

202/16–19 Fayth that will not woorke when oportunitie serueth can not iustifie.

203/14–17 Abraham beleued gods promises & therefore was iustified.

203/24–29 Hee that seeth hys neighbour in necessitie & hath no compassion on him, hath no fayth.

204/5–9 The Papistes preach workes that are profitable to them selues.

204/24–30 When we haue offended God we must returne quickly by repentaunce and call vpon God to heare vs for Christ our Sauiours sake.

205/9–14 As we haue receaued at the hand of God mercy, so must we shewe mercy to our neyghbours.

205/31–206/1 He that loueth hys neighbour for Christs sake the same is righteous.

206/17–20 All our workes if they procede not of loue are nothyng.

206/26–29 Fayth in Christ maketh our small workes acceptable.

207/8–10 The righteous lyueth by faith.

207/16–18 Faith in Christes bloud doth onely iustifie vs.

207/32–208/3 Iohn Baptist and our Lady also were sinners & looked for the redemption in Christ.

208/12–16 There was neuer any but Christ that was without sinne.

209/18–20 The blinde and fond reasoning of More.

209/32–210/3 The difference betwene Peters fall & the fall of Iudas.

210/9–10 Iudas perished in desperation.

210/18–21 By Adam we are all made the children of the wrath of God.

211/9–13 God worketh by diuers to make vs to call vpon and to trust in his mercy.

212/8–9 Mores wittes are captiuated.

212/16 A prety example.

213/4–6 King Henry the 4. was an vsurper of the crowne.

213/12–13 The Turk is to be resisted.

213/20–22 The vnion of Doctors a good booke.

214/12–13 Eare confession.

215/13–15 Paule dyd excommunicate, but our Byshops do burne.

GLOSSARY

This glossary of the 1531 edition of *Answer to More* is based on *The Compact Edition of the Oxford English Dictionary* (1971). All references with dates have been checked against *The Oxford English Dictionary* Second Edition [1989] *on Compact Disk* (1994). The glossary defines words whose meanings and forms are not easily recognizable, but it does not attempt to cover such normal 16c variants as *c* for *t*, *e* for *o*, *i* for *e*, *o* for *a*, *th* for *d*, *u* for *v* and *v* for *u*, *y* for *i* and *i* for *y*, etc. It usually limits itself to the spelling and location of the first occurrence of a word, with *etc.* indicating a later use in the text. Thus, plurals of nouns and different tenses of verbs are omitted, unless another meaning is recorded. In listing page and line numbers, it gives precedence to a word in the body of the text over a sidenote because the latter might be the work of the 16c editor. Half a dozen Northern usages (*ane, leppe, pleasant, power, shone, wauntage*) may shed light on the origins of Tyndale's family. The glossary also contains: two entries found, not in the text but in the sidenotes (*figured, soules slepe*); two variants from *1573* with substantially different meanings from *1531* (*inough, naught*); problematic words from the sidenotes of *1573* (*blasing, fast, frequented, lay, naughty, preferred, surely, swinge, wil*). The glossary further includes: instances from *Answer* later (c10) than in OED; words, senses, phrases, and forms earlier than in OED for Tyndale (c40) and for More (c20); quotations from *Answer* (c50) used as examples by OED; and new usages in *Answer* (c10) not found in OED. Because OED gives conflicting dates for many works cited, this account follows the revised STC for Tyndale and CWM for More. The abbreviation *see n.* refers the reader to the Commentary.

abode *v. pa.* stood firm 22/28 *etc.*
aboute *prep.* somewhere on or near the person 59/22, *first use (I. B. 4.), 1567.*
ace *sb.* single point, a jot 178/7, *first use (3. fig.): More,* Dialogue, *1529.*
actually *adv.* in reality not mystically 150/13 *etc., first use (3.), 1587.* with deeds, practically 211/11, *first use (1.), 1587.*
adamand *adj.* very hard 13/5
advoutrye *sb.* adultery 219/19 *etc.*
affeccion *sb. of affeccion* from passion 18/13
after as *conj.* according as 197/29
aftir *prep.* according to 62/4 *etc. Only three instances (B. IV. 12. c.): 1483, 1586, 1601.*
agayne *adv.* in return 196/31 *etc.*
agenst *conj.* by the time that 153/25; in anticipation of 133/11 *etc.*

albe *sb.* white vestment reaching to feet 73/19 *etc.*

all *adj.* + *pronoun* the whole substance 155/22

all *sb. all to one* to the same thing 16/25

allegeth *v. pr. 3 s.* cites 115/25 *etc.*

al to *adv. phr.* asunder *to al to breake* to break asunder 111/16

alwaye *adv.* after all, still 151/11, *last use (3.), 1475.*

al wayes *adv. phr.* in all directions, every which way 104/26

amice *sb.* oblong vestment of white linen worn around the shoulders over the alb 73/13 *etc., first use (2.): this instance; second use: More,* Confutation, *1532–33.*

amonge *adv.* all the while 54/12

and *conj.* if 108/29; *but and* but if 120/26 *etc.*

and . . . and *conj.* [1] both . . . and 40/26, *last use (B. 5.), c1520.*

ane *numeral adj. Northern variant for* one 189/28

antistrephon *sb.* antistrophon, i.e. an argument that is retorted upon an opponent 222/10, *first use, 1611.*

aparte *adv.* aside 199/27

apayde *ppl. a.* pleased 66/2

appelled *v. pa.* appealed to a higher authority for deliverance from the adverse decision of a lower 186/10 *etc.*

apperinge *ppl. a.* apparent, seeming 164/27, *first use (4.), 1656.*

apposed *v. pa.* questioned 71/23 *etc.; pp.* confronted with hard questions 208/24–25 *etc.*

appoyntement *sb.* agreement, pact, contract 25/27 *etc.*

arow *adv.* in succession 99/28

as *adv.* as if, as though 209/23

a slepe *adv. brought a slepe* caused to become asleep 54/3 *etc.*

assoyled *pp.* resolved, solved 99/21

at *prep.* on the occasion of 200/31

attendeth *v. pr. 3 s.* listens 34/19

autenticke *adj.* authoritative 130/5 *etc.*

awaye *adv.* absent, wanting 125/10 *etc.*

a worth *adv. take(n) a worth* borne patiently 106/32–107/1 *etc.*

axes *sb.* access, ague, intermitting fever 165/4

babe *sb.* a foolish fellow 95/9

bage *sb.* badge, sign 64/14, *first use (2.): Tyndale,* Acts 28.11, *1526.*

bald *adj.* destitute of meaning 96/28

barelie *adv.* poorly, baldly 15/3, *first use (6.): More,* Confutation, *1532–33.*

bate *sb. be at bate* like a chained bear attacked by dogs 142/15

be *aux. v.* Form of "be" with intrans. verb in perfect tenses to express the condition or state now attained, become [sic] 114/7 *etc.; is come* 199/31 *etc.; haue be pp. form, 14–15c.* 156/20 *etc.*

be *prep.* by 113/15 *etc.*

bedged *v. pa. (Form not in OED)* begged 36/32; *vbl. sb.* 76/10; *v. inf.* beggar, impoverish 92/19

beestely *adv.* irrational 101/7 *etc.*

beestlynesse *sb.* unintelligence 139/4–5

before *adv.* beforehand 209/19

before *conj.* previous to the time when 193/7

behinde *adv.* in the past 26/8

beleue *v. beleue in* rely upon 181/5 *etc.*

belie *v.* tell lies about 197/10

bely *adj.* fleshly, carnal 61/21, *first use (III. 15. c.): Tyndale,* Obedience, *1528.*

bere *v. bere . . . in hand* delude 160/26 *etc.*

beshrew *v.* curse 20/2

besydes *adv.* in addition 169/17, *first use (A. 2.), 1564.*

besydes *prep.* away from 156/14; over and above 165/29

betell *sb.* ² insect taken as a type of blindness 7/34 *etc., first use (3.), 1548.*

betimes, be tymes *adv.* before it is too late 108/30, 14/19 *etc.*

bigamus *adj.* remarried after death of first wife 167/6

bisshopes, busshopes *sb. pl. Translation of NT* "episkopos," overseers, a class of officers in the early Christian church 16/4 *etc.*

blasing *vbl. sb².* blazing, boasting *first use (1. b.), 1563.* ppl. *a.²* boasting, *OED (1. b.) mistakenly cites octavo of 1531, not folio of 1573, where word occurs in side-note for 105/30–32*

blere *v. inf.* deceive, hoodwink 160/16

bogge *sb.* bugbear, terror 108/28

bolles *sb. pl.* bulls, papal edicts 129/31

bosh *sb* ¹. ivy bush as sign of tavern 75/29, *first use (5.): More,* Confutation, *1532–33, see n.*

bottes *sb. pl.* parasitical worms or maggots 21/21

brestes *sb. pl.* private thoughts and feelings 21/10

briddes *sb. pl. Metathesis for* birds 191/27, *last use of this spelling (I. 2.): Tyndale,* Matt. 8.20, *1526.*

bringeth *v. pr. 3 s.* adduces (a statement or argument) 87/23 *etc.*

brode *sb.* brood, crew 99/23, *first use (3.), 1581.*

busy *adj.* actively engaged 180/24

by and by *adv. phr.* immediately 154/26

by *v.* be 39/31

byde *v. byde out* endure to the end 129/15, *only use of this phrase (II. 9. b.), 1637.*

bydeth *v. pr. 3 s.* remains 62/16; endures 202/13 *etc.*

bye *adv.* near 206/32 *etc.*

bysshoped *pp.* confirmed 72/25

canvesed *v.* ² *pp.* solicited 120/18, *first use as trans. v. (7. a.), c1768.*

canvesynge *pres. part.* soliciting 160/3, *first use as intrans. v. (6.), c1555.*

captiue *v.* captivate, enthrall 140/28 *etc., first use (1. b. fig.):* More, Dialogue, *1529.*

cast *v. cast . . . in the teeth* reproach, upbraid 152/19, *first use (XII. 65.):* Tyndale, Jas. 1.5, *1526.*

castynge *pres. part.* devising, scheming 160/3

cauellacions *sb. pl.* cavils, frivolous objections 167/27, *first use (1. c.):* More, Letter against Frith, *1532.*

causes *sb. pl.* law cases, suits 59/24 *etc.*

cautels *sb. pl.* strategems, sleights 7/30 *etc.*

certifie *v. pres.* assure 121/9 *etc.*

chammeth *v. pr. 3 s.* chews 164/12–13, *this instance in OED.*

chamminge *vbl. sb.* chewing 164/16

charge *sb.* responsibility 151/22

charite *sb. done my charite* given alms 20/1; *saint charite* Christian love personified 19/29 *etc.;* patience 20/2

charite *v. Tyndale's coinage* 20/23

charmes *sb. pl.* incantations 108/11

chaunces *sb. pl.* mischances, mishaps, 208/17 *etc.*

chauntrees *sb. pl.* chapels endowed for the maintenance of one or more priests to sing daily mass for the souls of the founders or others specified by them 77/32

chresom cloth *sb. phr.* chrisom-cloth, a white robe put on infant at baptism 19/3 *etc., this instance (2. a.):* More, Confutation, *1532–33, see n.*

church *sb. Translation of NT "ekklesia,"* a building for public Christian worship 10/2 *etc.;* officers of an ecclesiastical organization, especially the clergy 8/29 *etc.;* "Holy Church" as opposed to "State" 8/10 *etc.;* a local congregation 11/26 *etc.;* the Church Universal 12/3 *etc.;* the Invisible Church of the elect 12/26, *first use (II. 4. c.), 1561;* any group having a common belief 13/25 *etc.*

churlishnesse *sb.* rudeness, harshness 104/2, *first use: Tyndale,* Mammon, *1528.*

clame *v. pa.* climbed 185/3

cleane *adv. cleane contrary adv. phr.* entirely contrary 106/28 *etc., first use (II. 5. d.), 1538, see* **playne.**

clerkes *sb. pl.* scholars 96/19

clocke *sb.* cloak, a bell-shaped cape. Clocks originally featured a bell for sriking the time. 155/27

combred *pp.* perplexed 36/19; overthrown, routed 188/21

come *v. pres. come . . . to* result in 195/2, *first use (III. 48. g.), 1568;* **come** *v. pa.* came 159/21 *etc., this form rare after 1500.*

comen *adj. comen charges* ordinary expenses 92/21; *comen wemen* prostitutes 156/14

commissaries *n. pl.* officers exercising spiritual jurisdiction as the representative of the bishop in parts of his diocese 11/19

companie *sb. Translation of "ekklesia" in Acts 19.32,* band 14/5, *see n.;* persons casually brought together 33/4

compasynge *pres. part.* contriving 160/3

compelled *ppl. a. compelled with* constrained by 193/33

complayne *v. pres.* lament 118/28

complayntes *sb. pl.* grounds of complaint 119/32–120/1, *first use (5.), c1699.*

complexcyon *sb.* bodily constitution 51/20; disposition of mind, nature 89/9 *etc.*

comprehended *pp.* included in a book 98/10

conclude *v.* infer 140/32; *v. pr. 3 s.* decides 184/19; *pp.* confuted 194/17

condicions *sb. pl.* morals, behavior 122/28

condicyon *v.* make dependent on a condition to be fulfilled 161/28

contrary *adj.* the opposite 51/2, *see* **cleane** and **playne.**

conuersation *sb.* behavior, mode of life 48/13; consorting 152/22 *etc.*

conveyaunce *sb.* sleight of hand 147/12

conynge *adj.* learned 168/27

corage *sb.* inclination 33/23; sexual inclination, lust 166/5, *first use (3. e.), 1541.*

corne *sb.* grain 60/27

corosy *sb.* a corrosive drug, remedy 195/28

corporiscloth *sb.* a linen cloth upon which the consecrated elements are placed during the celebration of the Mass 73/25 *etc.*

coude *v. past subj. had they coude* had they been able 46/12

counseled *v. pa.* recommended a plan 183/31; took counsel with 224/12

course *sb.* turn 166/13

craft *sb.* trade 163/6

credence *sb. credence of* belief in 211/21

credible *adj.* trustworthy 168/4

cropen *pp.* crept 100/22

dastard *sb.* a dullard 119/31

daunger *sb.* jurisdiction, power to inflict physical injury 186/30

declareth *v. pr. 3 s.* explains, makes clear 195/15 *etc.*

degrees *sb. pl.* ranks, grades, orders 11/26 *etc.*

departe *v.* share 32/21; be severed 94/8

depe *adj.* intense 122/19

depely *adv.* solemnly 18/29

describeth *v. pres.* gives a detailed account of 195/5

deserued *pp.* merited 192/19

deuocion *sb.* reverence 131/6

deuoure *sb.* duty, appointed task 139/13

diligenterly *adv.* more assiduously 97/4–5, *this instance in OED.*

diote *v. inf.* to regulate a person's food as a punishment 186/30 *etc., first use (I. 2. b.):Tyndale,* Prelates, *1530.*

disanull *v. inf.* make null and void 169/18

disceaueablenesse *sb.* deceivableness, deceitfulness 102/3, *first use:Tyndale,* 2 Thess. 2.10, *1526.*

disceueable *adj.* deceitful 154/1

discharged *pp. discharged of* exempted from 188/5

disconsent *v.* refuse consent 142/15, *first use: this instance.*

dispicience *sb.* disputation 95/31, *first use: this instance; second use: More,* Confutation, *1532–33.*

dispicions *sb. pl.* disputations 194/12, *first use: More,* Life of Pico, *c1510; second use:Tyndale,* Prologue to NT, Acts 28.29, *1526; third use: More,* Dialogue, *1529.*

doctrine *sb.* knowledge 118/26; teaching 121/19

domme *adj.* meaningless, stupid, senseless 9/2, *first use (7. a.):Tyndale,* 1 John, *1531.*

done *adv.* down 125/14

doo *v. to doo sb. phr.* ado, business, fuss 148/4, *first use (B. IV. 33. b.), 1570–76.*

doucheland Germany 38/24; **douchlonde** 97/28, 112/15, *first use, 1547.*

draffe *sb.* dregs 75/10

dresse *v. inf. dresse . . . meate* prepare for use as food 156/30

dulia *sb.* veneration given to saints and angels 55/11 *etc., first use, 1613, see n.*

dunce disciple of Duns Scotus, subtle reasoner 46/33, *see n.; first use:Tyndale,* Mammon, *1528; poss.* 75/9, *this instance in OED (headnote).*

dutie *sb.* due, debt 203/2 *etc.*

eare *sb. eareconfession sb. phr.* auricular confession 133/18–19 *etc., only instance (III. 16.), 1549.*

elder *sb.³ Translation of NT "presbyteros,"* a class of officers in the early Christian church 15/7 *etc., first use (B. 4.):Wyclif,* Acts 15.6, *1382; second use:Tyndale,* Titus 1.5, *1526, see n.*

electe *pp.* chosen by God for salvation 105/7, *first use (4.), c1617.*

electe *sb.²* one chosen by God for salvation 33/31 *etc., first use (B. 1.): More,* Confutation, *1532–33.*

endeuoure *sb.* effort, strenuous attempt 210/17 *etc.*

endeuoure *v. refl.* exert 140/28 *etc.*

endoted *pp.* endow 16/30–31, *only use:Tyndale,* Obedience, *1528.*

enforme *v. inf.* form 15/24

enserch *v.* investigate 172/27, *this instance (3.) in OED.*

entreted *pp.* treated (a subject) 12/1 *etc., first use (I. 3.): More,* Richard III, *c1513.*

enuye *sb.* hostile feeling, ill-will 184/23 *etc.*

envye *v. inf.* vie with 162/16

etherother *pron.* each other 171/23

evidently *adv.* clearly 16/15

excepte *ppl. a.* excepted, exempted 190/8 *etc.*

excomunicat *pp.* excluded by an authoritative sentence from participation in the sacraments 108/27, *first use: Tyndale,* John 16.2, *1526.*

executed *pp.* carried into effect 151/24

excercice *sb.* disciplinary suffering, fasting 80/13 *etc.*

exercised *v. pa.* gained skill by practice 96/25; *pp.* employed habitually, practised 207/24

experte *adj.* experienced 207/24

expresly *adv.* explicitly 24/29

faces *sb. pl.* pretences 9/23

faintie *adj.* faint, sickly 51/7, *first use: Tyndale,* Prelates, *1530.*

faith *sb. felinge faith* conviction practically operative on the character and will 12/28 *etc., first use (I. 3. b.): Wyclif,* Jas. 2.17, *1382: second use: Tyndale,* Prologue to Pentateuch, *1530. geue faith* yield belief to 46/31. *See* **historicall, historicall faith.**

fall *sb* ¹. *(Sense not in OED) abbreviated form of* offal: refuse, waste 42/9

fanon *sb.* short band corresponding with the stole, originally a kind of napkin worn on left wrist of celebrant at Mass 73/22 *etc.*

fareth *v.* ¹ *pr. 3 s. fareth . . . foule with him selfe* behaves in an ugly manner 152/2. *See "fare fayre" (II. 4. c.): Tyndale,* 2 Cor. 5.11, *1526.*

fautie *adj.* guilty of wrong-doing 168/12

faine *adj.* glad under the circumstances 36/23 *etc.*

fast *adv.* vigorously, *1573 sidenote for* 99/33–100/3

fayne *v.* fain, wish, desire 204/12

fayne *v.* feign *fayne them* conjure up 205/14

faynedly *adv.* feignedly, deceitfully 101/18, *first use, 1535.*

feare *v. inf.* frighten 26/16 *etc.*

feleable *adj.* manifest 211/17, *this instance in OED.*

fenix *sb.* phoenix 151/8

ferre forth *adv.* to the specified extent and no more 37/8 *etc.*

fett *v. pa. fett out* fetched out, drew forth 66/29 *etc., first use (II. 17.), 1644; v. inf.* obtain 179/28

figure *sb.* in logic, a form determined by the different position of the middle term in the premises of a syllogism 98/23, *first use (V. 23.), 1551; sb. pl.* in rhetoric, the various forms of expression, deviating from the normal arrangment or use of words, adopted to give beauty, variety or force to a composition 14/6

figured *pp.* represented typically, symbolically 154/S3 *etc.*

fine *v. pres.* pay a penalty 172/20

fled *pp.* hastened for protection 198/5

for *prep.* as a precaution against 93/19

fore- *prefix foresinnes sb. pl.* previous sins 111/23–24 *etc., this instance (II. 4. a.)*
in OED.

for that *conj.* for the reason that 122/28

forth on *adv.* forwards, onwards 76/26, *first use: More,* Dialogue, *1529.*

forthynke *v.* be sorry for, repent of 22/4 *etc.*

forthynkynge *vbl. sb.* repentance 22/3–4

fought *pp.* engaged in conflict 220/9

found *pp.* set up, originated 212/25.

frame *adj. (Form and meaning not in OED)* square 104/27

framed *ppl. a.* fashioned 37/30

frequented *pp.* practised, *1573 sidenote for* 6/27–29

frowardnesse *sb.* perversity 176/10

fynde *v.* support 12/17 *etc.; pp.* supported 156/21 *etc.*

gather *v.* infer 95/16

gaye *adj.* bright, showy 6/9 *etc., see 81/20n.*

generacion *sb.* breed, kind 28/12 *etc.*

geue *v. pres.* concede, yield 133/14, *first use (B. XI. 39. a.), 1548.*

gloses *sb. pl.* marginal notes, expositions 37/18 *etc.*

goeth *v. pr. 3 s. goeth to* get to work 144/31

goo *v. subj. 3 s.* walk 47/14 *etc.*

good *adj.* effectual 79/14, *this instance (A. V. 17. b.) in OED.*

gorge *sb. cast his gorge* express extreme disgust 50/9, *first use (I. 5. b.): More,*
Confutation, *1532–33.*

grace *sb.* Divine influence which regenerates and sanctifies humans 5/1 *etc.;*
(meaning not in OED) sexual favor 21/2, *see n. sb. pl.* dispensations from
some of the statuable conditions required for a university degree 21/3,
see n.

graunt *sb.* admission, acknowledgment 211/22

graunte *v. inf.* to yield 194/16

greate *adj.* eminent 182/20

grote *sb.* groat, English coin issued 1351–1662 equal to four pence 141/14
etc.

gulden *sb.* gold coin formerly current in the Netherlands and part of Germany 38/24

gylden *adj.* overlaid with a thin coat of gold. *Mistake for* gilded, *first use (3.),*
this instance. wonne his gylden spores to gain knighthood by some act of val-
or, to attain distinction 16/18 *etc.*

gyse *sb.* custom 156/9 *etc.*

halt *v. inf.* limp 28/15

halowenges *v.* ¹ *vbl. sb. pl.* consecrate (2.) 10/13; *v.* ² *vbl. sb. pl.* shout, in order to urge on dogs to the chase (2.) 10/13

hange on *v. inf.* depend upon 169/5

happly *adv.* perhaps 27/28 *etc.*

hard *adj.* deep 35/15

hardye *adj.* bold 39/13 *etc.*

haxeth *v. pr. 3 s.* asks 211/17

heedinesse *sb.* headiness, rashness, obstinacy 104/11

hedy *adj.* headstrong, impetuous 103/1 *etc.*

henge *v. pa.* hung 124/25. *Inflection of "hang," 13–15c.*

herber *sb.* harbor, shelter 103/31

here of *adv.* from this 196/27 *etc.*

here vn to *adv.* to this matter 169/12

hertes *sb.* intents, desires 167/29 *etc.*

heue *v. inf.* strive, press with force 77/4

his *poss. adj.* its 136/20 *etc.*

historicall *adj. historicall faith* intellectual belief or assent 48/28 *etc., first use (2. a.), 1513; second use, this instance; third use: Tyndale,* 1 John, *1531.* See **faith, felinge faith;** **storifaith.**

hold *v. pres. hold harde* maintain one's position vigorously 160/19

holde *sb.* refuge 100/3

honeste *adj.* chaste 17/15

honestye *sb.* honorable character 147/16 *etc.*

howseled *pp.* administered the Eucharist 180/18

hye minded *adj.* arrogant 102/31 *etc.*

Iack off napis *sb.* jackanapes, name for a tame ape or monkey 60/7 *etc., first use: Skelton,* Why Come Ye Not to Court, *1522; second use: Tyndale,* Obedience, *1528; third use: Tyndale,* 1 John, *1531.*

Idole *sb.* idol; applied polemically to any material object of worship in a Christian church 205/17, *first use (I. 1. b.), 1545.*

ieopardy *sb.* risk of loss 121/11 *etc.*

iesteth *v. pr. 3 s.* mocks 168/2, *first use (2.): Tyndale,* 3 John 1.10, *1526.* See **out.**

imageseruice *sb. phr. (Phrase not in OED)* idolatry 82/16 *etc.* See **image-worship,** *first use, 1628.*

imaginacion *sb.* a mental image (often with the implication that the conception is false) 5/16 *etc.*

impassible *adj.* incapable of suffering 164/14

improueth *v. pr. 3 s.* disproves 18/22 *etc.; pp. (meaning not in OED)* discovered the false attribution of 135/18 *etc.*

inconuenientes *sb. pl.* morally unfitting acts, abuses 148/6–7 *etc.*

indifferent *adj.* impartial 146/13 *etc.*

indurat *ppl. a.* hardened 13/5 *etc., first use, this instance.*

in lyke wyse *adv. phr.* in like manner 14/24–25, *only use, 1542.*

inough *adj. modifying sb. pl.* enough 161/4—*1573 Variant. See* **ynow.**

instantly *adv.* urgently, persistently 201/27

interdyte *v. pres.* cut off authoritatively from religious functions or privileges 138/18

inveyeth *v. pr. 3 s.* violently reproaches 190/29, *first use (II. 5.): More, Dialogue, 1529.*

Irish *sb. pl. the wild Irish* The tribes who lived "beyond the pale," not subject to English rule 125/6

iugled *v. pa.* played tricks so as to cheat or deceive 21/16 *etc., first use (3. fig.): Tyndale, Obedience, 1528.*

iuglinge *ppl. a.* deceptive 13/21 *etc.*

iugulars *sb. pl.* jugglers, tricksters 104/21

iustifienge *vbl. sb.* the action of making or accounting just 195/18 *etc., first use: Wyclif, Rom. 4.25, 1382.*

knowlege *sb.* acknowledgement 21/6

kynd *sb.* gender 172/6; *sb. pl.* kin, kindred 33/7

kynde *adj.* grateful 103/29

lade *v. inf.* load, chiefly in immaterial sense 92/5 *etc., first use (I. 1. c.), 1538.*

late *adj.* belonging to a recent period 97/20

later *adj. later end* latter end, concluding part 15/5 *etc.*

lawe *sb. pl.* laws 196/11

lay *v.* [1] *inf.* attack, *1573 sidenote for* 99/33—100/3

legendes *sb. pl.* stories of lives of saints 102/14

leppe *v. Northern variant for* leap 53/12

lerninge *vbl. sb.* teaching 142/3 *etc.*

lett *sb.* hindrance 152/30

lette *pp.* prevent 7/1 *etc.; v. inf.* leave undone 163/33

like *adj.* likely, probable 212/10

like *adv.* likely 44/9 *etc., first use (B. 8.), 1563;* equally 84/15 *etc.*

like *v. subj. and it like* if it please 108/29

limeteriers *sb. pl.* 60/25, *see n.*

liste *v. pres. what him liste* what is pleasing to him 185/5; wish 189/11 *etc.; v. pr. 3 s.* pleases 194/17 *etc.*

liuely *adj.* living 87/30 *etc.;* vigorous 173/17 *etc.*

liuely *adv.* as a living person 63/17; vigorously 177/3

liuynge *vbl. sb.* manner of life 11/11 *etc.; vbl. sb.* income 146/24

longe *adj.* tall 179/15

louely *adj.* loving 69/20

lubboures *sb. pl.* clumsy stupid fellows, especially those who live in idleness; frequently applied to monks 76/13

lucre *sb.* profit 14/14 *etc.*

lust *sb.* pleasure 67/17; *sb. pl.* desires 33/12 *etc.*

lust *v.* desire, choose, wish 160/1 *etc.*

lye *v. pres. lye on* tell lies about 174/4 *etc.*

lyenge *vbl. sb.* sojourning 138/5

lyeth *v. pr. 3 s.* exists, is found 159/14

mahometrie Mahometry, idolatry 25/20–21, *first use, 1481; second use, this instance.*

maior *adj. used absolutely* premise of a syllogism which contains the major term 79/17, *first use (A. I. 2.), 1533.*

malapertenesse *sb.* impudence 119/21 *etc.*

manchetes *sb. pl.* small loaves of finest wheaten bread 180/26

manifest *adj.* open to view or comprehension 127/12 *etc.*

marchaundice *sb. make marchaundice of* traffic in 23/10–11 *etc.;* article of commerce 189/9

mary *sb.* marrow 5/28 *etc.*

mastrie *sb.* mastery, victory 112/18

mater *sb. maketh no mater* it is of no importance 118/10

mayny *sb.* meinie, multitude of persons 149/21

meane *v. pres.* think, imagine 199/18

meates *sb. pl.* foods in general 172/1. *See* **dresse.**

members *sb. pl.* parts of the body 191/22

memory *sb. in a memory* as a memorial, memento 59/5 *etc.*

mend *v. Aphetic form of* amend 120/9 *etc.*

mendesmakynge *vbl. sb.* reparation 172/12, *only two examples: c1400 and this instance.*

might *sb. aboue might* beyond their strength 201/18

minde *sb.* judgment, opinion 82/34

ministre *v. pres.* supply 120/13; *v. inf.* direct, manage 161/6; *v. pr. 3 s.* administers 56/15

minor *adj. used absolutely* premise of a syllogism which contains the minor term 79/18, *first use (A. II. 4.), 1581.*

mischeue *sb.* evil-doing, wickedness 11/10 *etc.*

mischevouse *adj.* intending harm 13/13; miserable 130/31

misteries *sb. pl.* secrets 152/31, *see n.*

misticall *adj.* allegorical, symbolical 110/14. *misticall body* the Church 114/13, *first use: More,* Supplication of Souls, *1529; earlier use: Fisher,* Sermon against Luther, *1521.*

moare *adj.* greater 19/8 *etc.;* to a greater extent 84/13

moare *adv.* rather 88/14

mollyfye *v. inf.* to soften in disposition 196/7

mornynge *vbl. sb.* mourning 69/21

moue *v. inf.* bring forward, propound (a question) 194/15

mowseth *v. pr. 3 s.* tears like a cat with a mouse 152/3, *first use (3.), this instance.*

multitude *sb.* numerousness 151/7

Nai *adv.* Used *after affirmative clause* 81/28 *etc. See* **No.**

namely *adv.* especially, particularly 64/17 *etc.*

napken *sb.* pocket-handkerchief 123/22 *etc.*

naturall *adj.* unregenerate 5/20 *etc., first use (I. 4. a.): Tyndale,* 1 Cor. 2.14, *1526;* lawfully begotten 69/24; actually begotten, not adopted 189/3

naught *adj.* worthless, useless 12/25—*1573 Variant.*

naughty *adj.* bad, wrong, *1573 sidenote for* 176/7–14

necessite *sb.* want, poverty 76/10

nede *sb.* necessity 17/22 *etc.; at nede* a time of difficulty 76/19 *etc.; of nede* of necessity 75/5

nedeth *v. pr. 3 s. what nedeth to* what need is there (to do something) 121/9

nere *adv. neuer the nere* never the nearer 206/28

neuer the later *adv.* nevertheless 33/13 *etc.*

No *adv.* Used *after negative clause* 204/16 *etc.*

noseld *pp.* nuzzled, nurtured (a person) in some opinion 68/28

nother *adv.* neither 151/17

nother *pron.* neither 115/4 *etc.*

no nother wise *adv.* not other wise 86/12 *etc.*

nother . . . ner *adv.* neither . . . nor 59/31–32 *etc.*

nought *adj.* worthless, useless 12/25, *see n.;* immoral, vicious 114/17 *etc.;* injurious 144/26, *first use (B. 3.), 1532.*

nought *sb.* nothing 43/32 *etc.; to doo noughte* to do wrong 39/26 *etc., first use (A. 8. c.), 1538. See* **worth.**

noughty *adj.* vile, bad 149/26

nurtoure *sb.* discipline 32/27, *first use (1. b.): Tyndale,* Eph. 6.4, *1526.*

occasions *sb. pl.* opportunities (of sin) 30/27 *etc.; sb.* ¹ affairs, business 62/9, *first use (II. 6. a.), 1594.*

occupienge *vbl. sb.* engaging, busying 172/3

occupye *v.* employ 182/11; *v. pa.* seized 36/12

of *prep.* from, out of 88/31 *etc.*

office *sb.* moral obligation, duty towards others 185/25

olde *adj.* olden, bygone 133/28 *etc.; (meaning not in OED)* grown-up 142/27; long established 169/2 *etc.*

olders *sb. pl.* elders 134/28, *only example (B. 1.), c1470.*

on *adj.* the numeral one 125/3 *etc.;* the same 197/23

one *adv.* on 58/8

open *adj.* public 149/3

opened *pp.* revealed 182/10; *v. pr. 3 s.* reveals 15/6

opinatiue *adj.* adhering obstinatively to one's own opinion 160/26, *first use, this instance.*

or *adv.* ere, before, formerly 209/18, *last use of this spelling of "ere" (A. 4. β),* 15 . . .

ordeyned *pp.* predestined 139/28 *etc.; v. pa.* set up to continue in a certain order 176/30

ordinary *sb.* customary fare 170/11; *sb. pl.* bishops 38/29 *etc.*

ordinaunce *sb.* a religious usage authoritatively prescribed 163/15

other *adj. other . . . or* either . . . or 55/30

other *adv.* otherwise 164/20

other *pron. pl.* others 36/3 *etc.*

out *adv. Transforms v. intr. into a compound v. trans.* 78/10 *etc., first use of this function (I. 7. b.), 1535. See* **iesteth.**

parchment *sb. vn to the parchment* in writing 104/1

parte *sb.* interest, concern 159/14

partie *sb.* side 207/17; *sb. pl.* parts of the world, regions 136/18

pateringe *vbl. sb.* repeating prayers, e.g., Pater Noster, in a rapid mechanical manner 9/5, *first use of form: Tyndale,* Matthew, *1533; v. pr. 3 s.* 60/4

pax *sb.* disk marked with a symbol of Christ which the priest and people kissed before receiving communion 70/29, *see n.*

pedelery *sb.* pedlary, trumpery, rubbish 171/8–9, *first use (2.), this instance.*

peperith *v. pr. 3 s.* seasons (writing) 140/27, *first use (6. b.), 1600.*

peperinge *vbl. sb.* sprinkling with pepper 141/2, *first use of form, 1580.*

perfecter *sb.* one who perfects, completes 93/30

pickquareles *sb. pl.* quarrelsome persons 102/33, *first use: Tyndale,* Prelates, *1530.*

pied *ppl. a.* parti-colored 100/22 *etc.*

playne *adj.* level, calm 47/14

playne *adv. playne contrary adv. phr.* entirely contrary 95/17 *etc. See* **cleane.**

pleasant *adj. Northern variant for* pleasing 163/20

pluralities *sb. pl.* the holding of two or more benefices concurrently by one person 186/18

pocke *sb.* a disease characterized by eruptive spots 103/18, *this instance (2. b. β in sing.) in OED.*

poetisse *sb.* female poet 91/24, *first use, this instance.*

polaxes *sb. pl.* axes on a long pole 81/32–33 *etc., see n.*

pole *sb.* pool 87/25

poll *v. pres.* rob, despoil, fleece 38/31

pollynge *vbl. sb.* extortion, spoliation 138/14

pope holy *adj. used absolutely* sanctimonious 34/13

popetrie *sb.* puppetry, make believe 25/20, *first use: Tyndale,* Obedience, *1528; second use, this instance.* popery, the papal ecclesiastical system 25/20, *first use: Tyndale,* Matthew, *1533; see n.*

popiniaye *sb.* parrot; a type of empty conceit, in allusion to the bird's . . . mechanical repetition of words and phrases, and thus applied contemptuously to a person 72/19, *first use (4. b.): Tyndale,* Obedience, *1528.*

popish *adj.* pertaining to popery (hostile term) 76/2 *etc.; used absolutely* 79/21 *etc.*

popishnesse *sb.* popish doctrine or practice 80/24, *first use, this instance.*

pore *adj.* unfortunate 78/7

pose *v.* ² *Aphetic form of* appose; interrogate 102/26, *first use: Tyndale,* Luke 2.48, *1526.*

potte *sb.* ¹ *goeth . . . to potte* be cut in pieces like meat for the pot, be ruined 109/3, *first use (13. f.), this instance.*

power *v. pres. Northern variant for* pour 196/26

poynte *v. inf.* point out, direct attention to 104/21

praye *v.* ask earnestly 16/19 *etc.*

precession *sb. Error for* procession 60/27, *last use (1.) of this error, 1529.*

precyselye *adv.* absolutely 190/8

preferred *pp.* advanced, promoted, *1573 sidenote for* 17/23–26 *etc.*

prepare *v.* incline, dispose 22/12

present *adj.* instant 208/25, *first use (A. II. 9. a.), 1563.*

preuelye *adv.* privately, secretly 222/7

preuented *pp.* anticipated by God's grace 37/13–14 *etc., first use (I. 4.): Tyndale,* 1 John, *1531; v.* provide beforehand against the recurrence of something 158/3 *etc., first use (II. 8.), 1548;* act before 175/10; act more quickly than 192/24

priapish *adj.* obscene 172/30. From the classical god of procreation, represented with erect phallus, *only instance (5.) in* OED.

price *sb.* esteem, regard 151/1

probacion *sb.* proof, demonstration 97/30 *etc.*

profession *sb.* declaration of belief in and obedience to religion 30/31 *etc., first use (II. 5.): Tyndale,* Heb. 3.1, *1526.*

promocions *sb. pl.* preferments 187/1–2

pronounceth *v. pr. 3 s.* announces authoritatively 206/12

prophete *v. imp.* prophesy 73/15, *only two examples: c1450, 1582.*

proue *v. inf.* test 89/24; *v. pa.* experienced 166/28

prouoke *v. inf. prouoke vn to* rouse, spur on 83/15 *etc.;* invite 117/14

purchace *v. inf. intr.* become rich 72/8

purchasynge *vbl. sb.* obtaining, procuring 29/12

put *v. put . . . downe* abolish 28/4 *etc.; put out pp.* abolished 194/1; *put to* add 45/15 *etc.; v. pr. 3 s.* assumes 182/1; *v. pr. 3 pl.* posit 182/3 *etc.*

quarters *poss. sb.* a quarter of a year 146/23
qui(c)keneth *v. pr. 3 s.* gives life 179/32; stirs up 206/7
quite *adj.* quit, free 143/9 *etc.*
quite *adv.* entirely, altogether 117/21

rable *sb.* a disorderly collection of immaterial things 74/26, *first use (A. 3. b.), 1549.*
rascall *sb.* rabble, mob 11/7 *etc.*
rather *adv.* more correctly 61/14
raueshed *pp.* transported 90/20
raylars *sb. pl.* revilers 102/31
rayle *v.* ⁴ abuse 100/26, *first use of trans. form (3. a.), 1596; rayleth on v. pr. 3 s.* utters abusive language 13/15 *etc.*
reherse *v.* repeat 194/18; *v. pa.* recited aloud in a formal manner 179/24; *v. pr. 3 s.* gives an account 183/23
reioce *v. inf.* rejoyce 202/32
rekened *pp.* attributed 203/10 *etc., first use (I. 7.): Tyndale,* Rom. 4.9, *1526.*
reporte *v. refl. reporte me* appeal 13/18; *pres. part. refl.* 207/25
reserued *pp.* preserved 37/20
revell *sb.* noisy merry-making 91/4
reuerence *sb. wythe reuerence* apologetic phrase introducing offensive remark 60/6.
right *adj.* equitable 6/14; veritable 30/10 *etc.;* rightful, lawful 212/31
ryght *sb. of right* rightfully, with justice 209/9 *etc.;* justifiable claim 213/2
roules *sb. pl.* scrolls 124/29
rowme *sb.* office, function; situation, employment 17/24 *etc., in whose rowmes satt* occupied some administrative function 40/11
ruffeleth *v.* ¹ *pr. 3 s. ruffeleth vpp* involves in obscurity or perplexity 194/22, *this instance (II. 7. b.) in OED.*
ryme *sb. with out ryme or reason* without good sense 91/26, *first use of phrase (3. b.), 1664.*
ryott *v. runne . . . at ryott* act without restraint 113/9, *only two examples (3. c.): this instance and 1579.*

sacrament *sb.* a sign, symbol 25/26 *etc., first use (3. b.): More,* Treatise on the Passion, *1534–35; used absolutely* the Eucharist 104/7
sacrithe *v. pr. 3. s.* blesses 19/9, *this instance (3.) in OED.*
sad *adj.* serious 16/25
sadnesse *sb.* seriousness 16/11
santifie *v. inf. Variant of* sanctify: purify, free from sin 112/23, *first use (5. a.): Tyndale,* 1 Cor. 6.11, *1526.*

satisfactory *sb.* place of atonement 144/4, *only example (B. a.) in OED, this instance.*

saue *conj.* except 93/24. *See 139/8–9n.*

saye *sb. ² Aphetic form of* assay; a trial specimen, a sample 79/4, *first use (9.), this instance.*

sauereth *v. pr. 3 s. sauereth not* has a disagreeable taste 143/27 etc.

sauinge *prep.* without offense to 20/2, *this instance (2.) in OED.*

scace *adv. Variant of* scarce: barely 61/31, *first use (B. 2. β.): Tyndale,* Acts 14.18, *1526.*

scacely *adv. Variant of* scarcely: barely 138/6

schryuen *pp.* confessed sins 173/2, *last use (5.), c1450.*

sclenderly *adv.* feebly, ineffectively 157/21, *only two examples (2. a.): 1533 and 1577.*

scolars *sb. pl.* pupils 107/2 etc.

season *sb. a greate season* an indefinite period of time 69/5; *the meane season* intervening time 33/12 etc.

selfe *pronominal adj. following the sb. thinges selfe* 40/21, *workes selfe* 41/12, *scripture selfe* 136/6

selfeminded *ppl. a.* obstinate in one's opinion 160/26, *only two examples in OED: this instance and 1579.*

sene *ppl. a. well sene* well versed 5/22, *first use (2.): Tyndale,* Obedience, *1528; very common in 16–17c.*

sercheth *v. pr. 3 s.* makes himself thoroughly acquainted with 6/3

serue *v. pres.* offer prayer to 182/31

serues *sb.* service, public worship 178/22

sete *sb.* seat, authority 98/18; *sb. pl.* thrones 119/5

seuerall *adj.* separate 51/10

shameth *v. pr. 3 s.* feels shame 213/12

shauen *pp.* tonsured 98/22

shewenge *vbl. sb.* manner of putting a case 136/24

shewes, showes *sb. ¹ pl.* feigned or misleading appearances 9/22, *first use (I. 7. a.): Tyndale,* Introduction to Romans, *1526;* pageants, processions, or similar displays on a large scale 92/16, *first use (II. 13. a.), 1561.*

shyne *v. shyne to* shine on 191/26

shone *sb. pl. Northern form of* shoes 61/32

shore *v. pa.* fleeced used satirically 13/10, *first use (5. c. fig.), 1570;* **shoren** *pp.* shorn, tonsured 146/16

shoteancre *sb.* sheet anchor, the largest anchor, used only in emergencies; last reliable hope 44/1

showe *sb.* shoe 105/30 etc.

shriue *v. inf. refl.* to make one's confession 21/30

silogismus *sb.* syllogism, argument in form of major premise, minor premise and conclusion 98/24, *this instance in OED; More,* Dialogue, *1529;*

More, Confutation, 1532–33; **sylogismoses** *sb. pl.* 160/22

sily, syly *adj.* silly: unlearned 78/7, *first use (A. 3. a.), c1547;* deserving of compassion 141/12

similitude *sb.* parable 104/29–30 *etc.;* comparison between two things 118/17; likeness 119/6 *etc.;* symbolic representation 176/17–18

sindon *sb.* shroud, specifically Christ's 73/25

singular *adj.* separate 213/13

sith *conj.* seeing that, since 186/27

skill *v.* ¹ *skill of* have knowledge of 170/8, *first use (4. b.), 1540.*

slake *v. inf.* lessen 95/24

sleues *sb. pl. in their sleues* at their disposal 75/15

sneveled *ppl. a.* soiled with snivel (mucus from nose) 123/22, *first use of form, this instance.*

so *adv. so moch as* to such an extent as 35/13

so *conj.* so long as, if only 120/9 *etc.*

sodomitrie *sb.* sodomy 158/18, *first use, this instance.*

so euer *adv.* whatsoever *used with emphatic force* 66/4, *first use (2.), 1557.*

sofre *v. pres.* are the object of an action 175/28; *refl.* allow themselves to be treated 201/18

solue *v. inf.* resolve, explain, answer 23/16 *etc., first use (3.), 1533.*

solutions *sb. pl.* explanations, answers 79/1 *etc.*

sondry *adj.* distinct, different 24/22 *etc.*

sore *adj.* difficult to bear 93/20 *etc.;* oppressively heavy 34/35 *etc.*

sore *adv.* greatly 5/22 *etc.*

Soules slepe *sb. phr. (Phrase not in OED)* doctrine that soul sleeps between death and Last Judgment 181/S7 *etc. See 118/3–6n and "psychopannychism" in OED.*

sowed *pp.* attached 41/20

soyle *v.* expound, explain 99/20; refute 194/15 *etc.*

space *sb.* extent of time 41/1

spare *v.* refrain from 180/20

sped *pp. sped of* to be provided with 10/30, *first use (I. 6. d.), this instance.*

spede *v. spede wel* thrive 97/1 *etc.*

spite *sb. in spite of (mine) herte* despite (my) desire 20/10 *etc.*

splayenge *vbl. sb.* ¹ extension 73/27, *only example of this sense in OED, this instance.*

stablish *v. Variant of* establish: reinforce, strengthen *rather than* found or set up 9/10 *etc.*

starke *adj. starke deed* quite dead 144/27–28

stere *v. stere . . . vpp* rouse to action, set in motion 17/31; *stere op* stir up 178/22; *v. pa.* raised up, called into being 47/8, *first use (III. 16. c.): Tyndale,* Rom. 9.17, *1526; second use: More,* Confutation, *1532–33.*

stinte *sb.* allotted amount, customary portion 138/7, *see n.*

stole *sb.* vestment consisting of a narrow strip of silk or linen, worn over the shoulders (over the left shoulder only for a deacon) and hanging down to the knees 73/24 *etc.*

stonde *v. stonde with* agree with 26/18 *etc.; v. pr. 3 s.* remains in a specified condition 82/7; *how stondeth* what is the relation 117/3; continues unimpaired 193/20; remains valid 195/16

stoppeth *v. pr. 3 s. stoppethout* shuts out, excludes 191/30, *first use (I. 10. b.): Tyndale,* Jonas, *1531.*

storifaith *sb. phr.* 69/30 *etc.* See **historicall,** *historicall faith.*

storyes *sb. pl.* historical relations, especially from the Bible 8/34 *etc.*

stronge *adj.* having great moral power 209/26 *etc.*

studie *v. inf.* to endeavor 80/23 *etc.; v.* meditate upon 197/13

studyed *ppl. a.* learned, skilled 5/22. *First use (2.), this instance.*

stues *sb.*[2] stews, brothel 50/21 *etc.; first use of plural form construed as sing. (I. 4. b.),* 172/5.

stycke *v.*[1] *stycke with* haggle with 200/18, *first use (IV. 27. b.), this instance.*

sundrie *adj.* different, distinct 127/32 *etc.*

surely *adv.* steadfastly, *1573 sidenote for* 10/7–13

swapp *v. pres.* strike, hit 73/2

swere *v. swere . . . for* answer for under oath 85/8, *only two uses (III. 14.): 1579, 1611.*

swinge *sb.*[1] sway, authority, *1573 sidenote for* 11/11–14, *first use, Tyndale,* Exposition of 1 John, *1531.*

take *pp. Variant of* taken 206/29

teeth *sb. pl.* 152/19. See **cast.** *tethes* the teeth of several persons 51/22

temperaltie *sb.* the temporal peers and the commons as opposed to the spirituality, i.e., clergy 159/27

termes *sb. pl.* technical expressions 207/23

testament *sb.* a covenant between God and man 25/29 *etc.*

that *rel. pron.* what, that which 147/8 *etc.*

the *def. art. in place of poss. pron. for a part of the body* his 199/23

then *conj. Ellipsis for* other than: except 160/28 *etc.*

therby *adv.* by that, because of that 26/28 *etc. come therby* get possession of that 111/31

therfore *adv.* on that account 39/26 *etc.*

therin *adv.* upon that 198/26

therof *adv.* of that 18/14; from that 181/15

therthorow *adv.* by reason of that, thereby 184/32

therto *adv.* besides 13/28 *etc.;* to that thing 23/30 *etc.;* for that purpose 34/4 *etc.*

therwith *adv.* because of that 179/10; with that act 178/5

thither *adv.* to that place 211/10

thryftes *sb. pl.* savings 38/31

thynge *sb.* attribute, property 156/18; business, matter 161/21

to *adv. added to* expressing addition 177/24; *seled to* expressing contact especially with verbs of shutting 99/31

tot quottes *sb. pl.* dispensations to hold as many ecclesiastical benefices as the holder can get, *from Lt.* "*tot quot,*" "*as many as there may be*" 51/14–15 *etc., see n.*

tough *adj.* viscous, sticky 212/17, *this instance (2.) in OED.*

towarde *prep.* with regard to 193/30 *etc.*

towardnesse *sb.* inclination, willingness 209/18 *etc.; this instance (1.) in OED,* 210/25.

towseth *v. pr. 3 s.* tears at like a dog 152/3

trie *v.* test the truth of 110/3 *etc.*

trueth *sb.* fidelity 209/7

turmoyled *pp.* agitated 160/8, *first use: Tyndale,* Preface to Genesis, *1530; second use: this instance.*

twich *Obsolete form of* touch; *v. inf.* rebuke 77/7 *etc.; pres. subj.* allude to 171/19; *v. pa.* came in contact with 83/26 *etc.*

tyme *sb.* the general state of affairs at a particular period 158/8

variaunce *sb.* discord, dissension 206/25

vauntage *sb. Aphetic form of* advantage: an additional amount 121/13

vayne *adj.* unprofitable, unavailing 123/29; foolish 199/17

vertu *sb.* moral efficacy 173/15 *etc.*

verye *adj.* true 5/14 *etc.;* veritable 8/25

visett *v. inf.* supply (with some benefit) 82/33

vnexecuted *ppl. a.* not carried out 151/30, *first use, 1585.*

vnions *sb. pl.* the uniting of two or more benefices into one 51/14 *etc., see n.*

vnkyndnesse *sb.* unnatural conduct 102/11 *etc.*

vnprouided *ppl. a.* unprepared (to make a reply) 160/17

vnsensible *adj.* insensible, not having the faculty of sensation 77/14 *etc., first use (3. a.), this instance.*

vnto *prep.* with regard to 191/24

vnwashe *pp.* unwashed 164/8, *common till end of 16c.*

volowed *pp.* baptised 72/25, *only two examples in OED: Tyndale,* Obedience, *1528 and this instance.*

vplondish *adj.* rustic, rude 188/13 *etc., see n.*

vpp come *pp.* risen up 145/28

vse *sb. the vse* custom 153/9 *etc.; sb. pl.* functions, offices 56/25 *etc.*

vttereth *v.* [1] *pr. 3 s.* gives expression to 110/25, *this instance (II. 6. c.) in OED;* **vttur** *v.* make known the character of 128/1, *first use (II. 8. a.): Tyndale,*

Mark 3.12, *1526; second use: More,* Treatise on the Passion, *1534–35;* make manifest 134/3 *etc.;* describe, report 194/10

-warde *suffix* having a specified direction to, *(vn)to godwarde* 21/25 *etc., to vs warde* 197/3

wauntage *sb. Northern variant for* vantage: advantage, profit 138/21

wayte *v.* ¹ *inf. wayte on* to attend to a duty 57/8 *etc., only example (II. 14. d.):* Tyndale, Rom. 12.7, *1526;* be in readiness to receive orders 103/28 *etc., first example (I. 9. a.):* Tyndale, 1 Cor. 9.13, *1526; v. pr. 3 s. wayteth on* 223/25, *wayteth vppon* 34/26 *(meaning not in OED)* awaits the religious conversion of

we(a)lth *sb.* well-being 32/30 *etc.*

were *rel. adv.* where, in the place in which 195/8

were with *rel. adv.* where with, whereby 166/1 *etc.*

werketh, worketh *v. pr. 3 s.* brings about, produces 196/19; does, performs 196/23

weyhousse *sb.* a public building to which commodities are brought to be weighed 76/16

what someuer *pron.* whoever 62/24

w(h)erfore *rel. adv.* for which 14/32 *etc.; this instance (II. 3.) in OED,* 135/24; on which account 37/24 *etc.*

wher(e)of *adv.* wherewith, whereby 202/32; *interrog. adv.* whence 211/21

whether *pron.* which of the two 121/19

which *rel pron. introducing a defining clause* who 74/1

whom *sb.* home 166/13

whother *rel. adv.* whither, to whatever place 88/10 *etc.*

why *sb.* reason, cause 50/13

wife *sb.* woman 49/28

wil *adj.* wild, erring, *1573 sidenote for* 122/28–31, *last use (2. fig. a.), c1375; now only Scottish.*

with al(l) *adv.* with that 79/3 *etc.; prep. in post-position* with 220/9

with out *adv.* outside of the inward being 113/29

with out *prep.* beyond 16/27 *etc.;* outside 119/31

witte *sb.* intellect 7/15 *etc.; sb. pl.* mental faculties 191/25 etc.

wold *optative v.* would that by . . . *wold to christes bloude* 176/22, *wold too christes passyon* 176/29

wolward *adv. wolward goinge* wearing wool next to one's skin as a penance 80/12

wonderful *adj.* astonishing 7/16 *etc.*

wondred *v. pa.* marvelled 36/27

wordlie *adj.* worldly 7/25, *OED ("worldly" 2. b.) gives alternate spelling up to mid-16c, see n.*

worke *v.* cause, produce 206/18

worlde *sb. the worldes ende* the end of time 145/5–6

worshepful *adj.* imposing, honorable 77/6

worsheple *adj.* worshiply, honorable 123/25–26, *only instance of adj. form in OED, 1340.*

worshepe *v. pres.* honor 76/3 *etc.*

worth *adj.* of spiritual value, *moch worth* worth much 64/18, *nought worth* worth nothing 117/28

wother *adj. Variant of* other 106/2 *etc.*

wo(o)ther *pron. Variant of* other 190/19; *pl.* others 208/24

wother *rel. adv.* whither 194/17, *this spelling not in OED.*

wother wise *adv. Variant of* otherwise 76/30

wrought *pp.* performed 17/1 *etc.; v. pa.* acted, caused 37/9 *etc.;* labored 203/7 *etc.; pp.* changed, converted 203/34

wyll *sb.* desire 193/14

wyll *v.* ¹ *inf. not to wyll vse* to persist in not using 162/18; *v. pr. 3 s.* means, maintains 209/1 *etc., only two examples (B. I. 4.):Tyndale,* Prologue to James, *1534; 1602.*

yee *adv.* yea, *used after affirmative clause* 97/25. *See* **yes.**

yeldeth *v. pr. 3 s. refl.* surrenders, submits 168/10

yere *sb. partitive gen.* years 108/23

yes *adv. Used after negative clause* 136/29

yet *adv.* in addition, furthermore 178/27

ynow *adj. pl. of* enough 161/4

yperdulia *sb.* hyperdulia; superior veneration given to Mary 55/11, *etc., see n.; first use,* 55/14–15.

INDEX OF PROPER NAMES
MENTIONED IN
ANSWER TO MORE, 1531

References to the following are omitted because they occur so frequently: the apostles as a group, books of the Bible, the name "Christ," Christians, the name "God," More, Paul, and Tyndale. Included are references to the Father, the Holy Ghost, Jesus, Mary, ethnic groups, languages, and religious groups. Since proper names may or may not be capitalized, whichever form occurs first is given first.

SCRIPTURE INDEX

Because it translates from the original languages and is widely available, we follow the KJV for the titles of books, the numbers of the psalms, and the use of verse numbers in general. Readers who wish to consult both the KJV and the Vulgate can use *The Jerusalem Bible,* which gives the numbers for the Hebrew and the Latin versions.

Synoptic Entries

INDEX TO MAJOR
POST-SCRIPTURAL AUTHORS

GENERAL INDEX

Major entries are indicated by bold numbers. Cross references to the Index of Proper Names are indicated by "IPN."

The Independent Works of William Tyndale, Volume 3 was designed in 10.75/12 Bembo and produced by Kachergis Book Design in Pittsboro, North Carolina. This book was printed on sixty-pound House Natural and bound by Sheridan Books in Ann Arbor, Michigan.